Programming Languages
Principles and Practice
Second Edition

Kenneth C. Louden
San Jose State University

THOMSON

BROOKS/COLE

Australia • Canada • Mexico • Singapore • Spain
United Kingdom • United States

Editor: *Kallie Swanson*
Senior Editorial Assistant: *Carla Vera*
Technology Project Manager: *Burke Taft*
Executive Marketing Manager: *Tom Ziolkowski*
Marketing Assistant: *Darcie Pool*
Advertising Project Manager: *Laura Hubrich*
Project Manager, Editorial Production:
   Kelsey McGee
Print/Media Buyer: *Vena M. Dyer*

Permissions Editor: *Elizabeth Zuber*
Production Service: *Helen Walden*
Copy Editor: *Monique Calello*
Cover Designer: *Roy R. Neuhaus*
Cover Image: *David Bishop*
Cover Printing, Printing and Binding:
   Phoenix Color Corporation
Compositor: *Better Graphics, Inc.*

For more information about our products,
contact us at:
Thomson Learning Academic
Resource Center
1-800-423-0563
For permission to use material from this text,
contact us by:
Phone: 1-800-730-2214
Fax: 1-800-730-2215
Web: http://www.thomsonrights.com

Brooks/Cole–Thomson Learning
511 Forest Lodge Road
Pacific Grove, CA 93950
USA

Asia
Thomson Learning
5 Shenton Way #01–01
UIC Building
Singapore 068808

Australia
Nelson Thomson Learning
102 Dodds Street
South Melbourne, Victoria 3205
Australia

Canada
Nelson Thomson Learning
1120 Birchmount Road
Toronto, Ontario M1K 5G4
Canada

Europe/Middle East/Africa
Thomson Learning
High Holborn House
50/51 Bedford Row
London WC1R 4LR
United Kingdom

Latin America
Thomson Learning
Seneca, 53
Colonia Polanco
11560 Mexico D.F.
Mexico

Spain
Paraninfo Thomson Learning
Calle/Magallanes, 25
28015 Madrid, Spain

Library of Congress Control Number: 2002105363

ISBN 0-534-95341-7

Contents

10   Object-Oriented Programming   409

11   Functional Programming   471

Preface

This book is an introduction to the broad field of programming languages. It combines a general presentation of principles with considerable detail about many modern languages, including some of the newest functional and object-oriented languages. Unlike many introductory texts, it contains significant material on implementation issues, the theoretical foundations of programming languages, and a large number of exercises. All of these features make this text a useful bridge to compiler courses and to the theoretical study of programming languages. However, it is a text specifically designed for an advanced undergraduate programming languages survey course that covers most of the programming languages requirements specified in the 2001 ACM/IEEE-CS Joint Curriculum Task Force Report, and the CS8 course of the 1978 ACM Curriculum.

My goals in preparing this new edition are to bring the language-specific material in line with the changes in the popularity and use of programming languages since the publication of the first edition in 1993, to improve and expand the coverage in certain areas, and to improve the presentation and usefulness of the examples and exercises, while retaining as much of the original text and organization as possible.

Students are not expected to know any one particular language. However, experience with at least one language is necessary. A certain degree of "computational sophistication," such as that provided by a course in data structures and a discrete mathematics course, is also expected. Major languages used in this edition include C, C++, Java, Ada, ML, Haskell, Scheme, and Prolog; many other languages are discussed more briefly.

Overview and Organization

In most cases, each chapter largely is independent of the others without artificially restricting the material in each. Cross references in the text allow the student or instructor to fill in any gaps that might arise even if a particular chapter or section is skipped.

Chapter 1 surveys the concepts studied in later chapters, and introduces the different language paradigms with simple examples in typical languages.

Chapters 2 and 3 provide overviews of the history of programming languages and language design principles, respectively. Chapter 3 could serve well as a culminating chapter for the book, but I find it arouses interest in later topics when covered here.

Chapter 4 treats syntax in some detail, including the use of BNF, EBNF, and syntax diagrams. A brief section views recursive definitions (like BNF) as set equations to be solved, a view that recurs periodically throughout the text. One section is devoted to recursive-descent parsing and the use of parsing tools.

Chapters 5, 6, 7, and 8 cover the central semantic issues of programming languages: declaration, allocation, evaluation; the symbol table and runtime environment as semantic functions; data types and type checking; procedure activation and parameter passing; and exceptions and exception handling.

Chapter 9 gives an overview of modules and abstract data types, including language mechanisms and equational, or algebraic, specification.

Chapters 10, 11, 12, and 13 address language paradigms, beginning with the object-oriented paradigms in Chapter 10. I use Java to introduce the concepts in this chapter. Individual sections feature C++ and Smalltalk. Chapter 11 deals with the functional paradigm. Each of the languages Scheme, ML, and Haskell are covered in some detail. This chapter also introduces the lambda calculus and the theory of recursive function definitions. Chapter 12, on logic programming, offers an extended section on Prolog, and devotes one section to equational languages such as OBJ.

Chapter 13 introduces the three principal methods of formal semantics: operational, denotational, and axiomatic. This is somewhat unique among introductory texts in that it gives enough detail to provide a real flavor for the methods.

Chapter 14 treats the major ways parallelism has been introduced into programming languages: coroutines, threads, semaphores, monitors, and message passing, with examples primarily from Java and Ada. Its final section surveys recent efforts to introduce parallelism into LISP and Prolog.

Use as a Text

I have used this text for more than ten years in my CS 152 classes of upper division computer science majors and graduate students at San Jose State University. I have taught the course using two completely different organizations, which could loosely be called the "principles" approach and the "paradigm" approach. Two suggested organizations of these approaches in a semester-long course are as follow:

> *The principles approach*: Chapters 1, 4, 5, 6, 7, 8, and 9. If there is extra time, Chapters 2 and 3.

> *The paradigm approach*: Chapters 1, 10, 11, 12, 13, and 14 (not neces-
> sarily in that order). If there is extra time, Chapters 2 and 3, or
> selected topics from the remaining chapters.

In a two-semester or two-quarter sequence it should be possible to cover
most of the book.

Selected answers for many of the exercises at the end of each chapter may be found at www.brookscole.com or on the author's Web site,
www.cs.sjsu.edu/faculty/louden. Many are programming exercises (none
extremely long) in languages discussed in the text. Conceptual exercises
range from the short-answer type that test understanding of the material
to longer, essay-style exercises and challenging "thought" questions. A few
moments' reflection should give the reader adequate insight into the
potential difficulty of a particular exercise. Further knowledge can be
gained by reading the on-line answers, which I treat as an extension of the
text and sometimes provide additional information beyond that required
to solve the problem. Occasionally the answer to an exercise on a particular language requires the reader to consult a language reference manual
or have knowledge of the language not specifically covered in the text.
Throughout the book I have tried to improve the usefulness of the code
examples by adding line numbers where appropriate, and by augmenting
many examples with main program drivers that allow them to be executed
to demonstrate their described behavior. All such examples, as well as a
number of others (in which, for space or other reasons, such extra code
was suppressed), are available through www.brookscole.com or the
author's Web site listed above. These Web sites also contain links to free,
downloadable translators for all the major languages of the book, many of
which I have used to test the examples. Other materials may also be available.

Summary of Changes between
the First and Second Editions

In the first edition, I used examples from the most widely known imperative languages, including C, Pascal, Ada, Modula-2, and FORTRAN, as
well as some of the less widely known languages representing other language paradigms, such as Scheme, ML, Miranda, C++, Eiffel, Smalltalk,
and Prolog. The most extensive change in the current edition is the
replacement of Pascal and Modula-2 largely by C, C++, and Java in the
examples. Modula-2 has disappeared, except for a "historical" section in
Chapter 9, on ADTs; a few examples in Pascal remain. I also use Ada
quite a bit, especially for features that are not well represented in
C/C++/Java (e.g., subranges, arrays and slices, name equivalence of data
types). Java replaces Simula as the primary example in Chapter 10, on
object-oriented programming languages, and I eliminated the section on
Eiffel. I devote considerably more space to ML and Haskell in Chapter 11,
on functional languages, and I added ML examples liberally throughout
the book. Finally, I use Java threads as the basic example of concurrency

in Chapter 14, on parallel programming languages. Additional significant changes are as follows:

- I split off procedures and environments from the rest of the control material, so Chapter 7 now treats control expressions and statements, and the new Chapter 8 treats control procedures and environments. I moved expressions from the end of Chapter 5, on basic semantics, to the beginning of Chapter 7. Because in most cases some implicit or explicit control is inherent in evaluating expressions, this topic fits well with other control issues.

- I include overloading with the symbol table material in Chapter 5, because it essentially is a symbol table task to disambiguate overloaded identifiers. While this presents a "phase order" problem with Chapter 6, on data types—the type signature being the primary attribute used in overload resolution—the amount of data type information needed to understand overload resolution is not great, and the material seems more natural presented in this way.

- I include parametric polymorphism with the discussion of type checking in Chapter 6, in which I also give a more extensive account of Hindley-Milner polymorphic type checking. Parametric polymophism comes up again in Chapter 9 in discussing Ada packages, and in Chapter 10 in discussing C++ class templates.

- I rewrote Chapter 9 on ADTs and modules to emphasize modules a bit more and changed its title to include modules. This topic is more challenging than most to present concisely, because the design of ADT and module mechanisms differs more widely among common languages than any other feature except, possibly, concurrency mechanisms. I use ML and Ada as the major examples here, with some additional material on C++ namespaces and Java packages. I defer the use of classes to represent ADTs and modules to Chapter 10 on object-oriented programming.

- I do not mention the scripting languages, such as Perl, JavaScript, and Tcl, extensively in this text (except for a brief section in Chapter 2). While the use of such languages is widespread and increasing, particularly for Web applications, and student interest in them is intense, I still consider them somewhat too special-purpose for this text. However, nothing would prevent the interested instructor from providing examples in these languages of virtually every major language feature.

- I also do not cover any "visual" languages or component assembly tools, such as Visual Basic or various JavaBean tools. My view is that these "languages" are better studied in a GUI or software engineering course. Similarly, I only mention the various markup languages such as XML, SGML, and HTML, in passing.

Acknowledgments

I would like to thank all those persons too numerous to mention who, over the years, have emailed me with comments, corrections, and suggestions. I especially thank the reviewers of this edition for their many useful suggestions and comments: Leonard M. Faltz of Arizona State University, Jesse Yu of the College of St. Elizabeth, Mike Frazier of Abilene Christian University, Ariel Ortiz Ramírez of ITESM Campus Estado de Mexico, James J. Ball of Indiana State University, Samuel A. Rebelsky of Grinnell College, and Arthur Fleck of the University of Iowa.

I also thank Eran Yahav of Tel-Aviv University for reading and commenting on Chapter 14 on concurrency, and Hamilton Richards of the University of Texas for his comments and suggestions on survey Chapter 1 and Chapter 11, on functional programming.

I remain grateful to the many students in my CS 152 sections at San Jose State University for their direct and indirect contributions to this edition and to the previous edition; to my colleagues at San Jose State, Michael Beeson, Cay Horstmann, and Vinh Phat, who read and commented on individual chapters in the first edition; and to the reviewers of that edition, Ray Fanselau of American River College, Larry Irwin of Ohio University, Zane C. Motteler of California Polytechnic State University, Tony P. Ng of the University of Illinois-Urbana, Rick Ruth of Shippensburg University of Pennsylvania, and Ryan Stansifer of the University of North Texas.

Of course, I alone am responsible for the shortcomings and errors in this book. I am happy to receive reports of errors and any other comments from readers at louden@cs.sjsu.edu.

I particularly thank Kallie Swanson, computer science editor at Brooks/Cole, for her encouragement and patience during the seemingly endless process of revision. A special thanks is owed to Marjorie Schlaikjer, who first convinced me to write this book.

Finally, I give my thanks and appreciation, as ever, for the patience, support, and love of my wife, Margreth, and my sons, Andrew and Robin. Without you, much of this would never have happened.

1 Introduction

How we communicate influences how we think, and vice versa. Similarly, how we program computers influences how we think about them, and vice versa. Over the last several decades a great deal of experience has been accumulated in the design and use of programming languages. Although there are still aspects of the design of programming languages that are not completely understood, the basic principles and concepts now belong to the fundamental body of knowledge of computer science. A study of these principles is as essential to the programmer and computer scientist as the knowledge of a particular programming language such as C or Java. Without this knowledge it is impossible to gain the needed perspective and insight into the effect programming languages and their design have on the way we communicate with computers and the ways we think about computers and computation.

It is the goal of this text to introduce the major principles and concepts underlying all programming languages without concentrating on one particular language. Specific languages are used as examples and illustrations. These languages include C, Java, C++, Ada, ML, LISP, FORTRAN, Pascal, and Prolog. It is not necessary for the reader to be

1

familiar with all these languages, or even any of them, to understand the concepts being illustrated. At most the reader is required to be experienced in only one programming language and to have some general knowledge of data structures, algorithms, and computational processes.

In this chapter we will introduce the basic notions of programming languages and outline some of the basic concepts. We will also briefly discuss the role of language translators. However, the techniques used in building language translators will not be discussed in detail in this book.

1.1 What Is a Programming Language?

A definition often advanced for a programming language is "a notation for communicating to a computer what we want it to do."

But this definition is inadequate. Before the 1940s computers were programmed by being "hard-wired": switches were set by the programmer to connect the internal wiring of a computer to perform the requested tasks. This effectively communicated to the computer what computations were desired, yet switch settings can hardly be called a programming language.

A major advance in computer design occurred in the 1940s, when John von Neumann had the idea that a computer should not be "hard-wired" to do particular things, but that a series of codes stored as data would determine the actions taken by a central processing unit. Soon programmers realized that it would be a tremendous help to attach symbols to the instruction codes, as well as to memory locations, and **assembly language** was born, with instructions such as

```
LDA #2
STA X
```

But assembly language, because of its machine dependence, low level of abstraction, and difficulty in being written and understood, is also not what we usually think of as a programming language and will not be studied further in this text. (Sometimes, assembly language is referred to as a **low-level language** to distinguish it from the **high-level languages**, which are the subject of this text.) Indeed, programmers soon realized that a higher level of abstraction would improve their ability to write concise, understandable instructions that could be used with little change from machine to machine. Certain standard constructions, such as assignment, loops, and selections or choices, were constantly being used and had nothing to do with the particular machine; these constructions should be expressible in simple standard phrases that could be translated into machine-usable form, such as the C code for the previous assembly language instructions (indicating assignment of the value 2 to the location with name X)

```
X = 2
```

Programs thus became relatively machine independent, but the language still reflected the underlying architecture of the von Neumann model of a machine: an area of memory where both programs and data are stored and a separate central processing unit that sequentially executes instructions fetched from memory. Most modern programming languages still retain the flavor of this processor model of computation. With increasing abstraction, and with the development of new architectures, particularly parallel processors, came the realization that programming languages need not be based on any particular model of computation or machine, but need only describe computation or processing in general.

A parallel evolution has also led away from the use of programming languages to communicate solely from humans to computers to the use of such languages to communicate from human to human. Indeed, while it is still an important requirement that a programming language allows humans to easily *write* instructions, in the modern world of very large programming projects, it is even more important that other programmers be able to *read* the instructions as well.

This leads us to state the following definition.

Definition: A **programming language** is a notational system for describing computation in machine-readable and human-readable form.

We will discuss the three key concepts in this definition.

Computation.   Computation is usually defined formally using the mathematical concept of a **Turing machine**, which is a kind of computer whose operation is simple enough to be described with great precision. Such a machine needs also to be powerful enough to perform any computation that a computer can, and Turing machines are known to be able to carry out any computation that current computers are capable of (though certainly not as efficiently). In fact, the generally accepted **Church's thesis** states that it is not possible to build a machine that is inherently more powerful than a Turing machine.

Our own view of computation in this text is less formal. We will think of computation as any process that can be carried out by a computer. Note, however, that computation does not mean simply mathematical calculation, such as the computation of the product of two numbers or the logarithm of a number. Computation instead includes *all* kinds of computer operations, including data manipulation, text processing, and information storage and retrieval. In this sense, computation is used as a synonym for processing of any kind on a computer. Sometimes a programming language will be designed with a particular kind of processing in mind, such as report generation, graphics, or database maintenance. Although such **special-purpose languages** may be able to express more general kinds of computations, in this text we will concentrate on the **general-purpose**

languages that are designed to be used for general processing and not for particular purposes.

Machine Readability.   For a language to be machine-readable, it must have a simple enough structure to allow for efficient translation. This is not something that depends on the notion of any particular machine, but is a general requirement that can be stated precisely in terms of definiteness and complexity of translation. First, there must be an **algorithm** to translate a language, that is, a step-by-step process that is unambiguous and finite. Second, the algorithm cannot have too great a complexity: Most programming languages can be translated in time that is proportional to the size of the program. Otherwise, a computer might spend more time on the translation process than on the actual computation being described. Usually, machine readability is ensured by restricting the structure of a programming language to that of the so-called **context-free languages,** which are studied in Chapter 4, and by insisting that all translation be based on this structure.

Human Readability.   Unlike machine readability, this is a much less precise notion, and it is also less understood. It requires that a programming language provide **abstractions** of the actions of computers that are easy to understand, even by persons not completely familiar with the underlying details of the machine.[1] One consequence of this is that programming languages tend to resemble natural languages (like English or Chinese), at least superficially. This way, a programmer can rely on his or her natural understanding to gain immediate insight into the computation being described. (Of course, this can lead to serious misunderstandings as well.)

Human readability acquires a new dimension as the size of a program increases. (Some programs are now as large as the largest novels.) The readability of large programs requires suitable mechanisms for reducing the amount of detail required to understand the program as a whole. For example, in a large program we would want to localize the effect a small change in one part of the program would have—it should not require major changes to the entire program. This requires the collection of local information in one place and the prevention of this information from being used indiscriminately throughout the program. The development of such abstraction mechanisms has been one of the important advances in programming language design over the past two decades, and we will study such mechanisms in detail in Chapter 9.

Large programs also often require the use of large groups of programmers, who simultaneously write separate parts of the programs. This substantially changes the view that must be taken of a programming language. A programming language is no longer a way of describing compu-

---

[1] Human *writability* also requires such abstractions to reduce the effort of expressing a computation. Writability is related to but not the same as readability. See Chapter 3.

tation, but it becomes part of a **software development environment** that promotes and enforces a software design methodology. Software development environments not only contain facilities for writing and translating programs in one or more programming languages, but also have facilities for manipulating program files, keeping records of changes, and performing debugging, testing, and analysis. Programming languages thus become part of the study of **software engineering**. Our view of programming languages, however, will be focused on the languages themselves rather than on their place as part of such a software development environment. The design issues involved in integrating a programming language into a software development environment can be treated more adequately in a software engineering text.

1.2 Abstractions in Programming Languages

We have noted the essential role that abstraction plays in providing human readability of programs. In this section we briefly describe common abstractions that programming languages provide to express computation and give an indication of where they are studied in more detail in subsequent chapters. Programming language abstractions fall into two general categories: **data abstraction** and **control abstraction**. Data abstractions abstract properties of the data, such as character strings, numbers, or search trees, which is the subject of computation. Control abstractions abstract properties of the transfer of control, that is, the modification of the execution path of a program based on the situation at hand. Examples of control abstractions are loops, conditional statements, and procedure calls.

Abstractions also fall into **levels**, which can be viewed as measures of the amount of information contained in the abstraction. **Basic abstractions** collect together the most localized machine information. **Structured abstractions** collect more global information about the structure of the program. **Unit abstractions** collect information about entire pieces of a program.

In the following paragraphs we classify common abstractions according to the levels of abstraction, for both data abstraction and control abstraction.

1.2.1 Data Abstractions

Basic Abstractions.   Basic data abstractions in programming languages abstract the internal representation of common data values in a computer. For example, integer data values are often stored in a computer using a two's complement representation, and standard operations such as addition and multiplication are provided. Similarly, a real, or floating-point, data value is usually provided. Locations in computer memory that contain data values are abstracted by giving them names and are called **variables**. The kind of data value is also given a name and is called a **data**

type. Data types of basic data values are usually given names that are variations of their corresponding mathematical values, such as `int` or `integer` and `real` or `float`. Variables are given names and data types using a **declaration**, such as the Pascal

```
var x : integer;
```

or the equivalent C declaration

```
int x;
```

In this example, `x` is established as the name of a variable and is given the data type *integer*. Data types are studied in Chapter 6 and declarations in Chapter 5.

Structured Abstractions.   The **data structure** is the principal method for abstracting collections of data values that are related. For example, an employee record may consist of a name, address, phone number, and salary, each of which may be a different data type, but together represent the record as a whole. Another example is that of a group of items, all of which have the same data type and which need to be kept together for purposes of sorting or searching. A typical data structure provided by programming languages is the **array**, which collects data into a sequence of individually indexed items. Variables can be given a data structure in a declaration, as in the C

```
int a[10];
```

or the FORTRAN

```
INTEGER a(10)
```

which establish the variable **a** as containing an array of ten integer values. Data structures can also be viewed as new data types that are not internal, but are constructed by the programmer as needed. In many languages these types can also be given type names, just as the basic types, and this is done in a **type declaration**, such as the C

```
typedef int Intarray[10];
```

which defines the new name `Intarray` for the type *array of integer*, with space for ten values. Such data types are called **structured types**. The different ways of creating and using structured types are studied in Chapter 6.

Unit Abstractions.   In a large program, it is useful and even necessary to collect related code into specific locations within a program, either as separate files or as separate language structures within a file. Typically such abstractions include access conventions and restrictions, which traditionally have been referred to as **data encapsulation** and **information hiding**. These mechanisms vary widely from language to language, but are often associated with structured types in some way, and thus are related (but not identical) to **abstract data types**. Examples include the **module** of ML and Haskell and the **package** of Ada and Java. A somewhat intermediate abstraction more closely related to abstract data types is the **class** mechanism of object-oriented languages, which could be categorized as either a structured abstraction or a unit abstraction (or both), depending on the language. Classes generally offer data encapsulation and possibly also information hiding, and may also have some of the characteristics of modules or packages. In this text we study modules and abstract data types in Chapter 9, whereas classes (and their relation to abstract data types) are studied in Chapter 10.

An additional property of a unit data abstraction that has become increasingly important is its **reusability**—the ability to reuse the data abstraction in different programs, thus saving the cost of writing abstractions from scratch for each program. Typically such data abstractions represent **components** (operationally complete pieces of a program or user interface) or **containers** (data structures containing other user-defined data) and are entered into a library of available components and containers. As such, unit data abstractions become the basis for language **library** mechanisms (the library mechanism itself, as well as certain standard libraries, may or may not be part of the language itself), and their ability to be easily combined with each other (their **interoperability**) is enhanced by providing standard conventions for their interfaces. Many interface standards have been developed, either independent of the programming language, or sometimes tied to a specific language. Most of these apply to the class structure of object-oriented languages, since classes have proven to be more flexible for reuse than most other language structures (see the next section and Chapter 10). Two language independent standards for communicating processes (that is, programs that are running separately) are Microsoft's Component Object Model (COM) and the Common Object Request Broker Architecture (CORBA) recognized as an international standard. A somewhat different interface standard is the JavaBeans application programming interface tied to the Java programming language. A study of such interface standards is beyond the scope of this book, however.

1.2.2   Control Abstractions

Basic Abstractions.   Typical basic control abstractions are those statements in a language that combine a few machine instructions into a more understandable abstract statement. We have already mentioned the **assignment statement** as a typical instruction that abstracts the computation and storage of a value into the location given by a variable, as for example,

```
x = x + 3
```

This assignment statement represents the fetching of the value of the variable x, adding the integer 3 to it, and storing the result in the location of x. Assignment is studied in Chapter 5.

Another typical basic control statement is the **goto** statement, which abstracts the jump operation of a computer or the transfer of control to a statement elsewhere in a program, such as the FORTRAN

```
        . . .
        GOTO 10
C       this part skipped
        . . .
C       control goes here
10      CONTINUE
        . . .
```

Goto statements today are considered too close to the actual operation of a computer to be a useful abstraction mechanism (except in special situations), so most modern languages provide only very limited forms of this statement. See Chapter 7 for a discussion.

Structured Abstractions.   Structured control abstractions divide a program into groups of instructions that are nested within tests that govern their execution. Typical examples are selection statements, such as the **if-statement** of many languages, the **case-statement** of Pascal, and the **switch-statement** of C. For example, in the following C code,

```
if (x > 0)
{   numSolns = 2;
    r1 = sqrt (x);
    r2 = - r1;
}
else
{   numSolns = 0;
}
```

the three statements within the first set of curly brackets are executed if x > 0, and the single statement within the second set of curly brackets otherwise. (C allows the second set of brackets to be deleted, since they only surround a single statement.)

Some languages provide additional support for such structured control by, for example, allowing indentation to substitute for the curly brackets, as in the Haskell

```
case numSolns(x) of
   0  -> []
   2  -> [sqrt(x),-sqrt(x)]
```

which is shorthand for

```
case numSolns(x) of
{ 0  -> [] ;
```

```
    2   -> [sqrt(x),-sqrt(x)]
}
```

(This is called the *layout rule* in Haskell.)

Ada goes one step farther in structured control, in that the opening of a group of nested statements is automatic and does not require a "begin":

```
if x > 0.0 then
    numSolns := 2;
    r1 := sqrt(x);
    r2 := -r1;
else
    numSolns := 0;
end if;
```

(Note the required keywords **end** if at the end of the if-statement.)

One advantage of structured control structures is that they can be **nested** within other control structures, usually to any desired depth, as in the following C code (which is a modification of the foregoing example):

```
if (x > 0)
{   numSolns = 2;
    r1 = sqrt (x);
    r2 = - r1;
}
else
{   if (x == 0)
    { numSolns = 1;
    r1 = 0.0;
    }
    else
    { numSolns = 0;
    }
}
```

which is usually written more compactly as

```
if (x > 0)
{   numSolns = 2;
    r1 = sqrt (x);
    r2 = - r1;
}
else if (x == 0)
{   numSolns = 1;
    r1 = 0.0;
}
else numSolns = 0;
```

or the Ada,

```
if x > 0.0 then
  numSolns := 2;
  r1 := sqrt (x);
  r2 := r1;
elsif x = 0.0 then
  numSolns := 1;
  r1 := 0.0;
else
  numSolns := 0;
end if;
```

Structured looping mechanisms come in many forms, including the while, for, and do loops of C and C++, the repeat loops of Pascal, and the loop statement of Ada. For example, the following program fragments, first in C and then Ada, both compute x to be the greatest common divisor of u and v using Euclid's algorithm (for example, the greatest common divisor of 8 and 20 is 4, and the greatest common divisor of 3 and 11 is 1):

```
/* C example */
x = u;
y = v;
while (y != 0) /* not equal in C */
{ t = y;
  y = x % y; /* the integer remainder operation in C */
  x = t;
}

-- Ada example
x := u;
y := v;
loop
  exit when y = 0;
  t := y;
  y := x mod y; -- modulo, similar to % in C
  x := t;
end loop;
```

Structured selection and loop mechanisms are studied in Chapter 7.

A further, powerful mechanism for structuring control is the **procedure**, sometimes also called a **subprogram** or **subroutine**. This allows a programmer to consider a sequence of actions as a single action and to control the interaction of these actions with other parts of the program. Procedure abstraction involves two things. First, a procedure must be defined by giving it a name and associating with it the actions that are to be performed. This is called **procedure declaration**, and it is similar to variable and type declaration, mentioned earlier. Second, the procedure must actually be called at the point where the actions are to be performed. This is sometimes also referred to as procedure **invocation** or procedure **activation**.

As an example, consider the sample code fragment that computes
the greatest common divisor of integers u and v. We can make this into a
procedure in Ada with the procedure declaration as given in Figure 1.1:

```
(1)  procedure gcd (u, v: in integer; x: out integer) is
(2)     y, t, z: integer;
(3)  begin
(4)     z := u;
(5)     y := v;
(6)     loop
(7)        exit when y = 0;
(8)        t := y;
(9)        y := z mod y;
(10)       z := t;
(11)    end loop;
(12)    x := z;
(13) end gcd;
```

Figure 1.1   An Ada gcd procedure

In this declaration, u, v, and x have become **parameters** to the procedure (line 1), that is, things that can change from call to call. This procedure can now be **called** by simply naming it and supplying appropriate
actual parameters or **arguments**, as in

```
gcd (8, 18, d);
```

which gives d the value 2. (The parameter x is given the out label in line
1 to indicate that its value is computed by the procedure itself and will
change the value of the corresponding actual parameter of the caller.)

In FORTRAN, by contrast, a procedure is declared as a subroutine,

```
SUBROUTINE gcd (u, v, x)
. . .
END
```

and is called using an explicit call-statement:

```
CALL gcd (a, b, d)
```

Procedure call is a more complex mechanism than selection or looping, since it requires the storing of information about the condition of the
program at the point of the call and the way the called procedure operates.
Such information is stored in a **runtime environment**. Procedure calls,
parameters, and runtime environments are all studied in Chapter 8. (The
basic kinds of runtime environments are also mentioned in Section 1.5 of
this chapter.)

An abstraction mechanism closely related to procedures is the **function**, which can be viewed simply as a procedure that returns a value or
result to its caller. For example, the Ada code for the gcd procedure in
Figure 1.1 can be more appropriately be written as a function as given in
Figure 1.2.

```
(1)   function gcd (u, v: in integer) return integer is
(2)      y, t, z: integer;
(3)   begin
(4)      z := u;
(5)      y := v;
(6)      loop
(7)         exit when y = 0;
(8)         t := y;
(9)         y := z mod y;
(10)        z := t;
(11)     end loop;
(12)     return z;
(13) end gcd;
```

Figure 1.2   An Ada gcd function

In some languages, procedures are viewed as special cases of functions that return no value, as in C and C++, where procedures are called **void functions** (since the return value is declared to be void, or nonexistent). However, the importance of functions is much greater than this correspondence to procedures implies, since functions can be written in such a way that they correspond more closely to the mathematical abstraction of a function, and thus, unlike procedures, can be understood independently of any concept of a computer or runtime environment. This is the basis for the functional programming paradigm and the functional languages mentioned in the next section, and discussed in detail in Chapter 11.

Unit Abstractions.   Control can also be abstracted to include a collection of procedures that provide logically related services to other parts of a program and that form a **unit**, or stand-alone, part of the program. For example, a data management program may require the computation of statistical indices for stored data, such as mean, median, and standard deviation. The procedures that provide these operations can be collected into a program unit that can be translated separately and used by other parts of the program through a carefully controlled interface. This allows the program to be understood as a whole without needing to know the details of the services provided by the unit.

Note that what we have just described is essentially the same as a unit-level data abstraction, and is usually implemented using the same kind of module or package language mechanism. The only difference is that here the focus is on the operations rather than the data, but the goals of reusability and library building remain the same.

One kind of control abstraction that is difficult to fit into any one abstraction level is that of parallel programming mechanisms. Many modern computers have several processors or processing elements and are capable of processing different pieces of data simultaneously. A number of programming languages include mechanisms that allow for the parallel execution of parts of programs, as well as providing for synchronization and communication among such program parts. Java has mechanisms for declaring **threads** (separately executed control paths within the Java system) and **processes** (other programs executing outside the Java system). Ada provides the **task** mechanism for parallel execution. Ada's tasks are essentially a unit abstraction, whereas Java's threads and processes are classes and so are structured abstractions, albeit part of the standard `java.lang` package. Other languages provide different levels of parallel abstractions, even down to the statement level. Parallel programming mechanisms are surveyed in Chapter 14.

It is worth noting that almost all abstraction mechanisms are provided for human readability. If a programming language needs to describe only computation, then it needs only enough mechanisms to be able to describe all the computations that a Turing machine can perform, since, as we noted previously, a Turing machine can perform any known computation on a computer. Such a language is called **Turing complete**. As the following property shows, Turing completeness can be achieved with very few language mechanisms:

> A programming language is Turing complete provided it has integer variables and arithmetic and sequentially executes statements, which include assignment, selection (if) and loop (while) statements.

1.3 Computational Paradigms

Programming languages began by imitating and abstracting the operations of a computer. It is not surprising that the kind of computer for which they were written had a significant effect on their design. In most cases the computer in question was the von Neumann model mentioned in Section 1.1: a single central processing unit that sequentially executes instructions that operate on values stored in memory. Indeed, the result on Turing completeness of the previous section explicitly referred to sequential execution and the use of variables and assignment. These are typical features of a language based on the von Neumann model: variables represent memory values, and assignment allows the program to operate on these memory values.

A programming language that is characterized by these three properties—the sequential execution of instructions, the use of variables representing memory locations, and the use of assignment to change the values of variables—is called an **imperative** language, since its primary feature is a sequence of statements that represent commands, or imperatives. Sometimes such languages are also called **procedural**, but this has nothing explicitly to do with the concept of procedures discussed earlier.

Most programming languages today are imperative. But it is not necessary for a programming language to describe computation in this way. Indeed, the requirement that computation be described as a sequence of instructions, each operating on a single piece of data, is sometimes referred to as the **von Neumann bottleneck**, since it restricts the ability of a language to indicate parallel computation, that is, computation that can be applied to many different pieces of data simultaneously, and nondeterministic computation, or computation that does not depend on order.[2] Thus, it is reasonable to ask if there are ways to describe computation that are less dependent on the von Neumann model of a computer. Indeed there are, and these will be described shortly. Imperative programming languages therefore become only one **paradigm**, or pattern, for programming languages to follow.

Two alternative paradigms for describing computation come from mathematics. The **functional** paradigm comes from mathematics and is based on the abstract notion of a function as studied in the lambda calculus. The **logic** paradigm is based on symbolic logic. Each of these will be the subject of a subsequent chapter, but we will discuss them in a little more detail here. The importance of these paradigms is their correspondence to mathematical foundations, which allows for program behavior to be described abstractly and precisely, thus making it much easier to judge (even without a complete theoretical analysis) that a program will execute correctly, and permitting very concise code to be written even for very complex tasks.

A fourth programming paradigm has also become of enormous importance over the last ten years, and that is the **object-oriented** paradigm. Languages using this paradigm have been very successful in allowing programmers to write reusable, extensible code that operates in a way that mimics the real world, thus allowing programmers to use their natural intuition about the world to understand the behavior of a program and construct appropriate code (as with "natural language" syntax, this can also lead to misunderstanding and confusion, however, if relied on too extensively). In a sense, though, the object-oriented paradigm is an extension of the imperative paradigm, in that it relies primarily on the same sequential execution with a changing set of memory locations. The difference is that the resulting programs consist of a large number of very small pieces whose interactions are carefully controlled and yet easily changed. Still, the behavior of object-oriented programs is often even harder to understand fully and especially to describe abstractly, so that along with practical success comes a certain difficulty in precisely predicting behavior and determining correctness. Still, the object-oriented paradigm has essentially become the new standard, much as the imperative paradigm was in the past, and so will feature prominently throughout this book.

We treat each of these paradigms in a little more detail in the following, in roughly decreasing order of importance in current practice: object-oriented programming first, then functional programming, and finally logic programming. Later, an entire chapter will be devoted to each of these paradigms.

Object-oriented Programming.

The object-oriented paradigm is based on the notion of an object, which can be loosely described as a collection of memory locations together with all the operations that can change the values of these memory locations. The standard simple exam-

---

[2] Parallel and nondeterministic computations are related concepts; see Chapter 14.

ple of an object is a variable, with operations to assign it a value and to fetch its value. It represents computation as the interaction among, or communication between, a group of objects, each of which behaves like its own computer, with its own memory and its own operations. In many object-oriented languages, objects are grouped into **classes** that represent all the objects with the same properties. Classes are defined using declarations, much as structured types are declared in a language like C or Pascal. Objects are then created as particular examples, or **instances**, of a class.

Consider the example of the greatest common divisor of two integers from the previous section, which we wrote as either a procedure or a function with two incoming integer values and an outgoing integer result. The object-oriented view of the gcd is to consider it to be an operation, or **method**, available for integer-like objects. Indeed, in Java, such a gcd method is already available for BigInteger objects from the standard library (a BigInteger is an integer with an arbitrarily large number of digits). Here, we would like to show an implementation of gcd for ordinary integers in Java. Unfortunately, ordinary integers in Java are not "real" objects (an efficiency tradeoff, similar to C++, but unlike Smalltalk, in which all data values are implicitly objects).[3] Thus, we must include the integers themselves in the class that defines integer objects with a gcd method, as in the Java code in Figure 1.3.

```
(1)   public class IntWithGcd
(2)   { public IntWithGcd( int val ) { value = val; }
(3)     public int intValue() { return value; }
(4)     public int gcd ( int v )
(5)     { int z = value;
(6)       int y = v;
(7)       while ( y != 0 )
(8)       { int t = y;
(9)         y = z % y;
(10)        z = t;
(11)      }
(12)      return z;
(13)    }
(14)    private int value;
(15) }
```

Figure 1.3   A Java class with gcd method.

This class defines four things within it. First, a **constructor** is defined on line 2 (by definition it has the same name as the class, but no return type). A constructor allocates memory and provides initial values for the data of an object. In this case, the constructor needs to be provided with an integer, which is the "value" of the object. Second, a method is

---

[3] For those who know Java, it may appear reasonable to use the standard Integer class already available. Unfortunately, this class is defined to be "final," so a gcd method cannot be added to it. See, however, the BigInteger class in Java, which contains a gcd method similar to this one.

provided to access (but not change) this value (the `intValue` method on line 3). Third, the `gcd` method is defined in lines 4–11, but with only *one* integer parameter (since the first parameter is implicitly the value of the object on which `gcd` will be called). Finally, the integer `value` is defined on line 14 (this is called a *field* in Java). Note also that the constructor and methods are defined to have `public` access on lines 2, 3, and 4 (so they can be called by users), while the data field on line 14 is defined to be `private` (and thus inaccessible to the "outside world"). This is a feature of Java classes that relate to the encapsulation and information hiding properties of unit abstractions discussed in the previous section.

The `IntWithGcd` class can be used by defining a variable name to hold an object of the class as follows:

```
IntWithGcd x;
```

At first there is no actual object contained in x;[4] we must create, or **instantiate**, the object with the following statement:

```
x = new IntWithGcd(8);
```

Then we can ask x to provide the greatest common divisor of its own value and that of another integer by calling the `gcd` method (using a familiar *dot notation*):

```
int y = x.gcd(18); // y is now 2, the gcd of 8 & 18
```

Internally, the `gcd` method works essentially the same as the Ada procedure or function of Figures 1.1 and 1.2 of the previous section. The main difference is that the data object—in this case the one contained in x—is emphasized by placing it first in the call: `x.gcd(18)` instead of `gcd(x,18)`, and then giving `gcd` only one parameter instead of two (since the data in the first parameter of the imperative version of `gcd` is now already stored in the object contained in x).

We examine object-oriented languages in more detail in Chapter 10, including Java, C++, and Smalltalk.

Functional Programming. The functional paradigm bases the description of computation on the evaluation of functions or the application of functions to known values. For this reason, functional languages are sometimes called **applicative** languages. A functional programming language has as its basic mechanism the evaluation of a function, or the **function call**. This involves, besides the actual evaluation of functions, the passing of values as parameters to functions and the obtaining of the resultant values as **returned values** from functions. The functional paradigm involves no notion of variable or assignment to variables. In a sense, functional programming is the opposite of object-oriented programming: It concentrates on values and functions rather than memory locations. Also, repetitive operations are not expressed by loops (which require con-

---

[4] To be precise, x does not actually contain an object, but a reference to an object. This is studied in detail in Chapters 5 and 10.

trol variables to terminate) but by recursive functions. Indeed, the study of **recursive function theory** in mathematics has established the following property:

> A programming language is Turing complete if it has integer values, arithmetic functions on those values, and if it has a mechanism for defining new functions using existing functions, selection, and recursion.

It may seem surprising that a programming language can completely do away with variables and loops, but that is exactly what the functional paradigm does, and there are advantages to doing so. We have already stated two: that the language becomes more independent of the machine model, and that, because functional programs resemble mathematics, it is easier to draw precise conclusions about their behavior. Exactly how this is possible is left to later chapters. We content ourselves here with one example of functional programming.

Returning to the Ada procedure to compute the greatest common divisor of two integers that we gave in the last section, a functional version of this procedure is given in Figure 1.4.

```
(1) function gcd (u, v: in integer) return integer is
(2) begin
(3)    if v = 0 then
(4)       return u;
(5)    else
(6)       return gcd(v, u mod v);
(7)    end if;
(8) end gcd;
```

Figure 1.4   A functional version of the gcd function in Ada.

Note that this code does not use any local variables or loops, but does use recursion (it calls itself with a different set of parameters on line 6).

In an even more functionally oriented programming language, such as LISP, this function would be written as in Figure 1.5 (here and throughout the book we use the Scheme dialect of LISP).

```
(1) (define (gcd u v)
(2)    (if (= v 0) u
(3)        (gcd v (modulo u v))))
```

Figure 1.5   A gcd function in the Scheme dialect of LISP.

A few comments about this Scheme code may be worthwhile.

In LISP, programs are list expressions, that is, sequences of things separated by spaces and surrounded by parentheses, as in (+ 2 3). Programs are run by evaluating them as expressions, and expressions are evaluated by applying the first item in a list, which must be a function, to the rest of the items as arguments. Thus, (gcd 8 18) applies the gcd function to arguments 8 and 18. Similarly 2 + 3 is written (+ 2 3), which applies the + function to the values 2 and 3.

In the definition of the gcd function we have used the if-then-else function (lines 2 and 3 in Figure 1.5), which is just called "if"—the "then" and "else" are dispensed with. Thus, (if a b c) means "if *a* then *b* else *c*." Note that the "if" function represents control as well as the computation of a value: first a is evaluated and, depending on the result, either b or c is evaluated, with the resulting value becoming the returned value of the function. (This differs from the "if" statement of C or Ada, which does not have a value.)

Finally, LISP does not require a return-statement to indicate the value returned by a function. Simply stating the value itself implies that it is returned by the function.

An even more succinct version of this function can be written in the functional language Haskell:

```
gcd u v = if v == 0 then u else gcd v (u `mod` v)
```

Note the minimal use of parentheses (no parentheses are needed for parameters) and the use of backquotes (`mod`) to allow a function name to be used as an infix operator (written between its arguments).

Chapter 11 examines functional programming in detail, including Scheme and Haskell.

Logic Programming.   This language paradigm is based on symbolic logic. In a logic programming language, a program consists of a set of statements that describe what is true about a desired result, as opposed to giving a particular sequence of statements that must be executed in a fixed order to produce the result. A pure logic programming language has no need for control abstractions such as loops or selection. Control is supplied by the underlying system. All that is needed in a logic program is the statement of the properties of the computation. For this reason, logic programming is sometimes called **declarative programming**,[5] since properties are declared, but no execution sequence is specified. (Since there is such a removal from the details of machine execution, these languages are sometimes also referred to as **very-high-level languages**.)

In our running example of the greatest common divisor, we can state the properties of gcd in a form similar to that of a logic program as follows:

The gcd of *u* and *v* is *u* if *v* = 0.

The gcd of *u* and *v* is the same as the gcd of *v* and *u* mod *v* if *v* is not = 0.

A number of logic programming languages have been developed, but only one has become widely used: Prolog. The gcd statements given translate into Prolog as in Figure 1.6.[6]

---

[5] Functional programming is sometimes also referred to as "declarative," for similar reasons.

[6] A Prolog programmer would actually write this program in a somewhat more efficient form; see Chapter 12.

```
(1) gcd(U, V, U) :- V = 0.
(2) gcd(U, V, X) :- not (V = 0),
(3)                  Y is U mod V,
(4)                  gcd (V, Y, X).
```

Figure 1.6   Prolog clauses defining a gcd function.

In Prolog, the form of a program is a sequence of statements, called **clauses**, which are of the form

    a :- b, c, d

Such a clause roughly corresponds to the assertion that a is true if b and c and d are true. Unlike functional programming (and more like imperative programming), Prolog requires values to be represented by variables. However, variables do not represent memory locations as they do in imperative programming, but behave more as names for the results of partial computations, as they do in mathematics.

In the Prolog program of Figure 1.6, gcd has three parameters instead of two: The third represents the computed value (much as if gcd were a procedure), since gcd itself can only be true or false (that is, it can only succeed or fail). Note also the use of uppercase names for variables. This is a requirement in Prolog, where variables must be syntactically distinct from other language elements.

The first of the two clauses for gcd in (Figure 1.6, line 1) states that the gcd of U and V is U, provided V is equal to 0. The second clause (lines 2, 3, and 4) states that the gcd of U and V is X, provided V is not equal to 0 (line 2), and that X is the result of the gcd of V and Y (line 4), where Y is equal to U mod V (line 3). (The "is" clause for Y in line 3 is somewhat like assignment in an ordinary programming language and gives Y the value of U mod V.)

Details of Prolog and logic programming are treated in Chapter 12.

It needs to be stressed that, even though a programming language may exhibit most or all of the properties of one of the four paradigms just discussed, few languages adhere purely to one paradigm, but usually contain features of several paradigms. Indeed, as we saw, we were able to write a functional version of the gcd function in Ada, a language that is considered to be more of an imperative language. Nevertheless, it and most other modern imperative languages permit the definition of recursive functions, a mechanism that is generally considered to be functional. Similarly, the Scheme dialect of LISP, which is considered to be a functional language, does permit variables to be declared and assigned to, which is definitely an imperative feature. Scheme programs can also be written in an object-oriented style that closely approximates the object-oriented paradigm. Thus, we can refer to a programming **style** as following one (or more) of the paradigms. In a language that permits the expression of several different paradigms, which one is used depends on the kind of computation desired and the requirements of the development environment.

1.4 Language Definition

A programming language needs a complete, precise description. As obvious as that sounds, in the past many programming languages began with only informal English descriptions. Even today most languages are defined by a **reference manual** in English, although the language in such manuals has become increasingly formalized. Such manuals will always be needed, but there has been increasing acceptance of the need for programming languages to have definitions that are formally precise. Such definitions have, in a few cases, been completely given, but currently it is customary to give a formal definition only of parts of a programming language.

The importance of a precise definition for a programming language should be clear from its use to describe computation. Without a clear notion of the effect of language constructs, we have no clear idea of what computation is actually being performed. Moreover, it should be possible to reason mathematically about programs, and to do this requires formal verification or proof of the behavior of a program. Without a formal definition this is impossible.

But there are other compelling reasons for the need for a formal definition. We have already mentioned the need for machine or implementation independence. The best way to achieve this is through standardization, which requires an independent and precise language definition that is universally accepted. Standards organizations such as ANSI (American National Standards Institute) and ISO (International Organization for Standardization) have published definitions for many languages, including Pascal, FORTRAN, C, C++, Ada, and Prolog.

A further reason for a formal definition is that, inevitably in the programming process, difficult questions arise about program behavior and interaction. Programmers need an adequate reference to answer such questions besides the often-used trial-and-error process: It can happen that such questions need to be answered already at the design stage and may result in major design changes.

Finally, the requirements of a formal definition provide discipline during the design of a language. Often a language designer will not realize the consequences of design decisions until he or she is required to produce a clear definition.

Language definition can be loosely divided into two parts: **syntax**, or structure, and **semantics**, or meaning. We discuss each of these categories in turn.

Language Syntax.   The syntax of a programming language is in many ways like the grammar of a natural language. It is the description of the ways different parts of the language may be combined to form other parts. As an example, the syntax of the if-statement in C may be described in words as follows:

An if-statement consists of the word "if" followed by an expression inside parentheses, followed by a statement, followed by an optional else part consisting of the word "else" and another statement.

The description of language syntax is one of the areas where formal definitions have gained acceptance, and the syntax of almost all languages is now given using **context-free grammars**. For example, a context-free grammar rule for the C if-statement can be written as follows:

$$<\text{if-statement}> ::= \text{if } (<\text{expression}>) <\text{statement}>$$
$$[\text{else } <\text{statement}>]$$

or (using special characters and formatting):

$$\textit{if-statement} \rightarrow \texttt{if } (\textit{expression}) \textit{ statement}$$
$$[\texttt{else } \textit{statement}]$$

An issue closely related to the syntax of a programming language is its **lexical structure**. This is similar to spelling in a natural language. The lexical structure of a programming language is the structure of the words of the language, which are usually called **tokens**. In the example of a C if-statement, the words "if" and "else" are tokens. Other tokens in programming languages include identifiers (or names), symbols for operations, such as "+" and "<=" and special punctuation symbols such as the semicolon (";") and the period (".").

In this book we shall consider syntax and lexical structure together, and a more detailed study is found in Chapter 4.

Language Semantics.   Syntax represents only the surface structure of a language and thus is only a small part of a language definition. The semantics, or meaning, of a language is much more complex and difficult to describe precisely. The first difficulty is that "meaning" can be defined in many different ways; typically describing the meaning of a piece of code involves some kind of description of the effects of executing it, and there is no standard way to do this. Moreover, the meaning of a particular mechanism may involve interactions with other mechanisms in the language, so that a comprehensive description of its meaning in all contexts may become extremely complex.

To continue with our example of the C if-statement, its semantics may be described in words as follows (adapted from Kernighan and Richie [1988]):

An if-statement is executed by first evaluating its expression, which must have arithmetic or pointer type, including all side effects, and if it compares unequal to 0, the statement following the expression is executed. If there is an else part, and the expression is 0, the statement following the "else" is executed.

This description in itself points out some of the difficulty in specifying semantics, even for a simple mechanism such as the if-statement. The description makes no mention of what happens if the condition evaluates to 0, but there is no else part (presumably nothing happens; that is, the program continues at the point after the if-statement). Another important question is whether the if-statement is "safe" in the sense that there are no other language mechanisms that may permit the statements inside an if-statement to be executed without the corresponding evaluation of the if expression. If so, then the if-statement provides adequate protection from errors during execution, such as division by zero:

```
if (x != 0) y = 1 / x;
```

Otherwise, additional protection mechanisms may be necessary (or at least the programmer must be aware of the possibility of circumventing the if expression).

The alternative to this informal description of semantics is to use a formal method. However, no generally accepted method, analogous to the use of context-free grammars for syntax, exists here either. Indeed, it is still not customary for a formal definition of the semantics of a programming language to be given at all. Nevertheless, several notational systems for formal definitions have been developed and are increasingly in use. These include **operational semantics**, **denotational semantics**, and **axiomatic semantics**.

Language semantics are implicit in many of the chapters of this book, but semantic issues are more specifically addressed in Chapters 5 and 9. Chapter 13 discusses formal methods of semantic definition, including operational, denotational, and axiomatic semantics.

1.5 Language Translation

For a programming language to be useful, it must have a **translator**, that is, a program that accepts other programs written in the language in question and that either executes them directly or transforms them into a form suitable for execution. A translator that executes a program directly is called an **interpreter**, while a translator that produces an equivalent program in a form suitable for execution is called a **compiler**.

Interpretation is a one-step process, in which both the program and the input are provided to the interpreter, and the output is obtained:

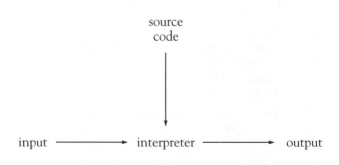

An interpreter can be viewed as a simulator for a machine whose "machine language" is the language being translated.

Compilation, on the other hand, is at least a two-step process: the original program (or **source program**) is input to the compiler, and a new program (or **target program**) is output from the compiler. This target program may then be executed, if it is in a form suitable for direct execution (i.e., in machine language). More commonly, the target language is assembly language, and the target program must be translated by an **assembler** into an object program, and then **linked** with other object programs, and **loaded** into appropriate memory locations before it can be executed. Sometimes the target language is even another programming language, in which case a compiler for that language must be used to obtain an executable object program.

The compilation process can be visualized as follows:

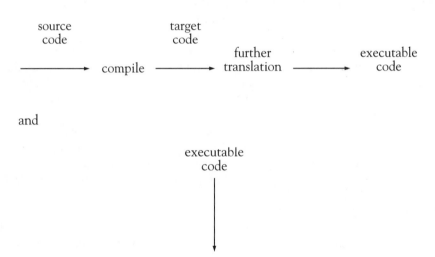

and

It is also possible to have translators that are intermediate between interpreters and compilers: a translator may translate a source program into an intermediate language and then interpret the intermediate language. Such translators could be called **pseudointerpreters**, since they execute the program without producing a target program, but they process the entire source program before execution begins.

It is important to keep in mind that a language is different from a particular translator for that language. It *is* possible for a language to be defined by the behavior of a particular interpreter or compiler (a so-called **definitional** translator), but this is not common (and even problematic, in view of the need for a formal definition discussed in the last section). More often, a language definition exists independently, and a translator may or may not adhere closely to the language definition (one hopes the former). When writing programs one must always be aware of those features and properties that depend on a specific translator and are not part of the language definition. There are significant advantages to be gained from avoiding nonstandard features as much as possible.

Both compilers and interpreters must perform similar operations when translating a source program. First, a **lexical analyzer**, or **scanner**, must convert the textual representation of the program as a sequence of characters into a form that is easier to process, typically by grouping characters into **tokens** representing basic language entities, such as keywords, identifiers, and constants. Then a **syntax analyzer** or **parser** must determine the structure of the sequence of tokens provided to it by the scanner. Finally, a **semantic analyzer** must determine enough of the meaning of a program to allow execution or generation of a target program to take place. Typically, these **phases** of translation do not occur separately but are combined in various ways. A language translator must also maintain a **runtime environment**, in which suitable memory space for program data is allocated, and that records the progress of the execution of the program. An interpreter usually maintains the runtime environment internally as a part of its management of the execution of the program, while a compiler must maintain the runtime environment indirectly by adding suitable operations to the target code. Finally, a language may also require a **preprocessor**, which is run prior to translation to transform a program into a form suitable for translation.

The properties of a programming language that can be determined prior to execution are called **static** properties, while properties that can be determined only during execution are called **dynamic** properties. This distinction is not very useful for interpreters, but it is for compilers: A compiler can *only* make use of a language's static properties. Typical static properties of a language are its lexical and syntactic structure. In some languages, such as C and Ada, important semantic properties are also static: data types of variables are a significant example; see Chapter 6.

A programming language can be designed to be more suitable for interpretation or compilation. For instance, a language that is more dynamic, that is, has fewer static properties, is more suitable for interpretation and is more likely to be interpreted. On the other hand, a language with a strong static structure is more likely to be compiled. Historically, imperative languages have had more static properties and have been compiled, while functional and logic programming languages have been more dynamic and have been interpreted. Of course, a compiler or interpreter can exist for any language, regardless of its dynamic or static properties.

The static and dynamic properties of a language can also affect the nature of the runtime environment. In a language with **static allocation** only—all variables are assumed to occupy a fixed position in memory for the duration of the program's execution—a **fully static** environment may be used. For more dynamically oriented languages, a more complex **fully dynamic** environment must be used. Midway between these is the typical

stack-based environment of languages like C and Ada, which has both static and dynamic aspects. (Chapter 8 describes these in more detail.)

Efficiency may also be an issue in determining whether a language is more likely to be interpreted or compiled. Interpreters are inherently less efficient than compilers, since they must simulate the actions of the source program on the underlying machine. Compilers can also boost the efficiency of the target code by performing code improvements, or **optimizations**, often by making several **passes** over the source program to analyze its behavior in detail. Thus, a programming language that needs efficient execution is likely to be compiled rather than interpreted.

Situations may also exist when an interpreter may be preferred over a compiler. Interpreters usually have an interactive mode, so that the user can enter programs directly from a terminal and also supply input to the program and receive output using the interpreter alone. For example, a Scheme interpreter can be used to provide immediate input to a procedure as follows:

```
> (gcd 8 18)  ;; calls gcd with the values 8 and 18
2             ;; the interpreter prints the returned
              ;; value
```

By contrast, in a compiled language, such as C, Ada, or Java,[7] the programmer must write out by hand the interactive input and output. For example, we provide complete runnable code for the gcd example in these three languages in Figures 1.7, 1.8, and 1.9, respectively.[8] Note in particular the code overhead to get line-oriented input in Java (window-oriented input is actually easier, but not covered here). This overhead, plus the lack of the compilation step, makes an interpreter more suitable than a compiler in some cases for instruction and for program development. By contrast, a language can also be designed to allow **one-pass** compilation, so that the compilation step is efficient enough for instructional use (C has this property).

An important property of a language translator is its response to errors in a source program. Ideally, a translator should attempt to correct errors, but this can be extremely difficult. Failing that, a translator should issue appropriate error messages. It is generally not enough to issue only one error message when the first error is encountered, though some translators do this for efficiency and simplicity. More appropriate is **error recovery**, which allows the translator to proceed with the translation, so that further errors may be discovered.

---

[7] Java code is compiled to a machine-independent set of instruction codes called bytecode (because each instruction code occupies a single byte). The **bytecode** is then interpreted by the **Java Virtual Machine** (JVM). This allows compiled Java code to be run on any machine that has an available JVM.

[8] We do not explain this code here, but it can be used with very little modification to run most of the examples from this book in these languages.

```
#include <stdio.h>

int gcd(int u, int v)
{ if (v == 0) return u;
  else return gcd (v, u % v);
}

main()
{ int x, y;
  printf("Input two integers:\n");
  scanf("%d%d",&x,&y);
  printf("The gcd of %d and %d is %d\n",x,y,gcd(x,y));
  return 0;
}
```

Figure **1.7**   A Complete C Program with a gcd function

```
with Text_IO; use Text_IO;
with Ada.Integer_Text_IO;
use Ada.Integer_Text_IO;

procedure gcd_prog is

  function gcd (u, v: in integer) return integer is
  begin
    if v = 0 then
      return u;
    else
      return gcd(v, u mod v);
    end if;
  end gcd;

  x: Integer;
  y: Integer;
begin
  put_line("Input two integers:");
  get(x);
  get(y);
  put("The gcd of ");
  put(x);
  put(" and ");
  put(y);
  put(" is ");
  put(gcd(x,y));
  new_line;
end gcd_prog;
```

Figure **1.8**   A Complete Ada Program with a gcd function.

```
import java.io.*;

class IntWithGcd
{ public IntWithGcd( int val ) { value = val; }
  public int getValue() { return value; }
  public int gcd ( int v )
  { int z = value;
    int y = v;
    while ( y != 0 )
    { int t = y;
      y = z % y;
      z = t;
    }
    return z;
  }
  private int value;
}

class GcdProg
{ public static void main (String args[])
  { System.out.println("Input two integers:");
    BufferedReader in =
      new BufferedReader(new
      InputStreamReader(System.in));
    try
      { IntWithGcd x = new
        IntWithGcd(Integer.parseInt(in.readLine()));
        int y = Integer.parseInt(in.readLine());
        System.out.print("The gcd of " + x.getValue()
                        + " and " + y + " is ");
        System.out.println(x.gcd(y));
      }
    catch ( Exception e)
    { System.out.println(e);
      System.exit(1);
    }
  }
}
```

Figure 1.9 A Complete Java Program with an `IntWithGcd` class

Errors may be classified according to the stage in translation at which they occur. Lexical errors occur during lexical analysis; these are generally limited to the use of illegal characters. An example in C is

```
x@ = 2
```

The character @ is not a legal character in the language.

Misspellings such as "whille" for "while" are often not caught by a lexical analyzer, since it will assume that an unknown character string is an identifier, such as the name of a variable. Such an error will be caught

by the parser, however. Syntax errors include missing tokens and malformed expressions, such as

```
if (scaleFactor != 0   /* missing right parenthesis */
```

or

```
adjustment = base + * scaleFactor
            /* missing operand between + and * */
```

Semantic errors can be either static (i.e., found prior to execution),
such as incompatible types or undeclared variables, or dynamic (found
during execution), such as an out-of-range subscript or division by zero.

A further class of errors that may occur in a program are **logic** errors.
These are errors that the programmer makes that cause the program to
behave in an erroneous or undesirable way. For example, the following C
fragment

```
x = u;
y = v;
while (y != 0)
{ t = y;
  y = x * y;
  x = t;
}
```

will cause an infinite loop during execution if u and v are 1. However, the
fragment breaks no rules of the language and must be considered semantically correct from the language viewpoint, even though it does not do
what was intended. Thus, logic errors are not errors at all from the point
of view of language translation.[9]

A language definition will often include a specification of what
errors must be caught prior to execution (for compiled languages), what
errors must generate a runtime error, and what errors may go undetected.
The precise behavior of a translator in the presence of errors is usually
unspecified, however.

Finally, a translator needs to provide user options for debugging, for
interfacing with the operating system, and perhaps with a software development environment. These options, such as specifying files for inclusion,
disabling optimizations, or turning on tracing or debugging information,
are the **pragmatics** of a programming language translator. Occasionally,
facilities for pragmatic directives, or **pragmas**, are part of the language definition. For example, in Ada the declaration

```
pragma LIST(ON);
```

turns on the generation of a listing by a compiler at the point it is encountered, and

---

[9] Syntax and semantic errors could be described as inconsistencies between a
program and the specification of the language, while logic errors are inconsistencies between a program and its own specification.

```
pragma LIST(OFF);
```

turns listing generation off again.

1.6 Language Design

We have spoken of a programming language as a tool for describing computation; we have indicated that differing views of computation can result in widely differing languages but that machine and human **readability** are overriding requirements. It is the challenge of programming language design to achieve the power, expressiveness, and comprehensibility that human readability requires while at the same time retaining the precision and simplicity that is needed for machine translation.

Human readability is a complex and subtle requirement. It depends to a large extent on the facilities a programming language has for abstraction. A. N. Whitehead emphasized the power of abstract notation in 1911: "By relieving the brain of all unnecessary work, a good notation sets it free to concentrate on more advanced problems. . . . Civilization advances by extending the number of important operations which we can perform without thinking about them."

A successful programming language has facilities for the natural expression of the structure of data (**data abstraction**) and for the structure of the computational process for the solution of a problem (**control abstraction**). A good example of the effect of abstraction is the introduction of recursion into the programming language Algol60. C. A. R. Hoare, in his 1980 Turing Award Lecture, describes the effect his attendance at an Algol60 course had on him: "It was there that I first learned about recursive procedures and saw how to program the sorting method which I had earlier found such difficulty in explaining. It was there that I wrote the procedure, immodestly named QUICKSORT, on which my career as a computer scientist is founded."

The overriding goal of abstraction in programming language design is **complexity control**. A human being can retain only a certain amount of detail at once. To understand and construct complex systems, humans must control how much detail needs to be understood at any one time.

Abelson and Sussman, in their book *Structure and Interpretation of Computer Programs* [1996], have emphasized the importance of complexity control as follows: "We control complexity by building abstractions that hide details when appropriate. We control complexity by establishing conventional interfaces that enable us to construct systems by combining standard, well-understood pieces in a 'mix and match' way. We control complexity by establishing new languages for describing a design, each of which emphasizes particular aspects of the design and deemphasizes others."

In Chapter 3 we study additional language design issues that help to promote readability and complexity control.

Exercises

1.1 The following is a C function that computes the number of (decimal) digits in an integer:

```
int numdigits(int x)
{ int t = x, n = 1;
  while (t >= 10)
  { n++;
    t = t / 10;
  }
  return n;
}
```

Rewrite this function in functional style.

1.2 Write a `numdigits` function (as in the previous exercise) in any of the following languages (or in any language for which you have a translator): **(a)** Pascal, **(b)** Scheme, **(c)** Haskell, **(d)** Prolog, **(e)** Ada, **(f)** FORTRAN, **(g)** Java, and **(h)** BASIC.

1.3 Rewrite the `numdigits` function of Exercise 1.1 so that it will compute the number of digits to any base (such as base 2, base 16, base 8). You may do this exercise for any of the following languages or any other language for which you have a translator: **(a)** C, **(b)** Pascal, **(c)** Ada, **(d)** Java, **(e)** FORTRAN, **(f)** Scheme, **(g)** Haskell, **(h)** Prolog, and **(i)** BASIC.

1.4 Write a program similar to those in Figures 1.7, 1.8, or 1.9 that tests your `numdigits` function from Exercises 1.1, 1.2, or 1.3 in C, Ada, Java, or C++.

1.5 The C and Java versions of the greatest common divisor calculation in this chapter have used the remainder operation %, while the Ada, Scheme, Haskell, and Prolog versions have used the modulo operation. **(a)** What is the difference between remainder and modulo? **(b)** Can this difference lead to any differences in the result of a gcd computation?

1.6 The `numdigits` function of Exercise 1.1 will not work for negative integers. Rewrite it so that it will.

1.7 The following C function computes the factorial of an integer:

```
int fact (int n)
{ if n <= 1) return 1;
  else return n * fact (n - 1);
}
```

Rewrite this function into imperative style (i.e., using variables and eliminating recursion).

1.8 Write a factorial function in any of the following languages (or in any language for which you have a translator): **(a)** Pascal, **(b)** Scheme, **(c)** Prolog, **(d)** Java, **(e)** Ada, **(f)** FORTRAN, and **(g)** BASIC.

1.9 Write a program similar to those in Figures 1.7, 1.8, or 1.9 that tests your factorial function from Exercises 1.8 or 1.9 in C, Ada, Java, or C++.

1.10 Factorials grow extremely rapidly, and overflow is soon reached in the factorial function of Exercise 1.7. What happens during execution when overflow occurs? How easy is it to correct this problem in C? In any of the languages you have used in Exercise 1.8?

1.11 For any of the languages of Exercise 1.8, find where (if anywhere) it is specified in your translator manual what happens on integer overflow. Compare this, if possible, to the requirements of the language standard.

1.12 Rewrite the `IntWithGcd` Java class of Section 1.3 to use recursion in the computation of the greatest common divisor.

1.13 The `IntWithGcd` Java class of Section 1.3 has a possible design flaw in that the `gcd` method takes an integer parameter rather than another object of class `IntWithGcd`. Rewrite the `IntWithGcd` class to correct this. Discuss whether you think this new design is better or worse than the one given in the text.

1.14 For any of the following languages, determine if strings are part of the language definition and whether your translator offers string facilities that are not part of the language definition: **(a)** C, **(b)** Pascal, **(c)** Ada, **(d)** C++, **(e)** Java, **(f)** Scheme, **(g)** Haskell, **(h)** FORTRAN, and **(i)** BASIC.

1.15 Add explicit interactive input and output to the Scheme gcd function of Section 1.3 (that is, make it into a "compiler-ready" program in a similar manner to the programs in Figures 1.7, 1.8, and 1.9).

1.16 Add explicit interactive input and output to the Prolog program for gcd in Section 1.3.

1.17 The following C program differs from Figure 1.7 in that it contains a number of errors. Classify each error as to whether it is lexical, syntactic, static semantic, dynamic semantic, or logical:

```
(1)  #include <stdio.h>

(2)  int gcd(int u#, double v);
(3)  { if (v = 0) return 0;
(4)     else return gcd (v, u# % v);
(5)  }

(6)  main()
(7)  {  int x, y;
(8)     printf("Input two integers: ");
(9)     scanf("%d%d",&x,&y);
(10)    printf("The gcd of %d and %d is %d\n",
                 x,y,Gcd(x,y));
(11)    return;
(12) }
```

1.18 Describe the syntax of the do-while-statement in C.

1.19 Describe the semantics of the do-while-statement in C.

1.20 Is it possible in any of the following languages to execute the statements inside an if-statement without evaluating the expression of the if? **(a)** C, **(b)** Pascal, **(c)** FORTRAN, **(d)** Ada, and **(e)** Java? Why or why not?

1.21 What are the reasons for the inclusion of many different kinds of loop statements in a programming language? (Address your answer in particular to the need for the while-, do-while-, and for-statements in C and Java, or the while-, loop-, and for-statements in Ada.)

1.22 Given the following properties of a variable in C (or Java or Ada), state which are static and which are dynamic, and why: **(a)** its value, **(b)** its data type, and **(c)** its name.

1.23 Given the following properties of a variable in Scheme, state which are static and which are dynamic, and why: **(a)** its value, **(b)** its data type, and **(c)** its name.

1.24 Prove that a language is Turing complete if it contains integer variables, integer arithmetic, assignment, and while-statements. (*Hint:* Use the characterization of Turing completeness stated at the end of Section 1.2, and eliminate the need for if-statements.)

1.25 Pick one of the following statements and argue both for and against it:
  (a) A programming language is solely a mathematical notation for describing computation.
  (b) A programming language is solely a tool for getting computers to perform complex tasks.
  (c) A programming language should make it easy for programmers to write code quickly and easily.
  (d) A programming language should make it easy for programmers to read and understand code with a minimum of comments.

1.26 Since most languages can be used to express any algorithm, why should it matter which programming language we use to solve a programming problem? (Try arguing both that it should and that it shouldn't matter.)

1.27 Java and C++ are both considered object-oriented languages. To what extent is it possible to write imperative-style code in either of these languages? Functional-style code?

1.28 Stroustrup [1997] contains the following statement (page 9): "A programming language serves two related purposes: it provides a vehicle for the programmer to specify actions to be executed, and it provides a set of concepts for the programmer to use when thinking about what can be done." Compare and contrast this statement to the definition of a programming language given in this chapter.

Notes and References

An early description of the von Neumann architecture and the use of a program stored as data to control the execution of a computer is in Burks, Goldstine, and von Neumann [1947]. A similar view of the definition of a programming language we have used is given in Horowitz [1984]. Human readability is discussed in Ghezzi and Jazayeri [1997], but with more emphasis on software engineering. Attempts have been made to study readability from a psychological, or cognitive, perspective, where it is called **comprehension**. See Rosson [1997] for a survey of research in this direction.

References for the major programming languages used as examples in this text are as follows. A reference for the C programming language is Kernighan and Ritchie [1988]. The latest C standard is ISO 9899 [1999]. C++ is described in Stroustrup [1994] [1997], and Ellis and Stroustrup [1990]; an introductory text is Lippman and Lajoie [1998]; the international standard for C++ is ISO 14882-1 [1998]. Java is described in many books, including Horstmann and Cornell [1999], Arnold, Gosling, and Holmes [2000], and Flanagan [1999]; the Java language specification is given in Gosling, Joy, Steele and Bracha [2000]. Ada exists in two versions: The original is sometimes called Ada83, and is described by its reference manual (ANSI-1815A [1983]); a newer version is Ada95,[10] and is described by its international standard (ISO 8652 [1995]). Standard texts for Ada include Cohen [1996], Barnes [1998], and Feldman and Koffman [1999]. Pascal is described in Cooper [1983]. FORTRAN also exists in several versions: Fortran77, Fortran90 and Fortran95. An introductory text that covers all three is Chapman [1997]; a more advanced reference is Metcalf and Reid [1999]. Scheme is described in Dybvig [1996] and Abelson and Sussman [1996]; a language definition can be found in Abelson et al. [1998]. Haskell is covered in Hudak [2000] and Thompson [1999]. The ML functional language (related to Haskell) is covered in Paulson [1996] and Ullman [1997]. The standard reference for Prolog is Clocksin and Mellish [1994]. The logic paradigm is discussed in Kowalski [1979], and the functional paradigm in Backus [1978] and Hudak [1989]. Smalltalk is presented in Lewis [1995] and Sharp [1997].

The Turing completeness property for imperative languages stated on page 13 is proved in Böhm and Jacopini [1966]. The Turing completeness result for functional languages on page 17 can be extracted from results on recursive function theory in such texts as Sipser [1997] and Hopcroft and Ullman [1979]. Language translation techniques are described in Louden [1997] and Aho, Sethi, and Ullman [1986]. The quote from A. N. Whitehead in Section 1.6 is in Whitehead [1911], and Hoare's Turing Award Lecture quote is in Hoare [1981].

---

[10] Since Ada95 is an extension of Ada83, we will indicate only those features that are specifically Ada95 when they are not part of Ada83.

2 History

Programming languages describe computation for use by computers, particularly electronic digital computers with stored program capability. The history of programming languages is therefore tied to the evolution of these kinds of machines, which began in the 1940s. It is remarkable that the subject has developed so richly in such a few short years.

In the sections that follow we discuss the half century or so of programming language history that followed the development of the modern computer, plus the one significant attempt to construct a mechanical general-purpose computer that predated this development. This is a very brief history that leaves out many interesting programming languages and developments. The interested reader is encouraged to consult the primary references at the end of the chapter and the further references contained in those.

There is, however, also a history of "programming languages" that developed independently of the existence of appropriate machines. This history is closely tied to the second important function of programming languages: the need to describe computation and algorithms for human use. It is also tied to the development of mathematics and mathematical notation. Two examples of this kind that appeared just before the devel-

opment of the modern computer include the **Plankalkül** of Konrad Zuse
and the **lambda calculus** of Alonzo Church. The second of these has had
an important influence on functional programming languages and is
studied further in Chapter 11.

But the need to describe computation goes back to early antiquity,
for of course there was a need to calculate even then: sizes of land
parcels, sums of money, amounts of property. It is interesting that one of
the earliest uses of written human language was to describe computational methods for performing such calculations, something programming languages do so well today. In fact, right through the Greek flower-
ing of mathematics, mathematical processes were seen primarily in terms
of algorithms: how to calculate to get certain results. Indeed, the stylized
language used to describe algorithms on cuneiform tablets resembles very
much a "programming language" in which sample data are used to
describe a general computation. Here is an example of such a description, adapted from Knuth [1972]:

> A cistern.
> The length equals the height.
> A certain volume of dirt has been excavated.
> The cross-sectional area plus this volume comes to 120.
> The length is 5. What is the width?
> Add 1 to 5, getting 6.
> Divide 6 into 120, obtaining 20.
> Divide 5 into 20, obtaining the width, 4.
> This is the procedure.

As mathematics developed, the description of algorithms became
less important in relation to the theorems and proofs that became the
primary content of modern mathematics. Mathematicians concentrated
on the "what" rather than the "how." Now, however, with the expand-
ing interest in computers and computation, there has been a renewed
interest in computational mathematics and constructive methods, that
is, algorithms that construct mathematical objects, as opposed to proofs
that establish their properties without actual constructions.

2.1 Early History: The First Programmer

The first computers with stored programs and a central processor that executed instructions provided by users were built in the late 1940s by a team
led by John von Neumann. "Real" programming could be said to date from
these machines. Yet there were many previous machines that could be
"programmed" in the sense that data could be supplied, usually in the form

of cards or paper tape, that would affect what the machine did. One example is the Jacquard loom of the early 1800s, which automatically translated card patterns into cloth designs.

The first machine of this type devoted entirely to computation was invented by Charles Babbage in the 1830s and 1840s. "Programs" for his Analytical Engine consisted of a sequence of cards with data and operations. Although only parts of the machine were ever built,[1] several examples of the computations it could perform were developed by Ada Augusta, Countess Lovelace, a daughter of Lord Byron. For this reason, she is considered to be the first programmer, and the language Ada has been named after her.

Ada Lovelace had a remarkable and somewhat tragic life. Perhaps the most remarkable thing about her was her keen grasp of the significance of the concept of a computer, and particularly that of the stored program, building on the idea of the cards of the Jacquard loom:

> The distinctive characteristic of the Analytical Engine, and that which has rendered it possible to endow mechanism with such extensive faculties as bid fair to make this engine the executive right-hand of abstract algebra, is the introduction into it of the principle which Jacquard devised for regulating, by means of punched cards, the most complicated patterns in the fabrication of brocaded stuffs. . . . We may say most aptly, that the Analytical Engine weaves algebraical patterns just as the Jacquard loom weaves flowers and leaves. . . . In enabling mechanism to combine together general symbols in successions of unlimited variety and extent, a uniting link is established between the operations of matter and the abstract mental processes of the most abstract branch of mathematical science. A new, a vast, and a powerful language is developed for the future use of analysis, in which to wield its truths so that these may become of more speedy and accurate practical application for the purposes of mankind than the means hitherto in our possession have rendered possible. (Morrison and Morrison [1961], p. 252)

A further quote shows the extent to which she also understood the basic symbolic nature of computation, something that has been only slowly reunderstood in the modern computing community:

> Many persons who are not conversant with mathematical studies, imagine that because the business of the engine is to give its results in numerical notation, the nature of its processes must consequently be arithmetical and numerical, rather than algebraical and analytical. This is an error. The engine can arrange and combine its numerical quantities exactly as if they were letters or any other general symbols; and in fact it might bring out its results in algebraical notation, were provisions made accordingly. (Ibid., p. 273)

---

[1] In 1991 Babbage's Difference Engine, a simpler computer than the Analytical Engine, but which was also never completed, was constructed at the National Museum of Science in London, England, from drawings he left. The success of this project indicates that the Analytical Engine, had it been built, would probably have worked—100 years before its electronic counterpart was invented.

2.2 The 1950s: The First Programming Languages

With the advent of general-purpose digital computers with stored programs in the early 1950s, the task of programming became a significant challenge. Early programs were written directly in machine codes or sequences of bit patterns. This soon gave way to assembly languages, which use symbols and mnemonics to express the underlying machine codes. However, assembly languages are highly machine dependent and are written using a syntax very unlike natural language. They are sometimes referred to as "low-level" languages.

The first high-level language was **FORTRAN**, developed between 1954 and 1957 by a team at IBM led by John Backus. It was designed primarily for scientific and computational programming, as its name implies (FORmula TRANslation), and its descendants are still significant in scientific applications today. However, it has also been used for general-purpose programming, and many new features taken from other languages have been added through the years (FORTRAN II, FORTRAN IV, FORTRAN66, FORTRAN77, FORTRAN90). The survival of FORTRAN has been at least partially due to the fact that compilers for it are still among the most efficient available, in that they produce very fast code. This emphasis on efficiency was in fact a major goal of the initial design effort, since the general belief at the time was that translators for high-level languages would produce such inefficient code that writing programs in such languages would be of little practical use. FORTRAN proved, at least partially, that this was not the case: Though the machine code generated by a FORTRAN compiler was somewhat less efficient than what a human could produce directly, its speed was still comparable, and the modest sacrifice in execution efficiency was more than offset by the huge increase in the speed with which a program could be written using the higher-level language.

Since FORTRAN was the first high-level programming language, most of its features were new. Some of them have become standard in later languages. These include the array, loops controlled by an indexed variable, and a branching if-statement. Following FORTRAN, two other languages were developed that also had a major impact on programming and the use of computers: COBOL and Algol60.

COBOL (COmmon Business-Oriented Language) was developed by the U.S. Department of Defense (1959–1960) by a team led by Grace Hopper of the Navy. This language was quickly adopted by banks and corporations for large-scale record-keeping and other business applications. It is perhaps still the most widely used programming language but has been largely ignored by the academic community. (Business schools often offer courses on COBOL programming, but computer science departments generally do not.) This is partially due to the extreme wordiness of the language. (The design was supposed to permit nonprogrammers to read and understand programs, but it only complicated the syntax without providing true readability.) Complex algorithms are also extremely difficult to program in COBOL, and the language has added only a few new features to language design. However, those features are significant. Features that COBOL did pioneer were: (1) the record structure for organizing data, (2) the separation of data structures from the execution section of a program, and (3) versatile formatting for output using "pictures," or examples of the desired format (still used in some database languages today).

Algol60 (ALGOrithmic Language) was developed by a committee (1958–1960) to provide a general, expressive language for describing algorithms, both in research and in practical applications. It is hard to overestimate the influence and importance of this language for future language development. Most of the current imperative languages are derivatives of Algol, including Pascal, C, and Ada. Research papers today still often use Algol or Algol-like syntax to describe algorithms. It achieved widespread practical acceptance in Europe for general programming tasks, but was rarely used outside of academic circles in the United States.

Algol60 introduced many concepts into programming, including free-format, structured statements, begin-end blocks, type declarations for variables, recursion, and pass-by-value parameters. It also implicitly introduced the stack-based runtime environment for block-structured languages, which is still the major method for implementing such languages today. (See Chapter 8.) And it was the first to use Backus-Naur forms (BNF) notation to define syntax. (See Chapter 4.)

At the same time that these three languages were created, based on the standard von Neumann architecture of computers, other languages were being developed based on the mathematical concept of function. Two major examples of such languages are LISP and APL.

LISP (LISt Processor) was designed at MIT in the late 1950s by John McCarthy, based on general list structures and function application. It and its many variants are still in use today in many artificial intelligence applications. (Some common variants are MacLisp, Franz Lisp, Common LISP, and Scheme.) It was based on a uniform data structure, the S-expression, and function application as the fundamental notion of computation. It pioneered general notions of computation and environment and introduced "garbage collection," or automatic reclamation of memory no longer in use, as a method of maintaining runtime storage allocation. Since it is based on a computational principle that is very different from the usual von Neumann architecture, it could not run efficiently on existing machines. However, machine architectures have been developed that are specifically designed to run LISP programs, and many practical decision-making systems have been written in LISP. Recent improvements in translation techniques and machine execution speed have made functional languages and functional techniques much more useful for general programming, and the influence of LISP has grown with time. Now almost all programming languages include features such as recursion that originated with LISP.

APL (A Programming Language) was designed by K. Iverson at Harvard University in the late 1950s and at IBM in the early 1960s as a language for programming mathematical computations, particularly those involving arrays and matrices. It is also functional in style and has a large set of operators that allow most iterations to be performed completely automatically. In the 1960s a version of APL was used as the basis for one of the first time-sharing systems, on an IBM 360. Its major drawbacks were that it has no structuring and that it uses a Greek symbol set that requires the use of a special terminal. Programs written in APL are also extremely difficult to read. Nevertheless, the power of its operations have given it a loyal following, and it strongly influenced the language FP (see Section 2.5), which itself significantly influenced modern functional languages. Since 1990 its development continues in the language J, which extends APL with structured features and dispenses with the special symbols so it can run on standard displays.

It is interesting to note how rapidly programming languages developed in the short period 1955–1960. Three major imperative languages (FORTRAN, COBOL, Algol60) had come into existence, revolutionizing the view of computing and programming. All three are, in modified form, still in use today. And programming outside the von Neumann model—in particular, functional programming—had already begun with LISP, also still much in use today. The same can certainly not be said about the period to follow: the 1960s.

2.3 The 1960s: An Explosion in Programming Languages

After the tremendous success of the first few programming languages, "everyone" tried to get into the act. The 1960s saw the development of literally hundreds of programming languages, each incorporating its designer's particular interests or concerns (some of these were so-called **special-purpose languages**, used for particular programming situations such as graphics, communications, report generation, etc.). Most of these languages have now vanished, and only a few had a significant effect on the development of programming languages. Figure 2.1 contains a list of many of the programming languages in existence in 1967. As a comparison, a similar list can be obtained by looking at the language newsgroups in comp.lang on the Internet; these are given in Figure 2.2.

Some of the designers involved in the original efforts of the 1950s began also to dream grandiosely of more general and universal languages, perhaps a "language to end all languages." In many ways such a project was the **PL/I** project at IBM: designed in 1963–1964 and intended for use with a new family of computers (the 360 family), it was supposed to combine all the best features of FORTRAN, COBOL, and Algol60 and to add concurrency and exception handling as well. Although it is still supported by IBM, it can be considered to be a failure: translators were difficult to write, slow, huge, and unreliable (at least in the beginning), and the language was difficult to learn and error prone to use, due to the large number of unpredictable interactions among language features. Some consider PL/I to have been simply ahead of its time: a number of its features, such as

ADAM	DIAMAG	MADCAP
AED	DIMATE	MAP
AESOP	DOCUS	MATHLAB
AIMACO	DSL	MATH-MATIC
ALGOL	DYANA	META
ALGY	DYNAMO	MILITRAN
ALTRAN	DYSAC	MIRFAC
AMBIT	FACT	NELIAC
AMTRAN	FLAP	OCAL
APL	FLOW-MATIC	OMNITAB
APT	FORMAC	OPS
BACIAC	FORTRAN	PAT
BASEBALL	FORTRANSIT	PENCIL
BASIC	FSL	PL/I
BUGSYS	GAT	PRINT
C-10	GECOM	QUIKTRAN
CLIP	GPL	SFD-ALGOL
CLP	GPSS	SIMSCRIPT
COBOL	GRAF	SIMULA
COGENT	ICES	SNOBOL
COGO	IDS	SOL
COLASL	IPL-V	SPRINT
COLINGO	IT	STRESS
COMIT	JOSS	STROBES
CORAL	JOVIAL	TMG
CORC	L	TRAC
CPS	LDT	TRANDIR
DAS	LISP	TREET
DATA-TEXT	LOLITA	UNCOL
DEACON	LOTIS	UNICODE
DIALOG	MAD	

Figure 2.1 Selected Languages from the 1967 Tower of Babel (Sammet [1969], pp. xi–xii. Adapted by permission of Prentice-Hall, Inc., Englewood Cliffs, N.J.)

concurrency and exception handling, were not well enough understood at the time. Yet a case could be made that it attempted to do too much, provide too many features, and satisfy too many users.

An analogous situation occurred with the development of Algol, but in a completely different direction. **Algol68** (1963–1968) attempted to improve on Algol60, not by incorporating many new features from different sources, but by creating a more expressive and theoretically completely consistent structure. It included a general type system and adopted an expression orientation without arbitrary restrictions—a so-called completely **orthogonal** language; see Chapter 3. Moreover, in the interest of

ADA	FOR	PERL
ALGOL	FORTH	PL1
APL	FORTRAN	PLB
ASM	HERMES	POP
AWK	ICON	POSTSCRIPT
BASIC	IDL	PROGRAPH
BETA	JAVA	PROLOG
C	JAVASCRIPT	PYTHON
C++	LABVIEW	REXX
CLARION	LIMBO	SATHER
CLIPPER	LISP	SCHEME
CLOS	LOGO	SIMULA
CLU	MH	SMALLTALK
COBOL	ML	SNOBOL
CPLU	MODULA2	TCL
CRASS	MODULA3	VERILOG
DFL	MUMPS	VHDL
DYLAN	OBERON	VRML
EBONICS	OBJECTIVE-C	YORICK
EIFFEL	OCCAM	
ESTEREL	PASCAL	

Figure 2.2   Language newsgroups, June 2000.

precision the Algol68 committee developed a new terminology with precise definitions to describe the language. Hence the language reference manual became almost unreadable to the average computer scientist or programmer. Although this language is still an extremely interesting example for its design consistency, type system, and runtime environment, it was rarely used, often maligned, and not readily available on popular computers.

Not all languages developed in the 1960s were failures, however. A few became widely used and made significant and lasting contributions to the development of programming languages. Such a language was, for example, **SNOBOL** (StriNg Oriented symBOlic Language, an intentionally humorous extreme of acronym building), developed in the early 1960s by R. Griswold at Bell Labs. It was one of the first string processing languages, and in its revised form SNOBOL4 provides sophisticated and powerful pattern matching facilities.

Another influential language is **Simula67**, created by Kristen Nygaard and Ole-Johan Dahl at the Norwegian Computing Center in Oslo, Norway, during the period 1965–1967. It is based on an earlier language, Simula I, designed in the early 1960s, and includes Algol60 as a subset. Designed originally for simulations, it contributed fundamentally to the understanding of abstraction and computation through its introduction of the class concept fundamental to most object-oriented languages. Indeed, Simula67 can be called the first object-oriented language; see Chapter 10.

An often overlooked contribution of the 1960s is the functional language **ISWIM** designed by Peter Landin. More even than LISP, this language has deeply influenced the modern functional languages ML and Haskell. Indeed, it was probably the first language that was completely based on mathematical formalisms and whose behavior was described with complete precision.

A final example from the 1960s is the **BASIC** (Beginners All-purpose Symbolic Instruction Code) programming language. Initially designed in 1964 by John Kemeny and Thomas Kurtz at Dartmouth College, its original purpose was as a simple language for the new time-sharing systems of the time. It made a natural transition some ten years later to microcomputers, and it is still widely used in schools, businesses, and homes. BASIC is, in fact, not one language, but a family of languages. There are even two separate BASIC standards issued by ANSI: the 1978 "minimal BASIC" standard and the more elaborate 1988 version of full Standard BASIC, which dispenses with the line numbers of the earlier standard and adds structured control, variable declarations, and procedures. However, because of its simplicity the earlier version of BASIC continues to be in wide use as an instructional language and as a language for microcomputer applications despite its lack of modern language constructs.

2.4 The 1970s: Simplicity, Abstraction, Study

After the turmoil of the 1960s, language designers returned to the "drawing boards" chastened and with a new appreciation for simplicity and consistency of language design. Niklaus Wirth in particular was, along with a few others, vigorous in his rejection of the Algol68 design. He and C. A. R. Hoare published **Algol-W** as a response, and then in 1971 Wirth described the programming language **Pascal**, which distilled the ideas of Algol into a small, simple, efficient, structured language that was intended for use in teaching programming. It was amazingly successful, gaining acceptance not only for instruction, but for many practical uses as well, despite its smallness and the omission of important practical features such as separate compilation, adequate string handling, and expandable input-output capabilities.

In 1972 another outgrowth of Algol was being designed by Dennis Ritchie at Bell Labs that was to become tremendously successful as well: the **C** programming language. C tries for simplicity in different ways from Pascal: by retaining and restricting the expression orientation, by reducing the complexity of the type system and runtime environment, and by providing more access to the underlying machine. For this latter reason, C is sometimes called a "middle-level" programming language, as opposed to a high-level language. This it shares with a number of other languages that are used for operating system programming, most notably BLISS (1971) and FORTH (1971). In part, the success of C has been due to the popularity of the Unix operating system with which it is associated, but it has been adapted to many other operating environments as well.

In themselves, C and Pascal have contributed few new concepts to programming language design. Their success has been principally due to their simplicity and overall consistency of design, perhaps as a result of having been designed by very small groups of people.

In the mid- and late 1970s language designers experimented extensively with mechanisms for data abstraction, concurrency, and verification (proving programs correct). Some of the more notable efforts include the following languages:

CLU.   Designed between 1974 and 1977 at MIT by a team led by Barbara Liskov, CLU aims for a consistent approach to abstraction mechanisms for the production of high-quality software systems. Abstraction mechanisms in CLU include data abstraction, control abstraction, and exception handling. In CLU, the **cluster** data abstraction mechanism is similar to the class construct of Simula. CLU also provides an **iterator** construct, which is a very general control abstraction. CLU's exception handling mechanism was carefully designed and became the basis for a similar facility in Ada (discussed shortly). Indeed, CLU was a major influence on many of the important languages of the 1980s (see Section 2.5). The cluster mechanism of CLU is studied briefly in Chapter 9.

Euclid.   Designed by a committee based at the University of Toronto in 1976–1977, it extends Pascal to include abstract data types and aids program verification by suppressing aliasing and other undesirable programming features. Its principal goal was that of formal verification of programs, perhaps the first imperative language to be so oriented.

Mesa.   Another experimental language designed by a team at the Xerox Palo Alto Research Center from 1976 to 1979, Mesa integrated a Pascal-like base language with a module facility, exception handling, and added mechanisms for concurrency, or parallel programming, to allow it to be used to write operating systems. (See Chapter 14 for a discussion of parallel programming.) Mesa's module facility strongly influenced the design of a similar mechanism in Modula-2 (discussed shortly).

2.5 The 1980s: New Directions and the Rise of Object-Orientation

After the experimentation of the 1970s, particularly with ADTs, it is not surprising that the 1980s began with the introduction of two languages with ADT mechanisms: **Ada** and **Modula-2**.

Ada's design was fixed in 1980 after a lengthy design effort by the Department of Defense (an international standard was adopted in 1983, so this language is sometimes referred to as Ada83, to distinguish it from the newer Ada95). A group led by J. Ichbiah developed a number of carefully designed and interesting features, including an abstract data type mechanism (the **package**), a concurrency or parallel programming facility (the **task**), and exception handling. Initially, there was tremendous enthusiasm for Ada, since it was carefully designed, contained mechanisms based on the best research of the 1970s, and because it was expected that most government projects would eventually be written in it. However, its size and complexity, and the U.S. government's attempt to maintain strict control over it, made the development of Ada compilers and systems slow and difficult, particularly for small machines (just as the PC revolution was occurring). Indeed, Ada has been called the PL/I of the 1980s, and a similar fate was predicted for it. However, it is still in use today and is an important and influential language on account of its careful design. Thus, we use it for a number of examples in this book.

Modula-2 can be thought of as Ada's more modest cousin. Designed in the early 1980s as a successor to Pascal by Niklaus Wirth, Modula-2 was based on an earlier language, Modula, that was created for constructing operating systems. Modula-2 was given its first published definition in 1982, with subsequent revisions in 1985 and 1988. It contains a **module** mechanism, similar but more restricted than the Ada package, and also has a limited form of concurrency called the **coroutine**, which makes it suitable for systems programming on a single-processor system, as well as for simulations. Because of its simplicity (Wirth's continuing major design goal), it could run even on very small personal computers and was a popular replacement for Pascal in education. However, its limited support for abstract data types, its restrictive type system, and a number of other design decisions, such as the lack of an exception mechanism, made it difficult to use for the larger software projects that became standard in the late 1980s and 1990s, and its popularity has declined. It still remains a historically interesting and influential language.

What perhaps most held Ada and Modula-2 to their modest successes, however, was the tremendous rise of interest in object-oriented programming during the 1980s. It began with the release of the final version of **Smalltalk** in 1980 (sometimes referred to as Smalltalk-80 to distinguish it from its predecessors) and was given even more impetus by the rise of **C++** in the latter half of the decade. Both of these languages reached back to Simula67 for their inspiration, and were able to capitalize on the use of the class concept of Simula as a more flexible substitute for the abstract data type mechanisms of the 1970s and their successors, the package of Ada and the module of Modula-2.

Smalltalk was developed over the period 1972–1980 by Alan Kay, Dan Ingalls, and others at Xerox Corporation's Palo Alto Research Center. Smalltalk was designed to apply the object-oriented approach in a completely consistent way and is the purest example of an object-oriented language. However, Smalltalk was developed in conjunction with many other new computing features that have since become commonplace, in particular the use of a "personal computer" with a bitmap display, a graphics windowing system, and a mouse. As such it represented an amazing advance, not just as a programming language, but as a complete man-machine interface. Unfortunately, it was in part this very fact that also limited its use for much of the 1980s: It was tied to a particular kind of operating system on specialized hardware that was not yet generally available. It also suffered from a number of additional problems, such as an unusual notation and a somewhat inefficient implementation. But it did create a wave of interest in object-orientation that helped propel C++ into the spotlight, and which in turn moved object-oriented methods into the forefront of computing.

C++ was developed by Bjarne Stroustrup at Bell Labs, beginning in 1980. It is perhaps unique in that it was specifically designed "to make programming more enjoyable for the serious programmer" [Stroustrup 1997, p. ix]. It started as a modest extension of C using ideas from Simula67 and was originally called "C with Classes." Building on the popularity and portability of C (and Unix), it was very efficient and could run almost anywhere. It has since added many features, an enormous number of libraries, and has been ported to virtually every platform. An ISO standard was finally established in 1998, which is likely to aid in its continued popularity and use. However, it has also become a very large language, it is difficult to implement (at this writing almost no compiler conforms completely to the 1998 standard), and is also difficult to understand thoroughly.

With the rise of object-oriented programming, many other object-oriented languages were created in the mid- to late 1980s. Some of the more noteworthy include Objective C, Object Pascal, Modula-3, Oberon, and Eiffel. Some of these continue to have devoted users, but none have achieved the success enjoyed by C++. Object-oriented languages are studied in Chapter 10.

A further development of the 1980s over the 1970s was the renewed interest in functional programming and alternative language paradigms. Two new functional languages that had their origins already in the late 1970s are **Scheme** and **ML**. Scheme, a version of LISP, was developed from 1975 to 1978 by Gerald J. Sussman and Guy L. Steele, Jr., at MIT (like the original LISP). However, it did not become popular until the mid-1980s, with the publication of an influential book by Abelson and Sussman [1985]. Scheme provides a version of LISP that is more uniform than other versions and that was designed to resemble more closely the lambda calculus. Another version of LISP that appeared in the 1980s is **Common LISP**, which attempts to define a standard for the LISP family.

In another direction, the language **ML** (for metalanguage), was developed by Robin Milner at Edinburgh University beginning in 1978. ML is substantially different from previous functional languages in that it has a syntax more closely related to Pascal, and it also has a mechanism for type checking similar to Pascal, but much more flexible and powerful. A related language is **Miranda**, developed by David Turner at Manchester University (England) in 1985–1986. Scheme and ML are studied in Chapter 11.

Some of the renewed interest and increasing popularity of functional languages in the 1980s can also be traced to a famous talk delivered by John Backus (the chief developer of FORTRAN) in 1978 (Backus [1978]), in which he advocated the abandonment of imperative languages (like FORTRAN) in favor of functional languages and proposed a functional language schema called **FP** (for "Functional Programming"). FP was strongly influenced by APL and in turn influenced the further development of functional languages in the 1980s.

Many attempts to use mathematical logic more or less directly as a programming language have been made over the years, but the language **Prolog** has become the main practical example of logic programming; see Chapter 12. Developed by a group at Marseille led by A. Colmerauer beginning in 1972, it slowly developed into an efficient implementation and began to become popular with the development of Edinburgh Prolog in the early 1980s. It received tremendous publicity in the mid-1980s when it was chosen as the principal language of the so-called fifth-generation project of Japan. With the ending of that project, general interest in Prolog has waned, but it is still used widely in artificial intelligence and as a prototyping language. It exists in many interesting extensions, such as Prolog IV and Parlog.

2.6 The 1990s: Consolidation, the Internet, Libraries, and Scripting

The early 1990s was a period in which few new languages received the attention surrounding the ADT and object-oriented languages of the 1980s. After the introduction of so many object-oriented languages, this was a period, perhaps more than any other, in which languages competed in the arenas of publicity and marketplace. Not coincidentally, this was also a period in which personal computing and windowing operating systems expanded rapidly, becoming for the first time an important consumer market. The consumerization of computing received even greater impetus with the rapid expansion of the Internet during the same period. And after the first Web browser (Mosaic) was released in 1993, this rapid expansion became a virtual explosion. Meanwhile, C++ was gradually winning the object-oriented language "wars," with an estimated 1 million or more programmers using it by 1993. Then, in 1995, came the most amazing event in the history of programming languages: the introduction of **Java**.

Java was originally developed by James Gosling at Sun Microsystems, not for the Internet, but for embedded consumer-electronic applications; its original name was Oak. With the increasing use of the Internet, and the advent of the Web, Sun developers revised it for Web and network use, and Sun began a publicity campaign for it that put it before the eyes of the public like no other programming language. Not surprisingly, Java is an object-oriented language. Additionally, it has the real virtues of being relatively simple, cleanly designed, easily portable, and furnished from the start with a large library of windowing, networking, and concurrency utilities. Correspondingly, the growth in the use of Java over its first five years has been nothing short of phenomenal. It is currently being used not only for Internet and networked applications, but also for ordinary applications and for instruction in universities, and these uses are growing daily. However, questions about its future remain. First, its use in stand-alone applications has not yet been proven: Such applications typically run significantly more slowly than, say, C++ versions, are larger, and use more hardware resources—but that could easily change with new development tools. Second, Sun Microsystems has chosen to maintain tight proprietary control over Java. This means that there is unlikely to be an independent ISO or ANSI standard for the language, and all use of Java is subject to permission, a fact that may seriously impede its acceptance by other companies. Nevertheless, its future in networked/Internet applications and education seems already assured. Java and C++ are covered in some detail in Chapter 10, and of course we use these languages liberally for examples in other chapters.

However, the history of programming languages in the 1990s is certainly not just that of C++ and Java; significant developments have occurred elsewhere as well. We mention two as being relatively mature after a few years: the functional language **Haskell** and the new Ada95 standard.

Haskell is a purely functional language similar to ML and Miranda, but with a number of more advanced features, many implementations, and a growing library and interface capabilities. It began as an international university research effort around 1989, supported principally at Yale and Glasgow Universities. It is named after the mathematical logician Haskell B. Curry. A current standard, Haskell98, is supported at several locations worldwide. Closely related smaller languages **Gofer** and **HUGS** are currently used widely in education and for smaller applications. We cover Haskell in some detail in Chapter 11.

Ada95 is essentially a superset of Ada83 with additional facilities for object-oriented programming and parallelism, among many additional features. It brings Ada up to date with respect to experience with the language since 1983, as well as with the revolution in object-oriented methods, and should help maintain Ada as a viable language well into the next decade. We will use Ada95 for several examples where appropriate (Ada examples that are not specifically marked as Ada95 can be assumed to be valid for both Ada83 and Ada95).

One additional language issue that developments of the 1990s has brought into greater focus is that of **libraries**. Historically, libraries were given secondary importance in language design, since, strictly speaking, they were not part of the language itself, but more an "interface" issue with the operating system and hardware. In some languages, such as Pascal, libraries were even ignored (as was the separate compilation and linking issues that libraries bring up): basic input-output and utility functions (such as math functions) were built into the language itself, leaving all additional capabilities as nonstandard extensions. Other languages, such as C, did provide a standard, but extremely minimal, library, again leaving everything else to proprietary, nonstandard systems. Today this approach is no longer adequate, and the need for a rich library of capabilities, written in a system-independent way, and integrated well into the language itself, is central for the success of a programming language. Java is the primary example of this: Java without the Java API ("Application Program Interface"—really a set of libraries) would likely have been "just another language." Similarly, C++ also has a standard library containing many utilities, though not the windowing systems and networking of the Java libraries. Haskell, too, has a large and growing set of libraries, as does Ada95.

With the increasing importance of libraries has come a corresponding increase in the number and importance of so-called **scripting languages**, including AWK, Perl, Tcl, Javascript, Rexx, and Python. A scripting language is a language that ties together utilities, library components, and operating system commands into complete programs; it can be viewed as a kind of special-purpose language. Typical characteristics of a scripting language are the brevity of its programs, highly dynamic behavior, built-in high-level data structures, extendable syntax, and lack of type checking. An early example of a scripting language is the Job Control Language (JCL) on IBM computers of the 1960s. More modern examples of such operating system command languages include the various Unix shell languages and the DOS command language. Such OS-based languages tend, however, to be limited in scope and operationality. AWK, Perl, and Tcl were all developed to compensate for the limitations of Unix shell languages: AWK contains powerful text and file processing primitives, including pattern matching and arrays indexed by strings ("associative" arrays, implemented as hash tables). As a simple example of an AWK script, consider the following single-line AWK program:

```
{ print NR, $0 }
```

This program prints any text file with line numbers (NR is the line or "record" number, $0 represents each line of text). Perl has similar facilities, but is somewhat more general than AWK in that it is targeted at all systems administration tasks (as well as text processing). Perl has also become popular as an alternative to C for writing so-called CGI scripts that provide dynamic behavior for Internet server applications. Tcl ("tool command language") was developed as an *embeddable* language; that is, it is easily called from within programs and scripts written in other languages. Tcl has become popular because of a very powerful windowing library that accompanies it, called Tk ("tool kit"), which allows graphics user interfaces to be built very quickly in Unix (and more recently Windows and MacIntosh computers). For example, here is a simple Tcl/Tk command:

```
button .b -text Hello! -font {Times 16} -command
{puts hello}
```

This command creates a button on the screen labelled "Hello!" (in 16 point Times) which, when clicked with the mouse, prints the message "hello" to the standard output.

Another example of an embedded scripting language is Javascript (only vaguely related to Java), which is used to embed (client-side) dynamic behavior inside Web pages. A final example of a scripting language is Visual Basic, which is actually three things: a programming language, a scripting language, and a visually-oriented Windows development environment.

2.7 The Future

In the 1960s some computer scientists dreamed of a single universal programming language that would meet the needs of all computer users. Attempts to design and implement such a language, however, resulted in frustration and failure. In the late 1970s and early 1980s a different dream emerged—a dream that programming languages themselves would become obsolete, that new **specification languages** would be developed that would allow computer users to just say what they wanted, and the system itself would find out how to implement the requirements. A succinct exposition of this view is contained in Winograd [1979]:

> Just as high-level languages enabled the programmer to escape from the intricacies of a machine's order code, higher level programming systems can provide help in understanding and manipulating complex systems and components. We need to shift our attention away from the detailed specification of algorithms, towards the description of the properties of the packages and objects with which we build. A new generation of programming tools will be based on the attitude that what we say in a programming system should be primarily declarative, not imperative: the fundamental use of a programming system is not in creating sequences of instructions for accomplishing tasks (or carrying out algorithms), but in expressing and manipulating descriptions of computational processes and the objects on which they are carried out. (Ibid., p. 393)

In a sense, he is just describing what logic programming languages attempt to do. But as we will see in Chapter 12, even though these languages can be used for quick prototyping, programmers still need to specify algorithms step by step when efficiency is needed. Little progress has been made in designing systems that can on their own construct algorithms to accomplish a set of given requirements.

Programming has thus not become obsolete. In a sense it has become even more important, since it now can occur at so many different levels, from assembly language to specification language. And with the development of faster, cheaper, and easier-to-use computers, the "software crisis" has if anything increased: there is a tremendous demand for more and better programs to solve a variety of problems. Perhaps this crisis is already

being solved, but by organizational rather than strictly linguistic techniques: by greater reuse of existing code, by increasing the portability and
reusability of code, and by mechanical systems such as syntax-directed editors to increase programmer productivity.

Where will programming language design be in the years to come?
Predicting the future is notoriously difficult. The first edition of this book
stated that "it does not seem now as though there will be any really overwhelming new developments, but rather a steady process of increasing
understanding and refinement, based primarily on existing languages." In
an important sense, this prediction was very wrong: Java can easily be
called an "overwhelming new development." In another sense, however,
the statement can also be defended (at least at the time of this writing),
since Java itself does not represent any astoundingly new techniques or
ideas (as far as the language itself is concerned), but is a well-designed
combination of the best ideas of the previous decades. Nevertheless, as
long as new computer technologies arise (such as the Internet), and as
long as the field of computing remains as dynamic as it is today, there will
be room for new languages and new ideas, and the study of programming
languages will remain as fascinating and exciting as it is today.

Exercises

2.1 The Babylonian algorithm involving a cistern given at the beginning of
this chapter expresses the solution to a particular algebraic equation.

(a) Write down the equation and solve it for the width. Show how the
Babylonian algorithm corresponds to your solution.

(b) Write a procedure (in one or more languages) that implements the
Babylonian algorithm, making the length and the sum of the area
and volume into parameters to the procedure. Is your procedure easier to understand than the Babylonian description? Why?

2.2 Write out a description of Euclid's algorithm in the style of the
Babylonian algorithm of the text.

2.3 Here is another algorithm in the Babylonian style:

A rectangle.
The perimeter is 2 less than the area.
The area is 20.
What are the dimensions?
Divide 2 into 20, giving 10.
Divide 2 into 2, giving 1.
Subtract 1 from 10, giving 9.
Multiply 9 by 9, giving 81.
Multiply 20 by 4, giving 80.

Subtract 80 from 81, giving 1.
Subtract 1 from 9, giving 8.
Divide 8 by 2, giving 4.
The width is 4.
Divide 20 by 4, giving 5.
The length is 5.
This is the procedure.

What famous mathematical formula is used by this algorithm? What special numeric requirement is necessary for this algorithm to work?

2.4 Pick a programming language you know or have heard of that was not mentioned in this chapter. Write a short report on its development, its major features, and its place in the history of programming languages.

2.5 Each of the following languages is historically related to a language or languages mentioned in this chapter. Determine and briefly describe this relationship.

JOVIAL
Euler
BCPL
Alphard
HOPE

2.6 What does it mean for a language to "exist" at a particular time? Determine what criteria Sammet used for the languages in Figure 2.1, and compare these to the criterion used in Figure 2.2. What criteria would you use?

2.7 Dates of origin of particular programming languages are difficult to determine and specify with precision. Give at least five different ways to specify the date of origin of a programming language. How is this related to your answer to Exercise 2.6?

2.8 One area of special-purpose languages that has been very active since the 1960s has been algebraic or formula manipulation languages. Write a brief report on the history of these languages, including the following languages: FORMAC, MATLAB, REDUCE, Macsyma, Scratchpad, and Maple.

2.9 Here are some more "special-purpose" languages (some of them scripting languages, some of them mentioned in the text). Determine their area of specialty and briefly describe each: RPG, APT, SPSS, GPSS, DCDL, TeX, Rexx, Python, VBScript.

2.10 This chapter did not mention so-called **markup** languages, such as SGML, HTML, and XML. These languages have, like scripting languages, been given special importance by the Internet.
   (a) Briefly describe each of these languages, and compare their uses.
   (b) Are these languages special-purpose programming languages? Why or why not?

2.11 Language developments often occur as a result of or in step with new hardware or machine developments. Discuss one or more of the following hardware developments and its relationship to and effect on programming language development.

> Time sharing
> Personal computers
> Cheap, fast random access memory
> Disk drives
> Multiple processors
> Video display terminals
> Fast computer networks
> The Internet

2.12 **(a)** Name the languages that are listed in both Figures 2.1 and 2.2.
    (b) For each of the languages in (a), state why you think they have survived from 1967 to 2000.

2.13 In Backus et al. [1957] it is stated that FORTRAN was developed "to enable the programmer to specify a numerical procedure using a concise language like that of mathematics." But in Backus [1978], the author complains that languages like FORTRAN "lack useful mathematical properties" and proposes his FP language schema in part to make programming look more like mathematics. Thus, one interpretation of the history of programming languages is as a series of successive attempts to make programs look more and more like mathematics. Is this view supported by the historical overview given in this chapter? Why or why not?

2.14 A mathematical definition for the gcd of two numbers is often given as follows: x is the gcd of u and v if x divides both u and v, and given any other y that divides u and v, y divides x.
    (a) Discuss the difference between this definition and Euclid's algorithm (the algorithm of the gcd procedure of Chapter 1).
    (b) Is it possible to use this definition in a procedure to compute the gcd? Why or why not?
    (c) Based on this example, can you draw any conclusions about the relation of programming to mathematics? Explain.

2.15 Here is a quote from Gelernter and Jagannathan [1990], pp. 150–151:

> Programming after all is a kind of machine-building, not the derivation of formulas. No matter how great the superficial resemblance between a program and a mathematical derivation, the derivation has to be true, whereas the program has to work when you turn it on. It simply does not follow that by making a program look like a mathematical formula, programming takes on the characteristics of mathematics.

    (a) Discuss the validity of this point of view.
    (b) Discuss the relationship of this statement to the questions raised in Exercises 2.12 and 2.13.

Notes and References

Wexelblat [1981] is a collection of papers presented at an Association for Computing Machinery (ACM) conference on the history of programming languages in 1978 (called HOPL or HOPL-I). A second conference was held in 1993 (called HOPL-II), and the papers and discussion from that conference have been published in Bergin and Gibson [1996]. Preliminary versions of the HOPL-II papers only were published in the March 1993 issue of the ACM SIGPLAN Notices (Vol. 28, No. 3). Many of the papers are by original designers of the languages discussed, and these two books are the primary references for the history of many major languages. (Articles by individual authors will also be mentioned in the following.) Sammet [1969] is an earlier book that discusses some of the same languages but with a focus on the details of the languages themselves. Another book that includes history with descriptions of a number of the languages mentioned is Birnes [1989]. Survey articles on programming language history include Wegner [1976], Sammet [1976], Rosen [1972], and Sammet [1972]. The early history of programming languages is discussed in Knuth and Trabb Pardo [1977].

Zuse's Plankalkül was developed in 1945 but did not appear until later (Zuse [1972]). A brief description of the Plankalkül is given in Sebesta [1996]. Ancient Babylonian algorithms are discussed in Knuth [1972]. For an introduction into constructive mathematics, that is, the mathematics of algorithmic computation, see Martin-Löf [1979] or Bridges and Richman [1987]. Charles Babbage and his machines are described in Morrison and Morrison [1961], which also contains the writings of Ada Lovelace. Biographies of Ada Lovelace include those by Stein [1985] and Moore [1977]. For an account of the construction of Babbage's Difference Engine at the National Science Museum in London, England, see Dane [1992].

The history of FORTRAN is given in Backus [1981], of Algol60 in Naur [1981] and Perlis [1981], of LISP in McCarthy [1981] and Steele and Gabriel [1996], of COBOL in Sammet [1981], of Simula67 in Nygaard and Dahl [1981], of BASIC in Kurtz [1981], of PL/I in Radin [1981], of SNOBOL in Griswold [1981], of APL in Falkoff and Iverson [1981], of Pascal in Wirth [1996], of C in Ritchie [1996], of C++ in Stroustrup [1994] [1996], of Smalltalk in Kay [1996], of Ada in Whitaker [1996], of Prolog in Colmerauer and Roussel [1996], of Algol68 in Lindsey [1996], and of CLU in Liskov [1996]. Other references for languages more frequently used in this text are given at the end of Chapter 1; these include FORTRAN, Scheme, Pascal, Modula-2, Ada, C, C++, Simula67, Prolog, and Smalltalk. Articles and books on some of the other languages mentioned in this chapter are as follows: COBOL—Schneiderman [1985], Ashley [1980]; Algol60—Naur [1963a,b], Knuth [1967]; Algol68—Tanenbaum [1976]; Algol-W—Hoare and Wirth [1966]; APL—Iverson [1962]; SNOBOL—Griswold, Poage, and Polonsky [1971], Griswold and Griswold [1973]; CLU—Liskov et al. [1984], Liskov et al. [1977], Liskov and Snyder [1979]; Euclid—Lampson et al. [1981];

Mesa—Geschke, Morris, and Sattherthwaite [1977], Lampson and Redell [1980], Mitchell, Maybury, and Sweet [1979]; FP—Backus [1978]; J (APL derivative)—Hui [1990]; and Miranda—Turner [1986].

Some references for the scripting languages mentioned at the end of Section 2.6 are as follows. AWK is described in Aho et al. [1988]; Perl is described in Wall et al. [2000]; Tcl/Tk is covered in Welch [2000]. The sample Tcl/Tk program given on page 48 is taken from Ousterhout [1998].

Some interesting languages not mentioned in this chapter are Icon, a successor to SNOBOL which is described in Griswold and Griswold [1983] [1996]; Cedar, a successor to Mesa, described in Lampson [1983], Teitelman [1984], and Swinehart et al. [1986]; the "middle-level" languages BLISS (Wulf, Russell, and Habermann [1971]) and FORTH (Brodie [1981], Colburn, Moore, and Rather [1996]); and Concurrent Pascal (Brinch Hansen [1996]), which influenced Ada's task mechanism.

3 Language Design Principles

Language design is one of the most difficult and poorly understood areas of computer science. In Chapter 1 we emphasized human readability and mechanisms for abstraction and complexity control as key requirements for a modern programming language. Judging a language by these criteria is difficult, however, since the success or failure of a language may depend on complex interactions among the language mechanisms.

Practical matters not directly connected to language definition also have a major effect on the success or failure of a language. These include the availability, price, and quality of translators. Even politics, geography, timing, and markets have an effect. The C programming language has been a success at least partially because of the success of the Unix operating system, which promoted its use. COBOL, though chiefly ignored by the computer science community, continues as a significant language because of its use in industry, and because of the large number of "legacy" applications (old applications that continue to be maintained). The language Ada achieved immediate influence because of its required use in certain U.S. Defense Department projects. And Java has achieved instant importance through the growth of the Internet.

Languages have been successes for as many different reasons as they have been failures. Language designers have noted the importance of the consistency of "feel" of a language and the uniformity of design concept that can be achieved when a language is designed by a single individual or a small group of individuals. This has been true, for example, with Pascal, C, C++, APL, SNOBOL, and LISP. But languages designed by committees have also been successful: COBOL, the Algols, and Ada.

We mentioned in Chapter 2 the attempts to achieve even greater abstraction in programming languages—even to make programming obsolete with the use of specification languages and very-high-level constructs. These efforts did not succeed, and we still find it necessary to specify algorithms and computation at a level considerably more detailed than the theorists had hoped. Why? A partial answer is that almost every programming application is different and requires different abstractions. Thus, we must either provide suitable abstractions for particular situations with the design of the language or provide general facilities for the creation of these abstractions on demand. Thus, programming language design depends heavily on the intended use and the requirements of this use. In this it is similar to programming itself—it is a goal-oriented activity.

Keeping the goal of the design in mind is particularly important for special-purpose languages, such as database languages, graphics languages, and real-time languages, since the particular abstractions for the application should be built into the language design. But it is true for general-purpose languages as well, where design goals can be less obvious. In most of the successful languages, particular design goals were constantly kept in mind during the design process. In FORTRAN it was efficiency of execution. In COBOL it was to provide an English-like nontechnical readability. In Algol60 it was to provide a block-structured language for describing algorithms. In Pascal it was to provide a simple instructional language to promote top-down design. In C++ it was the needs of the users for greater abstraction while preserving efficiency and compatibility with C.

Nevertheless, with all this in mind, it is still extremely difficult to say what good programming language design is. Even noted computer scientists and successful language designers offer conflicting and even contradictory advice. Niklaus Wirth, the designer of Pascal, advises that simplicity is paramount (Wirth [1974]). C. A. R. Hoare, a prominent computer scientist and co-designer of a number of languages, emphasizes the design of individual language constructs (Hoare [1973]). Bjarne Stroustrup, the designer of C++, notes that a language cannot be merely a collection of "neat" features (Stroustrup [1994], page 7). Fred Brooks, a computer science pioneer, maintains that language design is similar to any other design problem, such as that of a building (Brooks [1996]). Often, hazy-sounding qualities such as "design philosophy" or "expressiveness" are used in descriptions of language design issues. In the sections that follow we will collect some proposed general criteria and a list of more detailed principles that are potential aids to the language designer. We will also give some specific examples to emphasize possible good and bad choices, with the understanding that there often is no general agreement on these issues. (Sometimes it will be necessary to read further sections of the book to understand fully the examples.)

3.1 History and Design Criteria

When programming languages began, there was one principal design criterion: **efficiency of execution**. (Machines were extremely slow, and program speed was a necessity; also, there was a generally held belief that language translators could not produce efficient executable code.) FORTRAN, for example, had as its most important goal the compactness and speed of the executable code. Indeed, the FORTRAN code was designed to resemble as much as possible the machine code that needed to be generated. Of course one could not forget that the whole reason for the existence of a high-level language was to make it easier to write than machine or assembly language. But this **writability**—the quality of a language that enables a programmer to use it to express a computation clearly, correctly, concisely, and quickly—was always subservient to efficiency. And the fact that programs should be readable by humans as well as machines was hardly appreciated, simply because programs at that time tended to be short, written by one or a few people, and rarely revised or updated except by their creators.

Both COBOL and Algol60 can be viewed as steps toward more general criteria than the efficiency of the generated code. The block structure and the availability of recursion in Algol60 made it more suitable for expressing algorithms in a logically clear and concise way, thus promoting even greater writability of the language. (We noted in Chapter 1 that C. A. R. Hoare understood how to express his QUICKSORT algorithm clearly only after learning Algol60.) But Algol60 was also designed as a language for communicating algorithms among people, not just from people to machines. Thus **readability**—the quality of a language that enables a programmer to understand and comprehend the nature of a computation easily and accurately—was also an important design goal.

COBOL attempted to improve the readability of programs by trying to make programs look like ordinary written English. In a sense this was not a success, since it did not improve the ability of the reader to understand the logic or behavior of the program and, in fact, decreased the writability of programs by making them long and verbose. But human readability was perhaps for the first time a clearly stated design goal.

With the growing complexity of languages in the 1960s, language designers became aware of a greater need for abstraction mechanisms and for reducing the rules and restrictions programmers had to learn. Both of these were expressions of the need for complexity control. On the one hand, abstractions allow the programmer to control the complexity of a programming task. On the other hand, reducing the rules and restrictions of a language reduces the complexity of its definition and makes the language easier to use actually to solve the task. Simula67 had as a goal the provision of more powerful abstraction mechanisms, and Algol68 attempted to reduce the complexity of the language by being completely **general** and **orthogonal**: the language features were designed to have as few restrictions as possible and be combinable in any meaningful way; see Section 3.3. Simula67's class concept was an innovation that influenced the abstraction mechanisms provided by many languages of the 1970s and 1980s. Algol68's generality and orthogonality, however, were less of a success. Wirth [1974] has pointed out that generality can in fact increase complexity even as it reduces the number of special rules, because extremely general constructs are more difficult to understand, their effects may be less predictable, and the underlying computational model is conceptually more difficult. Stroustrup [1994] [1996] also notes that the pursuit of conceptual unity and elegance represented by Algol68 and Simula67 led to inefficient implementations that made them unusable in certain contexts.

With the 1970s and early 1980s came a greater emphasis on simplicity and abstraction, as exhibited by Pascal, C, Euclid, CLU, Modula-2, and Ada. Attempts were also made to improve the reliability of programs by introducing mathematical definitions for constructs and providing a language with mechanisms that would permit a translator to prove the correctness of a program as it performed the translation. However, program proof systems have had limited success—due primarily to the added complexity they introduce, not only to the language design and the task of programming in the language, but to the translator itself. One offshoot of these efforts—strong typing—has become a standard part of most languages, and indeed is part of all five of the above-named languages, to a greater or lesser degree.

In the 1980s and 1990s interest has continued in improving the logical or mathematical precision of languages, as well as attempts to make logic into a programming language itself. Interest in functional languages has also been rekindled with the development of ML and Haskell and the continued popularity of Lisp/Scheme.

But the most important development of the last 15 years has been the practical success of the object-oriented languages Smalltalk, C++, and Java, and the proof by experience of the object-oriented approach to abstraction that these languages have brought with them. The design goals that proved most successful here have been the correspondence of abstraction mechanisms to the needs of real-world programming tasks, the use of libraries to extend language mechanisms to solve specific tasks, and the use of object-oriented techniques to increase the flexibility and reuse of existing code.

Thus, we see that the emphasis on different design goals has changed through the years both as a response to experience with previous language designs and as the nature of the problems addressed by computer science have changed. Still, readability, abstraction, and complexity control are issues that are involved in almost every design question.

3.2 Efficiency

We want to list some of the more specific principles mentioned in the last section and give examples of good and bad design choices with respect to each. We start with the ubiquitous requirement that can apply in many different guises—efficiency.

This principle can encompass almost all the other principles in various forms. We usually think of efficiency of target code first: the language design should be such that a translator can generate **efficient executable code**. Sometimes this is referred to as **optimizability**. As an example, statically typed variables allow code to be generated that efficiently allocates and references them. As another example, in C++ the design of the class mechanism is such that, in the absence of more advanced object-oriented features, no extra memory or code is required over the simpler struct mechanism of C.

A second kind of efficiency is **efficiency of translation**: Does the language design permit the source code to be translated efficiently, that is, quickly and by a reasonably sized translator? For example, does the language design allow a one-pass compiler to be written? This is the case in Pascal and C, since variables must be declared before they are used. In C++, however, this restriction is relaxed, so that a compiler must make a second pass over (at least some of) the code to resolve identifier references. Sometimes language designs include rules that are extremely difficult to check at translation time or even at execution time. One example of this is the rule in Algol68 that prohibits dangling reference assignments. Occasionally, language designers will try to escape such inefficiencies by allowing translators to fail to check such rules. Indeed, error checking in general can be a problematic efficiency issue, since to check for an error at translation time can cause the translator to be inefficient, while generating code to check the error during execution can cause the target code to be inefficient. On the other hand, ignoring error checking violates another design principle—**reliability**—the assurance that a program will not behave in unexpected or disastrous ways during execution.

There are many more views of efficiency than just these two, however. One is **implementability**, or the efficiency with which a translator can be written. This is related to efficiency of translation, but it is also a function of the complexity of the language definition. The success of a language can be impaired simply because it is too difficult to write a translator or because algorithms to perform the translation are not sufficiently well understood. One of the reasons Algol60 was not used more in the United States may have been that the stack-based structure needed for the runtime system was not widely known at the time. Type inference without declarations, as in the programming language ML, had to await the application of the unification algorithm to type inference. And the size and complexity of Ada was a hindrance to the development of compilers and has impaired its availability and use. Occasionally, a language will even be designed with a requirement that cannot be met by a known method—the language is then untranslatable except by magic! Wirth [1974] states the principle of implementability particularly forcefully: "Language design is compiler construction."

Another view of efficiency is **programming efficiency**: How quickly and easily can programs be written in the language? This is essentially writability, as discussed earlier. One of the qualities involved in this is the **expressiveness** of the language: How easy is it to express complex processes and structures? Or, to put it another way: How easily can the design in the programmer's head be mapped to actual code? This is clearly related to the power and generality of the abstraction mechanisms of the language. The conciseness of the syntax and the avoidance of unnecessary detail, such as variable declarations, are often considered to be important factors in this kind of efficiency as well. From this point of view, LISP and Prolog are ideal languages, since the syntax is extremely concise, no declarations are necessary, and many of the details of computations can be left to the runtime system. Of course, this can compromise other language principles, such as readability, efficiency of execution, and reliability.

Indeed, reliability can be viewed as an efficiency issue itself. A program that is not reliable causes many extra costs—modifications to isolate or remove the erroneous behavior, extra testing time, plus the time required to correct the effects of the erroneous behavior. If the program is extremely unreliable, it may even cause a complete waste of the development and coding time. This kind of efficiency is a resource consumption issue in software engineering. In this sense the efficiency with which software can be created depends on readability and **maintainability**—the ease with which errors can be found and corrected and new features added—while writability is less important. Software engineers estimate that much more time is spent on debugging and maintenance than on the original coding of a program. Thus readability and maintainability may ultimately be the most important efficiency issues of all.

3.3 Regularity

Regularity is a somewhat ill-defined quality of a language that expresses how well the features of a language are integrated—greater regularity implies fewer unusual restrictions on the use of particular constructs, fewer strange interactions between constructs, and fewer surprises in general in the way language features behave. Often regularity is subdivided into three more definite concepts: generality, orthogonality, and uniformity. A language achieves **generality** by avoiding special cases in the availability or use of constructs and by combining closely related constructs into a single more general one. Orthogonality is a term borrowed from mathematics, where it means perpendicularity or in a completely independent direction. **Orthogonality** in a programming language means that language constructs can be combined in any meaningful way and that the interaction of constructs, or the context of use, should not cause unexpected restrictions or behavior. **Uniformity** means that similar things should look similar and have similar meanings and, inversely, that different things should look different.

We give next a series of examples of these three principles (mainly of constructs that violate them). The examples will also make clear that distinctions between the three are sometimes more a matter of viewpoint than actual substance, and one can always classify a feature or construct as simply irregular if one of these three subcategories does not seem to fit adequately.

Generality.   Here is a list of a few of the features in common programming languages that show a lack of generality:

- Pascal has nested functions and procedures, and these can be passed as parameters to other procedures, but there are no procedure variables, and so procedures lack generality. C lacks nested procedure/ function definitions, and so procedures also lack generality in C. On the other hand, C permits procedure parameters, variables, and returned values (called function pointers by the C community). By contrast, most functional languages such as Scheme and ML have a completely general procedure/function construct, as one would expect.

- Pascal has no variable-length arrays, so arrays lack generality. C and Ada do have variable-length arrays, and FORTRAN has the ability to pass variable-length array parameters, but cannot define variable-length array types.

- In C, two structures or arrays cannot be directly compared using the equality operator "==" but must be compared element by element. Thus, the equality operator lacks generality. This restriction has been removed in Ada and (partially) in C++. More generally, many languages have no facility for extending the use of predefined operators (like == or +) to new data types. Some languages, however, (like Haskell) even allow new operators to be created by the user (unlike even Ada and C++). In such languages, operators can be viewed as having achieved complete generality.

- In FORTRAN, named constants do not exist. In Pascal, constants may not be expressions, while in Modula-2, constant expressions may not include function calls. Ada, however, has a completely general constant declaration facility (constants may even be dynamic quantities).

Orthogonality.   Here the viewpoint is that language constructs should not behave differently in different contexts. Thus, restrictions that are context dependent are nonorthogonalities, while restrictions that apply regardless of context are nongeneralities. In fact, the nongenerality of constants in Modula-2 mentioned above could be interpreted instead as a nonorthogonality of expressions: in constant declarations expressions can be only of restricted form. Similarly, the nongenerality of comparison for equality could be viewed as a nonorthogonality, since the applicability of equality depends on the types of the values being compared. Here are some further examples of lack of orthogonality:

- In Pascal, functions can return only scalar or pointer types as values. In C and C++, values of all data types, except array types, can be returned from a function (indeed, arrays are treated in C and C++ differently from all other types). In Ada and most functional languages this nonorthogonality is removed.

- In C, local variables can only be defined at the beginning of a block (compound statement),[1] while in C++ variable definitions can occur at any point inside a block (but, of course, before any uses).

- In C there is a nonorthogonality in parameter passing: C passes all parameters by value except arrays, which are passed by reference.

Orthogonality was a major design goal of Algol68, and it remains the best example of a language where constructs can be combined in all meaningful ways.

Uniformity.   This principle focuses on the consistency of appearance and behavior of language constructs. Nonuniformities are of two types: Similar things do not look similar or behave similarly, and dissimilar things actually look similar or behave similarly when they should not. Examples of nonuniformities include:

- In C++, a semicolon is necessary after a class definition but forbidden after a function definition:

```
class A { ... } ; // semicolon required

int f () { ... }  // semicolon forbidden
```

- Returned values from functions in Pascal look like assignments:

```
function f : boolean;
begin
  ...
  f := true;
end;
```

Most languages use the return-statement for this operation. This is a case where different things should look different, but instead look confusingly

---

[1] The new ISO C Standard (ISO 9899 [1999]) removes this restriction.

alike. A similar situation occurs in C with the operators "&" and "&&": The first operator is "bitwise and," while the second operator is "logical and." These two operators yield very different results, yet look confusingly similar.

Nonuniformities can in some cases be thought of as nonorthogonalities too, since nonuniformities occur in particular contexts and can be seen as interactions between constructs.

Why do languages exhibit such nonregularities at all? Surely the language designers did not intentionally set out to create strange restrictions, interactions, and confusions? Indeed, many nonregularities are case studies in the difficulties of language design, with obscure, sometimes historical, but often very practical issues coming into play.

Take, for example, the problem with semicolons in C++, noted as a nonuniformity above. Since C++ was attempting to deviate from C as little as possible, this nonregularity was essentially forced, as it is required for compatibility with C.

The nongenerality of functions in C and Pascal was essentially forced as well (although different choices were made in what restrictions to impose), since both of these languages opt for a simple stack-based run-time environment; see Chapter 8. Without some restriction on functions, a more general environment is required, and that would compromise the simplicity and efficiency of implementations.

Finally, it is also worth noting that too great a desire to impose a goal, such as generality or orthogonality on the design of a language, can itself be dangerous. A case in point is Algol68. While this language was largely successful in meeting the goals of generality and orthogonality, many language designers have felt that this in itself led to obscurity and complexity in the language.

Readability and reliability can also be seriously affected without some restrictions on the use of certain features. In Pascal, for instance, pointers are specifically restricted to reduce aliasing and insecurities, while in C they are permitted to be much more general, and thus much more prone to misuse and error. In Java, pointers have been eliminated altogether (they are implicit in all object allocation), but at some cost: The runtime environment is more complicated, and changes to variables and arguments can sometimes occur in obscure ways.

In assessing whether a nonregularity is reasonable, one must relate it to the basic design goals of the language and the possible complications that might occur if it were removed. If a nonregularity cannot be clearly justified in this way, then it is probably a design flaw.

3.4 Further Language Design Principles

We have seen efficiency and regularity as design principles in the previous sections. Further principles, some of which we have discussed briefly in Section 3.2, are the following:

Simplicity.   We have mentioned this principle already several times. It was one of the major design goals of Pascal, after experience with the complexity of Algol68 and PL/I. It is also a feature of C, although simplicity was only an indirect goal of the design of C to permit efficient target code (for writing Unix operating system code) and small compilers (to fit on a small computer). Simplicity is perhaps the major reason Pascal became so successful. Simplicity seems like an easy principle to achieve, but it is surprisingly difficult in practice. For one thing, regularity is not simplicity. Algol68 is one of the most regular languages, but it is not simple. Nor is simplicity merely a matter of very few basic constructs (though this does help): LISP and Prolog have only a few basic constructs but depend on a complex runtime system. On the other hand, overly simple programming languages can actually make the task of using them more complex. BASIC is a simple language, but the lack of some fundamental constructs, such as declarations and blocks, makes it much more difficult to program large applications. Pascal itself suffers from oversimplicity: It lacks good string handling, separate compilation, and reasonable input-output facilities, and it has many nonuniformities, such as the use of the assignment for function return. Indeed, Pascal's oversimplicity has been a major factor in its replacement by C, C++, and Java. Thus, C might be regarded as a more successful attempt at simplicity, though it too has a number of major flaws: poor string handling (as in Pascal), somewhat obscure type and operator syntax, unusual array semantics, and weak type checking.

Perhaps it is worth repeating here the famous remark of Einstein:

> Everything should be made as simple as possible, but not simpler.

Oversimplicity can make a language cumbersome to use, lacking in expressiveness, readability, or security, and subject to too many restrictions.

Expressiveness.   We have mentioned this before as an aid to programming efficiency: Expressiveness is the ease with which a language can express complex processes and structures. One of the original advances in expressiveness was the addition of recursion to programming languages (LISP and Algol60). LISP is also expressive in that both data and program can change during execution in arbitrary ways. This is especially useful in complex situations where the size and form of data may not be known. But as we have noted, expressiveness can conflict with simplicity: LISP, Prolog, and Algol68 are extremely expressive languages that are not simple—partially as a result of their expressiveness.

Expressiveness has also been one of the reasons for the rise of popularity of object-oriented languages, since object-oriented features can dramatically improve the ability of programmers to write code that imitates their designs. Stroustrup [1996] notes how impressed he was with Simula67, which led him to design C++: "I was particularly impressed by the way the concepts of the language helped me think about the problems in my application."[2] Such expressiveness, he notes, also leads directly to readability: "The class concept allowed me to map my application con-

---

[2] Ibid., page 700.

cepts into the language constructs in a direct way, that made my code more readable than I had seen in any other language."[3]

Sometimes expressiveness is viewed as conciseness, which can, however, actually compromise readability. The C language is expressive in this sense, yet many programmers do not find C expressions, such as

```
while (*s++ = *t++);
```

easy to understand.[4]

Extensibility.   This principle advocates that there should be some general mechanism for the user to add features to a language. What one means by "add new features" varies, however, with one's point of view. It could mean simply to be able to define new data types, which most languages allow. At a different level it could mean to add new functions from a library, which many languages permit as well. It could also mean to be able to add keywords and constructs to the translator itself. In functional languages such as LISP, this is not too difficult, especially when, as in LISP, language constructs can be defined in terms of the language itself. Thus, LISP is an extensible language in that it has a small number of built-in constructs, or **primitives**, and further operations are added to the environment as needed. In an imperative language, however, this is more difficult. The current trend in such languages is to settle for a little less than full extensibility: to permit the user to define new data types plus operations that apply to these types and to allow these operations to appear just as though they had been defined in the language in the first place.

As an example, the matrix data type can be added to Ada in such a way that matrix operations can be written just as ordinary integer or floating-point operations. Given the declarations

```
type MATRIX is
 array (POSITIVE range <>, POSITIVE range <>) of FLOAT;
function "+" (LEFT,RIGHT: MATRIX) return MATRIX;
A, B, C: MATRIX (1..10, 1..10);
```

we can write

```
C := A + B;
```

The "+" operation is said then to be **overloaded**. A similar definition can be given in C++ through the use of classes; see Chapters 5 and 10 for more discussion.

In C++ and Ada, overloading of operators such as "+" is limited to the existing operators, and one must accept the same syntactic features of these operators (such as left associativity and precedence level; see Chapter 4). In a few languages, particularly functional languages such as ML and Haskell, one can even add user-defined operators, such as, say,

---

[3] Ibid., page 700.

[4] A famous example of code used to copy one string to another; see Kernighan and Ritchie [1988], p. 105.

"+++" by including a definition in a program, such as the following in Haskell:

```
infixr 6 +++
a +++ b = ...
```

which defines +++ to be an "infix" operator (i.e. written between its two operands), with right associativity (the "r" tacked on to "infix"), and with precedence level 6 (the same as + in this particular language).

Extensibility has become of major importance as a language property over the last ten years, as the range of applications and their interactivity has grown. In particular, simplicity without extensibility, at least in terms of the ability to add libraries and interact with other languages and systems, virtually guarantees that a language will not survive in the contemporary computing world.

Extensibility also permits language designers to make different choices in which features to make available in the core language, which to make available in a standard library, and which to not specify at all (but to allow as a third-party library), and not to have to worry too much about a wrong choice. For example, Ada includes concurrent programming features right in the core language (the task mechanism), Java puts such features in a standard library (the thread library), and C++ does not specify any particular concurrency features at all.

Restrictability.   A language design should make it possible for a programmer to program usefully using a minimal knowledge of the language and a minimum number of language constructs. Thus, the language design should promote the ability to define language subsets. This can be useful in two ways: First, a programmer need not learn the whole language to use it effectively; second, a translator writer could choose to implement only a subset if implementing the whole language is too costly or unnecessary. With the increasing size and complexity of modern languages such as C++ and Java, restrictability becomes as important as extensibility. Of course, one could well ask, with an eye on simplicity: If one can program effectively using only a subset of the language, why not make the subset the whole language in the first place, and leave everything else to, say, a library? For a general-purpose language it is difficult to decide what should be included and what should not, since different applications may require different facilities. For example, concurrency and exception handling may be of critical importance only for certain applications. Also, certain features are much more easily included in the core language itself, rather than left to a library. For example, it is sometimes useful to have different versions of the same kind of constructs available—such as repeat-statements as well as while-statements—because of the greater expressiveness of each under certain circumstances. Strictly speaking, such **syntactic sugar** is unnecessary, but it may aid the understanding of a program. On the other hand, if there are ten or fifteen different ways of doing one thing, the complexity of the language increases substantially, with diminishing payoff in expressiveness.

One aspect of restrictability that is often overlooked is efficiency: In principle, if a program does not use certain features of a language, then there should be no performance penalty as a result of those unused features. In other words, a program in C++ that doesn't use exception handling should not run slower than an equivalent program in C (which doesn't have exception handling), simply because exception handling is available in C++. This was, in fact, a major design goal of C++.

Consistency with Accepted Notations and Conventions. A programming language should be easy to learn and understand for the experienced programmer. One aspect of this is that language design should incorporate as much as possible features and concepts that have become standard. Standard concepts such as program, function, and variables should be clearly recognizable. Standard forms for if-then-else and other control structures have evolved. Algol68 violates this principle in a number of ways—for example, in the use of the reserved word **mode** instead of **type**. White-space conventions can also be considered part of this design principle, since Algol60's free format has become the rule, FORTRAN notwithstanding. Blank lines should be allowed. Delimiters of reserved words and identifiers should make the program clear and readable. FORTRAN's ignoring of blanks can cause major problems in readability and security, as the following famous example shows:

```
DO 99 I = 1.10
```

Despite appearances, this assigns the value 1.1 to the variable DO99I. Such surprises are quite aptly referred to as violations of the **law of least astonishment**: Things should not act or appear in completely unexpected ways.

Preciseness. Sometimes called definiteness, preciseness is the existence of a precise definition for a language, so that the behavior of programs can be predicted. A precise language definition is an aid not only to reliability of programs but also to the reliability of translators: A precisely defined language will have more predictable translators, so that program behavior will not vary as much from machine to machine. One step in achieving preciseness is the publication of a language manual or report by the designer. Another is the adoption of a standard by a national or international standards organization, such as the American National Standards Institute (ANSI) or the International Organization for Standardization (ISO). Published standards exist for many languages, including LISP, FORTRAN, Ada, Pascal, COBOL, C, and C++. These are major assets for the usability of these languages. A language standard or reference manual, to be useful, must be not only as precise as possible but also comprehensible to most language users. The Algol68 designers, in attempting to gain greater precision, invented many new terms to describe the language. As a result, the reference manual was extremely difficult to read, and the language lost acceptance.

Machine Independence.   This principle is aided by a language definition that is independent of a particular machine. The primary method for achieving machine independence is the use of predefined data types that do not involve details of memory allocation or machine architecture. Unfortunately, these data types can never be entirely free from machine issues. For example, the real data type consists of numbers that may need infinite precision to specify exactly, while only finite precision can ever be implemented on a computer. Such questions of precision are difficult to specify in a completely machine-independent way. The design of a language must try therefore to isolate and identify whatever machine dependencies cannot be avoided, so that the programmer knows exactly where difficulties might arise. The implementation-defined constants in the C standard libraries `limits.h` and `float.h` are an example of a useful way of isolating machine dependencies. The Ada language goes one step further in that it contains many facilities for actually specifying the precision of numbers within a program and thus removing dependencies on the precision of the operations of a particular machine.

Security.   This principle promotes a language design that both discourages programming errors and allows errors to be discovered and reported. Security is closely related to reliability and preciseness. It was this principle that led language designers to introduce types, type checking, and variable declarations into programming languages. The idea was to "maximize the number of errors that could not be made" by the programmer (Hoare [1981]). In this, it can compromise both the expressiveness and conciseness of a language, and typically puts the onerous task on the programmer of having to specify as many things as possible in the actual code. A debate still exists over the advisability of introducing features that promote security into a language. LISP and Prolog programmers often feel that static type-checking and variable declarations cause major complications when attempting to program complex operations or provide "generic" utilities that work for a wide variety of data. On the other hand, in industrial, commercial, and defense applications, there is often a call for even greater security. Perhaps the real issue is how to design languages that are secure and yet allow for maximal expressiveness and generality. An example of an advance in this direction are the languages ML and Haskell, which are functional in approach, allow multityped objects, do not require declarations, and yet perform static type-checking.

3.5   C++: A Case Study in Language Design

The history and design of most programming languages have tended to be not well documented, and except for the two *History of Programming Languages* books (Wexelblatt [1981]; and Bergin and Gibson [1996]), little published literature exists on how individual programming languages have come into being. There are probably several reasons for this, including: the rapid pace of computer technological development, leaving little time for documentation (a common problem in the software industry, which spills over into language design); little interest in history on the part of language developers; and a general reluctance on the part of developers to reveal their behind-the-scenes secrets, including mistakes and failures (a common attitude among scientists of all kinds).

One exception to this lack of historical information is C++, whose origins, design, and evolution have been richly documented by its developer, Bjarne Stroustrup (Stroustrup [1994] and Stroustrup [1996]). Indeed, Stroustrup's interest in history and philosophy, as well as his extraordinary openness about the design process, provide a unique picture of one of the major language design successes. Some of the important issues in the design of C++ are summarized in the next section; refer to Stroustrup's own accounts for more detail, which are rewarding reading for anyone seriously interested in programming language design.

Background

Stroustrup's interest in designing a new programming language came from his experience as a graduate student at Cambridge, England, in the 1970s. His research focused on a simulator for software running on a distributed system, which he first wrote in Simula67, having found its abstraction mechanisms (primarily the class construct) to be ideal for expressing the conceptual organization of his simulator. In addition, he found the strong type-checking of Simula to be of considerable help in correcting conceptual flaws in the program design. He also found that the larger his program grew, the more helpful these features became.

Unfortunately, he also found that his large program was hard to compile and link in a reasonable time, and so slow as to be virtually impossible to run. The compilation and linking problems were annoying, but the runtime problems were catastrophic, since he was unable to obtain the runtime data necessary to complete his Ph.D. thesis. After some study, he concluded that the runtime inefficiencies were an inherent part of Simula67, and that he would have to abandon that language in order to complete the project. He then rewrote his entire program in BCPL (a low-level predecessor of C), which was a language totally unsuited for the proper expression of the abstractions in his program. This effort was such a painful experience that he felt he should never again attempt such a project with the languages that were then in existence.

But, in 1979, as a new employee at Bell Labs in New Jersey, Stroustrup was again faced with a similar task: simulating a Unix kernel distributed over a local area network. He immediately decided that a new programming language was necessary, and he decided to base it on C, with which he had become familiar at Bell Labs (the "home" of C and Unix), and to add the class construct from Simula67 that he had found so useful.

Stroustrup's reasons for choosing C were flexibility, efficiency, availability, and portability (Stroustrup [1994], page 43). These qualities also fit nicely with the perceived design goals of the new language (ibid., page 23):

1. Support for good program development in the form of classes, inheritance, and strong type-checking
2. Efficient execution on the order of C or BCPL
3. Highly portable, easily implemented, and easily interfaced with other tools

First Implementations

Stroustrup's first implementation of the new language came in 1979–80, in the form of a preprocessor Cpre that transformed the code into ordinary C. The language itself was called C with Classes. It added features that met most of the three goals listed above, and Stroustrup called it a "medium success" (ibid., page 63). However, it did not include several important features, such as dynamic binding of methods ("virtual functions"; see Chapter 10), type parameters ("templates"; see Chapters 6 and 10), or general overloading (see Chapter 5). Stroustrup decided to expand the language in these and other directions, and to replace the preprocessor by a more sophisticated true compiler (which still generated C code as its target, for portability). The language that emerged in 1985 was now called C++, and its compiler was called Cfront (still the basis for many compilers today). He also expanded on the basic goals of the language development effort, to explicitly include the following:

1. C compatibility should be maintained as far as practical, but should not be an end in itself ("there would be no *gratuitous* incompatibilities," ibid., page 101).
2. The language should undergo incremental development based firmly in practical experience; that is, C++ should undergo an evolution driven by real programming problems, not theoretical arguments, while at the same time avoiding "featurism" (adding "neat" features just because it is possible).
3. Any added feature must be implementable at essentially zero cost in runtime efficiency, or, if not, there should be no extra cost to programs that do not use the new feature (the "zero-overhead" rule, ibid., page 121).
4. The language should not force any one style of programming on a programmer; that is, C++ should be a "multiparadigm" language.
5. The language should maintain and strengthen its stronger type-checking (as opposed to C). ("No implicit violations of the static type system," ibid., page 201.)
6. The language should be learnable in stages; that is, it should be possible to program in C++ using some of its features, without knowing anything about other, unused, features.
7. The language should maintain its compatibility with other systems and languages.

The language now included dynamic binding, function and operator over-loading, and improved type-checking, but not type parameters, exceptions, or multiple inheritance (these would all come later).

Growth

In late 1985, Stroustrup published the first edition of his book on C++ (Stroustrup [1997] is the much-changed third edition of this book). In the meantime, Cpre and Cfront had already been distributed for educational purposes essentially at no cost, and interest in the language had begun to grow in industry. Thus, a first commercial implementation was made available in 1986, and in 1987, the first conference specifically on C++ was organized by USENIX (the Unix users' association). By October 1988, Stroustrup estimates that there were about 15,000 users of the language, with PC versions of C++ compilers appearing that same year (between October 1979, when Stroustrup first began using Cpre himself and October 1991, Stroustrup estimates that the number of C++ users doubled every $7\frac{1}{2}$ months). The success of the language indicated to Stroustrup and others that a concerted attempt at a standard language definition was necessary, including possible extensions that had not yet been implemented.

Standardization

Since C++ was rapidly growing in use, was continuing to evolve, and had a number of different implementations, the standardization effort would not be easy. Moreover, because of the growing user pool, there was some pressure to undertake and complete the effort as quickly as possible, while, at the same time, Stroustrup felt that the evolution of the language was not yet complete and should be given some more time.

Nevertheless, Stroustrup produced a reference manual in 1989 (the Annotated Reference Manual, or ARM; Ellis and Stroustrup [1990]) that included all of C++ up to that point, including proposals for new exception handling and template (type parameter) mechanisms (multiple inheritance had already been added to the language and Cfront that same year). In 1990 and 1991, respectively, ANSI and ISO standards committees were convened; these soon combined their efforts and accepted the ARM as the "base document" for the standardization effort.

Then began a long process of clarifying the existing language, producing precise descriptions of its features, and adding features and mechanisms (mostly of a minor nature after the ARM) whose utility was agreed upon. In 1994, a major development was the addition of a standard library of containers and algorithms (the Standard Template Library, or STL). The standards committees produced two drafts of proposed standards in April 1995 and October 1996 before adopting a proposed standard in November 1997. This proposal became the actual ANSI/ISO standard in August 1998.

Retrospective

Obviously, C++ was a success—a particularly striking success in terms of user growth and total number of users. Why has it been such a success? Probably the most significant reason is that, just as interest in object-oriented techniques was exploding, it was able to bring object-oriented features into the mainstream of computing, in that it used straightforward syntax based on C, was not tied to a particular operating environment, and had no associated performance penalty. Additional characteristics of C++ that have probably also contributed to its popularity include its flexibility and multiparadigm nature and the willingness of its designer to extend its features based on practical experience (Stroustrup lists Algol68, CLU, Ada, and ML as major influences after C and Simula67).

Is it possible to point to any "mistakes" in the design of C++? Many people consider C++ to be, like Ada and PL/I before it, a "kitchen-sink" language, with too many features and too many ways of doing similar things. Stroustrup justifies the size of C++ as follows (Stroustrup [1994], page 199):

> The fundamental reason for the size of C++ is that it supports more than one way of writing programs. . . . This flexibility is naturally distasteful to people who believe that there is exactly one right way of doing things. . . . C++ is part of a trend towards greater language complexity to deal with the even greater complexity of the programming tasks attempted.

Stroustrup does, however, list one fact in the "biggest mistake" category (ibid., page 200)—namely, that C++ was first defined and implemented without any standard library (even without strings). This has, of course, been corrected with the 1998 C++ standard, but Java has shown that an important feature of new languages will be an extensive library that includes graphics, user interfaces, networking, and concurrency. That is perhaps the biggest challenge for C++ to face in the future. Stroustrup himself comments (ibid., page 208): "In the future, I expect to see the major activity and progress shift from the language proper . . . to the tools, environments, libraries, applications, etc., that depend on it and build on it."

Exercises

3.1 Give your own examples of features in a language of your choice that promote or violate the following design principles:

Efficiency
Expressiveness
Maintainability
Readability

Reliability
Security
Simplicity
Writability

3.2 Give your own examples to distinguish among the concepts of orthogonality, generality, and uniformity.

3.3 In Ada there is a `loop` ... `exit` construct, and in PL/I there is a similar `loop` ... `break` construct. Is there a similar construct in C or Java? Is this an example of any of the design principles?

3.4 In Java, integers can be assigned to real variables, but not vice versa. What design principle does this violate? In C, this restriction does not exist. What design principle does this violate?

3.5 Choose a feature from a programming language of your choice that you think should be removed. Why should the feature be removed? What problems might arise as a result of the removal?

3.6 Choose a feature that you think should be added to a programming language of your choice. Why should the feature be added? What needs to be stated about the feature to specify completely its behavior and interaction with other features?

3.7 In Ada the `end` reserved word must be qualified by the kind of block that it ends: `if` ... `then` ... `end if`, `loop` ... `end loop`, and so on. In Algol68, the `end` is replaced by writing a reserved word backward: `if` ... `then` ... `fi`, `while` ... `do` ... `od`, and so on. Discuss the effect these conventions have on readability, writability, and security.

3.8 Should a language require the declaration of variables? Languages such as FORTRAN and BASIC allow variable names to be used without declarations, while C, Java, and Ada require all variables to be declared. Discuss the requirement that variables should be declared from the point of view of readability, writability, efficiency, security, and expressiveness.

3.9 Compare and contrast the views expressed in Hoare [1973], Hoare [1981], and Wirth [1974].

3.10 The semicolon was used as an example of a nonuniformity in C++. Discuss the use of the semicolon in C. Is its use entirely uniform?

3.11 Two opposing views on comments in programs could be stated as follows:
   (a) A program should always contain elaborate comments to make it readable and maintainable.
   (b) A program should be as much as possible self-documenting, with comments added sparingly only where the code itself might be unclear.

   Discuss these two viewpoints from the point of view of language design. What design features might aid one viewpoint but not the other? What might aid both?

3.12 Here are two more opposing statements:

    (a) A program should never run with error checking turned off. Turning off error checking after a program has been tested is like throwing away the life preserver when graduating from the pool to the ocean.

    (b) A program should always have error checking turned off after the testing stage. Keeping error checking on is like keeping training wheels on a bike after you've entered a race.

Discuss (a) and (b) from the point of view of language design.

3.13 Discuss the following two views of language design:

    (a) Language design is compiler construction.

    (b) Language design is software engineering.

3.14 Two contrasting viewpoints on the declaration of comments in a programming language are represented by Ada and C: In Ada, comments begin with adjacent hyphens and end with the end of a line:

```
-- this is an Ada comment
```

In C, comments begin with "/*" and proceed to a matching "*/":

```
/* this is a C comment */
```

Compare these two comment features with respect to readability, writability, and reliability. C++ added a comment convention (two forward slashes) similar to that of Ada.[5] Why didn't C++ use exactly the Ada convention?

3.15 The **principle of locality** maintains that variable declarations should come as close as possible to their use in a program. What language design features promote or discourage this principle? How well do Ada, C, C++, and Java promote this principle?

3.16 Often a language can be much more easily learned and used if there exists a good symbolic runtime debugger. Compare the language systems you know with regard to the existence and/or quality of a debugger. Can you think of any language constructs that would aid or discourage the use of a debugger?

3.17 One of the major problems in programming language design is the lack of understanding of many human factors that affect language use, from psychology to human-machine interaction ("ergonomics"). One example of this is that programming errors made by humans are far from random, and language design should attempt to prevent the most common errors. Keep a record of the kinds of errors you have made most frequently in learning a new language, or look up the study by Ripley and

---

[5] The 1999 ISO C Standard adds the C++ comment convention to C as well.

Druseikis [1978] for the case of Pascal. How could the most common errors have been prevented by the language design?

3.18 Most programming languages now use the **free format** pioneered by Algol60: Statements can begin anywhere and end not with the end of a line of text but with an explicit end symbol, such as a semicolon. By contrast, FORTRAN and a few other languages use **fixed format**: Statements must begin in a particular column and are ended by the physical end of the line, unless continuation marks are provided. Discuss the effect of fixed or free format on readability, writability, and security.

3.19 Here is a quote from D. L. Parnas [1985]: "Because of the very large improvements in productivity that were noted when compiler languages were introduced, many continue to look for another improvement by introducing better languages. Better notation always helps, but we cannot expect new languages to provide the same magnitude of improvement that we got from the first introduction of such languages. . . . We should seek simplifications in programming languages, but we cannot expect that this will make a big difference." Discuss.

3.20 A possible additional language design principle is **learnability**, that is, the ability of programmers to learn to use the language quickly and effectively. Describe a situation in which learnability may be an important requirement for a programming language to have. Describe ways in which a language designer can improve the learnability of a language.

3.21 In most language implementations the integer data type has a fixed size, which means that the maximum size of an integer is machine dependent. In some languages like Scheme, however, integers may be of any size, and so become machine independent. Discuss the advantages and disadvantages of making such "infinite-precision" integers a requirement of a language definition. Is it possible to also implement "infinite-precision" real numbers? Can real numbers be made machine independent? Discuss.

3.22 Brooks [1996] lists five basic design principles:

    1. Design, don't hack.

    2. Study other designs.

    3. Design top-down.

    4. Know the application area.

    5. Iterate.

(a) Explain what each of these means in terms of programming language design.

(b) Describe to what extent the C++ design effort (Section 3.5) appears to meet each of the above design criteria.

3.23 Here is another quote from Stroustrup (Stroustrup [1994], page 45):

> . . . language design is not just design from first principles, but an art that requires experience, experiments, and sound engineering tradeoffs. Adding a major feature or concept to a language should not be a leap of faith, but a deliberate action based on experience and fitting into a framework of other features and ideas of how the resulting language can be used.

Compare this view of language design with the list of five principles in the previous exercise.

3.24 In Chapter 1 we discussed how the von Neumann architecture affected the design of programming languages. It is also possible for a programming language design to affect the design of machine architecture as well. Describe one or more examples of this.

Notes and References

Horowitz [1984] gives a list of programming language design criteria similar to the ones in this chapter, which he partially attributes to Barbara Liskov. For an extensive historical perspective on language design, see Wegner [1976] (this paper and the papers by Wirth [1974] and Hoare [1973] mentioned in this chapter are all reprinted in Horowitz [1987]). The unification algorithm for type-checking mentioned in Section 3.2 is described in Hindley [1969] and Milner [1978]. The rationale for the design of Ada is discussed in Ichbiah et al. [1979], where many design principles are discussed. Many design issues in modern languages are discussed in Bergin and Gibson [1996], especially the articles on Pascal (Wirth [1996]), C (Ritchie [1996]), C++ (Stroustrup [1996]), Lisp (Steele and Gabriel [1996]), CLU (Liskov [1996]), Algol68 (Lindsey [1996]), and Prolog (Colmerauer and Roussel [1996]). Another article in that collection (Brooks [1996]) gives general advice on language design. Stroustrup [1994] is a significantly expanded version of the C++ paper in that collection and gives a detailed analysis of design issues in C++. See also Hoare [1981] for some wry comments on designing languages, compilers, and computer systems in general.

4 Syntax

Syntax is the structure of a language. In Chapter 1 we noted the difference between the syntax and semantics of a programming language. In the early days of programming languages, both the syntax and semantics of a language were described by lengthy English explanations and many examples. While the semantics of a language are still usually described in English, one of the great advances in programming languages has been the development of a formal system for describing syntax that is now almost universally in use. In the 1950s Noam Chomsky developed the idea of context-free grammars, and John Backus, with contributions by Peter Naur, developed a notational system for describing these grammars that was used for the first time to describe the syntax of Algol60. These **Backus-Naur forms—BNFs** for short—have subsequently been used in the definition of many programming languages, including C, Java, and Ada. Indeed, every modern programmer and computer scientist needs to know how to read, interpret, and apply BNF descriptions of language syntax. These BNFs occur with minor textual variations in three basic forms: original BNF; extended BNF (EBNF), popularized by Niklaus Wirth; and syntax diagrams.

In Section 4.1, we briefly look at the lexical structure of programming languages—the building blocks on which syntax is often based, and the process of scanning, or recognizing lexical structure. In Section 4.2, we introduce context-free grammars and their description in BNF. In Section 4.3, we describe the representation of syntactic structure using trees. In Section 4.4, we consider a few of the issues that arise in constructing BNFs for a programming language. EBNFs and syntax diagrams are introduced in Section 4.5. In Section 4.6, we discuss the basic technique of recursive-descent parsing and its close relationship to EBNF and syntax diagrams and briefly look at YACC/Bison, a standard tool for analyzing grammars and constructing parsers. Finally, in Section 4.7, we examine the sometimes hazy boundaries among the lexical, syntactic, and semantic structures of a programming language.

4.1 Lexical Structure of Programming Languages

The lexical structure of a programming language is the structure of its words, or **tokens**. Lexical structure can be considered separately from syntactic structure, but it is closely related to and, in some cases (depending on the design of the language), can be an inextricable part of syntax. Typically, the **scanning** phase of a translator collects sequences of characters from the input program into tokens, which are then processed by a **parsing** phase, which determines the syntactic structure.

Tokens generally fall into several distinct categories. Typical token categories include the following:

> **reserved words**, sometimes called **keywords**, such as `if` and `while`
>
> **literals** or **constants**, such as 42 (a numeric literal) or `"hello"` (a string literal)
>
> **special symbols**, such as ";", "<=", or "+"
>
> **identifiers**, such as `x24`, `monthly_balance`, or `putchar`

Reserved words are so named because an identifier cannot have the same character string as a reserved word. Thus, in C, the following variable declaration is illegal because `if` is a reserved word:

```
double if;
```

Sometimes confusion can occur in a language between reserved words and **predefined identifiers**, or identifiers that have been given an initial meaning for all programs in the language, but which are capable of redefinition. (To add to the confusion, sometimes these identifiers are also called keywords.) Examples are all standard data types in Pascal and Ada, such as `integer` and `boolean`. See Section 4.7 for more on this phenomenon.

In some languages identifiers have a fixed maximum size, while in most newer languages identifiers can have arbitrary length. Occasionally, even when arbitrary-length identifiers are allowed, only the first six or eight characters are guaranteed to be significant. (This is guaranteed to be confusing to the programmer.)

A problem arises in determining the end of a variable-length token such as an identifier and in distinguishing identifiers from reserved words. As an example, the sequence of characters

```
doif
```

in a program could be either the two reserved words do and if, or it could be the identifier doif. Similarly, the string x12 could be a single identifier or the identifier x and the numeric constant 12. To eliminate this ambiguity, it is a standard convention to use the **principle of longest substring** in determining tokens (sometimes called the principle of "maximum munch"): At each point, the longest possible string of characters is collected into a single token. This means that doif and x12 are always identifiers. It also means that intervening characters, even blanks, can make a difference. Thus, in most languages

```
do if
```

is not an identifier but becomes the two reserved words do and if.

The format of a program can affect the way tokens are recognized. For example, as we just saw, the principle of longest substring requires that certain tokens be separated by **token delimiters** or **white space**. The end of a line of text can be doubly meaningful: It can be white space, and it can also mean the end of a structural entity. Indentation can also be used in a programming language to determine structure. A **free-format** language is one in which format has no effect on the program structure (other than to satisfy the principle of longest substring). Most modern languages are free format, but a few have significant format restrictions. Rarely is a language **fixed format**, in which all tokens must occur in prespecified locations on the page.

FORTRAN is the primary example of a language that violates many of these format and token conventions (perhaps its age is showing). In the last chapter we mentioned the following example in FORTRAN:

```
DO 99 I = 1.10
```

This statement is equivalent to the C

```
DO99I = 1.10;
```

In other words, it assigns the value 1.1 to the variable DO99I. On the other hand, the FORTRAN

```
DO 99 I = 1, 10
```

is equivalent to the C

```
for (I = 1; I <= 10; I++)
```

That is, it begins a loop by giving the bounds of the index I. Thus, the first FORTRAN statement contains three tokens: an identifier, the assignment operator ("="), and the real constant 1.1. The second FORTRAN statement, on the other hand, contains seven tokens. The reason for this is that FORTRAN ignores spaces completely—they are removed before processing begins. Furthermore, FORTRAN has *no* reserved words at all: DO, IF, or any other word describing a structure can also be an identifier; the FORTRAN statements

```
IF = 2
IF(IF.LT.0) IF = IF + 1
ELSE IF = IF + 2
```

are perfectly legal. In FORTRAN, the token structure and the syntax are inextricably entwined.

As a final example of lexical structure in a programming language, we quote the description of the token conventions of the C language from the reference manual in Kernighan and Ritchie [1988]:

> There are six classes of tokens: identifiers, keywords, constants, string literals, operators, and other separators. Blanks, horizontal and vertical tabs, newlines, formfeeds, and comments as described below (collectively, "white space") are ignored except as they separate tokens. Some white space is required to separate otherwise adjacent identifiers, keywords, and constants. If the input stream has been separated into tokens up to a given character, the next token is the longest string of characters that could constitute a token.

Thus, C adheres to the principle of longest substring.

Tokens in a programming language are often described in English, but they can also be described formally by **regular expressions**, which are descriptions of patterns of characters. Regular expressions have three basic operations: concatenation, repetition, and choice or selection. Repetition is indicated by the use of an asterisk after the item to be repeated; choice is indicated by a vertical bar between the items from which the selection is to be made; and concatenation is given simply by sequencing the items without an explicit operation. Parentheses are also often included to allow for the grouping of operations. For example, (a|b)*c is a regular expression indicating 0 or more repetitions of either the characters a or b (choice), followed by a single character c (concatenation); strings that match this regular expression include ababaac, aac, babbc, and just c itself, but not aaaab or bca.

Regular expression notation is often extended by additional operations and special characters to make them easier to write. For example, square brackets with a hyphen indicate a range of characters, + indicates one or more repetitions, ? indicates an optional item, and a period indicates any character. With these notations, we can write compact regular expressions for even fairly complex tokens. For example,

```
[0-9]+
```

is a regular expression for simple integer constants consisting of one or more digits (characters between 0 and 9). Also, the regular expression

```
[0-9]+(\.[0-9]+)?
```

describes simple (unsigned) floating-point literals consisting of one or more digits followed by an optional fractional part consisting of a decimal point (with a backslash "escape" character in front of it to remove the special meaning of a period as matching any character), followed again by one or more digits.

Many utilities exist that use regular expressions in text searches, including most modern text editors, and various file search utilities, such as Unix grep ("global regular expression print"). The Unix lex utility can also be used to turn a regular expression description of the tokens of a language into a scanner automatically. (A successor to lex, called flex, or "fast lex," is freely available and runs on most operating systems.)

While a study of lex/flex and the use of regular expressions to construct scanners is beyond the scope of this text, in simple cases scanners can be relatively easily constructed by hand. To show the flavor of such a scanner construction, we present C code for a simple scanner in Figure 4.1. There are six tokens in this language (represented as constants of an enumeration type, lines 4–5): integer constants consisting of one or more digits; the special characters +, *, (, and); and the end of line token (represented in C or Java as the special character '\n', or newline). Such a language may be used to specify a simple integer arithmetic expression with addition and multiplication on a single line of input, such as

```
(2 + 34) * 42
```

Blanks are to be skipped, and any character (such as a or # or -) that is not specified is to be considered an error (thus, the need for the additional ERROR token on line 5).

Before closing this section and moving on to the study of syntax and parsing, we note the following additional features of the code in Figure 4.1. First, the code contains a main program (lines 32–47) to demonstrate the scanner (which is represented by the getToken function, lines 8–31): Given a line of input, the program simply calls getToken repeatedly and prints out each token as it is recognized; a number is also printed with its numeric value, and an error is printed with the offending character. Second, we note that the scanner communicates the additional numeric and character information to the main program via the global variables numval and curr_char (lines 6 and 7). A more sophisticated design would eliminate these globals and package this information into a data structure containing all token information; see Exercise 4.7. Given the input line

```
* + ( ) 42 # 345
```

(text continues on page 83)

```
(1)   #include <ctype.h>
(2)   #include <stdio.h>

(3)   /* the tokens as an enumerated type */
(4)   typedef enum {PLUS,TIMES,LPAREN,RPAREN,
(5)                   EOL,NUMBER,ERROR} TokenType;

(6)   int numval; /* computed numeric value of a NUMBER token
      */
(7)   int curr_char; /* current character */

(8)   TokenType getToken(void)
(9)   { while ((curr_char = getchar()) == ' '); /* skip
      blanks */
(10)    if (isdigit(curr_char)) /* recognize a NUMBER token
        */
(11)   { numval = 0;
(12)     while (isdigit(curr_char))
(13)     { /* compute numeric value */
(14)        numval = 10 * numval + curr_char - '0';
(15)        curr_char = getchar();
(16)     }
(17)     /* put back last character onto input */
(18)     ungetc(curr_char,stdin);
(19)     return NUMBER;
(20)   }
(21)   else /* recognize a special symbol */
(22)   { switch (curr_char)
(23)     { case '(': return LPAREN; break;
(24)       case ')': return RPAREN; break;
(25)       case '+': return PLUS; break;
(26)       case '*': return TIMES; break;
(27)       case '\n': return EOL; break;
(28)       default: return ERROR; break;
(29)     }
(30)   }
(31) }

(32) main()
(33) { TokenType token;
(34)   do
(35)   { token = getToken();
(36)     switch (token)
(37)     { case PLUS: printf("PLUS\n"); break;
(38)       case TIMES: printf("TIMES\n"); break;
```

Figure 4.1   A Scanner for Simple Integer Arithmetic Expressions

```
(39)        case LPAREN: printf("LPAREN\n"); break;
(40)        case RPAREN: printf("RPAREN\n"); break;
(41)        case EOL: printf("EOL\n"); break;
(42)        case NUMBER: printf("NUMBER: %d\n", numval);
            break;
(43)        case ERROR: printf("ERROR: %c\n", curr_char);
            break;
(44)    }
(45)  } while (token != EOL);
(46)  return 0;
(47) }
```

Figure 4.1   (*continued*)

the program of Figure 4.1 produces the following output:

```
TIMES
PLUS
LPAREN
RPAREN
NUMBER: 42
ERROR: #
NUMBER: 345
EOL
```

Note that no order for the tokens is specified by the scanner—defining and recognizing an appropriate order is the subject of syntax and parsing, studied in the remainder of this chapter.

4.2 Context-Free Grammars and BNFs

We begin our description of grammars and BNFs with the example in Figure 4.2 (the numbers are for reference purposes).

(1) *sentence* → *noun-phrase verb-phrase* .

(2) *noun-phrase* → *article noun*

(3) *article* → a | the

(4) *noun* → girl | dog

(5) *verb-phrase* → *verb noun-phrase*

(6) *verb* → sees | pets

Figure 4.2   A Grammar for Simple English Sentences

In English, simple sentences consist of a noun phrase and a verb phrase followed by a period. We express this as the grammar rule 1 in Figure 4.2.

Rules 2 through 6 describe in turn the structure of noun phrases, verb phrases, and other substructures that appear in previous rules. Each of these grammar rules consists of a name in italics (the name of the structure being described), followed by an arrow (which can be read as "consists of" or "is the same as,"), followed by a sequence of other names and symbols. The italics serve to distinguish the names of the structures from the actual words, or tokens, that may appear in the language (which, in our examples are also indicated in a different typeface). For instance, we would not wish to confuse the keyword `program` in Pascal with the program structure itself:

$$\textit{program} \rightarrow \texttt{program} \dots$$

Typically, of course, we would prefer also to use different names to distinguish structures from tokens.

The symbol "$\rightarrow$" is a **metasymbol** that serves to separate the left-hand side from the right-hand side of a rule. The vertical bar "|" is also a metasymbol and means "or" or choice (similar to its use in regular expressions). Thus, rule 6 above states that a verb is either the word "`sees`" or the word "`pets.`" Sometimes a metasymbol is also an actual symbol in a language. In that case the symbol can be surrounded by quotes to distinguish it from the metasymbol, or the metasymbol can be written in a different typeface, or both. Often it is a good idea to do this for special symbols like punctuation marks, even when they are not also metasymbols. For example, rule 1 has a period in it. While a period is not part of any metasymbol described, it can easily be mistaken for one. Hence, it might be better to write the rule as follows:

$$\textit{sentence} \rightarrow \textit{noun-phrase verb-phrase} \text{ '.'}$$

(Of course, now the quotes also become metasymbols.) Some notations also rely on metasymbols (such as angle brackets) rather than italics or fonts to distinguish structures from tokens, which can also be useful in situations where formatting is not available (such as in text files or handwritten text). In that case, the arrow is also often replaced by a metasymbol that is also pure text (such as two colons and an equal sign). For example, one might see rule 1 of Figure 4.2 written as follows:

$$\text{<sentence>} ::= \text{<noun-phrase> <verb-phrase> "."}$$

Here the angle brackets also become metasymbols, and double quotes have been used instead of single quotes to mark the period as a token.

Indeed, there are many different, often personal, preferences in the notational conventions used in writing grammar rules. There is also an ISO standard format for BNF notation (ISO 14977 [1996]), which is almost universally ignored, perhaps because, by the time of its adoption (1996), other conventions such as the above were already entrenched. For example, the grammar rule for a sentence would appear in standard ISO form as

$$\textit{sentence} = \textit{noun phrase} , \textit{verb phrase} \text{ "." } ;$$

Any legal sentence according to the foregoing grammar can be constructed as follows: We start with the symbol *sentence* (the **start symbol** for the grammar) and proceed to replace left-hand sides by choices of right-hand sides in the foregoing rules. This process creates a **derivation** in the language. Thus, we could construct, or derive, the sentence "`the girl sees a dog.`" as in Figure 4.3, where each step is annotated by the number of the rule from Figure 4.2 that is used in that step.

sentence ⇒ *noun-phrase verb-phrase* . (rule 1)
        ⇒ *article noun verb-phrase* . (rule 2)
        ⇒ `the` *noun verb-phrase* . (rule 3)
        ⇒ `the girl` *verb-phrase* . (rule 4)
        ⇒ `the girl` *verb noun-phrase* . (rule 5)
        ⇒ `the girl sees` *noun-phrase* . (rule 6)
        ⇒ `the girl sees` *article noun* . (rule 2)
        ⇒ `the girl sees a` *noun* . (rule 3)
        ⇒ `the girl sees a dog` . (rule 4)

Figure 4.3   A Derivation Using the Grammar of Figure 4.2

Conversely, we could start with the sentence "`the girl sees a dog.`" and work backward through the derivation of Figure 4.3 to arrive at *sentence* and so have shown that the sentence is legal in the language.

The simple grammar of Figure 4.2 already exhibits most of the properties of programming language grammars. Note that not all legal sentences actually make sense: "`the dog pets the girl.`" is one such. Note that there is also a subtle error: Articles that appear at the beginning of sentences should be capitalized. Such a "positional" property is often hard to deal with using context-free grammars. Also, we have written the tokens in the foregoing sentence with spaces in between the tokens, but the grammar does not specify whether such spaces are necessary (we might have easily written "`thegirlseesadog.`"). This question is left to a scanner, which recognizes the individual tokens or words, as noted in the previous section. (See also Exercise 4.9.) Finally, the grammar also does not specify additional requirements on input format, such as the fact that a sentence should be followed by some kind of termination symbol (such as a newline or end of file marker). Occasionally one needs to make this latter condition explicit in a grammar, and one typically writes a rule such as

input → *sentence* $

to indicate that a sentence is to be followed by some kind of end marker, indicated by the dollar sign (and which may or may not need to be generated explicitly). (Examples of this will occur later in this chapter.)

Here are some definitions for what we have seen. (We could give mathematically precise definitions, but we prefer a more informal approach.) A **context-free grammar** consists of a series of grammar rules as described: The rules consist of a left-hand side that is a single structure name, then the metasymbol "→", followed by a right-hand side consisting of a sequence of items that can be symbols or other structure names. The names for structures (like *sentence*) are called **nonterminals**, since they are broken down into further structures. The words or token symbols are also called **terminals**, since they are never broken down. Grammar rules are also called **productions**, since they "produce" the strings of the language using derivations. Productions are in **Backus-Naur form** if they are as given using only the metasymbols "→" and "|". (Sometimes parentheses are also allowed to group things together.)

A context-free grammar also has a distinguished nonterminal called the **start symbol**, as noted above. This nonterminal stands for the entire structure being defined (such as a sentence or a program), and is the symbol that all derivations begin with. A context-free language defines a language, called the **language of the grammar**. This language is the set of all strings of terminals for which there exists a derivation beginning with the start symbol and ending with the string of terminals.

In Figure 4.2 there are seven terminals ("girl," "dog," "sees," "pets," "the," "a," and "."), six nonterminals, and six productions. The language defined by this grammar is also finite (see Exercise 4.8), but in general languages defined by grammars are not finite.

Typically there are as many productions in a context-free grammar as there are nonterminals, although one could eliminate the "|" metasymbol by writing each choice separately, such as

$$noun \rightarrow \texttt{girl}$$

$$noun \rightarrow \texttt{dog}$$

in which case each nonterminal would correspond to as many productions as there are choices.

Why is such a grammar **context-free**? The simple reason is that the nonterminals appear singly on the left-hand sides of productions. This means that each nonterminal can be replaced by any right-hand side choice, no matter where the nonterminal might appear. In other words, there is no **context** under which only certain replacements can occur. For example, in the grammar just discussed, it makes sense to use the verb "pets" only when the subject is "girl"; this can be thought of as a context-sensitivity. One could write out context-sensitive grammars by allowing "context strings" to appear on left-hand sides of the grammar rules, and some authors consider context-sensitivities to be syntactic issues. We shall adopt the view, however, that anything not expressible using context-free grammars is a semantic, not a syntactic issue. (Even some things that *are* expressible as context-free grammars are often better left to semantic descriptions, since they involve writing many extra productions; see Exercise 4.30.)

As an example of a context-sensitivity, we noted that articles that appear at the beginning of sentences in the preceding grammar should be capitalized. One way of doing this is to rewrite the first rule as

$$sentence \rightarrow beginning\ noun\text{-}phrase\ verb\text{-}phrase\ `.'$$

and then add the context-sensitive rule:

$$\textit{beginning article} \rightarrow \mathsf{The} \mid \mathsf{A}$$

Now the derivation would look as follows:

> *sentence* ⇒ *beginning noun-phrase verb-phrase* . (new rule 1)
>
> ⇒ *beginning article noun verb-phrase* . (rule 2)
>
> ⇒ The *noun verb-phrase* . (new context-sensitive rule)
>
> ⇒ . . .

Context-free grammars have been studied extensively by formal language theorists and are now so well understood that it is natural to express the syntax of any programming language in BNF form. Indeed, doing so makes it easier to write translators for the language, since the parsing stage can be automated; see Section 4.6.

A typical simple example of the use of a context-free grammar in programming languages is the description of simple integer arithmetic expressions with addition and multiplication given in Figure 4.4.

expr → *expr* + *expr* | *expr* * *expr* | (*expr*) | *number*
number → *number digit* | *digit*
digit → 0 | 1 | 2 | 3 | 4 | 5 | 6 | 7 | 8 | 9

Figure 4.4   A Simple Integer Arithmetic Expression Grammar

Note the recursive nature of the rules: An expression can be the sum or product of two expressions, each of which can be further sums or products. Eventually, of course, this process must stop by choosing the *number* alternative, or we would never arrive at a string of terminals.

Note also that the recursion in the rule for *number* is used to generate a repeated sequence of digits. For example, the number 234 is constructed as in Figure 4.5.

number ⇒ *number digit*
    ⇒ *number digit digit*
    ⇒ *digit digit digit*
    ⇒ 2 *digit digit*
    ⇒ 23 *digit*
    ⇒ 234

Figure 4.5   A Derivation for the *Number* 234 Using the Grammar of Figure 4.4

This process could actually be performed by a scanner, as we have noted in the previous section, since it deals only with sequences of characters. Indeed, the grammar above has as its terminals only single character tokens such as + and 9, and the question of white space is ignored. We will return to this question in Section 4.7, but for simplicity we ignore scanning questions for the moment.

As a more complex example of a grammar in BNF, Figure 4.6 shows the beginning of a BNF description for the C language:

translation-unit → *external-declaration*
   | *translation-unit external-declaration*

external-declaration → *function-definition* | *declaration*

function-definition → *declaration-specifiers declarator*
                         declaration-list compound-statement
   | *declaration-specifiers declarator compound-statement*
   | *declarator declaration-list compound-statement*
   | *declarator compound-statement*

declaration → *declaration-specifiers* ';'
   | *declaration-specifiers init-declarator-list* ';'

init-declarator-list → *init-declarator*
   | *init-declarator-list* ',' *init-declarator*

init-declarator → *declarator* | *declarator* '=' *initializer*
declarator → *pointer direct-declarator* | *direct-declarator*

pointer → '*' *type-qualifier-list pointer* | '*' *type-qualifier-list*
   | '*' *pointer* | '*'

direct-declarator → ID
   | '(' *declarator* ')' | *direct_declarator* '[' ']'
   | *direct_declarator* '[' *constant_expression* ']'
   | *direct_declarator* '(' *parameter_type_list* ')'
   | *direct_declarator* '(' *identifier_list* ')'
   | *direct_declarator* '(' ')'
. . .
. . .

Figure 4.6   Partial BNFs for C (Adapted from Kernighan and Ritchie [1988])

4.2.1 BNF Rules as Equations

An alternative way of explaining how BNF rules construct the strings of a language is as follows. Given a grammar rule such as

$$expr \rightarrow expr + expr \mid number$$

(abstracted from Figure 4.4), let **E** be the set of strings representing expressions, and let **N** represent the set of strings representing numbers. The preceding grammar rule can be viewed as a **set equation**

$$\mathbf{E = E + E \cup N}$$

where $\mathbf{E + E}$ is the set constructed by concatenating all strings from $\mathbf{E}$ with the "+" symbol and then all strings from E and "$\cup$" is set union. Assuming that the set $\mathbf{N}$ has already been constructed, this represents a recursive equation for the set $\mathbf{E}$. *The smallest set* $\mathbf{E}$ *satisfying this equation* can be taken to be the set defined by the grammar rule. Intuitively, this consists of the set

$$\mathbf{N \cup N + N \cup N + N + N \cup N + N + N + N \cup} \ldots$$

and we could actually prove that this is the smallest set satisfying the given equation; see Exercise 4.53. Solutions to recursive equations appear frequently in formal descriptions of programming languages, and are a major object of study in the theory of programming languages, where they are called **least fixed points** (a term that will be explained later). We will see them again from time to time in later chapters (for example, in the definition of recursive data types, recursive functions, and formal semantics).

4.3 Parse Trees and Abstract Syntax Trees

Syntax establishes structure, not meaning. But the meaning of a sentence (or program) must be related to its syntax. In English a sentence has a subject and a predicate, which are semantic notions, since the subject (the "actor") and the predicate (the "action") determine the meaning of the sentence. A subject generally comes at the beginning of a sentence and is given by a noun phrase. Thus, in the syntax of an English sentence, a noun phrase is placed first and is subsequently associated with a subject. Similarly, in the grammar for expressions, when we write

$$expr \rightarrow expr + expr$$

we expect to add the values of the two right-hand expressions to get the value of the left-hand expression. This process of attaching the semantics of a construct to its syntactic structure is called **syntax-directed semantics**. We must therefore construct the syntax so that it reflects the semantics we will eventually attach to it as much as possible. (Syntax-directed semantics could just as easily have been called semantics-directed syntax.)

To make use of the syntactic structure of a program to determine its semantics, we must have a way of expressing this structure as determined by a derivation. A standard method for doing this is with a **parse tree**. The parse tree describes graphically the replacement process in a derivation. For example, the parse tree for the sentence "the girl sees a dog." is as follows:

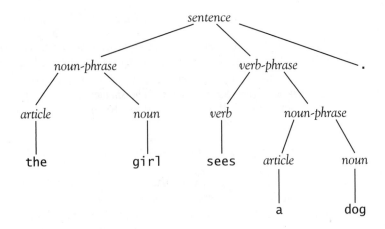

Similarly, the parse tree for the number 234 in the expression grammar is

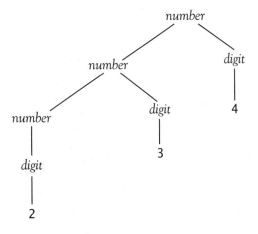

A parse tree is labeled by nonterminals at interior nodes and terminals at leaves. The structure of a parse tree is completely specified by the grammar rules of the language and a derivation of a particular sequence of terminals: The grammar rules specify the structure of each interior node, and the derivation specifies which interior nodes are constructed. For example, the tree for the number 234 is specified by the grammar rules for *number* and the derivation of 234 as given in the previous section. Indeed, the first two steps of the derivation are

$$number \Rightarrow number\ digit \qquad (step\ 1)$$
$$\Rightarrow number\ digit\ digit \qquad (step\ 2)$$

and correspond to the construction of the two children of the root (step 1) and the two children of the left child of the root (step 2). Not surprisingly, there are exactly as many steps in the derivation of 234 as there are interior nodes in the parse tree.

All the terminals and nonterminals in a derivation are included in the parse tree. But not all the terminals and nonterminals may be necessary to determine completely the syntactic structure of an expression or sentence. For example, the structure of the number 234 can be completely determined from the tree

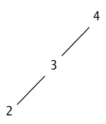

and a parse tree for 3 + 4 * 5 such as

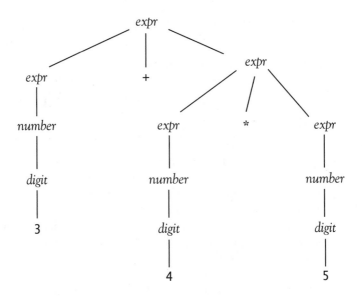

could be condensed to the tree

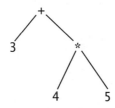

Such trees are called **abstract syntax trees** or just **syntax trees**, since they abstract the essential structure of the parse tree. Abstract syntax trees may also do away with terminals that are redundant once the structure of the tree is determined. For example, the grammar rule

if-statement → if (*expression*) *statement* else *statement*

gives rise to the parse tree

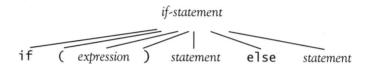

and the abstract syntax tree

It is possible to write out rules for abstract syntax in a similar way to the BNF rules for ordinary syntax. For example, the abstract syntax for an *if-statement* corresponding to the previous BNF rule could be written simply as

if-statement → *expression statement statement*

Of course, this can also be a little confusing, since this is not what we would see in an actual program. For this reason, abstract syntax is typically of less interest to the programmer and is often left unspecified. Sometimes ordinary syntax is distinguished from abstract syntax by calling it **concrete syntax**. Of course, abstract syntax is of great importance to the language designer and translator writer, since it is the abstract, not the concrete, syntax that expresses a language's essential structure, and a translator will often construct a syntax tree rather than a full parse tree because it is more concise. In this text, rather than specify both concrete and abstract syntax, we will focus on the concrete syntax and infer typical abstract structures for syntax trees directly from the concrete syntax.

4.4 Ambiguity, Associativity, and Precedence

Two different derivations can lead to the same parse tree or syntax tree: In the derivation for 234 in Figure 4.5, we could have chosen to replace the *digit* nonterminals first:

$$number \Rightarrow number\ digit$$
$$\Rightarrow number\ 4$$
$$\Rightarrow number\ digit\ 4$$
$$\Rightarrow number\ 34$$
$$. . .$$

but we would still have the same parse tree (and syntax tree). However, different derivations can also lead to different parse trees. For example, if we construct 3 + 4 * 5 from the expression grammar of Figure 4.4, we can use the derivation

$$expr \Rightarrow expr + expr$$
$$\Rightarrow expr + expr * expr$$
(replace the second *expr* with *expr* * *expr*)
$$\Rightarrow number + expr * expr$$
$$. . .$$

or the derivation

$$expr \Rightarrow expr * expr$$
$$\Rightarrow expr + expr * expr$$
(replace the first *expr* with *expr* + *expr*)
$$\Rightarrow number + expr * expr$$
$$. . .$$

and these lead to two distinct parse trees (dashed lines here and in the following trees indicate missing nodes in the parse trees that are unimportant for the structure being discussed):

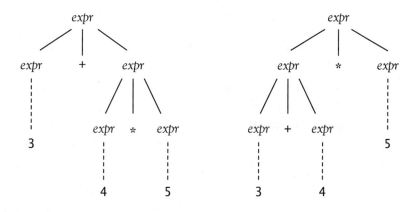

and the two distinct abstract syntax trees as given in Figure 4.7.

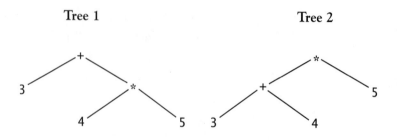

Figure 4.7 Two Abstract Syntax Trees for 3 + 4 * 5, Indicating Ambiguity of the Grammar of Figure 4.4

A grammar such as that in Figure 4.4, for which two distinct parse (or syntax) trees are possible for the same string, is **ambiguous**. Ambiguity can also be expressed directly in terms of derivations. Even though many derivations may in general correspond to the same parse tree, certain special derivations that are constructed in a special order can only correspond to unique parse trees. One kind of derivation that has this property is a **leftmost derivation**, where the leftmost remaining nonterminal is singled out for replacement at each step. For example, the derivations in Figures 4.3 and 4.5 are leftmost but the derivation at the beginning of this section (deriving the same string as Figure 4.5) is not. Each parse tree has a unique leftmost derivation, which can be constructed by a preorder traversal of the tree. Thus, the ambiguity of a grammar can also be tested by searching for two different leftmost derivations of the same string. If such leftmost derivations exist, then the grammar must be ambiguous, since each such derivation must correspond to a unique parse tree. For example, the ambiguity of the grammar of Figure 4.4 is also demonstrated by the two leftmost derivations for the string 3 + 4 * 5 as given in Figure 4.8.

Leftmost Derivation 1 (Corresponding to Tree 1 of Figure 4.7)	Leftmost Derivation 2 (Corresponding to Tree 2 of Figure 4.7)
$expr \Rightarrow expr + expr$	$expr \Rightarrow expr * expr$
$\Rightarrow number + expr$	$\Rightarrow expr + expr * expr$
$\Rightarrow digit + expr$	$\Rightarrow number + expr * expr$
$\Rightarrow 3 + expr$	$\Rightarrow \ldots$ (etc.)
$\Rightarrow 3 + expr * expr$	
$\Rightarrow 3 + number * expr$	
$\Rightarrow \ldots$ (etc.)	

Figure 4.8 Two Leftmost Derivations for 3 + 4 * 5, Indicating Ambiguity of the Grammar of Figure 4.4

Ambiguous grammars present difficulties, since no clear structure is expressed. To be useful, either the grammar must be revised to remove the ambiguity, or a **disambiguating rule** must be stated to establish which structure is meant.

Which of the two parse trees (or leftmost derivations) is the correct one for the expression 3 + 4 * 5? If we think of the semantics to be attached to the expression, we can understand what this decision means. The first syntax tree of Figure 4.7 implies that the multiplication operator "*" is to be applied to the 4 and 5 (resulting in the value 20), and this result is added to 3 to get 23. The second syntax tree, on the other hand, says to add 3 and 4 first (getting 7) and then multiply by 5 to get 35. Thus, the operations are applied in a different order, and the resulting semantics are quite different.

If we take the usual meaning of the expression 3 + 4 * 5 from mathematics, we would choose the first tree of Figure 4.7 over the second, since multiplication has precedence over addition. This is the usual choice in programming languages, although some languages (such as APL) make a different choice. How could we express the fact that multiplication should have precedence over addition? We could state a disambiguating rule separately from the grammar, or we could revise the grammar. The usual way to revise the grammar is to write a new grammar rule (called a "term") that establishes a "precedence cascade" to force the matching of the "*" at a lower point in the parse tree:

$$expr \rightarrow expr + expr \mid term$$
$$term \rightarrow term * term \mid (\ expr \ ) \mid number$$

But we have not completely solved the ambiguity problem: the rule for an *expr* still allows us to parse 3 + 4 + 5 as either (3 + 4) + 5 or 3 + (4 + 5). In other words, we can make addition either **right-** or **left-associative**:

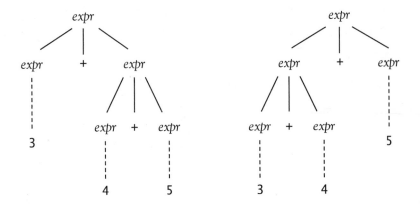

In the case of addition this does not affect the result, but if we were to include subtraction, it surely would: 8 − 4 − 2 = 2 if "−" is left-associative, but $8 - 4 - 2 = 6$ if "$-$" is right-associative. What is needed is to replace the rule

$$expr \rightarrow expr + expr$$

with either

$$expr \rightarrow expr + term$$

or

$$expr \rightarrow term + expr$$

The first rule is **left-recursive** while the second rule is **right-recursive**. A left-recursive rule for an operation causes it to left-associate, as in the parse tree

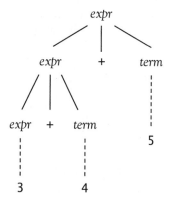

while a right-recursive rule causes it to right-associate:

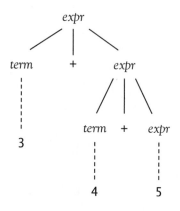

The revised grammar for simple integer arithmetic expressions that expresses both precedence and associativity is given in Figure 4.9.

expr → *expr* + *term* | *term*
term → *term* * *factor* | *factor*
factor→ (*expr*) | *number*
number → *number digit* | *digit*
digit → 0 | 1 | 2 | 3 | 4 | 5 | 6 | 7 | 8 | 9

Figure 4.9   Revised Grammar for Simple Integer Arithmetic Expressions

The grammar of Figure 4.9 is now unambiguous (a proof of this requires more advanced techniques from parsing theory). Moreover, the syntax trees generated by this grammar correspond to the semantics of the arithmetic operations as they are usually defined. Sometimes the process of rewriting a grammar to eliminate ambiguity causes the grammar to become extremely complex, and in such cases we prefer to state a disambiguating rule (see the if-statement discussion in Chapter 7).

4.5 EBNFs and Syntax Diagrams

We noted earlier that the grammar rule

number → *number digit* | *digit*

generates a number as a sequence of digits:

number ⇒ *number digit*
⇒ *number digit digit*
⇒ *number digit digit digit*
⇒ *digit* . . . *digit*

. . .

⇒ (arbitrary repetitions of *digit*)

Similarly, the rule

expr → *expr* + *term* | *term*

generates an expression as a sequence of terms separated by "+'s":

expr ⇒ *expr* + *term*
⇒ *expr* + *term* + *term*
⇒ *expr* + *term* + *term* + *term*

. . .

⇒ *term* + . . . + *term*

This situation occurs so frequently that a special notation for such grammar rules is adopted that expresses more clearly the repetitive nature of their structures:

number → *digit* {*digit*}

and

$$expr \rightarrow term \; \{+ \; term\}$$

In this notation the curly brackets "{ }" stand for "zero or more repetitions of." Thus, the rules express that a number is a sequence of one or more digits, and an expression is a term followed by zero or more repetitions of a "+" and another term. In this notation the curly brackets have become new metasymbols, and this notation is called **extended Backus-Naur form**, or **EBNF** for short.

This new notation obscures the left associativity of the "+" operator that is expressed by the left recursion in the original rule in BNF. We can get around this by simply assuming that any operator involved in a curly bracket repetition is left-associative. Indeed, if an operator were right-associative, the corresponding grammar rule would be right-recursive, and right-recursive rules are usually not written using curly brackets. (The reason for this is explained more fully in the next section.) This problem does point out a flaw in EBNF grammars: Parse trees and syntax trees cannot be written directly from the grammar, but assumptions must be made about their structure. Therefore, we will always use BNF notation to write parse trees.

A second common situation is for a structure to have an optional part, such as the optional else-part of an if-statement in C or Pascal, which is expressed in BNF notation for C as follows:

$$if\text{-}statement \rightarrow \texttt{if} \; (\; expression \;) \; statement \; |$$
$$\texttt{if} \; (\; expression \;) \; statement \; \texttt{else} \; statement$$

This is written more simply and expressively in EBNF as follows:

$$if\text{-}statement \rightarrow \texttt{if} \; (\; expression \;) \; statement \; [\; \texttt{else} \; statement \;]$$

where the square brackets "[ ]" are new metasymbols indicating optional parts of the structure.

Another example is the grammar rule for *function-definition* in the BNF grammar for C; see Figure 4.6:

$$function\text{-}definition \rightarrow declaration\text{-}specifiers \; declarator$$
$$declaration\text{-}list \; compound\text{-}statement$$
$$| \; declaration\text{-}specifiers \; declarator \; compound\text{-}statement$$
$$| \; declarator \; declaration\text{-}list \; compound\text{-}statement$$
$$| \; declarator \; compound\text{-}statement$$

Using EBNF, this can be much more simply expressed as

$$function\text{-}definition \rightarrow [\; declaration\text{-}specifiers \;] \; declarator$$
$$[\; declaration\text{-}list \;] \; compound\text{-}statement$$

Right-associative (binary) operators can also be written using these new metasymbols. For example, if "@" is a right-associative operator with BNF

$$expr \rightarrow term \; @ \; expr \; | \; term$$

then this rule can be rewritten in EBNF as follows:

$$expr \rightarrow term\ [\ @\ expr\ ]$$

For completeness, we write out the grammar of Figure 4.3 for simple integer arithmetic expressions in EBNF in Figure 4.10.

$expr \rightarrow term\ \{\ +\ term\ \}$
$term \rightarrow factor\ \{\ *\ factor\ \}$
$factor \rightarrow (\ expr\ )\ |\ number$
$number \rightarrow digit\ \{\ digit\ \}$
$digit \rightarrow 0\ |\ 1\ |\ 2\ |\ 3\ |\ 4\ |\ 5\ |\ 6\ |\ 7\ |\ 8\ |\ 9$

Figure 4.10   EBNF Rules for Simple Integer Arithmetic Expressions

A sometimes useful graphical representation for a grammar rule is the **syntax diagram**, which indicates the sequence of terminals and non-terminals encountered in the right-hand side of the rule. For example, syntax diagrams for *noun-phrase* and *article* of our simple English grammar of Section 4.2 would be drawn as

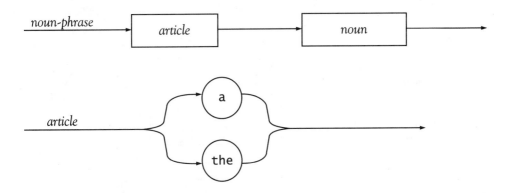

or, condensing the two rules into one,

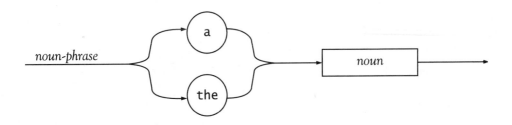

Syntax diagrams use circles or ovals for terminals and squares or rectangles for nonterminals, connecting them with lines and arrows to indicate appropriate sequencing. Syntax diagrams can also condense several grammar rules into one diagram.

Syntax diagrams for the expression grammar in Figure 4.10 are given in Figure 4.11. Note the use of loops in the diagrams to express the repetition given by the curly brackets in the EBNFs.

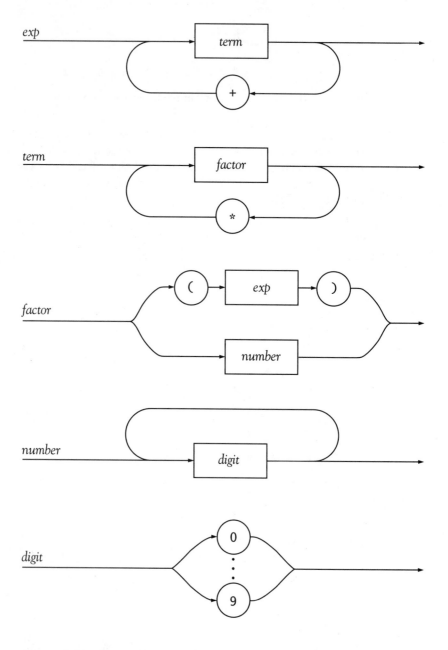

Figure 4.11   Syntax Diagrams for a Simple Integer Expression Grammar

As an example of how to express the square brackets [ ] in syntax diagrams, we give the syntax diagram for the *if-statement* in C:

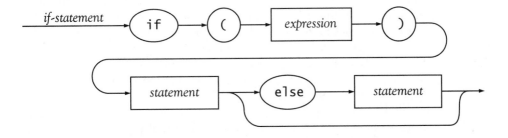

Syntax diagrams are always written from the EBNF notation, not the BNF notation, for reasons that are made clear in the next section. Thus, the following diagram for *expr* would be incorrect:

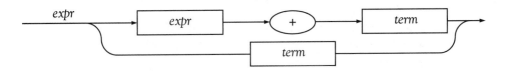

Syntax diagrams are visually appealing but take up a great deal of space. As more programmers have become familiar with rules written directly in BNF or EBNF, syntax diagrams have been used less frequently, and now are seen much more rarely than in the past.

4.6 Parsing Techniques and Tools

A grammar written in BNF, EBNF, or as syntax diagrams describes the strings of tokens that are syntactically legal in a programming language. The grammar thus also implicitly describes the actions that a parser must take to parse a string of tokens correctly, that is, construct, either implicitly or explicitly, a derivation or parse tree for the string. The simplest form of a parser is a **recognizer**—a program that accepts or rejects strings, based on whether they are legal strings in the language. More general parsers build parse trees (or, more likely, abstract syntax trees) and carry out other operations, such as calculating values for expressions.

Given a grammar in one of the forms we have discussed, how does it correspond to the actions of a parser? One method of parsing attempts to match an input with the right-hand sides of the grammar rules. When a match occurs, the right-hand side is replaced by, or **reduced** to, the non-terminal on the left. Such parsers are **bottom-up** parsers, since they construct derivations and parse trees from the leaves to the root. They are sometimes also called **shift-reduce** parsers, since they shift tokens onto a stack prior to reducing strings to nonterminals. The other major parse method is **top-down**: Nonterminals are expanded to match incoming tokens and directly construct a derivation. Both of these parsing techniques can be automated; that is, a program can be written that will automatically translate a BNF description into a parser. Since bottom-up parsing is somewhat more powerful than top-down parsing, it is usually the preferred method for such **parser generators** (historically also called **compiler compilers**). One such parser generator in wide use is YACC (yet another compiler compiler), or its freeware version Bison, which we will study later in this section.

However, there is an older method for constructing a parser by hand from a grammar that is very effective and is still often used. Essentially, it operates by turning the nonterminals into a group of mutually recursive procedures whose actions are based on the right-hand sides of the BNFs; hence its name: **recursive-descent parsing**.

The right-hand sides are interpreted in the procedures as follows. Tokens are matched directly with input tokens as constructed by a scanner. Nonterminals are interpreted as calls to the procedures corresponding to the nonterminals.

As an example, in our simplified English grammar, procedures for *sentence*, *noun-phrase*, and *article* would be written as follows (in C-like pseudocode):

```
void sentence(void)
{   nounPhrase();
    verbPhrase();
}

void nounPhrase(void)
{   article();
    noun();
}

void article(void)
{ if (token == "a") match("a");
  else if (token == "the") match("the");
  else error();
}
```

In this pseudocode, we are using strings to imitate tokens, and a global variable called `token` to hold the current token as constructed by a scanner. The `getToken` procedure of the scanner is called whenever a new token is desired. A `match` of a token corresponds to a successful test for that token, followed by a call to `getToken`:

```
void match(TokenType expected)
{ if (token == expected) getToken();
  else error();
}
```

Parsing starts with the variable `token` already holding the first token, so a call to `getToken` must precede the first call to the `sentence` procedure. We also assume there exists an `error` procedure that aborts the parse. (Note that errors need only be detected when actual tokens are expected, as in the procedure `article`. We could have checked for "a" or "the" in the `sentence` procedure, but in this scheme it is unnecessary.)

If we apply this process to the BNF description of Figure 4.9, we encounter a problem with the left-recursive rules such as the one for an expression:

$$expr \rightarrow expr + term \mid term$$

If we were to try to write this rule as a recursive-descent procedure, two fatal difficulties arise. First, the first choice in this rule ($expr \rightarrow expr + term$) would have the procedure immediately calling itself recursively, which would result in an infinite recursive loop. Second, there is no way to decide which of the two choices to take ($expr \rightarrow expr + term$ or $expr \rightarrow term$) until a $+$ is seen (or not) much later in the input. The problem is caused by the existence of the left recursion in the first alternative of the grammar rule, since the right-recursive rule

$$expr \rightarrow term + expr \mid term$$

has only a very modest problem and can be turned into a parsing procedure by simply calling `term()` and then testing for a "+":

```
void expr(void)
{ term();
  if (token == "+")
  { match("+");
    expr();
  }
}
```

Unfortunately, this grammar rule (and the associated parsing procedure) make + into a right-associative operator. How can we remove the problem caused by the left recursion, while at the same time retaining the left associative behavior of the + operation? The solution is implicit in the EBNF description of this same grammar rule, which expresses the recursion as a loop:

$$expr \rightarrow term \{ + term\}$$

This form of the grammar rule for *expr* corresponds to the recursive-descent code:

```
void expr(void)
{ term();
  while (token == "+")
  { match("+");
    term();
    /* perform left associative operations here */
  }
}
```

While this form of the grammar does suppress the explicit left associativity of +, the corresponding code *does* provide the opportunity for
enforcing left associativity by timing whatever operations are to be performed (tree building or expression calculation) right after the second
call to term() (at the end of the body of the loop, as indicated by the
comment).

Thus, the curly brackets in EBNF represent **left recursion removal**
by the use of a loop. While there are more general mechanisms than this
for left recursion removal, this simple use of EBNF usually suffices in practice.

Right-recursive rules on the other hand, as we have already noted,
present no such problem in recursive-descent parsing. However, the code
that we write for a right-recursive rule such as

$$expr \rightarrow term \text{ @ } expr \mid term$$

(we change the name of the operation to @ to avoid confusion with +) also
corresponds to the use of square brackets in EBNF to express an optional
structure:

$$expr \rightarrow term \text{ [@ } expr \text{]}$$

This process is called **left factoring,** since it is as if the *term* in both alternatives of the grammar rule is "factored out," leaving either @ *expr* or nothing (thus making @ *expr* optional).

Another typical left factoring situation is that of an if-statement
with an optional else-part:

$$\textit{if-statement} \rightarrow \text{if (} \textit{expression} \text{) } \textit{statement} \mid$$
$$\text{if (} \textit{expression} \text{) } \textit{statement} \text{ else } \textit{statement}$$

This cannot be translated directly into code, since both alternatives
begin with the same prefix. As in the previous example, in EBNF this is
written with square brackets, and the common parts of the alternatives are
"factored out":

$$\textit{if-statement} \rightarrow \text{if (} \textit{expression} \text{) } \textit{statement} \text{ [else } \textit{statement} \text{]}$$

This corresponds directly to the recursive-descent code to parse an
if-statement:

```
void ifStatement()
{ match("if");
  match("(");
  expression();
  match(")");
  statement();
  if (token == "else")
  {   match("else");
    statement();
  }
}
```

Thus, in both left recursive and left factoring situations, EBNF rules or syntax diagrams correspond naturally to the code of a recursive-descent parser, and this is one of the main reasons for their use.

As a demonstration of the power and ease of recursive-descent parsing, we give in Figure 4.12 the complete code in C for an integer calculator based on the grammar of Figure 4.10. This program accepts a single line of input containing a simple integer arithmetic expression consisting of numbers, the operators + and *, and parentheses, and prints out the computed value of the expression, or an error message if the expression is not syntactically correct. As in the grammar, the calculator assumes all tokens are characters, and it does not permit spaces to appear in an expression. To make it easy to print the computed value, and also to make sure only a single expression is entered in the input line, a new grammar rule is added to the grammar of Figure 4.10 (and the start symbol is changed to *command*):

$$command \rightarrow expr \; '\backslash n'$$

In effect, this grammar rule makes the newline character ('\n') into the marker for the end of the input (just like the $ token discussed elsewhere in this chapter).

Finally, we note that the timing of the computation of the results in each procedure ensures that the operators + and * are left-associative.

```
(1)   #include <ctype.h>
(2)   #include <stdlib.h>
(3)   #include <stdio.h>

(4)   int token; /* holds the current input character for the
      parse */

(5)   /* declarations to allow arbitrary recursion */
(6)   void command(void);
(7)   int expr(void);
(8)   int term(void);
(9)   int factor(void);
(10)  int number(void);
(11)  int digit(void);

(12)  void error(void)
(13)  { printf("parse error\n");
(14)      exit(1);
(15)  }

(16)  void getToken(void)
(17)  { /* tokens are characters */
(18)      token = getchar();
(19)  }
```

(continues)

(continued)

```
(20) void match(char c)
(21) { if (token == c) getToken();
(22)   else error();
(23) }

(24) void command(void)
(25) /* command -> expr '\n' */
(26) { int result = expr();
(27)   if (token == '\n') /* end the parse and print the
       result */
(28)       printf("The result is: %d\n",result);
(29)   else error();
(30) }

(31) int expr(void)
(32) /* expr -> term { '+' term } */
(33) { int result = term();
(34)   while (token == '+')
(35)   { match('+');
(36)     result += term();
(37)   }
(38)   return result;
(39) }

(40) int term(void)
(41) /* term -> factor { '*' factor } */
(42) { int result = factor();
(43)   while (token == '*')
(44)   { match('*');
(45)     result *= factor();
(46)   }
(47)   return result;
(48) }

(49) int factor(void)
(50) /* factor -> '(' expr ')' | number */
(51) { int result;
(52)   if (token == '(')
(53)   { match('(');
(54)     result = expr();
(55)     match(')');
(56)   }
(57)   else
(58)     result = number();
(59)   return result;
(60) }
```

```
(61) int number(void)
(62) /* number -> digit { digit } */
(63) { int result = digit();
(64)    while (isdigit(token))
(65)    /* the value of a number with a new trailing digit
(66)       is its previous value shifted by a decimal place
(67)       plus the value of the new digit
(68)    */
(69)       result = 10 * result + digit();
(70)    return result;
(71) }

(72) int digit(void)
(73) /* digit -> '0' | '1' | '2' | '3' | '4'
(74)                  | '5' | '6' | '7' | '8' | '9' */
(75) { int result;
(76)    if (isdigit(token))
(77)    { /* the numeric value of a digit character
(78)       is the difference between its ascii value and the
(79)       ascii value of the character '0'
(80)    */
(81)       result = token - '0';
(82)       match(token);
(83)    }
(84)    else
(85)       error();
(86)    return result;
(87) }

(88) void parse(void)
(89) { getToken(); /* get the first token */
(90)    command(); /* call the parsing procedure for the
          start symbol */
(91) }

(92) main()
(93) { parse();
(94)    return 0;
(95) }
```

Figure 4.12   A Calculator for Simple Integer Arithmetic Expressions
                 Using Recursive-Descent Parsing

In this method for converting a grammar into a parser, the resulting parser bases its actions only on the next available token in the input stream (stored in the token variable in the code). This use of a single token to direct a parse is called **single-symbol lookahead**, and a parser that commits itself to a particular action based only on this lookahead is called a **predictive parser** (sometimes laboriously referred to as a top-down parser with single-symbol lookahead and no backtracking). Predictive parsers require that the grammar to be parsed satisfies certain conditions so that this decision-making process will work.

The first condition that predictive parsing requires is the ability to choose among several alternatives in a grammar rule. Suppose that a non-terminal A has the following choices:

$$A \rightarrow \alpha_1 \mid \alpha_2 \mid \ldots \mid \alpha_n$$

(each α_i stands for a string of tokens and nonterminals). To decide which choice to use, the tokens that begin each of the α_i must be different. Given a string α of tokens and nonterminals, we define **First(α)** to be the set of tokens that can begin the string α. For example, given the grammar rules

$$factor \rightarrow (\ expr \ ) \mid number$$
$$number \rightarrow digit \ \{ \ digit \ \}$$
$$digit \rightarrow 0 \mid 1 \mid \ldots \mid 9$$

we have

$$First(\ (\ expr \ ) \ ) = \{ \ (\ \}$$
$$First(\ number \ ) = First(\ digit \ )$$
$$= First(0) \cup First(1) \cup \ldots First(9)$$
$$= \{ \ 0, \ldots, 9 \ \}$$

and then

$$First(\ factor \ ) = First(\ (\ expr \ ) \ ) \cup First(\ number \ )$$
$$= \{ \ (, 0 \ , \ 1, \ldots, 9 \ \}$$

The requirement that a predictive parser be able to distinguish between choices in a grammar rule can be stated in terms of First sets, as follows. Given the grammar rule

$$A \rightarrow \alpha_1 \mid \alpha_2 \mid \ldots \mid \alpha_n$$

the First sets of any two choices must not have any tokens in common; that is,

$$First(\alpha_i) \cap First(\alpha_j) = \varnothing \text{ for all } i \neq j$$

$$(\varnothing \text{ denotes the empty set})$$

In the example of the grammar rule for a factor:

$$factor \rightarrow (\ expr \ ) \mid number$$

this condition for predictive parsing is satisfied, since

$$First(\ (\ expr \ ) \ ) \cap First(\ number \ ) = \{ \ (\ \} \cap \{ \ 0, \ldots, 9 \ \} = \varnothing$$

There is a second condition for predictive parsing that arises when structures are optional. For example, to parse the grammar rule

$$expr \rightarrow term \; [\; @ \; expr \;]$$

we must test for the presence of the token "@" before we can be sure that the optional part is actually present:

```
void expr(void)
{ term();
  if (token == '@')
  { match('@');
    expr();
  }
}
```

However, if the token @ can also come after an expression, this test is insufficient: If @ is the next token in the input, it may be the start of the optional "@ expr" part, or it may be a token that comes after the whole expression. Thus, the second requirement for predictive parsing is that, for any optional part, no token beginning the optional part can also come after the optional part.

We can formalize this condition in the following way. For any string α of tokens and nonterminals that appears on the right-hand side of a grammar rule, define **Follow(α)** to be the set of tokens that can follow α. The second condition for predictive parsing can now be stated in terms of Follow sets. Given a grammar rule in EBNF with an optional α,

$$A \rightarrow \beta \; [\alpha] \; \sigma$$

we must have

$$\text{First}(\alpha) \cap \text{Follow}(\alpha) = \varnothing$$

As an example of the computation of Follow sets, consider the grammar of Figure 4.10. Follow sets for the nonterminals can be computed as follows. From the rule

$$factor \rightarrow (\; expr\;)$$

we get that the token ")" is in Follow(*expr*). Since *expr* can also comprise a whole expression, *expr* may be followed by the end of the input, which we indicate by the special symbol $. Thus, Follow(*expr*) = {), $ }. From the rule

$$expr \rightarrow term \; \{\; +\; term\}$$

we obtain that "+" is in Follow(*term*). Since a *term* also appears as the last thing in an *expr*, anything that follows an *expr* can also follow a *term*. Thus,

$$\text{Follow}(term) = \{\;),\; \$,\; +\; \}$$

Finally, Follow(*factor*) = {), $, +, * } by a similar computation.

Note that the grammar of Figure 4.10 automatically satisfies the second condition for predictive parsing since there are no optional structures inside square brackets. A more instructive example comes from Figure 4.6 (a small part of a BNF grammar for C), where the grammar rule for a *declaration* in EBNF is written as

$$declaration \rightarrow declaration\text{-}specifiers\ [\ init\text{-}declarator\text{-}list\ ]\ `;'$$

By tracing through the rules for *init-declarator-list* in Figure 4.6, we can determine that First(*init-declarator-list*) = { ID, *, (} and Follow(*init-declarator-list*) = { ';', ',' }, so that

$$\text{First}(init\text{-}declarator\text{-}list) \cap \text{Follow}(init\text{-}declarator\text{-}list) = \varnothing$$

thus satisfying the second condition for predictive parsing in this case also.

The computation of First and Follow sets can also be useful in recursive-descent parsing to obtain appropriate tests; see Exercise 4.49.

We mentioned at the beginning of this section that the process of converting grammar rules into a parser can be automated; that is, a program can be written that will translate a grammar into a parser. Such parser generators or "compiler-compilers" take as their input a version of BNF or EBNF rules and generate an output that is a parser program in some language. This program can then be compiled to provide an executable parser. Of course, providing only a grammar to the parser generator will result in a recognizer. To get the parser to construct a syntax tree or perform other operations, we must provide operations or actions to be performed that are associated with each grammar rule, that is, a syntax-directed scheme.

One of the more common and popular of the parser generators is YACC, which is available on most Unix systems, or its freeware version Bison, which is available for many different systems (including all versions of Unix). YACC was written by Steve Johnson in the mid-1970s; it generates a C program that uses a bottom-up algorithm to parse the grammar. The format of a YACC specification is as follows:

```
%{ /* code to insert at the beginning of the parser */
%}
/* other YACC definitions, if necessary */
%%
/* grammar and associated actions */
%%
/* auxiliary procedures */
```

The grammar is given in a BNF-like form, and associated actions are written in C. Figure 4.13 shows a complete YACC/Bison description of a simple integer expression interpreter using the grammar of Figure 4.9 (Section 4.4). Note that it uses the original left-recursive BNF grammar—bottom-up parsers are not bothered by left recursion. The actions provided with the rules are essentially the same as in the recursive-descent calculator of Figure 4.12 (and the C program generated by YACC behaves exactly as that program from the user's perspective). The YACC/Bison convention for constructing values from a parse is that the value of the left-hand side of a production is indicated by the symbol "$$," while the value of the nth symbol of the right-hand side is given by $n. (These values are always integers unless specified otherwise.) For example, on line 7 of Figure 4.13, $1 + $3 represents the sum of the first and third symbols of the right-hand side of the rule

```
expr : expr '+' term
```

so that the value of exp and term on the right are added. Note the different conventions for metasymbols, nonterminals, and tokens.

```
(1)   %{
(2)   #include <stdio.h>
(3)   %}

(4)   %%
(5)   command : expr '\n' { printf("The result is: %d\n",$1); }
(6)           ;

(7)   expr      : expr '+' term { $$ = $1 + $3; }
(8)             | term { $$ = $1; }
(9)             ;
(10)  term      : term '*' factor { $$ = $1 * $3; }
(11)            | factor { $$ = $1; }
(12)            ;

(13)  factor  : number { $$ = $1; }
(14)          | '(' expr ')' { $$ = $2; }
(15)          ;

(16)  number  : number digit { $$ = 10 * $1 + $2; }
(17)          | digit { $$ = $1; }
(18)          ;

(19)  digit   : '0' { $$ = 0; }
(20)          | '1' { $$ = 1; }
(21)          | '2' { $$ = 2; }
(22)          | '3' { $$ = 3; }
(23)          | '4' { $$ = 4; }
(24)          | '5' { $$ = 5; }
(25)          | '6' { $$ = 6; }
(26)          | '7' { $$ = 7; }
(27)          | '8' { $$ = 8; }
(28)          | '9' { $$ = 9; }
(29)          ;                              (continues)
```

(continued)

```
(30) %%

(31) main()
(32) { yyparse();
(33)    return 0;
(34) }

(35) int yylex(void)
(36) { static int done = 0; /* flag to end parse */
(37)    int c;
(38)    if (done) return 0; /* stop parse */
(39)    c = getchar();
(40)    if (c == '\n') done = 1; /* next call will end parse */
(41)    return c;
(42) }

(43) int yyerror(char *s)
(44) /* allows for printing error message */
(45) {    printf("%s\n",s);
(46) }
```

Figure 4.13   YACC/Bison Specification of a Calculator for Simple Integer
Arithmetic Expressions

YACC/Bison generates a procedure yyparse from the grammar, so we have to provide a main procedure that calls yyparse (lines 31–34). YACC/Bison also assumes that tokens (aside from individual characters) are recognized by a scanner procedure called yylex similar to the getToken procedure of Figure 4.12. Thus, we provide a yylex in C that reads and returns a character (lines 35–42). One difference, however, between yylex and getToken is that YACC/Bison will only end a parse when yylex returns 0 (in the recursive-descent version we could write special code that ended the parse on a newline character). Thus, yylex includes code to remember when a newline is reached and to return 0 on the next call after a newline (allowing the generated parser to match the newline directly before finishing; see Exercise 4.28). It would also be possible to generate yylex automatically from a **scanner generator** such as LEX/Flex (see the Notes and References), but we will not study this here. Finally, an error procedure yyerror is needed to print error messages.

YACC/Bison is useful not only to the translator writer, it is also useful to the language designer: Given a grammar, it provides a description of possible problems and ambiguities. However, to read this information we must have a more specific knowledge of bottom-up parsing techniques. The interested reader may consult the references at the end of this chapter.

4.7 Lexics versus Syntax versus Semantics

A context-free grammar typically includes a description of the tokens of a language by including the strings of characters that form the tokens in the grammar rules. For example, in the partial English grammar of Section 4.2, the tokens are the English words "a," "the," "girl," "dog," "sees," and "pets," plus the "." character, and in the simple integer expression grammar of Section 4.3 the tokens are the arithmetic symbols "+" and "*," the parentheses "(" and ")," and the digits 0 through 9. Specific details of formatting, such as the white-space conventions mentioned in Section 4.1, are left to the scanner and need to be stated as lexical conventions separate from the grammar.

Some typical token categories, such as literals or constants and identifiers, are not fixed sequences of characters in themselves, but are built up out of a fixed set of characters, such as the digits 0..9. These token categories can have their structure defined by the grammar, as for example the grammar rules for *number* and *digit* in the expression grammar. However, it is possible and even desirable to use a scanner to recognize these structures, since the full recursive power of a parser is not necessary, and the scanner can recognize them by a simple repetitive operation. This is more efficient—it makes the recognition of numbers and identifiers faster and simpler, and it reduces the size of the parser and the number of grammar rules.

To express the fact that a number in the expression grammar should be a token rather than represented by a nonterminal, we can rewrite the grammar of Figure 4.10 as in Figure 4.14.

expr → *term* { + *term*}
term → *factor* { * *factor* }
factor → (*expr*) | NUMBER

Figure 4.14 Numbers as Tokens in Simple Integer Arithmetic

By making the string NUMBER uppercase in the new grammar, we are saying that it is not a token to be recognized literally, but one whose structure is determined by the scanner. The structure of such tokens must then be specified as part of the lexical conventions of the language. As noted in Section 4.1, the structure of such tokens can be specified using regular expressions. However, many language designers choose to include the structure of such tokens as part of the grammar, with the understanding that an implementor may include these in the scanner instead of the parser. Thus, a description of a language using BNF, EBNF, or syntax diagrams may include not only the syntax but most of the lexical structure (or **lexics**) of a programming language as well. The boundary, therefore, between syntactic and lexical structure is not always clearly drawn but depends on the point of view of the designer and implementor.

The same is true for syntax and semantics. We have been taking the approach that syntax is anything that can be defined with a context-free grammar and semantics is anything that cannot. However, many authors include properties that we would call semantic as syntactic properties of a language. Examples include such rules as declaration before use for variables and no redeclaration of identifiers within a procedure. These are rules that are context-sensitive and cannot be written as context-free rules. Hence we prefer to think of them as semantic rather than syntactic rules.

Another conflict between syntax and semantics arises when languages require certain strings to be **predefined identifiers** rather than **reserved words**. Recall (from Section 4.1) that reserved words are fixed strings of characters that are tokens themselves and that cannot be used as identifiers, while a predefined identifier is a fixed string that is given a predefined meaning in a language, but this meaning can be changed by redefining the string as a name within a program. As we have noted, the strings if, while, and do are reserved words in C, Java, Pascal, and Ada. But in Pascal and Ada all of the basic data type names, such as integer and boolean, are predefined identifiers that can be redefined. For example, the following declaration in Ada is perfectly legal:

```
integer: boolean;
```

After this declaration, the name integer has become a variable of type boolean—guaranteed to be confusing!

C, C++, and Java,[1] on the other hand, make the basic types such as int, double, and bool (in C++) or boolean (in Java) reserved words that cannot be redefined. This is probably a better approach, since then these names have a fixed semantics in every program that we would hardly want to change even if we could.

Finally, it can also happen that syntax and semantics become interdependent in languages when semantic information must be used to distinguish ambiguous parsing situations. A simple situation where this occurs is in C, where type names and variable names must be distinguishable during parsing. Consider, for example, the C expression

```
(x)-y
```

If x is a type name, this is a cast of the value -y to type x. But if x is a variable name, then this is subtraction of y from x. Thus, a parser must have context information on identifiers available to disambiguate such situations. One might view this as a design flaw in the grammar of C (Java has the same problem, but not Pascal or Ada). However, it is a relatively easy problem to overcome in practice.

---

[1] Java does have predefined identifiers, too, which are placed in a library (called the **java.lang package**) and which are visible in every Java program, but which can be redefined.

Exercises

4.1 **(a)** The C programming language distinguishes character constants from string constants by using single quotes for characters and double quotes for strings. Thus, `'c'` is the character c, while `"c"` is a string of length 1 consisting of the single character c. Why do you think this distinction is made? Is it useful?

    (b) Pascal, on the other hand, uses single quotes for both characters and strings (thus `'c'` is either a character or string, depending on context). Discuss the advantages and disadvantages of these two approaches.

4.2 Devise a test in one or more of the following languages to determine whether comments are considered white space: **(a)** C, **(b)** Java, **(c)** Ada, and **(d)** FORTRAN. What is the result of performing your test?

4.3 Discuss the pros and cons of ignoring or requiring "white space" (i.e., blanks, end-of-lines, and tabs) when recognizing tokens.

4.4 Many programming languages (like C) do not allow nested comments. Why is this requirement made? Modula-2 and a few other languages do allow nested comments. Why is this useful?

4.5 **(a)** Describe the strings that are represented by the regular expression

    `[0-9]+((E|e)(\+|\-)?[0-9]+)?`

    (b) Write a regular expression for C identifiers consisting of letters, digits, and the underscore character '_', and starting with a letter or underscore.

4.6 **(a)** Numeric constants may be signed or unsigned in a programming language (e.g., `123` is an unsigned integer constant, but `-123` is a signed integer constant). However, there is a problem associated with signed constants. Describe it. (*Hint:* Consider expressions involving subtraction.)

    (b) Can you think of a solution to the problem of part (a)?

4.7 Rewrite the scanner program of Figure 4.1 to eliminate the global variable `numval` and `curr_char` by using a data structure for tokens.

4.8 In the simplified English grammar of Figure 4.2 there are only finitely many legal sentences. How many are there? Why?

4.9 **(a)** Suppose white space was completely ignored (as in FORTRAN) in the grammar of Figure 4.2, so that sentences could be written as, for example, "`thegirlseesadog.`" Can this grammar still be parsed? Explain.

    (b) Answer the previous question again, assuming that the nouns `theorist` and `orator` are added to the grammar.

4.10 Translate the BNF rules of Figure 4.6 into EBNF.

4.11 Add subtraction and division to the **(a)** BNF, **(b)** EBNF, and **(c)** syntax diagrams of simple integer arithmetic expressions (Figures 4.9, 4.10, and 4.11). Be sure to give them the appropriate precedences.

4.12 Add the integer remainder and power operations to (a) the arithmetic BNF or (b) EBNF of Figures 4.9 or 4.10. Use % for the remainder operation and ∧ for the power operation. Recall that the remainder operation is left-associative and has the same precedence as multiplication, but that power is right-associative (and has greater precedence than multiplication, so 2 ∧ 2 ∧ 3 = 256, not 64.)

4.13 Unary minuses can be added in several ways to the arithmetic expression grammar of Figure 4.9 or Figure 4.10. Revise the BNF and EBNF for each of the cases that follow so that it satisfies the stated rule:
  (a) At most one unary minus is allowed in each expression, and it must come at the beginning of an expression, so -2 + 3 is legal (and equals 1) and -2 + (-3) is legal, but -2 + -3 is not.
  (b) At most one unary minus is allowed before a number or left parenthesis, so -2 + -3 and -2 * -3 are legal but --2 and -2 + --3 are not.
  (c) Arbitrarily many unary minuses are allowed before numbers and left parentheses, so everything above is legal.

4.14 Using the grammar of Figure 4.9, draw parse trees and abstract syntax trees for the arithmetic expressions:
  (a) ((2))
  (b) 3 + 4 * 5 + 6 * 7
  (c) 3 * 4 + 5 * 6 + 7
  (d) 3 * (4 + 5) * (6 + 7)
  (e) (2 + (3 + (4 + 5)))

4.15 Finish writing the pseudocode for a recursive-descent recognizer for the English grammar of Section 4.2 that was begun in Section 4.6.

4.16 Translate the pseudocode of the previous exercise into a working recognizer program in C or another programming language of your choice. (*Hint:* This will require a scanner to separate the text into token strings.)

4.17 Revise the program of the previous exercise so that it randomly *generates* legal sentences in the grammar. (This will require the use of a random number generator.)

4.18 Modify the recursive-descent calculator program of Figure 4.12 to use the grammar of Figure 4.14 and the scanner of Figure 4.1 (so that the calculator also skips blanks appropriately).

4.19 Add subtraction and division to either **(a)** the calculator program of Figure 4.12, or **(b)** your answer to the previous exercise.

4.20 Add the remainder and power operations as described in Exercise 4.12 to **(a)** the program of Figure 4.12; **(b)** your answer to Exercise 4.18; or **(c)** your answer to Exercise 4.19.

4.21 Rewrite the program of Figure 4.12 or your answer to any of the previous three exercises (except for the remainder operation) to produce floating-point answers, as well as accept floating-point constants using the following revised grammar rules (in EBNF):

... (rules for *expr* and *term* as before)
factor → (*expr*) | *decimal-number*
decimal-number → *number* [. *number*]
... (rules for *number* and *digit* as before)

4.22 To eliminate the left recursion in the simple integer arithmetic grammar one might be tempted to write:

expr → *term* + *term*

Why is this wrong?

4.23 Modify the YACC/Bison program of Figure 4.13 to use the grammar of Figure 4.14 and the scanner of Figure 4.1 (so that the calculator also skips blanks appropriately). This will require some additions to the YACC definition and changes to the scanner, as follows. First, YACC already has a global variable similar to the numval variable of Figure 4.1, with the name yylval, and so numval must be replaced by this variable. Second, YACC must define the tokens itself, rather than to use an enum such as in Figure 4.1; this is done by placing a definition as follows in the YACC definition:

```
%{ /* code to insert at the beginning of the
parser */
%}
#token NUMBER PLUS TIMES ...
%%
etc....
```

4.24 Add subtraction and division to either **(a)** the YACC/Bison program of Figure 4.13, or **(b)** your answer to the previous exercise.

4.25 Add the remainder and power operations as described in Exercise 4.12 to **(a)** the YACC/Bison program of Figure 4.13; **(b)** your answer to Exercise 4.23; or **(c)** your answer to Exercise 4.24.

4.26 Repeat Exercise 4.21 for the YACC/Bison program of Figure 4.13. This will require that the type of the parsing result be redefined to double, and this requires the insertion of a new definition into the YACC definition as follows:

```
%{
#define YYSTYPE double
...
%}
...
%%
etc....
```

4.27 (a) Explain why the code for a command in Figure 4.12 (lines 23–29) does not call `match('\n')`.

(b) Explain what the behavior of the code of Figure 4.12 *would* be if command *did* call `match('\n')`.

4.28 The YACC/Bison code of Figure 4.13 could be simplified by using a newline to end the parse, as in the code of Figure 4.12: We would simply change the grammar rule for `command` (Figure 4.13, line 5) to remove the newline:

```
command : expr { printf("The result is: %d\n",$1); }
```

and change the `yylex` procedure (Figure 4.13, lines 35–42) to:

```
int yylex(void)
{ int c;
  c = getchar();
  if (c == '\n') return 0; /* newline will end
  parse */
  return c;
}
```

Unfortunately, this changes the behavior of the YACC/Bison parser so that it is no longer the same as that of the recursive-descent version.

(a) Describe the different behavior. (*Hint:* Consider a missing operator, as in "3 4".)

(b) Explain why you think this different behavior occurs.

4.29 Capitalization of articles at the beginning of a sentence was viewed as a context-sensitivity in the text. However, in the simple English grammar of Figure 4.2, capitalization can be achieved by adding only context-free rules. How would you do this?

4.30 It was stated in this chapter that it is not possible to include in the BNF description the rule that there should be no redeclaration of variables. Strictly speaking, this is not true if only finitely many variable names are allowed. Describe how one could include the requirement that there be no redeclaration of variables in the grammar for a language, if only finitely many identifiers are allowed. Why isn't it a good idea?

4.31 The text notes that it is more efficient to let a scanner recognize a structure such as an unsigned integer constant, which is just a repetition of digits. However, an expression is also just a repetition of terms and pluses:

$$expr \rightarrow term \ \{ + term\}$$

Why can't a scanner recognize all expressions?

4.32 Write a BNF description for a statement-sequence as a sequence of statements separated by semicolons. (Assume that statements are defined elsewhere.) Then translate your BNF into EBNF and/or syntax diagrams.

4.33 Write a BNF description for a statement-sequence as a sequence of statements in which each statement is terminated by a semicolon. (Assume that statements are defined elsewhere.) Then translate your BNF into EBNF and/or syntax diagrams.

4.34 C uses the semicolon as a statement terminator (as in the previous exercise), but also allows a statement to be empty (that is, consisting of only a semicolon), so that the following is a legal C program:

```
main()
{ ;;;;;;;;
  return 0;
}
```

Discuss the advantages and disadvantages of this.

4.35 (a) List the predefined identifiers in Pascal and describe their meanings.
(b) Does C have predefined identifiers? Explain.
(c) Does Ada have predefined identifiers? Explain.

4.36 (a) One measure of the complexity of a language is the number of reserved words in its syntax. Compare the number of reserved words in C, C++, Pascal, Ada, and Java.
(b) One could argue that the preceding comparison is misleading because of the use of predefined identifiers in Pascal and standard (predefined) libraries in C++, Java, and Ada. Discuss the pros and cons of adding the number of predefined identifiers or the number of library identifiers into the comparison.

4.37 Here is a legal Pascal program:

```
program yecch;
var true, false: boolean;
begin
  true := 1 = 0;
  false := true;
      ...
      ...
end.
```

What values do **true** and **false** have in this program? What design principle does this violate? Is this program possible in Ada? In C? In C++? In Java?

4.38 Is it possible to have a language without any reserved words? Discuss.

4.39 Some languages use format to distinguish the beginning and ending of structures, as follows:

```
if (x == 0)
    (* all indented statements here are part of
      the if *)
else
    (* all indented statements here are part of
      the else *)
(* statements that are not indented are outside
the else *)
```

Discuss the advantages and disadvantages of this for **(a)** writing programs in the language, and **(b)** writing a translator. (This rule is sometimes called the **Offside rule**; it is used in Haskell; see Landin [1966].)

4.40 A number is defined in the grammar of Figure 4.9 using a left-recursive rule. However, it could also be defined using a right-recursive rule:

$$number \rightarrow digit\ number\ |\ digit$$

Which is better, or does it matter? Why?

4.41 In Exercise 4.21 a decimal constant was defined using the rule

$$decimal\text{-}number \rightarrow number\ [\ .\ number\ ]$$

This causes a problem when computing the value of the fractional part of a decimal number (to the right of the decimal point), because of the left-recursive rule for a *number*.

(a) Describe the problem. Is this problem as significant when a scanner recognizes a decimal number as it is when a parser does the recognition?

(b) A solution to the problem of part (a) is to write the fractional number as a right-recursive rule, as in the previous exercise. Write out BNF rules expressing this solution, and explain why it is better.

(c) Implement your solution of part (b) in the code of Exercise 4.21 or Exercise 4.26.

4.42 Given the following BNF:

$$expr \rightarrow (\ list\ )\ |\ a$$
$$list \rightarrow list\ ,\ expr\ |\ expr$$

(a) Write EBNF rules and/or syntax diagrams for the language.
(b) Draw the parse tree for ((a, a), a, (a)).
(c) Write a recursive-descent recognizer for the language.

4.43 One way of defining the abstract syntax for the expressions of Figure 4.9 is as follows:

$$expr \rightarrow expr + expr\ |\ expr * expr\ |\ number$$
$$number \rightarrow digit\ \{\ digit\ \}$$
$$digit \rightarrow 0\ |\ 1\ |\ 2\ |\ 3\ |\ 4\ |\ 5\ |\ 6\ |\ 7\ |\ 8\ |\ 9$$

(a) Why are there no precedences or associativities expressed in this grammar?

(b) Why are there no parentheses in this grammar?

(c) The rule for *number* is written in EBNF in this grammar, yet we stated in the text that this obscures the structure of the parse tree. Why is the use of EBNF legitimate here? Why did we not use EBNF in the rule for *expr*?

4.44 Write data type definitions in C, C++, or Java for an *expr* abstract syntax tree, as given in the text and the previous exercise.

4.45 Some languages, like ML and Haskell, allow the abstract syntax tree to be defined in a way that is virtually identical to syntax rules. Write data type definitions in ML or Haskell that follow the abstract syntax for *expr* described in Exercise 4.43.

4.46 Compute First and Follow sets for the nonterminals of the grammar of Exercise 4.42.

4.47 Show that any left-recursive grammar rule does not satisfy the first condition for predictive parsing.

4.48 Show that the following grammar does not satisfy the second rule of predictive parsing:

$$stmt \rightarrow \textit{if-stmt} \mid \texttt{other}$$
$$\textit{if-stmt} \rightarrow \texttt{if } stmt \, [\texttt{else } stmt \,]$$

4.49 Given the following grammar in EBNF:

$$expr \rightarrow (\, list \,) \mid \texttt{a}$$
$$list \rightarrow expr \, [\, list \,]$$

(a) Show that the two conditions for predictive parsing are satisfied.

(b) Write a recursive-descent recognizer for the language.

4.50 In Section 4.7 the definition of Follow sets was somewhat nonstandard. More commonly Follow sets are defined for nonterminals only rather than for strings, and optional structures are accommodated by allowing a nonterminal to become empty. Thus, the grammar rule

$$\textit{if-statement} \rightarrow \texttt{if } (\, expression \,) \; statement$$
$$\mid \texttt{if } (\, expression \,) \; statement \; \texttt{else} \; statement$$

is replaced by the two rules

$$\textit{if-statement} \rightarrow \texttt{if } (\, expression \,) \; statement \; \textit{else-part}$$
$$\textit{else-part} \rightarrow \texttt{else} \; statement \mid \varepsilon$$

where the symbol "ε" (Greek epsilon) is a new metasymbol standing for the empty string. A nonterminal A can then be recognized as optional if it either becomes ε directly, or there is a derivation beginning with A that derives ε. In this case we add ε to First(A). Rewrite the second condition for predictive parsing using this convention, and apply this technique to the grammars of Exercises 4.42 and 4.49.

4.51 The second condition for predictive parsing, involving Follow sets, is actually much stronger than it needs to be. In fact, for every optional construct β:

$$A \rightarrow \alpha \, [\, \beta \,] \, \gamma$$

a parser only needs to be able to tell when β is present and when it isn't. State a condition that will do this without using Follow sets.

4.52 The second condition for predictive parsing is suspect (even more than the previous exercise indicates) because there is a natural disambiguating rule in those cases where it is not satisfied. What is it? Explain what its effect would be on when parsing the grammar of Exercise 4.48.

4.53 Given the following grammar in BNF:

$$string \rightarrow string \; string \mid \mathsf{a}$$

This corresponds to the set equation

$$S = SS \cup \{a\}$$

Show that the set $S_0 = \{a, aa, aaa, aaaa, \ldots\}$ is the smallest set satisfying the equation. [*Hint:* First show that S_0 does satisfy the equation by showing set inclusion in both directions. Then show that, given any set S' that satisfies the equation, S_0 must be contained in S' (this can be done using induction on the length of strings in S_0).]

4.54 According to Wirth [1976], data structures based on syntax diagrams can be used by a "generic" recursive-descent parser that will parse any set of grammar rules that satisfy the two conditions for predictive parsing. A suitable data structure is given by the following C declarations:

```
typedef int TokenKind;
typedef struct RuleRec * RulePtr;
typedef struct RuleRec
{  RulePtr next, other;
   int isToken;
   union
   { TokenKind name;
     RulePtr rule;
   } token_or_rule;
} RuleRec;
```

The **next** field is used to point to the next item in the grammar rule, and the **other** field is used to point to choices given by the "|" meta-symbol. Thus, the data structure for the grammar rule

$$factor \rightarrow (\; expr \;) \mid number$$

from Figure 4.10 would look as follows:

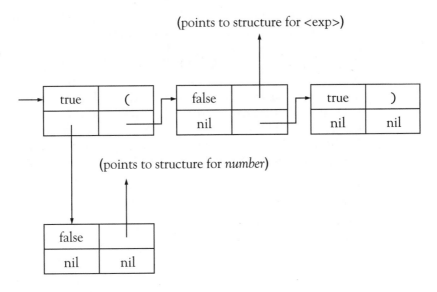

where the fields of the record structure are shown as follows:

isToken	name/rule
other	next

(a) Draw the data structures for the rest of the grammar rules in Figure 4.10. (*Hint:* For repetitive and optional structures you will need a special token to represent the empty string.)

(b) Write a generic parse procedure that uses these data structures to recognize an input string, assuming the existence of *getToken* and *error* procedures.

(c) Write a parser-generator that reads EBNF rules (either from a file or standard input) and generates the preceding data structures.

Notes and References

Many of the topics discussed in this chapter are treated in more detail in Louden [1997]. An overview similar to this chapter but with a little more depth is in Louden [1997b]. EBNF and syntax diagrams are studied in Wirth [1976] and in Horowitz [1984]. Context-free grammars and regular expressions are studied in Hopcroft and Ullman [1979] and Sipser [1997]. The original description of context-free grammars is in Chomsky [1956]. An early use of BNF in the description of Algo160 is in Naur [1963a]. A description of general algorithms to compute First and Follow sets, and to perform left-recursion removal, are found in Louden [1997], Aho, Sethi, and Ullman [1986], and Wirth [1976]. Our description of Follow sets is for EBNF grammars and is slightly nonstandard; see Exercise 4.50. YACC is described in more detail in Johnson [1975] and LEX in Lesk [1975]. A BNF description of C can be found in Kernighan and Ritchie [1988], for C++ in Stroustrup [1997], for Java in Gosling et al. [2000], for Pascal in Cooper [1983], and for Ada in Horowitz [1987]. All of these BNF descriptions can be found in many other places as well.

5 Basic Semantics

In Chapter 1 we made the distinction between the syntax of a programming language—what the language constructs look like—and its semantics—what the language constructs actually do. In Chapter 4 we saw how the syntactic structure of a language can be precisely specified using context-free grammar rules in Backus-Naur form (BNF). In this chapter we will introduce the major features of the semantics of programming languages.

Specifying the semantics of a programming language is a more difficult task than is specifying syntax, as we might expect when we talk about meaning as opposed to form or structure. In Chapter 1 we noted that there are several ways to specify semantics:

1. *By a language reference manual.* This is the most common method. Experience with the use of English descriptions has made reference manuals clearer and more precise over the years, but they still suffer from the lack of precision inherent in natural language descriptions and also may have omissions and ambiguities.

2. *By a defining translator.* This has the advantage that questions about a language can be answered by experiment (as in chemistry or physics).

A drawback is that questions about program behavior cannot be answered in advance—we must execute a program to discover what it does. Another drawback is that bugs and machine dependencies in the translator become parts of the language semantics, possibly unintentionally. Also, the translator may not be portable to all machines and may not be generally available.

3. *By a formal definition.* Such mathematical methods are precise, but are also complex and abstract, and require study to understand. Different formal methods are available, with the choice of method depending on its intended use. Perhaps the best formal method to use for the description of the translation and execution of programs is denotational semantics, which describes semantics using a series of functions.

In this chapter we will use an adaptation of informal description as it might occur in a manual, together with a simplified use of functions as in denotational descriptions. We will provide abstractions of the operations that occur during the translation and execution of programs in general, whatever the language, but will concentrate on the details of Algol-like languages, such as C, C++, Java, Pascal, and Ada. More formal methods of describing semantics are studied in Chapter 13.

5.1 Attributes, Binding, and Semantic Functions

A fundamental abstraction mechanism in a programming language is the use of **names**, or **identifiers**, to denote language entities or constructs. In most languages, variables, procedures, and constants can have names assigned by the programmer. A fundamental step in describing the semantics of a language is to describe the conventions that determine the meaning of each name used in a program.

In addition to names, a description of the semantics of a programming language needs the concepts of **location** and **value**. Values are any storable quantities, such as the integers, the reals, or even array values consisting of a sequence of the values stored at each index of the array. Locations are places where values can be stored. Locations are like addresses in the memory of a computer, but we can think of them more abstractly than as the addresses of a particular computer. If necessary, we can think of locations being numbered by integers starting at 0 and going up to some maximum location number. Most of the time we will not need to be that specific.

The meaning of a name is determined by the properties, or **attributes** associated with the name. For example, the C declaration[1]

```
const int n = 5;
```

makes n into an integer constant with value 5, that is, associates to the name n the data type attribute "integer constant" and the value attribute 5. (In C, the "constant" attribute—that n can never change its value—is part of the data type; in other languages this may be different.) The C declaration

```
int x;
```

associates the attribute "variable" and the data type "integer" to the name x. The C declaration

```
double f(int n)
{
  ...
}
```

associates the attribute "function" to the name f and the following additional attributes:

1. The number, names, and data types of its parameters (in this case, one parameter with name n and data type "integer")
2. The data type of its returned value (in this case, "double")
3. The body of code to be executed when f is called (in this case, we have not written this code but just indicated it with three dots)

We should also note here that attributes should not be confused with keywords—just as syntactic structures should not be confused with keywords. Thus, we have referred to the attribute "constant" rather than the keyword const above, and the attribute "integer" instead of the keyword int. Sometimes, where there is no danger of confusion, we may refer to an attribute by the keyword that establishes it—so we might refer to the const attribute, by abuse of terminology.

Declarations are not the only language constructs that can associate attributes to names. For example, the assignment

```
x = 2;
```

associates the new attribute "value 2" to the variable x. And, if y is a pointer variable[2] declared as

```
int* y;
```

the C++ statement

```
y = new int;
```

---

[1] In C, C++, Pascal, and Ada, some declarations are called "definitions;" the distinctions will be explained later.

[2] Pointers are discussed more fully in Sections 5.5 and 5.7.

allocates memory for an integer variable (that is, associates a location attribute to it) and assigns this location to *y, that is, associates a new value attribute to y.

The process of associating an attribute to a name is called **binding**. In some languages, constructs that cause values to be bound to names (such as the C constant declaration earlier) are in fact called bindings rather than declarations. For example, in the ML code

```
let val x = 2; val y = 3 in x + y
```

this is a `let` expression which binds the value 2 to x and the value 3 to y (these are called let-bindings).

An attribute can be classified according to the time during the translation/execution process when it is computed and bound to a name. This is called the **binding time** of the attribute. Binding times can be classified into two general categories: **static binding** and **dynamic binding**. Static binding occurs prior to execution, while dynamic binding occurs during execution. An attribute that is bound statically is a static attribute, while an attribute that is bound dynamically is a dynamic attribute.

Languages differ substantially in which attributes are bound statically and which are bound dynamically. Often, functional languages have more dynamic binding than imperative languages. Binding times can also depend on the translator. Interpreters, for example, translate and execute code simultaneously, and so will perform most bindings dynamically, while compilers will perform many bindings statically. To make the discussion of attributes and binding independent of such translator issues, we usually refer to the binding time of an attribute as the earliest time that the language rules permit the attribute to be bound. Thus, an attribute that *could* be statically bound, but which is dynamically bound by a translator, is still referred to as a static attribute.

As examples of binding times, consider the previous examples of attributes. In the declaration

```
const int n = 2;
```

the value 2 is bound statically to the name n, and in the declaration

```
int x;
```

the data type "integer" is bound statically to the name x. A similar statement holds for the function declaration.

On the other hand, the assignment x = 2 binds the value 2 dynamically to x when the assignment statement is executed. And the C++ statement

```
y = new int;
```

dynamically binds a storage location to *y and assigns that location as the value of y.

Binding times can be further refined into subcategories of dynamic and static binding. A static attribute can be bound during parsing or semantic analysis (translation time), during the linking of the program with libraries (link time), or during the loading of the program for execution (load time). For example, the body of an externally defined function will not be bound until link time, and the location of a global variable is bound at load time, since its location does not change during the execution of the program. Similarly, a dynamic attribute can be bound at different times during execution—for example, on entry or exit from a procedure, or on entry or exit from the entire program.

Names can be bound to attributes even prior to translation time. Predefined identifiers such as the Pascal data types `boolean` and `char` have their meanings (and hence attributes) specified by the language definition: Data type `boolean`, for example, is specified as having the two values `true` and `false`. Some predefined identifiers, such as data type `integer` and constant `maxint`, have their attributes specified by the language definition *and* by the implementation. The language definition specifies that data type `integer` has values consisting of a subset of the integers and that `maxint` is a constant, while the implementation specifies the value of `maxint` and the actual range of data type `integer`.[3]

Thus, we have the following possible binding times for attributes of names:

Language definition time
Language implementation time
Translation time ("compile-time")
Link time
Load time
Execution time ("run-time")

All binding times in this list, except for the last, represent static binding. (Differing binding times during execution will be studied more closely in Chapter 8.)

Bindings must be maintained by a translator so that appropriate meanings are given to names during translation and execution. A translator does this by creating a data structure to maintain the information. Since we are not interested in the details of this data structure, but only its properties, we can think of it abstractly as a function that expresses the binding of attributes to names. This function is a fundamental part of language semantics and is usually called the **symbol table**. Mathematically, the symbol table is a function from names to attributes, which we could write as SymbolTable : Names → Attributes, or more graphically as

SymbolTable

Names ——————————————→ Attributes

This function will change as translation and/or execution proceeds to reflect additions and deletions of bindings within the program being

---

[3] This assumes that a program does not redefine the meanings of these names in a declaration. Redefinition is a possibility since these predefined identifiers are not reserved words.

translated and/or executed. The symbol table will be studied in more detail in the next two sections.

A fundamental distinction exists between the way a symbol table is maintained by an interpreter and the way it is maintained by a compiler. A compiler can by definition compute only static attributes, since the program does not execute until after compilation is completed. Thus, the symbol table for a compiler can be pictured as follows:

SymbolTable

Names $\longrightarrow$ Static Attributes[4]

During the execution of a compiled program attributes such as locations and values must be maintained. A compiler generates code that maintains these attributes in data structures during execution. The memory allocation part of this process—that is, the binding of names to storage locations, is usually considered separately and is called the **environment**:

Environment

Names $\longrightarrow$ Locations

Finally, the bindings of storage locations to values is called the **memory**, since it abstracts the memory of an actual computer (sometimes it is also called the **store** or the **state**):

Memory

Locations $\longrightarrow$ Values

In an interpreter, on the other hand, the symbol table and the environment are combined, since static and dynamic attributes are both computed during execution. Usually, memory is also included in this function, and we have the following picture:

Environment

Names $\longrightarrow$ Attributes (including locations and values)

5.2 Declarations, Blocks, and Scope

Declarations are, as we have seen, a principal method for establishing bindings. Bindings can be determined by a declaration either **implicitly** or **explicitly**. For example, the C declaration

```
int x;
```

---

[4] Note that not all static attributes may be computed by the compiler; a linker and loader may also compute some static attributes, such as the code for an externally linked function or the location of a global variable.

establishes the data type of x explicitly using the keyword int, but the exact location of x during execution is only bound implicitly and indeed could be either static or dynamic, depending on the location of this declaration in the program (this will be discussed again later). Similarly, the value of x is either implicitly zero or undefined, depending on the location of the declaration. On the other hand, the declaration

```
int x = 0;
```

explicitly binds 0 as the initial value of x.

Not only can bindings be implicit in a declaration, but the entire declaration itself may be implicit. For example, in some languages simply using the name of the variable causes it to be declared. Languages with implicit declarations usually have name conventions to establish other attributes. For example, FORTRAN does not require variable declarations for simple variables. All variables in FORTRAN that are not explicitly declared are assumed to be integer if their names begin with "I," "J," "K," "L," "M," or "N," and real otherwise. A similar convention holds in some BASICs, where variables ending in "%" are integer, variables ending in "$" are strings, and all others are real. Other languages with implicit declarations are APL and SNOBOL.

Sometimes a language will have different names for declarations that bind certain attributes but not others. For example, in C and C++, declarations that bind *all* potential attributes are called **definitions**, while declarations that only *partially* specify attributes are called simply declarations. For example, the function declaration (or **prototype**)

```
double f(int x);
```

specifies only the data type of the function f (i.e., the types of its parameters and return value), but does not specify the code to implement f. Similarly,

```
struct x;
```

specifies an **incomplete type** in C or C++, so this declaration is also not a definition. (Such specialized declarations are used to resolve recursive definitions and in cases where the complete definition can only be found at link time—see subsequent remarks in this chapter.)

Declarations are commonly associated with particular language constructs and are syntactically and semantically attached to these constructs. One such standard language construct is typically called a **block**, and consists of a sequence of declarations followed by a sequence of statements, and surrounded by syntactic markers such as braces or begin-end pairs. In C, blocks are called **compound statements**, and appear as the body of functions in function definitions, and also anywhere an ordinary program statement could appear. Thus,

```
void p (void)
{ double r, z; /* the block of p */
   ...
  { int x, y; /* another, nested, block */        (continues)
```

(continued)

```
        x = 2;
        y = 0;
        x += 1;
    }
    ...
}
```

establishes two blocks, one of which represents the body of p, and the other nested inside the body of p.

In addition to declarations associated with blocks, C also has an "external" or "global" set of declarations outside any compound statement:

```
int x;
double y;
/* these are external to all functions
 and so global */

main()
{ int i, j; /* these are associated with the block of
  main only */
  ...
}
```

Declarations that are associated with a specific block are also called **local**, while declarations in surrounding blocks (or global declarations) are called **nonlocal** declarations. For example, in the previous definition of the procedure p, variables r and z are local to p but are nonlocal from within the second block nested inside p.

The notion of blocks with associated declarations that can be nested began with Algol60, and all Algol descendants exhibit this **block struc-ture** in various ways. For example, in Ada, a block is formed by a `begin-end` pair preceded by the keyword `declare`:

```
declare x: integer;
        y: boolean;
begin
  x := 2;
  y := true;
  x := x + 1;
  ...
end;
```

In Pascal, only those `begin-end` pairs associated with the main pro-gram or a procedure or function can have declarations:

```
program ex; (* main program *)
var x: integer; (* global declaration *)

procedure p; (* global declaration *)
var y: boolean; (* declaration local to p *)
begin
  if x = 2 then
```

```
(* no declarations allowed here *)
begin
  ...
 end;
end; (* p *)

begin (* main *)
(* no declarations allowed here *)
 ...
end. (* program *)
```

Note how the program declarations takes the place of the "external" declarations of C, allowing global declarations to look just like other block declarations (but at the same time identifying global declarations with those "local" to the main program).

Other language constructs besides blocks are important sources of declarations: All structured data types are defined using local declarations associated with the type. For example, in C, a struct definition is composed of local variable (or **member**) declarations within it:

```
struct A
{ int x; /* local to A */
  double y;
  struct
  { int* x; /* nested member declarations */
    char y;
  } z;
};
```

(Note how the syntax with braces is almost, but not quite, that of a block: There is an extra semicolon at the end.)

Similarly, in object-oriented languages, the **class** is an important source of declarations—indeed in pure object-oriented languages such as Java and Smalltalk the class is the *only* declaration that does not itself need to be inside another class declaration, thus making the class the *primary* source of declarations:

```
/* Java example of class declaration from Chapter 1 */
public class IntWithGcd
{ ...
  /* local declaration of intValue method */
  public int intValue()
  { return value;
  }

  /* local declaration of gcd method */
  public int gcd( int v )
  { ...
  }

  /* local declaration of value field */
  private int value;
}
```

(Note that in Java functions are called methods and members are called fields.)

Finally, declarations can also be collected into larger groups as a way of organizing programs and providing special behavior. **Ada packages** and **tasks** belong to this category, as do **Java packages** (rather different from Ada packages), ML and Haskell **modules**, and C++ **namespaces**. These will be treated in more detail in Chapter 9.

Declarations bind various attributes to names, depending on the kind of declaration. Each of these bindings itself has an attribute that is determined by the position of the declaration in the program and by the language rules for the binding. The **scope of a binding** is the region of the program over which the binding is maintained. We can also refer to the scope of a declaration if all the bindings established by the declaration (or at least all of the bindings we are interested in at a particular moment) have identical scopes. Sometimes, by abuse of language, we refer to the scope of a name, but this is dangerous, since the same name may be involved in several different declarations, each with a different scope. For example, the following C code contains two declarations of the name x, with different meanings and different scopes:

```
void p(void)
{ int x;
   ...
}

void q(void)
{ char x;
   ...
}
```

In a block-structured language like C (and most modern languages), where blocks can be nested, the scope of a binding is limited to the block in which its associated declaration appears (and other blocks contained within it). Such a scope rule is called **lexical scope**, since it follows the structure of the blocks as they appear in the written code. It is the standard scope rule in most languages (but see the next section for a discussion of a different scope rule).

A simple example of scope in C is given in Figure 5.1.

```
(1)   int x;

(2)   void p(void)
(3)   { char y;
(4)      ...
(5)   } /* p */

(6)   void q(void)
(7)   { double z;
(8)      ...
(9)   } /* q */
```

```
(10) main()
(11) { int w[10];
(12)    ...
(13) }
```

Figure 5.1 A Simple C Program Demonstrating Scope

In Figure 5.1, the declarations of variable x (line 1) and procedures p (lines 2–5), q (lines 6–9), and main (lines 10–13) are global. The declarations of y (line 3), z (line 7), and w (line 11), on the other hand, are associated with the blocks of procedures p, q, and main, respectively. They are local to these functions, and their declarations are valid only for those functions. C has the further rule that the scope of a declaration begins at the point of the declaration itself (this is the so-called **declaration before use** rule), so that we can state the following basic scope rule in C: The scope of a declaration extends from the point just after the declaration to the end of the block in which it is located.[5]

We repeat the example of Figure 5.1 in Figure 5.2, drawing brackets to indicate the scope of each declaration.

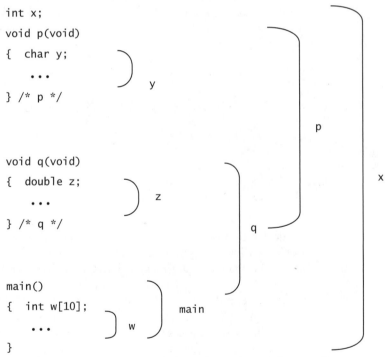

```
int x;
void p(void)
{   char y;
    ...
} /* p */
```
) y

```
void q(void)
{   double z;
    ...
} /* q */
```
) z

q

p

```
main()
{   int w[10];
    ...
}
```
) w

main

x

Figure 5.2 A Simple C Program with Brackets Indicating Scope

---

[5] C's scope rules are actually a bit more complicated, and we discuss a few of these complications further on in the chapter.

Blocks in other Algol-like languages establish similar scope rules. For example, in the following Ada code,

```
B1: declare
        x: integer;
        y: boolean;
     begin
        x := 2;
        y := false;
     B2: declare
             a, b: integer;
          begin
             if y then a := x;
             else b := x;
             end if;
          end B2;
        ...
     end B1;
```

the scope of the declarations of x and y is all of block B1 (including block B2), while the scope of the declarations of a and b is block B2 only.

One feature of block structure is that declarations in nested blocks take precedence over previous declarations. Consider the following example:

```
(1)  int x;

(2)  void p(void)
(3)  { char x;
(4)    x = 'a'; /* assigns to char x */
(5)    ...
(6)  }

(7)  main()
(8)  { x = 2; /* assigns to global x */
(9)    ...
(10) }
```

The declaration of x in p (line 3) takes precedence over the global declaration of x (line 1) in the body of p. Thus, the global integer x cannot be accessed from within p. The global declaration of x is said to have a **scope hole** inside p. For this reason, a distinction is sometimes made between the scope and the **visibility** of a declaration: Visibility includes only those regions of a program where the bindings of a declaration apply, while scope includes scope holes (since the bindings still exist, but are hidden from view). In C++, the **scope resolution operator** :: (double colon) can be used to access such hidden declarations (as long as they are global):

```
int x;

void p(void)
{ char x;
  x = 'a'; // assigns to char x
```

```
    ::x = 42; // assigns to global int x
    ...
}
main()
{ x = 2; // assigns to global x
    ...
}
```

This is an example of a widespread phenomenon in programming languages: Operators and declaration modifiers can alter the accessibility and scope of declarations. For example, Ada allows any named enclosing scope to be accessed using a dot notation similar to record structure access, so the above C++ behavior can also be achieved in Ada:

```
B1: declare
        a: integer;
        y: boolean;
    begin
      a := 2;
      y := false;
    B2: declare
            a, b: integer; -- local a now hides a in B1
          begin
            if y then a := B1.a; -- select the a in B1
            else b := B1.a;
            end if;
          end B2;
        ...
    end B1;
```

This is called **visibility by selection** in Ada.

C++ also uses the scope resolution operator to enter the scope of a class from the "outside" to provide missing definitions, since C++ only requires declarations, not complete definitions within a class declaration:

```
/* C++ example of class declaration similar to previous
   Java example */
class IntWithGcd
{
public:
  /* local declaration of intValue function - code for
     intValue() is not provided */
  int intValue();

  int gcd ( int v ); /* local declaration of gcd */

private:
  int value; /* local declaration of value member */
};                                                (continues)
```

(continued)

```
/* use scope resolution to give actual definition of
 intValue */
int IntWithGcd::intValue()
{ return value;
}
```

One further example in this vein is the way additional keyword modifiers in a declaration can alter the scope of the declaration. In C, global variable declarations can actually be accessed across files, using the extern keyword:

File 1:

```
extern int x; /* uses x from somewhere else */
...
```

File 2:

```
int x; /* a global x that can be accessed by
            other files */
...
```

Now if File 1 and File 2 are compiled separately and then linked together, the external x in File 1 will be identified by the linker with the x provided in File 2. If, on the other hand, when writing File 2, the programmer wishes to restrict the scope of x to File 2 alone, and thus prevent external references, the programmer may use the static keyword:

File 2:

```
/* a global x that can only be seen within this
   file */
static int x;
...
```

Now an attempt to link File 1 with File 2 will result in an error: undefined reference to x. This is a primitive version of the kind of scope-modifying access control that modules and classes provide, and which will be discussed in detail in Chapters 9 and 10.

Scope rules need also to be constructed in such a way that recursive, or self-referential declarations are possible when they make sense. Since functions must be allowed to be recursive, this means that the declaration of a function name has scope beginning *before* the block of the function body is entered:

```
int factorial (int n)
/* scope of factorial begins here */
{ /* factorial can be called here */

   ...
}
```

On the other hand, recursive variable declarations don't in general make sense:

```
int x = x + 1; /* ??? */
```

This declaration should probably be an error, and indeed Java and Ada flag this as an error, even though the scope of the x begins at the = sign: Ada, because self-references in variable declarations are specifically outlawed, and Java because the self reference is flagged as an uninitialized use. C and C++, however, do not flag this as an error if x is a local variable,[6] but simply add one to the (probably random) uninitialized value of x.

A special scoping situation, related to recursion, occurs in class declarations in object-oriented languages: Local declarations inside a class declaration generally have scope that extends backwards to include the entire class (thus partially suspending the declaration before use rule). For example, in the previous `IntWithGcd` example in Java, the local data `value` was referenced in the class declaration even before it was defined. This rule exists so that the order of declarations within a class does not matter.

The bindings established by declarations are maintained by the symbol table. The way the symbol table processes declarations must correspond to the scope of each declaration. Thus, different scope rules require different behavior by, and even different structure within, the symbol table. In the next section we examine the basic ways a symbol table can maintain scope in a block-structured language.

5.3 The Symbol Table

A symbol table is like a variable dictionary: It must support insertion, lookup, and deletion[7] of names with associated attributes, representing the bindings in declarations. A symbol can be maintained by any number of data structures to allow for efficient access and maintenance: Hash tables, trees, and lists are some of the data structures that have been used. However, the maintenance of scope information in a lexically scoped language with block structure requires that declarations be processed in a stacklike fashion: On entry into a block, all declarations of that block are processed and the corresponding bindings added to the symbol table; then, on exit from the block, the bindings provided by the declarations are removed, restoring any previous bindings that may have existed. Without restricting our view of a symbol table to any particular data structure, we may nevertheless view the symbol table schematically as a collection of names, each of which has a stack of declarations associated with it, such that the declaration on top of the stack is the one whose scope is currently active. To see how this works, consider the C program of Figure 5.3.

---

[6] Global variables in C and C++ cannot have such an initializer expression, since their initial values must be compile-time quantities; see Section 5.6.2.

[7] Deletion, of course, may not mean complete erasure from the symbol table, but simply marking as no longer active, since bindings may need to be revisited even after a scope is exited by the translator.

```
(1) int x;
(2) char y;

(3) void p(void)
(4) { double x;
(5)    ...
(6)    { int y[10];
(7)       ...
(8)    }
(9)    ...
(10) }

(11) void q(void)
(12) { int y;
(13)    ...
(14) }

(15) main()
(16) { char x;
(17)    ...
(18) }
```

Figure 5.3   A C Program Demonstrating Symbol Table Structure

The names in this program are x, y, p, q, and main, but x and y are each associated with three different declarations with different scopes. Right after the processing of the variable declaration at the beginning of the body of p (line 5 of Figure 5.3), the symbol table can be represented as in Figure 5.4. (Since all function definitions are global in C, we do not indicate this explicitly in the attributes of Figure 5.4 and subsequent figures.)

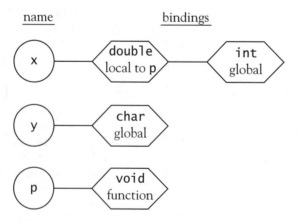

Figure 5.4   Symbol Table Structure at Line 5 of Figure 5.3

After the processing of the declaration of the nested block in p, with the local declaration of y (i.e., at line 7 of Figure 5.3), the symbol table is as shown in Figure 5.5.

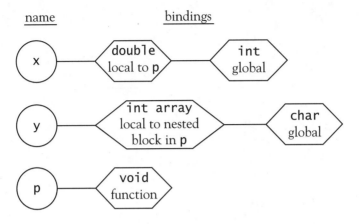

Figure 5.5   Symbol Table Structure at Line 7 of Figure 5.3

Then, when the processing of p has finished (line 10 of Figure 5.3), the symbol table becomes as in Figure 5.6 (with the local declaration of y popped from the stack of y declarations at line 8 and then the local dec-laration of x popped from the x stack at line 10).

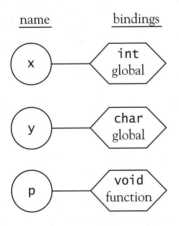

Figure 5.6   Symbol Table Structure at Line 10 of Figure 5.3

After q is entered (line 13), the symbol table becomes as in Figure 5.7.

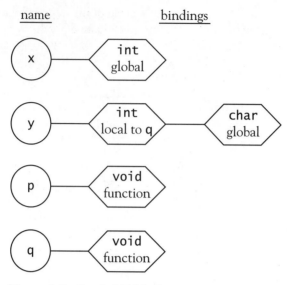

Figure 5.7   Symbol Table Structure at Line 13 of Figure 5.3

and when q exits (line 14), the symbol table is as in Figure 5.8.

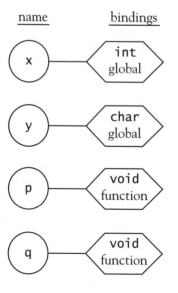

Figure 5.8   Symbol Table Structure at Line 14 of Figure 5.3

Finally, after main is entered (line 17), the symbol table is as in Figure 5.9.

name   bindings

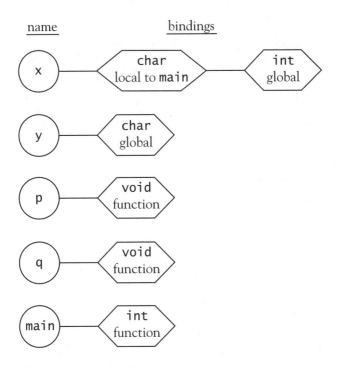

Figure 5.9   Symbol Table Structure at Line 17 of Figure 5.3

Note that this process maintains the appropriate scope information, including the scope holes for the global declaration of x inside p and the global declaration of y inside q.

This representation of the symbol table assumes that the symbol table processes the declarations statically, that is, prior to execution. This is the case if the symbol table is managed by a compiler, and the bindings of the declarations are all static. But if the symbol table is managed in this same way, but dynamically, that is, during execution, then declarations are processed as they are encountered along an execution path through the program. This results in a different scope rule, which is usually called **dynamic scoping**, and our previous lexical scoping rule is sometimes called **static scoping**.

To show the difference between static and dynamic scoping, let us add some code to the example of Figure 5.3, so that an execution path is established, and also give some values to the variables, so that some output can be generated to emphasize this distinction. The revised example is given in Figure 5.10.

```
(1) #include <stdio.h>

(2) int x = 1;
(3) char y = 'a';
```

(continues)

(continued)

```
(4) void p(void)
(5) { double x = 2.5;
(6)    printf("%c\n",y);
(7)    { int y[10];
(8)    }
(9) }

(10) void q(void)
(11) { int y = 42;
(12)    printf("%d\n",x);
(13)    p();
(14) }

(15) main()
(16) { char x = 'b';
(17)    q();
(18)    return 0;
(19) }
```

Figure 5.10   The C Program of Figure 5.3 with Added Code

Now consider what would happen if the symbol table for the code of Figure 5.10 were constructed dynamically as execution proceeds. First, execution begins with main, and all the global declarations must be processed before main begins execution, since main must know about all the declarations that occur before it. Thus, the symbol table at the beginning of the execution (line 17) is as in Figure 5.11.

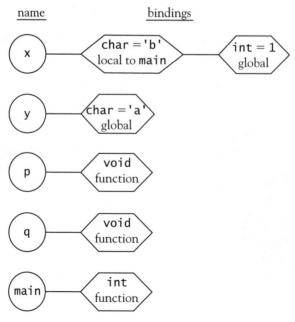

Figure 5.11   Symbol Table Structure at Line 17 of Figure 5.10 Using Dynamic Scope

Note that this is the same symbol table as when `main` is processed statically (Figure 5.9), except that we have now added value attributes to the picture. Note we have yet to process the bodies of any of the other functions.

Now `main` proceeds to call `q`, and we begin processing the body of `q`. The symbol table on entry into `q` (line 12) is then as in Figure 5.12.

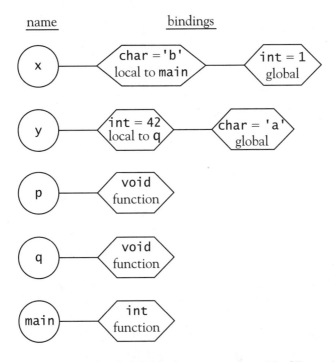

Figure 5.12   Symbol Table Structure at Line 12 of Figure 5.10 Using Dynamic Scope

This is now quite different from the symbol table on entry into `q` using static processing (Figure 5.7). Note also that *each* call to `q` may have a different symbol table on entry, depending on the execution path to that call, while using lexical scoping, each procedure has only one symbol table associated with its entry. (Since there is only one call to `q` in this example, this doesn't happen in this case.)

To continue with the example, `q` now calls `p`, and the symbol table becomes as shown in Figure 5.13.

Now consider how dynamic scope will affect the semantics of this program and produce different output. First, note that the actual output of this program (using lexical scoping, which is the standard for most languages, including C) is:

    1
    a

since in the first `printf` statement (line 6), the reference is to the global `y`, regardless of the execution path, and in the second `printf` statement (line 12) the reference is to the global x, again regardless of the execution path, and the values of these variables are 'a' and 1 throughout the program.

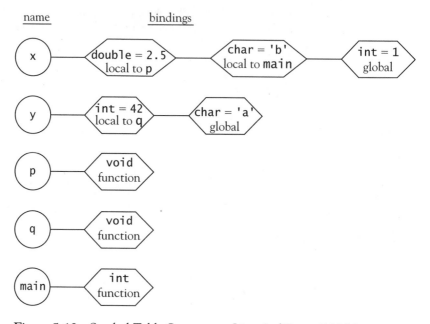

Figure 5.13   Symbol Table Structure at Line 6 of Figure 5.10 Using Dynamic Scope

However, using dynamic scoping,[8] the nonlocal references to y and x inside p and q, respectively, can change, depending on the execution path. In this program, the `printf` statement at line 12 of Figure 5.10 is reached with the symbol table as in Figure 5.12 (with a new declaration of x as the character 'b' inside `main`), and thus the `printf` statement will print this character interpreted as an integer (because of the format string `"%d\n"`), and this is the ASCII value 98. Second, the `printf` reference to y inside p (line 6 of Figure 5.10) is now the integer y with value 42 defined inside q, as shown in Figure 5.13. This value will now be interpreted as a character (ASCII 42 = '*'), and the program will print

```
92
*
```

This example brings up many of the issues that make dynamic scoping problematic, and why few languages use it. The first, and perhaps foremost problem, is that under dynamic scoping, when a nonlocal name is

---

[8] Of course, since C uses lexical scope, we cannot actually execute this program this way. We are using C syntax only as a convenience.

used in an expression or statement, the declaration that applies to that name cannot be determined by simply reading the program. Instead, the program must be executed, or its execution traced by hand, to find the applicable declaration (and different executions may lead to different results). Therefore the semantics of a function can change radically as execution proceeds. We saw this in the example above, where the reference to y in the `printf` statement on line 6 of Figure 5.10 cannot be known until execution time (we could if we wanted have rewritten this example to make the y reference actually depend on user input). Thus, the semantics of p change during execution.

Another serious problem is also shown by our example: Since nonlocal variable references cannot be predicted prior to execution, neither can the data types of these variables. In our example, the reference to y in the `printf` statement on line 6 of Figure 5.10 is assumed to be a character (from the data type of the global y), and we therefore write a character format directive "%c" in the format string of the `printf` function. However, with dynamic scoping, the variable y could have any type when p is executed, and so this formatting directive is likely to be wrong. In our example, we were lucky that C has very liberal conversion rules between two basic data types such as `char` and `int`. But imagine what would happen if the global y or the y local to q were a `double` or even a user-defined structure—we still are likely not to get a runtime error in C, but predicting the output can be difficult (and machine dependent!). In other, stricter languages like Ada or Pascal, this would definitely lead to a runtime error—not at all what we would like. Thus, static binding of data types ("static typing") and dynamic scoping are inherently incompatible. (See the next chapter for more on this issue.)

Nevertheless, dynamic scoping remains a possible option for highly dynamic, interpreted languages when we do not expect programs to be extremely large. The reason is that the runtime environment is made considerably simpler by using dynamic scoping in an interpreter. Indeed, at the end of Section 5.1, we noted that the environment in an interpreter includes the symbol table, so it may seem that it is impossible to maintain lexical scope in an interpreter, since, by definition, the symbol table is maintained dynamically. This is not the case. However, maintaining lexical scope dynamically does require some extra structure and bookkeeping; see Chapter 8. Thus, languages like APL, Snobol, and Perl (all interpreted languages with relatively small expected programs) have traditionally opted for dynamic scoping.[9]

Lisp, too, has traditionally been dynamically scoped (although we can hardly say that the typical Lisp program is small). The inventor of Lisp, John McCarthy, has stated that he felt this was a bug in the initial implementation of Lisp in 1958 (McCarthy [1981], page 180), but if so it has persisted to the present in many Lisp dialects. However, the popular

---

[9] Recent versions of Perl now offer lexical scoping.

Scheme dialect of Lisp (studied in Chapter 11) has used lexical scoping from its inception (Steele and Gabriel [1996], page 249), and Common Lisp (Steele [1982] [1984]) offers lexical scoping as an option.

Aside from the question of lexical versus dynamic scope, there is significant additional complexity surrounding the structure and behavior of the symbol table that we have not yet discussed. Indeed, the symbol table as we have discussed it so far—a single table for an entire program, with insertions on entry into a scope and deletions on exit—is appropriate only for the simplest languages, such as C and Pascal, with a strict declaration before use requirement, and where scopes cannot be reaccessed once they have been exited during processing by a translator.

Actually, even this description does not fully cover all situations in C and Pascal. Consider, for example, struct declarations in C (or record declarations in Pascal) as given in Figure 5.14.

Clearly, each of the two struct declarations in this code (lines 1–5 and 7–11 of Figure 5.14) must contain the further declarations of the data fields within each struct, and these declarations must be accessible (using the "dot" notation of member selection) whenever the struct variables themselves (x and y) are in scope. This means two things: (1) A struct declaration actually contains a local symbol table itself as an attribute (which contains the member declarations), and (2) this local symbol table cannot be deleted until the struct variable itself is deleted from the "global" symbol table of the program.

```
(1)    struct
(2)    { int a;
(3)      char b;
(4)      double c;
(5)    } x = {1,'a',2.5};

(6)    void p(void)
(7)    { struct
(8)      { double a;
(9)        int b;
(10)       char c;
(11)     } y = {1.2,2,'b'};
(12)     printf("%d, %c, %g\n",x.a,x.b,x.c);
(13)     printf("%f, %d, %c\n",y.a,y.b,y.c);
(14) }

(15) main()
(16) { p();
(17)   return 0;
(18) }
```

Figure 5.14 Code Example Illustrating Scope of Local Declarations in a C
struct

Thus, inside **p** (line 12 of Figure 5.14), the symbol table for the above code might look as shown in Figure 5.15 (with the symbol table attribute labeled as "symtab"):

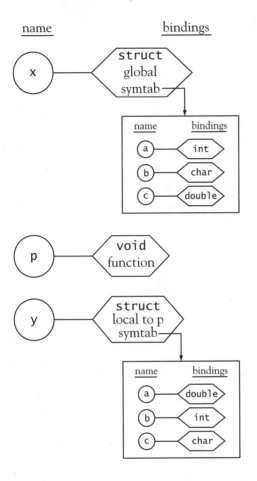

Figure 5.15   A Representation of the Symbol Table Structure at Line 12 of the Program of Figure 5.14 Showing Local **struct** Symbol Tables

Any scoping structure that can be referenced directly in a language must also have its own symbol table. Examples include all named scopes in Ada; classes, structs and namespaces in C++; and classes and packages in Java. Thus, a more typical structure for the symbol table of a program in any of these languages is to have a table for each scope, with nested scopes having their own tables within their enclosing tables. Again, these can be maintained in a stack-based fashion.

As a second example of this phenomenon, we rewrite the C example of Figure 5.10 into Ada as in Figure 5.16.

```
(1) with Text_IO; use Text_IO;
(2) with Ada.Integer_Text_IO; use Ada.Integer_Text_IO;

(3) procedure ex is
(4)    x: integer := 1;
(5)    y: character := 'a';

(6)    procedure p is
(7)    x: float := 2.5;
(8)    begin
(9)       put(y); new_line;
(10)   A: declare
(11)        y: array (1..10) of integer;
(12)       begin
(13)          y(1) := 2;
(14)          put(y(1)); new_line;
(15)          put(ex.y); new_line;
(16)       end A;
(17)   end p;

(18)   procedure q is
(19)      y: integer := 42;
(20)   begin
(21)      put(x); new_line;
(22)      p;
(23)   end q;

(24)     begin
(25)     declare
(26)       x: character := 'b';
(27)     begin
(28)        q;
(29)        put(ex.x); new_line;
(30)     end;
(31) end ex;
```

Figure 5.16   Ada Code Corresponding to Figure 5.10

A possible organization for the symbol table of this program after entry into block A inside p (line 12 of Figure 5.16) is as shown in Figure 5.17 (we ignore the question of how to represent the imported packages).

Note in Figure 5.17 that we no longer have to mention which specific scope each declaration belongs to, since membership in a particular symbol table already gives us that information. Also, note that if a lookup in an inner table fails, the lookup must proceed with the next outermost table. Thus, as indicated in the diagram with dotted arrows, there must be links from each inner scope to the next outer scope.

(global symbol table:)

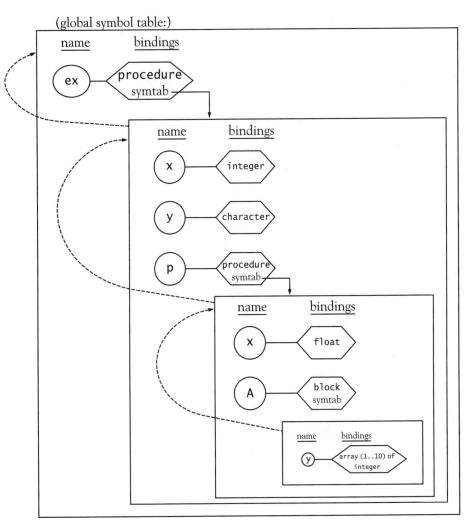

Figure 5.17   Symbol Table Structure at Line 12 of Figure 5.16

Consider, for example, how the lookup of ex.y in line 15 of Figure 5.16 would proceed from within block A in function p. First, ex would be looked up in the symbol table of A. Since this lookup fails, the next outermost symbol table would be consulted (the symbol table of p) by following the dotted line. This lookup also fails, and the next symbol table—that of ex—is consulted. This fails too, and finally the outermost symbol table is arrived at, which has only the entry for ex—which is the one we want. Once this entry is found, then the lookup of y proceeds (the "ex." in ex.y is stripped off for this lookup). The character variable y is found, and this is the variable that is meant in line 15.

A final question about symbol tables and scope is to what extent the same name can be reused for different functions, variables, and other entities within the same scope—such reuse is called overloading, and is discussed, along with related issues, in the next section.

5.4 Name Resolution and Overloading

An important question about declarations and the operation of the symbol table in a programming language is to what extent the same name can be used to refer to different things in a program. One might at first consider that this should not be allowed, as it can lead to serious confusion and unreadability. But consider, for example, the addition operation denoted by a "+" sign, which is typically a built-in binary infix[10] operator in most languages and whose result is the sum of its two operands. In virtually all languages, this simple "+" sign refers to at least two (and often more) completely different operations: integer addition and floating-point addition (typically denoted in assembly language by two different symbols ADDI and ADDF, or similar names). The "+" operator is then said to be **overloaded**. Clearly this reuse of the same symbol does not cause confusion, since these operations are closely related (and are even "the same" in some mathematical sense). Just as clearly, it would be a major annoyance if a programming language required programmers to use two different symbols for these operations (say +% for integer addition and +# for floating-point addition).

How does a translator disambiguate (tell apart) these two uses of the "+" symbol?

It does so by looking at the data types of the operands. For example, in C, if we write 2+3, we mean integer addition, and if we write 2.1+3.2 we mean floating-point addition. Of course, 2+3.2 is still potentially ambiguous, and the rules of a language must deal in some way with this case (most languages automatically convert 2 to 2.0, but Ada says this is an error).

It is, therefore, a major advantage for a language to allow overloading of operators and function names based in some way on data types. C++ and Ada allow extensive overloading of both function names and operators. Java also allows overloading, but only on function names, not operators.[11] The functional language Haskell also allows overloading of both functions and operators, and even allows new operators to be defined (which is not allowed in C++ or Ada). The latest versions of FORTRAN (Fortran90/95) also allow limited forms of overloading. We discuss overloading here using C++, Ada, and Java (which have similar, but not identical mechanisms). Overloading in Haskell will be described briefly in Chapter 11. See the Notes and References for overloading in Fortran 90/95.

---

[10] That is, written between its operands.

[11] At least, not in the current version of Java—a proposal exists to allow operator overloading in future versions.

The basic method for allowing overloaded functions is to expand the operation of the lookup operation in the symbol table to perform lookups based not only on the name of a function, but also on the number of its parameters and their data types. This process of choosing a unique function among many with the same name, which represents an expansion of the symbol table capabilities, is called **overload resolution**.

To see how overload resolution works, we consider the simple but useful example of a `max` function for numbers. This function can be defined for integers, doubles, and all other numeric types, and may have two, three, or four (or even more) parameters. For our purposes, we define only three of the possible `max` functions (in C++ syntax)[12] in Figure 5.18.

```
int max(int x, int y) // max #1
{ return x > y ? x : y; }

double max(double x, double y) // max #2
{ return x > y ? x : y; }

int max(int x, int y, int z) // max #3
{ return x > y ? (x > z ? x : z) : (y > z ? y : z); }
```

Figure 5.18   Three Overloaded `max` Functions in C++

We will refer to these as `max` #1, `max` #2, and `max` #3, respectively.

Now consider the following calls:

```
max(2,3); // calls max #1
max(2.1,3.2); // calls max #2
max(1,3,2); // calls max #3
```

The symbol table can easily determine the appropriate `max` function for each of these calls from the information contained in each call (the **calling context**)—it just needs to count the number of parameters, and then look (in the two-parameter case) to see if the parameter values are integers or doubles.

Difficulties do arise in determining which of several overloaded definitions should be used when several different definitions of an overloaded function are equally likely in a particular calling context under the rules of the language. Consider, for example, the following call:

```
max(2.1,3); // which max?
```

Here the answer depends on the language rules for converting a value of one type to another; see Chapter 6. In C++, for example, this call is **ambiguous**: C++ allows conversions both from integer to double and from double to integer (automatic truncation). Thus, the above call could be converted to either

```
max(2,3); // max #1
```

---

[12] These functions can be easily turned into Ada code, but Java does not have free-standing functions; to write this example in Java, we would write these functions as static methods inside the class containing the `main` function.

or to

```
max(2.1,3.0); // max #2
```

and the language rules do not say which conversion should be preferred. In Ada, too, the call max(2.1,3) is illegal, but for a different reason: No automatic conversions at all are allowed in Ada. In Ada, all parameter types must match a definition exactly. On the other hand, this call is perfectly legitimate in Java since Java permits conversions that do not lose information, and so Java would convert 3 to 3.0 and call max #2 since the other possible call involves converting 2.1 to 2 and would result in information loss (the fractional part would disappear). Note also that the call

```
max(2.1,4,3);
```

is legal in C++ (and results in 2.1 being truncated to 2), but not legal in either Ada or Java. On the other hand, suppose we add the definitions of Figure 5.19 to those of Figure 5.18.

```
double max(int x, double y) // max #4
{ return x > y ? (double) x : y; }

double max(double x, int y) // max #5
{ return x > y ? x : (double) y; }
```

Figure 5.19   Two More Overloaded max Functions in C++ (see Figure 5.18)

Then the calls max(2.1,3) and max(2,3.2) become legal in C++ and Ada, since now there is an exact match for each call. Of course, these extra definitions are unnecessary (but not harmful) in Java.

Thus, automatic conversions as they exist in C++ and Java significantly complicate the process of overload resolution (but less in Java than C++ because of Java's more restrictive conversion policy).

An additional issue in overload resolution is to what extent additional information in a calling context beside the number and types of the parameter values can be used. Ada, for example, allows the return type and even the names of the parameters in a definition to be used. Consider the Ada program in Figure 5.20.

```
(1)  procedure overload is

(2)    function max(x: integer; y: integer) -- max #1
(3)       return integer is
(4)    begin
(5)       if x > y then return x;
(6)       else return y;
(7)       end if;
(8)    end max;
```

```
(9)  function max(x: integer; y: integer) -- max #2
(10)     return float is
(11) begin
(12)    if x > y then return float(x);
(13)    else return float(y);
(14)    end if;
(15) end max;

(16) a: integer;
(17) b: float;
(18) begin -- max_test
(19)    a := max(2,3); -- call to max # 1
(20)    b := max(2,3); -- call to max # 2
(21) end overload;
```

Figure 5.20   An Example of max Function Overloading in Ada

Because line 19 of Figure 5.20 assigns the result of the max call to integer a, while line 20 assigns the result to float b, Ada can still resolve
the overloading since there are no automatic conversions. C++ and Java,
on the other hand, ignore the return type (if they didn't, the rules for
overload resolution would become even more complex, with more room
for ambiguity), and so this program would be an error in either of those
languages.

Both Ada and C++ (but not Java) also allow built-in operators to
be extended by overloading. For example, suppose we have a data structure in C++

```
typedef struct { int i; double d; } IntDouble;
```

We can then define a "+" and a "<" (less than) operation on IntDouble
as follows:

```
bool operator < (IntDouble x, IntDouble y)
{ return x.i < y.i && x.d < y.d; }

IntDouble operator + (IntDouble x, IntDouble y)
{ IntDouble z;
    z.i = x.i + y.i;
    z.d = x.d + y.d;
    return z;
}
```

Now code such as

```
IntDouble x, y;
...
if (x < y) x = x + y;
else y = x + y;
```

is possible. A complete runnable example of this C++ code is given in
Figure 5.21. A corresponding Ada example is given in Figure 5.22.

```cpp
#include <iostream>

using namespace std;

typedef struct { int i; double d; } IntDouble;

bool operator < (IntDouble x, IntDouble y)
{ return x.i < y.i && x.d < y.d;
}

IntDouble operator + (IntDouble x, IntDouble y)
{ IntDouble z;
  z.i = x.i + y.i;
  z.d = x.d + y.d;
  return z;
}

int main()
{ IntDouble x = {1,2.1}, y = {5,3.4};
  if (x < y) x = x + y;
  else y = x + y;
  cout << x.i << " " << x.d << endl;
  return 0;
}
```

Figure 5.21   A Complete C++ Program Illustrating Operator Overloading

```ada
with Text_IO; use Text_IO;
with Ada.Integer_Text_IO;
use Ada.Integer_Text_IO;
with Ada.Float_Text_IO;
use Ada.Float_Text_IO;

procedure opover is

type IntDouble is
record
  i: Integer;
  d: Float;
end record;

function "<" (x,y: IntDouble) return Boolean is
begin
  return x.i < y.i and x.d < y.d;
end "<";

function "+" (x,y: IntDouble) return IntDouble is
  z: IntDouble;
begin
  z.i := x.i + y.i;
  z.d := x.d + y.d;
  return z;
end "+";
```

```
    x, y: IntDouble;
begin
    x := (1,2.1);
    y := (5,3.4);
    if (x < y) then x := x + y;
    else y := x + y;
    end if;
    put(x.i); put(" "); put(x.d); new_line;
end opover;
```

Figure 5.22   A Complete Ada Program Illustrating Operator Overloading
                  Analagous to the C++ Program of Figure 5.21

Of course, when overloading a built-in operator, we must accept the syntactic properties of the operator—we cannot change their associativity or precedence. Indeed, there is no *semantic* difference between operators and functions, only the *syntactic* difference that operators are written in infix form, while function calls are always written in prefix form. In fact, in Ada, all operators also have a prefix form: "+"(3,2) means the same as 3 + 2. C++ also allows prefix form for operators, but only for overloaded ones applied to user-defined types:

```
    // x and y are IntDoubles as above
    x = operator + (x,y);
```

In Ada one can even redefine the built-in operators using overloading, while in C++ this is prohibited.

In Ada the operators that are allowed to be overloaded are those that traditionally have been viewed as infix or prefix mathematical operators. In C++, however, a much wider class of operations are viewed as overloadable operators. For example, the subscript operation can be viewed as a binary operator (with the "[" part of the operator symbol written infix and the "]" part of the operator symbol written postfix). These operations in C++ can only be overriden using object-oriented constructs (in the parlance of object-oriented programming, these overloaded functions must be "member functions" defined in a C++ class). Indeed, further opportunities for overloading are provided by object-oriented techniques; these will be studied in Chapter 10.

Up to this point, we have discussed only overloading of functions—by far the most important case. But an additional potential for overloading exists: Could we reuse the same name for things of completely different kinds? For example, could we use the same name to indicate both a data type and a variable, or both a variable and a function? In most langauges this is not permitted, and with good reason: It can be extremely confusing, and programs have little to gain by using such overloading (as opposed to function or operator overloading, which is very useful).

Occasionally, however, such overloading comes in handy as a way of limiting the number of names that one actually has to think about in a program. Take, for example, a typical C definition of a recursive type:

```
struct A
{  int data;
    struct A * next;
};
```

This is "old-style" C in which the data type is given by the `struct` name A, but the keyword `struct` must also always appear. Using a `typedef` one can remove the need for repeating the `struct`:

```
typedef struct A A;
struct A
{  int data;
    A * next;
};
```

Notice that we have used the same name A both for the `struct` name and the `typedef` name. This is legal in C, and is useful in this case, since it reduces the number of names that we need to remember.[13] This implies that `struct` names in C occupy a different symbol table than other names, so the principle of unique names for types (and variables) can be preserved.[14] Some languages have extreme forms of this principle, with different symbol tables for each of the major kinds of definitions, so that one could, for example, use the same name for a type, a function, and a variable (why this might be useful is another question).

Java is a good example of this extreme form of name overloading, where the code of Figure 5.23 is perfectly acceptable to a Java compiler.[15]

```
class A
{  A A(A A)
    {  A:
        for(;;)
        {  if (A.A(A) == A) break A; }
        return A;
    }
}
```

Figure 5.23   A Java Class Definition Showing Overloading of the Same Name for Different Language Constructs. (Adapted from Arnold, Gosling, and Holmes [2000], p. 153.)

In the example of Figure 5.22 there is a definition of a class, a method (a function), a parameter, and a label, all of which share the name A; see Exercise 5.20.

---

[13] In C++, the `typedef` is unnecessary, since the definition of `struct A` automatically creates a `typedef` named A.

[14] In fact, C implementations often simply add a prefix like `struct_` to a `struct` name and use the same symbol table, so the `struct` name A becomes `struct_A` and remains unique.

[15] In Java, the different symbol tables for different kinds of definitions are called **namespaces**, not to be confused with the namespaces of C++.

5.5 Allocation, Lifetimes, and the Environment

Having considered the symbol table in some detail, we need also to study the environment, which maintains the bindings of names to locations. We will introduce the basics of environments without functions here, as a comparison to the symbol table, but defer the study of environments in the presence of functions and procedures until Chapter 8.

Depending on the language, the environment may be constructed statically (at load time), dynamically (at execution time), or a mixture of the two. A language that uses a complete static environment is FORTRAN—all locations are bound statically. A language that uses a completely dynamic environment is LISP—all locations are bound during execution. C, C++, Ada, Java, and other Algol-style languages are in the middle—some allocation is performed statically, while other allocation is performed dynamically.

Not all names in a program are bound to locations. In a compiled language, names of constants and data types may represent purely compile-time quantities that have no existence at load or execution time. For example, the C global constant declaration

```
const int MAX = 10;
```

can be used by a compiler to replace all uses of MAX by the value 10. The name MAX is never allocated a location and indeed has disappeared altogether from the program when it executes.

Declarations are used to construct the environment as well as the symbol table. In a compiler, the declarations are used to indicate what allocation code the compiler is to generate as the declaration is processed. In an interpreter, the symbol table and the environment are combined, so attribute binding by a declaration in an interpreter includes the binding of locations.

Typically, in a block-structured language global variables are allocated statically, since their meanings are fixed throughout the program. Local variables, however, are allocated dynamically when execution reaches the block in question. In the last section we saw that in a block-structured language the symbol table uses a stack-like mechanism to maintain the bindings of the declarations. Similarly, the environment in a block-structured language binds locations to local variables in a stack-based fashion. To see how this takes place, consider the following C program fragment of Figure 5.24 with nested blocks.

```
(1) A: {  int x;
(2)       char y;
(3)       ...
(4)    B: {  double x;
(5)          int a;
(6)          ...
(7)       } /* end B */
```

(continues)

(continued)

```
(8)     C: {  char y;
(9)            int b;
(10)           . . .
(11)       D: {  int x;
(12)              double y;
(13)              . . .
(14)           } /* end D */
(15)           . . .
(16)       } /* end C */
(17)       . . .
(18)   } /* end A */
```

Figure 5.24   A C Program with Nested Blocks to Demonstrate Allocation
by the Environment

During execution of this code, when each block is entered, the variables declared at the beginning of each block are allocated, and when each block is exited, those same variables are deallocated. If we view the environment as a linear sequence of storage locations, with locations allocated from the top in descending order, then the environment at line 3 of Figure 5.24 (after the entry into A) looks as follows (ignoring the size of each allocated variable):

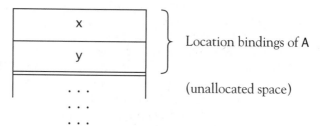

and the environment after entry into B is

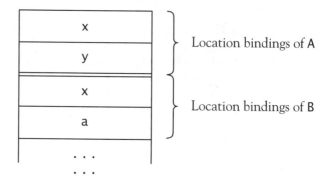

On exit from block B (line 7) the environment returns to the environment as it existed just after the entry into A. Then, when block C is entered (lines 8–9), the variables of C are allocated and the environment becomes

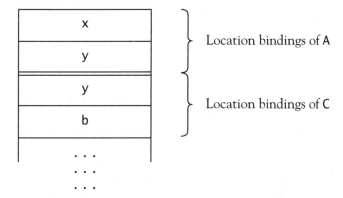

Notice that the variables y and b of block C are now allocated the same space that previously was allocated to the variables x and a of block B. This is okay, since we are now outside the scope of those variables, and they will never again be referenced.

Finally, on entry into block D (lines 11–12), the environment becomes

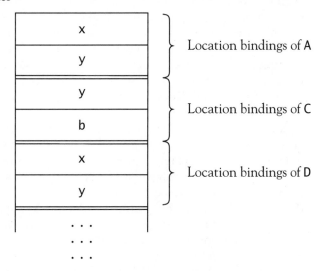

On exit from each block the location bindings of that block are successively deallocated, until, just prior to exit from block A, we have again recovered the original environment of A. In this way, the environment behaves like a stack. (Tradition has it that environments are drawn "upside down" from the usual way stacks are depicted.)

This behavior of the environment in allocating and deallocating space for blocks is relatively simple. Procedure and function blocks are more complicated. Consider the following procedure declaration in C syntax:

```
void p(void)
{ int x;
  double y;
    ...
} /* p */
```

During execution this declaration will not itself trigger an execution of the block of p, and the local variables x and y of p will not be allocated at the point of the declaration. Instead, the variables x and y will be allocated only when p is called. Also, each time p is called, new local variables will be allocated. Thus, every call to p results in a region of memory being allocated in the environment. We refer to each call to p as an **activation** of p and the corresponding region of allocated memory as an **activation record**. A more complete description of the structure of activation records, and the information necessary to maintain them, is postponed to the discussion of procedures in Chapter 8.

It should be clear from these examples that, in a block-structured language with lexical scope, the same name may be associated with several different locations (though only one of these can be accessed at any one time). For instance, in the environment of the previous nested blocks example, the name x is bound to two different locations during the execution of block D (lines 11–14), and the name y is bound to three different locations (though only the x and y of D are accessible at that time). We must therefore distinguish among a name, an allocated location, and the declaration that causes them to be bound. We will call the allocated location an object. That is, an object is an area of storage that is allocated in the environment as a result of the processing of a declaration. According to this definition, variables and procedures in C are objects, but global constants and data types are not (since type and global constant declarations do not result in storage allocation).[16] **The lifetime** or **extent** of an object is the duration of its allocation in the environment. The lifetimes of objects can extend beyond the region of a program where they may be accessed. For example, in the previous block example, the declaration of integer x in block A defines an object whose lifetime extends through block B, even though the declaration has a scope hole in B, and the object is not accessible from inside B. Similarly, it is possible for the reverse to happen: An object can be accessible beyond its lifetime; see Section 5.7.

When pointers are available in a language, a further extension of the structure of the environment is necessary. A **pointer** is an object whose stored value is a reference to another object.

---

[16] This notion of object is not the same as that in object-oriented programming languages; see Chapter 10.

In C, the processing of the declaration

```
int* x;
```

by the environment causes the allocation of a pointer variable x, but *not* the allocation of an object to which x points. Indeed, x may have an undefined value, which could be any arbitrary location in memory. To permit the initialization of pointers that do not point to an allocated object, and to allow a program to determine whether a pointer variable points to allocated memory, C allows the integer 0 to be used as an address that cannot be the address of any allocated object, and various C libraries give the name NULL to 0, so that one can write in C

```
int* x = NULL;
```

Other languages generally reserve a special symbol for this address (null in Java and Ada, nil in Pascal), so that it cannot be used as an identifier.[17] With this initialization, x can be tested to see if it points to an allocated object:

```
if (x != NULL) *x = 2;
```

For x to point to an allocated object, we must manually allocate it by the use of an allocation routine. Again, C is unusual in that there is no built-in allocation routine specified by the language, but the stdlib library module contains several functions to allocate and deallocate memory. The most commonly used of these are the malloc (for memory *allocation*) and free functions. Thus,

```
x = (int*) malloc(sizeof(int));
```

allocates a new integer variable and at the same time assigns its location to be the value of x. The malloc function returns the location it allocates and must be given the size of the data it is to allocate space for. This can be given in implementation-independent form using the built-in sizeof function, which is given a data type and returns its (implementation-dependent) size. The malloc function must also be cast to the data type of the variable its result is being assigned to, by putting the data type in parentheses before the function, since the address it returns is an *anonymous* pointer (a void* in C). (Casts and anonymous pointers are explained in Chapter 6.)

Once x has been assigned the address of an allocated integer variable, this new integer variable can be accessed by using the expression *x. The variable x is said to be **dereferenced** using the unary "*" operator.[18]

---

[17] Though technically, null is a literal, in practice there is little difference between this literal use and that of a reserved word.

[18] While this use of * is made to look similar to the way x is defined, this is an entirely different use of the * symbol from its purpose in a declaration.

We can then assign integer values to *x and refer to those values as we would with an ordinary variable, as in

```
*x = 2;
printf("%d\n",*x);
```

*x can be also be deallocated by calling the free procedure, as in

```
free(x);
```

(Note that dereferencing is not used here, although it is *x that is being freed, not x itself.)

C++ simplifies the dynamic allocation of C by adding built-in operators new and delete, which are reserved names. Thus, the previous code in C++ would become

```
int* x = new int; // C++
*x = 2;
cout << *x << endl; // output in C++
delete x;
```

Note the special syntax in this code—new and delete are used as unary operators, rather than functions, since no parentheses are required. Pascal is similar to C++, only the delete procedure is called dispose.

To allow for arbitrary allocation and deallocation using new and delete (or malloc and free), the environment must have an area in memory from which locations can be allocated in response to calls to new, and to which locations can be returned in response to calls to delete. Such an area is traditionally called a **heap** (although it has nothing to do with the heap data structure). Allocation on the heap is usually referred to as **dynamic allocation**, even though allocation of local variables is also dynamic, as we have seen. To distinguish these two forms of dynamic allocation, allocation of local variables according to the stack-based scheme described earlier is sometimes called **stack-based** or **automatic**, since it occurs automatically under control of the runtime system. (A more appropriate term for pointer allocation using new and delete might be *manual* allocation, since it occurs under programmer control.)

In a typical implementation of the environment, the stack (for automatic allocation) and the heap (for dynamic allocation) are kept in different sections of memory, and global variables are also allocated in a separate, static area. Although these three memory sections could be placed anywhere in memory, a common strategy is to place the three adjacent to each other, with the global area first, the stack next, and the heap last, with the heap and stack growing in opposite directions (to avoid stack/heap collisions in case there is no fixed boundary between them). This is usually depicted as in Figure 5.25.

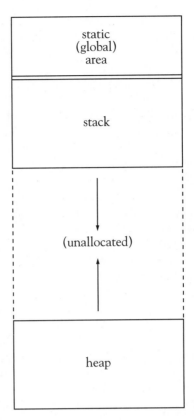

Figure 5.25   The Structure of a Typical Environment with a Stack and a Heap

Note that though the heap is shown as growing in only one direction, storage can be released anywhere in the allocated part of the heap, and that storage needs to be reusable; thus, a simple stack protocol will not work for the heap. Chapter 8 discusses this question in more detail.

A further complication in the management of the heap is that many languages require that heap deallocation be managed automatically (like the stack, except that allocation may still be under user control). For example, virtually all functional languages require that the heap be completely automatic, with no allocation or deallocation under programmer control. Java, on the other hand, allows allocation, but not deallocation, under programmer control. Java also further restricts heap allocation to objects only (in the sense of object-oriented programming), that is, variables of class type. Thus, our previous example would look as follows in Java:

```
// in Java must use class Integer, not int
// also, cannot allocate without assigning a value
Integer x = new Integer(2);
// print the actual integer value of x, i.e. 2
System.out.println(x);
// no delete operation allowed
```

Note how this code also does not have any explicit dereferencing (such as *x in C); Java forbids the use of such dereferencing—indeed it is not even part of Java's syntax, as there is no "dereference" operator.

The reason languages like Java and the functional languages (Scheme, ML, Haskell) do not allow much programmer control over heap allocation and deallocation, as well as explicit pointer manipulation (such as dereferencing) is that these are all inherently unsafe operations and can introduce seriously faulty runtime behavior that is very difficult to analyze and fix (as any C or C++ programmer can attest). Moreover, such faulty program behavior can, if extreme enough, compromise the entire operating system of a computer and cause an entire system or network to fail, or, worse, to act in malicious ways (such as a computer virus). This inherent lack of safety for heap allocation is studied further in Section 5.7.

One final, somewhat unusual example, of a language mechanism for heap allocation is that of Ada. Ada also has a **new** operation but no corresponding `delete` operation, similar to Java. However, Ada allows a `delete` operation to be user-defined using a standard language utility called `Ada.Unchecked_Deallocation`—thus making it more difficult to use by the programmer, as well as alerting anyone reading the code that this code is potentially unsafe, while at the same time allowing explicit programmer control of this feature as in C/C++. Figure 5.26 shows the above simple example rewritten in Ada (in its own block, to provide for the necessary declarations).

```
(1)   declare
(2)      type Intptr is access Integer;
(3)      procedure delete_int is
(4)         new Ada.Unchecked_Deallocation(Integer,Intptr);
(5)         -- generic procedure instantialtion in Ada
            -- see Chapter 6
(6)      x: Intptr := new Integer;
(7)   begin
(8)      x.all := 2;
(9)      put(x.all); new_line;
(10)     delete_int(x);
(11)  end;
```

Figure 5.26   Ada Code Showing Manual Dynamic Deallocation

Note how the keyword `access` is used in Figure 5.26 (line 2) to indicate a pointer, and the dereference operator (line 8 of Figure 5.26) is ".all"—this comes from the expectation of Ada (as with Java) that heap allocation will be used primarily for record (class) structures, and the .all refers to *all fields* (in our case, there are no fields, only an integer, but one must still use the dereferencer). Unlike Java, Ada does not require x to be a record, however.

To summarize, in a block-structured language with heap allocation, there are three kinds of allocation in the environment: static (for global

variables), automatic (for local variables), and dynamic (for heap allocation). These categories are also referred to as the **storage class** of the variable. Some languages, such as C, allow a declaration to specify a storage
class as well as a data type. Typically, this is used in C to change the allocation of a local variable to static:

```
int f(void)
{    static int x;
 ...
}
```

Now x is allocated only once, and it has the same meaning (and value) in
all calls to f. This combination of local scope with global lifetime can be
used to preserve local state across calls to f, while at the same time preventing code outside the function from changing this state. For example,
Figure 5.27 shows the code for a function in C that returns the number of
times it has been called, together with some interesting main program code.

```
(1)   int p(void)
(2)   { static int p_count = 0;
(3)             /* initialized only once - not each call! */
(4)       p_count += 1;
(5)       return p_count;
(6)   }

(7)   main()
(8)   { int i;
(9)     for (i = 0; i < 10; i++)
(10)    { if (p() % 3) printf("%d\n",p());
(11)    }
(12)    return 0;
(13) }
```

Figure 5.27   A C Program Demonstrating the Use of a Local Static Variable

5.6 Variables and Constants

5.6.1 Variables

A **variable** is an object whose stored value can change during execution.
A variable can be thought of as being completely specified by its attributes, which include its name, its location, its value, and other attributes
such as data type and size. A schematic representation of a variable can be
drawn as follows:

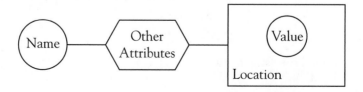

This picture singles out the name, location, and value of a variable as being its principal attributes. Often we will want to concentrate on these alone, and then we picture a variable in the following way:

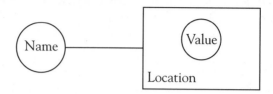

We will call this a **box-and-circle** diagram. The line drawn between the name and the location box can be thought of as representing the binding of the name to the location by the environment and the circle inside the box as representing the value bound by the memory—that is, the value stored at that location.

The principal way a variable changes its value is through the **assignment** statement x = e, where x is a variable name and e is an expression. The semantics of this statement are that e is evaluated to a value, which is then copied into the location of x. If e is a variable name, say, y, then the assignment (in C syntax)

    x = y

can be viewed as follows (the double arrow stands for copying):

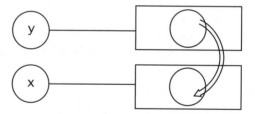

Since a variable has both a location and a value stored at that location, it is important to distinguish clearly between the two. However, this distinction is obscured in the assignment statement: y on the right-hand side stands for the value of y, while x on the left-hand side stands for the location of x. For this reason the value stored in the location of a variable is sometimes called its **r-value** (for right-hand side value), while the location of a variable is its **l-value** (for left-hand side value). A few languages make this distinction explicit. ML is one modern language that does so (Algol68 and BLISS are more historical examples). For example, in ML, variables are explicitly thought of as locations, or references to values. If x is an integer variable in ML, then its type is "reference to integer," and to obtain its value we must write !x, which dereferences x to produce its value. Thus, to increment x we must write in ML

    x := !x + 1;

and the assignment of the value of the variable y to x would be written in ML as

    x := !y;

More on this topic, and ML in general, can be found in Chapter 11.

In C, in addition to the standard automatic dereferencing of l-values to r-values, there is an explicit "address of" operator & that turns a reference into a pointer. This allows the address of a variable to be explicitly fetched as a pointer (which can then be dereferenced using the standard * operator on pointers). Thus, given the C declaration

```
int x;
```

&x is a pointer to x (the "address" of x) and *&x is again x itself (both as an l-value and an r-value; see Exercise 5.24). Also, C allows the mixing of expressions with assignments, where both the r-value and l-value of a variable are involved. Thus, to increment the integer x by 1, one can write either x = x + 1 or x += 1 (indicating that x is both added to 1 and reassigned). The mixing of r-values, l-values, and pointers in C can lead to confusing and unsafe situations. For example,

```
x + 1 = 2;
```

is illegal (x + 1 is not an l-value), but

```
*(&x + 1) = 2;
```

is legal (&x is a pointer, to which 1 is added using address arithmetic, and then 2 is stored at the resulting address—likely to be unsafe!).

These features of C—the mixing of references and values, the use of the & operator, and the distinction between a reference and a pointer—all make C vulnerable to extremely obscure and even dangerous or improper use of variables, many of which cannot easily be caught either during translation or execution. They are, however, a consequence of C's design goal as a fast, unsafe language for systems programming.

Ada95 also has an "address-of" operator: If x has an l-value, then x'access is a pointer to x (in Ada pointer types are called **access types**).[19] Ada95 applies strict rules, however, that limit the use of these types in ways that make it much more difficult to misuse them than in C. This will be discussed in further detail in Chapter 8 (environments).

In some languages a different meaning is given to assignment: locations are copied instead of values. In this case x = y has the result of binding the location of y to x instead of its value:

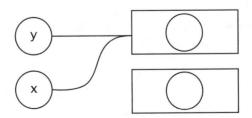

---

[19] The apostrophe is used in Ada to fetch various attributes of program entities; thus, x'access fetches the access attribute of the variable x, that is, the address of x as a pointer.

This is **assignment by sharing**. An alternative is to allocate a new location, copy the value of y, and bind x to the new location (this could be called **assignment by cloning**):[20]

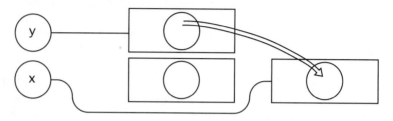

In both cases this interpretation of assignment is sometimes referred to as **pointer semantics** to distinguish it from the more usual semantics, which is sometimes referred to as **storage semantics**. Java, for example, uses assignment by sharing for all object variables, but not for simple data; see Section 5.7 for an example. Other languages that use pointer semantics are SNOBOL and LISP.

The figure for assigment by sharing shows the name x being associated directly to a new location (that of y). This is difficult to achieve for a compiler, since the symbol table commonly does not exist during execution. Standard implementations of assignment by sharing (such as in Java) use pointers and implicit dereferencing. In this view of assignment by sharing, x and y are implicitly pointers (with implicit automatically allocated pointer values):

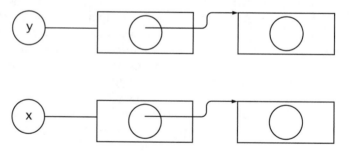

Then the assignment x = y has the following effect (the same as if one wrote *x = *y in C):

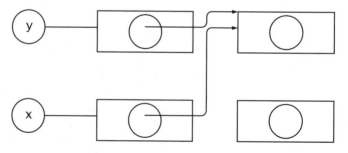

---

[20] A *clone* is an exact copy of an object in memory.

However, in the absence of address-of and dereference operators (& and *
in C), this implementation is indistiguishable from the original picture;
see Exercise 5.25 and Section 5.7.1.

5.6.2 Constants

A **constant** is a language entity that has a fixed value for the duration of
its existence in a program. A constant is like a variable, except that it has
no location attribute, but a value only:

We sometimes say that a constant has **value semantics** instead of
the storage semantics of a variable. This does not mean that a constant is
not stored in memory. It is possible for a constant to have a value that is
known only at execution time. In this case, its value must be stored in
memory, but, unlike a variable, once this value is computed, it cannot
change, and the location of the constant cannot be explicitly referred to
by a program.

This notion of constant is **symbolic**; that is, a constant is essentially
a name for a value. Sometimes representations of values, like the sequence
of digits 42 or the representation of a character such as "a," are called constants. To distinguish them from the constants in a constant declaration,
we sometimes refer to these representations of values as **literals**.

Many languages—especially the functional languages—emphasize
the use of constants over variables because of their much simpler semantics: Each constant name stands for only one value, and, once the value is
created, it remains the same regardless of the position or use of the name
within the code. Some languages like Haskell even prohibit variables altogether (the way some languages prohibit goto's) and rely entirely on constants for computations (how this is done will be studied in Chapter 11).

As we have noted, constants can be static or dynamic. A static constant is one whose value can be computed prior to execution, while a
dynamic constant has a value that can be computed only during execution. Static constants may also be of two kinds: Some constants can be
computed at translation time (compile-time), while others may only be
computable at load time (like the static location of a global variable), or
right at the beginning of the execution of the program. This distinction is
important, since a compile-time constant can, in principle, be used by a
compiler to improve the efficiency of a program and need not actually
occupy memory, while a load-time or dynamic constant must be computed
either on startup or as execution proceeds and must be stored in memory. Unfortunately, the word "static" is used sometimes to refer to
compile-time constants and sometimes to load-time constants. We shall
try to be precise in the following description by referring to static translation-time constants as **compile-time constants** (even though the language

may be interpreted rather than compiled), and we shall restrict the use of the term **static constant** to load-time constants. One can also make a distinction between general constants and **manifest constants**: a manifest constant is a name for a literal, while a constant can be more general.

Consider, for example, the following C code:

```
#include <stdio.h>
#include <time.h>

const int a = 2;
const int b = 27+2*2;
/* warning - illegal C code! */
const int c = (int) time(0);

int f( int x)
{   const int d = x+1;
    return b+c;
}
...
```

In this code a and b are compile-time constants (a is a manifest constant), while c is a static (load-time) constant, and d is a dynamic constant. In C, the const attribute can be applied to any variable in a program, and simply indicates that the value of a variable, once set, cannot be changed; other criteria determine whether a variable is static or not (such as the global scope in which a, b, and c are defined above). In C, however, load-time constants cannot be defined because of a separate rule restricting initial values of global variables to a narrow subset of compile-time expressions. Thus, in C, we cannot even write

```
const int a = 2;
int b = 27+a*a; /* also illegal in C */
```

in the above program, because the initial value of b is not allowed to be computed from the constant a, but must be computed from literals only (with a few small exceptions). C++, however, removes these restrictions, and the above program is legal C++.

Ada is similar to C++ in that a constant declaration such as

```
time : constant integer := integer(seconds(clock));
```

may appear anywhere in a program (and is static if global, and dynamic if local).

Java is similar to C++ and Ada, with two exceptions. First, in Java, a constant is indicated by using the keyword final (indicating that it gets only one, or a "final" value). Second, to get a static constant, one must use the keyword static (Java is structured so that there are no global variables as such). For example, the complete Java program in Figure 5.28 prints out the date and time at the moment when the program begins to run.

```
import java.util.Date;

class PrintDate
{  public static void main(String[] args)
   {  System.out.println(now);
   }
   static final Date now = new Date();
}
```

Figure 5.28   A Java Program Demonstrating a Load-Time ("static final")
                  Constant Variable

One issue often suppressed or overlooked in language discussions is that function definitions in virtually all languages are definitions of constants whose values are functions. Indeed, a C definition such as

```
int gcd( int u, int v)
{ if (v == 0) return u;
  else return gcd(v, u % v);
}
```

defines the name gcd to be a (compile-time) constant whose value is a function with two integer parameters, returning an integer result, and whose operation is given by the code of its body. Notice how this definition differs from that of a function *variable* in C, to which we could assign the value of gcd, as given in Figure 5.29.

```
(1) int (*fun_var)(int,int) = gcd;

(2) main()
(3) { printf("%d\n", fun_var(15,10));
(4)   return 0;
(5) }
```

Figure 5.29   C Code Showing the Use of a Function Variable

C is a little inconsistent in the code of Figure 5.29, in that we must define a function variable like fun_var as a pointer,[21] but when assigning it a value and calling it, use of pointer syntax is not required. C also has no way of writing a function *literal* (that is, a function value, without giving it a name such as gcd). As we would expect, functional languages do a much better job of making clear the distinction between function constants, function variables, and function literals (also called anonymous functions). For example, in ML, a function literal (in this case the integer "square" function) can be written as

```
fn(x:int) => x * x
```

---

[21] This is necessary because without the pointer syntax this would be a function declaration or prototype.

and the square function can be defined as a function constant (a constant is a val in ML) as:

```
val square = fn(x:int) => x * x;
```

as well as in more traditional C-like syntax:

```
fun square (x: int) = x * x;
```

An unnamed function literal can also be used directly in expressions without ever giving it a name. For example,

```
(fn(x:int) => x * x) 2;
```

evaluates the (unnamed) "square" function, passes it the value 2, and returns the value 4:

```
val it = 4 : int
```

Similar syntax is possible in Scheme and Haskell (see Chapter 11).

5.7 Aliases, Dangling References, and Garbage

This section describes several of the problems that arise with the naming and dynamic allocation conventions of programming languages, particularly the standard block-structured languages C, C++, and Ada. Language design solutions can be found to many of these problems (Java has found some)—as opposed to programmer solutions, which are to avoid the problematic situations—and a few of these will be discussed.

5.7.1 Aliases

An **alias** occurs when the same object is bound to two different names at the same time. Aliasing can occur in several ways. One is during procedure call and is studied in Chapter 8. Another is through the use of pointer variables. A simple example in C is given by the following code:

```
(1) int *x, *y;
(2) x = (int *) malloc(sizeof(int));
(3) *x = 1;
(4) y = x;     /* *x and *y now aliases */
(5) *y = 2;
(6) printf("%d\n",*x);
```

After the assignment of x to y (line 4), *y and *x both refer to the same variable, and the preceding code prints 2. We can see this clearly if we record the effect of the above code in our box-and-circle diagrams of Section 5.6, as follows.

After the declarations (line 1), both x and y have been allocated in the environment, but the values of both are undefined. We indicate that in the following diagram by shading in the circles indicating values:

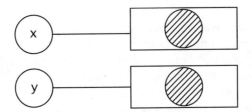

After line 2, *x has been allocated, and x has been assigned a value equal to the location of *x, but *x is still undefined:

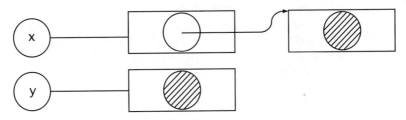

After line 3, the situation is as follows:

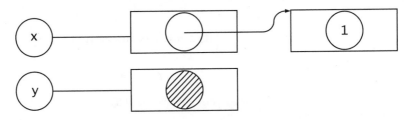

Line 4 now copies the value of x to y, and so makes *y and *x aliases of each other (note that x and y are not aliases of each other):

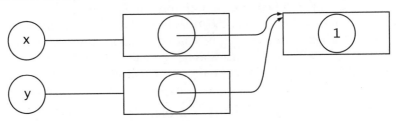

Finally, line 5 results in the following diagram:

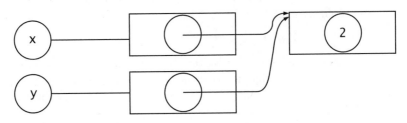

Aliases present a problem in that they cause potentially harmful **side effects**. For our purposes, we define a side effect of a statement to be any change in the value of a variable that persists beyond the execution of the statement.[22] From this definition, side effects are not all harmful, since an assignment is explicitly intended to cause one. However, side effects that are changes to variables whose names do not directly appear in the statement are potentially harmful in that the side effect cannot be determined from the written code. In the preceding example, the assignment *y = 2 also changed *x, even though no hint of that change appears in the statement that causes it (line 5). One must instead read the previous code to discover that this is happening.

Aliasing due to pointer assignment is difficult to control and is one of the reasons that programming with pointers is so difficult. One language that does attempt to limit aliasing, not only by pointers, but throughout the language, is Euclid. See the references at the end of the chapter.

A third way that aliases can be created is through assignment by sharing, as described in the previous section, since assignment by sharing implicitly uses pointers. Java is a major example of this kind of aliasing. Consider the following Java program:

```
(1) class ArrTest
(2) { public static void main(String[] args)
(3)   { int[] x = {1,2,3};
(4)     int[] y = x;
(5)     x[0] = 42;
(6)     System.out.println(y[0]);
(7)   }
(8) }
```

In line 3 an array named x is created with size 3, such that $x[0] = 1$, $x[1] = 2$, and $x[2] = 3$. In line 4 another array y is defined and initialized with x. In line 5, x[0] is changed to 42, and in line 6 y[0] is printed, which is now also 42, because of assignment by sharing.

Because of this aliasing problem in Java, Java has a mechanism for explicitly **cloning** any object, so that aliases are not created by assignment. For example, if we replace line 4 in the above code with

```
int[] y = (int[]) x.clone();
```

then the value printed in line 6 is 1, as we might reasonably expect.

FORTRAN also provides an explicit mechanism for aliasing: the EQUIVALENCE statement. Thus,

```
EQUIVALENCE X,Y
```

causes X and Y to be aliases of each other, so that an assignment to X causes an implicit assignment to Y, and vice versa. In the early days of programming, the EQUIVALENCE statement was used to reduce the amount of mem-

---

[22] Other definitions of side effect exist; see Exercise 5.22.

ory needed for a large program by sharing memory locations among variables that were not used at the same time. Today the use of this statement would be considered poor design. COMMON statements in FORTRAN can also cause aliasing; see Exercise 5.3.

5.7.2   Dangling References

Dangling references are a second problem that can arise from the use of pointers. A dangling reference is a location that has been deallocated from the environment, but that can still be accessed by a program. Another way of stating this is that a dangling reference occurs if an object can be accessed beyond its lifetime in the environment.

A simple example of a dangling reference is a pointer that points to a deallocated object. In C, the use of the free procedure can cause a dangling reference, as follows:

```
int *x , *y;
...
x = (int *) malloc(sizeof(int));
...
*x = 2;
...
y = x; /* *y and *x now aliases */
free(x); /* *y now a dangling reference */
...
printf("%d\n",*y); /* illegal reference */
```

In C, it is also possible for dangling references to result from the automatic deallocation of local variables when the block of the local declaration is exited. This is because, as noted previously, C has the "address of" operator & that allows the location of any variable to be assigned to a pointer variable. Consider the following C code:

```
(1) { int * x;
(2)      { int y;
(3)          y = 2;
(4)          x = &y;
(5)      }
(6)      /* *x is now a dangling reference */
(7) }
```

At line 5 when we exit the block in which y is declared, the variable x contains the location of y and the variable *x is an alias of y. But in the standard stack-based environment we described in Section 5.5, y has been deallocated on exit from the block. A similar example is the following C code:

```
int * dangle(void)
{  int x;
   return &x;
}
```

Whenever function `dangle` is called, it returns the location of its local automatic variable x, which has just been deallocated. Thus, after any assignment such as `y = dangle()` the variable *y will be a dangling reference.

Ada does not permit this kind of dangling reference, since it has no function equivalent to the "&" function of C. Ada *does* allow the first kind of dangling reference, but only if the program uses the `Unchecked_Deallocation` package (see Section 5.5, Figure 5.26).

Java does not allow dangling references at all, since there are no explicit pointers in the language, no "address of" operator, and no memory deallocation operators such as `free` or `delete`.

5.7.3 Garbage

One easy way to eliminate the dangling reference problem is simply to not perform any deallocation at all from the environment. This causes the third problem that we discuss in this section, namely, garbage. Garbage is memory that has been allocated in the environment but that has become inaccessible to the program.

A typical way for garbage to occur in C is to fail to call `free` before reassigning a pointer variable:

```
int *x;
...
x = (int *) malloc(sizeof(int));
x = 0;
```

At the end of this code, the location allocated to *x by the call to `malloc` is now garbage, since x now contains the null pointer, and there is no way to access the previously allocated object. A similar situation occurs when execution leaves the region of the program in which x itself is allocated, as in

```
void p(void)
{   int *x;
    x = (int *) malloc(sizeof(int));
    *x = 2;
}
```

When procedure p is exited, the variable x is deallocated and *x is no longer accessible by the program. A similar situation occurs in nested blocks.

Garbage is a problem in program execution because it is wasted memory. However, an argument can be made that programs that produce garbage are less seriously flawed than programs that contain dangling references. A program that produces garbage may fail to run because it runs out of memory, but it is internally correct; that is, if it does not exceed available memory, it will produce correct results (or at least not be incorrect because of the failure to deallocate inaccessible memory). A program that accesses dangling references, on the other hand, may run but produce incorrect results, may corrupt other programs in memory, or may cause runtime errors that are hard to locate.

For this reason it is useful to remove the need to deallocate memory explicitly from the programmer (which, if done incorrectly, can cause dangling references), while at the same time automatically reclaiming garbage for further use. Language systems that automatically reclaim garbage are said to perform **garbage collection**.

We should note that the stack-based management of memory in the environment of a block-structured language can already be called a kind of simple garbage collection: When the scope of an automatic variable declaration is exited, the environment reclaims the location allocated to that variable by "popping" the memory allocated for the variable.

Historically, functional language systems, particularly LISP systems, pioneered garbage collection as a method for managing the runtime deallocation of memory. Indeed, in LISP, all allocation as well as deallocation is performed automatically, and we have previously noted that (as a result) functional languages have no explicit pointers or operations like `malloc` and `free`. Object-oriented language systems also often rely on garbage collectors for the reclamation of memory during program execution. This is the case for Smalltalk and Java. C++ is the notable exception.[23]

Language design is a key factor in what kind of runtime environment is necessary for the correct execution of programs. Nevertheless, the language design itself may not explicitly state what kind of memory allocation is required. For example, the definition of Algol60 introduced block structure, and so implicitly advocated the use of a stack-based environment, without explicitly describing or requiring it. Definitions of LISP have also not mentioned garbage collection, even though a typical LISP system cannot execute reasonably without it.

One way for the designer of an Algol-like language to indicate the need for automatic garbage collection would be to include in the language definition a `new` procedure for pointers, but fail to include a corresponding `free` or `delete` procedure. Java takes this approach, as we have noted, and so does Ada, except that Ada allows the manual introduction of such a procedure using `Unchecked_Deallocation`. A further quirk of Ada is that, even with the use of `Unchecked_Deallocation`, a garbage collector may be called if a pointer is not correctly deallocated. Since one of Ada's key design goals was to be used in real-time situations where control of the speed of execution of a program is critical, Ada provides a further option to turn off any existing garbage collectors for variables of given data types:

```
-- Intptr defined as in Figure 5.26
-- Pragma is described in Chapter 1
Pragma CONTROLLED(Intptr);
```

---

[23] The C++ Standard does allow for nonstandard heap managers, however, and the new and delete operators can be overloaded (for example, delete may be redefined to do nothing at all). But all such redefinitions are nonstandard and currently not well supported by typical C++ implementations.

Exercises

5.1 Assume the language C, C++, or Java. Give as precise binding times as you can for the following attributes, and give reasons for your answers:

(a) The maximum number of significant digits in a real number

(b) The meaning of **char**

(c) The size of an array variable

(d) The size of an array parameter

(e) The location of a local variable

(f) The value of a constant

(g) The location of a function

5.2 Discuss the meaning of the following statement: Early binding promotes security and efficiency, while late binding promotes flexibility and expressiveness.

5.3 In FORTRAN, global variables are created using a COMMON statement, but it is not required that the global variables have the same name in each subroutine or function. Thus, in the code

```
FUNCTION F
COMMON N
   . . .
END

SUBROUTINE S
COMMON M
   . . .
END
```

Variable N in function F and variable M in subroutine S share the same memory, so they behave as different names for the same global variable.

(a) Compare this method of creating global variables to that of C. How is it better? How is it worse?

(b) Describe the difference between variables that are COMMON and variables that are EQUIVALENCEd.

5.4 Compare the advantages and disadvantages of C's declaration before use rule with C++'s relaxation of that rule to extend the scope of a declaration inside a class declaration to the entire class, regardless of its position in the declaration.

5.5 C++ relaxes C's rule that all declarations in a block must come at the beginning of the block: In C++, declarations can appear anywhere a statement can appear. Discuss this feature of C++ from the point of view of (a) the principle of locality (Chapter 3); (b) language complexity; (c) implementation complexity.

5.6 Describe the bindings performed by a C extern declaration. Why is such a declaration necessary?

5.7 As noted in this chapter, C and C++ make a distinction between a **declaration** and a **definition**. Which of the following are declarations only and which are definitions:

(a) `char * name;`
(b) `typedef int * IntPtr;`
(c) `struct rec;`
(d) `int gcd(int,int);`
(e) `double y;`
(f) `extern int z;`

5.8 Using the first organization of the symbol table described in the text (a single simple table), show the symbol table for the following C program at the three points indicated by the comments (a) using lexical scope and (b) using dynamic scope. What does the program print using each kind of scope rule?

```
#include <stdio.h>

int a,b;

int p(void)
{ int a, p;
  /* point 1 */
  a = 0; b = 1; p = 2;
  return p;
}

void print(void)
{   printf("%d\n%d\n",a,b);
}

void q (void)
{   int b;
    /* point 2 */
    a = 3; b = 4;
    print();
}

main()
{   /* point 3 */
    a = p();
    q();
}
```

5.9 Using the second organization of the symbol table described in the text (multiple nested tables), show the symbol table for the following Ada program at the three points indicated by the comments (a) using lexical scope and (b) using dynamic scope. What does the program print using each kind of scope rule?

```
procedure scope2 is
a, b: integer;
```

(continues)

(continued)

```
function p return integer is
a: integer;
begin -- point 1
  a := 0; b := 1; return 2;
end p;

procedure print is
begin -- point 2
  put(a); new_line; put(b); new_line; put(p);
    new_line;
end print;

procedure q is
b, p: integer;
begin -- point 3
  a := 3; b := 4; p := 5; print;
end q;

begin
  a := p;
  q;
end scope2;
```

5.10 Describe the problem with dynamic scoping and static typing. Does a similar problem exist with lexical (static) scoping and dynamic typing? Why?

5.11 Sometimes the symbol table is called the **static environment**. Discuss the validity of this viewpoint.

5.12 Is extent the same as dynamic scope? Why or why not?

5.13 An alternative organization for a simple symbol table in a block-structured language to that described in the text is to have only one stack, rather than a stack for each name. All declarations of all names are pushed onto this stack as they are encountered and popped when their scopes are exited. Then, given a name, its currently valid declaration is the first one found for that name in a top-down search of the stack.
(a) Redo Exercise 5.8 with this organization for the symbol table.
(b) Sometimes this organization of the symbol table is called **deep binding**, while the organization described in the text is called **shallow binding**. Discuss the reason for these terms. Should one of these organizations be required by the semantics of a programming language? Explain.

5.14 The following program prints two integer values; the first value typically is garbage (or possibly 0, if you are executing inside a debugger or other controlled environment), but the second value might be 2. Explain why.

```
#include <stdio.h>
```

```
void p(void)
{ int y;
  printf("%d\n", y);
  y = 2;
}

main()
{ p(); p();
  return 0;
}
```

5.15 The following program prints two integer values; the first value typically is garbage (or possibly 0, if you are executing inside a debugger or other controlled environment), but the second value might be 2. Explain why.

```
#include <stdio.h>

main()
{
  { int x;
    printf("%d\n",x);
    x = 2;
  }
  { int y;
    printf("%d\n",y);
  }
  return 0;
}
```

5.16 Explain the difference between aliasing and side effects.

5.17 Suppose the following function declarations (in C++ syntax) are available in a program:

(1) `int pow(int, int);`
(2) `double pow(double,double);`
(3) `double pow(int, double);`

and suppose the following code calls the **pow** function:

```
int x;
double y;
x = pow(2,3);
y = pow(2,3);
x = pow(2,3.2);
y = pow(2,3.2);
x = pow(2.1,3);
y = pow(2.1,3);
x = pow(2.1,3.2);
y = pow(2.1,3.2);
```

Given the language **(a)** C++; **(b)** Java; or **(c)** Ada, write down the number of the **pow** function called in each of the 8 calls, or write "illegal" if a call cannot be resolved in the language chosen, or if a data type conversion cannot be made.

5.18 Pointers present some special problems for overload resolution. Consider the following C++ code:

```
void f( int* x) { ... }
void f( char* x) { ... }

int main()
{ ...
   f(0);
   ...
}
```

What is wrong with this code? How might you fix it? Can this problem occur in Java? In Ada?

5.19 Default arguments in function definitions, such as:

```
void print( int x, int base = 10);
```

also present a problem for overload resolution. Describe the problem, and give any rules you can think of that might help resolve ambiguities. Are default arguments reasonable in the presence of overloading? Explain.

5.20 Figure 5.23 of the text illustrates Java "namespace" overloading: the same name can be used for different kinds of definitions, such as classes, methods (functions), parameters, and labels. In the code of Figure 5.23, there are 12 appearances of the name A. Describe which of these appearances represent definitions, and specify the kind of definition for each. Then classify which of the other appearances represent uses of each definition.

5.21 The text mentions that the lookup operation in the symbol table must be enhanced to allow for overloading. The insert operation must also be enhanced.
   (a) Describe in detail how both operations should behave using a standard interface for a dictionary data structure.
   (b) Should the symbol table itself attempt to resolve overloaded names, or should it leave that job to other utilities in a translator? Discuss.

5.22 Many programming languages (including C, C++, Java, and Ada) prohibit the redeclaration of variable names in the same scope. Discuss the reasons for this rule. Could not variables be overloaded the same way functions are in a language like C++ or Ada?

5.23 A common definition of side effect is a change to a nonlocal variable or to the input or output made by a function or procedure. Compare this definition of side effect to the one in the text.

5.24 (a) Which of the following C expressions are l-values, which are not, and why (assume x is an int variable and y is an int* variable):

(1) x + 2
(2) &x
(3) *&x
(4) &x + 2
(5) *(&x + 2)
(6) &*y

(b) Is it possible for a C expression to be an l-value but *not* an r-value? Explain.
(c) Is &(&z) ever legal in C? Explain.

5.25 Show how one could use an "address-of" operator such as & in C to discover whether a translator is implementing assignment by sharing or assignment by cloning as described in Section 5.6.1.

5.26 Given the following C program, draw box-and-circle diagrams of the variables after each of the two assignments to **x (lines 11 and 15). Which variables are aliases of each other at each of those points? What does the program print?

```
(1) #include <stdio.h>

(2) main()
(3) { int **x;
(4)     int *y;
(5)     int z;
(6)     x = (int**) malloc(sizeof(int*));
(7)     y = (int*) malloc(sizeof(int));
(8)     z = 1;
(9)     *y = 2;
(10)    *x = y;
(11)    **x = z;
(12)    printf("%d\n",*y);
(13)    z = 3;
(14)    printf("%d\n",*y);
(15)    **x = 4;
(16)    printf("%d\n",z);
(17)    return 0;
(18) }
```

5.27 Explain the reason for the two calls to malloc (lines 6 and 7) in the previous exercise. What would happen if line 6 were left out? Line 7?

5.28 Repeat Exercise 5.26 for the following code:

```
(1) #include <stdio.h>

(2) main()
(3) { int **x;
```

(continues)

(continued)

```
(4)    int *y;
(5)    int z;
(6)    x = &y;
(7)    y = &z;
(8)    z = 1;
(9)    *y = 2;
(10)   *x = y;
(11)   **x = z;
(12)   printf("%d\n",*y);
(13)   z = 3;
(14)   printf("%d\n",*y);
(15)   **x = 4;
(16)   printf("%d\n",z);
(17)   return 0;
(18) }
```

5.29 A generalization of the notion of a constant in a programming language is that of a **single-assignment variable**: a variable whose value can be computed at any point but that can be assigned to only once, so that it must remain constant once it is computed. Discuss the usefulness of this generalization compared to constant declarations in C, C++, Java, or Ada. How does this concept relate to that of a dynamic constant as discussed in Section 5.6?

5.30 In Ada, an object is defined as follows: "An object is an entity that contains a value of a given type." This is interpreted to mean that there are two kinds of objects: constants and variables. Compare this notion of object with that of Section 5.6.

5.31 Why is the following C code illegal:

```
{ int x;
  &x = (int *) malloc(sizeof(int));
   ...
}
```

5.32 Why is the following C code illegal:

```
{ int x[3];
  x = (int *) malloc(3*sizeof(int));
   ...
}
```

5.33 Here is a legal C program with a function variable:

```
(1)   #include <stdio.h>

(2)   int gcd( int u, int v)
(3)   { if (v == 0) return u;
(4)       else return gcd(v, u % v);
(5)   }
```

```
(6)  int (*fun_var)(int,int) = &gcd;
(7)  main()
(8)  { printf("%d\n", (*fun_var)(15,10));
(9)    return 0;
(10) }
```

Compare lines 6 and 8 of this code to the equivalent code of Figure 5.29 (lines 1 and 3). Why is this version of the code permitted? Why is it not required?

Notes and References

Most of the concepts in this chapter were pioneered in the design of Algol60 (Naur [1963a]), except for pointer allocation. Pointer allocation was, however, a part of the design of Algol68 (Tanenbaum [1976]). Some of the consequences of the design decisions of Algol60, including the introduction of recursion, may not have been fully understood at the time they were made (Naur [1981]), but certainly by 1964 full implementations of Algol60 existed, which used most of the techniques of today's translators (Randell and Russell [1964]). For more detail on these techniques, consult Chapter 8 and a compiler text such as Louden [1997] or Aho, Sethi, and Ullman [1986].

Structured programming, which makes use of the block structure in an Algol-like language, became popular some time later than the appearance of the concept in language design (Dahl, Dijkstra, and Hoare [1972]). For an interesting perspective on block structure, see Hanson [1981].

The distinction that C and C++ make between definition and declaration is explained in more detail in Stroustrup [1997] and Kernighan and Ritchie [1988]. The effect of a declaration during execution, including its use in allocation, is called **elaboration** in Ada and is explained in Cohen [1996].

The notion of an object has almost as many definitions as there are programming languages. For different definitions than the one used in this chapter, see Exercise 5.30 and Chapter 10. The notions of symbol table, environment, and memory also change somewhat from language to language. For a more formal, albeit simple, example of an environment function, see Chapter 13. For a more detailed discussion of the theoretical representation of environments, see Meyer [1990]. For a more detailed description of environments in the presence of procedure calls, see Chapter 8.

Overloading in C++ is discussed in detail in Stroustrup [1997]; overloading in Java in Arnold, Gosling, and Holmes [2000] and Gosling, Joy, Steele, and Bracha [2000]; overloading in Ada in Cohen [1996]; and overloading in Fortran90/95 in Chapman [1997] and Metcalf and Reid [1999]. As an aside, overloading rules and ambiguity resolution occupy a significant portion of the C++ language standard (more than 50 pages, including one entire chapter).

Aliases and the design of the programming language Euclid, which attempts to remove all aliasing, are discussed in Popek et al. [1977] (see also Lampson et al. [1981]). Techniques for garbage collection and automatic storage management have historically been so inefficient that their use in imperative languages has been resisted. With modern advances that has changed, and many modern object-oriented languages require it (Java, Modula-3, Eiffel) and do not suffer greatly from execution inefficiency. Functional languages too have improved dramatically in efficiency while maintaining fully automatic dynamic allocation. For an amusing anecdote on the early use of garbage collection, see McCarthy [1981, p. 183]. Garbage collection techniques are studied in Chapter 8.

For a perspective on the problem of dynamic scoping and static typing, see Lewis et al. [2000].

6 Data Types

Every program uses data, either explicitly or implicitly, to arrive at a result. Data in a program are collected into data structures, which are manipulated by control structures that represent an algorithm. This is clearly expressed by the following pseudoequation (an equation that isn't mathematically exact but expresses the underlying principles),

$$\text{algorithms} + \text{data structures} = \text{programs}$$

which comes from the title of a book by Niklaus Wirth (Wirth [1976]). How a programming language expresses data and control largely determines how programs are written in the language. The present chapter studies the concept of data type as the basic concept underlying the representation of data in programming languages, while the chapters that follow study control.

Data in its most primitive form inside a computer is just a collection of bits. A programming language could take this view as its basis and build up all data from it. This would in essence provide a virtual machine (that is, a simulation of hardware—though not necessarily the actual hardware being used) as part of the definition of the language.

But this would not provide the kinds of abstraction necessary for large or even moderately sized programs. Thus, most programming languages provide a set of simple data entities, such as integers, reals, and Booleans, as well as mechanisms for constructing new data entities from these. Such abstractions are an essential mechanism in programming languages and contribute to almost every design goal: readability, writability, reliability, and machine independence. However, we should also be aware of the pitfalls to which such abstraction can lead. One is that machine dependencies are often part of the implementation of these abstractions, and the language definition may not address these because they are hidden in the basic abstractions.

An example of this is the **finiteness** of all data in a computer, which is masked by the abstractions. For example, when we speak of integer data we often think of integers in the mathematical sense as an infinite set: ..., −2, −1, 0, 1, 2, ..., but in a computer's hardware there is always a largest and smallest integer. Sometimes this is ignored in the definition of a programming language, and it then becomes a machine dependency.[1]

A similar situation arises with the precision of real numbers and the behavior of real arithmetic operations. This is a difficult problem for the language designer to address, since simple data types and arithmetic are usually built into hardware. A positive development was the establishment in 1985 by the Institute of Electrical and Electronics Engineers (IEEE) of a floating-point standard that attempts to reduce the dependency of real number operations on the hardware (and encourages hardware manufacturers to ensure that their processors comply with the standard). C++, Ada, and Java all rely on some form of this standard to make floating-point operations more machine independent. Indeed, Java and Ada have, as part of their standards, strong requirements for all arithmetic operations, in an attempt to reduce machine dependencies to a minimum. C++, too, has certain minimal requirements as part of its standard, but is less strict than Ada and Java.

An even more significant issue regarding data types is that there is disagreement among language designers on the extent to which type information should be made explicit in a programming language and be

---

[1] In a few languages, particularly functional languages, integers can be arbitrarily large and integer arithmetic is implemented in software; while this removes machine dependencies, it usually means arithmetic is too slow for computationally intensive algorithms.

used to verify program correctness prior to execution. Typically the argument is clearest between those who emphasize maximal flexibility in the use of data types and who advocate no explicit typing or translation-time type verification, versus those who emphasize maximum restrictiveness and call for strict implementation of translation-time type checking. A good example of a language with no explicit types or translation-time typing is Scheme,[2] while Ada is a good example of a very strictly type-checked language (sometimes referred to as a **strongly-typed** language). There are many reasons to have some form of static (i.e., translation-time) type checking, however:

1. Static type information allows compilers to allocate memory efficiently and generate machine code that efficiently manipulates data, so **execution efficiency** is enhanced.

2. Static types can be used by a compiler to reduce the amount of code that needs to be compiled (particularly in a recompilation), thus improving **translation efficiency**.

3. Static type checking allows many standard programming errors to be caught early, improving **writability**, or efficiency of program coding.

4. Static type checking improves the **security** and **reliability** of a program by reducing the number of execution errors that can occur.

5. Explicit types in a programming language enhance **readability** by documenting data design, allowing programmers to understand the role of each data structure in a program, and what can and cannot be done with data items.

6. Explicit types can be used to **remove ambiguities** in programs. A prime example of this was discussed in the previous chapter (Section 5.4): Type information can be used to resolve overloading.

7. Explicit types combined with static type checking can be used by programmers as a **design tool**, so that incorrect design decisions show up as translation-time errors.

8. Finally, static typing of interfaces in large programs enhance the development of large programs by verifying **interface consistency** and **correctness**.

---

[2] To say that Scheme has no explicit types and no translation-time type checking is not to say that Scheme has no types. Indeed, every data value in Scheme has a type, and extensive checking is performed on the type of each value during execution.

Many language designers considered these arguments so compelling that they developed languages in which virtually every programming step required the exact specification in the source code of the data types in use and their properties. This led programmers and other language designers to complain (with some justification) that type systems were being used as mechanisms to force programmers into a rigid discipline that was actually *reducing* writability and good program design.[3]

Since these arguments were first made in the 1960s and 1970s, many advances have been made in understanding how to make static typing more flexible while at the same time preserving all or most of the above listed properties, and most modern languages (except for special-purpose languages such as scripting and query languages) use some form of static typing, while using techniques that allow for a great deal of flexibility.

Our viewpoint in this chapter will be to first describe the primary notion of **data type** (the basic abstraction mechanism, common to virtually all languages), and the principal types and type constructors available in most languages. After discussing these basic principles of data types, we will describe the mechanisms of static type checking and type inference, and discuss some of the modern methods for providing flexibility in a type system, while still promoting correctness and security. Other mechanisms that provide additional flexibility and security come from modules and object-oriented techniques, and will be studied in later chapters.

6.1 Data Types and Type Information

Program data can be classified according to their **types**. At the most basic level, virtually every data value expressible in a programming language has an implicit type. For example, in C the value -1 is of type `int`, 3.14159 is of type `double`, and `"hello"` is of type "array of `char`".[4] In Chapter 5 we saw that the types of variables are often explicitly associated with variables by a declaration, such as

```
int x;
```

---

[3] Bjarne Stroustrup, for example (Stroustrup [1994], p. 20), has written that he found Pascal's type system to be a "straightjacket that caused more problems than it solved by forcing me to warp my designs to suit an implementation-oriented artifact."

[4] This type is not expressible directly using C keywords, though the C++ type `const char*` could be used. In reality, we should distinguish the type from its keyword (or words) in a language, but we shall continue to use the simple expedient of using keywords to denote types whenever possible.

which assigns data type `int` to the variable `x`. In a declaration like this, a type is just a name (in this case the keyword `int`), which carries with it some properties, such as the kinds of values that can be stored, and the way these values are represented internally.

Some declarations *implicitly* associate a type with a name, such as the Pascal declaration

```
const PI = 3.14159;
```

which implicitly gives the constant `PI` the data type `real`, or the ML declaration

```
val x = 2;
```

which implicitly gives the constant `x` the data type `int`.

Since the internal representation is a system-dependent feature, from the abstract point of view, we can consider a type name to represent the possible values that a variable of that type can hold. Even more abstractly, we can consider the type name to be essentially identical to the set of values it represents, and we can state the following:

Definition 1. A **data type** is a set of values.

Thus, the declaration of `x` as an `int` says that the value of `x` must be in the set of integers as defined by the language (and the implementation), or, in mathematical terminology (using $\in$ for membership) the declaration

```
int x;
```

means the same as:

$$\text{value of } x \in \textit{Integers}$$

where *Integers* is the set of integers as defined by the language and implementation (in Java, for example, this set is always the set of integers from to $-2{,}147{,}483{,}648$ to $2{,}147{,}483{,}647$, since integers are always stored in 32-bit two's-complement form).

A data type as a set can be specified in many ways: It can be explicitly listed or enumerated; it can be given as a subrange of otherwise known values; or it can be borrowed from mathematics, in which case the finiteness of the set in an actual implementation may be left vague or ignored.[5] Set operations can also be applied to get new sets out of old (see below).

A set of values generally also has a group of operations that can be applied to the values. These operations are often not mentioned explicitly

---

[5] In C, these limits are defined in the standard header files `limits.h` and `float.h`. In Java, the classes associated with each of the basic data types record these limits (for example, `java.lang.Integer.MAX_VALUE` = 2147483647).

with the type, but are part of its definition. Examples include the arithmetic operations on integers or reals, the subscript operation "[ ]" on arrays, and the structure member operator "." on structure or record types. These operations also have specific properties that may or may not be explicitly stated [e.g., $(x + 1) - 1 = x$ or $x + y = y + x$]. Thus, to be even more precise, we revise our first definition to include explicitly the operations, as in the following definition:

> **Definition 2.** A **data type** is a set of values, together with a set of operations on those values having certain properties.

In this sense, a data type is actually a mathematical algebra, but we will not pursue this view to any great extent here. (For a brief look at algebras, see the mathematics of abstract data types in Chapter 9.)

As we have already noted, a language translator can make use of the set of algebraic properties in a number of ways to assure that data and operations are used correctly in a program. For example, given a statement such as

```
z = x / y;
```

a translator can determine whether x and y have the same (or related) types, and if that type has a division operator defined for its values (thus also specifying which division operator is meant, resolving any overloading). For example, in C and Java, if x and y have type int, then integer division is meant (with the remainder thrown away) and the result of the division also has type int, and if x and y have type double, then floating-point division is inferred.[6] Similarly, a translator can determine if the data type of z is appropriate to have the result of the division copied into it. In C, the type of z can be any numeric type (and any truncation is automatically applied), while in Java, z can only be a numeric type that can hold the entire result (without loss of precision).

The process a translator goes through to determine whether the type information in a program is consistent is called **type checking**. In the above example, type checking verifies that variables x, y, and z are used correctly in the given statement.

Type checking also uses rules for inferring types of language constructs from the available type information. In the example above, a type must be attached to the expression x / y so that its type may be compared to that of z (in fact, x / y may have type int or double, depending on the types of x and y). The process of attaching types to such expressions is called **type inference**. Type inference may be viewed as a separate opera-

---

[6] Ada, on the other hand, has different symbols for these two operations: div is integer division, while / is reserved for floating-point division.

tion performed during type checking, or it may be considered to be a part of type checking itself.

Given a group of basic types like `int`, `double`, and `char`, every language offers a number of ways to construct more complex types out of the basic types; these mechanisms are called **type constructors**, and the types created are called **user-defined types**. For example, one of the most common type constructors is the **array**, and the definition

```
int a[10];
```

creates in C (or C++) a variable whose type is "array of `int`" (there is no actual `array` keyword in C), and whose size is specified to be 10. This same declaration in Ada appears as

```
a: array (1..10) of integer;
```

Thus, the "array" constructor takes a base type (`int` or `integer` in the above example), and a size or range indication, and constructs a new data type. This construction can be interpreted as implicitly constructing a new set of values, which can be described mathematically, giving insight into the way the values can be manipulated and represented.

New types created with type constructors do not automatically get names. Names are, however, extremely important, not only to document the use of new types, but also for type checking (as we will describe in Section 6.6), and for the creation of recursive types (Section 6.3.5). Names for new types are created using a **type declaration** (called a **type definition** in some languages). For example, the variable a, created above as an array of 10 integers, has a type that has no name (an **anonymous type**). To give this type a name, we use a `typedef` in C:

```
typedef int Array_of_ten_integers[10];
Array_of_ten_integers a;
```

or a type declaration in Ada:

```
type Array_of_ten_integers is array (1..10) of integer;
a: Array_of_ten_integers;
```

With the definition of new user-defined types comes a new problem. During type checking a translator must often compare two types to determine if they are the same, even though they may be user-defined types coming from different declarations (possibly anonymous, or with different names). Each language with type declarations has rules for doing this, called **type equivalence** algorithms. The methods used for constructing types, the type equivalence algorithm, and the type inference and type correctness rules, are collectively referred to as a **type system**.

If a programming language definition specifies a complete type system that can be applied statically and that guarantees that all (unintentional) data-corrupting errors in a program will be detected at the earliest possible point, then the language is said to be **strongly typed**. Essentially, this means that all type errors are detected at translation time, with the exception of a few errors that can only be checked during execution (such as array subscript bounds), and in these cases code is introduced to produce a runtime error. Strong typing ensures that most **unsafe programs** (i.e., programs with data-corrupting errors) will be rejected at translation time, and those unsafe programs that are not rejected at translation time will cause an execution error prior to any data-corrupting actions. Thus, no unsafe program can cause data errors in a strongly typed language. Unfortunately, strongly typed languages often reject safe programs as well as unsafe programs, due to the strict nature of their type rules (that is, the set of **legal programs**—those accepted by a translator—is a *proper* subset of the set of safe programs). Strongly typed languages also place an additional burden on the programmer in that appropriate type information must generally be explicitly provided, in order for type checking to work properly. The main challenge in the design of a type system is to minimize both the number of illegal safe programs and the amount of extra type information that the programmer must supply, while still retaining the property that all unsafe programs are illegal.

Ada is a strongly typed language that, however, has a fairly rigid type system with a considerable programmer burden. ML and Haskell are languages that are also strongly typed, but with less of a burden on the programmer, and with fewer illegal safe programs (indeed ML has a completely formalized type system in which all properties of legal programs are mathematically provable). Pascal and its related languages (such as Modula-2) are usually also considered to be strongly typed, even though there are a few loopholes. C has even more loopholes and so is sometimes called a **weakly typed language**. (C++ has attempted to close some of the most serious type loopholes of C, but for compatibility reasons still is not completely strongly typed).

Languages without static type systems are usually called **untyped languages** (or **dynamically typed languages**). Such languages include Scheme and other dialects of Lisp, Smalltalk, and most scripting languages such as Perl. Note, however, that an untyped language does not necessarily allow programs to corrupt data—it just means that all safety checking is performed at execution time. For example, in Scheme *all* unsafe programs will generate runtime errors, and no safe programs are illegal—an enviable property from the point of view of strong typing, but one that comes with a significant cost (all type errors cause unpleasant runtime errors, and the code used to generate these errors causes slower execution times).

In the next section we study the basic types that are the building blocks of all other types in a language. In Section 6.3 we study basic type constructors and their corresponding set interpretations. In Section 6.4 we give an overview of typical type classifications and nomenclature. In Section 6.5 we study type equivalence algorithms, and in Section 6.6 type checking rules. Methods for allowing the programmer to override type checking are examined in Section 6.7. Sections 6.8 and 6.9 give an overview of **polymorphism**, in which names may have multiple types, while still permitting static type checking.

6.2 Simple Types

Algol-like languages (C, Ada, Pascal), even the object-oriented ones (C++, Java), all classify data types according to a relatively standard basic scheme, with minor variations. Unfortunately, the names used in different language definitions are often different, even though the concepts are the same. We will attempt to use a generic name scheme in this section and then point out differences among some of the foregoing languages in the next.

Every language comes with a set of **predefined types** from which all other types are constructed. These are generally specified using either keywords (such as `int` or `double` in C++ or Java) or predefined identifiers (such as `String` or `Process` in Java). Sometimes variations on basic types are also predefined, such as `short, long, long double, unsigned int,` etc. that typically give special properties to numeric types.

Predefined types are primarily **simple types**: types that have no other structure than their inherent arithmetic or sequential structure. All the foregoing types except `String` and `Process` are simple. However, there are simple types that are not predefined: **enumerated types** and **subrange types** are also simple types.

Enumerated types are sets whose elements are named and listed explicitly. A typical example (in C) is

```
enum Color {Red, Green, Blue};
```

or (the equivalent in Ada)

```
type Color_Type is (Red, Green, Blue);
```

or (the equivalent in ML)

```
datatype Color_Type = Red | Green | Blue;
```

In Ada, ML, and many other languages (Pascal, Modula-2), enumerations are defined in a type declaration, and are truly new types. In most languages (but not ML), enumerations are **ordered**, in that the order in which the values are listed is important, and there is often a predefined **successor** and **predecessor** operation defined for any enumerated type. Also, in most languages, no assumptions are made about how the listed values are represented internally, and the only possible value that can be printed is the value name itself. As a runnable example, the short program in Figure 6.1 demonstrates Ada's enumerated type mechanism, which comes complete with symbolic I/O capability so that the actual defined names can be printed (see line 6 below that allows enumeration values to be printed).

```
(1)  with Text_IO; use Text_IO;
(2)  with Ada.Integer_Text_IO; use Ada.Integer_Text_IO;

(3)  procedure Enum is
(4)    type Color_Type is (Red,Green,Blue);
(5)    -- define Color_IO so that Color_Type values can be
       -- printed
(6)    package Color_IO is new Enumeration_IO(Color_Type);
(7)    use Color_IO;
(8)    x : Color_Type := Green;
(9)  begin
(10)   x := Color_Type'Succ(x); -- x is now Blue
(11)   x := Color_Type'Pred(x); -- x is now Green
(12)   put(x); -- prints GREEN
(13)   new_line;
(14) end Enum;
```

Figure 6.1   An Ada Program Demonstrating the Use of an Enumerated Type

By contrast, in C an enum declaration defines a type "enum ...," but the values are all taken to be names of integers and are automatically assigned the values 0, 1, etc., unless the user initializes the enum values to other integers; thus, the C enum mechanism is really just a shorthand for defining a series of related integer constants, except that a compiler could use less memory for an enum variable. The short program in Figure 6.2, similar to the above Ada program, shows the use of C enums. Note the fact that the programmer can also control the actual values in an enum (line 3 of Figure 6.2), even to the point of creating overlapping values.

```
(1)  #include <stdio.h>

(2)  enum Color {Red,Green,Blue};
(3)  enum NewColor {NewRed = 3, NewGreen = 2, NewBlue = 2};

(4)  main()
(5)  { enum Color x = Green; /* x is actually 1 */
(6)    enum NewColor y = NewBlue; /* y is actually 2 */
(7)    x++; /* x is now 2, or Blue */
(8)    y--; /* y is now 1 -- not even in the enum */
(9)    printf("%d\n",x); /* prints 2 */
(10)   printf("%d\n",y); /* prints 1 */
(11)   return 0;
(12) }
```

Figure 6.2   A C Program Demonstrating the Use of an Enumerated Type, Similar to Figure 6.1

Java omits the enum construction altogether.[7]

---

[7] Java does have an Enumeration interface, but it is a different concept.

Subrange types are contiguous subsets of simple types specified by giving a least and greatest element, as in the following Ada declaration:

```
type Digit_Type is range 0..9;
```

The type `Digit_Type` is a completely new type that shares the values 0 through 9 with other integer types, and also retains arithmetic operations too, in so far as they make sense. This is useful if we want to distinguish this type in a program from other integer types, and if we want to minimize storage and generate runtime checks to make sure the values are always in the correct range. Languages in the C family (C, C++, Java) do not have subrange types, since the same effect can be achieved manually by writing the appropriate-sized integer type (to save storage), and by writing explicit checks for the values, such as the Java:

```
byte digit; // digit can contain -128..127
...
if (digit > 9 || digit < 0) throw new DigitException();
```

Subrange types are still useful, though, because they cause such code to be generated automatically, and because type checking need not assume that subranges are interchangeable with other integer types.

Typically subranges are defined by giving the first and last element from another type for which, like the integers, every value has a next element and a previous element. Such types are called **ordinal types** because of the discrete order that exists on the set. All numeric integer types in every language are ordinal types, and enumerations and subranges are also typically ordinal types. Ordinal types always have comparison operators (like < and >=), and often also have successor and predecessor operations (or ++ and −− operations). Not all types with comparison operators are ordinal types, however: real numbers are ordered (i.e., 3.98 < 3.99), but there is no successor or predecessor operation. Thus, a subrange declaration such as

```
type Unit_Interval is range 0.0..1.0;
```

is usually illegal in most languages—Ada is a significant exception.[8]

Allocation schemes for the simple types are usually conditioned by the underlying hardware, since the implementation of these types typically relies on hardware for efficiency. However, as noted previously, languages are calling more and more for standard representations such as the IEEE 754 standard, which also requires certain properties of the operators applied to floating-point types. Some languages like Java also require certain properties of the integer types, and if the hardware does not conform, then the language implementor must supply code to force compliance. For example, here is a description of the Java requirements for integers, taken from Arnold, Gosling, and Holmes [2000], page 156:

---

[8] In Ada, however, the number of digits of precision must also be specified, so we must write `type Unit_Interval is digits 8 range 0.0 .. 1.0;`.

Integer arithmetic is modular two's complement arithmetic—that is, if a value exceeds the range of its type (`int` or `long`), it is reduced modulo the range. So integer arithmetic never overflows or underflows, but only wraps.

Integer division truncates toward zero (7/2 is 3 and $-7/2$ is -3). For integer types, division and remainder obey the rule

```
(x/y)*y + x%y == x
```

So 7%2 is 1 and $-7\%2$ is -1. Dividing by zero or remainder by zero is invalid for integer arithmetic and throws `ArithmeticException`.

Character arithmetic is integer arithmetic after the `char` is implicitly converted to `int`.

6.3 Type Constructors

Since data types are sets, set operations can be used to construct new types out of existing ones. Such operations include Cartesian product, union, powerset, function set, and subset.

When applied to types these set operations are called **type constructors**. In a programming language all types are constructed out of the predefined types using type constructors. In the previous section we have already seen a limited form of one of these constructors—the subset construction—in subrange types. There are also type constructors that do not correspond to mathematical set constructions, with the principal example being pointer types, which involve a notion of storage not present in mathematical sets. There are also some set operations that do not correspond to type constructors, such as intersection (for reasons to be explained). In this section we will catalog and give examples of the common type constructors.

6.3.1 Cartesian Product

Given two sets U and V, we can form the Cartesian or cross product consisting of all ordered pairs of elements from U and V:

$$U \times V = \{(u, v) \mid u \text{ is in } U \text{ and } v \text{ is in } V\}$$

Cartesian products come with projection functions $p_1: U \times V \to U$ and $p_2: U \times V \to V$, where $p_1((u, v)) = u$ and $p_2((u, v)) = v$. This construction extends to more than two sets. Thus $U \times V \times W = \{(u, v, w) \mid u \text{ in } U, v \text{ in } V, w \text{ in } W\}$. There are as many projection functions as there are components.

In many languages the Cartesian product type constructor is available as the **record** or **structure construction**. For example, in C the declaration

```
struct IntCharReal
{ int i;
  char c;
  double r;
};
```

constructs the Cartesian product type int × char × double.

In Ada this same declaration appears as

```
type IntCharReal is record
     i: integer;
     c: character;
     r: float;
end record;
```

However, there is a difference between a Cartesian product and a record structure: The components have names in a record structure, while in a product they are referred to by position. The projections in a record structure are given by the **component selector** (or **structure member**) **operation**: If x is a variable of type IntCharReal, then x.i is the projection of x to the integers. Some authors therefore consider record structure types to be different from Cartesian product types. Indeed, most languages consider component names to be part of the type defined by a record structure. Thus,

```
struct IntCharReal
{ int j;
  char ch;
  double d;
};
```

can be considered different from the struct previously defined, even though they represent the same Cartesian product set.

Some languages have a purer form of record structure type that is essentially identical to the Cartesian product, where they are often called **tuples**. For example, in ML, we can define IntCharReal as

```
type IntCharReal = int * char * real;
```

(the asterisk takes the place of the ×, which is not a keyboard character). All values of this type are then written as tuples, such as (2,#"a",3.14) or (42,#"z",1.1).[9] The projection functions are then written as #1, #2, etc. (instead of the mathematical notation p_1, p_2, etc.), so that #3 (2,#"a",3.14) = 3.14.

A data type found in object-oriented languages that is related to structures is the **class**. Classes, however, include functions that act on the data in addition to the data components themselves, and these functions have special properties that will be studied in Chapter 10 (such functions are called **member functions** or **methods**). In fact, in C++, a struct is

---

[9] Characters in ML use double quotes preceded by a # sign.

really another kind of class, as will be noted in that chapter. The `class` data type is closer to our second definition of data type, which includes functions that act on the data, and we will explore how functions can be associated with data later in this chapter and in subsequent chapters.

A typical allocation scheme for product types is sequential allocation according to the space needed by each component. Thus, a variable of type `IntCharReal` might be allocated 13 bytes: the first four for an integer, the third byte for a character, and the last eight for a real number. Sometimes the space must be allocated in even or word-size chunks, so an implementation might allocate 14 or even 16 bytes instead of 13. Also, in languages (like Java) that support international character sets (so-called **Unicode** characters), the `char` data type occupies two bytes, not one.

6.3.2 Union

A second construction is the union of two types: It is formed by taking the set theoretic union of their sets of values. Union types come in two varieties: discriminated unions and undiscriminated unions. A union is **discriminated** if a **tag** or **discriminator** is added to the union to distinguish which type the element is, that is, which set it came from. Discriminated unions are similar to disjoint unions in mathematics. Undiscriminated unions lack the tag, and assumptions must be made about the type of any particular value (in fact, the existence of undiscriminated unions in a language makes the type system *unsafe*, in the sense discussed in Section 6.2).

In C (and C++) the `union` type constructor constructs undiscriminated unions:

```
union IntOrReal
{ int i;
  double r;
};
```

Note that, as with `structs`, there are names for the different components (`i` and `r`). These are necessary because their use tells the translator which of the types the raw bits stored in the union should be interpreted as; thus, if `x` is a variable of type `union IntOrReal`, then `x.i` is always interpreted as an `int`, and `x.r` is always interpreted as a `double`. These component names should not be confused with a discriminant, which is a separate component that indicates which data type the value *really* is, as opposed to which type we may think it is. A discriminant can be imitated in C as follows:

```
enum Disc {IsInt,IsReal};
struct IntOrReal
{   enum Disc which;
    union
    {   int i;
        double r;
    } val;
};
```

and could be used as follows:

```
IntOrReal x;
x.which = IsReal;
x.val.r = 2.3;
...
if (x.which == IsInt) printf("%d\n",x.val.i);
else printf("%g\n",x.val.r);
```

Of course, this is still unsafe, since it is up to the programmer to generate the appropriate test code (and the components can also be assigned individually and arbitrarily).

Ada has a completely safe union mechanism, called a **variant record**. The above C code written in Ada would look as follows:

```
type Disc is (IsInt, IsReal);
type IntOrReal (which: Disc) is
record
  case which is
    when IsInt =>  i: integer;
    when IsReal => r: float;
  end case;
end record;
...
x: IntOrReal := (IsReal,2.3);
```

Note how in Ada the IntOrReal variable x must be assigned both the discriminant and a corresponding appropriate value at the same time—it is this feature that guarantees safety. Also, if the code tries to access the wrong variant during execution (which cannot be predicted at translation time):

```
put(x.i); -- but x.which = IsReal at this point
```

then a CONSTRAINT_ERROR is generated and the program halts execution.

Functional languages that are strongly typed also have a safe union mechanism that extends the syntax of enumerations to include data fields. Recall from Section 6.2 that ML declares an enumeration as in the following example (using vertical bar for "or"):

```
datatype Color_Type = Red | Green | Blue;
```

This syntax can be extended to get an IntOrReal union type as follows:

```
datatype IntOrReal = IsInt of int | IsReal of real;
```

Now the "tags" IsInt and IsReal are used directly as discriminants to determine the kind of value in each IntOrReal (rather than as member or field names). For example,

```
val x = IsReal(2.3);
```

creates a value with a real number (and stores it in constant x), and to access a value of type IntOrReal we must use code that tests which kind of value we have. For example, the following code for the printIntOrReal function uses a case expression and **pattern matching** (i.e., writing out a sample format for the translator, which then fills in the values if the actual value matches the format):

```
fun printInt x =
    (print("int: "); print(Int.toString x);
    print("\n"));

fun printReal x =
    (print("real: "); print(Real.toString x);
    print("\n"))

fun printIntOrReal x =
  case x of
    IsInt(i) => printInt i |
    IsReal(r) =>printReal r ;
```

The printIntOrReal function can now be used as follows:

```
printIntOrReal(x); (* prints "real: 2.3" *)
printIntOrReal (IsInt 42); (* prints "int: 42" *)
```

The "tags" IsInt and IsReal in ML are called **data constructors**, since they construct data of each kind within a union; they are similar to the object constructors in an object-oriented language. (Data constructors and the pattern matching that goes with them are studied in more detail in Chapter 11.)

Unions can be useful in reducing memory allocation requirements for structures when different data items are not needed simultaneously. This is because unions are generally allocated space equal to the maximum of the space needed for individual components, and these components are stored in overlapping regions of memory. Thus, a variable of type IntOrReal (without the discriminant) might be allocated 8 bytes: the first four would be used for integer variants, and all 8 would be used for a real variant. If a discriminant field is added, 9 bytes would be needed (probably rounded to 10 or 12).

Unions, however, are not needed in object-oriented languages, since a better design is to use inheritance to represent different nonoverlapping data requirements (see Chapter 10). Thus, Java does not have unions. C++ does retain unions, presumably primarily for compatibility with C.

Even in C, however, unions have a small but significant problem, in that typically unions are used as a "variant part" of a struct, and this requires that an extra level of member selection must be used, as in the struct IntOrReal definition above, where we had to use x.val.i and x.val.r to address the overlapping data. C++ offers a new option here— the **anonymous union** within a struct declaration, and we could write struct IntOrReal in C++ as follows:

```
enum Disc {IsInt,IsReal};
struct IntOrReal    // C++ only!
{ enum Disc which;
  union
  { int i;
    double r;
  }; // no member name here
};
```

Now we can address the data simply as x.i and x.r. Of course, Ada already has this built into the syntax of the variant record.

6.3.3 Subset

In mathematics a subset can be specified by giving a rule to distinguish its elements, such as pos_int = {x | x is an integer and x > 0}. Similar rules can be given in programming languages to establish new types that are subsets of known types. Ada, for example, has a very general **subtype** mechanism. By specifying a lower and upper bound, subranges of ordinal types can be declared in Ada, as for example:

```
subtype IntDigit_Type is integer range 0..9;
```

(Compare this with the simple type defined in Section 6.2:

```
type Digit_Type is range 0..9;
```

which is a completely new type, *not* a subtype of integer.)

Variant parts of records can also be fixed using a subtype. For example, consider the Ada declaration of IntOrReal on page 203; a subset type can be declared that fixes the variant part (which then must have the specified value):

```
subtype IRInt is IntOrReal(IsInt);
subtype IRReal is IntOrReal(IsReal);
```

Such subset types **inherit** operations from their parent types. Most languages, however, do not have ways in which a user can specify which operations are inherited and which are not. Instead operations are automatically or implicitly inherited. In Ada, for example, subtypes inherit all the operations of the parent type. It would be nice to be able to exclude operations that do not make sense for a subset type; for example, unary minus makes little sense for a value of type IntDigit_Type.

An alternative view of the subtype relation is to *define* it in terms of sharing operations. That is, a type S is a subtype of a type T if and only if all of the operations on values of type T can also be applied to values of type S. With this definition, a subset may not be a subtype, and a subtype may not be a subset. This, however, is a little more abstract a view than we are taking in this chapter.

Inheritance in object-oriented languages can also be viewed as a subtype mechanism, in the same sense of sharing operations as just described, with a great deal more control over which operations are inherited; see Chapter 10.

6.3.4 Arrays and Functions

The set of all functions $f: U \to V$ can give rise to a new type in two ways: as an **array type** or as a **function type**. When U is an ordinal type, the function f can be thought of as an **array** with **index type** U and **component type** V: if i is in U, then $f(i)$ is the ith component of the array, and the whole function can be represented by the sequence or tuple of its values $(f(low), \ldots, f(high))$, where low is the smallest element in U and $high$ is the largest. (For this reason, array types are sometimes referred to as **sequence types**.) In C, C++, and Java the index set is always a positive integer range beginning at zero, while in Ada any ordinal type can be used as an index set.

Typically array types can be defined either with or without sizes, but to define a *variable* of an array type a size must typically be specified at translation time, since arrays are normally allocated statically or on the stack (and thus a translator needs to know the size).[10] For example, in C we can define array types as follows:

```
typedef int TenIntArray [10];
typedef int IntArray [];
```

and we can now define variables as follows:

```
TenIntArray x;
int y[5];
int z[] = {1,2,3,4};
IntArray w = {1,2};
```

Note that each of these variables has its size determined statically, either by the array type itself or by the initial value list: x has size 10, y 5, z 4, and w 2. Also, it is illegal to define a variable of type IntArray without giving an initial value list:

```
IntArray w; /* illegal C! */
```

Indeed, in C the size of an array cannot even be a computed constant—it must be a literal:

```
const int Size = 5;
int x[Size]; /* illegal C, ok in C++ (see Section
              5.6.2) */
int x[Size*Size] /* illegal C, ok in C++ */
```

---

[10] Arrays can be allocated dynamically on the stack, but this complicates the runtime environment; see Chapter 8.

And of course any attempt to dynamically define an array size is illegal (in both C and C++):[11]

```
int f(int size)
{ int a[size]; /* illegal */
  ...
}
```

C does allow arrays without specified size to be parameters to functions (these parameters are essentially pointers—see later in this section):

```
int array_max (int a[] , int size)
{ int temp, i;
  assert(size > 0);
  temp = a[0];
  for (i = 1; i < size; i++)
  { if (a[i] > temp) temp = a[i];
  }
  return temp;
}
```

Note in this code that the size of the array a had to be passed as an additional parameter—the size of an array is not part of the array (or of an array type) in C (or C++).

Java takes a rather different approach to arrays, although, like C, Java array indexes must be nonnegative integers starting at 0. However, unlike C, Java arrays are always dynamically (heap) allocated, and the size of an array can be specified completely dynamically (but once specified cannot change unless reallocated). While the size is not part of the array type, the size *is* part of the information stored when an array is allocated (and is called its **length**). Arrays can also be defined using C-like syntax, or in alternate form that associates the "array" property more directly with the component type. Figure 6.3 contains an example of some array declarations and array code in Java packaged into a runnable example.

```
(1)    import java.io.*;

(2)    class ArrayTest
(3)    { static int array_max (int[] a) // note location of []
(4)       { int temp;
(5)          temp = a[0];
           // size is part of a
(6)          for (int i = 1; i < a.length; i++)
(7)          { if (a[i] > temp) temp = a[i];
(8)          }
(9)          return temp;
(10)   }
```
(continues)

---

[11] This restriction has been removed in the 1999 C Standard.

(continued)

```
(11)    public static void main (String args[])
(12)    // this placement of [] also allowed
(13)    { System.out.print("Input a positive integer: ");
            // Java code to get formatted input
(14)      BufferedReader in =
(15)        new BufferedReader(new InputStreamReader (System.in));
(16)      try // must catch exceptions
(17)      { int u = Integer.parseInt(in.readLine());
(18)        int[] x = new int[u] ; // Dynamic array allocation
(19)        for (int i = 0; i < x.length; i++) x[i] = i;
(20)        System.out.println(array_max(x));
(21)      }
(22)      catch ( IOException e)
(23)      { System.out.println("Invalid input.");  }
(24)      catch (NumberFormatException e)
(25)      { System.out.println("Invalid input.");  }
(26)   }
(27) }
```

Figure 6.3   A Java Program Demonstrating the Use of Arrays

Ada, like C, allows array types to be declared without a size (so-called **unconstrained arrays**), but requires that a size be given when array variables (but not parameters) are declared. For example, the declaration

```
type IntToInt is array (integer range <>) of integer;
```

creates an array type from a subrange of integers to integers. The brackets "<>" indicate that the precise subrange is left unspecified. When a variable is declared, however, a range must be given:

```
table : IntToInt(-10..10);
```

Unlike C (but like Java), array ranges in Ada can be given dynamically. Unlike Java, Ada does not allocate arrays on the heap, however (see Chapter 8). Figure 6.4 represents a translation of the Java program of Figure 6.3, showing how arrays are used in Ada.

```
(1)   with Text_IO; use Text_IO;
(2)   with Ada.Integer_Text_IO;
(3)   use Ada.Integer_Text_IO;

(4)   procedure ArrTest is

(5)   type IntToInt is array (INTEGER range <>) of INTEGER;

(6)   function array_max(a: IntToInt) return integer is
(7)   temp: integer;
(8)   begin
(9)     temp := a(a'first); -- first subscript value for a
              -- a'range = set of legal subscripts
```

```
(10)    for i in a'range loop
(11)      if a(i) > temp then
(12)         temp := a(i);
(13)      end if;
(14)    end loop;
(15)    return temp;
(16) end array_max;

(17) size: integer;

(18) begin
(19)    put_line("Input a positive integer: ");
(20)    get(size);
(21)    declare
(22)      x: IntToInt(1..size); -- dynamically sized array
(23)      max: integer;
(24)    begin
(25)      for i in x'range loop -- x'range = 1..size
(26)        x(i) := i;
(27)      end loop;
(28)      put(array_max(x));
(29)      new_line;
(30)    end;
(31) end ArrTest;
```

Figure 6.4   An Ada Program Demonstrating the Use of Arrays, Equivalent
to the Java Program of Figure 6.3

Multidimensional arrays are also possible, with C/C++ and Java
allowing arrays of arrays to be declared:

```
int x[10][20]; /* C code */
int[][] x = new int [10][20]; // Java code
```

Ada and Fortran have separate multidimensional array constructs as in
the following Ada declaration:

```
type Matrix_Type is
      array (1..10,-10..10) of integer;
```

In Ada this type is viewed as different from the type

```
type Matrix_Type is
      array (1..10) of array (-10..10) of integer;
```

Variables of the first type must be subscripted as x(i,j), while variables
of the second type must be subscripted as x(i)(j). (Note that square
brackets are never used in Ada.)

Arrays are perhaps the most widely used type constructor, since their
implementation can be made extremely efficient: Space is allocated sequentially in memory, and indexing is performed by an offset calculation from
the starting address of the array. In the case of multidimensional arrays,

allocation is still linear, and a decision must be made about which index to use first in the allocation scheme: If x is defined (in Ada) as follows:

```
x: array (1..10,-10..10) of integer;
```

then x can be stored as x[1,-10], x[1,-9], x[1,-8], ..., x[1,10], x[2,-10], x[2,-9], and so on (**row-major form**) or as x[1,-10], x[2,-10], x[3,-10], ..., x[10,-10], x[1,-9], x[2,-9] and so on (**column-major form**). Note that if the indices can be supplied separately (from left to right), as in the C declaration

```
int x[10][20];
```

then row-major form *must* be used. Only if all indices must be specified together can column-major form be used (in FORTRAN this is the case, and column-major form is generally used).

Multidimensional arrays have a further quirk in C/C++ because of the fact that the size of the array is not part of the array, and is not passed to functions (see the previous array_max function in C). If a parameter is a multidimensional array, then the size of all the dimensions **except the first** must be specified in the parameter declaration:

```
int array_max (int a[][20] , int size)
        /* size of second dimension required ! */
```

The reason is that, using row-major form, the compiler must be able to compute the distance in memory between a[i] and a[i+1], and this is only possible if the size of subsequence dimensions is known at compile-time. This is not an issue in Java or Ada, since the size of an array is carried with an array value dynamically.

Functional languages usually do not supply an array type, since arrays are specifically designed for imperative rather than functional programming. Some functional languages have imperative constructs, though, and those that do often supply some sort of array mechanism. Scheme has, for example, a **vector** type, and some versions of ML have an array module. Typically, functional languages use the **list** in place of the array, and this will be discussed in Chapter 11.

General function and procedure types can also be created in some languages. For example, in C we can define a function type from integers to integers as follows:

```
typedef int (*IntFunction)(int);
```

and we can use this type to define either variables or parameters:

```
int square(int x) { return x*x; }
IntFunction f = square;
int evaluate(IntFunction g, int value)
{ return g(value); }
...
printf("%d\n", evaluate(f,3)); /* prints 9 */
```

Note that, as we remarked in the previous chapter, C requires that we define function variables, types, and parameters using pointer notation, but then does not require that we perform any dereferencing (this is to distinguish function definitions from function types).

Of course, functional languages have very general mechanisms of this kind as well. For example, in ML we can define a function type as above in the following form:

```
type IntFunction = int -> int;
```

and we can use it in a similar way to the previous C code:

```
fun square (x: int) = x * x;
val f = square;
fun evaluate (g: IntFunction, value: int) = g value;
...
evaluate(f,3); (* evaluates to 9 *)
```

In Ada95 we can also write function parameters and types. Here is the evaluate function example in Ada95:

```
type IntFunction is
            access function (x:integer) return integer;
-- "access" means pointer in Ada

function square (x: integer) return integer is
begin
  return x * x;
end square;

function evaluate (g: IntFunction; value: integer)
      return integer is
begin
  return g(value);
end evaluate;

f: IntFunction := square'access;
// note use of access attribute to get pointer to square
...
evaluate(f,3); -- evaluates to 9
```

By contrast, most pure object-oriented languages, such as Java and Smalltalk, have no function variables or parameters: their focus is on objects, rather than functions.

The format and space allocation of function variables and parameters depend on the size of the address needed to point to the code representing the function and on the runtime environment required by the language. See Chapter 8 for more details.

6.3.5 Pointers and Recursive Types

A type constructor that does not correspond to a set operation is the **reference** or **pointer** constructor, which constructs the set of all addresses that refer to a specified type. In C the declaration

```
typedef int* IntPtr;
```

constructs the type of all addresses where integers are stored. If x is a variable of type IntPtr, then it can be **dereferenced** to obtain a value of type integer: *x = 10 assigns the integer value 10 to the location given by x. Of course, x must have previously been assigned a valid address; this is usually accomplished dynamically by a call to an allocation function such as malloc in C. (Pointer variables were discussed in Chapter 5.)

The same declaration as the foregoing in Ada is

```
type IntPtr is access integer;
```

Pointers are implicit in languages that perform automatic memory management. For example, in Java all objects are implicitly pointers that are allocated explicitly (using the new operator like C++) but deallocated automatically by a garbage collector. Functional languages like Scheme, ML, or Haskell also use implicit pointers for data but do both the allocation and deallocation automatically, so that there is no syntax for pointers (and no new operation).

Sometimes languages make a distinction between pointers and **references**, a reference being the address of an object under the control of the system, which cannot be used as a value or operated on in any way (although it may be copied), while a pointer can be used as a value and manipulated by the programmer (including possibly using arithmetic operators on it). In this sense, pointers in Java are actually references (since, except for copying and the new operation they are under the control of the system). C++ is perhaps the only language where both pointers and references exist together (in a somewhat uneasy relationship). Reference types are created in C++ by a **postfix & operator** (not to be confused with the *prefix* address-of & operator, which returns a pointer):

```
double r = 2.3;
double& s = r; // s is a reference to r - C++ only!
              // so they share memory
s += 1; // r and s are now both 3.3
cout << r << endl; // prints 3.3
```

This can also be implemented in C++ (also valid in C) using pointers:

```
double r = 2.3;
double* p = &r; // p has value = address of r
*p += 1; // r is 3.3
cout << r << endl; // prints 3.3
```

References in C++ are essentially constant pointers that are derefer-enced every time they are used (Stroustrup [1997], p. 98). For example, in the above code, s += 1 is the same as r += 1 (s is dereferenced first), while p +=1 increments the *pointer* value of p, so that p is now pointing to a different location (actually 8 bytes higher, if a **double** occupies 8 bytes).

A further complicating factor in C++ and C is that arrays are implicitly constant pointers to their first component. Thus, we can write code in C or C++ as follows:

```
int a[] = {1,2,3,4,5}; /* a[0] = 1, etc. */
int* p = a; /* p points to first component of a */
printf("%d\n", *p); /* prints value of a[0], so 1 */
printf("%d\n", *(p+2)); /* prints value of a[2]= 3 */
printf("%d\n", *(a+2)); /* also prints 3 */
printf("%d\n", 2[a]); /* also prints 3! */
```

Indeed, a[2] in C is just a shorthand notation for a + 2, and, by the com-mutativity of addition, we can equivalently write 2[a]!

Pointers are most useful in the creation of **recursive types**: a type that uses itself in its declaration. Recursive types are extremely important in data structures and algorithms, since they naturally correspond to recur-sive algorithms, and represent data whose size and structure is not known in advance, but may change as computation proceeds. Two typical exam-ples are lists and binary trees. Consider the following C-like declaration of lists of characters:

```
struct CharList
{ char data;
   struct CharList next; /* not legal C! */
};
```

There is no reason in principle why such a recursive definition should be illegal; recursive functions have a similar structure. However, a close look at this declaration indicates a problem: Any such data must contain an infinite number of characters! In the analogy with recursive functions, this is like a recursive function without a "base case," that is, a test to stop the recursion:

```
int factorial (int n)
{ return n * factorial (n - 1); /* oops */
}
```

This function lacks the test for small n and results in an infinite number of calls to fact (at least until memory is exhausted). We could try to remove this problem in the definition of CharList by providing a base case using a union:

```
union CharList
{ enum { nothing } emptyCharList; /* no data */
  struct
  { char data;
    union CharList next; /* still illegal */
  } charListNode;
};
```

Of course, this is still "wishful thinking" in that, at the line noted, the code is still illegal C. However, consider this data type as an abstract definition of what it means to be a CharList as a set, and then it actually makes sense, giving the following recursive equation for a CharList:

CharList = {nothing} ∪ char × CharList

where ∪ is union and × is Cartesian product. In Section 4.2.1, we described how BNF rules could be interpreted as recursive set equations that define a set by taking the smallest solution (or **least fixed point**). The current situation is entirely analogous, and one can show that the least fixed point solution of the preceding equation is

{nothing} ∪ char ∪ (char × char) ∪
                    (char × char × char) ∪. . .

That is, a list is either the empty list or a list consisting of one character or a list consisting of two characters, and so on; see Exercise 6.7. Indeed, ML allows the definition of CharList to be written virtually the same as the above illegal C:

```
datatype CharList
    = EmptyCharList | CharListNode of char * CharList ;
```

Why is this still illegal C? The answer lies in C's data allocation strategy, which requires that each data type have a fixed maximum size determined at translation time. Unfortunately, a variable of type CharList has no fixed size and cannot be allocated prior to execution. This is an insurmountable obstacle to defining such a data type in a language without a fully dynamic runtime environment; see Chapter 8. The solution adopted in most imperative languages is to use pointers to allow manual dynamic allocation. Thus, in C, the direct use of recursion in type declarations is prohibited, but indirect recursive declarations through pointers is allowed, as in the following (now legal) C declarations:

```
struct CharListNode
{ char data;
  struct CharListNode* next; /* now legal */
};
typedef struct CharListNode* CharList;
```

With these declarations each individual element in a CharListNode now has a fixed size, and they can be strung together to form a list of arbitrary size. Note that the union has now disappeared, because we represent the empty list simply with a null pointer (the special address 0 in C). Nonempty CharLists are constructed using manual allocation; for example the list containing the single character 'a' can be constructed as follows:

```
CharList cl
    = (CharList) malloc(sizeof(struct CharListNode));
(*cl).data = 'a'; /* can also write cl->data = 'a'; */
(*cl).next = 0;   /* can also write cl->next = 0; */
```

and this can be changed to a list of two characters as follows:

```
(*cl).next
        = (CharList) malloc(sizeof(struct CharListNode));
(*(*cl).next).data = 'b'; /*or cl->next->data = 'b'; */
(*(*cl).next).next = 0;   /* or cl->next->next = 0; */
```

6.3.6 Data Types and the Environment

At a number of points in this section, we have referred the reader to the discussion in Chapter 8 on environments, when the structure of a data type required space to be allocated dynamically. This is the case for pointer types, recursive types, and general function types. In their most general forms, these types require fully dynamic environments with automatic allocation and deallocation ("garbage collection") as exemplified by the functional languages and the more dynamic object-oriented languages (such as Smalltalk). More traditional languages such as C++ and Ada carefully restrict these types so that a heap (a dynamic address space under programmer control) suffices, in addition to a traditional stack-based approach to nested blocks (including functions), as discussed in Chapter 5. While it would make sense to discuss these general environment issues at this point and relate them directly to data structures, we opt to delay a full discussion to Chapter 8, where all environment issues, including those of procedure and function calls, can be addressed.

More generally, there is in fact a duality in the requirements of recursive data and recursive functions—indeed, in a language with very general function constructs (such as the functional languages of Chapter 11), recursive data can be modeled entirely by functions. Similarly, object-oriented languages (Chapter 10) can model recursive functions entirely by recursive data objects. While we do not focus on this duality in detail in this book, specific examples can be found in Chapters 10 and 11 and their exercises.

6.4 Type Nomenclature in Sample Languages

Although we have presented the general scheme of type mechanisms in Sections 6.2 and 6.3, various language definitions use different and confusing terminology to define similar things. In this section we give a brief description of the differences among three of the languages used in previous examples: C, Java, and Ada.

6.4.1 C

An overview of C data types is given in Figure 6.5. The simple types are called **basic types** in C, and types that are constructed using type constructors are called **derived types**. The basic types include the void type (in a sense the simplest of all types, whose set of values is empty) and the **numeric types**: the **integral types**, which are ordinal, and the **floating types**. There are three kinds of floating types and 12 possible kinds of integral types—four basic kinds, all of which can also have either signed or unsigned attributes given them (indicated in Figure 6.5 by listing the four basic types with signed and unsigned in parentheses above them). Of course, not all of the 12 possible integral types are distinct—for example, signed int is the same as int, and some of the other possibilities may be the same as well.

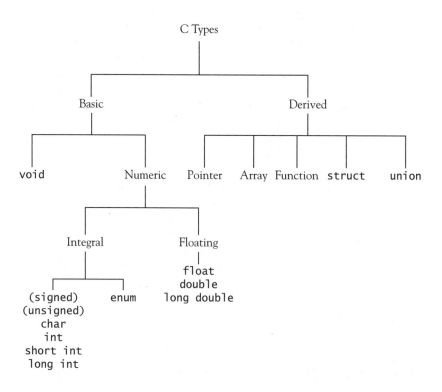

Figure 6.5   The Type Structure of C

6.4.2 Java

The Java type structure is shown in Figure 6.6. In Java the simple types are called **primitive types**, and types that are constructed using type constructors are called **reference types** (since they are all implicitly pointers or references). The primitive types divide into the single type boolean (which is *not* a numeric or ordinal type) and the numeric types, which split as in C into the integral (ordinal) and floating-point types (five integral and two floating point). There are only three type constructors in Java: the array (with no keyword as in C), the **class**, and the **interface**. The class and interface constructors will be described in Chapter 10.

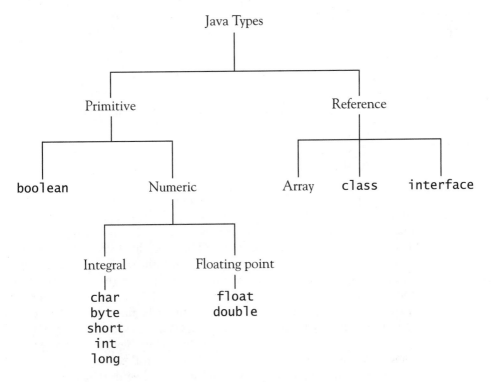

Figure 6.6   The Type Structure of Java

6.4.3 Ada

Ada has a rich set of types, a condensed overview of which is given in Figure 6.7. Simple types are called **scalar types** in Ada, and these are split into several overlapping categories. Ordinal types are called **discrete** types in Ada; **numeric types** comprise the **real** and **integer** types. Pointer types are called access types. Array and record types are called **composite types**.

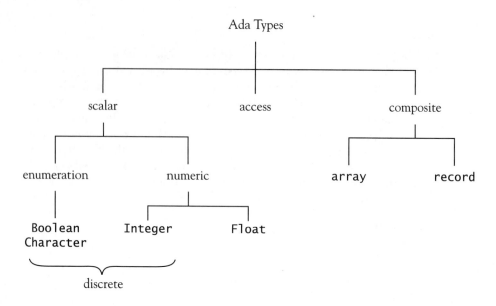

Figure 6.7 The Type Structure of Ada (somewhat simplified)

6.5 Type Equivalence

A major question involved in the application of types to type checking is that of **type equivalence**: When are two types the same? One way of trying to answer this question is to compare the sets of values simply as sets. Two sets are the same if they contain the same values: For example, any type defined as the Cartesian product $A \times B$ is the same as any other type defined in the same way. On the other hand, if we assume type B is not the same as type A, then a type defined as $A \times B$ is not the same as a type defined as $B \times A$, since $A \times B$ contains the pairs (a, b) but $B \times A$ contains the pairs (b, a). This view of type equivalence is that two data types are the same if they have the same structure: They are built in exactly the same way using the same type constructors from the same simple types. This form of type equivalence is called **structural equivalence** and is one of the principal forms of type equivalence in programming languages.

EXAMPLE

In a C-like syntax, the types struct Rec1 and struct Rec2 defined as follows are structurally equivalent, but struct Rec1 and struct Rec3 are not (the char and int fields are reversed in the definition of struct Rec3):

```
struct Rec1
{ char x;
  int y;
  char z[10];
};
```

```
struct Rec2
{ char x;
  int y;
  char z[10];
};
struct Rec3
{ int y;
  char x;
  char z[10];
};
```

∎

Structural equivalence is relatively easy to implement (except for recursive types—see below) and provides all the information needed to perform error checking and storage allocation. It is used in such languages as Algol60, Algol68, FORTRAN, COBOL, and a few modern languages such as Modula-3; it is also used selectively in such languages as C, Java and ML (we will describe how shortly). To check structural equivalence, a translator may represent types as trees and check equivalence recursively on subtrees; see Exercise 6.36. Questions still arise, however, in determining how much information is included in a type under the application of a type constructor. For example, are the two types A1 and A2 defined by

```
typedef int A1[10];
typedef int A2[20];
```

structurally equivalent? Perhaps yes, if the size of the index set is not part of an array type, otherwise no. A similar question arises with respect to member names of structures. If structures are taken to be just Cartesian products, then, for example, the two structures

```
struct RecA
{ char x;
  int y;
};
```

and

```
struct RecB
{ char a;
  int b;
};
```

should be structurally equivalent; typically, however, they are not equivalent, because variables of the different structures would have to use different names to access the member data.

A complicating factor is the use of **type names** in declarations. As noted previously, type expressions in declarations may or may not be given explicit names. For example, in C, variable declarations may be given using **anonymous types** (type constructors applied without giving them names), but names can also be given right in `structs` and `unions`, or by using a `typedef`. For example, consider the C code:

```
struct RecA
{ char x;
  int y;
} a;

typedef struct RecA RecA;

typedef struct
{ char x;
  int y;
} RecB;

RecB b;

struct
{ char x;
  int y;
} c;
```

Variable a has a data type with two names: struct RecA and RecA (as given by the typedef). Variable b's type has only the name RecB (the struct name was left blank). And variable c's type has no name at all! (Actually, c's type still has a name, but it is internal and cannot be referred to by the programmer). Of course, the types struct RecA, RecA, RecB, and c's anonymous type are all structurally equivalent.

Structural equivalence in the presence of type names remains relatively simple—simply replace each name by its associated type expression in its declaration—*except* for recursive types, where this rule would lead to an infinite loop (recall that a major reason for introducing type names is to allow for the declaration of recursive types). Consider the following example (a variation on an example used previously):

```
typedef struct CharListNode* CharList;
typedef struct CharListNode2* CharList2;

struct CharListNode
{ char data;
  CharList next;
};

struct CharListNode2
{ char data;
  CharList2 next;
};
```

Clearly CharList and CharList2 are structurally equivalent, but a type checker that simply replaces type names by definitions will get into an infinite loop trying to verify it! The secret is to *assume* that CharList and CharList2 are structurally equivalent to start with. Then it follows easily that CharListNode and CharListNode2 are structurally equivalent, and then that CharList and CharList2 are indeed themselves equivalent. Of course, this seems like a circular argument, and it must be done carefully to give correct results. The details can be found in Louden [1997].

To avoid this problem, a different, much stricter, type equivalence algorithm was developed that focuses on the type names themselves (rather than trying to eliminate the names as in structural equivalence): Two types are the same only if they have the same name. For obvious reasons, this is called **name equivalence**.

EXAMPLE

In the following C declarations,

```
struct RecA
{ char x;
  int y;
};

typedef struct RecA RecA;

struct RecA a;
RecA b;
struct RecA c;

struct
{ char x;
  int y;
} d;
```

all of the variables a, b, c, and d are structurally equivalent. However, a and c are name equivalent (and not name equivalent to b or d), while b and d are not name equivalent to any other variable. Similarly, given the declarations

```
typedef  int Ar1[10];
typedef Ar1 Ar2;
typedef int Age;
```

types Ar1 and Ar2 are structurally equivalent but not name equivalent, and Age and int are structurally equivalent but not name equivalent.

■

Name equivalence in its purest form is even easier to implement than structural equivalence, as long as we *force* every type to have an explicit name (this can actually be a good idea, since it *documents* every type with an explicit name): Two types are the same only if they are the same name, and two variables are type equivalent only if their declarations use exactly the same type name. We can also invent **aliases** for types (e.g., Age above is an alias for int), and the type checker forces the programmer to keep uses of aliases distinct (this is also a very good *design tool*).

The situation becomes slightly more complex if we allow variable or function declarations to contain new types (i.e., type constructors) rather than existing type names only. Consider, for example, the declarations

```
struct
{ char x;
  int y;
} d,e;
```

Are d and e name equivalent? Here there are no visible type names from which to form a conclusion, so a name equivalence algorithm could say either yes or no. A language might say that a combined declaration as this is equivalent to separate declarations:

```
struct
{ char x;
  int y;
} d;

struct
{ char x;
  int y;
} e;
```

in which case d and e are clearly *not* name equivalent (since new internal names are generated for each new struct). On the other hand, using a single struct in a combined declaration could be viewed as constructing only *one* internal name, in which case d and e *are* equivalent.

Ada is one of the few languages to implement a very pure form of name equivalence. The only time Ada allows type constructors to be used in variable declarations is with the array constructor:

```
a: array (1..10) of integer;
```

The following is illegal Ada:

```
a: record
      x: integer;
      y: character;
   end record;
```

Instead, we must write:

```
type IntChar is record
        x: integer;
        y: character;
     end record;
a: IntChar;
```

Thus, ambiguity is avoided in Ada by requiring type names in variable and function declarations in virtually all cases. (Ada views simultaneous array variable declarations without type names as having separate, inequivalent types.)

One small special rule is made in Ada for aliases and subtypes: Writing

```
type Age is integer;
```

is illegal, since Ada wants to know whether we want an actual new type, or just an alias that should be considered equivalent to the old type. Here we must write either

```
type Age is new integer;
        -- Age is a completely new type
```

or

```
subtype Age is integer;
        -- Age is just an alias for integer
```

(As noted previously, the subtype designation is also used to create subset types, which are also not new types, but indications for runtime value checking.)

C uses a form of type equivalence that falls between name and structural equivalence, and which can be loosely described as "name equivalence for structs and unions, structural equivalence for everything else." What is really meant here is that applying the struct or union type constructor creates a new, nonequivalent, type, while applying any other type constructor, or using a typedef, does not create a new type but one that is equivalent to every other type with the same structure (taking into account the special rule for structs and unions).

EXAMPLE

```
struct A
{ char x;
   int y;
};

struct B
{ char x;
   int y;
};

typedef struct A C;
typedef C* P;
typedef struct B * Q;
typedef struct A * R;
typedef int S[10];
typedef int T[5];
typedef int Age;
typedef int (*F)(int);
typedef Age (*G)(Age);
```
■

Types struct A and C are equivalent, but they are not equivalent to struct B; types P and R are equivalent, but not to Q; types S and T are equivalent; types int and Age are equivalent, as are function types F and G.

Pascal adopts a similar rule to C, except that almost all type constructors, including arrays, pointers, and enumerations, lead to new, inequivalent types.[12] However, new names for existing type names are, as in C's typedefs, equivalent to the original types. (Sometimes this rule is referred to as **declaration equivalence**.) Thus, in

```
type
    IntPtr = ^integer;
    Age = integer;
var
    x: IntPtr;
    y: ^integer;
    i: Age;
    a: integer;
```

x and y are not equivalent in Pascal, but i and a are.

Java has a particularly simple approach to type equivalence. First, there are no typedefs, so naming questions are minimized. Second, class and interface declarations implicitly create new type names (the same as the class/interface names), and name equivalence is used for these types. The only complication is that arrays (which cannot have type names) use structural equivalence, with special rules for establishing base type equivalence (we do not further discuss Java arrays in this text—see the Notes and References for more information).

Last, we mention the type equivalence rule used in ML. ML has *two* type declarations—datatype and type, but only the former constructs a new type, while the latter only constructs aliases of existing types (like the typedef of C). For example

```
type Age = int;
datatype NewAge = NewAge int;
```

Now Age is equivalent to int, but NewAge is a new type not equivalent to int (indeed, we reused the name NewAge to also stand for a data constructor for the NewAge type, so that (NewAge 2) is a value of type NewAge, while 2 is a value of type int (or Age).

One issue we have left out in this discussion of type equivalence is the interaction the type equivalence algorithm has with the type checking algorithm (since, as explained earlier, type equivalence comes up in type checking and can be given a somewhat independent answer). In fact, some type equivalence questions may never arise because of the type checking rules, and so we might never be able to write code in a language that would answer a particular type equivalence question. In such cases we might sensibly adopt an operational view and simply disregard the question of type equivalence for these particular cases (an example of this is discussed in Exercise 6.25).

---

[12] Subrange types in Pascal are implemented as runtime checks, not new types.

6.6 Type Checking

Type checking, as we have said at the beginning of the chapter, is the process a translator goes through to verify that all constructs in a program make sense in terms of the types of its constants, variables, procedures, and other entities. It involves the application of a type equivalence algorithm to expressions and statements, and the type checking algorithm can vary the use of the type equivalence algorithm to suit the context. (Thus, a strict type equivalence algorithm such as name equivalence could be relaxed by the type checker if the situation warrants.)

Type checking can be divided into **dynamic** and **static** checking: If type information is maintained and checked at runtime, the checking is dynamic. Interpreters by definition perform dynamic type checking. But compilers can also generate code that maintains type attributes during runtime in a table or as type tags in an environment. A LISP compiler, for example, would do this. Dynamic type checking is required when the types of objects can only be determined at runtime.

The alternative to dynamic typing is static typing: The types of expressions and objects are determined from the text of the program, and type checking is performed by the translator before execution. In a strongly typed language, all type errors must be caught before runtime, so these languages must be statically typed, and type errors are reported as compilation error messages that prevent execution. However, a language definition may leave unspecified whether dynamic or static typing is to be used.

EXAMPLE 1

C compilers apply static type checking during translation, but C is not really strongly typed since many type inconsistencies do not cause compilation errors but are automatically removed through the generation of conversion code, either with or without a warning message. Most modern compilers, however, have error level settings that do provide stronger typing if it is desired. C++ also adds stronger type checking to C, but also mainly in the form of compiler warnings rather than errors (for compatibility with C). Thus, in C++ (and to a certain extent also in C), many type errors appear only as warnings and do not prevent execution. Thus, ignoring warnings can be a "dangerous folly" (Stroustrup [1994], p. 42). ∎

EXAMPLE 2

The Scheme dialect of LISP (see Chapter 10) is a dynamically typed language, but types *are* rigorously checked, with all type errors causing program termination. There are no types in declarations, and there are no explicit type names. Variables and other symbols have no predeclared types, but take on the type of the value they possess at each moment of execution. Thus, types in Scheme must be kept as explicit attributes of values. Type checking consists of generating errors for functions requiring certain values to perform their operations. For example, `car` and `cdr` require their operands to be lists: `(car 2)` generates an error. Types can be checked explicitly by the programmer, however, using predefined test functions. Types in Scheme include lists, symbols, atoms, and numbers. Predefined test functions include `number?` and `symbol?`. (Such test functions are called **predicates** and always end in a question mark.)   ■

EXAMPLE 3

Ada is a strongly typed language, and all type errors cause compilation error messages. However, even in Ada, certain errors, like range errors in array subscripting, cannot be caught prior to execution, since the value of a subscript is not in general known until runtime. However, the Ada standard guarantees that all such errors will cause exceptions and, if these exceptions are not caught and handled by the program itself, program termination. Typically, such runtime type checking errors result in the raising of the predefined exception `Constraint_Error`.   ■

An essential part of type checking is **type inference**, where the types of expressions are inferred from the types of their subexpressions. Type checking rules (that is, when constructs are type correct) and type inference rules are often intermingled. For example, an expression $e1 + e2$ might be declared type correct if $e1$ and $e2$ have the same type, and that type has a "+" operation (type checking), and the result type of the expression is the type of $e1$ and $e2$ (type inference). This is the rule in Ada, for example. In other languages this rule may be softened to include cases where the type of one subexpression is automatically convertible to the type of the other expression—see the next section.

As another example of a type checking rule, in a function call, the types of the actual parameters or arguments must match the types of the formal parameters (type checking), and the result type of the call is the result type of the function (type inference).

Type checking and type inference rules have a close interaction with the type equivalence algorithm. For example, the C declaration

```
void p ( struct { int i; double r; } x )
{ ...
}
```

is an error under C's type equivalence algorithm, since no actual parameter can have the type of the formal parameter `x`, and so a type mismatch will be declared on every call to `p`. As a result, a C compiler will usually issue a warning here (although, strictly speaking, this is legal C).[13] Similar situations occur in Pascal and Ada.

---

[13] This has been raised to the level of an error in C++.

The process of type inference and type checking in statically typed languages is aided by explicit declarations of the types of variables, functions, and other objects. For example, if x and y are variables, the correctness and type of the expression x + y is difficult to determine prior to execution unless the types of x and y have been explicitly stated in a declaration. However, explicit type declarations are not an absolute requirement for static typing: The languages ML and Haskell perform static type checking but do not require types to be declared. Instead, types are inferred from context using an inference mechanism that is more powerful than what we have described (it will be described in Section 6.8).

Type inference and correctness rules are often one of the most complex parts of the semantics of a language. Nonorthogonalities are hard to avoid in imperative languages such as C. In the remainder of this section we will discuss major issues and problems in the rules of a type system.

6.6.1 Type Compatibility

Sometimes it is useful to relax type correctness rules so that the types of components need not be precisely the same according to the type equivalence algorithm. For example, we noted earlier that the expression $e1 + e2$ may still make sense even if the types of $e1$ and $e2$ are different. In such a situation, two different types that still may be correct when combined in certain ways are often called **compatible** types. In Ada, any two subranges of the same base type are compatible (of course, this can result in errors, as we shall see in Section 6.6.3.). In C and Java, all numeric types are compatible (and conversions are performed such that as much information as possible is retained).

A related term, **assignment compatibility**, is often used for the type correctness of the assignment $e1 = e2$ (which may be different from other compatibility rules because of the special nature of assignment). Initially, this statement may be judged type correct when x and e have the same type. But this ignores a major difference: The left-hand side must be an **l-value** or **reference**, while the right-hand side must be an **r-value**. Many languages solve this problem by requiring the left-hand side to be a variable name, whose address is taken as the l-value, and by automatically **dereferencing** variable names on the right-hand side to get their r-values. In ML this is made more explicit by saying that the assignment is type correct if the type of the left-hand side (which may be an arbitrary expression) is ref t (a reference to a value of type t), and the type of the right-hand side is t. ML also requires explicit dereferencing of variables used on the right-hand side:

```
val x = ref 2; (* type of x is ref int *)
x = !x + 1;  (* x dereferenced using ! *)
```

As with ordinary compatibility, assignment compatibility can be expanded to include cases where both sides do not have the same type. For example, in Java the assignment x = e is legal when e is a numeric type whose value can be converted to the type of x without loss of information (for example, char to int, or int to long, or long to double, etc.). On the other hand, if *e* is a floating-point type and *x* is an integral type, then this is a type error in Java (thus, assignment compatibility is different from the compatibility of other arithmetic operators). Such assignment compatibilities may or may not involve the conversion of the underlying values to a different format; see Section 6.7.

6.6.2 Implicit Types

As noted at the beginning of this chapter, types of basic entities such as constants and variables may not be given explicitly in a declaration. In this case the type must be inferred by the translator, either from context information or from standard rules. We say that such types are **implicit**, since they are not explicitly stated in a program, though the rules that specify their types must be explicit in the language definition.

As an example of such a situation in C, variables are implicitly integers if no type is given,[14] and functions implicitly return an integer value if no return type is given:

```
x; /* implicitly integer */

f(int x) /* implicitly returns an int */
{ return x + 1; }
```

As another example, in Pascal named constants are implicitly typed by the literals they represent:

```
const
      PI = 3.14156; (* implicitly real *)
      Answer = 42; (* implicitly integer *)
```

Indeed, literals are the major example of implicitly typed entities in all languages. For example, 123456789 is implicitly an int in C, unless it would overflow the space allocated for an int, in which case it is a long int (or perhaps even an unsigned long int, if necessary). On the other hand, 1234567L is a long int by virtue of the "L" suffix. Similarly, any sequence of characters surrounded by double-quotes such as "Hello" (a "C string") is implicitly a character array of whatever size is necessary to hold the characters plus the delimiting null character that ends every such literal. Thus, "Hello" is of type char[6].

When subranges are available as independent types in a language (such as Ada), new problems arise in that literals must now be viewed as potentially of several different types. For instance, if we define

```
type Digit_Type is range 0..9;
```

then the number 0 could be an integer or a Digit_Type. Usually in such cases the context of use is enough to tell a translator what type to choose (or alternatively, one can regard 0 as immediately convertible from integer to Digit_Type).

---

[14] This has been made illegal by the 1999 ISO C Standard.

6.6.3 Overlapping Types and Multiply-typed Values

As just noted, types may overlap in that two types may contain values in common. The above `Digit_Type` example shows how subtyping and sub-ranges can create types whose sets of values overlap. Normally, it is prefer-able for types to be disjoint as sets, so that every expressible value belongs to a unique type, and no ambiguities or context-sensitivities arise in determining the type of a value. However, enforcing this restric-tion absolutely would be far too restrictive, and would in fact eliminate one of the major features of object-oriented programming—the ability to create subtypes through inheritance that refine existing types yet retain their membership in the more general type (this will be discussed in Chapter 10). But even at the most basic level of predefined numeric types, overlapping values are difficult to avoid. For instance, in C the two types `unsigned int` and `int` have substantial overlap, and in Java, a small integer could be a `short`, an `int`, or a `long`. Thus, rules such as the following are necessary (Arnold, Gosling, and Holmes [2000], p. 143):

> Integer constants are long if they end in L or l, such as 29L; L is pre-ferred over l because l (lowercase L) can easily be confused with 1 (the digit one). Otherwise, integer constants are assumed to be of type `int`. If an `int` literal is directly assigned to a `short`, and its value is within the valid range for a `short`, the integer literal is treated as if it were a `short` literal. A similar allowance is made for integer liter-als assigned to `byte` variables.

Also, as already noted, subranges and subtypes are the source of range errors during execution that cannot be predicted at translation time, and thus a source of program failure that type systems were in part designed to prevent. For example, the Ada declarations

```
subtype SubDigit is integer range 0..9;
subtype NegDigit is integer range -9..-1;
```

create two subranges of integers that are in fact disjoint, but the language rules allow code such as

```
x: SubDigit;
y: NegDigit;
...
x := y;
```

without a compile-time error. Of course, this code cannot execute with-out generating a `CONSTRAINT_ERROR` and halting the program. Similar results hold for other languages that allow subranges, like Pascal and Modula-2.

Sometimes, however, overlapping types and multiply-typed values can be of very direct benefit in simplifying code. For example, in C the lit-eral 0 is not only a value of every integral type, but is also a value of every pointer type, and represents the null pointer that points to no object. In

Java too there is a single literal value `null` that is, in essence, a value of every reference type.[15]

6.6.4 Shared Operations

Types have a set of operations associated with them, usually implicitly. Often these operations are shared among several types or have the same name as other operations that may be different. For example, the operator + can be real or integer addition or set union. Such operators are said to be **overloaded**, since the same name is used for essentially different operations. In the case of an overloaded operator, a translator must decide which operation is meant from the types of its operands. In Chapter 5 we studied in some detail how this can be done using the symbol table. In that discussion we assumed the argument types of an overloaded operator are disjoint as sets, but problems can arise if they are not, or if subtypes are present with different meanings for these operations. Of course there should be no ambiguity for built-in operations, since the language rules should make clear which operation is applied. For example, in Java, if two operands are of integral type, then integer addition is *always* applied (and the result is an `int`) regardless of the type of the operands, *except* when one of the operands has type `long`, in which case `long` addition is performed (and the result is of type `long`). Thus, in the following Java code, 40000 is printed (since the result is an `int`, not a `short`):

```
short x = 20000;
System.out.println(x+x);
```

On the other hand,

```
x = x + x;
```

is now illegal in Java—it requires a cast (see next section):

```
x = (short) (x + x);
```

Thus, there is no such thing as `short` addition in Java (or other kinds of arithmetic on any integral types other than `int` and `long`).

Ada, as usual, allows a much finer control over what operations are applied to data types—as long as these are indeed new types and not simply subranges (subranges simply inherit the operations of their base types). Consider, for example, the following Ada code:

---

[15] This is not quite accurate, according to the Java Language specification (Gosling et al. [2000], p. 32): "There is also a special null type, the type of the expression `null`, which has no name. Because the null type has no name, it is impossible to declare a variable of the null type or to cast to the null type. The null reference is the only possible value of an expression of null type. The null reference can always be cast to any reference type. In practice, the programmer can ignore the null type and just pretend that `null` is merely a special literal that can be of any reference type."

```
type Digit_Type is range 0..9;

function "+"(x,y: Digit_Type) return Digit_Type is
   a: integer := integer(x);
   b: integer := integer(y);
begin
   return Digit_Type((a+b) mod 10);
end "+";
```

This defines a new addition operation on Digit_Type that wraps its result so that it is always a digit. Now, given the code

```
a: Digit_Type := 5+7;
```

it may seem surprising, but Ada knows enough here to call the new "+" function for Digit_Type, rather than use standard integer addition, and a gets the value 2 (otherwise a Constraint_Error would occur here). The reason is (as noted in Chapter 5) since there are no implicit conversions in Ada, Ada can use the result type of a function call, as well as the parameter argument types, to resolve overloading, and since the result type is Digit_Type, the user-defined "+" must be the function indicated.

C++ does not allow this kind of overloading: Operator overloading must involve new, user-defined types. For example, the following definition:

```
int * operator+(int* a, int* b) // illegal in C++
{ int * x = new int;
  *x = *a+*b;
  return x;
}
```

is illegal in C++, as would be any attempt to redefine the arithmetic operators on any built-in type.

6.7 Type Conversion

In every programming language there is a need to convert one type to another under certain circumstances. Such **type conversion** can be built into the type system so that conversions are performed automatically, as in a number of examples discussed previously. For example, in the following C code:

```
int x = 3;
...
x = 2.3 + x / 2;
```

at the end of this code x still has the value 3: x / 2 is integer division, with result 1, then 1 is converted to the double value 1.0 and added to 2.3 to obtain 3.3, and then 3.3 is truncated to 3 when it is assigned to x.

In this example, two automatic, or **implicit conversions** were inserted by the translator: The conversion of the int result of the division to `double` ($1 \rightarrow 1.0$) before the addition and the conversion of the `double` result of the addition to an `int` ($3.3 \rightarrow 3$) before the assignment to x. Such implicit conversions are sometimes also called **coercions**. The conversion from `int` to `double` is an example of a **widening** conversion, where the target data type can hold all of the information being converted without loss of data, while the conversion from `double` to `int` is a **narrowing** conversion that may involve a loss of data.

Implicit conversion has the benefit that the programmer does not have to write extra code to perform an obvious conversion. However, implicit conversion can have unpleasant effects as well: It can weaken type checking so that errors may not be caught. This compromises the strong typing and the reliability of the programming language. Implicit conversions can also cause unexpected behavior in that the programmer may expect a conversion to be done one way, while the translator actually performs a different conversion. A famous example in (early) PL/I is the expression

```
1/3 + 15
```

which was converted to the value 5.33333333333333 (on a machine with 15-digit precision): The leading 1 was lost by overflow because the language rules state that the precision of the fractional value must be maintained.

An alternative to implicit conversion is **explicit conversion**: the writing of conversion directives right into the code. Such conversion code is typically called a **cast**, and is commonly written in one of two varieties of syntax. The first variety is used in C and Java and consists of writing the desired result type inside parentheses before the expression to be converted. Thus, in C we can write the previous implicit conversion example as explicit casts in the following form:

```
x = (int) (2.3 + (double) (x / 2));
```

The other variety of cast syntax is to use function call syntax, with the result type used as the function name and the value to be converted as the parameter argument. C++ and Ada use this form, and the above conversions would be written in C++ as:

```
x = int( 2.3 + double( x / 2 ) );
```

(C++ also uses a newer form for casts, which will be discussed shortly.)

The advantange to using casts is that the conversions being performed are documented precisely in the code, and there is less likelihood of unexpected behavior, or of readers misunderstanding the code. For this reason, a few languages prohibit implicit conversions altogether, forcing programmers to write out casts in all cases. Ada is such a language. Additionally, eliminating implicit conversions makes it easier for the translator (and the reader) to resolve overloading. For example, in C++ if we have two function declarations

```
double max (int, double);
double max (double,int);
```

then the call max(2,3) is ambiguous because of the possible implicit conversions from int to double (which could be done either on the first or second parameter). If implicit conversions were not allowed, then the programmer is forced to specify which conversion is meant. (A second example of this phenomenon was just seen in Ada in the previous section.)

A middle ground between the two extremes of eliminating all implicit conversions and allowing conversions that could potentially be errors, is to allow only those implicit conversions that are guaranteed not to corrupt data. For example, Java follows this principle and only permits widening implicit conversions for arithmetic types. C++, too, adopts a more cautious approach than C toward narrowing conversions, generating warning messages in all cases except the int to char narrowing implicit conversion.[16]

Even explicit casts need to be restricted in various ways by languages. Often, casts are restricted to simple types, or even just the arithmetic types. If casts are permitted for structured types, then clearly a restriction must be that the types have identical sizes in memory, and then the translation merely **reinterprets** the memory as a different type, without changing the bit representation of the data. This is particularly true for pointers, which are generally simply reinterpreted as pointing to a value of a different type. This kind of explicit conversion also allows for certain functions such as memory allocators and deallocators to be defined using a "generic pointer." For example, in C the malloc and free functions are declared using the generic or **anonymous pointer type** void*:

```
void* malloc (size_t );
void free( void*);
```

and casts may be used to convert from any pointer type[17] to void* and back again:

```
int* x = (int*) malloc(sizeof(int));
...
free( (void*)x );
```

(Actually, C allows both of these conversions to be implicit, while C++ allows implicit conversions from pointers to void*, but not vice versa.)

Object-oriented languages also have certain special conversion requirements, since inheritance can be interpreted as a subtyping mechanism, and conversions from subtypes to supertypes and back are necessary in some cases. This kind of conversion will be discussed in more detail in Chapter 10. However, we mention here that C++, because of its mixture of object-oriented and nonobject-oriented features, as well as its compatibility with C, identifies four different kinds of casts, and has invented new

---

[16] Stroustrup [1994], pp. 41–43, discusses why warnings are not generated in this case.

[17] Not "pointers to functions," however.

syntax for each of these casts: `static_cast`, `dynamic_cast`, `reinterpret_cast`, and `const_cast`. The first, `static_cast`, corresponds to the casts we have been describing here[18] (static, since the compiler interprets the cast, generates code if necessary, and the runtime system is not involved). Thus, the previous explicit cast example would be written using the C++ standard as follows:

```
x = static_cast<int>(2.3 + static_cast<double>(x / 2));
```

An alternative to casts is to have predefined or library functions that perform conversions. For example, in Ada casts between integers and characters are not permitted. Instead, two predefined functions (called **attribute functions** of the `character` data type) allow conversions between characters and their associated ASCII values:

```
character'pos('a') -- returns 97, the ASCII value of 'a'
character'val(97) -- returns the character 'a'
```

Conversions between strings and numbers are also often handled by special conversion functions. For example, in Java the `Integer` class in the `java.lang` library contains the conversion functions `toString`, which converts an `int` to a `String`, and `parseInt`, which converts a `String` to an `int`:

```
String s = Integer.toString(12345); // s becomes "12345"
int i = Integer.parseInt("54321"); // i becomes 54321
```

A final mechanism for converting values from one type to another is provided by a loophole in the strong typing of some languages: Undiscriminated unions can hold values of different types, and without a discriminant or tag (or without runtime checking of such tags) a translator cannot distinguish values of one type from another, thus permitting indiscriminate reinterpretation of values. For example, the C++ declaration

```
union
{ char c;
  bool b;
} x;
```

and the statements

```
x.b = true;
cout << static_cast<int>(x.c) << endl;
```

would allow us to see the internal value used to represent the Boolean value `true` (in fact, the C++ standard says this should always be 1).

---

[18] The `reinterpret_cast` is not used for `void*` conversions, but for more dangerous conversions such as `char*` to `int*` or `int` to `char*`.

6.8 Polymorphic Type Checking

Most statically typed languages require that explicit type information be given for all names in each declaration (with certain exceptions about implicitly typed literals, constants, and variables noted previously). However, it is also possible to use an extension of type inference to determine the types of names in a declaration *without explicitly giving those types.* Indeed, a translator can collect information on *uses* of a name, and infer from the set of all uses a probable type that is the *most general type* for which all uses are correct (or declare a type error because some of the uses are incompatible with others). In this section we will give an overview of this kind of type inference and type checking, called **Hindley-Milner type checking** for its coinventors (Hindley [1969], Milner [1978]). It is a major feature of the strongly typed functional languages ML and Haskell.

First, consider how a conventional type checker works; for purposes of discussion, consider the expression (in C syntax) a[i] + i. For a normal type checker to work, both a and i must be declared, a as an array of integers, and i as an integer, and then the result of the expression is an integer.

Using syntax trees shows us this in more detail. The type checker starts out with a tree such as the following:

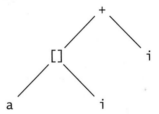

First, the types of the names (the leaf nodes) are filled in from the declarations:

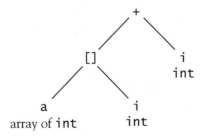

Then the type checker checks the subscript node (labeled []): The left operand must be an array, and the right operand must be an int; indeed they are, so the operation type checks correctly. Then the inferred type of the subscript node is the component type of the array, which is int, and so this type is added to the tree:

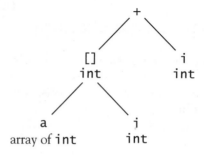

Finally, the + node is type checked: The two operands must have the same type (we assume no implicit conversions here) and this type must have a + operation; indeed they are both int, so the + operation is type correct, and the result is the type of the operands, which is int:

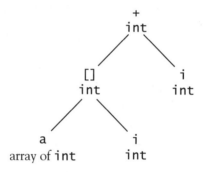

Could the type checker have come to any other conclusion about the types of the five nodes in this tree? No, not even if the declarations of a and i were missing. Here's how it would do it.

First, the type checker would assign **type variables** to all the names for which it did not already have types. Thus, if a and i do not yet have types, we need to assign some type variable names to them. Since these are internal names that should not be confused with program identifiers, let us use a typical convention and assign the Greek letters α and β as the type variables for a and i:

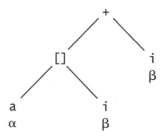

(Note in particular that both occurences of i have *the same type variable* β).

Now the type checker visits the subscript node, and infers that, for this to be correct, the type of a must actually be an array (in fact, array of γ, where γ[19] is another type variable, since we don't yet have any information about the component type of a). Also, the type checker infers that the type of i must be int (we assume that the language only allows int subscripts in this example). Thus β is replaced by int in the entire tree, and the situation becomes:

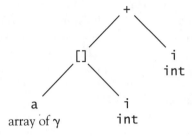

Finally, the type checker concludes that, with these assignments to the type variables, the subscript node is type correct and has the type γ (the component type of a):

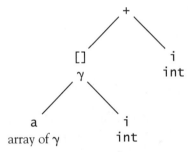

Now the type checker visits the + node, and concludes that, for it to be type correct, γ must be int (the two operands of + must have the same type), and so γ is replaced by int *everywhere* it appears, and the result of the + operation is also int, and we have arrived at the same typing of this expression as before, without using any prior knowledge about the types of a and i:

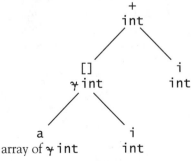

---

[19] Greek letter gamma.

This is the basic form of operation of Hindley-Milner type checking.

We note two things about this form of type checking. First, as we have indicated, once a type variable is replaced by an actual type (or a more specialized form of a type), then *all* instances of that variable must be updated to that same new value for the type variable. This process is called **instantiation** of type variables, and it can be achieved using various forms of indirection into a table of type expressions that is very similar to a symbol table. The second thing to note is that when new type information becomes available, the type expressions for variables can change form in various ways. For example, in the previous example α became "array of γ," β became int, and then γ became int as well. This process can become even more complex. For example, we might have two type expressions "array of α" and "array of β" that need to be the same for type checking to succeed. In that case, we must have α == β, and so β must be changed to α everywhere it occurs (or vice versa). This process is called **unification**; it is a kind of pattern matching that appears frequently in programming languages: Versions of it exist in several contexts in functional languages like ML and Haskell (to handle type checking and pattern matching code), logic languages like Prolog (to handle variables and to direct execution), and even C++ compilers (to handle template instantiation). These other uses will be discussed elsewhere in this book. Unification involves essentially three cases (here described in terms of types):

1. Any type variable unifies with any type expression (and is instantiated to that expression).

2. Any two type constants (that is, specific types like int or double) unify only if they are the same type.

3. Any two type constructions (that is, applications of type constructors like "array" or struct) unify only if they are applications of the same type constructor and all of their component types also (recursively) unify.

For example, unifying type variable β with type expression "array of α" is case 1 above, and β is instantiated to "array of α." Unifying int to int is an example of case 2. Unifying "array of α" with "array of β" is case 3, and we must recurse on the component types of each expressions (which are α and β, and thus unify by case 1). On the other hand, by case 2, int cannot unify with "array of α," and by case 3 "array of int" cannot unify with "array of char."

Hindley-Milner type checking can be extremely useful in that it simplifies tremendously the amount of type information that the programmer must write down in code[20]. But if this were the only advantage it would

---

[20] Of course, this must be balanced with the advantage of documenting the desired types directly in the code: It is often useful to write explicit type information even when unnecessary in a language like ML, for documentation purposes.

not be an overwhelming one (see previous footnote). In fact, Hindley-Milner type checking gives an enormous advantage over simple type checking in that *types can remain as general as possible*, while still being strongly checked for consistency.

Consider, for example, the following expression (again in C syntax):

    a[i] = b[i]

This assigns the value of b[i] to a[i] (and returns that value). Suppose again that we know nothing in advance about the types of a, b, and i. Hindley-Milner type checking will then establish that i must be an int, a must be an "array of α" and b must be an "array of β," and then (because of the assignment, and assuming no implicit conversions), $\alpha == \beta$. Thus, type checking concludes with the types of a and b narrowed to "array of α," but α is still a completely unconstrained type variable that could be *any* type. This expression is said to be **polymorphic**, and Hindley-Milner type checking implicitly implements **polymorphic type checking**—that is, we get such polymorphic type checking "for free" as an automatic consequence of the implicit type variables introduced by the algorithm.

In fact, there are several different interpretations for the word "polymorphic" that we need to separate here. Polymorphic is a Greek word meaning "of many forms." In programming languages it applies to names that (simultaneously) can have more than one type. We have already seen situations in which names can have several different types simultaneously—namely, the **overloaded functions**. So overloading is one kind of polymorphism. However, overloaded functions have only a finite (usually small) set of types, each one given by a different declaration. The kind of polymorphism we are seeing here is different: The type "array of α" is actually a set of *infinitely many* types, depending on the (infinitely many) possible instantiations of the type variable α. This type of polymorphism is called **parametric polymophism** because α is essentially a *type parameter* that can be replaced by any type expression. In fact, so far in this section we have seen only **implicit parametric polymorphism**, since the type parameters (represented by Hindley-Milner type variables) are *implicitly introduced* by the type checker, rather than being explicitly written by the programmer. (In the next section we will discuss **explicit parametric polymorphism**.) To distinguish overloading more clearly from parametric polymorphism, it is sometimes called **ad hoc polymorphism**: "ad hoc" means "to this" in Latin, and refers to anything that is done with a specialized goal or purpose in mind. Indeed, overloading is always represented by a set of distinct declarations, each with a special purpose. Finally, there is a third form of polymorphism that occurs in object-oriented languages: Objects that share a common ancestor can also either share or redefine the operations that exist for that ancestor. Some authors refer to this as **pure polymorphism**; in keeping with modern terminology we shall call it **subtype polymorphism**, since it is closely related to the view of subtypes as sharing operations (see Section 6.3.3). Subtype polymorphism will be discussed in Chapter 10.

Finally, a language that exhibits no polymorphism, or an expression or function that has a unique, fixed type, is said to be **monomorphic** (Greek for "having one form").

The previous example of a polymorphic expression was somewhat too simple to show the true power of parametric polymorphism and Hindley-Milner type checking. Polymorphic functions are the real goal of this kind of polymorphism, so consider an example that appeared in the discussion of overloading in Chapter 5—namely, that of a max function such as:

```
int max (int x, int y)
{ return x > y ? x : y; }
```

We note two things about this function. First, the body for this function is the same, regardless of the type (double or any other arithmetic type could be substituted for int without changing the body). Second, the body *does* depend on the existence of a greater-than operator > for each type used in overloading this function, and the > function itself is over-loaded for a number of types. Thus, to *really* remove the dependency of this function on the type of its parameters, we should add a new parame-ter representing the greater-than function:[21]

```
int max (int x, int y, int (*gt)(int a,int b) )
{ return gt(x,y) ? x : y; }
```

Now let us consider a version of this function that does not specify the type of x, y, or gt. We could write this in C-like syntax as

```
max (x, y, gt)
{ return gt(x,y) ? x : y; }
```

or, to use the syntax of ML (where this is legal code):

```
fun max (x, y, gt) = if gt(x,y) then x else y;
```

Let us invent a syntax tree for this definition and assign type variables to the identifiers:

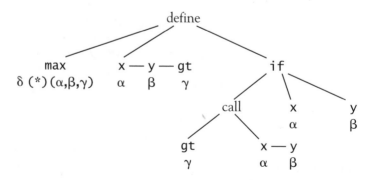

---

[21] Actually, leaving the dependency on the > function is also possible; it is called **constrained parametric polymorphism** and will be briefly discussed in the next section and in Chapter 9.

Note that we are using C notation for the type of the function max, which is a function of three parameters with types α, β, γ, and returns a value of type δ.

We now begin type checking, and visit the call node. This tells us that gt is actually a function of two parameters of types α and β, and returns a type ε (which is as yet unknown). Thus, $\gamma = \varepsilon$ (*)(α, β) and we get the tree

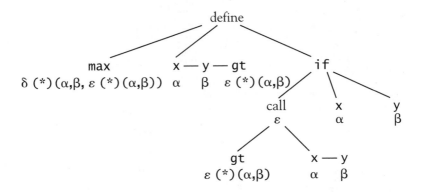

Note that the result of the call has type ε, the return type of the gt function.

Now type checking continues with the if node. Typically, such a node requires that the test expression return a Boolean value (which doesn't exist in C), and that the types of the "then" part and the "else" part must be the same (C will actually perform implicit conversions in a ?: expression, if necessary). We will assume the stronger requirements (and the existence of a bool type), and we get that $\alpha = \beta = \delta$ and $\varepsilon = $ bool, with the following tree:

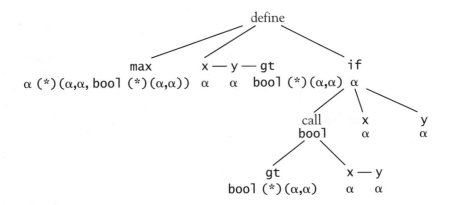

($\delta = \alpha$ because the result type of the if expression is now α, and this is the type of the body of the function; hence the return type of the body.) Thus, max has been determined to have type α (*)(α, α, bool (*)(α, α)), where α is *any* type—in other words, a type parameter that can have any actual type substituted for it. In ML this type is printed as

```
'a * 'a * ('a * 'a -> bool) -> 'a
```

where 'a is used instead of the type variable α, a function type is indicated by the arrow ->, and the multiple parameters are represented by a tuple (or Cartesian product) type[22] (the Cartesian product A $\times$ B in ML is printed as A*B and values of this type are written as tuples (a, b) with $\alpha \in$ A and b $\in$ B).

With this typing for the function max, we can use max in any situation where the actual types unify with the polymorphic type. For example, if we provide the following definitions in ML:

```
fun gti (x:int,y) = x > y;
fun gtr (x:real,y) = x > y;
fun gtp ((x,y),(z,w)) = gti (x,z);
```

we can call the max function as follows:

```
max(3,2,gti); (* returns 3 *)
max(2.1,3.2,gtr); (* returns 3.2 *)
max((2,"hello"),(1,"hi"),gtp); (* returns (2,"hello") *)
```

Note that α (*)(α, α, bool (*)(α, α)) really is the most general type possible for the max function with the given implementation (called its **principal type**), and that each call to max **specializes** this principle type to a monomorphic type, which may also implicitly specialize the types of the parameters. For example, the type of the gtp function is bool (*) ((int, α),(int,β)) (or (int * 'a) * (int * 'b) -> bool in ML syntax), with two type variables for the types of y and w, since these two variables are not used in the body of gtp, and so each can be of any type. Now, in the call to max above, we still could not use two different types for y and w, since the max function insists on the same type for the first two parameters:

```
max((2,"hello"),(1,2),gtp); (* illegal! *)
```

so in any call to max the gtp function is specialized to the type bool(*) ((int,α),(int,α)).

An extension of this principle is that any polymorphically typed object that is passed into a function as a parameter must have a fixed specialization for the duration of the function. Thus, if gtp were called again within the max function, it would still have to retain the above specialization. The same is not true for nonlocal references to polymorphic functions. For example, the following code is legal ML:

```
fun ident x = x;
fun makepair (x,y) = (ident x,ident y);
makepair(2,3.2);
  (* ok -- ident has two different types, one for each
  call *)
```

---

[22] In fact, we have written the parameters (x, y, gt) in tuple notation in the definition. It is possible to write them differently, resulting in what is called a **Curried function**. This is discussed in Chapter 11.

but making ident into a parameter results in a type error:

```
fun makepair2 (x,y,f) = (f x, f y);
makepair2(2,3.2,ident);
        (* type error -- ident cannot have general type *)
```

This restriction on polymorphic types in Hindley-Milner type systems is called (for technical reasons) **let-bound polymorphism**.

Let-bound polymorphism complicates Hindley-Milner type checking because it requires that type variables be divided into two separate categories. The first category is the one in use during type checking, whose value is everywhere the same and is universally changed with each instantiation/specialization. The second is part of a polymorphic type in a non-local reference, which can be instantiated differently at each use. Sometimes these latter type variables are called **generic** type variables. Citations for futher detail on this issue can be found in the Notes and References.

An additional problem with Hindley-Milner type checking arises when an attempt is made to unify a type variable with a type expression that contains the variable itself. Consider the following function definition (this time in ML syntax):

```
fun f (g) = g (f);
```

Now consider what will happen to this definition during type checking. First, g will be assigned the type variable α, and f will be assigned the type $\alpha \rightarrow \beta$ (a function of one parameter of type α returning a value of type β, using ML-like syntax for function types). Then the body of f will be examined, and it indicates that g is a function of one parameter whose type must be the type of f, and whose return type is also the return type of f. Thus, α (the type of g) should be set equal to $(\alpha \rightarrow \beta) \rightarrow \beta$. But trying to establish the equation $\alpha = (\alpha \rightarrow \beta) \rightarrow \beta$ will cause an infinite recursion, because α will contain itself as a component. Thus, before any unification of a type variable with a type expression is attempted, the type checker must make sure that the type variable is not itself a part of the type expression it is to become equal to. This is called the **occur-check**, and must be a part of the unification algorithm for type checking to operate correctly (and declare such a situation a type error). Unfortunately, this is a difficult check to perform in an efficient way, and so in some language contexts where unification is used (such as in versions of Prolog) the occur-check is omitted. However, for Hindley-Milner type checking to work properly, the occur-check is essential.

Finally, we want to mention the issue of translating code with polymorphic types. Consider the previous example of a polymorphic max function. Clearly the values x and y of arbitrary type will need to be copied from location to location by the code, since gt is to be called with arguments x and y, and then either x or y is to be returned as the result. But without knowing the type of x (and y), a translator cannot determine the size of these values, which must be known in order to make copies. How can a translator effectively deal with the problem?

There are several solutions. Two standard ones are as follows:

1. *Expansion*: Examine all the calls of the max function, and generate a copy of the code for each different type used in these calls, using the appropriate size for each type.

2. *Boxing and tagging*: Fix a size for all data that can contain any scalar value such as integers, floating-point numbers, and pointers; add a bit field that tags a type as either scalar or not, with a size field if not. All structured types then are represented by a pointer and a size, and copied indirectly, while all scalar types are copied directly.

In essence, solution 1 makes the code look as if separate, overloaded functions had been defined by the programmer for each type (but with the advantage that the compiler generates the different versions, not the programmer). This is efficient but can cause the size of the target code to grow very large (sometimes called **code bloat**), unless the translator can use target machine properties to combine the code for different types. Solution 2 avoids code bloat, but at the cost of many indirections, which can substantially affect performance. Of course, this indirection may be necessary anyway for purposes of memory management, but there is also the increase in data size required by the tag and size fields, even for simple data.

6.9 Explicit Polymorphism

Implicit parametric polymorphism is fine for defining polymorphic functions, but it doesn't help us if we want to define polymorphic data structures. Suppose, for example, that we want to define a stack that can contain any kind of data (here implemented as a linked list):

```
typedef struct StackNode
{  ?? data;
    struct StackNode * next;
} * Stack;
```

Here the double question mark stands for the type of the data, which must be written in for this to be a legal declaration. Thus, to define such a data type, it is impossible to make the polymorphic type *implicit*; instead, we must write the type variable *explicitly* using appropriate syntax. This is called **explicit parametric polymorphism**.

Explicit parametric polymorphism is allowed in ML, of course (it would be foolish to have implicit parametric polymorphism for functions without explicit parametric polymorphism for data structures), and the same notation is used for type parameters as in the types for implicitly polymorphic functions: 'a, 'b, 'c can be used in data structure declarations to indicate arbitrary types. Here is a Stack declaration in ML that imitates the above C declaration, but with an explicit type parameter:

```
datatype 'a Stack = EmptyStack
                  | Stack of 'a * ('a Stack);
```

First, note that this is unusual syntax, in that the type parameter 'a is written *before* the type name (Stack) rather than after it (presumably in imitation of what one does without the parameter, which is to define various stacks such as IntStack, CharStack, StringStack, etc.). Second, this declaration incorporates the effect of the pointer in C by expressing a stack as a union of the empty stack with a stack containing a pair of components—the first the data (of type 'a), and the second another stack (the tail or rest of the original stack). We can now write values of type Stack as follows:

```
val empty = EmptyStack; (* empty has type 'a Stack *)
val x = Stack(3, EmptyStack); (*x has type int Stack *)
```

Note that EmptyStack has no values, so is still of polymorphic type, while x, which contains the single value 3, is specialized by this value to int Stack.

Explicit parametric polymorphism creates no special new problems for Hindley-Milner type checking, which can operate in the same way on explicitly parameterized data as it did on implicitly parameterized functions. Indeed, polymorphic functions can be declared using an explicitly parameterized type, as for instance:

```
fun top (Stack p) = #1(p);
```

which (partially) defines top as a function 'a Stack -> 'a by using the projection function #1 on the pair p to extract its first component, which is the data. Thus, for the x previously defined, top x = 3.

Explicitly parameterized polymorphic data types fit nicely into languages with Hindley-Milner polymorphic type checking, but in fact they are nothing more than a mechanism for creating **user-defined type constructors**.

Recall that a type constructor, like array or struct, is a *function* from types to types, in that types are supplied as parameter values (these are the component types), and a new type is returned. For example, the array constructor in C, denoted by the brackets [ ], takes a component type (int, say) as a parameter and constructs a new type (array of int). This construction can be expressed directly in C as a typedef, where the syntactic ordering of the type parameter and return type is different from that of a function but entirely analogous:

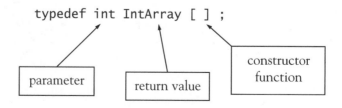

A type declaration in ML using the type constructor Stack is essentially the same kind of construction:

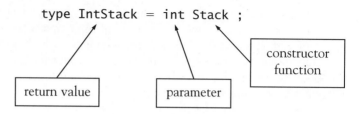

When comparing an explicitly parameterized polymorphic type construction such as Stack in ML to equivalent constructs in C or other languages, we do need to remain aware of the difference between the uses of the name Stack in a declaration like

```
datatype 'a Stack = EmptyStack
                  | Stack of 'a * ('a Stack);
```

The first occurrence of Stack (to the left of the = sign) defines the Stack type constructor, while the second occurrence of Stack (after the |) defines the *data* or *value constructor* Stack (the third occurrence of Stack is a recursive *use* of the type constructor meaning of Stack). Value constructors correspond precisely to the constructors of an object-oriented language; reusing the same name for the value and type constructor is standard practice in a number of languages. In C++ and Java, for example, constructors always have the same name as their associated class (and type); see Chapter 10 for more detail.

C++ is, in fact, an example of a language with explicit parametric polymorphism, but without the associated implicit Hindley-Milner type checking. The mechanism for explicit polymorphism is the **template**, which can be used either with functions or the class or struct type constructor (thus, unlike ML,[23] both functions and data structures have explicit type parameters).

Here, for example, is the Stack data structure in C++ using an explicit type parameter T:[24]

```
template <typename T>
struct StackNode
{ T data;
  StackNode<T> * next;
};
template <typename T>
struct Stack
{ StackNode<T> * theStack;
};
```

[23] Actually, ML functions *can* be written with explicit type parameters (e.g., ident (x: 'a) = x), but it is unusual to do so, since Hindley-Milner type checking introduces them automatically.

[24] The keyword class was used instead of typename in older versions of C++; the new keyword much more clearly denotes the actual meaning of T as a type parameter.

(Notice how we must also use a `struct` definition in C++ to get a `Stack` type as essentially a pointer to `StackNode`—there are no template `type-defs` in C++.)

Now we can define an explicitly parameterized `top` function equivalent to the previous ML definition as follows:

```
template <typename T>
T top (Stack<T> s)
{ return s.theStack->data;
}
```

We can use these definitions in some sample code as follows:

```
Stack<int> s;
s.theStack = new StackNode<int>;
s.theStack->data = 3;
s.theStack->next = 0;
int t = top(s); //  t is now 3
```

Note that the call to `top(s)` does not require that the type parameter of `top` be explicitly given—the type parameter is inferred to be `int` by the compiler from the type of `s`. On the other hand, whenever a `Stack` variable is defined, an actual (nonparameterized) type must be written as the type parameter—writing a definition such as

```
Stack s; // illegal C++
```

in C++ is not allowed.

An explicitly parameterized `max` function can also be written in C++ that is equivalent to the implicitly parameterized ML version:

```
template <typename T>
T max (T x, T y, bool (*gt)(T,T))
{ return gt(x,y) ? x : y ;
}
```

To use this function, we can define a function such as

```
int gti (int x, int y)
{ return x > y; }
```

and then we can call the `max` function as follows:

```
int larger = max(2,3,gti); // larger is now 3
```

In fact, we can also define a `max` function that depends implicitly on the existence of a `>` operator for its type parameter T:

```
template <typename T>
T max (T x, T y)
{ return x > y ? x : y ; }
```

We can call this function using values of any type for which the `>` operator exists:

```
int larger_i = max(2,3); // larger_i is now 3
int larger_d = max(3.1,2.9); // larger_d is now 3.1
Stack<int> s,t,u;
u = max(s,t);
        // Error! operator > not defined for Stack types
```

This form of parametric polymorphism is called **(implicitly) constrained parametric polymorphism**, because it implicitly applies a constraint to the type parameter T—namely, that only a type with the > operator defined for its values can be substituted for the type parameter T. (This is a form of parametric polymorphism that ML does not have).[25]

Ada also allows explicitly parameterized functions and, somewhat indirectly, also explicitly parameterized types. The essential difference between Ada and C++ or ML is that Ada allows parameterization only for program **units**, which are separately compiled program segments that can either be a subprogram (i.e., a function or a procedure) or an Ada **package**. An Ada package is essentially a **module**, and in Chapter 9 we discuss modules and their relation to data types. Here we will only briefly sketch how parametric polymorphism can be achieved using Ada units; see Chapter 9 for more detail on Ada units.

An Ada unit that includes parameters is called a **generic unit**. Type parameters must be specified as `private`, indicating that no specific information is available about which types will be used with the unit. Here is a **package specification** in Ada that implements the same `Stack` structure example as before, parameterized by a type T:

```
generic
   type T is private;
package Stacks is
   type StackNode;
   type Stack is access StackNode;
   type StackNode is
   record
     data: T;
     next: Stack;
   end record;
   function top( s: Stack ) return T ;
end Stacks;
```

Note that the `Stack` data type and the package name are not the same, and that the `top` function is also declared (but not implemented) here, since it is parameterized on the same type T. This package specification needs an associated **package body** that provides the actual implementation of the `top` function:

---

[25] A functional language that *does* have implicitly constrained parametric polymorphism is Haskell (see Chapter 11).

```
package body Stacks is
   function top( s: Stack ) return T is
   begin
      return s.data;
   end top;
end Stacks;
```

Now this Stacks package can be used by a program as follows:

```
with Stacks; -- import the Stacks package
...
package IntStacks is new Stacks(integer);
      -- instantiate the parameterized package
      -- with type integer

use IntStacks;
      -- without this, we must write use the package name
      -- before all of its components, e.g.
      -- IntStacks.Stack,
      -- IntStacks.StackNode, IntStacks.pop, etc.

s: Stack := new StackNode;
t: integer;
...
s.data := 3;
s.next := null;
t := top(s); -- t is now 3
```

Explicitly parameterized polymorphic functions can also be defined in Ada using generic units, but since functions are themselves compilation units, a package is not required (unless we wanted to define more than one function at a time in the same place). For example, here is the specification of the max function of previous examples in Ada:

```
generic
   type T is private;
   with function gt(x,y:T) return boolean;
function max (x,y:T) return T;
```

Notice that, rather than making the gt function a parameter to the max function itself, we have included it as a "generic" parameter to the unit; this is **explicitly constrained parametric polymorphism**, which, unlike the implicitly contrained polymorphism of C++, makes explicit that the max function depends on the gt function, even though it is not in the list of parameters to the function call itself.

The max function unit requires also a body, where the actual code for the max function is written:

```
-- body of max unit
function max (x,y:T) return T is
begin
```

(continues)

(continued)

```
        if gt(x,y) then return x;
        else return y;
        end if;
    end max;
```

Now the max function can be used by an Ada program as follows:

```
    with max; -- import the max unit
    ...
    function maxint is new max(integer,">");
    -- instantiate the max function for integers,
    -- using the ">" function as the gt function.

    integer i;
    ...
    i := maxint(1,2); -- i is now 2
```

As is generally true with Ada, everything must be done explicitly in the code: Polymorphism must always be explicit, parameterization must make all dependencies explicit, and instantiation must be made explicit (even to the extent of requiring a new name—e.g., maxint above).

Exercises

6.1 Compare the flexibility of the dynamic typing of LISP with the reliability of the static typing of Ada, ML, C++, or Java. Think of as many arguments as you can both for and against static typing as an aid to program design.

6.2 Look up the implementation details on the representation of data by your C/C++ compiler (or other non-Java compiler) that you are using and compare them to the sketches of typical implementations given in the text. Where do they differ? Where are they the same?

6.3 **(a)** The Boolean data type may or may not have an order relation, and it may or may not be convertible to integral types, depending on the language. Compare the treatment of the Boolean type in at least two of the following languages with regard to these two issues: Java, C++, Ada, ML.

(b) Is it useful for Booleans to be ordered? Convertible to integers?

6.4 **(a)** Given the C declarations

```
    struct
    { int i;
      double j;
    } x, y;
```

```
struct
{ int i;
  double j;
} z;
```

the assignment x = z generates a compilation error, but the assignment x = y does not. Why?

(b) Give two different ways to fix the code in part (a) so that x = z works. Which way is better and why?

6.5 Suppose we have two C arrays:

```
int x[10];
int y[10];
```

Why won't the assignment x = y compile in C? Can the declarations be fixed so the assignment will work?

6.6 Given the following variable declarations in C/C++:

```
enum { one } x;
enum { two } y;
```

the assignment x = y is fine in C, but generates a compiler error in C++. Explain.

6.7 Given the following function variable declarations in C/C++:

```
int (*f)(int);
int (*g)(int);
int (*h)(char);
```

the assignment f = g is fine in C and C++, but the assignment h = g generates a compiler warning in C and a compiler error in C++. Explain.

6.8 Show that the set

```
{emptylist} ∪ char ∪ (char × char) ∪
(char × char × char) ∪ ...
```

is the smallest solution to the set equation

```
CharList = {emptylist} ∪ char × CharList
```

(See Section 6.3.5 and Exercise 4.53.)

6.9 Consider the set equation

$$X \times \text{char} = X$$

(a) Show that any set X satisfying this equation must be infinite.

(b) Show that any element of a set satisfying this equation must contain an infinite number of characters.

(c) Is there a smallest solution to this equation?

6.10 Consider the following declaration in C syntax:

```
struct CharTree
{ char data;
   struct CharTree left, right;
};
```

(a) Rewrite CharTree as a union, similar to the union CharList declaration of Section 6.3.5.

(b) Write a recursive set equation for your declaration in part (a).

(c) Describe a set that is the smallest solution to your equation of part (b).

(d) Prove that your set in part (c) is the smallest solution.

(e) Rewrite this as a valid C declaration.

6.11 Here are some type declarations in C:

```
typedef struct Rec1 * Ptr1;
typedef struct Rec2 * Ptr2;
struct Rec1
{ int data;
   Ptr2 next;
};
struct Rec2
{ double data;
   Ptr2 next;
};
```

Should these be allowed? Are they allowed? Why or why not?

6.12 (a) What is the difference between a subtype and a derived type in Ada?

(b) What C type declaration is the following Ada declaration equivalent to?

```
subtype New_Int is integer;
```

(c) What C type declaration is the following Ada declaration equivalent to?

```
type New_Int is new integer;
```

6.13 In Ada the equality test (x = y in Ada syntax) is legal for all types, as long as x and y have the same type. In C, however, the equality test (x == y in C syntax) is only permitted for variables of a few types; however, the types of x and y need not always be the same.

(a) Describe the types of x and y for which the C comparison x == y is legal.

(b) Why does the C language not allow equality tests for variables of certain types?

(c) Why does the C language allow comparisons between certain values of different types?

6.14 Describe the type correctness and inference rules in C for the conditional expression

```
e1 ? e2 : e3
```

Must e2 and e3 have the same type? If they have the same type, can it be any type?

6.15 Suppose we used the following C++ code that attempts to avoid the use of a **static_cast** to print out the internal value of **true** (see the code at the end of Section 6.7):

```
union
{ int i;
   bool b;
} x;
...
x.b = true;
cout << x.i << endl;
```

Why is this wrong? (*Hint:* Try the assignment x.i=20000 before x.b=true.)

6.16 Programmers often forget that numeric data types such as int are only approximations of mathematical number systems. For example, try the following two divisions in C or C++ or Java on your system, and explain the result: -2147483648 / -1; -2147483647 / -1.

6.17 The chapter makes no mention of the initialization problem for variables. Describe the rules for variable initialization in C, Ada, ML, or other similar language. In particular, are variables of all types initialized when a program starts running? If so, how is the initial value constructed?

6.18 Here are some type and variable declarations in C syntax:

```
typedef char* Table1;
typedef char* Table2;

Table1 x,y;
Table2 z;
Table2 w;
```

State which variables are type equivalent under **(a)** structural equivalence, **(b)** name equivalence, and **(c)** the actual C equivalence algorithm. Be sure to identify those cases that are ambiguous from the information at hand.

6.19 Given the declarations:

```
int x[10];
int y[5];
```

are x and y type equivalent in C?

6.20 Given the following C declaration:

```
const PI = 3.14159;
```

if we then use the constant `PI` in a geometry formula (like `A = PI*r*r`), we get the wrong answer. Why?

6.21 Given the following Java declaration:

```
short i = 2;
```

the Java compiler generates an error for the statement

```
i = i + i;
```

Why?

6.22 Here are some type and variable declarations in C syntax:

```
typedef struct
{ int x;
  char y;
} Rec1;
typedef Rec1 Rec2;
typedef struct
{ int x;
  char y;
} Rec3;
Rec1 a,b;
Rec2 c;
Rec3 d;
```

State which variables are type equivalent under **(a)** structural equivalence, **(b)** name equivalence, and **(c)** the actual C equivalence algorithm. Be sure to identify those cases that are ambiguous from the information at hand.

6.23 In C++ the equality test `==` can be applied to arrays, but tests the wrong thing, and the assignment operator `=` cannot be applied to arrays at all. Explain.

6.24 Can equality and assignment be applied to Ada arrays? Do they test the right thing?

6.25 By the type rules stated in the text, the array constructor in C does not construct a new type; that is, structural equivalence is applied to arrays. How could you write code to test this? (*Hint:* Can we use an equality test? Are there any other ways to test compatibility?)

6.26 Can a union in C be used to convert `ints` to `doubles` and vice versa? `longs` to `floats`? Why or why not?

6.27 In a language in which "/" can mean either integer or real division and that allows coercions between integers and reals, the expression `I + J / K` can be interpreted in two different ways. Describe how this can happen.

6.28 Show how Hindley-Milner type checking determines that the following function (in ML syntax) takes an integer parameter and returns an integer result (i.e., is of type int -> int in ML terminology):

```
fun fac n = if n = 0 then 1 else n * fac (n-1);
```

6.29 Here is a function in ML syntax:

```
fun f (g,x) = g (g(x));
```

(a) What polymorphic type does this function have?
(b) Show how Hindley-Milner type checking infers the type of this function.
(c) Rewrite this function as a C++ template function.

6.30 Write a polymorphic **swap** function that swaps the values of two variables of the same type in
(a) C++; (b) ML

6.31 Write a polymorphic **max** function in C++ that takes an array of values of any type and returns the maximum value in the array, assuming the existence of a ">" operation.

6.32 Repeat the previous exercise, but add a parameter for a **gt** function that takes the place of the ">" operation.

6.33 Can both functions of the previous two exercises exist (and be used) simultaneously in a C++ program? Explain.

6.34 Explicit parametric polymorphism need not be restricted to a single type parameter. For example, in C++ one can write:

```
template <typename First, typename Second>
struct Pair
{ First first;
  Second second;
};
```

Write a C++ template function makePair that takes two parameters of different types and returns a Pair containing its two values.

6.35 Write the Pair data structure of the previous exercise as an Ada generic package, and write a similar makePair function in Ada.

6.36 Is C++ parametric polymorphism let-bound? (*Hint:* See the functions makepair and makepair2 on pages 242–243).

6.37 Does the occur-check problem occur in C++? Explain.

6.38 A problem related to let-bound polymorphism in ML is that of **polymorphic recursion**, where a function calls itself recursively, but on different types at different points in the code. For example, consider the following function (in ML syntax):

```
fun f x = if x = x then true else (f false);
```

What type does this function have in ML? Is this the most general type it could have? Show how ML arrived at its answer.

6.39 Does the polymorphic recursion problem of the previous exercise exist in C++? Explain.

6.40 Data types can be kept as part of the syntax tree of a program and checked for structural equivalence by a simple recursive algorithm. For example, the type

```
struct
{ double x;
   int y[10];
};
```

might be kept as the tree

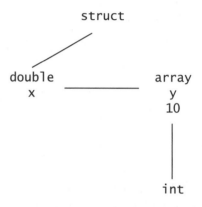

Describe a tree node structure that could be used to express the types of C or a similar language as trees. Write out a TypeEqual function in pseudocode that would check structural equivalence on these trees.

6.41 How could the trees of the previous exercise represent recursive types? Modify your TypeEqual function to take recursive types into account.

6.42 The language C uses structural type equivalence for arrays and pointers, but declaration equivalence for structs and unions. Why do you think the language designers did this?

6.43 Compare the BNFs for type declarations in C (Java, Ada) with the type tree of Figure 6.5 (6.6, 6.7). To what extent is the tree a direct reflection of the syntax?

6.44 What new type constructors does C++ add to those of C? Add these to the type tree of Figure 6.5. (*Hint:* Use the BNFs for C++ as motivation.)

6.45 The type tree for Ada (Figure 6.7) is somewhat simplified, with a number of constructors omitted. Add the missing constructors. Are there any missing simple types?

6.46 What operations would you consider necessary for a string data type? How well do arrays of characters support these operations?

6.47 Given the following C++ declarations,

```
double* p = new double(2);
void* q;
int* r;
```

which of the following assignments does the compiler complain about?

```
q = p;
p = q;
r = p;
p = r;
r = q;
r = (int*)q;
r = static_cast<int*>(q);
r = static_cast<int*>(p);
r = reinterpret_cast<int*>(p);
```

Try to explain the behavior of the compiler. Will *r ever have the value 2 after one of the assignments to r? Why?

6.48 In Java, the following local variable declaration results in a compiler error:

```
float x = 2.1;
```

Why? Find two ways of removing this error.

6.49 Should the equality test be available for floating-point types (explain)? Is it available in Java? Ada? ML?

6.50 Should the equality test be available for function types (explain)? Is it available in C? Ada? ML?

6.51 The conversion rules for an arithmetic expression such as $e1 + e2$ in C are stated in Kernighan and Ritchie [1978] as follows (these are the pre-ANSI rules, which are simpler than the ANSI rules, but have the same result in many cases):

> First, any operands of type char or short are converted to int, and any of type float are converted to double. Then, if either operand is double, the other is converted to double and that is the type of the result.
>
> Otherwise, if either operand is long, the other is converted to long and that is the type of the result.
>
> Otherwise, if either operand is unsigned, the other is converted to unsigned and that is the type of the result.
>
> Otherwise, both operands must be int, and that is the type of the result.

Given the following expression in C, assuming x is an `unsigned` with value 1, describe the type conversions that occur during evaluation and the type of the resulting value. What is the resulting value?

```
'0' + 1.0 * (-1 + x)
```

6.52 In C there is no Boolean data type. Instead, comparisons such as a == b and a <= b return the integer value 0 for false and 1 for true. On the other hand, the if-statement in C considers any nonzero value of its condition to be equivalent to true. Is there an advantage to doing this? Why not allow the condition a <= b to return any nonzero value if it is true?

6.53 The text mentions in Section 6.2 that a subrange can be allocated more efficiently if it is packed into the minimum space necessary to store its values. For example, the subrange 0 . . 7 could be stored in just three bits instead of the full allocated space of its integer base type. This creates type conversion problems, however, since now values of the subranges 0 . . 7 and 1 . . 8 are stored differently and cannot be directly copied to each other or to an integer variable. Explain how these conversions can be done. Is it possible for a translator to insert code to perform these?

Notes and References

Data type systems in Algol-like languages such as Pascal, C, and Ada seem to suffer from excessive complexity and many special cases. In part, this is because a type system is trying to balance two opposing design goals: expressiveness and security. That is, a type system tries to make it possible to catch as many errors as possible while at the same time allowing the programmer the flexibility to create and use as many types as are necessary for the natural expression of an algorithm. ML (as well as Haskell) escapes from this complexity somewhat by using structural equivalence for predefined structures but name equivalence for user-defined types; however, this does weaken the effectiveness of type names in distinguishing different uses of the same structure. An interesting variant on this same idea is Modula-3, an object-oriented modification of Modula-2 that uses structural equivalence for ordinary data and name equivalence for objects (Cardelli et al. [1989a,b]; Nelson [1991]). Ada has perhaps the most consistent system, albeit containing many different ideas and hence extremely complex.

One frustrating aspect of the study of type systems is that language reference manuals rarely state the underlying algorithms explicitly. Instead, the algorithms must be inferred from a long list of special rules, a time-consuming investigative task. There are also few references that give detailed overviews of language type systems. Two that do have considerable detail are Cleaveland [1986] and Bishop [1986]. A lucid description of Pascal's type system can be found in Cooper [1983]. A very detailed description of Ada's type system can be found in Cohen [1996]. Java's type system is described in Gosling et al. [2000]; C's type system in Kernighan and Ritchie [1988]; C++'s type system in Stroustrup [1997]; and ML's type system in Ullman [1998] and Harper and Mitchell [1993].

For a study of type polymorphism and overloading, see Cardelli and Wegner [1985]. The Hindley-Milner algorithm is clearly presented in Cardelli [1987], together with Modula-2 code that implements it for a small sample language; let-bound polymorphism and the occur-check are also discussed. Let-bound polymorphism is also described in Ullman [1998], Section 5.3, where "generic" type variables are called "generalizable." C++ templates are amply described in Stroustrup [1997]. Ada "generics" are described in Cohen [1996]. Polymorphic recursion (Exercise 6.38) is described in Henglein [1993].

The IEEE floating-point standard, mentioned in Section 6.2, appears in IEEE [1985].

Control I— Expressions and Statements

In Chapter 6 we discussed basic and structured abstraction of data through the use of data types. In this chapter we discuss the basic and structured abstraction of control through the use of expressions and statements. Structured control through the use of procedures and functions, and the organization of runtime environments, will be studied in the next chapter. As noted in Chapter 1, unit-level data and control converge to the same kinds of language mechanisms, and they will be studied in the chapter on modules.

Expressions represent the most fundamental computation mechanism in programs. An **expression**, in its pure (mathematical) form, returns a value and produces no side effect (that is, no change to program memory), while a **statement** is executed for its side effects and returns no value. Many languages, however, do not make such a clear distinction and allow expressions to contain side effects. In functional languages—sometimes also called **expression languages**—virtually all language constructs are expressions. Even in nonfunctional languages expressions play a significant role, and in some languages, like C (which could be called an **expression-oriented language**), expressions make up a much larger portion of the language than statements. Expressions are also the parts of programming languages that are closest in appearance to mathematics, and in the absence of side effects, program expressions have very similar semantics to mathematical expressions, which leads to semantic simplicity and precision. Unfortunately, in the presence of side effects, expressions can behave in ways that are very different from their mathematical counterparts, and this can be a source of confusion and error. In fact, the semantics of expressions with side effects have a significant control component: The way that such expressions are evaluated, including the order in which subexpressions are computed, can have a major impact on their meaning, something that is never true for mathematical expressions. That is why we discuss them along with more explicit forms of control in this chapter.

Explicit control structures began in programming languages as GOTOs, which are simple imitations of the jump statements of assembly language, transferring control directly, or after a test, to a new location in the program. With Algol60 came the improvement of **structured control**, in which control statements transfer control to and from sequences of statements that are (at least in principle) **single-entry, single-exit**, that is, those that enter from the beginning and exit from the end. Examples of such single-entry, single-exit constructs are the **blocks** of Algol60, Algol68, C, and Ada, which may also include declarations, and which we studied in Chapter 5.[1]

Structured programming led to an enormous improvement in the readability and reliability of programs, and structured control constructs are part of most major languages today. Some languages do away with GOTOs altogether, although a (now somewhat muted) debate continues to this day on the utility of GOTOs within the context of structured programming.

In this chapter we will first discuss expressions and the variety of control questions that can arise during their evaluation. Then we discuss structured control mechanisms (the assignment statement was already studied in Chapter 5), after which we review the GOTO issue. In the last section of this chapter we begin a discussion of exception handling, which is essentially a preemptive control mechanism, causing the

---

[1] All these languages contain certain relaxations of the single-entry, single-exit property of these constructs, but the principle of controlling entry and exit points remains.

explicit control structure of a program to be disturbed. In that section we discuss the appearance and operation of exceptions in several languages; implementation issues are postponed to the next chapter, since they involve the runtime environment.

7.1 Expressions

As we saw in Chapters 4 and 5, basic expressions are the literals (manifest constants) and identifiers. More complex expressions are built up recursively from the basic expressions by the application of operators and functions, sometimes involving grouping symbols such as parentheses. For example, in the simple arithmetic expression 3 + 4 * 5, the + **operator** is applied to its two **operands**, consisting of the integer literal 3 and the (sub)expression 4 * 5, which in its turn represents the application of the * operator to its operands, consisting of the integer literals 4 and 5. Operators can take one or more operands: An operator that takes one operand is called a **unary operator**; an operator that takes two is a **binary operator**. Operators can be written in **infix, postfix,** or **prefix** notation, corresponding to an inorder, postorder, or preorder traversal of the syntax tree of the expression. For example, the infix expression 3 + 4 * 5 with syntax tree (see Chapter 4)

is written in postfix form as 3 4 5 * + and in prefix form as + 3 * 4 5. Postfix and prefix forms have the advantage that parentheses are not necessary to express the order in which operators are applied, so operator precedence (see Chapter 4) is not required to disambiguate an unparenthesized expression. For instance, (3 + 4) * 5 is written in postfix form as 3 4 + 5 * and in prefix form as * + 3 4 5. Associativity of operators is also expressed directly in postfix and prefix form without the need for a rule. For example, the postfix expression 3 4 5 + + right associates and 3 4 + 5 + left associates the infix expression 3 + 4 + 5.

Many languages make a distinction between operators and functions: Operators are predefined and (if binary) written in infix form, with specified associativity and precedence rules, while functions, which can be either predefined or user-defined, are written in prefix form and the operands are viewed as **arguments** or **actual parameters** to calls of the functions. For example, in C, if we wrote the expression 3 + 4 * 5 with user-defined addition and multiplication operations, it would appear as add(3,mul(4,5)). In fact, the distinction between operators and functions is arbitrary, since they are equivalent concepts. Historically, however, the distinction *was* significant, since built-in operators were implemented using highly optimized **inline code** (code for the function body that is inserted directly at the point where the function would be called),[2] while function calls required the building of sometimes time-consuming **activations** (described in the next chapter). Modern translators, however, often inline even user-defined functions, and in any case the performance penalty of activations has largely disappeared in modern architectures.

Programming languages, too, have increasingly allowed programmers to overload the built-in operators and even to define new infix operators with arbitrary associativity and precedence, as we have seen in Sections 3.4 and 5.4. Some languages even allow all operators to be written in either prefix or infix form. For example, 3 + 4 * 5 can be just as well written in Ada as "+"(3,"*"(4,5)), and a few languages use either prefix or postfix form exclusively, for both predefined and user-defined operations. For example, stack-based languages such as PostScript and FORTH use postfix notation exclusively, while Lisp uses prefix notation. Lisp also requires expressions to be **fully parenthesized**; that is, all operators and operands must be enclosed in parentheses. This is because LISP operators can take variable numbers of arguments as operands. Thus, 3 + 4 * 5 and (3 + 4) * 5 would look as follows in LISP:

```
(+ 3 (* 4 5))
(* (+ 3 4) 5)
```

Each programming language has rules for evaluating expressions. A common evaluation rule is that all operands are evaluated first and then operators are applied to them. This is called **applicative order evaluation**, or sometimes **strict** evaluation, and is the most common rule in programming languages. It corresponds to a bottom-up evaluation of the values at nodes of the syntax tree representing an expression. For example, the expression (3 + 4) * (5 − 6) is represented by the syntax tree

In applicative order evaluation, first the "+" and "−" nodes are evaluated to 7 and −1, respectively, and then the "*" is applied to get −7.

Let us also consider how this would appear in terms of user-defined functions, written in prefix form in C syntax:

```
mul(add(3,4),sub(5,6))
```

---

[2] Code inlining is an important optimization technique for translators; indeed, C++ has an inline keyword to allow the programmer to specifically request inlining, if possible; see Chapter 10. Inlining of operators and nonrecursive functions with no nonlocal references is relatively easy, but in the most general case inlining may be difficult or impossible. For an example of the difficulties of inlining, see Exercise 8.14.

Applicative order says evaluate the arguments first. Thus, calls to `add` (3,4) and `sub(5,6)` are made, which are also evaluated using applicative order. Then, the calls are replaced by their returned values, which are 7 and -1. Finally, the call

```
mul(7,-1)
```

is made. Note that this process corresponds to a bottom-up "reduction" of the syntax tree to a value: First the $+$ and $-$ nodes are replaced by their values 7 and -1, and finally the root $*$ node is replaced by the value -7, which is the result of the expression.

One question to be answered is in which order the subexpressions $(3 + 4)$ and $(5 - 6)$ are computed, or in which order the calls `plus(3,4)` and `minus(5,6)` are made. A natural order is left to right, corresponding to a left-to-right traversal of the syntax tree. However, many languages explicitly state that there is no specified order for the evaluation of arguments to user-defined functions, and the same is often true for predefined operators as well.

There are several reasons for this. One is that different machines may have different requirements for the structure of calls to procedures and functions. Another is that a translator may attempt to rearrange the order of computation so that it is more efficient. For example, consider the expression $(3 + 4) * (3 + 4)$. A translator may discover that the same subexpression, namely, $3 + 4$, is used twice and will evaluate it only once. And in evaluating a call such as `max(3,4+5)`, a translator may evaluate $4 + 5$ before 3 because it is more efficient to evaluate more complicated expressions first.

If the evaluation of an expression causes no side effects, then the expression will yield the same result, regardless of the order of evaluation of its subexpressions. In the presence of side effects, however, the order of evaluation can make a difference. Consider, for example, the C program of Figure 7.1.

```
(1)   #include <stdio.h>

(2)   int x = 1;

(3)   int f(void)
(4)   { x += 1;
(5)      return x;
(6)   }

(7)   int p( int a, int b)
(8)   { return a + b;
(9)   }

(10)  main()
(11)  { printf("%d\n",p(x,f()));
(12)     return 0;
(13)  }
```

Figure 7.1   C Program Showing Evaluation Order Matters in the Presence of Side Effects

If the arguments of the call to p on line 11 are evaluated left to right, this program will print 3. If the arguments are evaluated right to left, the program will print 4. The reason is that a call to the function f has a side effect: It changes the value of the global variable x.

In a language that explicitly states that the order of evaluation of expressions is unspecified, programs that depend on the order of evaluation for their results (such as the one above) are incorrect, even though they may have predictable behavior for one or more translators.

In spite of the problems side effects cause in expression evaluation, sometimes expressions are explicitly constructed with side effects in mind. For example, in C, assignment (a quintessential side effect) is an expression, not a statement: x = y not only assigns the value of y to x, but also returns the copied value as its result.[3] Thus, assignments can be combined in expressions, so that

```
x = (y = z)
```

assigns the value of z to both x and y. Note that in languages with this kind of construction, assignment can be considered to be a binary operator similar to arithmetic operators. In that case its precedence is usually lower than other binary operators, and it is made right associative. Thus,

```
x = y = z + w
```

in C assigns the sum of z and w to both x and y (and returns that value as its result).

C and other expression languages also have a **sequence operator**, which allows several expressions to be combined into a single expression and evaluated sequentially. In C, the sequence operator is the comma operator, which has precedence lower than any other operator. Unlike most other operators in C, the order of evaluation is specified to be left to right, and the value of the right-most expression is the value returned by the entire expression. For example, given that x and y are integer variables with values 1 and 2, respectively, the C expression

```
x = (y+=1,x+=y,x+1)
```

returns the value 5 and leaves x with the value 5 and y with the value 3.

The evaluation of an expression can sometimes be performed even without the evaluation of all its subexpressions. An interesting case is that of the Boolean, or logical, expressions. For example, the Boolean expressions (in Ada or C++ syntax)

```
true or x
```

and

```
x or true
```

are true regardless of whether x is true or false. Similarly,

```
false and x
```

---

[3] When a type conversion occurs, the type of the copied value is that of x, not y.

and

```
x and false
```

are clearly false regardless of the value of x. In a programming language one can specify that Boolean expressions are to be evaluated in left to right order, up to the point where the truth value of the entire expression becomes known and then the evaluation stops. A programming language that has this rule is said to possess **short-circuit evaluation** of Boolean or logical expressions.

Short-circuit evaluation has a number of benefits. One is that a test for the validity of an array index can be written in the same expression as a test of its subscripted value, as long as the range test occurs first:

```
if (i <= lastindex and a[i] >= x)  ... // C++ code
```

Without short-circuit evaluation, the test `i <= lastindex` will not prevent an error from occurring if `i > lastindex`, since the expression `a[i]` in the second part of the expression will still be computed. (This assumes, of course, that an out-of-range array subscript *will* produce an error.) Without short-circuit evaluation, the test must be written using nested `if`'s:

```
if (i <= lastindex) if (a[i] >= x) ...
```

Similarly, a test for a null pointer can be made in the same expression as a dereference of that pointer, using short-circuit evaluation:

```
if (p != 0 and p->data == x) ...  // C++ code
```

Note that the order of the tests becomes important in short-circuit evaluation. Short-circuit evaluation will protect us from a runtime error if we write

```
// ok:  y % x requires x != 0
if (x != 0 and y % x == 0) ...
```

but not if we write

```
if (y % x == 0 and x != 0) ... // not ok!
```

Most languages require Boolean operators to be short-circuit: C/C++, Java, and ML all have short-circuit Boolean operators (but not Pascal!). Typically, Ada offers both kinds: and and or are not short-circuit, but the operators (two keywords each) "and then" and "or else" *are* short-circuit:

```
-- Ada short circuit code:
if (i <= lastindex) and then (a(i) = x) then ...
```

While we are on the subject of Boolean operators, we note that there is unfortunately little agreement on the names of these operators. C and Java use the somewhat obscure notation && for and, || for or, and ! for not. C++ allows these same operators, but also allows the more common keywords and, or, and not. ML's names for the binary logical operators are andalso and orelse, presumably to call attention to their short-circuit nature. (ML has another, completely separate use for the keyword and, and the keyword or does not exist in ML.) Other languages occasionally use imitations of the operations as they are written in mathematical logic: /\ (forward slash followed by backslash) for and, \/ (the reverse of /\) for or, and ~ (tilde) for not.

Boolean expressions are not the only expressions whose subexpressions may not all be evaluated: Many languages have expressions that mimic control statements but return values; two of these are **if-expressions** and **case-expressions**.

An if (or if-then-else) operator is a **ternary operator**—that is, it has *three* operands: the conditional test expression (which is typically Boolean), the "then" expression (whose value is the result of the entire expression if the test expression is true), and the "else" expression (whose value is the result of the entire expression if the test expression is false). As a prefix function it would be written as

    if(*test-exp*,*then-exp*,*else-exp*)

but most languages use a **mix-fix** form that distributes parts of the syntax of the operator throughout the expression in traditional style. For example, in ML the if-expression appears as

    if *e1* then *e2* else *e3*

while in C the same expression appears as

    e1 ? *e2* : *e3*

Note that an if-expression may not have an optional else-part (unlike an if-statement), since there would be no value to return if the test expression were to evaluate to false.

If-expressions *never* have all of their subexpressions evaluated: *e1* (the test expression) is *always* evaluated first, but, based on that value, only one of *e2* and *e3* is ever evaluated (this is the only reason for the if-expression to exist at all).

ML and some other functional languages (but not C) also have a **case-expression**

    case *e1* of
      a => *e2* |
      b => *e3* |
      c => *e4* ;

which is more or less equivalent to a series of nested if-expressions: if e1 = a then e2 else if e1 = b then e3 .... Case-expressions have some special properties, however, and will be discussed again in Chapter 11.

Interestingly, the short-circuit Boolean operations can be defined using if-expressions as follows:

    e1 and *e2* = if *e1* then *e2* else false (* short circuit
                                                          and *)
    e1 or *e2* = if *e1* then true else *e2*   (* short cir-
                                                     cuit or *)

Short-circuit Boolean and if operators are a special case of operators that **delay** evaluating their operands. The general situation is called **delayed evaluation**, or sometimes **non-strict evaluation**. In the case of the short-circuit operators, *e1* and *e2* and *e1* or *e2*, both delay the evaluation of *e2* until *e1* is evaluated. Similarly, the if operator delays the evaluation of both *e2* and *e3* until *e1* is evaluated.

It is worth restating the fact that, in the absence of side effects (changes to variables in memory, input and output), the order of evaluation of expressions is immaterial to the final value of the expression.[4] In fact, in a language in which side effects do not exist or are carefully controlled, such as the pure functional languages (Chapter 11), expressions in programs share an important property with mathematical expressions, which we could call the **substitution rule** (it is often also called **referential transparency**): Any two expressions in a program that have the same value may be substituted for each other anywhere in the program—in other words, their values always remain equal, regardless of the context in which they are evaluated. For example, if x and y have the same value at one point in a referentially transparent program, then they *always* have the same value[5] and may be freely substituted for each other anywhere. (Note that this prohibits x and y from being variables in the programming language sense—they must be constants).

Referential transparency allows for a very strong form of delayed evaluation to be used that has important theoretical and practical consequences. It is called **normal order evaluation**. A precise mathematical definition can be given in the context of the lambda calculus, and this is explained briefly in Chapter 11. For our purposes in this section, normal order evaluation of an expression means that each operation (or function) begins its evaluation *before* its operands are evaluated, and each operand is evaluated only if it is needed for the calculation of the value of the operation.

As an example of normal order evaluation, consider the following functions (in C syntax):

```
int double( int x)
{ return x + x; }

int square( int x)
{ return x * x; }
```

Now consider the expression square(double(2)). Using normal order evaluation, the call to square is replaced by double(2)*double(2) without evaluating double(2), and then double(2) is replaced by 2 + 2, so that the following sequence of replacements occur:

$$square(double(2)) \Rightarrow double(2)*double(2) \Rightarrow (2 + 2)*(2 + 2)$$

---

[4] As long as it actually *has* a value, see Chapter 5.

[5] As long as we are in the scope of a particular declaration of these variables. Obviously, different declarations may cause different values to be associated with these names.

Only after these replacements occur is the expression evaluated, typically in left-to-right order:

$$(2 + 2)*(2 + 2) \Rightarrow 4 * (2 + 2) \Rightarrow 4 * 4 \Rightarrow 16$$

Note how this differs from applicative order evaluation, which evaluates the call to `double` before the call to `square`, and would result in the following sequence of replacements (with evaluation intermingled):

$$\text{square}(\text{double}(2)) \Rightarrow \text{square}(2 + 2) \Rightarrow \text{square}(4) \Rightarrow 4 *$$
$$4 \Rightarrow 16$$

Normal order evaluation implements a kind of code inlining, in which the bodies of functions are substituted at their call sites *before* evaluation occurs; see Footnote 2.

In the absence of side effects, normal order evaluation does not change the semantics of a program, and, while it might seem inefficient (e.g., 2+2 gets evaluated twice instead of once in the previous example), it can be made efficient, and it has a number of good properties that make it useful, particularly for functional languages. As a simple example, if C used normal order evaluation, the C if-expression *e1 ? e2 : e3* can be written (for each data type) as an ordinary C function, instead of needing special syntax in the language:

```
int if_exp (int x, int y, int z)
{ if (x) return y; else return z; }
```

Here y and z are only evaluated if they are needed in the code of `if_exp`, which is the behavior that we want.

On the other hand, the presence of side effects can mean that normal order evaluation substantially changes the semantics of a program. Consider for example the C function

```
int get_int(void)
{ int x;
  /* read an integer value into x from standard input
  */
  scanf("%d",&x);
  return x;
}
```

This function has a side effect (input).

Now consider what would happen to the expression `square(get_int())` using normal order evaluation: It would be expanded into `get_int()*get_int()`, and *two* integer values, rather than just one, would be read from standard input—a very different outcome from what we would expect.

Normal order evaluation appears as so-called **lazy evaluation** in the functional language Haskell, and will be studied in more detail in Chapter 11. Normal order evaluation appears also as a parameter passing technique for functions in Algol60, where it is known as **pass by name**; this will be studied briefly in the next chapter.

7.2 Conditional Statements and Guards

The most typical form of structured control is execution of a group of statements only under certain conditions. This involves making a Boolean, or
logical, test before entering a sequence of statements. The well-known **if-
statement** is the most common form of this construct. The various ways
such a conditional can be introduced will be discussed shortly.

First, however, we want to describe a general form of conditional
statement that encompasses all the various conditional constructs: the
guarded if statement introduced by E. W. Dijkstra:

```
if B1 -> S1
|   B2 -> S2
|   B3 -> S3
        . . .
|   Bn -> Sn
fi
```

The semantics of this statement are as follows: the B_i's are all Boolean
expressions, called the **guards**, and the S_i's are statement sequences. If
one of the B_i's evaluates to true, then the corresponding statement
sequence S_i is executed. If more than one of the B_i's is true, then one and
only one of the corresponding S_i's is selected for execution. If none of the
B_i's is true, then an error occurs.

There are several interesting features in this description. First, it
does not say that the first B_i that evaluates to true is the one chosen.
Thus, the guarded if introduces nondeterminism into programming, a
feature that becomes very useful in concurrent programming (Chapter 14). Second, it leaves unspecified whether all the guards are evaluated. Thus, if the evaluation of a B_i has a side effect, the result of the
execution of the guarded if may be unknown. Of course, the usual deterministic implementation of such a statement would sequentially evaluate the B_i's until a true one is found, whence the corresponding S_i is
executed and control is transferred to the point following the guarded
statement.

The two major ways that programming languages implement conditional statements like the guarded if are as if-statements and case-state-
ments.

7.2.1 If-statements

The basic form of the if-statement is as given in the extended Backus-
Naur form (EBNF) rule for the if-statement in C, with an optional "else"
part:

if-statement → if (*expression*) *statement* [else *statement*]

where *statement* can be either a single statement or a sequence of statements surrounded by braces:

```
if (x > 0) y = 1/x;
else
{ x = 2;
  y = 1/z;
}
```

This form of the `if` (which also exists in Java and Pascal) has a problem, however: It is ambiguous in the syntactic sense described in Chapter 4. Indeed, the statement

```
if (e1) if (e2) S1 else S2
```

has two different parse trees according to the BNF:

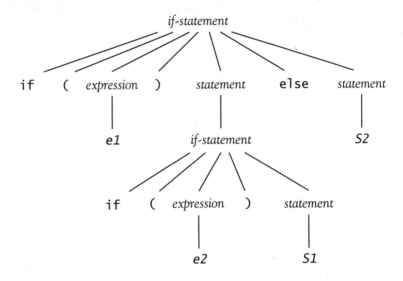

and

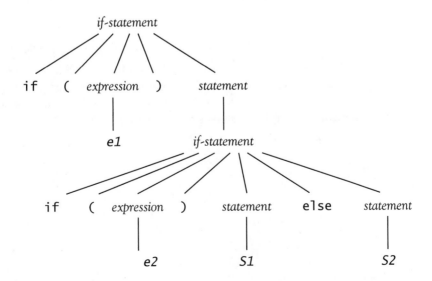

This ambiguity is called the **dangling-else** problem: The syntax does not tell us whether an else after two if-statements is to be associated with the first or second if. C (as well as Pascal) solves this problem by stating a **disambiguating rule**: The else is to be associated with the closest prior if that does not already have an else part. This rule is also referred to as the **most closely nested rule** for if-statements. It states that the second parse tree is the correct one.

The dangling-else problem is somewhat questionable language design from two points of view: It makes us state a new rule to describe what is essentially a syntactic feature, and it makes the interpretation of the if-statement by the reader more difficult; that is, it violates the readability design criterion. As an illustration, if we want actually to associate the else with the first if in the preceding statement, we would have to write either

```
if ( e1 ) { if ( e2 ) S1 } else S2
```

or

```
if ( e1 ) if ( e2 ) S1 else ; else S2
```

There are other ways to solve the dangling-else than by using a disambiguating rule. In fact, it is possible to write out BNF rules that specify the association precisely, but these rules make the grammar somewhat more complex (Java does this—see Exercises 7.28 and 7.29). A better way is to use a **bracketing keyword** for the if-statement, such as the Ada rule:

> *if-statement* → if *condition* then *sequence-of-statements*
>   [else *sequence-of-statements*] end if ;

The two bracketing keywords end if (together with the semicolon) close the if-statement and remove the ambiguity, since we must now write either

```
if e1 then if e2 then S1 end if ; else S2 end if;
```

or

```
if e1 then if e2 then S1 else S2 end if ; end if ;
```

to decide which if is associated with the else part. This also removes the necessity of using brackets (or a begin - end pair) to open a new sequence of statements: the if-statement can open its own sequence of statements and thus becomes fully structured:

```
if x > 0.0 then
    y := 1.0/x;
    done := true;
else
    x := 1.0;
    y := 1.0/z;
    done := false;
end if;
```

A similar approach was taken in the historical (but influential) language Algol68, which suggestively uses keywords spelled backwards as bracketing keywords:

```
if e1 then S1 else S2 fi
```

Thus, the bracketing keyword for if-statements is `fi`. (One still sees this convention in theoretical language design publications—witness the guarded if of Dijkstra, described above.)

An extension of the if-statement simplifies things when there are many alternatives. Multiple `else`'s would have to be written in Ada as

```
if e1 then S1
else if e2 then S2
else if e3 then S3
end if ; end if ; end if;
```

with many "`end if`"s piled up at the end to close all the if-statements. Instead the "`else if`" is compacted into a new reserved word `elsif` that opens a new sequence of statements at the same level:

```
if e1 then S1
elsif e2 then S2
elsif e3 then S3
end if ;
```

An additional question regarding the if-statement is what type the controlling expression must be (we have written the test variously as Bi or ei above, indicating possibly Boolean or not). In Java and Ada (as well as Pascal), the test must always have Boolean type. C has no Boolean type, and in C (as well as C++), the controlling expression can have either integral type (see Figure 6.1) or pointer type. The resulting value is then compared to 0 (the null pointer in the case of pointer type); unequal comparison is equivalent to true, equal comparison is equivalent to false. Thus, in C a test such as

```
if (p != 0 && p->>data == x) ...
```

can be written as

```
if (p && p->data == x) ...
```

7.2.2 Case- and Switch-Statements

The case-statement (or switch-statement in C/C++/Java) was invented by C. A. R. Hoare as a special kind of guarded if, where the guards, instead of being Boolean expressions, are ordinal values that are selected by an ordinal expression. An example in C is given in Figure 7.2.

```
(1)   switch (x - 1)
(2)   { case 0:
(3)       y = 0;
```

(continues)

(continued)

```
(4)        z = 2;
(5)          break;
(6)      case 2:
(7)      case 3:
(8)      case 4:
(9)      case 5:
(10)        y = 3;
(11)        z = 1;
(12)        break;
(13)     case 7:
(14)     case 9:
(15)        z = 10;
(16)        break;
(17)     default:
(18)        /* do nothing */
(19)        break;
(20) }
```

Figure 7.2   An Example of the Use of the Switch Statement in C

The semantics of this statement are to evaluate the controlling expression (x - 1 on line 1 in Figure 7.2), and to transfer control to the point in the statement where the value is listed. These values must have integral types in C (and conversions occur, if necessary, to bring the types of the listed cases into the type of the controlling expression). No two listed cases may have the same value after conversion. Case values may be literals as in the above example, or they can be constant expressions as C defines them (that is, compile-time constant expressions with no identifiers; see Chapter 5). If the value of the controlling expression is not listed in a case label, then control is transferred to the `default` case (line 17 in Figure 7.2), if it exists. If not, control is transferred to the statement following the `switch` (the switch-statement **falls through**).

The structure of this statement in C has a number of somewhat novel features. First, the `case` labels are treated syntactically as ordinary labels, which allows for potentially bizarre placements; see Exercise 7.30. Second, without a `break` statement, execution falls through to the next case. This allows cases to be listed together without repeating code (such as the cases 2 through 5, lines 6–9 in Figure 7.2); it also results in incorrect execution if a `break` statement is left out.

Java has a `switch` statement that is virtually identical to that of C, except that it tightens up the positioning of the `case` labels to eliminate bizarre situations.

A somewhat more "standard" version of a case statement (from the historical point of view) is that of Ada. The C example of Figure 7.2 is written in Ada in Figure 7.3.

```
(1)   case x - 1 is
(2)      when 0 =>
(3)             y := 0;
(4)             z := 2;
(5)      when 2 .. 5 =>
(6)             y := 3;
(7)             z := 1;
(8)      when 7 | 9 =>
(9)             z := 10;
(10) when others =>
(11)    null;
(12) end case;
```

Figure 7.3   An Example of the Use of the Case Statement in Ada,
            Corresponding to the C Example of Figure 7.2.

In Ada, case values can be grouped together, either by listing them individually, separated by vertical bars (as in line 8 of Figure 7.3), or by listing a range (such as 2 . . 5 in line 5 of Figure 7.3). Also, in Ada case values must not only be distinct but they must also be exhaustive: If a legal
value is not listed and there is no default case (called others in Ada, as
on line 10 of Figure 7.3), a compile-time error occurs (i.e., there is no fall
through as in C). An implication of this is that the complete set of possible values for the controlling expression must be known at compile time.
Thus, enumerations and small subranges are typically used to control case
statements.

     The functional language ML also has a **case** construct, but it is an
expression that returns a value, rather than a statement (as is usual in
functional languages). An example of a function in ML whose body is a
case expression is given in Figure 7.4.

```
(1) fun casedemo x =
(2)    case x - 1 of
(3)      0 => 2 |
(4)      2 => 1 |
(5)      _ => 10
(6)    ;
```

Figure 7.4   An Example of a Case Expression in ML

The syntax of a case expression in ML is similar to that of Ada, except
that cases are separated by vertical bars (and there is no **when** keyword).
Further, cases in an ML case expression are patterns to be matched, rather
than ranges or lists of values. In Figure 7.4, the only patterns are the numbers 0, 2, and the **wildcard pattern** (the underscore in line 5 of Figure 7.4),
which functions as a default case. For example, the function definition of
Figure 7.4 would result in the following evaluations in ML:

```
- casedemo 1;
val it = 2 : int
- casedemo 9;
val it = 10 : int
```

ML permits the cases of a case expression to be not exhaustive, but generates a warning in that case (since no value can be returned if an unlisted case occurs, and a runtime error must occur):

```
val casedemo = fn : int -> int
- fun casedemo x =
=    case x - 1 of
=        0 => 2 |
=        2 => 1
=    ;
stdIn:18.3-20.11 Warning: match nonexhaustive
            0 => ...
            2 => ...

val casedemo = fn : int -> int
```

Pattern matching and the case expression in ML are discussed again in Chapter 11.

7.3 Loops and Variations on WHILE

Loops and their use to perform repetitive operations, especially using arrays, have been one of the major features of computer programming since the beginning—computers were in a sense invented to make the task of performing repetitive operations easier and faster. A general form for a loop construct is given by the corresponding structure to Dijkstra's guarded if, namely, the **guarded do**:

```
do  B1 - > S1
 |  B2 - > S2
 |  B3 - > S3
    ...
 |  Bn -> Sn
od
```

This statement is repeated until all the Bi's are false. At each step, one of the true Bi's is selected nondeterministically, and the corresponding Si is executed.

The most basic form of loop construct, which is essentially a guarded do with only one guard (thus eliminating the nondeterminism), is the while-loop of C/C++/Java,

```
while (e) S
```

or the while-loop of Ada,

```
while e loop S1 ... Sn end loop;
```

In these statements e (the test expression, which must be Boolean in Ada and Java, but not C or C++) is evaluated first. If it is true (or nonzero), then the statement S (or statement sequence S1 ... Sn) is executed. Then e is evaluated again, and so on. Note that if e is false (or zero) to begin with, then the code inside is never executed. Most languages have an alternative statement that ensures that the code of the loop is executed at least once. In C and Java this is the do (or do-while statement):

```
do S while (e);
```

Of course, this is exactly equivalent to the following code,

```
S;
while (e) S
```

so the do-statement is "**syntactic sugar**" (a language construct that is completely expressible in terms of other constructs). But it does express a common situation.

The while and do constructs have the property that termination of the loop is explicitly specified only at the beginning (while-statement) or end (do-statement) of the loop. Often it is also convenient to exit from inside a loop at one or more intermediate points. For this reason, C (and Java) provide two options: A break statement can be used inside a loop (in addition to its use inside a switch statement) to exit the loop completely (and continue execution with the statement immediately following the loop); and a continue statement that skips the remainder of the body of the loop, resuming execution with the next evaluation of the control expression. The break statement is called an exit statement in Ada (Ada has no continue statement).

Multiple termination points complicate the semantics of loops, so some languages (like Pascal) prohibit them. A typical idiom in C is to indicate the presence of internal termination points (which might otherwise be overlooked) by writing 1 (or true in C++ or Java) for the test in a while-loop:

```
while (1) /* always succeeds */
{ ...
    if (...) break;
}
```

This same effect is achieved in Ada by simply omitting the while at the beginning of a loop:

```
loop S1... exit when e; ... Sn end loop;
```

A common special case of a looping construct is the **for-loop** of C/C++/Java:

```
for ( e1; e2; e3 ) S;
```

This is completely equivalent in C to

```
e1;
while (e2)
{ S;
   e3;
}
```

The expression *e1* is the **initializer** of the for-loop, *e2* is the **test**, and *e3* is the **update**. Typically, a for-loop is used in situations where we want an index to run through a set of values from first to last, as in processing the elements of an array:

```
for (i = 0; i < size; i++)
      sum += a[i];
```

Note that the **index** variable i is declared outside of the for-loop. C++, Java, and the 1999 ISO C Standard offer the additional feature that a for-loop initializer may contain declarations, so that a loop index can be defined right in the loop:

```
for ( int i = 0; i < size; i++)
      sum += a[i];
```

The scope of such declarations is limited to the rest of the loop; it is as if the for-loop code were inside its own block:[6]

```
{   // for loop in C++, Java, and 1999 ISO C
    e1; // may contain local declarations
    while (e2)
    {   S;
        e3;
    }
}
```

Many languages severely restrict the format of the for-loop (which, as noted, is just syntactic sugar in C), so that it can *only* be used for indexing situations. For example, in Ada the for-loop can *only* be written as a process controlled by a single local index variable, which is implicitly defined by the loop. Thus, the previous C for-loop would be written in Ada as

```
for i in 0 .. size - 1 loop
       sum := sum + a(i);
end loop;
```

and i is implicitly defined and is local to the code of the loop. Even more, i is viewed as a *constant* within the body of the loop, so assignments to i are illegal (because this would disrupt the normal loop progression):

---

[6] Many C++ compilers as of this writing do not implement this correctly.

```
for i in 0 .. size - 1 loop
    sum := sum + a(i);
    if sum > 42 then i := size; -- illegal in Ada
    end if;
end loop;
```

This form of loop is often included in languages because it can be more effectively optimized than other loop constructs. For example, the control variable (and perhaps the final bound) can be put into registers, allowing extremely fast operations. Also, many processors have a single instruction that can both increment a register, test it, and branch, so that the loop control and increment can occur in a single machine instruction. To gain this efficiency, however, many restrictions must be enforced, such as those for Ada mentioned above. Most of the restrictions involve the control variable i. Typical restrictions are the following:

- The value of i cannot be changed within the body of the loop.
- The value of i is undefined after the loop terminates.
- i must be of restricted type and may not be declared in certain ways, for example, as a parameter to a procedure, or as a record field, or perhaps it must even be a local variable.

Further questions about the behavior of loops include:

- Are the bounds evaluated only once? If so, then the bounds may not change after execution begins.
- If the lower bound is greater than the upper bound, is the loop executed at all? Most modern languages perform a bound test at the beginning rather than the end of the loop, so the loop behaves like a while-loop. Some older FORTRAN implementations, however, have loops that always execute at least once.
- Is the control variable value undefined even if an exit or break statement is used to leave the loop before termination? Some languages permit the value to be available on "abnormal termination," but not otherwise.
- What translator checks are performed on loop structures? Some language definitions do not insist that a translator catch assignments to the control variable, which can cause unpredictable results.

Some languages, such as CLU, have a general form of for-loop construct that involves a new language object, called an **iterator**. Abstractly, an iterator must provide for the definition of control variables, an iteration scheme for these control variables (that is, a way of assigning a new value given its current value), and a facility for making termination tests. Thus, an iterator becomes something like a new type declaration (and can be put into the scheme of abstract data types in Chapter 9). An example taken from Liskov et al. [1977] is given in Figure 7.5.

```
(1)   numcount = proc (s: string) returns (int);
(2)      count: int = 0;
(3)      for c: char in stringchars(s) do
(4)         if numeric (c) then
(5)            count := count + 1;
(6)         end;
(7)      end;
(8)      return (count);
(9)   end numcount;

(10) stringchars = iter (s: string) yields (char);
(11)    index: int := 1;
(12)    limit: int := string$size(s);
(13)    while index <= limit do
(14)       yield (string$fetch(s, index))
(15)          index := index + 1;
(16)    end;
(17) end stringchars;
```

Figure 7.5   An Example of a CLU Iterator (Liskov et al. [1977], Figure 5)

The iterator is `stringchars` (Figure 7.5, lines 10–17). Iterators are defined like functions with a returned value (in this case, `char`—see the `yields` clause on line 10 of Figure 7.5). However, the effect of calling an iterator is as follows.

The first time an iterator is called, the values of its parameters are saved. The iterator then commences to execute, until it reaches a `yield` statement (as on line 14 of Figure 7.5), when it suspends execution and returns the value of the expression in the `yield`. Upon subsequent calls it resumes execution after the `yield`, suspending whenever it reaches another `yield`, until it exits, whence the loop from which it is called also is terminated.

7.4 The GOTO Controversy

Gotos are still the mainstay of a number of programming languages, such as Fortran77 and BASIC. For example, the Fortran77 code

```
10 IF (A(I).EQ.0) GOTO 20
   ...
   I  = I + 1
   GOTO 10
20 CONTINUE
```

is the Fortran77 equivalent of the C:

```
while (a[i] != 0)  i++;
```

With the increasing use of structured control in the 1960s, as pioneered by Algol60, computer scientists began a debate about the usefulness of gotos, since they can so easily lead to unreadable "spaghetti" code, as in Figure 7.6.

```
    IF (X.GT.0) GOTO 10
    IF (X.LT.0) GOTO 20
    X = 1
    GOTO 30
10  X = X + 1
    GOTO 30
20  X = -X
    GOTO 10
30  CONTINUE
```

Figure 7.6   An Example of "Spaghetti" Code in Fortran77

Then, in 1966, Böhm and Jacopini produced the theoretical result (mentioned in Chapter 1) that gotos were in fact *completely unnecessary*, since *every* possible control structure could be expressed using structured control constructs (although of course with the possible addition of a significant number of extra tests). Finally, in 1968, the computer scientist E. W. Dijkstra published a famous note ("GOTO Statement Considered Harmful," Dijkstra [1968]) in which he forcefully argued that not only were goto statements unnecessary, but that their use was damaging in many ways.

The goto statement is very close to actual machine code. As Dijkstra pointed out, its "unbridled" use can compromise even the most careful language design and lead to undecipherable programs. Dijkstra proposed that its use be severely controlled or even abolished. This unleashed one of the most persistent controversies in programming, which raged up until the late 1980s (and even occasionally causes outbursts to this day). At first, a large number of programmers simply refused to believe the theoretical result and considered programming without gotos to be impossible. However, the academic community began campaigning vigorously for Dijkstra's position, teaching goto-less programming whenever possible, and with the increasing influence of Pascal, which applies strong limits on the use of gotos, programmers gradually became used to the idea of only using gotos in rare situations, where the flow of control seems difficult to write in a natural way using standard loops and tests.

However, programmers continued to cling to the idea that the use of gotos *was* justified in certain cases, and that academicians were doing a disservice to the programming community by not teaching the "proper" use of gotos. This view was succinctly expressed in a letter in 1987 ("'Goto considered harmful' considered harmful," Rubin [1987]) which unleashed a new flurry of controversy over whether there was sufficient justification for the complete abolition of goto statements in high-level languages.

Nowadays, depending on the audience and point of view, this controversy may seem quaint. To this author's knowledge, no one has complained that Java takes the "extreme" position and abolishes the goto (in fact, Java makes goto into a reserved word, so that it cannot be used under any circumstances in a Java program). Part of the reason for the lack of complaints may be that Java provides significant alternatives to the use of gotos in those cases that have been used most frequently as arguments for the use of gotos. One such situation is the return of control to an outer nesting level from a deeply nested location (here written using a legal C goto):

```
if (ok)
  while (more)
  {   ...
      while(!found)
      {  ...
        if (disaster) goto 99;
        ...
      }
  }
99: ...
```

This can be written in Java using a **labeled break** statement:

```
ok_block:
if (ok)
  while (more)
  {   ...
      while(!found)
      {  ...
        if (disaster) break ok_block;
        ...
      }
  }
  ...
```

Labeled breaks are severely restricted in Java: The labels must be to an enclosing block within the same function (method); thus, they cannot be used to jump forward or nonlocally; they can only be used to jump "out" locally. On the other hand, a labeled break need not appear inside a loop or switch block.

Java also has a corresponding **labeled continue** statement, with the same restrictions on its use. A labeled continue statement must also be inside a loop, and the label must be on an enclosing loop (though not necessarily the nearest one).

Other modern languages that elect to retain the goto, such as Ada, also place significant Java-like restrictions on its use (unlike C and FORTRAN).

7.5 Exception Handling

So far all the control mechanisms we have studied have been **explicit**: At the point where a transfer of control takes place, there is a syntactic indication of the transfer. For example, in a **while**-loop, the loop begins with the keyword `while`. In a procedure call, the called procedure with its arguments is named at the point of call. There are situations, however, where transfer of control is **implicit**: The transfer is set up at a different point in the program than that where the actual transfer takes place. At the point where the transfer actually occurs, there may be then no syntactic indication that control will transfer at that point.

Such a situation is **exception handling**: the control of error conditions or other unusual events during the execution of a program. Exception handling involves the declaration of both exceptions and exception handlers. An exception is any unexpected or infrequent event. When an exception occurs, it is said to be **raised** or **thrown**. Typical examples of exceptions include runtime errors, such as out-of-range array subscripts or division by zero. In interpreted languages exceptions can also include static errors, such as syntax and type errors. (These errors are not exceptions for compiled languages, since a program containing them cannot be executed.) But exceptions need not be restricted to errors: An exception can be any unusual event, such as input failure or a timeout. An **exception handler** is a procedure or code sequence that is designed to be executed when a particular exception is raised and that is supposed to make it possible for normal execution to continue in some way. An exception handler is said to **handle** or **catch** an exception.

Exception handling was pioneered by the language PL/I in the 1960s and significantly advanced by CLU in the 1970s. However, it was only in the 1980s and early 1990s that design questions were largely resolved, and virtually all major current languages, including C++, Java, Ada, ML, and Common Lisp have built-in exception handling mechanisms (but not C, Scheme, or Smalltalk). Exception handling has in particular been integrated very well into object-oriented mechanisms in Java and C++, and into functional mechanism in ML and Common Lisp. Also, languages that do not have built-in mechanisms sometimes have libraries available that provide them, or have other built-in ways of simulating them. Still, exception handling techniques are often ignored when programming is taught and deserve more widespread use by working programmers.

In this chapter we will use C++ as our main example for exception handling, with additional overviews of Ada and ML exceptions.

Exception handling is an attempt to imitate in a programming language the features of a hardware interrupt or error trap, in which the processor transfers control automatically to a location that is specified in advance according to the kind of error or interrupt. It is reasonable to try to build such a feature into a language, since it is often unacceptable for a program to allow the underlying machine or operating system to take control. This usually means that the program is aborted, or "crashes." Programs that exhibit this behavior fail the test of **robustness**, which is part of the design criteria of security and reliability: A program must be able to recover from errors and continue execution.

But even in a language with a good exception mechanism, it is unreasonable to expect a program to be able to catch and handle every possible error that can occur. The reason is that too many possible failures can occur at too low a level—the failure of a hardware device, memory allocation problems, communication problems—all can lead to situations in which the underlying operating system may need to take drastic action to terminate a program, without the program being able to do anything about it. Such errors are sometimes referred to as **asynchronous** exceptions, since they can occur at any moment, not just in response to the execution of program code. By contrast, errors that a program can definitely catch are called **synchronous** exceptions: Exceptions that occur in direct response to actions by the program (such as trying to open a file, perform a particular calculation, or the like). User-defined exceptions can only be synchronous (since they must be raised directly in program code), but predefined or library exceptions may include a number of asynchronous exceptions, since the runtime environment for the language can cooperate with the operating system to allow a program to trap some asynchronous errors.

It is helpful in studying exception handling mechanisms to recall how exceptions can be dealt with in a language without such facilities. Exception conditions in such languages have to be found before an error occurs, and this assumes it is possible to test for them in the language. One can then attempt to handle the error at the location where it occurs, as in the following C code:

```
if (y == 0)
    handleError("denominator in ratio is zero");
else
    ratio = x / y;
```

Or, if the error occurs in a procedure, one can either pass an error condition back to the caller, as in the C code

```
enum ErrorKind {OutOfInput, BadChar, Normal};
  ...
ErrorKind getNumber ( unsigned* result)
{ int ch = fgetc(input);
  if (ch == EOF) return OutOfInput;
  else if (! isdigit(ch)) return BadChar;
  /* continue to compute */
  ...
  *result = ... ;
  return Normal;
}
```

or, alternatively, one could pass an exception handling procedure into the procedure as a parameter,

```
enum ErrorKind {OutOfInput, BadChar, Normal};
typedef void (*ErrorProc)(ErrorKind);
  ...
unsigned value;
  ...
```

```
void handler (ErrorKind error)
{
  ...
}
  ...
unsigned getNumber (ErrorProc handle)
{ unsigned result;
   int ch = fgetc(input);
   if (ch == EOF) handle(OutOfInput);
   else if (! isdigit(ch)) handle(BadChar);
   /* continue to compute */
   ...
   return result;
}
  ...
  ...
value = getNumber (handler);
```

Explicit exception testing makes a program more difficult to write, since the programmer must test in advance for all possible exceptional conditions. We would like to make this task easier by declaring exceptions in advance of their occurrence and specifying what a program is to do if an exception occurs. In designing such program behavior we must consider the following questions:

Exceptions. What exceptions are predefined in the language? Can they be disabled? Can user-defined exceptions be created? What is their scope?

Exception handlers. How are they defined? What is their scope? What default handlers are provided for predefined exceptions? Can they be replaced?

Control. How is control passed to a handler? Where does control pass after a handler is executed? What runtime environment remains after an error handler executes?

We will discuss each of these topics in turn with examples from C++, Ada, and ML, and then conclude with a more extensive example from C++.

7.5.1 Exceptions

Typically an exception occurrence in a program is represented by a data object, and this data object may be either predefined or user-defined. Not surprisingly, in a functional language this data object is a *value* of some type, while in a structured or object-oriented language it is a variable or object of some structured type. Typically the *type* of an exception value or object is predefined, and exceptions themselves are given in a special declaration that creates a value or variable of the appropriate type. For example, in ML or Ada an exception is declared using the reserved word `exception`:

```
exception Trouble; (* a user-defined exception *)
exception Big_Trouble; (* another user-defined excep-
                                                    tion *)
```

Unusually, in C++ there is no special exception type, and thus no reserved word to declare them. Instead, any structured type (struct or class) may be used to represent an exception:[7]

```
struct Trouble {} trouble;
struct Big_Trouble {} big_trouble;
```

Now, these declarations as shown are minimal, since they only provide simple values or objects that represent the occurrence of an exception. Typically, we would want also some additional information to be attached to these exceptions, such as an error message (a string) and also perhaps a summary of the data or program state that led to the exception (such as a numeric value that led to an invalid computation, or an input character that was unexpected). It is easy to see how to do this in C++—we simply add data members to the defined data structure:

```
struct Trouble
{ string error_message;
  int wrong_value;
} trouble;
```

In ML this can also be done:

```
exception Trouble of string * int;
```

Unusually, in Ada this cannot be done directly: Exception objects are constants that contain no data.[8]

Exception declarations such as the above typically observe the same scope rules as other declarations in the language. Thus, in Ada, ML, and C++ lexical, or static, scope rules are observed for exception declarations. Since exceptions occur during runtime and, as we shall see below, can cause execution to exit the scope of a particular exception declaration, it can happen that an exception cannot be referred to by name when it is handled, and the design of a handler must take this into account. Typically, one wishes to minimize the trouble that this causes by declaring user-defined exceptions globally in a program. Local exceptions may under certain circumstances make sense, however, to avoid creating a large number of superfluous global exceptions. Note also that, when data are included in an exception, we want to separate the exception *type* declaration from the exception *object/value* declaration, since in general different instances of the same exception type may exist simultanously with

---

[7] Since we do not discuss the object-oriented features of C++ until Chapter 11, we write C++ code that is as close to C as possible in this section, even though somewhat unidiomatic.

[8] Ada95 does add a library Ada.Exceptions that has mechanisms for passing information along with exceptions, but it is not as clean as adding data to the exception objects themselves.

different data, so the objects/values must be created as the exceptions occur. As long as the exception types themselves are global, no scope issues result, as we will see below. Thus, the C++ declaration above (which defines a variable as well as a type) should be amended to only declare a type:

```
struct Trouble
{ string error_message;
  int wrong_value;
} ; // declare exception object later
```

Most languages also provide some predefined exception values or types. For instance, in Ada there are the following predefined exceptions:

Constraint_Error: Caused by exceeding the bounds of a subrange or array; also caused by arithmetic overflow and division by zero.

Program_Error: This includes errors that occur during the dynamic processing of a declaration.

Storage_Error: This is caused by the failure of dynamic memory allocation.

Tasking_Error: This occurs during concurrency control.

In ML there are a number of similar predefined exceptions, such as Div (division by 0), Overflow (arithmetic), Size (memory allocation), and Subscript (array subscript out of bounds); additional predefined exceptions exist that have to do with specific program constructs in ML and which correspond roughly to Ada's Program_Error. There also is a predefined value constructor Fail of string that allows a program to construct exception values containing an error message, without having to define a new exception type.

In C++, in keeping with usual practice, there are no predefined exception types or exceptions in the language proper. However, many standard library modules provide exceptions and exception mechanisms. Some of these standard exceptions are:

bad_alloc: Failure of call to new.

bad_cast: Failure of a dynamic_cast (see Chapter 10).

out_of_range: Caused by a checked subscript operation on library containers (the usual subscript operation is not checked).

overflow_error, underflow_error, range_error: Caused by math library functions and a few others.

We also mention below another standard exception, bad_exception, which can be useful in handling exceptions in C++.

7.5.2 Exception handlers

In C++ exception handlers are associated with **try-catch** blocks, which can appear anywhere a statement can appear. A sketch of a C++ try-catch block appears in Figure 7.7.

```
(1)   try
(2)   { // to perform some processing
(3)      ...
(4)   }
(5)   catch (Trouble t)
(6)   { // handle the trouble, if possible
(7)      displayMessage(t.error_message);
(8)      ...
(9)   }
(10)  catch (Big_Trouble b)
(11)  { // handle big trouble, if possible
(12)     ...
(13)  }
(14)  catch (...) // actual three dots here, not an ellipsis!
(15)  { // handle any remaining uncaught exceptions
(16)  }
```

Figure 7.7   A C++ Try-catch Block

Here the compound statement after the reserved word `try` is required (the curly brackets on lines 2 and 4 of Figure 7.7), and any number of `catch` blocks can follow the initial `try` block. Each `catch` block also requires a compound statement, and is written as a function of a single parameter whose type is an exception type (which can be any class or structure type). The exception parameter may be consulted to retrieve appropriate exception information, as in line 7 of Figure 7.7. Note also in Figure 7.7 that there is a "catch-all" catch block at the end that catches any remaining exceptions, as indicated by the three dots inside the parentheses on line 14.

The syntax of try-catch blocks in C++ is really overkill, since catch blocks could have been associated with any statement or block. Indeed in Ada and ML that is exactly the case. For example, in Ada the reserved word `exception` is reused to introduce handlers, and these can appear at the end of any block, as shown in Figure 7.8, which contains Ada code corresponding to the C++ code of Figure 7.7. Note also the similarity of the syntax of the `exception` list (lines 5–13 of Figure 7.8) to that of the Ada `case` statement.

```
(1)   begin
(2)      -- try to perform some processing
(3)      ...
(4)   exception
(5)      when Trouble =>
(6)         --handle trouble, if possible
(7)         displayMessage("trouble here!");
(8)         ...
(9)      when Big_Trouble =>
(10)        -- handle big trouble, if possible
(11)        ...
(12)     when others =>
```

(13)   -- handle any remaining uncaught exceptions
(14) end;

Figure 7.8   An Ada Try-catch Block Corresponding to Figure 7.7

In ML, the reserved word handle can come at the end of any expression, and introduces the handlers for exceptions generated by that expression, as shown in Figure 7.9.

```
(1)   val try_to_stay_out_of_trouble =
(2)   (* try to compute some value *)
(3)   handle
(4)      Trouble (message,value) =>
(5)          ( displayMessage(message); ... ) |
(6)      Big_Trouble =>   ...   |
(7)      _ =>
(8)          (* handle any remaining uncaught exceptions *)
(9)          ...
(10) ;
```

Figure 7.9   An Example of ML Exception Handling Corresponding to
              Figures 7.7 and 7.8

Exceptions in ML are distinguished by pattern-matching/unification within the handle clause (see Chapters 6 and 11), and the syntax is again similar to that of the case expression in ML (Section 7.2, Figure 7.4). In particular, the underscore character on line 7 of Figure 7.9 in the handler is again a wildcard pattern as in Figure 7.4, and has the same effect as the Ada others clause or the C++ catch(...): It will match any exception not previously handled.

The scope of handlers defined as above extends of course only to the statements/expression that they are attached to. If an exception reaches such a handler, it replaces whatever handlers may exist elsewhere, including predefined handlers.

Predefined handlers typically simply print a minimal error message, indicating the kind of exception, and possibly some information on the program location where it occurred, and terminate the program. None of the three languages we are considering here require any additional behavior. Also, in Ada and ML there is no way to change the behavior of default handlers, except to write a handler as we have just indicated.

C++, on the other hand, offers a way to replace the default handler by a user-defined handler, using the <exceptions> standard library module. One does this by calling the set_terminate function, passing it an argument consisting of a void function taking no parameters. This function will then be called as the default handler for all exceptions not explicitly caught in the program code.

In Ada it is not possible to replace the default handling action with a different one, but it is possible to *disable* the default handler by telling the compiler not to include code to perform certain checks, such as bounds or range checking. This is done using the **suppress** pragma (compiler directive), as in:

```
pragma suppress(Overflow_Check, On => Float);
```

which turns off all overflow checking for floating-point numbers throughout this pragma's scope (such a pragma is viewed as a declaration with standard scope rules). This can mean that such an Ada program runs to completion and produces incorrect results without any error message being generated. Normally, this is precisely the kind of program behavior that Ada was designed to prevent. However, in those cases where maximum efficiency is needed and the programmers are certain of the impossibility of an exception occurring, this feature can be helpful.

7.5.3 Control

Finally, in this subsection we discuss how exceptions are reported, and how control may pass to a handler. Typically, a predefined or built-in exception is either automatically raised by the runtime system, or it can be manually raised by the program. User-defined exceptions can, of course, only be raised manually by the program.

C++ uses the reserved word **throw** and an exception object to raise an exception:

```
if (/* something goes wrong */)
{ Trouble t; // create a new Trouble var to hold info
  t.error_message = "Bad news!";
  t.wrong_value = current_item;
  throw t;
}
else if (/* something even worse happens */)
    throw big_trouble; // can use global var, since no info
```

Ada and ML both use the reserved word **raise**:

```
-- Ada code:
if -- something goes wrong
then
    raise Trouble; -- use Trouble as a constant
elsif -- something even worse happens
then
    raise Big_Trouble; -- use Big_Trouble as a constant
end if;

(* ML code: *)
if (* something goes wrong *)
then (* construct a Trouble value *)
    raise Trouble("Bad news!",current_item)
else if (* something even worse happens *)
    raise Big_Trouble (* Big_Trouble is a constant *)
else ... ;
```

When an exception is raised, typically the current computation is abandoned, and the runtime system begins a search for a handler. In Ada and C++, this search begins with the handler section of the block in which the exception was raised. If no handler is found, then the handler section of the next enclosing block is consulted, and so on (this process is called **propagating the exception**). If the outermost block of a function or procedure is reached without finding a handler, then the call is exited to the caller, and the exception is re-raised in the caller as though the call itself had raised the exception. This proceeds until either a handler is found, or the main program is exited, in which case the default handler is called. The process is similar in ML, with expressions and subexpressions replacing blocks.

The process of exiting back through function calls to the caller during the search for a handler is called **call unwinding** or **stack unwinding**, the stack being the call stack whose structure is described in detail in the next chapter.

Once a handler has been found and executed, there remains the question of where to continue execution. One choice is to return to the point at which the exception was first raised, and begin execution again with that statement or expression. This is called the **resumption model** of exception handling, and it requires that, during the search for a handler and possible call unwinding, the original environment and call structure must be preserved and re-established prior to the resumption of execution.

The alternative to the resumption model is to continue execution with the code immediately following the block or expression in which the handler that is executed was found. This is called the **termination model** of exception handling, since it essentially discards all the unwound calls and blocks until a handler is found.

Virtually all modern languages, including C++, ML, and Ada, use the termination model of exception handling. The reasons are not obvious, but experience has shown that termination is easier to implement and fits better into structured programming techniques, while resumption is rarely needed and can be sufficiently simulated by the termination model when it is needed.

Here is an example of how to simulate the resumption model using termination in C++. Suppose a call to new failed because there was not enough free memory left, and we wished to call a garbage collector and then try again. We could write the code as follows:

```
while (true)
    try
    { x = new X; // try to allocate
      break; // if we get here, success!
    }
    catch (bad_alloc)
    { collect_garbage(); // can't exit yet!
      if ( /* still not enough memory */)
        // must give up to avoid infinite loop
        throw bad_alloc;
    }
```

Finally, we mention also that exception handling often carries substantial runtime overhead (see the next chapter for details). For that reason, and also because exceptions represent a not very structured control alternative, we want to avoid overusing exceptions to implement ordinary control situations, where simple tests would do the job. For example, given a binary search tree data structure (containing, e.g., integers), such as

```
struct Tree
{  int data;
    Tree * left;
    Tree * right;
};
```

we could write a search routine as in Figure 7.10.

```
void fnd (Tree* p, int i) // helper procedure
{ if (p != 0)
     if (i == p->data) throw p;
     else if (i <p->data) fnd(p->left,i);
     else fnd(p->right,i);
}

Tree * find (Tree* p, int i)
{   try
    { fnd(p,i);
    }
    catch(Tree* q)
    {   return q;
    }
    return 0;
}
```

Figure 7.10   A Binary Tree find Function in C++ Using Exceptions (Adapted from Stroustrup [1997], pp. 374–375.)

However, this code is likely to run much more slowly than a more standard search routine that does not use exceptions. Also, more standard code is probably easier to understand.

7.5.4   Exception specifications and an example in C++

Since exception handling is rarely taught with sufficient detail, we present here a relatively complete example of a program in C++ using exception handling. The program we use as the basis for our example is the recursive-descent calculator for simple integer arithmetic listed in Figure 4.12. This example, rewritten as a complete C++ program with exception handling added, is given in Figure 7.11. We will discuss it in detail shortly. However, we have used in that program an additional exception feature available in C++ and Java, (but not Ada or ML) that we have not previously discussed: exception specifications. We wish to discuss this feature first.

An **exception specification** is a list of exceptions added to the declaration of a function guaranteeing that the function will only throw the exceptions in the list, and no others. The syntax in C++ is as in the following example:

```
int f (int x) throw (Trouble,BigTrouble) ...
```

In this example, the list of exception types in parentheses after `throw` indicates that the function f will only throw the two exceptions `Trouble` and `Big_Trouble`, and no others.

Exception specifications represent important guarantees about what exceptions can appear in which contexts. Without them, we can only determine which exceptions can occur at a particular point in a program by examining the code for all functions that may directly or indirectly be called at that point. Indeed, without an exception specification, a function in C++ is assumed to be capable of throwing *any* exception, clearly an unhappy state of affairs.[9] In a program with strong exception handling, one expects that at the top level (`main` or the functions `main` calls), functions should throw no exceptions. One can announce that in an exception specification too:

```
// g should not throw an exception
int g( int x) throw () ...
```

Of course, since C++ does not *require* the use of exception specifications, a C++ compiler cannot check that an exception specification is correct, since a function might call other functions without exception specifications, and the compiler cannot in general tell which exceptions those functions might generate. Indeed, in C++ an exception specification is not part of the type of a function.[10] However, exception specifications can be used by the compiler in two important ways. First, the compiler can perform some optimizations that make exception handling more efficient. Second, the compiler can rewrite the code of a function in such a way that it *cannot* throw any exceptions other than the ones listed. Indeed, in C++ a compiler is *required* to convert any violation of an exception specification into a call to a special standard library function `unexpected()`, which takes no parameters and which also does not return (its default behavior is to call `abort()`). Thus, when calling a function with an exception specification, it is useless to try to catch exceptions that are not listed in the specification, since they cannot occur. This is an important check on the correctness of exception specifications. Of course, C++ allows the default behavior of the `unexpected()` function to be changed, and it can be used as a significant debugging tool.

---

[9] Java's view is exactly the opposite: A function without an exception specification is *not allowed* to throw synchronous exceptions, and in general Java is much stricter than C++ in enforcing exception specifications, as we would expect.

[10] C++ compilers *do* check for consistency in the exception specifications of multiple declarations of the same function.

We now turn to a discussion of the example program using exceptions in Figure 7.11.

```
(1)    #include <iostream>
(2)    #include <string>

(3)    using namespace std;

(4)    int token;

(5)    struct InputError {} inputError;
(6)    struct UnexpectedChar { char got; };
(7)    struct NumberExpected { char got; };
(8)    struct ExtraChars { string chars; };
(9)    struct Unwind {} unwind;

(10)   void command() throw (Unwind,InputError);
(11)   int expr() throw (Unwind, InputError);
(12)   int term() throw (Unwind, InputError);
(13)   int factor() throw (Unwind, InputError);
(14)   int number() throw (NumberExpected,InputError);
(15)   int digit() throw (NumberExpected,InputError);

(16)   void getToken() throw (InputError)
(17)   { token = cin.get();
(18)     if (cin.fail()) throw inputError;
(19)   }

(20)   void match(char c) throw (InputError,UnexpectedChar)
(21)   { if (token == c) getToken();
(22)     else
(23)     { UnexpectedChar u; // struct not required in C++
(24)       u.got = token;
(25)       throw u;
(26)     }
(27)   }

(28)   void command() throw (Unwind,InputError)
(29)   { try
(30)     { int result = expr();
(31)       if (token != '\n')
(32)       { ExtraChars e; // struct not required
(33)         while (token != '\n')
(34)         { e.chars += token;
(35)           getToken();
(36)         }
(37)         throw e;
(38)       }
(39)       else
```

Figure 7.11   Recusive Descent Calculator for Simple Integer Arithmetic
              Expressions—Exception Handling Version

```
(40)            cout << "The result is: " << result;
(41)    }
(42)    catch (ExtraChars e)
(43)    { cout << "Extra characters found in command: "
(44)             << e.chars << endl
(45)             << "(missing op or extra right paren?)\n";
(46)      throw unwind;
(47)    }
(48)    catch (Unwind u)
(49)    { cout << "Unwinding command\n";
(50)      throw;
(51)    }
(52)  }

(53)  int expr() throw (Unwind,InputError)
(54)  { try
(55)    { int result = term();
(56)      while (token == '+')
(57)      { match('+');
(58)        result += term();
(59)      }
(60)      return result;
(61)    }
(62)    catch (Unwind u)
(63)    { cout << "Unwinding expression\n";
(64)      throw;
(65)    }
(66)  }

(67)  int term() throw (Unwind,InputError)
(68)  { try
(69)    { int result = factor();
(70)      while (token == '*')
(71)      { match('*');
(72)        result *= factor();
(73)      }
(74)      return result;
(75)    }
(76)    catch (Unwind u)
(77)    { cout << "Unwinding term\n";
(78)      throw;
(79)    }
(80)  }
(81)  int factor() throw (Unwind,InputError)
(82)  { try
(83)    { int result;
(84)      if (token == '(')
(85)      { match('(');                          (continues)
```

(continued)

```
(86)          result = expr();
(87)          match(')');
(88)        }
(89)      else
(90)        result = number();
(91)      return result;
(92)    }
(93)    catch (UnexpectedChar u)
(94)    { cout << "Expected right parenthesis in factor\n"
(95)          << "found: " << u.got << endl;
(96)      throw unwind;
(97)    }
(98)    catch (Unwind u)
(99)    { cout << "Unwinding factor\n";
(100)     throw;
(101)   }
(102)   catch (NumberExpected n)
(103)   { cout << "Number expected in factor\n"
(104)         << "found: " << n.got << endl;
(105)     throw unwind;
(106)   }
(107) }

(108) int number() throw (NumberExpected,InputError)
(109) { int result = digit();
(110)   while (isdigit(token))
(111)     result = 10 * result + digit();
(112)   return result;
(113) }

(114) int digit() throw (NumberExpected,InputError)
(115) { if (isdigit(token))
(116)   { int result = token - '0';
(117)     match(token);
(118)     return result;
(119)   }
(120)   else
(121)   { NumberExpected n; // struct not required
(122)     n.got = token;
(123)     throw n;
(124)   }
(125) }

(126) void parse() throw (InputError)
(127) { try
(128)   { getToken();
(129)     command();
(130)   }
```

```
(131)    catch (Unwind u)
(132)    { cout << "Unwinding parse\n";
(133)    }
(134) }

(135) int main()
(136) { try
(137)    { parse();
(138)    }
(139)    catch (InputError i)
(140)    { cout << "Input error in parse\n";
(141)    }
(142)    return 0;
(143) }
```

Figure 7.11   Recusive Descent Calculator for Simple Integer Arithmetic
Expressions—Exception Handling Version

First, consider the original program of Figure 4.12. It handles errors by calling an `error` procedure that simply prints a generic error message and calls `exit`. Thus, no information about errors is transmitted. We would like to replace the `error` procedure by exception handlers, and the calls to `error` by throws of exceptions with appropriate information. In the listing of Figure 4.12, `error` is called three times: inside `match`, inside `command`, and inside `digit`. We will deal with each of these calls in turn.

The `match` procedure calls `error` when it is called to match a character that is not the current one. We will call this error `UnexpectedChar`. The `command` procedure calls `error` when the check for an end of line fails, indicating extra trailing characters after an expression has been parsed. We will call this error `ExtraChars`. Finally, the call to `error` inside `digit` means that a character other than a left parenthesis or digit is encountered in the input. We will call this exception `NumberExpected`.

There is one other possibility for an error to occur, and that is when the `getToken` procedure fails to get a character from the input when it is called. Typically, this only happens if an end of file or system error occurs in the input, but this is still a synchronous error and we should handle it as an exception. We will call it `InputError`.

Finally, reporting errors is not the only thing that exception handling is good at—it can also be used to generate debugging information about the program state when the error was encountered. One very useful piece of information is a **call trace** (or **stack trace**), indicating which procedures had been called when the error occurred. Some language processors even add a call trace to the information printed by the default handler when an uncaught exception is generated by a program (Java interpreters always do this). In our case, we can use the unwinding process during the handler search to print such a call trace. Since we want to do this regardless of the error generated, we will convert the other exceptions into an `Unwind` exception after the initial error handling—except for `InputError`, which rarely occurs, and for which we will print no call trace.

We therefore have a total of five different exceptions to define. The next step is to consider what kind of data to associate with each exception. An error message string is a natural piece of data to include with all exceptions, but in this case the exceptions themselves are sufficiently distinct so that the handlers themselves can construct appropriate error messages. It remains to decide what data are appropriate for each exception to contain. Clearly UnexpectedChar and NumberExpected are errors that occur when an input character (in the token variable) is not what we expect; thus these should record the character that was actually encountered when the exception was raised. ExtraChars will want to record the extra characters seen in the input, and so should contain a string of these extra characters (we use the C++ string class here rather than char*). Finally, InputError and Unwind have no particular data associated with them, so we leave them as empty structures. The final definitions are (lines 5–9 in Figure 7.11):

```
struct InputError {} inputError;
struct UnexpectedChar { char got; };
struct NumberExpected { char got; };
struct ExtraChars { string chars; };
struct Unwind {} unwind;
```

Note that we also define global variables for InputError and Unwind, which (because there are no data that would require distinct objects) we use to generate these exceptions.

The next step is to decide on the exception specifications for all of the functions. Clearly all mutually recursive procedures will need to throw Unwind. Procedure digit and number, however, are not recursive and do not need to do so.[11] Procedure command is the top-level parsing procedure, and for consistency it will also throw Unwind, even though it is not recursive. All functions will have to throw InputError, since they all implicitly or explicitly call getToken, and we do not trap this error locally. The only UnexpectedChar error that can occur in this particular parse is in factor (the call to match(')') on line 87), and the only NumberExpected error occurs in digit (and will be propagated to number). Thus, the procedures that throw these exceptions is limited. The complete specifications are listed in the declarations on lines 10–15, and in the individual function definitions.

Finally, we need to insert appropriate try/catch blocks and throw statements. For instance, factor will catch three possible exceptions—UnexpectedChar (for a missing right parenthesis), Unwind (for recursive calls to expr), and NumberExpected (for a failed call to number). All three will be rethrown as Unwind exceptions. (InputError will be ignored and passed through to main.) Note in all of the catches of Unwind how it is rethrown by using the throw keyword without an exception object

---

[11] As we noted in Chapter 4, digit and number are more appropriately part of a scanner.

(lines 50, 64, and 78)—this implicitly reraises the exception with the same exception object in the caller.

Finally, we note some of the output produced by the program of Figure 7.11:

Input:

```
()
```

Output:

```
Number expected in factor
found: )
Unwinding term
Unwinding expression
Unwinding factor
Unwinding term
Unwinding expression
Unwinding command
Unwinding parse
```

Input:

```
2+3*4   5*6
```

Output:

```
Extra characters found in command:    5*6
(missing oper or extra right paren?)
Unwinding parse
```

Input:

```
(23#
```

Output:

```
Expected right parenthesis in factor
found: #
Unwinding term
Unwinding expression
Unwinding command
Unwinding parse
```

Exercises

7.1 Rewrite the following infix expression in prefix and postfix and draw the syntax tree:

$$(3 - 4) / 5 + 6 * 7$$

7.2 Write a BNF description of **(a)** postfix arithmetic expressions and **(b)** prefix arithmetic expressions.

7.3 Modify the recursive descent calculator of Figure 4.12 to translate infix expressions to postfix expressions.

7.4 In LISP the following unparenthesized prefix expression is ambiguous:

    + 3 * 4 5 6

Why? Give two possible parenthesized interpretations.

7.5 Examples were given in the text that show the usefulness of a short-circuit and operation. Give an example to show the usefulness of a short-circuit or operation.

7.6 Write a program to prove that short-circuit evaluation is used for the logical operators of C/C++.

7.7 Write a program to determine the order of evaluation of function arguments for your C/C++/Ada compiler.

7.8 Java specifies that all expressions, including arguments to calls, are evaluated left to right. Why does Java do this, while C/C++ does not?

7.9 We noted in Chapter 4 that the "+" operator is left associative, so that in the expression $a + b + c$, the expression $a + b$ is computed and then added to c. Yet we stated in Section 7.1 that an expression $a + b$ may be computed by computing b before a. Is there a contradiction here? Does your answer also apply to the subtraction operator? Explain.

7.10 Suppose we were to try to write a short-circuit version of and in C as the following function:

```
int and (int a, int b)
{   return a ? b : 0
}
```

(a) Why doesn't this work?
(b) Would it work if normal order evaluation were used? Why?

7.11 Describe one benefit of normal order evaluation. Describe one drawback.

7.12 Consider the expressions

    (x != 0) and (y % x == 0)

and

    (y % x == 0) and (x != 0)

In theory, both these expressions could have value false if x == 0.
(a) Which of these expressions has a value in C?
(b) Which of these expressions has a value in Ada?
(c) Would it be possible for a programming language to require that both have values? Explain.

7.13 Describe the difference between the C/C++ operators **&&** and **||** and the operators **&** and **|**. Are these latter operators short-circuit? Why or why not?

7.14 Given the two functions (in C syntax):

```
int cube (int x) { return x*x*x; }
int sum (int x, int y, int z) { return x + y + z; }
```

describe the process of normal order evaluation of the expression `sum(cube(2),cube(3),cube(4))`, and compare it to applicative order evaluation. In particular, how many additions and multiplications are performed using each method?

7.15 A problem exists in normal order evaluation of recursive functions. Describe the problem using as an example the recursive factorial function

```
int factorial (int n)
{ if (n == 0) return 1; else return n * factorial
( n - 1 ); }
```

Propose a possible solution to the problem, and illustrate it with the above function, using the call `factorial(3)`.

7.16 Describe the process of evaluating the expression `factorial(5)` using normal order. When are the subtractions (such as $5 - 1$) performed? When are the multiplications (such as $5 * 24$) performed?

7.17 C insists that a sequence of statements be surrounded by braces { ... } in structured statements such as while-statements:

while-stmt → `while` (*expression*) *statement*

statement → *compound-statement* | ...

compound-statement → { [*declaration-list*] [*statement-list*] }

statement-list → *statement-list statement* | *statement*

Suppose that we eliminated the braces in compound statements and wrote the grammar as follows:

while-stmt → `while` (*expression*) *statement*

statement → *compound-statement* | ...

compound-statement → [*declaration-list*] [*statement-list*]

statement-list → *statement-list statement* | *statement*

Show that this grammar is ambiguous. What can be done to correct it without going back to the C convention?

7.18 The **default** case in a **switch** statement in C/C++ corresponds in a way to the else-part of an if-statement. Is there a corresponding "dangling-default" ambiguity similar to the dangling-else ambiguity in C/C++? Explain.

7.19 Since the `default` case in a `switch` statement in C/C++ is similar to the else-part of an if-statement, why not use the reserved word `else` instead of the new keyword `default`? What design principles apply here?

7.20 Show how to imitate a while-statement in C/C++ with a do-statement.

7.21 Show how to imitate a for-statement in C/C++ with a do-statement.

7.22 Show how to imitate a while-statement in C/C++ with a for-statement.

7.23 Show how to imitate a do-statement in C/C++ with a for-statement.

7.24 We saw in this chapter (and in Exercise 6.14) that it makes sense to have an if-expression in a language.
 (a) Does it make sense to have a while-expression; that is, can a while-expression return a value, and if so, what value?
 (b) Does it make sense to have a case-or switch-expression; that is, can a case-expression return a value, and if so, what value?
 (c) Does it make sense to have a do-or repeat-expression; that is, can a do-expression return a value, and if so, what value?

7.25 We noted in the text that, in a language that uses normal order evaluation, an if-expression can be written as an ordinary function. Can a while-expression be written in such a language? Explain.

7.26 Show how to write repeat and loop-exit statements in Fortran77 using GOTO statements.

7.27 An important difference between the semantics of the case-statement in C/C++ and Ada is that an unlisted case causes a runtime error in Ada, while in C/C++, execution "falls through" to the statement following the case-statement. Compare these two conventions with respect to the design principles of Chapter 3. Which principles apply?

7.28 (Aho, Sethi, and Ullman [1986])   The problem with the dangling else in C/C++ can be fixed by writing more complicated syntax rules. One attempt to do so might be as follows:

statement → `if` `(` *expression* `)` *statement* | *matched-statement*

matched-statement →

   `if` `(` *expression* `)` *matched-statement* `else` *statement* | ...

 (a) Show that this grammar is still ambiguous.
 (b) How can it be fixed so that the grammar expresses the most closely nested rule unambiguously?

7.29 Locate a grammar for the Java language, and describe how it fixes the dangling else ambiguity. How many extra grammar rules does it use to do this?

7.30 Here are three possible switch-statements in C/C++/Java syntax:

```
int x = 2;
switch (x) x++;

int x = 2;
switch (x)
{ x ++; }

int x = 2;
switch (x)
{ case 1: if (x > 2)
  case 2:    x++;
  default: break;
}
```

(a) Which of these are legal in C/C++? For those that are legal, what is the value of x after each is executed?

(b) Which of these are legal in Java? For those that are legal, what is the value of x after each is executed?

7.31 Here is a legal switch-statement in C/C++:

```
int n = ...;
int q = (n + 3) / 4;
switch (n % 4)
{ case 0:  do {  n++;
  case 3:       n++;
  case 2:       n++;
  case 1:       n++;
  } while (--q > 0);
}
```

Suppose n has the value **(a)** 0; **(b)** 1; **(c)** 5; **(d)** 8. What is the value of n in each case after the execution of the above switch-statement? Can you state a general rule for the value of n after this code executes? If so, state it. If not, explain why not.

7.32 Describe the effect of the FORTRAN "spaghetti code" of Figure 7.6, Section 7.4. Write C/C++ statements without GOTOs that are equivalent to the FORTRAN code.

7.33 Clark [1973] humorously describes a "come from" statement as a replacement for the GOTO statement:

```
10 J = 1
11 COME FROM 20
12 PRINT *, J
   STOP
13 COME FROM 10
20 J = J + 2
```

This sample program in FORTRAN syntax prints 3 and stops. Develop a description of the semantics of the COME FROM statement. What problems might a translator have generating code for such a statement?

7.34 Rubin [1987] used the following example to "prove" that GOTOs are essential to clear and concise code:

```
for (i = 0; i < n; i++)
{ for (j = 0; j < n; j++)
    if (x[i][j] != 0) goto reject;
  printf("First all-zero row is: %d\n",i);
  break;
reject:
}
```

This program is supposed to find the first zero row in a matrix x[n][n], with n >= 0.

(a) Rewrite this program without goto or break statements.

(b) Rewrite this program without the goto statement, but with break or continue statements.

(c) Do you agree with Rubin? Why or why not?

7.35 The labeled break in Java was discussed in this chapter using the following example:

```
ok_block:
if (ok)
  while (more)
  {   ...
      while(!found)
      {   ...
          if (disaster) break ok_block;
          ...
      }
  }
```

This seems difficult to read—it should look like

```
if (ok)
while (more)
{   ...
    while(!found)
    {   ...
        if (disaster) break ok_block;
        ...
    }
}
ok_block:
```

(a) Why is this latter form illegal in Java?

(b) Would it be possible to relax the rules for Java labeled breaks to allow this form? Explain.

7.36 Rewrite the code of Exercise 7.34 in Java using labeled breaks. Does this improve its readability and writability?

7.37 C++ and Java loops are often written with empty bodies by placing all side effects into the tests, such as in the following two examples:

```
i = 0;
while (a[i++] != 0);

for (i = 0; a[i] != 0; i++);
```

(a) Are these loops equivalent?

(b) Are there any advantages or disadvantages to using this style of code? Explain.

7.38 Test each of the following C/C++ code fragments with a translator of your choice (or rewrite it into another language and test it) and explain its behavior:

(a)

```
int i, n = 3;
for (i = 1; i <= n; i++)
{ printf ("i = %d\n", i);
   n = 2;
}
```

(b)

```
int i;
for (i = 1; i <= 3; i++)
{ printf ("i = %d\n", i);
   i = 3;
}
```

7.39 Rewrite the program of Figure 7.11 in Ada.

7.40 Consider the C++ simple expression calculator of Figure 7.11. Trace the behavior of the program and describe its output for the following inputs:

(a) ((3+))

(b) +2

(c) <enter> (i.e., empty input)

7.41 Consider the C++ simple expression recognizer of Figure 7.11. Suppose we replaced the exception specification of factor (lines 13 and 81 of Figure 7.11) with the following:

```
void factor() throw (InputError)
```

What would the output of the program be then, when given the input "( )"?

7.42 Some software engineers feel that exception specifications are too difficult to use in practice and have little benefit.

(a) Eliminate the exception specification for `factor` and compare the behavior of the program with that of the previous exercise for the given input.

(b) Do you agree with the above statement about exception specifications? Explain.

7.43 The simple expression calculator of Figure 7.11 gives reasonably complete error messages and a call trace, but it still doesn't *recover* from any errors. Add the following simple error recovery to the program: Have the program skip over any characters other than digits, the arithmetic operators (+ and *) and the parentheses, and continue to recognize an expression as if those characters were not there. Thus, your new recognizer will generate no error messages given an expression such as "&(2#+@3) *4$5!"

7.44 Note that the suggestion given in the previous exercise allows white space (blanks and tabs) to be skipped, along with other extraneous characters.

(a) Would it be possible to limit the characters skipped to *just* white space?

(b) Would this be a reasonable alternative to skipping white space in a scanner, as described in Chapter 4?

7.45 Give an example in C++ or Ada of an exception that is propagated out of its scope.

7.46 In Section 7.5 three alternatives to simulating exceptions were discussed: (1) testing for an error condition before the error occurs; (2) passing a flag (an enumerated type) back as well as a value to indicate success or various failure outcomes; or (3) passing an error-handling function as a parameter. A fourth alternative is a variation on (2), where instead of passing two values back, one of which is a flag, we indicate an error by using an actual value, such as −1 or 999 that is not a legal value for the computation, but is still a legal value for the result type. Discuss the advantages and disadvantages of this method compared to the use of an enumerated flag. What design principles from Chapter 3 apply?

7.47 Suppose in a C++ `try` block you had some code that you wanted to execute on exit, regardless of whether an exception occurred or not. Where would you have to place this code? What if the code needed to be executed only if an exception did *not* occur?

7.48 (a) Rewrite the binary search tree `find` function of Figure 7.10, Section 7.5.3 to eliminate the use of an exception.

(b) Compare the running times of your version of `find` in part (a) with the version in the text.

7.49 Suppose we wrote the following `try` block in C++:

```
try
{ // do something
}
catch (...) { cout << "general error!\n"; }
catch (range_error) { cout << "range error\n"; }
```

What is wrong with this code?

Notes and References

Normal and applicative order evaluation is described in Abelson and Sussman [1996] and Paulson [1996]. We will see normal order evaluation again in Chapter 8 in the pass by name parameter passing mechanism of Algol60 and also in Chapter 11 when discussing delayed evaluation and the lambda calculus.

Dijkstra's guarded if and guarded do commands are described in Dijkstra [1975]. Hoare describes his design of the case-statement in Hoare [1981]. Labeled breaks in Java are discussed in detail in Arnold et al. [2000]; Java also has labeled `continue` statements, and their use is also discussed in that reference. The unusual use of a C switch-statement in Exercise 7.31 is called Duff's device in Gosling et al. [2000, page 289]. The dangling-else ambiguity is discussed in Louden [1997], Aho, Sethi, and Ullman [1986], and Gosling et al. [2000]; these references describe a number of different approaches to the problem.

The iterators of CLU are described in Liskov et al. [1977] and Liskov et al. [1984]. Dijkstra's famous letter on the `GOTO` statement appears in Dijkstra [1968a]. A letter by Rubin [1987] rekindled the argument (see Exercise 7.34), which continued in the letters of the *Communications of the* ACM throughout most of 1987. Dijkstra's letter, however, was not the earliest mention of the problems of the `GOTO` statement. Naur [1963b] also comments on their drawbacks. For the disciplined use of `GOTO`s, see Knuth [1974]. For an amusing takeoff on the `GOTO` controversy, see Clark [1973] and Exercise 7.33.

An early seminal paper on exception handling is Goodenough [1975]. Exception handling in CLU, which also was a major influence on modern-day methods, is described and comparisons with other languages are given in Liskov and Snyder [1979]. See also Liskov et al. [1984]. Exception handling in Ada is discussed in Cohen [1996] and in Luckam and Polak [1980]. Exception handling in C++ is described in Stroustrup [1997]; Stroustrup [1994] gives a detailed view of the choices made in designing the exception handling of C++, including an extensive history of termination versus resumption semantics. Exception handling in ML is described in Ullman

[1998], Paulson [1996], Milner and Tofte [1991], and Milner et al. [1997]. A control structure related to exceptions is the **continuation** of the Scheme dialect of LISP. For a description of this mechanism see Springer and Friedman [1989], and Friedman, Haynes, and Kohlbecker [1985].

8 Control II— Procedures and Environments

In the previous chapter, we discussed statement-level control structures and simple structured control mechanisms. In this chapter we extend the study of blocks to the study of procedures and functions, which are blocks whose execution is deferred and whose interfaces are clearly specified.

Many languages make strong syntactic distinctions between procedures and functions, and a case can be made for a significant semantic distinction as well: Functions should (in an ideal world) produce a value only and have no side effects (thus sharing semantic properties with mathematical functions), while procedures produce no values and operate by producing side effects. Indeed, the distinction between procedures and functions is in essence the same as the difference between expressions and statements as discussed in the previous chapter: Procedure calls are statements, while function calls are expressions. However, most languages do not enforce semantic distinctions, and functions can produce side effects as well as return values, while procedures may be written as functions "in disguise"—producing values through their parameters, while causing no other side effects. Thus, we shall not make a significant distinction between procedures and functions in this chapter, since in most languages their semantic properties are similar, even when their syntax is not.[1]

Procedures began when memory was scarce as a way of splitting a program up into small separately compiled pieces, and it is not uncommon even today to see FORTRAN or C code in which every procedure is compiled separately. However, in modern use, separate compilation is more closely associated with modules (see the next chapter), while procedures are used as a mechanism to abstract a group of related operations into a single operation that can be used repeatedly without repeating the code. Procedures can also represent recursive processes that are not as easily represented by other control structures, and they can imitate or replace loop operations (as noted in Chapter 1, and of particular interest in functional languages).

While virtually all programming languages have some notion of procedure or function, the generality of procedures varies tremendously from language to language, and this generality has a major impact on the structure and complexity of the runtime environment needed for proper execution of programs. Fortran77 has a relatively simple notion of procedure as a static entity without recursion, and this leads directly to the notion of a static environment in which all memory allocation is performed prior to the start of execution. Algol60 pioneered the idea of a recursive, dynamic procedure, and this led directly to the stack-based environments common in most imperative and object-oriented languages today. LISP and other functional languages generalized the notion of function to the point that functions are "first-class" data objects themselves—they can be dynamically created and used as values just like any other data structure—and this led to even more dynamic environments that are not restricted to a stack-like structure, and that require dynamic memory management, including garbage collection. On the other hand, the basic notion of an **activation record** as the collection of data needed to maintain a single execution of a procedure, is common to virtually all runtime environments.

We begin this chapter with a review of the various syntactic ways of defining and calling procedures and functions. We continue with an

---

[1] C/C++ make virtually no syntactic difference between expressions and statements: Any expression can be turned into a statement by tacking on a semicolon (a so-called **expression statement**); the value of the expression is then simply thrown away.

investigation into the basic semantic properties of procedures and why they represent a significantly more complex notion of block structure than that covered in the previous chapter. We then study the major parameter passing techniques that lead to different semantic behavior, and outline the structure of activation records and the three basic varieties of runtime environments, including mechanisms for implementing exception handling. We conclude with an overview of methods for maintaining dynamically allocated environments with garbage collection.

8.1 Procedure Definition and Activation

A **procedure** is a mechanism in a programming language for abstracting a group of actions or computations. The group of actions is called the **body** of the procedure, and the body of the procedure is represented as a whole by the name of the procedure. A procedure is defined by providing a **specification** or **interface** and a body. The specification gives the name of the procedure, a list of the types and names of its **parameters**, and the type of its returned value, if any:

```
// C++ code
void intswap (int& x, int& y) // specification
{ int t = x;    // body
  x = y;        // body
  y = t;        // body
}
```

Procedure intswap swaps the values of its parameters x and y, using a local variable t.

In some languages, and in some situations, a procedure specification can be separated from its body, when the specification must be available in advance:

```
void intswap (int&, int&); // specification only
```

Note that this specification does not require the names of the parameters to be specified.[2] In C++ such a specification is called (confusingly) a *declaration*, while the complete definition (including the body) is called a *definition*. (In C, declarations are called *prototypes*.) Typically, even when a specification precedes a definition, it must be repeated with the body.

A procedure is **called** or **activated** by stating its name, together with **arguments** to the call, which correspond to its parameters:

```
intswap (a, b);
```

---

[2] They can of course be supplied if the programmer wishes, but they need not agree with names in other specifications or definitions.

A call to a procedure transfers control to the beginning of the body of the called procedure (the **callee**). When execution reaches the end of the body, control is returned to the **caller**. In some languages, control can be returned to the caller before reaching the end of the callee's body by using a **return-statement**:

```
// C++ code
void intswap (int& x, int& y)
{ if (x == y) return;
   int t = x;
   x = y;
   y = t;
}
```

In some languages, such as FORTRAN, to call a procedure one must also include the keyword CALL, as in

```
CALL INTSWAP (A, B)
```

(In FORTRAN, procedures are called **subroutines**.)

As we have noted, a programming language may make a distinction between procedures, which carry out their operations by changing their parameters or nonlocal variables, and **functions**, which appear in expressions and compute **returned values**. Functions may or may not also change their parameters and nonlocal variables. In C and C++, all procedures are implicitly functions; those that do not return values are declared void (such as the swap function above), while ordinary functions are declared to have the (return) type of the value that they return:

```
int max (int x, int y)
{ return x > y ? x : y;
}
```

In some languages, such as Ada and FORTRAN, different keywords are used for procedures and functions:

```
-- Ada procedure
procedure swap ( x,y: in out integer) is
   t: integer;
begin
   if (x = y) then return;
   end if;
   t := x;
   x := y;
   y := t;
end swap;

-- Ada function
function max ( x,y: integer ) return integer is
begin
   if (x > y) then return x;
   else return y;
   end if;
end max;
```

In some languages, there are only functions (that is, all procedures must return values). Functional languages in particular have this property; see Chapter 11.

In some languages, procedure and function declarations are written in a form similar to constant declarations, using an equal sign, as in the following ML function declaration for a `swap` procedure:[3]

```
(* ML code *)
fun swap (x,y) =
  let val t = !x
  in
      x := !y;
      y := t
  end;
```

The use of an equal sign to declare procedures is justified, because a procedure declaration gives the procedure name a meaning that remains constant during the execution of the program. We could say that a procedure declaration creates a **constant procedure value** and associates a symbolic name—the name of the procedure—with that value.

A procedure communicates with the rest of the program through its parameters and also through **nonlocal references,** that is, references to variables declared outside of its own body. The **scope rules** that establish the meanings of nonlocal references were introduced in Chapter 5.

8.2 Procedure Semantics

A procedure is a block whose declaration is separated from its execution. In Chapter 5, we saw examples of blocks in C and Ada that are not procedure blocks; these blocks are always executed immediately when they are encountered. For example, in C, blocks A and B in the following code are executed as they are encountered:

```
A:
{ int x,y;
   ...
  x = y * 10;
  B:
  { int i;
     i = x / 2;
     ...
  } /* end B */
} /* end A */
```

In Chapter 5, we saw that the **environment** determines the allocation of memory and maintains the meaning of names during execution. In

---

[3] This procedure in ML has type `'a ref * 'a ref -> unit` and is polymorphic; see Chapter 6. Note that its return type is `unit`, which is the equivalent of the C `void` type.

a block-structured language, when a block is encountered during execution, it causes the allocation of local variables and other objects corresponding to the declarations of the block. This memory allocated for the local objects of the block is called the **activation record** (or sometimes **stack frame**) of the block, and the block is said to be **activated** as it executes under the bindings established by its activation record. As blocks are entered during execution, control passes from the activation of the surrounding block to the activation of the inner block. When the inner block exits, control passes back to the surrounding block, and the activation record of the inner block is released, returning to the environment of the activation record of the surrounding block.

For example, in the preceding C code, during execution x and y are allocated in the activation record of block A:

Activation record of A

When block B is entered, space is allocated in the activation record of B:

Activation record of A

Activation record of B

When B exits, the environment reverts to the activation record of A. Thus, the activation of B must retain some information about the activation from which it was entered.

In the preceding code, block B needs to access the variable x declared in block A. A reference to x inside B is a **nonlocal** reference, since x is not allocated in the activation record of B, but in the activation record of the surrounding block A. This, too, requires that B retain information about its surrounding activation.

Now consider what would happen if B were a procedure called from A instead of a block entered directly from A. Suppose, for the sake of a concrete example, that we have the following situation, which we give in C syntax:

```
(1)   int x;

(2)   void B(void)
(3)   { int i;
(4)      i = x / 2;
(5)      ...
(6)   } /* end B */
```

```
(7)   void A(void)
(8)   { int x, y;
(9)     ...
(10)    x = y * 10;
(11)    B();
(12) } /* end A */

(13) main()
(14) { A();
(15)    return 0;
(16) }
```

B is still entered from A (line 11), and the activation of B must retain some information about the activation of A so that control can return to A on exit from B. But there is now a difference in the way nonlocal references are resolved: Under the lexical scoping rule (see Chapter 5), the x in B (line 4) is the global x of the program (line 1),[4] not the x declared in A (line 8). In terms of activation records, we have the following picture:

The activation of B must retain information about the global environment, since the nonlocal reference to x will be found there instead of in the activation record of A. This is because the global environment is the **defining environment** of B, while the activation record of A is the **calling environment** of B. (Sometimes the defining environment is called the **static environment** and the control environment the **dynamic environment**.) For blocks that are not procedures, the defining environment and the calling environment are always the same. By contrast a procedure has different calling and defining environments. Indeed, a procedure can have any number of calling environments during which it will retain the same defining environment.

The actual structure of the environment that keeps track of defining and calling environments will be discussed in the next section. What we are interested in this section is the way an activation of a block **communicates** with the rest of the program.

_____

[4] Technically, x is called an **external** variable, but, by the scope rules of C, such a variable has scope extending from its declaration to the end of the file in which it is declared; thus (ignoring separate compilation issues) it is global to the program.

Clearly, a nonprocedure block communicates with its surrounding block via nonlocal references: Lexical scoping allows it access to all the variables in the surrounding block that are not redeclared in its own declarations. By contrast, under lexical scoping, a procedure block can communicate only with its *defining* block via references to nonlocal variables. It has no way of directly accessing the variables in its calling environment. In the sample C code, procedure B cannot directly access the local variable x of procedure A. Nevertheless, it may need the value of x in A to perform its computations.

The method of communication of a procedure with its calling environment is through **parameters**. A **parameter list** is declared along with the definition of the procedure, as in the max procedure of the previous section:

```
int max (int x, int y)
{ return x > y ? x : y;
}
```

Here x and y are parameters to the max function. They do not take on any value until max is called, when they are replaced by the arguments from the calling environment, as in

```
z = max(a+b,10);
```

In this call to max, the parameter x is replaced by the argument a + b, and the parameter y is replaced by the argument 10. To emphasize the fact that parameters have no value until they are replaced by arguments, parameters are sometimes called **formal parameters**, while arguments are called **actual parameters**.

A strong case can be made that procedures should communicate with the rest of the program using *only* the parameters—that is, a procedure or function should *never* use or change a nonlocal variable. The reason is that such use or change represents a dependency (in the case of a use) or a side effect (in the case of a change) that is invisible from a reading of the procedure specification—it can only be determined from examining the body of the procedure (which could be very long, or even missing in the case of a library procedure). While this rule is generally a good one with regard to *variables* (e.g., a global variable should still be a parameter if it is changed), it is too much to expect with regard to *functions* and *constants*. In general, the body of a procedure will need to call other procedures in the program, library procedures, and may also need to use constants (such as PI). These are all nonlocal references, but we would not want to clutter up the parameter list with all such references (particularly since they are *all* essentially constants). Thus, nonlocal *uses* cannot be avoided.

Nevertheless, some procedures may depend only on parameters and fixed language features, and these are said to be in **closed form**, since they contain no nonlocal dependencies. An example is the max function above, which has no dependencies on nonlocal definitions—it depends entirely on fixed language features and its parameters.

On the other hand, a polymorphic definition of the same function in C++ (using templates):

```
template <typename T>
T max (T x, T y)
{ return x > y ? x : y ; }
```

is *not* in closed form, since the ">" operator can be overloaded for non-built-in types. Thus, to write this function in closed form, we would have to include the ">" operation in the parameter list:

```
template <typename T>
T max (T x, T y, bool (*gt)(T,T))
{ return gt(x,y) ? x : y ;
}
```

(These examples were discussed in detail in Section 6.9.)

If we choose not to do this, then the semantics of this function can only be determined relative to its enclosing environment (its environment of definition assuming static scoping), and the code of this function together with a representation of its defining environment is called a **closure**, because it can be used to resolve all outstanding nonlocal references relative to the body of the function. It is one of the major tasks of a runtime environment to compute closures for all functions in cases where they are needed.[5]

An additional issue affecting the semantics of a procedure is the nature of the correspondence between the parameters and the arguments during a call. In the foregoing, we stated that parameters are "replaced by" the arguments during a call, but the nature of this "replacement" was not specified. In fact, this association is a binding that can be interpreted in many different ways, and this interpretation is called the **parameter passing mechanism**. In the next section we discuss this topic in some detail.

8.3 Parameter Passing Mechanisms

As noted at the end of the previous section, the nature of the bindings of arguments to parameters has a significant effect on the semantics of procedure calls, and languages differ substantially on the kinds of parameter passing mechanisms available and the range of permissible implementation effects that may occur (we have already seen one of these implementation effects in Chapter 7, namely the effect different evaluation orders of the arguments can have in the presence of side effects). Some languages offer only one basic kind of parameter passing mechanism (C, Java, functional languages), while others may offer two (C++) or more. In languages

---

[5] In this particular example, the reference to ">" can be resolved at compile time, and no closure needs to be computed, as we will see later in this chapter.

with one mechanism it is also often possible to imitate other mechanisms using indirection or other language features.

In this section we will discuss four important parameter passing mechanisms: pass by value, pass by reference, pass by value-result, and pass by name.[6] Some variations on these will be discussed in the exercises.

8.3.1 Pass by Value

This is by far the most common mechanism for parameter passing. In this mechanism, the arguments are expressions that are evaluated at the time of the call, and their values become the values of the parameters during the execution of the procedure. In its simplest form, this means that value parameters behave as constant values during the execution of the procedure, and one can interpret **pass by value** as replacing all the parameters in the body of the procedure by the corresponding argument values. For instance, we can think of the call max (10, 2 + 3) of the preceding max function as executing the body of max with x replaced by 10 and y replaced by 5:

```
10 > 5 ? 10 : 5
```

This form of pass by value is usually the only parameter passing mechanism in functional languages. Pass by value is also the default mechanism in C++ and Pascal, and is essentially the only parameter passing mechanism in C and Java. However, in these languages a slightly different interpretation of pass by value is used: The parameters are viewed as local variables of the procedure, with initial values given by the values of the arguments in the call. Thus, in C, Java, and Pascal, value parameters may be assigned to, just as with local variables (but cause no changes outside the procedure), while Ada in parameters may not be assigned to (see the discussion of Ada parameters in Section 8.3.5).

Note that pass by value does not imply that changes cannot occur outside the procedure through the use of parameters. If the parameter has a pointer or reference type, then the value is an address, and can be used to change memory outside the procedure. For example, the following C function definitely changes the value of the integer pointed to by the parameter p:

```
void init_p (int* p)
{ *p = 0; }
```

On the other hand, directly assigning to p does *not* change the argument outside the procedure:

```
void init_ptr (int* p)
{ p = (int*) malloc(sizeof(int)); /* error - has no
                                            effect! */

}
```

---

[6] Parameter passing mechanisms are often referred to using the words "call by" rather than "pass by," as in "call by value," "call by reference," etc. We prefer "pass by" and use it consistently in this text.

In addition, in some languages certain values are implicitly pointers or references. For example, in C arrays are implicitly pointers (to the first location of the array), and so an array value parameter can always be used to change the values stored in the array:

```
void init_p_0 (int p[])
{ p[0] = 0; }
```

In Java, too, objects are implicitly pointers, so any object parameter can be used to change its data:

```
void append_1 (Vector v)
// adds an element to Vector v
{ v.addElement( new Integer(1)); }
```

But, as in C, direct assignments to parameters also do not work:

```
void make_new (Vector v)
{ v = new Vector(); /* error - has no effect! */ }
```

8.3.2 Pass by Reference

With this mechanism, an argument must in principle be a variable with an allocated address. Instead of passing the value of the variable, pass by reference passes the location of the variable, so that the parameter becomes an **alias** for the argument, and any changes made to the parameter occur to the argument as well. In FORTRAN, pass by reference is the only parameter passing mechanism. In C++ and Pascal, pass by reference (instead of the default pass by value) can be specified using extra syntax: An ampersand (&) after the data type in C++, and a var keyword before the variable name in Pascal:

```
void inc(int& x) // C++
{ x++ ; }

procedure inc(var x: integer); (* Pascal *)
begin
   x :=    x + 1;
end;
```

After a call to inc(a) the value of a has increased by 1, so that a side effect has occurred. Multiple aliasing is also possible, such as in the code

```
int a;

void yuck (int& x, int& y)
{ x = 2;
   y = 3;
   a = 4;
}
...
yuck (a, a);
```

Inside procedure yuck after the call, the identifiers x, y, and a all refer to the same variable, namely, the variable a.

As noted previously, C can achieve pass by reference by passing a reference or location explicitly as a pointer (C uses the operator "&" to indicate the location of a variable and the operator "*" to dereference a pointer):

```
void inc (int* x) /*C imitation of pass by reference */
{ (*x)++; /* adds 1 to *x */ }
...
int a;
...
inc(&a); /* pass the address of a to the inc function */
```

This code has the same effect as the previous C++ or Pascal code for the inc procedure. Of course, there is the annoying necessity here of explicitly taking the address of the variable a, and then explicitly deferencing it again in the body of inc.

A similar effect can be achieved in ML by using reference types to imitate pass by reference (ML has, like C, only pass by value available):

```
fun inc (x: int ref) = x := !x + 1;
```

One additional issue that must be resolved in a language with pass by reference is the response of the language to reference arguments that are not variables (and thus do not have known addresses within the run-time environment). For example, given the C++ code

```
void inc(int& x)
{ x++; }
...
inc(2); // ??
```

what should the response of the compiler be to the call inc(2)? In FORTRAN, in which pass by reference is the *only* available parameter mechanism, this is legal code, and the response of the compiler is to create a temporary integer location, initialize it with the value 2, and then apply the inc function (so this actually mimics pass by value, since the change to the temporary should not affect the rest of the program). In C++ and Pascal, however, this is an error—reference arguments *must* be l-values (that is, they must have known addresses).

8.3.3 Pass by Value-Result

This mechanism achieves a similar result to pass by reference, except that no actual alias is established: The value of the argument is copied and used in the procedure, and then the final value of the parameter is copied back out to the location of the argument when the procedure exits. Thus, this method is sometimes known as **copy-in, copy-out**—or **copy-restore**.

Pass by value-result is only distinguishable from pass by reference in the presence of aliasing. Thus, in the following code (written for convenience in C syntax):

```
void p(int x, int y)
{ x++;
  y++;
}

main()
{ int a = 1;
  p(a,a);
  ...
}
```

a has value 3 after p is called if pass by reference is used, while a has the value 2 if pass by value-result is used.

Issues left unspecified by this mechanism, and possibly differing in different languages or implementations, are the order in which results are copied back to the arguments and whether the locations of the arguments are calculated only on entry and stored or whether they are recalculated on exit.

A further option is that a language can offer a **pass by result** mechanism as well, in which there is no incoming value, but only an outgoing one.

8.3.4   Pass by Name and Delayed Evaluation

Pass by name is the term used for this mechanism when it was introduced in Algol60. At the time it was intended as a kind of advanced inlining process for procedures, so that the semantics of procedures could be described simply by a form of textual replacement, rather than an appeal to environments and closures; see Exercise 8.14. It turned out to be essentially equivalent to the normal order delayed evaluation described in the previous chapter. It also was discovered to be difficult to implement, and to have complex interactions with other language constructs, particularly arrays and assignment. Thus, it was rarely implemented and was dropped in all Algol60 descendants (AlgolW, Algol68, C, Pascal, etc.). Advances in delayed evaluation in functional languages, particularly pure functional languages such as Haskell (where interactions with side effects are avoided), has increased interest in this mechanism, however, and it is worthwhile to understand it as a basis for other delayed evaluation mechanisms, particularly the more efficient **lazy evaluation** studied in Chapter 11.

The idea of pass by name is that the argument is not evaluated until its actual use (as a parameter) in the called procedure. Thus, the *name* of the argument, or its textual representation at the point of call, replaces the name of the parameter it corresponds to. As an example, in the code (in C syntax)

```
void inc(int x)
{   x++; }
```

if a call such as `inc(a[i])` is made, the effect is of evaluating `a[i]++`. Thus, if `i` were to change before the use of `x` inside `inc`, the result would be different from either pass by reference or pass by value-result:

```
int i;
int a[10];

void inc(int x)
{ i++;
  x++;
}

main()
{ i = 1;
  a[1] = 1;
  a[2] = 2;
  p(a[i]);
  return 0;
}
```

This code has the result of setting `a[2]` to 3 and leaving `a[1]` unchanged.

Pass by name can be interpreted as follows. The text of an argument at the point of call is viewed as a function in its own right, which is evaluated every time the corresponding parameter name is reached in the code of the called procedure. However, the argument will always be evaluated in the environment of the caller, while the procedure will be executed in its defining environment. To see how this works, consider the example in Figure 8.1.

```
(1)   #include <stdio.h>
(2)   int i;

(3)   int p(int y)
(4)   { int j = y;
(5)     i++;
(6)     return j+y;
(7)   }

(8)   void q(void)
(9)   { int j = 2;
(10)    i = 0;
(11)    printf("%d\n", p(i + j));
(12)  }

(13) main()
(14) { q();
(15)    return 0;
(16) }
```

Figure 8.1   Pass by name example (in C syntax)

The argument i + j to the call to p from q is evaluated every time the parameter y is encountered inside p. The expression i + j is, however, evaluated as though it were still inside q, so on line 4 in p it produces the value 2. Then, on line 6, since i is now 1, it produces the value 3 (the j in the expression i + j is the j of q, so it hasn't changed, even though the i inside p has). Thus, if pass by name is used for the parameter y of p in the program, the program will print 5.

Historically, the interpretation of pass by name arguments as functions to be evaluated during the execution of the called procedure was expressed by referring to the arguments as **thunks**.[7] For example, the above C code could actually imitate pass by name using a function, except for the fact that it uses the local definition of j inside q. If we make j global, then the following C code will actually print 5, just as if pass by name were used in the previous code:

```
#include <stdio.h>
int i,j;

int i_plus_j(void)
{ return i+j; }

int p(int (*y)(void))
{ int j = y();
  i++;
  return j+y();
}

void q(void)
{ j = 2;
  i = 0;
  printf("%d\n", p(i_plus_j));
}

main()
{ q();
  return 0;
}
```

Pass by name is problematic when side effects are desired. Consider the intswap procedure we have discussed before:

```
void intswap (int x, int y)
{ int t = x;
  x = y;
  y = t;
}
```

---

[7] Presumably, the image was of little machines that "thunked" into place each time they were needed.

Suppose that pass by name is used for the parameters x and y and that we call this procedure as follows,

```
intswap(i,a[i])
```

where i is an integer index and a is an array of integers. The problem with this call is that it will function as the following code:

```
t = i;
i = a[i];
a[i] = t;
```

Note that by the time the address of a[i] is computed in the third line, i has been assigned the value of a[i] in the previous line, and this will not assign t to the array a subscripted at the original i, unless i = a[i].

It is also possible to write bizarre (but possibly useful) code in similar circumstances. One of the earliest examples of this is called **Jensen's device** after its inventor J. Jensen. Jensen's device uses pass by name to apply an operation to an entire array, as in the following example, in C syntax:

```
int sum (int a, int index, int size)
{ int temp = 0;
   for (index = 0; index < size; index++)   temp += a;
   return temp;
}
```

If a and index are pass by name parameters, then in the following code

```
int x[10], i, xtotal;
...
xtotal = sum(x[i],i,10);
```

the call to sum computes the sum of all the elements x[0] through x[9].

8.3.5 Parameter Passing Mechanism versus Parameter Specification

One can fault these descriptions of parameter passing mechanisms in that they are tied closely to the internal mechanics of the code that is used to implement them. While one can give somewhat more theoretical semantic descriptions of these mechanisms, all of the questions of interpretation that we have discussed still arise in code that contains side effects. One language that tries to address this issue is Ada. Ada has two notions of parameter communication, in parameters and out parameters. Any parameter can be declared in, out, or in out (i.e., both). The meaning of these keywords is exactly what you expect: An in parameter specifies that the parameter represents an incoming value only; an out parameter specifies an outgoing value only; and an in out parameter specifies both an incoming and an outgoing value. (The in parameter is the default, and the keyword in can be omitted in this case.)

Any parameter implementation whatsoever can be used to achieve these results, as long as the appropriate values are communicated properly (an in value on entry and an out value on exit). Ada also declares that any program that violates the protocols established by these parameter specifications is **erroneous**. For example, an in parameter cannot legally be assigned a new value by a procedure, and the value of an out parameter cannot be legally used by the procedure. Thus, pass by reference could be used for an in parameter as well as an out parameter, or pass by value could be used for in parameters and copy out for out parameters.

Fortunately, many violations of these parameter specifications can be enforced by a translator—particularly the fact that an in parameter cannot be assigned to or otherwise have its value changed (it acts like a constant), and the fact that an out parameter can only be assigned to (its value can never be used). Unfortunately, in out parameters cannot be checked with this certainty, and in the presence of other side effects, as we have seen, different implementations (reference and copy in-copy out, for example) may have different results. Ada still calls such programs erroneous, but translators cannot in general check whether a program is erroneous under these conditions. Thus, the outcome of this specification effort is somewhat less than what we might have hoped for.

8.3.6   Type Checking of Parameters

In strongly typed languages, procedure calls must be checked so that the arguments agree in type and number with the parameters of the procedure. This means, first of all, that procedures may not have a variable number of parameters and that rules must be stated for the type compatibility between parameters and arguments. In the case of pass by reference, parameters usually must have the same type, but in the case of pass by value, this can be relaxed to assignment compatibility (Chapter 6), and can allow conversions, as is done in C, C++, and Java (Ada, of course, does not allow conversions).

8.4 Procedure Environments, Activations, and Allocation

In this section we want to give more detail on how information can be computed and maintained in an environment during procedure calls. We already saw in Chapter 5 and in Section 8.2 that the environment for a block-structured language with lexical scope can be maintained in a stack-based fashion, with an activation record created on the environment stack when a block is entered and released when the block is exited. We also saw how variables declared locally in the block are allocated space in this activation record.

In this section we want to see how this same structure can be extended to procedure activations, in which the defining environment and the calling environment differ, and we want to study the kinds of information necessary to maintain this environment correctly. We have already noted that some notion of **closure** is necessary in this case to resolve nonlocal references. A clear understanding of this **execution model** is often necessary to fully understand the behavior of programs, since the semantics of procedure calls are embedded in this model.

We also want to show that a completely stack-based environment is no longer adequate to deal with procedure variables and the dynamic creation of procedures, and that languages with these facilities, particularly functional languages, are forced to use a more complex fully dynamic environment with garbage collection.

But, first, by way of contrast, we want to give a little more detail about the fully static environment of FORTRAN, which is quite simple, yet completely adequate for that language. We emphasize that the structures that we present here are only meant to illustrate the general scheme. Actual details implemented by various translators may differ substantially from the general outlines given here.

8.4.1 Fully Static Environments

In a language like Fortran77,[8] all memory allocation can be performed at load time, and the locations of all variables are fixed for the duration of program execution. Function and procedure (or subroutine) definitions cannot be nested (that is, all procedures/functions are global, as in C),[9] and recursion is not allowed (unlike C).[10] Thus, all the information associated with a function or subroutine can be statically allocated. Each procedure or function has a fixed activation record, which contains space for the local variables and parameters, and possibly the return address for proper return from calls. Global variables are defined by COMMON statements, and are determined by pointers to a common area. Thus, the general form of the runtime environment for a FORTRAN program with subroutines S1...Sn is as follows:

---

[8] Fortran90 significantly extends the features of Fortran77, including allowing recursion and dynamically allocated variables.

[9] In Section 8.4.2 we will see why nested procedures present problems even for nonstatic environments.

[10] More precisely, recursive calls are permitted in Fortran77, but each new call overwrites the data of all previous calls, so recursion does not work. Procedures with this property are sometimes called **non-reentrant**.

COMMON area
Activation record of main program
Activation record of S1
Activation record of S2
etc.

Each activation record, moreover, is broken down into several areas:

space for local variables
space for passed parameters
return address
temporary space for expression evaluation

When a call to a procedure S occurs, the parameters are evaluated, and their locations (using pass by reference) are stored in the parameter space of the activation record of S. Then the current instruction pointer is stored as the return address, and a jump is performed to the instruction pointer of S. When S exits, a jump is performed to the return address. If S is a function, special arrangements must be made for the returned value; often it is returned in a special register, or space can be reserved for it in the activation record of the function or the activation record of the caller. Note that all nonlocal references must be to the global COMMON area, and so no closure is needed to resolve these references. Thus, no extra book-keeping information is necessary in an activation record to handle nonlocal references.

As an example, consider the following FORTRAN program:

```
REAL TABLE (10), MAXVAL
READ *, TABLE (1), TABLE (2), TABLE (3)
CALL LRGST (TABLE, 3, MAXVAL)
PRINT *, MAXVAL
END

SUBROUTINE LRGST (A, SIZE, V)
INTEGER SIZE
REAL A (SIZE), V
INTEGER K
V = A (1)
DO 10 K = 1, SIZE
IF (A( K) GT. V) V = A (K)
10 CONTINUE
RETURN
END
```

The environment of this program would look as follows, where we have added pointers indicating location references that exist immediately after the call to LRGST from the main program:

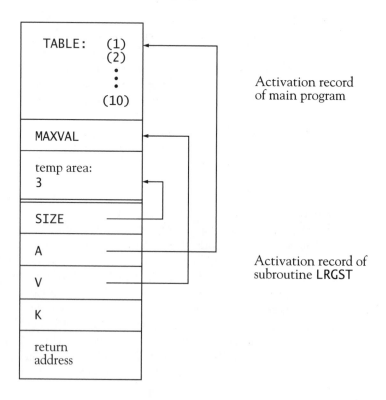

TABLE: (1)
(2)
⋮
(10)

Activation record
of main program

MAXVAL

temp area:
3

SIZE

A

Activation record of
subroutine **LRGST**

V

K

return
address

8.4.2   Stack-Based Runtime Environments

In a block-structured language with recursion, such as C and other Algol-like languages, activations of procedure blocks cannot be allocated statically, since a procedure may be called again before its previous activation is exited, and so a new activation must be created on each procedure entry. As we have seen, this can be done in a stack-based manner, with a new activation record created on the stack every time a block is entered and released on exit.

What information must be kept in the environment to manage a stack-based environment? As with the fully static environment of FORTRAN, space in an activation needs to be allocated for local variables, temporary space, and a return pointer. However, several additional pieces of information are required. First, a pointer to the current activation must be kept, since each procedure has no fixed location for its activation record, but the location of its activation record may vary as execution proceeds. This pointer to the current activation must be kept in a fixed location, usually a register, and it is called the **environment pointer** or **ep**, since it points to the current environment.

The second piece of information that needs to be kept in a stack-based environment is a pointer to the activation record of the block from which the current activation was entered. In the case of a procedure call, this is the activation of the caller. The reason this piece of information is necessary is that, when the current activation is exited, the current activation record needs to be removed (i.e., popped) from the stack of activation records. This means that the ep must be restored to point to the previous activation, and this can be done only if the old ep, which pointed to the previous activation record, is retained in the new activation record. This stored pointer to the previous activation record is called the **control link**, since it points to the activation record of the block from which control passed to the current block and to which control will return. Sometimes this control link is called the **dynamic link**.

A simple example is the following program, in C syntax:

```
void p(void)
{ ... }

void q(void)
{ ...
  p();
}

main()
{ q();
  ...
}
```

At the beginning of execution of the program, there is just an activation record for main and the ep points there (we ignore global data in this example):

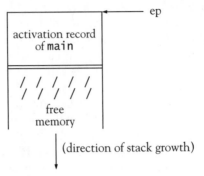

After the call to q, an activation record for q has been added to the stack, the ep now points to the activation record of q, and q has stored the old ep as its control link:

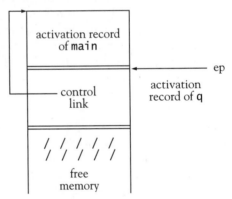

When p is called inside q, a new frame is added for p. Thus, after the call to p from within q, the activation stack looks as follows:

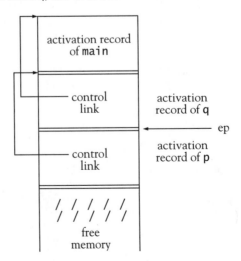

Now when p is exited, the activation record of p is returned to free memory, and the ep is restored from the control link of the activation record of p, so that it points to the activation record of q again. Similarly, when q is exited, the ep is restored to point to the original environment of the main program.

With this new requirement, the fields in each activation record need to contain the information in Figure 8.2.

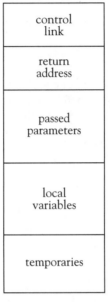

Figure 8.2   An Activation Record

Consider now how the environment pointer can be used to find variable locations. Local variables are allocated in the current activation record, which is pointed to by the ep. Since the local variables are allocated as prescribed by the declarations of the block, and these declarations are static, each time the block is entered the same kinds of variables are allocated in the same order. Thus, each variable can be allocated the same position in the activation record relative to the beginning of the record.[11] This position is called the **offset** of the local variable. Each local variable can be found using its fixed offset from the location pointed to by the ep.

Consider the following additions to our previous example:

```
int x;
void p( int y)
{ int i = x;
  char c;
  ...
}
```

(continues)

---

[11] This assumes that each variable has a constant size. Variable-length arrays are an exception to this requirement; see Exercise 8.22.

(continued)

```
void q ( int a)
{ int x;
  ...
  p(1);
}

main()
{ q(2);
  return 0;
}
```

Any activation record of p will have a format such as Figure 8.3. Each time p is called, the parameter y and the local variables i and c will be found in the same place relative to the beginning of the activation record.

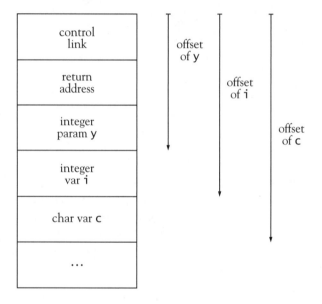

Figure 8.3   An Activation Record of p

Now consider the case of nonlocal references, such as the reference to x in p indicated in the foregoing code. How is x found? Fortunately, in C as in FORTRAN, procedures cannot be nested, so all nonlocal references outside a procedure are actually global and are allocated statically. Thus, additional structures to represent closures are not required in the activation stack: Any nonlocal reference is found in the global area and can actually be resolved prior to execution.

However, many languages *do* permit procedures to be nested: Pascal, Ada, Modula-2, to cite a few. With nested procedures, nonlocal references now may be to local variables in a surrounding procedure scope as in the following Ada code:

```
procedure q is
  x: integer;

  procedure p (y: integer) is
    i: integer := x;
  begin
    ...
  end p;

  procedure r is
  x: float;
  begin
    p(1);
    ...
  end r;

begin
  r;
end q;
```

Here is what the activation stack looks like during the execution of p:

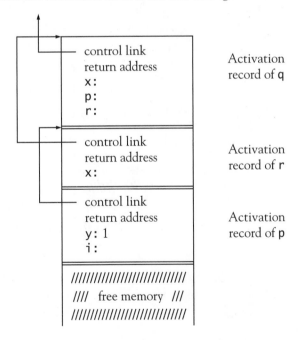

How is it possible to find the nonlocal reference to the x of q from inside p? One idea would be to follow the control link to the activation record of r, but this would find the x local to r.[12] This would achieve

---

[12] This would actually require that the full symbol table be maintained during execution, rather than replacing names by fixed offsets, since the offset (or even the existence) of a name in an arbitrary caller cannot be predicted to be at any fixed offset.

dynamic scope rather than lexical scope. To achieve lexical scope, a procedure such as p must maintain a link to its **lexical** or **defining environment**. This link is called the **access link**, since it provides access to nonlocal variables. (Sometimes the access link is called the **static link**, since it is designed to implement lexical, or static, scope.) Since p is defined inside q, the access link of p is the ep that exists when p is defined, so the access link of p points to the activation of q. Now each activation record needs a new field, the access link field, and the complete picture of the environment for our example is as follows:

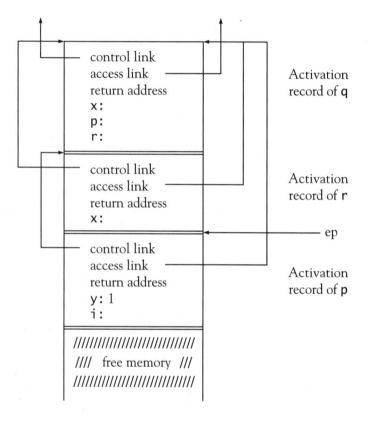

When blocks are deeply nested, it may be necessary to follow more than one access link to find a nonlocal reference. For example, in the Ada code

```
procedure ex is
  x: ... ;

  procedure p is
    ...
    procedure q is
    begin
       ... x ... ;
    end q;
```

```
     begin -- p
        ...
     end p;

  begin -- ex
     ...
  end ex;
```

to access x from inside q requires following the access link in the activation record of q to its defining environment, which is an activation record of p, and then following the access link of p to the global environment. This process is called **access chaining**, and the number of access links that must be followed corresponds to the difference in nesting levels, or **nesting depth**, between the accessing environment and the defining environment of the variable being accessed.

With this organization of the environment, the closure of a procedure—the code for the procedure, together with a mechanism for resolving nonlocal references—becomes significantly more complex, since every time a procedure is called, the defining environment of that procedure must be included as part of the activation record. Thus, a function or procedure in a language like Ada or Pascal must be represented not just by a pointer to the code for the procedure, but by a closure consisting of a pair of pointers: the code or instruction pointer, which we denote by ip, and the access link, or environment pointer of its defining environment, which we denote by ep; we write this closure as **<ep, ip>** and we use it as the representation of procedures in the following discussion.

We finish this section with an example of an Ada program with nested procedures and a diagram of its environment at one point during execution (Figures 8.4 and 8.5). Note in the diagram that the nested procedure show has two different closures, each corresponding to the two different activations of p in which show is defined.

```
(1)    with Text_IO; use Text_IO;
(2)    with Ada.Integer_Text_IO;
(3)    use Ada.Integer_Text_IO;

(4)    procedure lastex is

(5)      procedure p(n: integer) is

(6)        procedure show is
(7)        begin
(8)          if n > 0 then p(n - 1);
(9)          end if;
(10)         put(n);
(11)         new_line;
(12)       end show;

(13)     begin -- p
(14)       show;
(15)     end p;
```

(continues)

(continued)

```
(16) begin -- lastex
(17)     p(1);
(18) end lastex;
```

Figure 8.4 An Ada Program with Nested Procedures

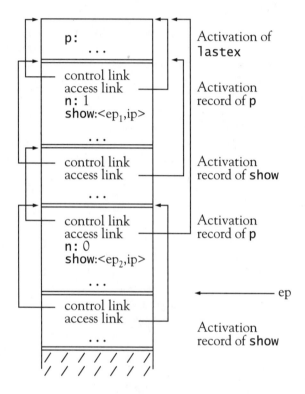

Figure 8.5 Environment of `lastex` during the Second Call to `show` (line 8 of Figure 8.4)

8.4.3 Dynamically Computed Procedures and Fully Dynamic Environments

The stack-based runtime environment shown is completely adequate for almost all block-structured languages with lexical scope. The use of <ep, ip> closures for procedures makes this environment even suitable for languages with parameters that are themselves procedures, as long as these parameters are value parameters: A procedure that is passed to another procedure is passed as a closure (an <ep, ip> pair), and when it is called, its access link is the ep part of its closure. Examples of languages for which this organization is necessary are Ada and Pascal.

A stack-based environment does have its limitations, however, which we already noted in Chapter 5. For instance, any procedure that can return a pointer to a local object, either by returned value or through a pass by reference parameter, will result in a **dangling reference** when the procedure is exited, since the activation record of the procedure will be deallocated from the stack. The simplest example of this is when the address of a local variable is returned, as for instance in the C code:

```
int * dangle(void)
{ int x;
   return &x;
}
```

An assignment addr = dangle() now causes addr to point to an unsafe location in the activation stack.

This situation cannot happen in Java, however, since the address of a local variable is unavailable. Ada95 also makes this an error by stating the **Access-type Lifetime Rule:** An attribute x'access yielding a result belonging to an access type T (i.e., a pointer type) is only allowed if x can remain in existence at least as long as T. Thus, the Ada code equivalent to the above C code

```
type IntPtr is access Integer;

function dangle return IntPtr is
   x: Integer;
begin
   return x'access;
end dangle;
```

is illegal because the IntPtr type definition occurs in an outer scope relative to x (as it must to allow the definition of dangle), and so violates the Access-type Lifetime Rule.

However, there are situations where a compiler cannot check for this error statically (see the Notes and References). In Ada an exception will still occur during execution (Program_Error), but in C/C++ and a few other languages this error will not be caught either statically or dynamically. In practice, it is easy for programmers who have an understanding of the environment to avoid this error.

A more serious situation occurs if the language designer wishes to extend the expressiveness and flexibility of the language by allowing procedures to be dynamically created, that is, allowing procedures to be returned from other procedures via returned value or reference parameters. This kind of flexibility is usually desired in a functional language (and even in some object-oriented languages, such as Smalltalk, where methods can be created dynamically), and in such a language, procedures become what are called **first-class values:** No "arbitrary" restrictions apply to their use. In such a language, a stack-based environment cannot be used, since the closure of a locally defined procedure will have an ep that points to the current activation record. If that closure is available outside the activation of the procedure that created it, the ep will point to an activation record that no longer exists. Any subsequent call to that procedure will have an incorrect access environment.

Consider the following example, in which we may reasonably want a procedure to create another procedure. We write this example in Ada95, since Ada95 has procedure types and parameters, and so can express the situation quite well (this example is adapted from Abelson and Sussman [1996]):

```
type WithdrawProc is
   access function (x:integer) return integer;

InsufficientFunds: exception;

function makeNewBalance (initBalance: integer)
    return WithDrawProc
is
   currentBalance: integer;

   function withdraw (amt: integer) return integer is
   begin
     if amt <= currentBalance then
        currentBalance := currentBalance - amt;
     else
        raise InsufficientFunds;
     end if;
     return currentBalance;
   end withdraw;

begin
   currentBalance := initBalance;
   return withdraw'access;
end makeNewBalance;
```

We now might want to make two different accounts from which to withdraw, one with an initial balance of 500 and the other with an initial balance of 100 dollars:

```
withdraw1, withdraw2: WithdrawProc;

withdraw1 := makeNewBalance(500);
withdraw2 := makeNewBalance(100);
```

The problem is that in a stack-based environment, the activation records in which both these functions were created have disappeared: Each time `makeNewBalance` returns, the local environment of `makeNewBalance` is released. For example,

```
newBalance1 := withdraw1(100);
newBalance2 := withdraw2(50);
```

should result in a value of 400 for `newBalance1` and a value of 50 for `newBalance2`, but if the two instances of the local `currentBalance` variable (with values 500 and 100) have disappeared from the environment, these calls will not work.

Pascal does not have this problem, since there are no procedure variables (procedures can only be value parameters). In C all procedures are global, so again this problem cannot arise. Ada considers this program to be similar to the dangling reference code, and calls this a violation of the Access-type Lifetime Rule. Thus, Ada will generate a compile-time error message in this case.

Nevertheless, we may want to be able to do things just like this in a language in which functions and procedures are first class values; that is, no nongeneralities or nonorthogonalities should exist for functions and procedures. Such a language, for example, is LISP. What kind of environment would we need to allow such constructs?

Now it is no longer possible for the activation record of procedure makeNewBalance to be removed from the environment, as long as there are references to any of its local objects. Such an environment is **fully dynamic** in that it deletes activation records only when they can no longer be reached from within the executing program. Such an environment must perform some kind of automatic reclamation of unreachable storage. Two standard methods of doing so are **reference counts** and **garbage collection**; these will be studied in Section 8.5.

This situation also means that the structure of the activations becomes treelike instead of stacklike: The control links to the calling environment no longer necessarily point to the immediately preceding activation. For example, in the two calls to makeNewBalance, the two activations remain, with their control links both pointing at the defining environment:

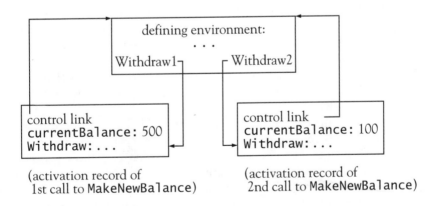

(activation record of
1st call to MakeNewBalance)

(activation record of
2nd call to MakeNewBalance)

Each activation of makeNewBalance can disappear only if withdraw1 or withdraw2 are reassigned or themselves disappear.

This is the model under which Scheme and other functional languages execute. In the next section we will discuss issues involved in maintaining such environments.

8.5 Dynamic Memory Management

In a typical imperative language such as C, the automatic allocation and deallocation of storage occurs only for activation records on a stack. This is a relatively easy process: Space is allocated for an activation record when a procedure is called and deallocated when the procedure is exited. Explicit dynamic allocation and use of pointers is also available under manual programmer control using a "heap" of memory separate from the stack, as we have described in Chapter 5. However, as we noted there, manual memory management on the heap suffers from a number of potential problems, including the creation of garbage and dangling references. Thus, languages with significant needs for heap storage, such as Java, are better off leaving nonstack dynamic storage to a memory manager that provides automatic garbage collection.

Now we have seen another reason to have automatic garbage collection: Any language that does not apply significant restrictions to the use of procedures and functions *must* provide it, since the stack-based system of procedure call and return is no longer correct. Since functional languages such as Scheme, ML, and Haskell are languages with first-class function values, they fall into this category, as do object-oriented languages such as Smalltalk and Java.

One might attempt to solve this problem by using a very simple approach: Simply do not deallocate any memory once it has been allocated! This means that every call to a function creates a new activation record in memory, but on exit this memory is not deallocated. This method has two advantages: It is correct, and it is easy to implement. While this method actually can work for small programs, functional and object-oriented languages have the property that large amounts of memory are dynamically allocated, since processing occurs primarily by function (or method) call, and the internal representation of data uses pointers and requires a substantial amount of indirection and memory overhead. Thus, performing no deallocation causes memory to be very quickly exhausted.

In fact, this method *has* been used in conjunction with virtual memory systems, since the address space for such systems is almost inexhaustible. This only pushes off the basic problem, however, since it causes the swap space of the operating system to become exhausted and can cause a serious degradation of performance due to page faults. These topics are beyond the scope of this book, but at least serve to point out that there is a strong interaction between memory management and operating system issues.

Automatic memory management actually falls into two categories: the **reclamation** of previously allocated but no longer used storage, sometimes called **garbage collection**, and the **maintenance** of the free space available for allocation. Indeed, maintenance of free space is needed even for manual heap operations in languages such as C; it is also a little more straightforward than is reclamation, so we discuss it first.

8.5.1 Maintaining Free Space

Generally, a contiguous block of memory is provided by the operating system for the use of an executing program. The free space within this block is maintained by a list of free blocks. One way to do this is via a linked list, such as the circular list in the following figure, indicating the total available space, with allocated blocks shaded and free blocks blank:

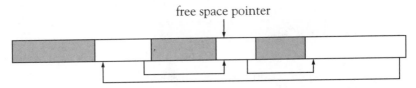

When a block of a certain size needs to be allocated, the memory manager searches the list for a free block with enough space, and then adjusts the free list to remove the allocated space, as in the following picture:

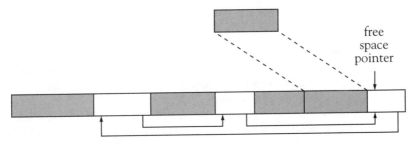

When memory is reclaimed, blocks are returned to the free list. For example, if the light-shaded areas are storage to be reclaimed,

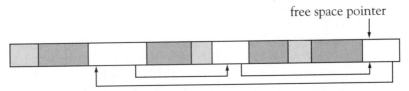

then the new free list after reclamation would look as follows:

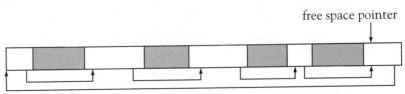

When blocks of memory are returned to the free list, they must be joined with immediately adjacent blocks to form the largest contiguous block of free memory. This process is called **coalescing**. In the preceding example, the small block freed in the middle of the memory area was coalesced with the free block adjacent to it on the right. Even with coalescing, however, a free list can become **fragmented**, that is, consist of a number of small-sized blocks. When this occurs, it is possible for the allocation of a large block to fail, even though there is enough total space available to allocate it. To prevent this, memory must occasionally be **compacted** by moving all free blocks together and coalescing them into one block. For example, the five blocks of free memory in the previous diagram could be compacted as follows:

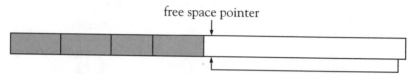

free space pointer

Compaction involves considerable overhead, since the locations of most of the allocated quantities will change and data structures and tables in the runtime environment will have to be modified to reflect these new locations.

8.5.2 Reclamation of Storage

Recognizing when a block of storage is no longer referenced, either directly or indirectly through pointers, is a much more difficult task than is the maintenance of the free list itself. Historically, two main methods have been used: reference counting and mark and sweep.

Reference counting is an "eager" method of storage reclamation, in that it tries to reclaim space as soon as it is no longer referenced. Each block of allocated storage contains an extra count field, which stores the number of references to the block from other blocks. Each time a reference is changed, these reference counts must be updated. When the reference count drops to zero, the block can be returned to the free list. In theory this seems like a simple and elegant solution to the problem, but in fact it suffers from serious drawbacks. One obvious one is the extra memory that it takes to keep the reference counts themselves. Even more serious, the effort to maintain the counts can be fairly large. For example, when making an assignment, which we will model by a C-like pointer assignment p = q, first the old value of p must be followed, and its reference count decremented by one. If this reference count should happen to drop to zero, it is not sufficient simply to return it to free storage, since it may itself contain references to other storage blocks. Thus, reference counts must be decremented recursively. Finally, when q is copied to p, its reference count must be incremented. A pseudocode description of assignment would therefore look as follows:

```
void decrement(p)
{ p->refcount--;
  if (p->refcount == 0)
  { for all fields r of *p that are pointers do
      decrement(r);
    deallocate(*p);
  }
}
```

```
void assign(p,q)
{ decrement(p);
  p = q;
  q->refcount++;
}
```

However, the overhead to maintain reference counts is not the worst flaw of this scheme. Even more serious is that circular references can cause unreferenced memory to never be deallocated.

For example, consider a circular list such as

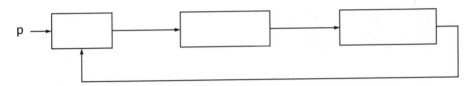

If p is deallocated, the reference count of the block pointed to by p will drop from 2 to 1. The entire list will never be deallocated at all.

The standard alternative to reference counts is **mark and sweep**. This method is a "lazy" method, in that it puts off reclaiming any storage until the allocator runs out of space, at which point it looks for all storage that can be referenced and moves all unreferenced storage back to the free list. It does this in two passes. The first pass follows all pointers recursively, starting with the current environment or symbol table, and marks each block of storage reached. This process requires an extra bit of storage for the marking. A second pass then sweeps linearly through memory, returning unmarked blocks to the free list.

This method, unlike reference counts, has no difficulty freeing blocks with circular references. However, it also requires extra storage, and it suffers from another serious problem: The double pass through memory causes a significant delay in processing, sometimes as much as a few seconds, each time the garbage collector is invoked, which can be every few minutes. This is clearly unacceptable for many applications involving interactive or immediate response. However, many modern LISP and Smalltalk implementations still suffer from this problem.

A bookkeeping improvement can be made by splitting available memory into two halves and allocating storage only from one half at a time. Then during the marking pass, all reached blocks are immediately copied to the second half of storage not in use; hence, this method is often called **stop and copy**. This means that no extra mark bit is required in storage, and only one pass is required. It also performs compaction automatically. Once all reachable blocks in the used area have been copied, the used and unused halves of memory are interchanged, and processing continues. However, this does little to improve processing delays during storage reclamation. In the 1980s a method was invented that reduces this delay significantly. Called **generational garbage collection**, it adds a permanent storage area to the reclamation scheme of the previous paragraph. Allocated objects that survive long enough are simply copied into permanent space and are never deallocated during subsequent storage reclamations. This means that the garbage collector needs to search only a very small section of memory for newer storage allocations, and the time for such a search is reduced to a fraction of a second. Of course, it is possible for permanent memory still to become exhausted with unreachable storage, but this is a much less severe problem than before, since temporary storage tends to disappear quickly, while storage that stays allocated for some time is small and tends to persist anyway. This process has been shown to work very well, especially with a virtual memory system.

8.6 Exception Handling and Environments

In the previous chapter we described exception handling in some detail in terms of its syntax, semantics, and use. In this section we give an introduction into implementation issues, particularly as they affect the structure and behavior of the runtime environment. Further detail can be found in the sources listed in the Notes and References.

In principle, the operations of raising and handling exceptions are similar to procedure calls, and can be implemented in similar ways. However, there are major differences as well. Primary among these are:

1. An activation cannot be created on the runtime stack to represent the raising of an exception, since this stack itself may be unwound as previously described when searching for a handler.

2. A handler must be found and "called" dynamically, rather than statically as with ordinary function calls.

3. The actions of a handler are based on the type of the exception, rather than the exception value itself; thus, exception type information must be retained during execution, contrary to standard practice for statically typed languages.[13]

The first difference can be easily overcome: When an exception is raised, no activation record is created, but the exception object (and its type information) are placed in a known location (a register or static memory), and a jump is performed to generic code that performs the process of looking for a handler (or calling exit code if one is not found). The return address (for successful handling of an exception) must also be stored in a known location, and this address is (under the termination model) the location following the block in which the exception occurred (or the return address of the most recent call if the block is a procedure).

---

[13] Of course, languages with dynamic types, such as LISP and Smalltalk, already have type information available at runtime. C++ and Java also have mechanisms available for preserving and extracting type information when necessary at runtime; in C++ the mechanism is called RTTI (for Run Time Type Information); in Java it is called Reflection.

The second difference is more problematic. Pointers to handlers must, at least in theory, be kept on some kind of stack. Each time code is entered that has an associated handler, a new handler pointer is pushed, and when that same code is exited, the pointer is popped again to reveal any previous handlers. If this stack is to be implemented directly, it must be maintained either on the heap or elsewhere in its own memory area (i.e., not on the runtime stack), and a pointer to the current stack top must be maintained, either in static memory or a register.

The third difference above is somewhat less problematic, but may involve some complexity that we do not describe here. The main issue is how to record the needed type information (essentially the type names) without added overhead in the exception structures themselves. One possibility is to have some sort of lookup table.

Once these issues have been addressed, the implementation of handlers is relatively straightforward. The basic idea is to collect all handler code attached to a particular block into a single handler implemented as a switch statement, based on the type of the exception parameter received, with a default case that pops the handler stack (adjusting the current return address) and, if necessary, pops the runtime stack before reraising the same exception. (Procedure blocks must at least have this latter default handler, even if no exceptions are explicitly handled.) For example, we saw the following handler code in Figure 7.11:

```
void factor() throw (Unwind,InputError)
{ try
  {...}
  catch (UnexpectedChar u)
  {...}
  catch (Unwind u)
  {...}
  catch (NumberExpected n)
  {...}
}
```

The handler for this `try` block might be implemented as in the following pseudocode:

```
switch (exception.type)
{ case UnexpectedChar: ...; break;
  case Unwind : ...; break;
  case NumberExpected: ... ; break;
  default: pop the runtime stack and reraise the excep-
  tion;
}
pop the runtime stack and return to caller;
```

The main problem with the implementation techniques described so far is that the maintenance of the handler stack causes a potentially significant runtime penalty, even for code that does not use exception handling. One would like to provide an alternative to the handler stack that can be statically generated, and thus cost nothing for code that does not use exception handling (this was a major design goal for C++). Such an alternative is a sorted table of code addresses that records the available handlers. When an exception occurs, the exception code performs a lookup based on the code address where the exception occurred (a binary search of the address table, for example). If no handler is found, the block in which the exception occurred is exited and the exit address is used for a new lookup.

Of course, such an address table has its own problems. First, the table itself can be quite large, causing the memory use of the program to grow significantly (a classic time-space tradeoff). Second, when an exception does occur, there can be an even greater execution speed penalty due to multiple searches of the address table. In a typical C++ system, for example, handling an exception may be as much as two orders of magnitude slower than a simple jump such as a loop exit. Thus, it makes even more sense in such systems to avoid using exceptions for routine control flow, and save them for truly unusual events.

Exercises

8.1 Beginning programmers often add a `return` statement at the end of each procedure:

```
void inc (int* x)
{ (*x)++;
    return;
}
```

The thinking is that, as with `switch` statements, there might be a "fall-through" if the `return` is not there. Could a function mechanism be designed that would allow this? Would it make sense to have such a mechanism?

8.2 What if we wrote an increment procedure in C as follows (removing the parentheses around `*x`):

```
void inc (int* x)
{ *x++;
}
```

Is this legal? If so, what does this procedure do? If not, why not?

8.3 Can a `swap` procedure that interchanges the values of its parameters be written in Java? Discuss.

8.4 (a) Consider the `intswap` C++ procedure of Section 8.1:

```
void intswap (int& x, int& y)
{ int t = x;
```

```
        x = y;
        y = t;
    }
```

Is this procedure in closed form? Why or why not?

(b) Is the following polymorphic `swap` procedure in C++ in closed form (why or why not)?

```
template <typename T>
void swap (T& x, T& y)
{ T temp = x;
    x = y;
    y = temp;
}
```

8.5 Suppose we tried to write a C procedure that would initialize an array to a certain size as follows:

```
void init(int a[], int size)
{ a = (int*) malloc(size*sizeof(int));
}
```

What, if anything, is wrong with this? Explain.

8.6 Here are some function declarations in C:

```
void f(int x, double y);
void f(int a, double);
void f(int, double z);
void f(int y, double q)
{ if (q > y) printf("ok!\n");
    else printf("not ok!\n");
}
```

Would it be legal to include all of the declarations in the same code file? Explain.

8.7 Suppose we tried to write a procedure in Java that would append "hello" to the end of a string:

```
class TestParams
{ public static void appendHello( String s)
    { s = s+"hello";
    }
    public static void main( String[] args)
    { String s = "Greetings! ";
        appendHello(s);
        System.out.println(s);
    }
}
```

Explain the behavior of this program. Can it be fixed?

8.8 Give the output of the following program (written in C syntax) using the four parameter passing methods discussed in Section 8.3:

```
int i;
int a[2];

void p( int x, int y)
{ x++;
  i++;
  y++;
}
main()
{ a[0] := 1;
  a[1] := 1;
  i = 0;
  p(a[i],a[i]);
  printf("%d\n",a[0]);
  printf("%d\n",a[1]);
  return 0;
}
```

8.9 Give the output of the following program using the four parameter passing methods of Section 8.3:

```
int i;
int a[3];

void swap( int x, int y)
{ x = x + y;
  y = x - y
  x = x - y
}

main()
{ i = 1;
  a[0] = 2;
  a[1] = 1;
  a[2] = 0;
  swap(i,a[i]);
  printf("%d %d %d %d\n", i, a[0], a[1], a[2]);
  swap(a[i],a[i]);
  printf("%d %d %d\n", a[0], a[1], a[2]);
  return 0;
}
```

8.10 FORTRAN has the convention that all parameter passing is by reference. Nevertheless, as described in the chapter, it is possible to call subroutines with nonvariable expressions as arguments, as in CALL P(X,X+Y,2).

(a) Explain how one can pass a variable X by value in FORTRAN.

(b) Suppose that subroutine P is declared as follows

```
SUBROUTINE P(A)
INTEGER A
```

```
PRINT *, A
A = A + 1
RETURN
END
```

and is called from the main program as follows:

```
CALL P(1)
```

In some FORTRAN systems this will cause a runtime error. In others, no runtime error occurs, but if the subroutine is called again with 1 as its argument, it may print the value 2. Explain how both behaviors might occur.

8.11 In Ada the compiler checks to make sure that the value of an in parameter is not changed in a procedure, and then allows in parameters to be implemented using pass by reference. Why not insist on pass by value for in parameters, so that the compiler check can be eliminated (as in C and Java)?

8.12 Ada restricts the parameters in a function declaration to be in parameters. Why is this?

8.13 A variation on pass by name is **pass by text**, in which the arguments are evaluated in delayed fashion, just as in pass by name, but each argument is evaluated in the environment of the called procedure, rather than in the calling environment. Show that pass by text can have different results from pass by name.

8.14 The Algol60 definition states the following **substitution rule** for pass by name:

1. Any formal parameter . . . is replaced, throughout the procedure body, by the corresponding actual parameter, after enclosing this latter in parentheses wherever syntactically possible. Possible conflicts between identifiers inserted through this process and other identifiers already present within the procedure body will be avoided by suitable systematic changes of the formal or local identifiers involved.
2. Finally the procedure body, modified as above, is inserted in place of the procedure statement and executed. If the procedure is called from a place outside the scope of any nonlocal quantity of the procedure body the conflicts between the identifiers inserted through this process of body replacement and the identifiers whose declarations are valid at the place of the procedure statement or function designator will be avoided through suitable systematic changes of the latter identifiers. (Naur [1963a], p. 12)

   (a) Give an example of an identifier conflict as described in rule 1.
   (b) Give an example of an identifier conflict as described in rule 2.
   (c) Carry out the replacement process described in these two rules on the program in Figure 8.1.

8.15 (a) Write a function that uses Jensen's device and pass by name to compute the scalar product of two vectors declared as array[1..n] of integer.

(b) The following sum procedure (in C syntax) was used as an example of pass by name and Jensen's device at the end of Section 8.3.4:

```
int sum (int a, int index, int size)
{ int temp = 0;
    for (index = 0; index < size; index++)   temp += a;
    return temp;
}
```

Rewrite this code using a function parameter for the parameter a to imitate pass by name, so that it actually executes like pass by name in C.

8.16 The text did not discuss the scope of parameter declarations inside function or procedure declarations.

(a) Describe the scope of the declaration of x in the following C procedure:

```
void p( int x)
{   int y, z;
    ...
}
```

(b) State whether the following C procedure declarations are legal, and give reasons:

```
void p( int p) { ... }
void p( int x) { int x; ... }
```

8.17 Draw the stack of activation records for the following C program after **(a)** the call to r on line 13 and **(b)** after the call to p on line 14. Show the control links, and fill in the local names in each activation record. **(c)** Describe how variables r and x are found on lines 4 and 5 during the execution of p.

```
(1)   int x;
(2)   void p(void)
(3)   { double r = 2;
(4)       printf("%g\n",r);
(5)       printf("%d\n",x);
(6)   }

(7)   void r(void)
(8)   { x = 1;
(9)       p();
(10)  }

(11)  void q(void)
(12)  { double x = 3;
(13)      r();
(14)      p();
(15)  }
```

```
(16) main()
(17) { p();
(18)    q();
(19)    return 0;
(20) }
```

8.18 Draw the stack of activation records for the following Ada program
(a) after the first call to procedure b; (b) after the second call to procedure b. Show the control links *and* the access links for each activation
record. (c) Indicate how b is found in procedure c.

```
procedure env is

  procedure a is

    procedure b is

      procedure c is
      begin
        b;
      end c;

    begin
      c;
    end b;

  begin
    b;
  end a;

begin
  a;
end env;
```

8.19 The following Ada program contains a function parameter.
(a) Draw the stack of activation records after the call to g in p.
(b) What does the program print and why?

```
with Text_IO; use Text_IO;
with Ada.Integer_Text_IO;
use Ada.Integer_Text_IO;

procedure params is
  procedure q is
  type IntFunc is access function (n:integer)
  return integer;
  m: integer := 0;

  function f (n: integer) return integer is
  begin
    return m + n;
  end f;
```

(continues)

(continued)

```
        procedure p (g: IntFunc) is
          m: integer := 3;
        begin
          put(g(2)); new_line;
        end p;

        begin
          p(f'access);
        end q;

  begin
    q;
  end params;
```

8.20 Show that the access link in an activation record (the "static" link) isn't static.

8.21 Suppose we tried to avoid adding an access link to each activation record in a language with nested procedures by devising a mechanism for counting our way through dynamic links until the appropriate activation was reached (dynamic links will always lead eventually to the correct lexical environment). Why can't this work?

8.22 FORTRAN allows the passing of variable-length arrays, as in the following examples:

```
SUBROUTINE P(A,I)
INTEGER I
REAL A(*)
...

SUBROUTINE Q(B,N)
INTEGER N,B(N)
...
```

Does this cause any problems for the activation records of P and Q, which in FORTRAN must have fixed size and location?

8.23 Some FORTRAN implementations use pass by value-result rather than pass by reference. Would this affect your answer to the previous exercise? Why?

8.24 In C, blocks that are not procedures, but have variable declarations, such as

```
{ int i;
    for (i=1; i<n; i++) a[i] = i;
}
```

can be allocated an activation record just as procedures. What fields in the activation record are unused or redundant in this case? Can such blocks be implemented without a new activation record?

8.25 Suppose we disallowed recursion in Ada. Would it be possible to construct a fully static environment for the language? Is the same true for C?

8.26 Describe how, in a language without procedure parameters, the environment pointer of a procedure closure does not need to be stored with the procedure, but can be computed when the procedure is called.

8.27 Suppose we wanted to state a rule that would make the C dangling reference created by the following function illegal:

```
int* dangle(void)
{ int x;
   return &x;
}
```

Suppose we decided to make the following statement: The address of a local variable cannot be a returned value and cannot be assigned to a nonlocal variable.
(a) Can this rule be checked statically?
(b) Does this rule solve the problem of dangling references created by the use of a stack-based environment?

8.28 The example program `params` of Exercise 8.19 remains valid from the point of view of a stack-based runtime environment if the definitions of procedure g and the `IntFunc` type are moved outside of procedure q, and yet Ada considers the new program to be erroneous.
(a) Draw the new runtime environment after the call to g in p that results from this change to show that it is still valid.
(b) Discuss the reasons that Ada declares error in this program (see the access-type lifetime rule discussion in Section 8.4.3).

8.29 The following program in Ada syntax has a function that has another function as its returned value, and so needs a fully dynamic runtime environment as described in Section 8.4.3. Draw a picture of the environment when g is called inside b. What should this program print?

```
with Text_IO; use Text_IO;
with Ada.Integer_Text_IO;
use Ada.Integer_Text_IO;

procedure ret is
   type IntFunc is
         access function (n:integer) return integer;

   function a return IntFunc is
   m: integer;

      function addm( n: integer) return integer is
      begin
         return (n + m);
      end addm;                                  (continues)
```

(continued)

```
            begin
              m := 0;
              return addm'access;
            end a;

            procedure b(g: IntFunc) is
            begin
              put(g(2));
            end b;

          begin
            b(a);
          end ret;
```

8.30 Compare the execution speeds of the simple arithmetic expression parser of Chapter 4 with the parser of the previous chapter that uses exceptions. Is there any difference under normal processing? Under abnormal processing?

8.31 Using a debugger, try to determine whether your C++ compiler uses static address tables to lookup exception handlers. Describe what the debugger tells you is occurring when an exception is raised.

8.32 Write declarations in a language of your choice for the maintenance of a free list of memory as **(a)** a circular singly linked list, and **(b)** a non-circular doubly linked list. Write procedures to deallocate a block using both of these data structures, being sure to coalesce adjacent blocks. Compare the ease of coalescing blocks in each case.

8.33 Show how compaction of memory can be accomplished by using a table to maintain an extra level of indirection, so that when a block of storage is moved, only one pointer needs to be changed.

8.34 In Section 8.5 a method of mark and sweep garbage collection was described in which memory is split into two sections, only one of which is used for allocation between calls to the garbage collector. It was claimed in the text that this eliminates the need for extra space to mark memory that has been previously seen. Describe how this can be accomplished.

8.35 In the generational method of garbage collection, it is still necessary eventually to reclaim "permanently" allocated storage after long execution times. It has been suggested that this could be made to interfere the least with execution by scheduling it to be performed "offline," that is, during periods when the running program is waiting for input or other processing. For this to be effective, the garbage collector must have a good interface with the operating system, especially if virtual memory is in use. Describe as many operating system issues as you can think of in this approach.

Notes and References

Structures of runtime environments are described in more detail in Louden [1997] and Aho, Sethi, and Ullman [1986]. Closures of procedures with non-local references are related to closures of lambda expressions with free variables; see Section 11.7. The access-type lifetime rule in Ada is discussed in more detail in Cohen [1996].

Dynamic memory management is treated in more detail in Horowitz and Sahni [1984] and Aho, Hopcroft, and Ullman [1983]. Traditionally, languages that have first-class procedures, and thus must use automatic memory management, have been thought to be highly inefficient for that reason. Advances in algorithms, such as generational garbage collection, and advances in translation techniques make this much less true. References dealing with efficiency issues are Steele [1977] and Gabriel [1985]; see also Louden [1987]. Overviews of garbage collection techniques can be found in Wilson [1992] or Cohen [1981]. Generational garbage collection was first described in Ungar [1984]. A generational garbage collector and runtime environment for the functional language ML is described in Appel [1992].

Exception handling implementation is discussed in Scott [2000] and Stroustrup [1994]. Details of two implementations can be found in Koenig and Stroustrup [1990] and Lenkov et al. [1992]. See also Lajoie [1994ab].

Abstract
9 Data Types
and Modules

In Chapter 6 we defined a data type as a set of values with certain operations on those values. Data types were divided into the predefined types of a language and user-defined types. Predefined types such as `integer` and `real` are designed to insulate the user of a language from the implementation of the data type, which is machine dependent. These data types can be manipulated by a set of predefined operations, such as the arithmetic operations, whose implementation details are also hidden from the user. Their use is completely specified by predetermined semantics, which are either explicitly stated in the language definition or are implicitly well known (like the mathematical properties of the arithmetic operations).

User-defined types, on the other hand, are built up from data structures created using the built-in types and type constructors of the language. Their structures are visible to the user, and they do not come with any operations other than the accessing operations of the data structures themselves (such as the field selection operation on a record structure). One can, of course, define functions to operate on these data structures, but with the standard procedure or function definitions available in most programming languages, these user-defined functions are not directly associated with the data type, and the implementation details of the data type and the operations are visible throughout the program.

It would be very desirable to have a mechanism in a programming language to construct data types that would have as many of the characteristics of a built-in type as possible. Such a mechanism should provide the following:

1. A method for defining a data type and at the same time operations on that type. The definitions should all be collected in one place, and the operations should be directly associated with the type. The definitions should not depend on any implementation details. The definitions of the operations should include a specification of their semantics.

2. A method for collecting the implementation details of the type and its operations in one place, and of restricting access to these details by programs that use the data type.

A data type constructed using a mechanism satisfying some or all of these two criteria is often called an **abstract data type** (or **ADT** for short). Note, however, that there is nothing really more abstract about such a type than a usual built-in type. It is just a more comprehensive way of creating user-defined types than the usual type declaration mechanism of Algol-like languages.

Criteria 1 and 2 promote three design goals that data types were originally introduced to assist with: modifiability, reusability, and security. Modifiability is enhanced by interfaces that are implementation independent, since changes can be made to an implementation without affecting its use by the rest of the program. Reusability is enhanced by standard interfaces, since the code can be reused by different programs. Security is enhanced by protecting the implementation details from arbitrary modification by other parts of a program.

Some authors, rather than using criteria 1 and 2, refer to **encapsulation** and **information hiding** as the essential properties of an abstract data type mechanism. Encapsulation refers to the collection of all definitions related to a data type in one location and restricting the use of the type to the operations defined at that location. Information hiding refers to the separation of implementation details from these definitions and the suppression of these details in the use of the data type. Since encapsulation and information hiding are sometimes difficult to separate in practice, we will use criteria 1 and 2 as our basis for studying abstract data types.

Confusion can sometimes result from the failure to distinguish a **mechanism** for constructing types in a programming language that has the foregoing properties, with the **mathematical concept** of a type, which is a conceptual model for actual types. This second notion is sometimes also called an abstract data type, or abstract type. Such mathematical models are often given in terms of an **algebraic specification**, which can be used to create an actual type in a programming language using an abstract data type mechanism with the foregoing properties.

Even more confusion exists over the difference between abstract data types and so-called **object-oriented programming**, the subject of the next chapter. Object-oriented programming emphasizes the capability of language entities to control their own use during execution and to share operations in carefully controlled ways. In an object-oriented programming language the primary language entity is the object, that is, something that occupies memory and has state. But these objects are also active: They control access to their own memory and state. This can include types, which control access to themselves in declarations and operations. In this sense, an abstract data type mechanism lends itself to the object-oriented approach, since information about a type is localized and access to this information is controlled. But abstract data type mechanisms do not provide the level of active control that represents true object-oriented programming. See Section 9.7 and the next chapter for more details.

The notion of abstract data type is in fact independent of the language paradigm (function, imperative, object-oriented) used to implement it, and languages from all three paradigms are used in this chapter as examples of different approaches to ADTs.

A further issue is that an ADT mechanism is often expressed in terms of a somewhat more general concept called a **module**, which is a collection of services that may or may not include a data type or types. Further, modules themselves are often related to indistinctly expressed notions of separate compilation and file structures.[1]

In the sections that follow we will first describe a method for specifying abstract data types and introduce some standard abstract data type

---

[1] "Indistinctly expressed" means that separate compilation and file structure issues may not be precisely specified in a language definition, since such a specification is difficult to do in an operating system-independent way.

mechanisms in programming languages. We then describe some aspects of modules and separate compilation and relate them to abstract data types, with examples from C, C++, and Java. Further sections will provide examples from Ada and ML. We also survey some of the limitations of these mechanisms. In the last section we discuss the mathematics of abstract data types.

9.1 The Algebraic Specification of Abstract Data Types

As an example of an abstract data type we will use the **complex** data type, which is not a built-in data type in most programming languages. Mathematically, complex numbers are well-known objects and are extremely useful in practice, since they represent solutions to algebraic equations. Complex numbers are usually represented as a pair of real numbers (x, y) in Cartesian coordinates, which is written as $x + iy$, where i is a symbol representing the complex number $\sqrt{-1}$. x is called the "real" part, and y is called the "imaginary" part. In fact, there are other representations for complex numbers, for example, as polar coordinates $(r,\ )$. In defining complex numbers, we shouldn't need to specify their representation, but only the operations that apply to them. These include the usual arithmetic operations "+," "−," "*," and "/." Also needed is a way of creating a complex number from a real and imaginary part and functions to extract the real and imaginary part from an existing complex number.

A general specification of a data type needs to include the name of the type and the names of the operations, including a specification of their parameters and returned values. This is the **syntactic specification** of an abstract data type, and is often also called the **signature** of the type. In a language-independent specification, it is appropriate to use the function notation of mathematics for the operations of the data type: Given a function f from set X to set Y, X is the domain, Y is the range, and we write $f: X \to Y$. For the complex data type, a signature looks like this:

type complex **imports** real

operations:

> +: complex $\times$ complex $\to$ complex
> −: complex $\times$ complex $\to$ complex
> *: complex $\times$ complex $\to$ complex
> /: complex $\times$ complex $\to$ complex
> −: complex $\to$ complex
> makecomplex: real $\times$ real $\to$ complex
> realpart: complex $\to$ real
> imaginarypart: complex $\to$ real

Note that the dependence of the complex data type on an already existing data type, namely, real, is made explicit by the "imports real" clause. (Do not confuse this imports clause with the `import` statement in some languages.) Note also that the negative sign is used for two different operations: subtraction and negation. Indeed, the usual names are used for all the arithmetic operations. Some means must eventually be used to distinguish these from the arithmetic operations on the integers and reals (or they must be allowed to be overloaded, as some languages provide).

The preceding specification lacks any notion of semantics, or the properties that the operations must actually possess. For example, $z * w$ might be defined to be always 0! In mathematics, the semantic properties of functions are often described by **equations** or **axioms**. In the case of arithmetic operations, examples of axioms are the associative, commutative, and distributive laws (in the equations that follow, x, y, and z are assumed to be variables of type complex; that is, they can take on any complex value):

$$x + (y + z) = (x + y) + z \quad \text{(associativity of +)}$$

$$x * y = y * x \quad \text{(commutativity of *)}$$

$$x * (y + z) = x * y + x * z \quad \text{(distributivity of * over +)}$$

Axioms such as these can be used to define the semantic properties of complex numbers, or the properties of the complex data type can be **derived** from those of the real data type by stating properties of the operations that lead back to properties of the real numbers. For example, complex addition can be based on real addition by giving the following properties:

$$realpart(x + y) = realpart(x) + realpart(y)$$

$$imaginarypart(x + y) = imaginarypart(x) + imaginarypart(y)$$

The appropriate arithmetic properties of the complex numbers can then be proved from the corresponding properties for reals. A complete algebraic specification of type complex combines signature, variables, and equational axioms:[2]

type complex **imports** real

operations:

+: complex $\times$ complex $\rightarrow$ complex

−: complex $\times$ complex $\rightarrow$ complex

*: complex $\times$ complex $\rightarrow$ complex

/: complex $\times$ complex $\rightarrow$ complex

−: complex $\rightarrow$ complex

makecomplex : real $\times$ real $\rightarrow$ complex

realpart : complex $\rightarrow$ real

imaginarypart : complex $\rightarrow$ real

---

[2] The variables section of a specification is a notational convenience that simply lists the names (and their types) over which the axioms are assumed to be universally quantified in the mathematical sense. Thus, the first axiom in this algebraic specification is actually "for all real r and s, realpart(makecomplex(r,s)) = s.

variables: x,y,z: complex; r,s: real

axioms:

>   realpart(makecomplex(r,s)) = r
>   imaginarypart(makecomplex(r,s)) = s
>   realpart($x+y$) = realpart(x) + realpart(y)
>   imaginarypart($x + y$) = imaginarypart(x) + imaginarypart(y)
>   realpart($x - y$) = realpart(x) - realpart(y)
>   imaginarypart($x - y$) = imaginarypart(x) - imaginarypart(y)

>   . . .

>   (more axioms)

>   . . .

Such a specification of a type is called an **algebraic specification** of an abstract data type. It provides a concise specification of a data type and its associated operations, and the equational semantics give a clear indication of implementation behavior, often containing enough information to allow coding directly from the equations. Finding an appropriate set of equations, however, can be a difficult task. Some indications of how this can be done are given in the paragraphs that follow.

Remember the difference in the foregoing specification between **equality** as used in the axioms and the **arrow** of the syntactic specification of the functions. Equality is of function values, while the arrows separate domain and range of the functions.

A second example of an algebraic specification of an abstract data type is the following specification of a queue:

type queue(element) **imports** boolean

operations:

>   createq: queue
>   enqueue: queue $\times$ element $\rightarrow$ queue
>   dequeue: queue $\rightarrow$ queue
>   frontq: queue $\rightarrow$ element
>   emptyq: queue $\rightarrow$ boolean

variables: q: queue; x: element

axioms:

>   emptyq(createq) = true
>   emptyq(enqueue(q,x)) = false
>   frontq(createq) = error
>   frontq(enqueue(q,x)) = if emptyq(q) then x else frontq(q)
>   dequeue(createq) = error
>   dequeue(enqueue(q,x)) = if emptyq(q) then q else
>   enqueue(dequeue(q),x)

This specification exhibits several new features. First, the data type queue is **parameterized** by the data type element, which is left unspecified. Such a type parameter can be replaced by any type and is indicated by placing its name inside parentheses, just as a function parameter would be. Second, there is a constant createq that is technically not a function. Such constants may also be a part of the algebraic specification; if desired, createq can be viewed as a function of no parameters that always returns the same value. Intuitively, createq is a new queue that has been initialized to empty. Third, there are now axioms that specify error values, such as

$$\text{frontq(createq)} = \text{error}$$

Such axioms can be called **error axioms**, and they provide limitations on the application of the operations. The actual error value of an error axiom is unspecified. Finally, the equations are specified using an if-then-else function, whose semantics are as follows:

$$\text{if true then } a \text{ else } b = a$$
$$\text{if false then } a \text{ else } b = b$$

Note also that the dequeue operation as specified does not return the front element of the queue, as in most implementations: It simply throws it away. Abstractly, this is simpler to handle and does not take away any functionality of the queue, since the frontq operation can extract the front element before a dequeue operation is performed.

The equations specifying the semantics of the operations in an algebraic specification of an abstract data type can be used not only as a specification of the properties of an implementation, and as a guide to the code for an implementation, but can also be used to prove specific properties about objects of the type. For example, the following applications of axioms shows that dequeuing from a queue with one element leaves an empty queue:

$$\text{emptyq(dequeue(enqueue (createq, } x)))$$
$$= \text{emptyq(createq)} \qquad \text{(by the sixth axiom above)}$$
$$= \text{true} \qquad \qquad \text{(by the first axiom)}$$

Note that the operations and the axioms are specified in a mathematical form that includes no mention of memory or of assignment. Indeed, enqueue is shown as returning a newly constructed queue every time a new element is added. These specifications are in fact in purely functional form, with no variables and no assignment (the variables in the specification are taken in the mathematical sense to be just names for values). This is important, since mathematical properties, such as the semantic equations, are much easier to express with purely functional constructions (see Chapter 11 for more on purely functional programming). In practice, abstract data type implementations often replace the specified functional behavior with a (hopefully) equivalent imperative one using explicit memory allocation and assignment or update operations. The question of how to infer that an imperative implementation is in some sense equivalent to a purely functional one such as the above is beyond the scope of our study here.

How do we find an appropriate axiom set for an algebraic specification? In general, this is a difficult question. One can, however, make some judgments about what kind and how many axioms are needed by looking at the syntax of the operations. An operation that creates a new object of the data type being defined is called a **constructor**, while an operation that retrieves previously constructed values is called an **inspector**. In the queue example, createq and enqueue are constructors, while frontq, dequeue, and emptyq are inspectors. Inspector operations can also be broken down into **predicates**, which return Boolean values, and selectors, which return non-Boolean values. Thus frontq and dequeue are selectors, while emptyq is a predicate.

In general, one needs one axiom for each combination of an inspector with a constructor. For the queue example, the axiom combinations are

$$emptyq(createq)$$
$$emptyq(enqueue(q,x))$$
$$frontq(createq)$$
$$frontq(enqueue(q,x))$$
$$dequeue(createq)$$
$$dequeue(enqueue(q,x))$$

According to this scheme, there should be six rules in all, and that is in fact the case.

As a final example of an algebraic specification of an abstract data type, we give a specification for the stack abstract data type, which has many of the same features as the queue ADT:

type stack(element) **imports** boolean

operations:

   createstk: stack
   push: stack × element → stack
   pop: stack → stack
   top: stack → element
   emptystk: stack → boolean

variables: s: stack; x: element

axioms:

   emptystk(createstk) = true
   emptystk(push(s,x)) = false
   top(createstk) = error
   top(push(s,x)) = x
   pop(createstk) = error
   pop(push(s,x)) = s

In this case, the operations createstk and push are constructors, the pop and top operations are selectors, and the emptystk operation is a predicate. By our proposed scheme, therefore, there should again be six axioms.

9.2 Abstract Data Type Mechanisms and Modules

9.2.1 Abstract Data Type Mechanisms

Some languages have a specific mechanism for expressing abstract data types. Such a mechanism must have a way of separating the specification or signature of the ADT (the name of the type being specified, and the names and types of the operations) from its implementation (a data structure implementing the type and a code body for each of the operations). Such a mechanism must also guarantee that any code outside the ADT definition cannot use details of the implementation, but can operate on a value of the defined type only through the provided operations.

ML is an example of a language with a special ADT mechanism, called abstype. It is viewed as a kind of type definition mechanism. An example of its use to specify a queue is given in Figure 9.1.

```
(1) abstype 'element Queue = Q of 'element list
(2) with
(3)   val createq = Q [];
(4)   fun enqueue (Q lis, elem) = Q (lis @ [elem]);
(5)   fun dequeue (Q lis) = Q (tl lis);
(6)   fun frontq (Q lis) = hd lis;
(7)   fun emptyq (Q []) = true | emptyq (Q (h::t)) = false;
(8) end;
```

Figure 9.1   A queue ADT as an ML abstype, implemented as an ordinary ML list

Here we have used an ordinary list in ML ('element list, line 1). Since an abstype must be a new type and not a type defined elsewhere, we also had to wrap 'element list in a constructor, for which we have used the single letter Q;[3] this constructor is not visible outside the definition of the abstype. Recall also that lists are written in ML using square brackets [...], @ is the append operator (line 4), h::t is a pattern for the list with head h and tail t (line 7), hd is the head function on lists (line 6), and tl is the tail function on lists (line 5). (For more on the details of the actual type constructor specification Q of 'element list see Chapter 6.)

_____

[3] It is a common practice to use the same name as the data type, namely Queue, for this constructor, but we have not done so in an attempt to make the code easier to understand.

When this definition is processed by the ML translator, it responds with essentially a description of the signature of the type:

```
type 'a Queue
val createq = - : 'a Queue
val enqueue = fn : 'a Queue * 'a -> 'a Queue
val dequeue = fn : 'a Queue -> 'a Queue
val frontq = fn : 'a Queue -> 'a
val emptyq = fn : 'a Queue -> bool
```

Since ML has parametric polymorphism, the Queue type can be parameterized by the type of the element that is to be stored in the queue, and we have done that with the type parameter 'element (reported as 'a by the ML system). Notice how ML refuses to specify the internal structure in this description, writing a dash for the actual representation of createq, and using only 'a Queue to refer to the type. Thus, all internal details of the representation of Queue, including its constructors, are suppressed and remain private to the code of the abstype definition.

With the above definition, the Queue type can be used in ML as follows:

```
- val q = enqueue(createq,3);
val q = - : int Queue
- val q2 = enqueue(q,4);
val q2 = - : int Queue
- frontq q2;
val it = 3 : int
- val q3 = dequeue q2;
val q3 = - : int Queue
- frontq q3;
val it = 4 : int
```

As a second example, a complex number ADT can be specified in ML as given in Figure 9.2.

```
(1) abstype Complex = C of real * real
(2) with
(3)   fun makecomplex (x,y) = C (x,y);
(4)   fun realpart (C (r,i)) = r;
(5)   fun imaginarypart (C (r,i)) = i;
(6)   fun +: ( C (r1,i1), C (r2,i2) ) = C (r1+r2, i1+i2);
(7)   infix 6 +: ;
(8)   (* other operations *)
(9) end;
```

Figure 9.2   A complex number ADT as an ML abstype

ML allows user-defined operators (they are called **infix functions** in ML), and they can use special symbols, but they cannot reuse the standard operator symbols, since ML does not allow user-defined overloading. Thus, in line 6 of Figure 9.2 we have defined the addition operator on complex numbers to have the name +: (a plus sign followed by a colon). Line 7 makes this into an infix operator (with left associativity), and gives it the precedence level 6, which is the ML precedence level for the built-in additive operators such as + and -. The Complex type can be used as follows:

```
- val z = makecomplex (1.0,2.0);
val z = - : Complex
- val w = makecomplex (2.0,~1.0); (* ~ is negation *)
val w = - : Complex
- val x = z +: w;
val x = - : Complex
- realpart x;
val it = 3.0 : real
- imaginarypart x;
val it = 1.0 : real
```

9.2.2 Modules

An ADT mechanism such as we have described in Section 9.2.1—essentially an extension of the definition of an ordinary data type—is completely adequate, even superior, as a way of implementing an abstract data type in a language with strong type abstractions such as ML. However, even in ML it is not the end of the story, since a pure ADT mechanism does not address the entire range of situations where an ADT-like abstraction mechanism is useful in a programming language.

Consider for example, a mathematical function package consisting of the standard functions such as sine, cosine, exponential, and logarithmic functions. These functions are closely related, and we might wish to encapsulate their definitions and implementations and hide the implementation details (which could then be changed without changing client code that uses these functions). However, such a package is not associated directly with a data type (or the data type, such as double, is built-in or defined elsewhere). Thus, such a package does not fit the format of an ADT mechanism as described in Section 9.2.1.

Similarly, a programming language compiler is a large program that is typically split into separate pieces corresponding to the phases described in Chapter 1:

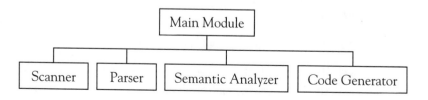

We would certainly wish to apply the principles of encapsulation and information hiding to each of the code pieces in this diagram. Here also, there is no special data type that can be associated directly with each phase. Instead, these examples demonstrate the need for an encapsulation mechanism that is viewed more generally as a provider of services, and that is given by the concept of a module:

> **Definition:** A *module* is a program unit with a public interface and a private implementation; all services that are available from a module are described in its public interface and are exported to other modules, and all services that are needed by a module must be imported from other modules.

As providers of services, modules can export any mix of data types, procedures, variables, and constants. Also, because modules have explicit (public) interfaces and separate (private) implementations, they are ideal mechansims to provide separate compilation and library facilities within a software development environment. Indeed, many languages, such as Ada and Java, tie the structure of modules to separate compilation issues (although the relationship is kept loose enough to allow for variation from system to system). Typically in a compiler-based system, the interface for each module in a library or program is kept in textual form, while the implementation may only be provided as object code, and is only needed at the link step to produce a running program.

Thus, modules are an essential tool in program decomposition, complexity control, and the creation of libraries for code sharing and reuse. Additionally, modules assist in the control of **name proliferation**: large programs have large numbers of names, and mechanisms to control access to these names, as well as preventing name clashes, are an essential requirement of a modern programming language. Nested scopes are only the first step in such name control, and modules typically provide additional scope features that make the task of name control more manageable. Indeed, one view of a module is that its main purpose is to provide controlled scopes, exporting only those names that its interface requires, and keeping hidden all others. At the same time, even the exported names should be **qualified** by the module name, to avoid accidental name clashes when the same name is used by two different modules. Typically this is done using the same dot notation used for structures, so that feature y from module X has the name X.y when imported into client code. (Note that the ML `abstype` mechanism discussed previously does not have this essential name control feature.)

Finally, a module mechanism can document the dependencies of a module on other modules by requiring explicit import lists whenever code from other modules is used. These dependencies can be used by a compiler to automatically recompile out-of-date modules and to automatically link in separately compiled code.

In the following sections, we will describe the mechanisms that several different languages (with very different approaches) offer to provide modular facilities.

9.3 Separate Compilation in C, C++ Namespaces, and Java Packages

We collect three different mechanisms in this section, because they are all less concerned with the full range of modular properties, but are aimed primarily at separate compilation and name control.

9.3.1 Separate Compilation in C and C++

The first language we consider is C. C does not have any module mechanisms as such, but it does have separate compilation and name control features that can be used to at least simulate modules in a reasonably effective way. Consider, for example, a queue data structure in C. A typical organization would be to place type and function specifications in a so-called **header file** queue.h as in Figure 9.3. Only type definitions and function declarations without bodies (called **prototypes** in C) go into this file. This file is used as a specification of the queue ADT by textually including it in client code as well as implementation code using the C preprocessor #include directive. Sample client code and implementation code is provided in Figures 9.4 and 9.5, respectively. Graphically, the separation of specification, implementation, and client code is as follows (with the inclusion dependencies represented by the arrows):

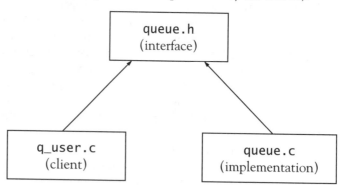

We make the following comments about the code of Figures 9.3–9.5.

The header file queue.h exhibits the standard C convention of surrounding the code with an #ifndef ... #endif preprocessor block (Figure 9.3, lines 1, 2, and 10). This causes the symbol QUEUE_H (a conventional modification of the file name) to be defined the first time the file is included, and all repeated inclusions to be skipped. This is a necessary feature of header files, since there may be multiple paths through which a header file is included, and the resulting repeated Queue type definition will cause a compilation error without it.

```
(1) #ifndef QUEUE_H
(2) #define QUEUE_H

(3) struct Queuerep;
(4) typedef struct Queuerep * Queue;

(5) Queue createq(void);
(6) Queue enqueue(Queue q, void* elem);
(7) void* frontq(Queue q);
(8) Queue dequeue(Queue q);
(9) int emptyq(Queue q);

(10) #endif
```

Figure 9.3   A queue.h header file in C

```
(1) #include "queue.h"
(2) #include <stdlib.h>
(3)   struct Queuerep
(4)   { void* data;
(5)     Queue next;
(6)   };

(7)   Queue createq(void)
(8)   { return 0;
(9)   }

(10) Queue enqueue(Queue q, void* elem)
(11) { Queue temp = malloc(sizeof(struct Queuerep));
(12)    temp->data = elem;
(13)    if (q)
(14)    { temp->next = q->next;
(15)      q->next = temp;
(16)      q = temp;
(17)    }
(18)    else
(19)    { q = temp;
(20)      q->next = temp;
(21)    }
(22)    return q;
(23) }

(24) void* frontq(Queue q)
(25) { return q->next->data;
(26) }

(27) Queue dequeue(Queue q)
(28) { Queue temp;
(29)    if (q == q->next)
(30)    { temp = q;
(31)      q = 0;
```

(continues)

(continued)

```
(32)   }
(33)   else
(34)   { temp = q->next;
(35)      q->next = q->next->next;
(36)   }
(37)   free(temp);
(38)   return q;
(39) }

(40) int emptyq(Queue q)
(41) { return q == 0;
(42) }
```

Figure 9.4 A queue.c implementation file in C

```
(1)   #include <stdlib.h>
(2)   #include <stdio.h>
(3)   #include "queue.h"

(4)   main()
(5)   {  int *x = malloc(sizeof(int));
(6)      int *y = malloc(sizeof(int));
(7)      int *z;
(8)      Queue q = createq();
(9)      *x = 2;
(10)     *y = 3;
(11)     q = enqueue(q,x);
(12)     q = enqueue(q,y);
(13)     z = (int*) frontq(q);
(14)     printf("%d\n",*z); /* prints 2 */
(15)     q = dequeue(q);
(16)     z = (int*) frontq(q);
(17)     printf("%d\n",*z); /* prints 3 */
(18)     return 0;
(19) }
```

Figure 9.5 A client code file q_user.c in C

The definition of the Queue data type is hidden in the implementation by defining Queue to be a pointer type (Figure 9.3, line 4), and leaving the actual queue representation structure (Queuerep, line 3) as an **incomplete type**. If this were not done, then the entire Queue data structure would have to be declared in the header file (since the compiler would need to know its size) and thus exposed to clients, and clients would then be able to write code that depends on the implementation, thus destroying the desired implementation independence of the interface. (On the other hand, making `Queue` into a pointer type has other drawbacks, since assignment and equality tests do not necessarily work as desired—see Section 9.7.)

Ideally, a `Queue` data type needs be parameterized by the data type of the elements it stores, as we have seen. However, C does not have user polymorphism of any kind. Nevertheless, parametric polymorphism can be effectively simulated by the use of `void*` elements, which are "pointers to anything" in C, and which can be used with casts to store any dynamically allocated object. Of course, there is the added burden of dynamically allocating all data and providing appropriate casts; also this code can be dangerous, since client code must always know the actual data type of the elements being stored; this is closely related to the based-object approach to parametric polymorphism in Java, noted in the next chapter.

The `queue.c` implementation file provides the actual definition for `Queuerep` (Figure 9.4, lines 3–6), and the code for the bodies of the interface functions. In the sample code we have used a singly-linked circular list with the queue itself represented by a pointer to the last element (the empty queue is represented by the null pointer 0).

The files `queue.c` and `q_user.c` can be separately compiled, and either can be changed without recompiling the other. For example, the queue implementation could be changed to a doubly-linked list with pointers to the first and last elements (Exercise 9.9), without affecting any client code. Also, after the `queue.c` file is compiled, no further recompilation is needed (and the implementation can be supplied to clients as header and object file only). This makes the implementation and client code reasonably independent of each other.

This mechanism for implementing abstract data types works fairly well in practice; it is even better suited to the definition of modules that do not export types, such as a math module (see the standard C `math.h` file), where the complications of incomplete types and dynamic allocation do not arise. However, the effectiveness of this mechanism depends entirely on convention, since neither C compilers nor standard linkers enforce any of the protection rules normally associated with module or ADT mechanisms. For example, a client could fail to include the header file `queue.h`, but simply textually copy the definitions in `queue.h` directly into the `q_user.c` file (by cut and paste, for instance). Then the dependence of the client code on the queue code is not made explicit by the `#include` directive. Worse, if changes to the `queue.h` file were made (which would mean all client code should be recompiled), these changes would not automatically be imported into the client code, but neither the compiler nor the linker would report an error: not the compiler, since the client code would be consistent with the now incorrect queue interface code, and not the linker, since the linker only ensures that some definition exists for every name, not that the definition is consistent with its uses. In fact, client code can circumvent the protection of the incomplete

Queuerec data type itself by this same mechanism: If the actual structure of Queuerec is known to the client, it can be copied into the client code and its structure used without any complaint on the part of the compiler or linker. This points out that this use of separate compilation is not a true module mechanism, but a simulation, albeit a reasonably effective one.

We note also that, while the #include directives in a source code file do provide some documentation of dependencies, this information cannot be used by a compiler or linker because there are no language rules for the structure of header files or their relationship to implementation files. Thus, all C systems require that the user keep track of out-of-date source code and manually recompile and relink.[4]

One might suppose that C++ improves significantly on this mechanism, and in some ways it does: Using the class mechanism of object-oriented programming (next chapter), C++ allows better control over access to the Queue data type. C++ also offers better control over names and name access through the namespace mechanism (next subsection). But C++ offers no additional features that would enhance the use of separate compilation to simulate modules.[5] In fact, such additional features would, as noted, place an extra burden on the linker to discover incompatible definitions and uses, and a strict design goal of C++ was that the standard C linker should continue to be used (Stroustrup [1994], page 120). Thus, C++ continues to use textual inclusion and header files to implement modules and libraries.

One might also imagine that the C++ template mechanism could be used to eliminate the use of void* to simulate parametric polymorphism in C. Unfortunately, templates in C++ do not mix well with separate compilation, since instantiations of template types requires knowledge of the separately compiled template code by the C++ compiler. Thus, the use of templates would not only force the details of the Queuerec data type to be included in the header file, but, using most compilers, even the code for the function implementations would have to be put into the header file (and thus the entire contents of queue.c would have to be moved to queue.h!). In fact, the standard template library of C++ exhibits precisely this property: Virtually all the code is in the header files only. Fortunately, the use of access control within the class mechanism still allows some form of protection, but the situation is far from ideal. The use of templates in data types is thus most effective in conjunction with the class construct. See Chapter 10 for an example.

---

[4] The lack of such a module facility in C led directly to the construction of tools to manage compilation and linking issues, such as the Unix make utility.

[5] Strictly speaking, the C++ standard does make it a violation of the "one definition rule" to have two different definitions of the same data structure that are not syntactically and semantically identical, but then allows linkers to fail to catch this error. See Stroustrup [1997], Section 9.2.3 for a discussion.

9.3.2 C++ Namespaces and Java Packages

One feature of C++ that does provide an effective supplement to the simulation of modules in C is the `namespace` mechanism. It is essentially a feature that allows the explicit introduction of a named scope to avoid name clashes among separately compiled libraries (although it is not explicitly tied to separate compilation).

Consider our previous example of a Queue ADT structure in C. A major problem with it is that there are likely to be other libraries available in a programming environment that could well include a different implementation of a queue, but with the same name. Additionally, it is likely that a programmer may want to include some code from that library as well as use the given Queue implementation. In C this is not possible. In C++ a namespace can be used to disambiguate such name clashes. Figure 9.6 lists the code for the `queue.h` file as it would look using a namespace in C++.

```
#ifndef QUEUE_H
#define QUEUE_H

namespace MyQueue
{ struct Queuerep;
  typedef Queuerep * Queue;
            // struct no longer needed in C++
  Queue createq();
  Queue enqueue(Queue q, void* elem);
  void* frontq(Queue q);
  Queue dequeue(Queue q);
  bool emptyq(Queue q);
}

#endif
```

Figure 9.6   The `queue.h` header file in C++ using a namespace

Inside the `queue.cpp` file, the definitions of the queue functions must now use the scope resolution operator, for example:

```
struct MyQueue::Queuerep
{ void* data;
  Queue next;
};
```

Alternatively, one could reenter the `MyQueue` namespace by surrounding the implementation code in `queue.cpp` with the same namespace declaration as in the header. (Namespaces can be reentered whenever one wishes to add definitions or implementations to a namespace.)

A client of MyQueue has three options:

1. After the appropriate #include, the user can simply refer to the MyQueue definitions using the qualified name (i.e., with MyQueue:: before each name used from the MyQueue namespace).

2. Alternatively, the user can write a using declaration for each name used from the namespace, and then use each such name without qualification.

3. Finally, one can "unqualify" all the names in the namespace with a single using namespace declaration.

Consider Figure 9.7, which lists C++ client code for the above C++ queue code. This code exhibits all three of the above options to reference names in a namespace. A using declaration (option 2) is given on line 3, allowing the standard library function endl from iostream to be used without qualification. A using namespace declaration (option 3) is given on line 4, allowing all names in MyQueue to be used without qualification. And the qualified name std::cout is used for the references to cout (lines 18 and 21).

```
(1)   #include <iostream>
(2)   #include "queue.h"

(3)   using std::endl;
(4)   using namespace MyQueue;

(5)   main()
(6)   {   int *x = new int;
(7)       int *y = new int;
(8)       int *z;
(9)       // explicit qualification unnecessary
(10)      // but permitted
(11)      Queue q = MyQueue::createq();
(12)      *x = 2;
(13)      *y = 3;
(14)      q = enqueue(q,x);
(15)      q = enqueue(q,y);
(16)      z = (int*) frontq(q);
(17)      // explicit qualification needed for cout
(18)      std::cout << *z << endl; // prints 2
(19)      q = dequeue(q);
(20)      z = (int*) frontq(q);
(21)      std::cout << *z << endl; // prints 3
(22)  }
```

Figure 9.7 A client code file q_user.cpp in C++ with using declarations

Java, too, has a namespace-like mechanism, called the **package**. Since Java emphasizes object-orientation and the class construct (see the next chapter), packages are constructed as groups of related classes. Each separately compiled file in a Java program is allowed to have only one public class, and this class can be placed in a package by writing a package declaration as the first declaration in the source code file:

```
package myqueue;
```

If the data type `Queue` is the public class in this file, `Queue` can now be used by other Java code files by referring to it by the name `myqueue.Queue`. This name can also be "dereferenced" in a similar manner to the C++ `using` declaration by the use of a Java `import` declaration:

```
import myqueue.Queue;
```

All names in a Java package can be imported by the use of an asterisk after the package name:

```
import myqueue.*;
```

This is similar to the C++ `using namespace` declaration.

Note here that the Java `import` declaration does *not* correspond to the abstract notion of an import in the definition of a module in the previous section. Indeed, an import in the latter sense represents a dependency on external code, and is more closely related to the C `#include` statement than to the Java `import` declaration. Code dependencies in Java are hidden by the fact that the compiler automatically searches for external code using the package name and, typically, a system search path (commonly called `CLASSPATH`). Package names can also contain extra periods, which are usually interpreted by Java as representing subdirectories. For example, the package `myqueue` might be best placed in a directory `mylibrary`, and then the package name would be `mylibrary.myqueue`. Using the fully qualified name of a library class allows any Java code to access any other public Java code that is locatable along the search path by the compiler, without use of an `import` declaration. Indeed, the compiler will also check for out-of-date source code files, and recompile all dependent files automatically. Thus, library dependencies can be well hidden in Java. Even the link step in Java does not need any dependency information, since linking is performed only just prior to execution by a utility called the **class loader**, and the class loader uses the same search mechanism as the compiler to find all dependent code automatically.

9.4 Ada Packages

Ada's module mechanism is the **package**, which was already briefly discussed in Chapter 6, because the package is used in Ada not only to implement modules but also to implement parametric polymorphism.[6] An Ada package is divided into a package **specification** and a package **body**.

---

[6] Ada packages should not be confused with Java packages, which are a rather different concept; see the previous section.

A package specification is the public interface to the package, and corresponds to the syntax or signature of an ADT (Section 9.1). Package specifications and package bodies also represent compilation units in Ada, and can be compiled separately.[7] Clients are also compiled separately and linked to compiled package bodies. A package specification in Ada for type Complex is given in Figure 9.8.

```
(1)   package ComplexNumbers is

(2)   type Complex is private;

(3)   function "+"(x,y: in Complex) return Complex;
(4)   function "-"(x,y: in Complex) return Complex;
(5)   function "*"(x,y: in Complex) return Complex;
(6)   function "/"(x,y: in Complex) return Complex;
(7)   function "-"(z: in Complex) return Complex;
(8)   function makeComplex (x,y: in Float) return Complex;
(9)   function realPart (z: in Complex) return Float;
(10)  function imaginaryPart (z: in Complex) return Float;

(11) private
(12)     type Complex is
(13)     record
(14)         re, im: Float;
(15)     end record;
(16) end ComplexNumbers;
```

Figure 9.8   A package specification for complex numbers in Ada

This specification of a complex number ADT uses oveloaded operators in Ada as studied in Chapter 6. Additionally, this specification uses a **private** declaration section (lines 11–16): Any declarations given in this section are inaccessible to a client. Type names, however, can be given in the public part of a specification and designated as private (line 2). Note, however, that an actual type declaration must still be given in the private part of the specification. This violates both criteria for abstract data type mechanisms: criterion 1, since the specification is still dependent on actual implementation details, and criterion 2, since the implementation details are divided between the specification and the implementation. However, the use of the private declarations at least prevents clients from making any use of the implementation dependency, although clients still must be recompiled if the implementation type changes. As in the C queue example of Section 9.2, this problem can be partially removed in

---

[7] Some implementations may not require the compilation of a package specification, since the compiled version is essentially a symbol table with the same information as the specification file itself.

Ada by using pointers, and a revised specification in Ada that removes the dependency of the specification on the implementation type (at the cost of introducing pointers) is as follows:

```
package ComplexNumbers is

type Complex is private;

-- functions as before

private
    type ComplexRecord;
    -- incomplete type defined in package body
    type Complex is access ComplexRecord;
    -- a pointer type
end ComplexNumbers;
```

A corresponding implementation for this somewhat improved package specification is given in Figure 9.9.

```
(1)   package body ComplexNumbers is

(2)   type ComplexRecord is record
(3)        re, im: Float;
(4)   end record;

(5)   function "+"(x,y: in Complex) return Complex is
(6)   t: Complex;
(7)   begin
(8)        t := new ComplexRecord;
(9)        t.re := x.re + y.re;
(10)       t.im := x.im + y.im;
(11)       return t;
(12)  end "+";

(13)  -- more operations here

(14)  function makeComplex (x,y: in Float)
(15)          return Complex is
(16)  begin
(17)      return new ComplexRecord'(re => x , im => y);
(18)  end makeComplex;

(19)  function realPart (z: in Complex) return Float is
(20)  begin
(21)      return z.re;
(22)  end realPart;
```
(continues)

(continued)

```
(23) function imaginaryPart (z: in Complex)
(24)     return Float is
(25) begin
(26)     return z.im;
(27) end imaginaryPart;

(28) end ComplexNumbers;
```

Figure 9.9   A package implementation for complex numbers in Ada using pointers

Note that pointers are automatically dereferenced in Ada by the dot notation and that fields can be assigned during allocation using the apostrophe attribute delimiter (the single quote in `makeComplex`, line 17). A client program can use the `ComplexNumbers` package by including a `with` clause at the beginning of the program, similar to a C `#include` directive:

```
with ComplexNumbers;

procedure ComplexUser is
    z,w: ComplexNumbers.Complex;
begin
    z := ComplexNumbers.makeComplex(1.0,-1.0);
    ...
    w := ComplexNumbers."+"(z,z);
end ComplexUser;
```

Packages in Ada are automatically namespaces in the C++ sense, and all referenced names must be referred to using the package name as a qualifier (the notation, however, is identical to field dereference in records or structures). Ada also has a `use` declaration analogous to the `using` declaration of C++ that dereferences the package name automatically:

```
with ComplexNumbers;
use ComplexNumbers;
procedure ComplexUser is
    z,w: Complex;
    ...
begin
    z := makeComplex(1.0,-1.0);
    ...
    w := z + z;
    ...
end ComplexUser;
```

Notice that the infix form of the overloaded "+" operator can only be used when the package name is dereferenced.

One of the major uses for the package mechanism in Ada is to implement parameterized types as discussed in Chapter 6; parameterized packages are called **generic packages** in Ada. As an example, we give an

implementation of a Queue ADT that is entirely analogous to the C
implementation of Section 9.2 (a queue given by a circularly linked list
with rear pointer). Figure 9.10 shows the package specification, Figure
9.11 shows the package implementation, and Figure 9.12 shows some sample client code.

```
(1)  generic
(2)     type T is private;
(3)  package Queues is
(4)     type Queue is private;
(5)     function createq return Queue;
(6)     function enqueue(q:Queue;elem:T) return Queue;
(7)     function frontq(q:Queue) return T;
(8)     function dequeue(q:Queue) return Queue;
(9)     function emptyq(q:Queue) return Boolean;
(10) private
(11)    type Queuerep;
(12)    type Queue is access Queuerep;
(13) end Queues;
```

Figure 9.10   A parameterized queue ADT defined as an Ada generic package specification

```
(1)  package body Queues is
(2)     type Queuerep is
(3)     record
(4)        data: T;
(5)        next: Queue;
(6)     end record;

(7)     function createq return Queue is
(8)     begin
(9)        return null;
(10)    end createq;

(11)    function enqueue(q:Queue;elem:T) return Queue is
(12)       temp: Queue;
(13)    begin
(14)      temp := new Queuerep;
(15)      temp.data := elem;
(16)      if (q /= null) then
(17)         temp.next := q.next;
(18)         q.next := temp;
(19)      else
(20)         temp.next := temp;
(21)      end if;
(22)      return temp;
(23)    end enqueue;
(24)    function frontq(q:Queue) return T is
(25)    begin
```

(continues)

(continued)

```
(26)        return q.next.data;
(27)     end frontq;

(28)     function dequeue(q:Queue) return Queue is
(29)     begin
(30)        if q = q.next then
(31)           return null;
(32)        else
(33)           q.next := q.next.next;
(34)           return q.next;
(35)        end if;
(36)     end dequeue;

(37)     function emptyq(q:Queue) return Boolean is
(38)     begin
(39)        return q = null;
(40)     end emptyq;

(41) end Queues;
```

Figure 9.11   Generic package implementation in Ada for the Queues
package specification of Figure 9.10

```
(1)   with Ada.Text_IO; use Ada.Text_IO;

(2)   with Ada.Float_Text_IO;
(3)   use Ada.Float_Text_IO;

(4)   with Ada.Integer_Text_IO;
(5)   use Ada.Integer_Text_IO;

(6)   with Queues;

(7)   procedure Quser is

(8)   package IntQueues is new Queues(Integer);
(9)   use IntQueues;

(10) package FloatQueues is new Queues(Float);
(11) use FloatQueues;

(12) fq: FloatQueues.Queue := createq;
(13) iq: IntQueues.Queue := createq;

(14) begin
(15)    fq := enqueue(fq,3.1);
(16)    fq := enqueue(fq,2.3);
(17)    iq := enqueue(iq,3);
(18)    iq := enqueue(iq,2);
(19)    put(frontq(iq)); -- prints 3
```

```
(20)    new_line;
(21)    fq := dequeue(fq);
(22)    put(frontq(fq));  -- prints 2.3
(23)    new_line;
(24) end Quser;
```

Figure 9.12   Sample Ada client code that uses the `Queues` generic package of Figures 9.10 and 9.11

We note the following about the code in Figure 9.12. First, lines 1–5 import and dereference standard Ada library IO functions. Line 6 imports the `Queues` package. Lines 8 and 10 create two different instantiations of the `Queues` generic package, one for integers and one for floating-point numbers; these are given the package names `IntQueues` and `FloatQueues`. These two packages are then dereferenced by the `use` declarations in lines 9 and 11. Note that this creates name ambiguities, since all of the names from each of these packages conflict with the names from the other package. Ada's overloading mechanism can, however, resolve most of these ambiguities, based on the data types of the parameters and results. Thus, the simple names such as `enqueue` are still able to be used instead of the qualified names `IntQueues.enqueue` and `FloatQueues.enqueue`. In one place, however, it is impossible to disambiguate the names, and that is when the data type `Queue` is used in the definitions of `fq` and `iq` (lines 12 and 13). In this case the qualified names `IntQueues.Queue` and `FloatQueues.Queue` are used to provide the necessary disambiguation.

9.5 Modules in ML

In Section 9.2 we demonstrated the ML `abstype` definition, which allows easy definition of abstract types with associated operations. ML also has a more general module facility, which consists of three mechanisms: **signatures**, **structures**, and **functors**. The signature mechanism is essentially an interface definition (it even adopts the name *signature* from the mathematical description of the syntax of an ADT as in Section 9.1). A structure is essentially an implementation of a signature; viewed another way, the signature is essentially the type of the structure. Functors are essentially functions from structures to structures (with the structure parameters having "types" given by signatures); functors allow for the parameterization of structures by other structures; functors will be discussed briefly in Section 9.7.4.

Figure 9.13 shows an ML signature for a queue ADT. The `sig ...` `end` expression (lines 2 and 9) produces a value of type `signature` by listing the types of the identifiers being defined by the signature. This signature value is then stored as the name `QUEUE`. Since a signature is not a type as such, we must export the type `Queue` as one of the identifiers; this is done in line 3 with the declaration `type 'a Queue`, which identifies the name `Queue` as an exported type, parameterized by the type variable `'a`. Thus, this signature allows queues to contain elements of arbitrary type (but each queue can only contain elements of a single type). The type `Queue` may be either a type synonym for a previously existing type, or a new type; making it a previously existing type can result in a loss of protection, however (see Exercise 9.29); thus, in our examples we will always use a new type.

```
(1)  signature QUEUE =
(2)      sig
(3)      type 'a Queue
(4)      val createq: 'a Queue
(5)      val enqueue: 'a Queue * 'a -> 'a Queue
(6)      val frontq: 'a Queue -> 'a
(7)      val dequeue: 'a Queue -> 'a Queue
(8)      val emptyq: 'a Queue -> bool
(9)      end;
```

Figure 9.13   A QUEUE signature for a queue ADT in ML

Figure 9.14 shows a structure `Queue1` that provides an implementation for the QUEUE signature. Using the QUEUE signature specification in the first line of this definition (after the colon but before the equal sign) restricts the public interface of this structure to only the features mentioned in the signature, and requires the structure to implement every feature in the signature in such a way that it has exactly the type specified in the signature. Line 1 of Figure 9.14 thus defines the name `Queue1` to have type `structure`, implementing the signature QUEUE. Lines 2 through 10 then provide the actual `structure` value, which is constructed by the `struct ... end` expression. This expression implements the `Queue` type in exactly the same way as in Figure 9.1, and the internal representation of the `Queue` as a list, including the constructor `Q`, is not accessible outside of the structure because it is not part of the QUEUE signature.

```
(1)   structure Queue1: QUEUE =
(2)       struct
(3)       datatype 'a Queue = Q of 'a list
(4)       val createq = Q [];
(5)       fun enqueue(Q lis, elem) = Q (lis @ [elem]);
(6)       fun frontq (Q lis) = hd lis;
(7)       fun dequeue (Q lis) = Q (tl lis);
(8)       fun emptyq (Q []) = true
(9)         | emptyq (Q (h::t)) = false;
(10)      end;
```

Figure 9.14   An ML structure `Queue1` implementing the QUEUE signature as an ordinary built-in list with wrapper

The structure `Queue1` can be used in ML as follows:

```
- val q = Queue1.enqueue(Queue1.createq,3);
val q = Q [3] : int Queue1.Queue
Queue1.frontq q;
val it = 3 : int
- val q1 = Queue1.dequeue q;
val q1 = Q [] : int Queue1.Queue
- Queue1.emptyq q1;
val it = true : bool
```

Note that the internal representation of Queue is not suppressed in the ML interpreter responses as it is with the `abstype` specification of Section 9.2. Also, all names in `Queue1` must be qualified by the name of the structure, unlike the `abstype` specification. As with other languages, this qualification can be removed if desired; in ML the expression that does so is the `open` expression:

```
- open Queue1;
opening Queue1
    datatype 'a Queue = ...
    val createq : 'a Queue
    val enqueue : 'a Queue * 'a -> 'a Queue
    val frontq : 'a Queue -> 'a
    val dequeue : 'a Queue -> 'a Queue
    val emptyq : 'a Queue -> bool
```

The ML interpreter responds to the `open` expression by listing the signature that `Queue1` implements. The features of `Queue1` can now be used without qualification:

```
- val q = enqueue (createq,3);
val q = Q [3] : int Queue
- frontq q;
val it = 3 : int
- val q1 = dequeue q;
val q1 = Q [] : int Queue
- emptyq q1;
val it = true : bool
```

Figure 9.15 shows a second implementation of the QUEUE signature, this time using a user-defined linked list instead of the built-in ML list structure. In the definition of the Queue data type (lines 3 and 4), we have used two constructors `Createq` and `Enqueue`; these constructors perform essentially the same operations as the functions `createq` and `enqueue`, so we have given them the same names (except for the uppercase first letter). With these names, the definitions of the functions `frontq`, `dequeue`, and `emptyq` look virtually identical to the equational axiomatic specification for the Queue ADT given in Section 9.1.

```
(1)   structure Queue2: QUEUE =
(2)      struct
(3)      datatype 'a Queue = Createq
(4)                        | Enqueue of 'a Queue * 'a ;
(5)      val createq = Createq;
(6)      fun enqueue(q,elem) = Enqueue (q,elem);
(7)      fun frontq (Enqueue(Createq,elem)) = elem
(8)                | frontq (Enqueue(q,elem)) = frontq q;
(9)      fun dequeue (Enqueue(Createq,elem)) = Createq
(10)               | dequeue (Enqueue(q,elem))
(11)                         = Enqueue(dequeue q, elem);
(12)     fun emptyq Createq = true | emptyq _ = false;
(13)     end;
```

Figure 9.15   An ML structure `Queue2` implementing the QUEUE signature as a user-defined linked list

The `Queue2` structure of Figure 9.15 can be used exactly as the `Queue1` structure of Figure 9.14:

```
- open Queue2;
opening Queue2
  datatype 'a Queue = ...
  val createq : 'a Queue
  val enqueue : 'a Queue * 'a -> 'a Queue
  val frontq : 'a Queue -> 'a
  val dequeue : 'a Queue -> 'a Queue
  val emptyq : 'a Queue -> bool
- val q = enqueue(createq,3);
val q = Enqueue (Createq,3) : int Queue
- frontq q;
val it = 3 : int
- val q1 = dequeue q;
val q1 = Createq : int Queue
- emptyq q1;
val it = true : bool
```

ML signatures and structures satisfy most of the requirements of criteria 1 and 2 for abstract data types from this chapter's introduction. A signature collects a type and its associated operations in one place, and the definitions do not depend on any implementation details. A structure collects the implementation details in one place and only exports the information contained in the associated signature. The main difficulty with the ML module mechanism from the point of view of abstract data types is that client code must explicitly state the implementation that is to be used in terms of the module name: code cannot be written to depend only on the signature, with the actual implementation structure to be supplied externally to the code. Thus, we cannot write

```
val x = QUEUE.createq;
```

Instead we must write

```
val x = Queue1.createq;
```

or

```
val x = Queue2.createq;
```

The main reason for this is that the ML language has no explicit or implicit separate compilation mechanism (or other code aggregation mechanism), and so there is no way to externally specify an implementation choice.[8]

9.6   Modules in Earlier Languages

Historically, modules and abstract data type mechanisms began with Simula67 and made significant progress in the 1970s through language design experiments at universities and research centers. Among the languages that have contributed significantly to module mechanisms in Ada, ML, and other languages, are the languages CLU, Euclid, Modula-2, Mesa, and Cedar. To indicate how module mechanisms have developed, we sketch briefly the approaches taken by Euclid, CLU, and Modula-2.

9.6.1   Euclid

In the Euclid programming language, modules are types, so a complex number module is declared as a type:

```
type ComplexNumbers = module
    exports(Complex, add, subtract, multiply,
            divide, negate, makeComplex,
            realPart, imaginaryPart)
    type Complex = record
        var re, im: real
    end Complex

    procedure add (x,y: Complex, var z: Complex) =
    begin
        z.re := x.re + y.re
        z.im := x.im + y.im
    end add

    procedure makeComplex
            (x,y: real, var z:Complex) =
    begin
        z.re := x
        z.im := y
    end makeComplex
        ...
end ComplexNumbers
```

---

[8] In fact, most ML systems have a compilation manager with separate compilation that can remove this problem, but such tools are not part of the language itself.

To be able to declare complex numbers, however, we need an actual object of type ComplexNumbers—a module type in itself does not exist as an object. Thus, we must declare

```
var C: ComplexNumbers
```

and then we can declare

```
var z,w: C.Complex
```

and apply the operations of C:

```
C.makeComplex(1.0,1.0,z)
C.Add(z,z,w)
```

Note that this implies that there could be two different variables of type ComplexNumbers declared and thus two different sets of complex numbers:

```
var C1,C2: ComplexNumbers
var x: C1.Complex
var y: C2.Complex

C1.makeComplex(1.0,0.0,x)
C2.makeComplex(0.0,1.0,y)
(* x and y cannot be added together *)
```

When module types are used in a declaration, this creates a variable of the module type, or **instantiates** the module. In Euclid two different instantiations of ComplexNumbers can therefore exist simultaneously, unlike languages such as Ada or ML, where modules are not types, but are objects on their own, with a single instantiation of each. (Ada generic package can of course have several different instantiations, even for the same type; see the discussion in Section 9.4 and Chapter 6.)

9.6.2 CLU

In CLU, modules are defined using the **cluster** mechanism. In the case of complex numbers, the data type Complex can be defined directly as a cluster:

```
Complex = cluster is add, multiply,...,
          makeComplex, realPart, imaginaryPart
  rep = struct [re,im: real]
  add = proc (x,y: cvt ) returns (cvt)
    return
    (rep${re: x.re+y.re, im: x.im+y.im})
  end add
     ...
  makeComplex = proc (x,y: real) returns (cvt)
    return (rep${re:x, im:y})
  end makeComplex

  realPart = proc(x: cvt) returns (real)
    return(x.re)
  end realPart

end Complex
```

The principal difference of this abstraction mechanism from the previous ones is that the datatype `Complex` is defined directly as a cluster. However, when we define

```
x,y: Complex
```

we do not mean that they should be of the cluster type, but of the representation type within the cluster (given by the **rep** declaration). Thus, a cluster in CLU really refers to two different things: the cluster itself and its internal representation type. Of course, the representation type must be protected from access by the outside world, so the details of the representation type can be accessed only from within the cluster. This is the purpose of the **cvt** declaration (for **convert**), which converts from the external type `Complex` (with no explicit structure) to the internal **rep** type and back again. **cvt** can be used only within the body of a cluster.

Clients can use the functions from `Complex` in a similar manner to other languages:

```
x := Complex$makeComplex(1.0,1.0)
x := Complex$add (x,x)
```

Note the use of the "$" to qualify the operations instead of the dot notation used in Ada and ML.

9.6.3   Modula-2

In Modula-2, the specification and implementation of an abstract data type are separated into a `DEFINITION MODULE` and an `IMPLEMENTATION MODULE`. For the type `Complex`, a Modula-2 specification module would look like this:

```
DEFINITION MODULE ComplexNumbers;

TYPE Complex;

PROCEDURE Add (x,y: Complex): Complex;
PROCEDURE Subtract (x,y: Complex): Complex;
PROCEDURE Multiply (x,y: Complex): Complex;
PROCEDURE Divide (x,y: Complex): Complex;
PROCEDURE Negate (z: Complex): Complex;
PROCEDURE MakeComplex (x,y: REAL): Complex;
PROCEDURE RealPart (z: Complex) : REAL;
PROCEDURE ImaginaryPart (z: Complex) : REAL;

END ComplexNumbers.
```

A Modula-2 `DEFINITION MODULE` contains only definitions or declarations, and only the declarations that appear in the `DEFINITION MODULE` are **exported**, that is, are usable by other modules. The incomplete type specification of type `Complex` in the `DEFINITION MODULE` is called an opaque type; the details of its declaration are hidden in an implementation module and are not usable by other modules. These features are all similar to those of Ada and ML.

A corresponding IMPLEMENTATION MODULE in Modula-2 for the DEF-INITION MODULE is as follows:

```
IMPLEMENTATION MODULE ComplexNumbers;

FROM Storage IMPORT ALLOCATE;

TYPE Complex = POINTER TO ComplexRecord
     ComplexRecord = RECORD
         re, im: REAL;
     END;

PROCEDURE add (x,y: Complex): Complex;
VAR t: Complex;
BEGIN
  NEW(t);
  t^.re := x^.re + y^.re
  t^.im := x^.im + y^.im;
  RETURN t;
END add;


    ...


PROCEDURE makeComplex (x,y: REAL): Complex;
VAR t: Complex;
BEGIN
  NEW(t);
  t^.re := x;
  t^.im := y;
  RETURN t;
END makeComplex;

PROCEDURE realPart (z: Complex) : REAL;
BEGIN
  RETURN z^.re;
END realPart;

PROCEDURE imaginaryPart (z: Complex) : REAL;
BEGIN
  RETURN z^.im;
END imaginaryPart;

END ComplexNumbers.
```

Because of the use of pointers and indirection, functions such as makeComplex have to include a call to NEW to allocate space for a new complex number, and this in turn requires that ALLOCATE be imported from a system `Storage` module. (The compiler converts a call to `NEW` to a call to `ALLOCATE`.)

A client module in Modula-2 uses type `Complex` by **importing** it and its functions from the `ComplexNumbers` module:

```
MODULE ComplexUser;

IMPORT ComplexNumbers;

VAR x,y,z: ComplexNumbers.Complex;

BEGIN
   x := ComplexNumbers.makeComplex(1.0,2.0);
   y := ComplexNumbers.makeComplex(-1.0,1.0);
   z := ComplexNumbers.add(x,y);
          . . .
END ComplexUser.
```

Note the qualification in the use of the features from `ComplexNumbers`. An alternative to this is to use a **dereferencing** clause. In Modula-2, the dereferencing clause is the `FROM` clause:

```
MODULE ComplexUser;

FROM ComplexNumbers IMPORT Complex,add,makeComplex:
VAR x,y,z: Complex;
. . .
BEGIN
   x := makeComplex(1.0,2.0);
   y := makeComplex(-1.0,1.0);
   . . .
   z := add(x,y);

END ComplexUser.
```

When a `FROM` clause is used, imported items must be listed by name in the `IMPORT` statement, and no other items (either imported or locally declared) may have the same names as those imported (Modula-2 does not support overloading).

The separation of a module into a `DEFINITION MODULE` and an `IMPLEMENTATION MODULE` in Modula-2 supports the first principle of an abstract data type mechanism: It allows the data type and operation definitions to be collected in one place (the `DEFINITION MODULE`) and associates the operations directly with the type via the `MODULE` name. The use of an opaque type in a `DEFINITION MODULE` supports the second principle of an abstract data type mechanism: the details of the `Complex` data type implementation are separated from its declaration and are hidden in an `IMPLEMENTATION MODULE` together with the implementation of the operations. Further, a client is prevented from using any of the details in the `IMPLEMENTATION MODULE`.

Since the DEFINITION MODULE is independent of any of the details of the IMPLEMENTATION MODULE, the implementation can be rewritten without affecting any use of the module by clients, in a similar manner to Ada and C.

9.7 Problems with Abstract Data Type Mechanisms

Abstract data type mechanisms in programming languages use separate compilation facilities to meet protection and implementation independence requirements. The specification part of the ADT mechanism is used as an interface to guarantee consistency of use and implementation. But ADT mechanisms are used to create types and associate operations to types, while separate compilation facilities are providers of services, which may include variables, constants, or any other programming language entities. Thus, compilation units are in one sense more general than ADT mechanisms. But at the same time they are less general, in that the use of a compilation unit to define a type does not identify the type with the unit, and thus is not a true type declaration. Furthermore, units are static entities—they retain their identity only before linking, which can result in allocation and initialization problems. Thus, the use of separate compilation units such as modules or packages to implement abstract data types is a compromise in language design—but a useful one, as it reduces the implementation question for ADTs to one of consistency checking and linkage.

In this section, we wish to catalog some of the major drawbacks of the ADT mechanisms we have studied (and others we have not). Of course, not all languages suffer from all the drawbacks we will list. Many, but not all, of these drawbacks have been corrected in object-oriented languages (studied in the next chapter). Thus, this section will serve as an indication of what to look for in object-oriented languages.

9.7.1 Modules Are Not Types

In C, Ada, and ML difficulties can arise because a module must export a type as well as operations. It would be helpful instead to define a module to *be a type*. Then there is no need to arrange to protect the implementation details of the type with an ad hoc mechanism such as incomplete or private declarations; the details are all contained in the implementation section of the type.

The fact that ML contains both an abstype and a module mechanism emphasizes this distinction. The module mechanism is more general, and it allows the clean separation of specification (signature) from implementation (structure), but a type must be exported. On the other hand, an abstype *is* a type, but the implementation of an abstype cannot be separated from its specification (although access to the details of the implementation is prevented), and clients of the abstype implicitly depend on the implementation.

9.7.2   Modules Are Static Entities

An attractive possibility for implementing an abstract data type is to simply not reveal a type at all, thus avoiding all possibility of clients depending in any way on implementation details, as well preventing clients from any misuse of a type. For example, in Ada one could write a Queue package specification as follows (note how the operations must change to never return a queue—this is pure imperative programming now):

```
generic
  type T is private;
package Queues is
  procedure enqueue(elem:T);
  function frontq return T;
  procedure dequeue;
  function emptyq return Boolean;
end Queues;
```

The actual queue data structure is then buried in the implementation:

```
package body Queues is

  type Queuerep;
  type Queue is access Queuerep;

  type Queuerep is
  record
    data: T;
    next: Queue;
  end record;

  q: Queue;

  procedure enqueue(elem:T) is
    temp: Queue;
  begin
    temp := new Queuerep;
    temp.data := elem;
    if (q /= null) then
        temp.next := q.next;
        q.next := temp;
    else
        temp.next := temp;
    end if;
    q := temp;
  end enqueue;

  function frontq return T is
  begin
    return q.next.data;
  end frontq;
```

(continues)

(*continued*)

```
        procedure dequeue is
        begin
          if q = q.next then
              q := null;
          else
              q.next := q.next.next;
              q := q.next;
          end if;
        end dequeue;

        function emptyq return Boolean is
        begin
          return q = null;
        end emptyq;

    begin
      q := null;
    end Queues;
```

Note that this allows us to write initialization code internally within the package body (the last three lines of the above code), which is executed on "elaboration," or allocation time (at the beginning of execution). This eliminates the need for user-supplied code to initialize a queue, and so there is no **createq** procedure.

Normally this would imply that there can only be one queue in a client, since otherwise the entire code must be replicated (try this using a C++ namespace—see Exercise 9.28). This results from the static nature of most module mechanisms (including those of Ada and ML). In Ada, however, the generic package mechanism offers a convenient way to obtain several different queues (even for the same stored type) by using multiple instantiations of the same generic package:

```
    with Ada.Text_IO; use Ada.Text_IO;
    with Ada.Integer_Text_IO;
    use Ada.Integer_Text_IO;
    with Queues;

    procedure Quser is

    package Queue1 is new Queues(Integer);
    package Queue2 is new Queues(Integer);

    begin
      Queue1.enqueue(3);
      Queue1.enqueue(4);
      Queue2.enqueue(1);
      Queue2.enqueue(2);
      put(Queue1.frontq); -- prints 3
      new_line;
      Queue2.dequeue;
```

```
    put(Queue2.frontq);  -- prints 2
    new_line;
  end Quser;
```

This is still a static alternative, and we could not create a new queue during execution. However, this can still be an extremely useful mechanism.

9.7.3 Modules That Export Types Do Not Adequately Control Operations on Variables of Such Types

In the C and Ada examples of data types Queue and Complex in Sections 9.3 and 9.4, variables of each type were pointers that had to be allocated and initialized by calling the procedure createq or makeComplex. But the exporting module cannot guarantee that this procedure is called before the variables are used; thus correct allocation and initialization cannot be ensured. Even worse, because queues and, most particularly, complex numbers are pointers in the sample implementations, copies can be made and deallocations performed outside the control of the module, without the user being aware of the consequences, and without the ability to return the deallocated memory to available storage. For instance, in the Ada code

```
  z := makeComplex(1.0,0.0);
  x := makeComplex(-1.0,0.0);
  x := z;
```

the last assignment has the effect of making z and x point to the same allocated storage and leaves the original value of x as garbage in memory. Indeed, the implementation of type Complex as a pointer type gives variables of this type pointer semantics, subject to problems of sharing and copying (see Chapter 5).

Even if we were to rewrite the implementation of type Complex as a record or struct instead of a pointer (which would wipe out some encapsulation and information hiding in both C and Ada), we would not regain much control. In that case, the declaration of a variable of type Complex would automatically perform the allocation, and calling makeComplex would perform initialization only. Still, we would have no guarantee that initializations would be properly performed, but at least assignment would have the usual storage semantics, and there would be no unexpected creation of garbage or side effects.

Part of the problem comes from the use of assignment. Indeed, when x and y are pointer types, x := y (x = y in C) performs assignment by sharing the object pointed to by y, with resulting potential unwanted side effects. This is another example of an operation that a module exporting types has no control of. Similarly, the comparison x = y tests pointer equality, identity of location in memory, which is not the right test when x and y are complex numbers:

```
  x := makeComplex(1.0,0.0);
  y := makeComplex(1.0,0.0);
  (* now a test of x = y returns false *)
```

We could write procedures `equal` and `assign` and add them to the operations in the package specification (or the header file in C), but, again, there would be no guarantee that they would be appropriately applied by a client.

In Ada, however, there is a mechanism for controlling the use of equality and assignment: the use of a **limited private type**:

```
package ComplexNumbers is

type Complex is limited private;

-- operations, including assignment and equality
   ...
function equal(x,y: in Complex) return Boolean;
procedure assign(x: out Complex; y: in Complex);

private
   type ComplexRec;
   type Complex is access ComplexRec;

end ComplexNumbers;
```

Now clients are prevented from using the usual assignment and equality operations, and the package body can ensure that equality is performed appropriately and that assignment deallocates garbage and/or copies values instead of pointers. Indeed, the "=" (and, implicitly, the inequality "/=") operator can be overloaded as described in Chapter 5, so the same infix form can be used after redefinition by the package. Assignment, however, cannot be overloaded in Ada. And there is still no automatic initialization and deallocation.

C++ has an advantage here, since it allows the overloading of *both* assignment (=) and equality (==). Additionally, object-oriented languages solve the initialization problem by the use of **constructors** (see the next chapter).

ML also is able to control equality testing by limiting the data type in an `abstype` or `struct` specification to types that do not permit the equality operation. Indeed, ML makes a distinction between types that allow equality testing and types that do not. Type parameters that allow equality testing must be written using a double apostrophe `''a` instead of a single apostrophe `'a`, and a type definition that allows equality must be specified as an `eqtype` rather than just a type:

```
signature QUEUE =
   sig
   eqtype ''a Queue
   val createq: ''a Queue
   ...etc.
   end;
```

Without this, equality cannot be used to test queues. Additionally, assignment in ML is much less of a problem, since standard functional programming practice does away with most uses of that operation (see Chapter 11).

9.7.4   Modules Do Not Always Adequately Represent How They Depend on Imported Types

Aside from assignment and equality testing, modules often depend on the existence of certain operations on type parameters and may also call functions whose existence is not made explicit in the module specification. A typical example is a data structure such as a binary search tree, priority queue, or ordered list, which all require that the type of the stored values have an order operation such as the less-than arithmetic operation "$<$" available. Frequently this is not made explicit in a module specification.

For example, C++ templates mask such dependencies in specifications. A simple example is of a template min function, which depends on an order operation. In C++ this could be specified as

```
template <typename T>
T min( T x, T y);
```

Naturally, the implementation of this function shows the dependency on the order operation (but the specification does not):

```
// C++ code
template <typename T>
T min( T x, T y)
// requires an available < operation on T
{ return x < y ? x : y;
}
```

(See Chapter 6 for a discussion on how to make this dependency explicit in C++.)

In Ada it is possible to specify this requirement using additional declarations in the generic part of a package declaration:

```
generic
type Element is private;
with function lessThan (x,y: Element) return Boolean;
package OrderedList is

...
end OrderedList;
```

Now an OrderedList package can be instantiated only by providing a suitable lessThan function, as in

```
package IntOrderedList is new
    OrderedList (Integer,"<");
```

Such a requirement is called **constrained parameterization**. Without explicit constraints in Ada, no operations are assumed for the type parameter except equality, inequality, and assignment (and, as noted in the previous section, even these are not assumed if the type is declared limited private).

ML also has a feature that allows structures to be explicitly parameterized by other structures; it is called a **functor**, because it is essentially a function on structures (albeit one that operates only statically). Given two signatures such as ORDER and ORDERED_LIST (lines 1–5 and 6–13 of Figure 9.16), a functor that takes an ORDER structure as an argument and produces an ORDERED_LIST structure as a result can be defined in the following way (see lines 14–28 of Figure 9.16):

```
functor OListFUN (structure Order: ORDER):
ORDERED_LIST =
    struct
    ...
    end;
```

Then, given an actual ORDER structure value, such as IntOrder (lines 29–33), the functor can be applied to create a new ORDERED_LIST structure IntOList:

```
structure IntOList =
    OlistFUN(structure Order = IntOrder);
```

This makes explicit the appropriate dependencies, but at the cost of requiring an extra structure (IntOrder) to be defined that encapsulates the required features.

```
(1)   signature ORDER =
(2)       sig
(3)       type Elem
(4)       val lt: Elem * Elem -> bool
(5)       end;

(6)   signature ORDERED_LIST =
(7)       sig
(8)       type Elem
(9)       type OList
(10)      val create: OList
(11)      val insert: OList * Elem -> OList
(12)      val lookup: OList * Elem -> bool
(13)      end;

(14) functor OListFUN (structure Order: ORDER):
(15) ORDERED_LIST =
(16)      struct
(17)      type Elem = Order.Elem;
(18)      type OList = Order.Elem list;
(19)      val create = [];
```

```
(20)      fun insert ([], x) = [x]
(21)        | insert (h::t, x) = if Order.lt(x,h) then x::h::t
(22)                                    else h:: insert (t, x);
(23)      fun lookup ([], x) = false
(24)        | lookup (h::t, x) =
(25)            if Order.lt(x,h) then false
(26)            else if Order.lt(h,x) then lookup (t,x)
(27)            else true;
(28)    end;
```

```
(29)  structure IntOrder: ORDER =
(30)      struct
(31)      type Elem = int;
(32)      val lt = (op <);
(33)      end;
```

```
(34)  structure IntOList =
(35)      OListFUN(structure Order = IntOrder);
```

Figure 9.16   The use of a functor in ML to define an ordered list

With the code of Figure 9.16, the IntOList structure can be used as
follows:

```
- open IntOList;
opening IntOList
  type Elem = IntOrder.Elem
  type OList = IntOrder.Elem list
  val create : OList
  val insert : OList * Elem -> OList
  val lookup : OList * Elem -> bool
- val ol = insert(create,2);
val ol = [2] : OList
- val ol2 = insert(ol,3);
val ol2 = [2,3] : OList
- lookup (ol2,3);
val it = true : bool
- lookup (ol,3);
val it = false : bool
```

9.7.5   Module Definitions Include No Specification of the Semantics of the Provided Operations

In the algebraic specification of an abstract data type, equations are given
that specify the behavior of the operations. Yet in almost all languages no
specification of the behavior of the available operations is required. Some
experiments have been conducted with systems that require semantic
specification and then attempt to determine whether a provided implementation agrees with its specification, but such languages and systems are
still unusual and experimental.

One example of a language that does allow the specification of semantics is Eiffel, an object-oriented language. In Eiffel, semantic specifications are given by preconditions, postconditions, and invariants. Preconditions and postconditions establish what must be true before and after the execution of a procedure or function. Invariants establish what must be true about the internal state of the data in an abstract data type. For more on such conditions, see Chapter 13 on formal semantics. For more on Eiffel, see the Notes and References.

A brief example of the way Eiffel establishes semantics is as follows. In a queue ADT as described in Section 9.1, the enqueue operation is defined as follows in Eiffel:

```
enqueue (x:element) is
require
     not full
ensure
     if old empty then front = x
     else front = old front;
     not empty
end; -- enqueue
```

The `require` section establishes preconditions—in this case, to execute the enqueue operation correctly, the queue must not be full (this is not part of the algebraic specification as given in Section 9.1; see Exercise 9.24). The `ensure` section establishes postconditions, which in the case of the `enqueue` operation are that the newly enqueued element becomes the front of the queue only if the queue was previously empty and that the queue is now not empty. These requirements correspond to the algebraic axioms

```
front(enqueue(q,x)) = if empty(q) then x else front(q)
empty(enqueue(q,x)) = false
```

of Section 9.1.

In most languages we are confined to giving indications of the semantic content of operations inside comments.

9.8 The Mathematics of Abstract Data Types

In the algebraic specification of an abstract data type, a data type, a set of operations, and a set of axioms in equational form are specified. Nothing is said, however, about the actual existence of such a type—such a type is still hypothetical until an actual type is constructed that meets all the requirements. In the parlance of programming language theory, an abstract data type is said to have **existential type**—it asserts the existence of an actual type that meets its requirements. Such an actual type is a set with operations of the appropriate form that satisfy the given equations. A set and operations that meet the specification is a **model** for the specification. Given an algebraic specification, it is possible for no model to exist, or many models. Therefore, it is necessary to distinguish an actual type (a model) from a potential type (an algebraic specification). Potential types are called sorts, and potential sets of operations are called signatures (this agrees with our previous use of the term signature to denote the syntax of prospective operations). Thus, a sort is the name of a type, which is not yet associated with any actual set of values. Similarly, a signature is the name and type of an operation or set of operations, which exists only in theory, having no actual operations yet associated with it. A model is then an actualization of a sort and its signature and is called an algebra (since it has operations).

For this reason, algebraic specifications are often written using the sort-signature terminology:

sort queue(element) **imports** boolean

signature:
    createq: queue
    enqueue: queue $\times$ element $\rightarrow$ queue
    dequeue: queue $\rightarrow$ queue
    frontq: queue $\rightarrow$ element
    emptyq: queue $\rightarrow$ boolean

axioms:
    emptyq(createq) = true
    emptyq (enqueue (q, x)) = false
    frontq(createq) = error
    frontq(enqueue(q,x)) = if emptyq(q) then x else front(q)
    dequeue(createq) = error
    dequeue(enqueue(q,x)) = if emptyq(q) then q else
    enqueue(dequeue(q), x)

Given a sort, a signature, and axioms, we would, of course, like to know that an actual type exists for that specification. In fact, we would like to be able to construct a *unique* algebra for the specification that we would then take to be *the* type represented by the specification.

How does one construct such an algebra? A standard mathematical method is to construct the **free algebra of terms** for a sort and signature and then to form the **quotient algebra** of the equivalence relation generated by the equational axioms. The free algebra of terms consists of all the legal combinations of operations. For example, the free algebra for sort queue(integer) and signature as above has terms such as the following:

    createq
    enqueue (createq, 2)
    enqueue (enqueue(createq, 2), 1)
    dequeue (enqueue (createq, 2))
    dequeue (enqueue(enqueue (createq, 2), -1))
    dequeue (dequeue (enqueue (createq, 3), 1))
    etc.

Note that the axioms for a queue imply that some of these terms are actually equal, for example,

$$\text{dequeue (enqueue (createq, 2))} = \text{createq}$$

In the free algebra, however, all terms are considered to be different; that is why it is called free. In the free algebra of terms, no axioms are true. To make the axioms true, and so to construct a type that models the specification, we need to use the axioms to reduce the number of distinct elements in the free algebra. The two distinct terms createq and dequeue(enqueue(createq,2)) need to be identified, for example, in order to make the axiom

$$\text{dequeue(enqueue}(q,x)) =$$
$$\text{if empty}(q) \text{ then } q \text{ else enqueue(dequeue}(q),x)$$

hold. This can be done by constructing an **equivalence relation** $==$ from the axioms: "$==$" is an equivalence relation if it is symmetric, transitive, and reflexive:

if $x == y$ then $y == x$ (symmetry)

if $x == y$ and $y == z$ then $x == z$ (transitivity)

$x == x$ (reflexivity)

It is a standard task in mathematics to show that, given an equivalence relation $==$ and a free algebra F, there is a unique, well-defined algebra $F/==$ such that $x = y$ in $F/==$ if and only if $x == y$ in F. The algebra $F/==$ is called the quotient algebra of F by $==$. Furthermore, given a set of equations, such as the axioms in an algebraic specification, there is a unique "smallest" equivalence relation making the two sides of every equation equivalent and hence equal in the quotient algebra. It is this quotient algebra that is usually taken to be "the" data type defined by an algebraic specification. This algebra has the property that the only terms that are equal are those that are provably equal from the axioms. Thus, in the queue example,

$$\text{dequeue(enqueue(enqueue(createq,2),3))} =$$
$$\text{enqueue (dequeue(enqueue(createq, 2)),3)} =$$
$$\text{enqueue(createq, 3)}$$

but

$$\text{enqueue(createq, 2)} \neq \text{enqueue(createq, 3)}.$$

For mathematical reasons (coming from category theory and universal algebra), this algebra is called the **initial algebra** represented by the specification, and using this algebra as the data type of the specification results in what are called **initial semantics**.

How do we know whether the algebra we get from this construction really has the properties of the data type that we want? The answer is that we don't, unless we have written the "right" axioms. In general, axiom systems should be **consistent** and **complete**. Consistency says that the axioms should not identify terms that should be different. For example, empty(createq) = true and empty(createq) = false are inconsistent axioms, because they result in false = true; that is, false and true become identified in the initial semantics. Consistency of the axiom system says that the initial algebra is not "too small." Completeness of the axiom system, on the other hand, says that the initial algebra is not "too big;" that is, elements of the initial algebra that should be the same aren't. (Note that adding axioms identifies more elements, thus making the initial algebra "smaller" while taking away axioms makes it "larger.") A further useful, but not as critical, property for an axiom system is for it to be **independent**: no axiom is implied by other axioms. For example, front(enqueue(enqueue(createq,x),y)) = x is not independent because it follows from other axioms:

$$\text{front(enqueue(enqueue(createq,}x\text{),}y\text{))} = \text{front(enqueue(enqueue(createq,}x\text{))}$$

since front(enqueue(q,y)) = front(q) for q = enqueue(createq,x), by the fourth axiom on page 361 applied to the case when $q \neq$ createq, and then

$$\text{front(enqueue (createq,}x\text{))} = x$$

by the same axiom applied to the case when q = createq.

Deciding on an appropriate set of axioms is in general a difficult process. In Section 9.1 we gave a simplistic method based on the classification of the operations into constructors and inspectors. Such methods, while useful, are not foolproof and do not cover all cases. Moreover, dealing with errors causes extra difficulties, which we do not study here.

Initial semantics for algebraic specifications are unforgiving because, if we leave out an axiom, we can in general get many values in our data type that should be equal but aren't. More forgiving semantics are given by an approach that assumes that any two data values that cannot be distinguished by inspector operations must be equal. An algebra that expresses such semantics is called (again for mathematical reasons) a **final algebra**, and the associated semantics are called **final semantics**.

A final algebra is also essentially unique, and can be constructed by means similar to the initial algebra construction. To see the difference between these two definitions, we take the example of an integer array abstract data type. An algebraic specification is as follows:

type IntArray **imports** integer

operations:

    createIA: IntArray

    insertIA: IntArray × integer × integer → IntArray

    extractIA: IntArray × integer → integer

variables: A: IntArray; i,j,k: integer;

axioms:

    extractIA(createIA,i) = 0

    extractIA (insertIA $(A, i, j), k)$ = if $i = k$ then j else extractIA(A, k)

This array data type is essentially an integer array type indexed by the entire set of integers: insertIA(A,i,j) is like $A[i] = j$, and extractIA(A, i) is like getting the value $A[i]$. There is a problem, however: In initial semantics, the arrays

$$\text{insertIA (insertIA (createIA, 1, 1), 2,2)}$$

and

$$\text{insertIA(insertIA(createIA,2,2),1,1)}$$

are not equal! (There is no rule that allows us to switch the order of inserts.) Final semantics, however, tells us that two arrays must be equal if all their values are equal:

$$A = B \text{ if and only if for all integers } i \text{ extractIA}(A,i) = \text{extractIA}(B,i)$$

This is an example of the **principle of extensionality** in mathematics: Two things are equal precisely when all their components are equal. It is a natural property and is likely to be one we want for abstract data types, or at least for the IntArray specification. To make the final and initial semantics agree, however, we must add the axiom:

$$\text{insertIA (insertIA}(A,i,j),k,m) = \text{insertIA (insertIA}(A,k,m),i,j)$$

In the case of the queue algebraic specification, the final and initial semantics already agree, so we don't have to worry: given two queues p and q,

$$p = q \text{ if and only if } p = \text{createq and } q = \text{createq}$$
$$\text{or front}(p) = \text{front}(q) \text{ and dequeue}(p) = \text{dequeue}(q)$$

Exercises

9.1 Discuss how the following languages meet or fail to meet criteria 1 and 2 for an abstract data type mechanism from the beginning of this chapter: **(a)** C; **(b)** Ada; **(c)** ML; **(d)** another language of your choice.

9.2 In the algebraic specification of the complex abstract data type in Section 9.1, axioms were given that base complex addition and subtraction on the corresponding real operations. Write similar axioms for **(a)** multiplication, and **(b)** division.

9.3 An alternative to writing axioms relating the operations of complex numbers to the corresponding operations of their real and imaginary parts is to write axioms for all the usual properties of complex numbers, such as associativity, commutativity, and distributivity. What problems do you foresee in this approach?

9.4 Finish writing the `abstype Complex` definition of Figure 9.1 in ML (Section 9.2).

9.5 Finish writing the implementation of `package ComplexNumbers` in Section 9.4.

9.6 Write a complex number module in C using the header file approach described in Section 9.3.

9.7 Use your implementation of Exercise 9.4, 9.5, or 9.6 to write a program to compute the roots of a quadratic equation $ax^2 + bx + c = 0$. (a, b, and c may be assumed to be either real or complex.)

9.8 Write a new implementation for complex numbers in C, Ada, or ML that uses polar coordinates. Make sure that your interface and client code (e.g., Exercise 9.7) does not change.

9.9 Write an implementation for the queue ADT in C or Ada that uses a doubly-linked list with front and rear pointers instead of the singly-linked list with rear pointer that was used in this chapter. Make sure that your interface and client code does not change.

9.10 Rewrite the abstype Complex in ML as a signature and structure.

9.11 Implement the Stack ADT as described in Section 9.1 in **(a)** C; **(b)** Ada; **(c)** ML.

9.12 A **double-ended queue**, or **deque**, is a data type that combines the actions of a stack and a queue. Write an algebraic specification for a deque abstract data type assuming the following operations: create, empty, front, rear, addfront, addrear, deletefront, deleterear.

9.13 Which operations of the complex abstract data type of Section 9.1 are constructors? Which are inspectors? Which are selectors? Which are predicates? Based on the suggestions in Section 9.1, how many axioms should you have?

9.14 Write the axioms for an algebraic specification for an abstract data type SymbolTable with the following operations:

> create: SymbolTable
>
> enter: SymbolTable × name × value → SymbolTable
>
> lookup: SymbolTable → name → value
>
> isin: SymbolTable × name → boolean

9.15 Which operations of the SymbolTable abstract data type in Exercise 9.14 are constructors? Which are inspectors? Which are selectors? Which are predicates? Based on the suggestions in Section 9.1, how many axioms should you have?

9.16 Write an algebraic specification for an abstract data type String; think up appropriate operations for such a data type and the axioms they must satisfy. Compare your operations to standard string operations in a language of your choice.

9.17 Write an algebraic specification for an abstract data type bstree (binary search tree) with the following operations:

create: bstree

make: bstree $\times$ element $\times$ bstree $\to$ bstree

empty: bstree $\to$ boolean

left: bstree $\to$ bstree

right: bstree $\to$ bstree

data: bstree $\to$ element

isin: bstree $\times$ element $\to$ boolean

insert: bstree $\times$ element $\to$ bstree

What does one need to know about the element data type in order for a bstree data type to be possible?

9.18 Write C, Ada, or ML implementations for the specifications of Exercises 9.12, 9.14, 9.16, or 9.17. (Use generic packages in Ada as appropriate; use type variables and/or functors in ML as appropriate.)

9.19 Describe the Boolean data type using an algebraic specification.

9.20 Show using the axioms for a queue from Section 9.1 that the following are true:
(a) front (enqueue(enqueue(create,x), y)) = x
(b) front(enqueue(dequeue(enqueue(create,x)), y)) = y
(c) front(dequeue(enqueue(enqueue(create,x), y))) = y

9.21 A delete operation in a SymbolTable (see Exercise 9.14),

$$\text{delete: SymbolTable} \times \text{name} \to \text{SymbolTable}$$

might have two different semantics, as expressed in the following axioms:

$$\text{delete(enter}(s,x,v),y) = \text{if } x = y \text{ then } s \text{ else}$$
$$\text{enter(delete}(s,y),x,v)$$

or

$$\text{delete(enter}(s,x,v),y) = \text{if } x = y \text{ then delete } (s,x)$$
$$\text{else enter (delete}(s,y),x,v)$$

(a) Which of these is more appropriate for a symbol table in a translator for a block-structured language? In what situations might the other be more appropriate?
(b) Rewrite your axioms of Exercise 9.14 to incorporate each of these two axioms.

9.22 Ada requires generic packages to be instantiated with an actual type before the package can be used. By contrast, some other languages (e.g., C++) allow for the use of a type parameter directly in a declaration as follows:

```
x: Stack(Integer);
```

Why do you think Ada did not adopt this approach?

9.23 One could complain that the error axioms in the stack and queue algebraic specifications given in this chapter are unnecessarily strict, since for at least some of them, it is possible to define reasonable nonerror values. Give two examples of such axioms. Is it possible to eliminate all error values by finding nonerror substitutes for error values? Discuss.

9.24 In the algebraic specification of a stack or a queue, no mention was made of the possibility that a stack or queue might become full:

$$\text{full: stack} \rightarrow \text{boolean}$$

Such a test requires the inclusion of another operation, namely,

$$\text{size: stack} \rightarrow \text{integer}$$

and a constant

$$\text{maxsize:} \rightarrow \text{integer}$$

Write out a set of axioms for such a stack.

9.25 The queue implementations of the text ignored the error axioms in the queue ADT specification (indeed, one of the ML implementations generated warnings as a result). Rewrite the queue implementations in **(a)** Ada or **(b)** ML to use exceptions to implement the error axioms.

9.26 If one attempts to rewrite the Complex abstype of ML as a signature and structure, a problem arises in that infix operators lose their infix status when used by clients, unlike the abstype definitions, which retain their infix status.
(a) Discuss possible reasons for this situation.
(b) Compare this to Ada's handling of infix operators defined in packages.

9.27 In C++, overloaded infix operators are exempt from any namespace membership.
(a) Write some code to demonstrate this fact.
(b) Discuss possble reasons for this situation.
(c) Compare this to Ada's handling of infix operators defined in packages.

9.28 Write a C++ namespace definition and implementation for a single queue that completely suppresses the queue data type itself. Compare this to the Ada `Queues` package in Section 9.7.2.

9.29 In the ML structure definition `Queue1` in Section 9.5 (Figure 9.14), we noted the problem that, even though the `Queue` data type was protected from misuse by clients, the actual details of the internal representation were still visible in the printed values. Even worse, if we had used the built-in list representation directly (instead of with a `datatype` definition with constructor `Q`), a client could arbitrarily change a `Queue` value without using the interface.

(a) Rewrite the `Queue1` implementation to use a list directly, and show that the internal structure of the data is not protected.

(b) A 1997 addition to the ML module system is the opaque signature declaration that uses the symbol `:>` instead of just the colon in a signature constraint:

```
structure Queue1:> QUEUE =
    struct
    ...
    end;
```

Show that the use of this opaque signature suppresses all details of the `Queue` type, and that an ordinary list can now be used with complete safety.

9.30 The functor `OListFUN` defined in Section 9.7.4 is not safe, in that it exposes the internal details of the `Queue` type to clients, and allows clients full access to these details.

(a) Explain why. (*Hint:* See the previous exercise.)

(b) Could we use an opaque signature declaration to remove this problem, as we did in the previous exercise? Explain.

9.31 An implementation of abstract data type bstree of Exercise 9.17 is unsafe if it exports all the listed operations: A client can destroy the order property by improper use of the operations.

(a) Which operations should be exported and which should not?

(b) Discuss the problems this may create for an implementation, and how it is best handled in C, Ada, or ML.

(c) Write an implementation in C, Ada, or ML based on your approach in part (b).

9.32 Can the integers be used as a model for the Boolean data type? How do the integers differ from the initial algebra for this data type?

9.33 A **canonical form** for elements of an algebra is a way of writing all elements in a standard, or canonical, way. For example, the initial algebra for the queue algebraic specification has the following canonical form for its elements:

$$\text{enqueue}(\text{enqueue}(\ldots \text{enqueue}(\text{create}, a_1). \ldots, a_{n-1}), a_n)$$

Show that any element of the initial algebra can be put in this form, and use the canonical form to show that the initial and final semantics of a queue are the same.

9.34 Given the following algebraic specification

type Item **imports** boolean

operations:

        create: $\to$ Item

        push: Item $\to$ Item

        empty: Item $\to$ boolean

variables: s: Item;

axioms:

        empty(create) = true

        empty(push(s)) = false

show that the initial and final semantics of this specification are different. What axiom needs to be added to make them the same?

9.35 Exercise 9.3 noted that Complex abstract data type may need to have all its algebraic properties, such as commutativity, written out as axioms. This is not necessary if one uses the principle of extensionality (Section 9.8) and assumes the corresponding algebraic properties for the reals. Use the principle of extensionality and the axioms of Exercise 9.2 to show the commutativity of complex addition.

9.36 The principle of extensionality (Section 9.8) can apply to functions as well as data.
(a) Write an extensional definition for the equality of two functions.
(b) Can this definition be implemented in a programming language? Why or why not?
(c) Does the language C, Ada, or ML allow testing of functions for equality? If so, how does this test differ from your extensional definition?

Notes and References

The earliest language to influence the development of abstract data types was Simula67, which introduced abstract data types in the form of classes. The algebraic specification of abstract data types described in Section 9.1 was pioneered by Guttag [1977] and Goguen, Thatcher, and Wagner [1978], who also developed the initial algebra semantics described in Section 9.9. The alternative final algebra semantics described there was developed by Kamin [1983]. A good general reference for abstract data type issues, including mathematical issues discussed in Section 9.8, is Cleaveland [1986]. Namespaces in C++

are discussed in Stroustrup [1997]. Packages in Java are described in Arnold et al. [2000]. More details on ADT specification and implementation in Ada (Section 9.4) can be found in Booch et al. [1993], Barnes [1998], and Cohen [1996]. The ML module mechanisms (signatures, structures, and functors) are described further in Paulson [1996], Ullman [1998], and MacQueen [1988]. CLU examples (Section 9.6) can be found in Liskov [1984]; Euclid examples (Section 9.6) can be found in Lampson et al. [1981]; Modula-2 examples can be found in Wirth [1988a] and King [1988]. Other languages with interesting abstract data type mechanisms are Mesa (Mitchell, Maybury, and Sweet [1979]; Geschke, Morris, and Satterthwaite [1977]) and Cedar (Lampson [1983], Teitelman [1984]).

For an interesting study of separate compilation and dependencies in ML with references to Ada, Modula-3, and C see Appel and MacQueen [1994].

10 Object-Oriented Programming

Object-oriented programming languages began in the 1960s with the Simula project, an attempt to design a programming language that extended Algol60 in a way suitable for performing computer simulations of real-world situations. One of the central ideas of this project was to incorporate into the language the notion of an object, which, similar to a real-world object, is an entity with certain properties, and with the ability to react in certain ways to events. A program then consists of a set of objects, which can vary dynamically, and which execute by acting and reacting to each other, in much the same way that a real-world process proceeds by the interaction of real-world objects. These ideas were incorporated into the general-purpose language Simula67.

Simula67's influence took two different directions during the 1970s. The first was the development of abstract data type mechanisms, which we have studied in the last chapter. The second was the development of the object paradigm itself, which considers a program to be a collection of interacting independent objects. The primary representative of this direction of development was the Dynabook Project, which culminated in the language Smalltalk-80, the first language to incorporate the object paradigm in a thorough and consistent way.

Beginning in the mid-1980s, **object-oriented programming**, not only as a language paradigm, but also as a methodology for program design, has experienced an explosion in interest and activity, much as structured programming and top-down design did in the early 1970s. Nowadays almost every language has some form of structured constructs, such as the if-then-else statement, as well as procedural abstraction, and it is well known that it is possible to apply structured programming principles even in a relatively unstructured language like FORTRAN. Similarly, the ideas of object-oriented programming can be applied, at least to a certain extent, in non-object-oriented languages. Nevertheless, the real power of the technique comes only in a language with true object-oriented constructs, and over the last decade object-oriented programming has proven itself to be an extremely effective mechanism for promoting code reuse and modifiability, so that it has essentially become the dominant paradigm for large software projects, despite certain drawbacks in a few areas, such as its ability to express abstract data types.

In the following sections we shall review the major concepts of object-oriented programming, using Java as our primary example. The concepts we will cover include the notions of object and class as a pattern for objects, inheritance of operations as a tool for code reuse and the maintenance of control over dependencies, and the dynamic nature of operations as an essential feature of reuse. We will also study two languages in addition to Java as major examples of the object-oriented paradigm: C++ and Smalltalk. Finally, we will look briefly at some issues of object-oriented design and techniques for implementation of object-oriented language features.

10.1 Software Reuse and Independence

Object-oriented programming languages address themselves to three issues in software design: the need to reuse software components as much as possible, the need to modify program behavior with minimal changes to existing code, and the need to maintain the independence of different components. In the last chapter we saw that abstract data type mechanisms can aid the independence of software components by separating interfaces from implementations and by controlling dependencies. In theory, abstract data type mechanisms should also provide for the reuse of software components. It turns out, however, that in practice each new programming problem tends to require a slightly different version of the services provided by a module. What is needed are different ways of varying the services a module offers to clients, while at the same time retaining control over access to those services. In this section we explore the principal ways that the services of software components can be varied and the ways that access to these services can be controlled. These can then be used to evaluate the versatility and effectiveness of an object-oriented mechanism in the subsequent sections.

There are five basic ways that a software component can be modified for reuse: extension, restriction, redefinition, abstraction, and "polymorphization," each of which we discuss in turn.

1. *Extension of the data and/or operations.* As an example of this kind of modification, consider a queue with operations create, enqueue, dequeue, front, and empty (as in Chapter 9). In a particular application, it may be necessary to extend the operations of a queue so that elements can be removed from the rear of the queue and added to the front of the queue. Such a data structure is called a double-ended queue or deque, with new operations addfront and deleterear. These two new operations need to be added to the basic queue structure without necessarily changing the underlying implementation data. As another example of modification by extension, a window is defined on a computer screen as a rectangle specified by its four corners, with operations that may include translate, resize, display, and erase. A text window can be defined as a window with some added text to be displayed. Thus, a text window extends a window by adding data, without necessarily changing the operations to be performed.

2. *Restriction of the data and/or operations.* This is essentially the opposite operation from the previous one. For example, if a double-ended queue is available, an ordinary queue can be obtained by restricting the operations, eliminating addfront and deleterear. More commonly, both queues and double-ended queues can be obtained from a general list structure by restricting the kinds of insertions and deletions available. Similarly (but less commonly), a new structure may be obtained by dropping a data item, while preserving the operations. For example, a rectangle has both a length and a width, but a square has length equal to width, so one piece of data can be dropped in creating a square. Restriction is a mechanism that is rarely seen in programming languages (perhaps because it is more natural to extend than restrict programs), and we will not see specific mechanisms for it in the languages we study. Nevertheless it is worth stating as a mechanism, since it does occasionally arise in practice as a contrast to extension.

3. *Redefinition of one or more of the operations.* Even if the operations of a new data item remain essentially the same, it may be necessary to redefine some of them to accommodate new behavior. For example, a text window may have the same operations on it as a general-purpose window, but the display operation needs redefinition in order to display the text in the window as well as the window itself. Similarly, if a square is obtained from a rectangle, an area or perimeter function may

need to be redefined to take into account the reduced data needed in the computation.

In several areas in computing (such as the windows examples), the basic structure of each application is so similar to others that software developers have begun using **application frameworks** that provide basic services in object-oriented form and that are used by software developers through redefinition and reuse to provide specific services for each particular application. Examples of such applications frameworks include the **Swing** windowing toolkit in Java and **Microsoft Foundation Classes** in C++. Both of these object-oriented libraries allow graphical user interfaces to be constructed, modified, and reused with a minimum of effort.

4. *Abstraction, or the collection of similar operations from two different components into a new component.* For example, a circle and a rectangle are both objects that have position and that can be translated and displayed. These properties can be combined into an abstract object called a figure, which has the common features of circles, rectangles, triangles, and so on. Specific examples of a figure are then forced to have each of these common properties.

5. *"Polymorphization," or the extension of the type of data that operations can apply to.* We have already seen examples of this in previous chapters as two kinds of polymorphism: overloading and parameterized types. Extending the types that an operation applies to can also be viewed as an example of abstraction, where common operations from different types are abstracted and collected together. A good example might be that of a print function, which should be applicable to any variable as long as its value is printable. (Indeed, the Pascal `write` function is polymorphic in this sense, even though polymorphism is not an available mechanism within the language.) We might call such variables printable-objects and define a print procedure for all printable-objects.[1]

Design for reuse is not the only goal of object-oriented languages. Restricting access to internal details of software components is another. As we have seen in Chapter 9, this requirement is necessary to ensure that clients use components in a way that is independent of the implementation details of the component and that any changes to the implementation of a component will have only a local effect.

The two goals of restricting access and modifiability for reuse can sometimes be mutually incompatible. For example, to add operations to a queue, one needs access to the internal implementation details of the queue data structure. Access restriction can also be complementary to the need for modification, since it forces operations to be defined in an abstract way, which may make it easier to modify their implementation without changing the definition.

---

[1] Indeed, the Java 2 Platform has a similar feature for printing graphical objects on a printer.

Control over access can take several forms. One way is to list explicitly all operations and data that are accessible to clients in an export list (as in the Euclid example in Chapter 9). A second is to list those properties of a component that are inaccessible in a private part, as in Ada. Most explicit of all is to insist that public and private entities both be explicitly declared.

Implicit export is another possibility, as with a C++ namespace, where all entities declared are implicitly exported.

It may also be possible to declare parts of a software component to be partially accessible, that is, accessible to some but not all outside components. This can be done either by explicitly naming the outside components or by implicitly allowing access to a group of components.

Correspondingly, clients may be required to declare explicitly their use of a component by an `import` (Java) or `using` (C++) statement. Or they may be able to use a component implicitly, which must then be located automatically by the language system or by instructions to an interface checker and linker.

Mechanisms for restricting access to internal details go by several names. Some authors call them encapsulation mechanisms, while others refer to them as information hiding mechanisms. As we noted in the last chapter, both of these terms are somewhat confusing. We shall instead refer in this chapter to **protection mechanisms**.

10.2   Java: Objects, Classes, and Methods

In this section we study the basic components of an object-oriented programming language: objects, classes, and methods. This terminology is taken primarily from Simula and Smalltalk and is somewhat unusual for those familiar only with imperative or functional languages, so part of the goal of this section is to relate these terms to more commonly known language constructs.

In Chapter 5, we gave a definition for an **object** as something that occupies memory and has a (modifiable) state. This is essentially what an object is in an object-oriented language, but with some modification. First, the state of an object in an object-oriented language is primarily **internal**, or **local** to the object itself. That is, the state of an object is represented by local variables declared as part of the object and inaccessible to components outside the object. Second, each object includes a set of functions and procedures through which the local state can be accessed and changed. These are called **methods**, but they are similar to ordinary procedures and functions, except that they can automatically access the object's data (unlike the "outside world") and therefore can be viewed as containing an implicit parameter representing the object itself. Calling a method of an object is sometimes called **sending the object a message**. We shall use the terminology "invoke a method" or "call a method" in this chapter.

Objects can be declared by creating a pattern for the local state and methods. This pattern is called a **class**, and it is essentially just like a data type. Indeed, in many object-oriented languages, a class *is* a type and is incorporated into the type system of the language in more or less standard ways (as described in Chapter 6). Objects are then declared to be of a particular class exactly as variables are declared to be of a particular type in a language like C or Pascal. An object is said to be an **instance of a class** (a terminology related to the instantiation of Ada generic packages or the instantiation of variables by allocating them appropriate memory locations). The local variables representing an object's state are called **instance variables**.

We pause to consider an example in Java. Consider the complex number data type, which was described as an abstract data type in Chapter 9 and implemented there using the mechanisms of the Ada package and ML module. In Java the type complex can be defined as a class as in Figure 10.1.

```
(1)   public class Complex
(2)   { public Complex()
(3)     { re = 0; im = 0; }

(4)     public Complex (double realpart, double imagpart)
(5)     { re = realpart; im = imagpart; }

(6)     public double realpart()
(7)     { return re; }
(8)     public double imaginarypart()
(9)     { return im; }

(10)    public Complex add( Complex c )
(11)    { return new Complex(re + c.realpart(),
(12)                          im + c.imaginarypart());
(13)    }
(14)    public Complex multiply (Complex c)
(15)    { return new
(16)        Complex(re * c.realpart() - im * c.imaginary part(),
(17)              re * c.imaginarypart() + im * c.real part())
(18)    }

(19)    private double re, im;
(20) }
```

Figure 10.1   A Java class for complex numbers

Instance variables for class Complex are re and im (line 19 of Figure 10.1). Methods are realpart, imaginarypart, add, multiply, and other operations not included in the foregoing declaration for brevity's sake. Note that, in the code for add (lines 11–13), the realpart and imaginarypart methods of the parameter c are accessed using a dot notation just like the record field reference of C or Pascal. Note also that the instance variables of the "current instance" are accessed directly as `re` and `im` by the `add` and `multiply` procedures.[2]

In addition to the instance variables and methods, the definition of `Complex` contains two **constructors** (lines 2 and 4). These are like methods, except that they have the same name as the class and have no return value. Constructors specify initial values for the instance variables, and can perform other operations required when an object is first constructed (hence the name). In the case of `Complex`, the first constructor (line 2) takes no parameters (it is a so-called **default constructor**), and initializes both `re` and `im` to 0. The second constructor (line 4), on the other hand, has two parameters that provide initial values for the instance variables.

The definition of `Complex` also includes a protection mechanism like that of ADT mechanisms: The instance variables `re` and `im` are declared `private`, while the constructors and methods (indeed, also the `Complex` class itself), are declared `public`.[3] In this definition of class `Complex`, we have provided methods `realpart` and `imaginarypart` to fetch the values of the instance variables `re` and `im`. Code outside the class definition cannot access these instance variables, since they are declared `private`. This is an important property of the class structure—instance variables should be inaccessible in all but exceptional cases. This ensures that the use of a class is independent of the internal representation of the data. For example, we could rewrite the class `Complex` to use polar coordinates without changing any of the method interfaces as in Figure 10.2.[4]

```
public class Complex
{   public Complex()
    { radius = 0; angle = 0; }

    public Complex (double realpart, double imagpart)
    { radius = Math.sqrt(realpart*realpart + imagpart*imagpart);
      angle = Math.atan2(imagpart,realpart);
    }

    public double realpart()
    { return radius * Math.cos(angle); }

    public double imaginarypart()
    { return radius * Math.sin(angle); }                          (continues)
```

---

[2] The instance variables of the parameter c in the code for `add` or `multiply` could also have been accessed directly in Java, but not all object-oriented languages permit this (it is illegal in Smalltalk, for instance), so we use the more general approach for this example.

[3] Java has two additional levels of protection—`protected` and package—which will be discussed later in the chapter.

[4] Note that even the code for `add` and `multiply` would not have changed from Figure 10.1 to Figure 10.2 if we had used the access methods `realpart` and `imaginarypart` instead of `re` and `im`.

(continued)

```
    public Complex add( Complex c )
    { return new Complex(realpart() + c.realpart(),
                           imaginarypart() + c.imaginary part());
    }
    public Complex multiply (Complex c)
    { return new
        Complex(realpart() * c.realpart()
                  - imaginarypart() * c.imaginarypart(),
                  realpart() * c.imaginarypart()
                   + imaginarypart() * c.realpart());
    }

    private double radius, angle;
}
```

Figure 10.2   A Java `Complex` class implemented using polar coordinates, but retaining the same public interface as Figure 10.1

Instances of class `Complex` are created in Java as follows:

```
    Complex z,w;
      . . .
    z = new Complex (1,2);
    w = new Complex (-1,1);
```

Note how this mechanism separates the declaration of the variables z and w from the creation (or instantiation) of `Complex` objects via the **new** statements. Note also that initialization of the objects z and w occurs at the same time as allocation—the parenthesized values in the new expressions become the parameters to constructor calls—so that after these statements, z.re == 1.0, z.im == 1.0, w.re == −1.0, and w.im == 1.0. In many object-oriented languages, objects are implicitly reference or pointer types, so that initialization can be explicitly controlled during allocation and so that assignment is by sharing (that is, pointer semantics are maintained as described in Chapter 5). This is, for example, the case with Java.

Methods for the objects z and w can be invoked after allocation by using the usual dot notation. For example,

```
    z = z.add(w);
```

adds w to z, creating a new `Complex` object in the process, and assigns this new object to z (throwing away the object previously pointed to by z). It is also possible to nest operations, so that for example

```
    z = z.add(w).multiply(z);
```

performs the computation z = (z + w) * z. In the process, a temporary object (t, say) is created to hold the value of z + w, and a new object is then created to hold the value t + z. This object is then stored in z and z's old object thrown away. This has essentially all the advantages of the ADT mechanisms studied in the previous chapter, and with overloading, can make the type Complex look just like a built-in type. (Unfortunately, Java does not allow operator overloading, but C++ does—see later in this chapter.)

The disadvantages to this mechanism are two-fold. First, without automatic garbage collection, serious space leaks become difficult to avoid. For this reason, most object-oriented languages require automatic garbage collection (Java, for example, but not C++). Second, this view of binary operations is not symmetric, since the left-hand operand is singled out as the target of the method call. In a mixed-paradigm language like C++, such operators could be implemented instead as ordinary functions. Alternatively, some object-oriented languages allow **multimethods**, in which more than one object can be the target of a method call. These options and their benefits and drawbacks will be discussed in greater detail later in this chapter.

A class can of course refer to itself in its definition (Complex already did this), and an object can contain another object of its own class as an instance variable. Consider, for example, the Java definition of a class of linkable objects, each of which contains a link field to an object of the same class, as shown in Figure 10.3.

```
(1)    public class LinkableObject
(2)    {   public LinkableObject()
(3)        { link = null; }
(4)        public LinkableObject(LinkableObject link)
(5)        { this.link = link; }
(6)        public LinkableObject next()
(7)        { return link; }
(8)        public void linkTo( LinkableObject p)
(9)        { link = p; }
(10)        private LinkableObject link;
(11) }
```

Figure 10.3   A Java class LinkableObject containing a LinkableObject instance variable

In this example, every LinkableObject contains (a reference to) an instance of another LinkableObject (line 10 of Figure 10.3), which is initialized by the default constructor to the null reference (that is, a reference to no object at all). An additional feature of the above code is the use of the this keyword to refer to the current instance (line 5). The reason for that code is that the second constructor (lines 4–5) has a link parameter that creates a scope hole for the link instance variable (a not unusual occurrence), which can still be accessed as this.link. Indeed, all direct references to instance variables and methods within the code of a class are implicitly accessed through this.

The methods next and linkTo (lines 6 and 8) allow fetching and assignment of the link variable. The statement

```
x = new LinkableObject();
```

creates x as a reference to a storage location with a single link field initialized to the null reference:

Alternatively, one could define a linkableObject that is initialized to point to itself by changing line 3 above to:

(3)   { link = this; }

Now x = new LinkableObject(); creates the following picture:

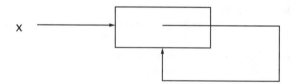

The concepts of class and object can be thought of as generalizing the notion of record or structure type and variable, respectively. Indeed, in a language with procedure and function types, such as C, the foregoing class definitions can be imitated as follows:

```
typedef struct ComplexStruct * Complex;
struct ComplexStruct
{   double re, im;
    double (*realpart)(Complex this);
    double (*imaginarypart)(Complex this);
    Complex (*add)(Complex this, Complex c);
    Complex (*multiply)(Complex this, Complex c);
};

typedef struct LinkStruct * LinkableObject;
struct LinkStruct
{   LinkableObject link;
    LinkableObject (*next)(LinkableObject this);
    void (*linkTo)(LinkableObject this, LinkableObject link);
};
```

There are major differences, however. For example, there is no initialization of the structure fields in C. In particular, the function fields need to be explicitly assigned values of global functions. There is also no way for a variable of type Complex or LinkableObject to refer to itself. Indeed, all methods above require an explicit this parameter, which must be used to refer explicitly to the current instance, so that we would have to write

```
z = z.add(z,w);
```

instead of

```
z = z.add(w);
```

(see Exercise 10.7). There are also no protection mechanisms available to limit access to the structure fields. Nevertheless, some object-oriented languages (such as C++) do treat classes as a form of structure declaration.

10.3 Inheritance

Inheritance is the major mechanism in object-oriented languages that allows the sharing of data and operations among classes, as well as the ability to redefine these operations without modifying existing code. A class B can **inherit** some or all of the instance variables and methods of another class A by declaring that class in its definition. In Java this is done by using the `extends` keyword in the definition of B:

```
public class B extends A
{
    ...
}
```

In Java, B inherits all the instance variables and methods of A, and B is called a **subclass** of A and A a **superclass** of B. Consider the example from Section 10.1 of a `Deque` as an extension of a `Queue` that adds the operations `addFront` and `removeRear`. A `Deque` can inherit from a `Queue` in Java as follows (for simplicity we assume that the data stored is integer):

```
public class Queue
{ // constructors and instance variables omitted
    // ...
    public void enqueue( int x) { ... }
    public void dequeue() { ... }
    public int front() { ... }
    public boolean empty() { ... }
}

public class Deque extends Queue
{ // ...
    public void addFront( int x) { ... }
    public void deleteRear() { ... }
}
```

Whenever we create a `Deque`, all six methods are available (four from `Queue` and the two added methods). A `Deque` is an **extension** of the class Queue, and all of the operations that apply to a Queue can also apply to a Deque.

Because class definitions in Java (and most object-oriented languages) are also type definitions, one can ask about the type relationship of a subclass such as Deque to a superclass such as Queue. In fact, because all the operations of Queue are inherited by Deque, Deque is a subtype of Queue as described in Chapter 6, Queue is a supertype of Deque, and all objects of a subclass such as Deque obey the **subtype principle**:

An object of a subtype may be used anywhere an object of its supertype is legal.

For example, if we define the following variables in Java,

```
Queue q;
Deque d;
```

and then create a Deque,

```
d = new Deque();
```

it is now possible to assign d to q:

```
q = d;
```

Now q.dequeue() and d.dequeue() perform exactly the same operation. The difference is that d.deleteRear() is a legal operation, but q.deleteRear() is not (see Exercise 10.8).

To state this another way, inheritance that obeys the subtype principle expresses the **is-a** relation: If A is a subclass of B, then every object belonging to A also belongs to B, or every A "is-a" B. In Java all objects obey the subtype principle, but in other languages (notably C++, as we will see), inheritance can be a more general concept, since it is in principle possible to restrict access to methods and data of a superclass. In this case the subtype principle may no longer hold.

By contrast with assignment to an object of a superclass, assignment to an object of a subclass is only reasonable if it is known that the object in question is really already an instance of the subclass in question. For example, assigning q to d above is inherently suspicious, even when q does contain a Deque object (as it would after the previous assignment):

```
q = d; // a compile-time error in Java
```

Thus, most object-oriented languages declare this to be an error (as does Java). In those cases where it is actually safe to assume that the object really is of the appropriate subtype, the desired effect can be achieved by a cast:

```
q = (Deque) d; // now no compiler error
```

This process is called **downcasting**, and, if incorrect, will generally result in a runtime error (Java will generate a ClassCastException).

Inheritance establishes a hierarchy of classes and their associated objects that can be used to share common behavior. At the top of Java's class hierarchy is the class `Object`, which establishes behavior that is common to all of Java's objects. By definition in Java all classes implicitly extend class `Object`:

```
class A
{  ... }
```

means

```
class A extends Object
{ ... }
```

Two examples of behaviors that are common to all objects in Java are the methods `equals` and `toString`, which are defined in Java's `Object` class:

```
class Object
{  ...
    public boolean equals( Object obj ) { ... }
    public String toString() { ... }
    ...
}
```

The `equals` method is designed to test for **value equality** of objects, as opposed to reference or pointer equality (see Chapter 5). Since all objects in Java are references, the == operator is usually the wrong equality test, because it tests identity in memory, rather than equality as values. For example, strings in Java should always be tested using `equals`, which tests that they are comprised of the same characters:

```
String s = "Hello";
String t = new String("Hello");
// now s == t is false, but s.equals(t) is true
```

Similarly, the `toString` function is used by many system utilities to convert an object into printable form. In particular, the `System.out.println` standard output method in Java implicitly calls the `toString` method of any object it is asked to print.

Unfortunately, the default behaviors for these methods (that is, their definitions in class `Object`) are usually not what we want. In fact, the default behavior for `equals` is the same as ==, since it doesn't know what instance variables might exist for subobjects. And the default behavior for `toString` is also not very useful—it prints out the class name and an internal index that has no meaning in terms of the value itself:

```
Complex z = new Complex(1,1);
System.out.println(z);
// prints something like Complex@73d6a5
```

Fortunately, inheritance not only allows the operations and data of objects to be extended, but also allows the behavior of methods to be *changed* or **overriden** in subclasses. Thus, in our earlier definition of Complex, we would want to add new definitions of equals and toString:

```
public class Complex
{  // ... previous code as before

    public boolean equals ( Complex c)
    { return re == c.realpart()
                    && im == c.imaginary part(); }

    public String toString()
    { return re + " + " + im + "i"; }
}
```

Now, given the following code:

```
Complex z = new Complex(1,1);
Complex x = new Complex(1,1);
if (x.equals(z)) System.out.println("ok!");
System.out.println(z);
```

The Java interpreter will print

```
ok!
1.0 + 1.0i
```

As another example of how inheritance promotes reuse, consider the situation of a graphics object that can be a circle or a rectangle. We might define these as in Figure 10.4:

```
public class Point
{  public Point (double x, double y)
    {  this.x = x;
       this.y = y;
    }
    // ...
    private double x;
    private double y;
}

public class Circle
{  public Circle( Point c, double r)
    { center = c;
      radius = r;
    }
    //...

    public double area()
    {  return Math.PI * radius * radius; }

    private Point center;
    private double radius;
}
```

```
public class Rectangle
{   public Rectangle (Point c, double w, double h)
    {   center = c;
        width = w;
        height = h;
    }
    // ...
    public double area()
    { return width * height; }

    private Point center;
    private double width;
    private double height;
}
```

Figure 10.4   A first pass at a definition of `Point`, `Circle`, and `Rectangle` in Java

Both `Circle` and `Rectangle` have things in common in Figure 10.4, however: a `Point` object (pointed to by `center`) describing its location, and the method `area`. Indeed, every closed figure will have these same properties, and we may abstract them as follows:

```
public abstract class ClosedFigure
{   public ClosedFigure (Point c)
    {   center = c; }
    // ...

    public abstract double area();

    private Point center;
}
```

Now the `area` method has become **abstract**, that is, a method that is always available for objects of the class but that is given different implementations for different subclasses. In the case of `area`, it cannot be given a general implementation for `ClosedFigure`, but an implementation must be deferred until a subclass is defined with enough properties to enable the area to be determined. Indeed, abstract methods are sometimes called **deferred**, and a class that has a deferred method is called a **deferred class**. The advantage to defining abstract or deferred methods is not only to consolidate code, but also to make it a requirement that any `ClosedFigure` have an `area` function, that is, to ensure that any object of a subclass of `ClosedFigure` has an area. To complete the example of `ClosedFigure`, we define `area` in the two subclasses `Circle` and `Rectangle` as in Figure 10.5.

```
(1)   public class Circle extends ClosedFigure
(2)   { public Circle( Point c, double r)
(3)     { super(c);                                        (continues)
```

(continued)

```
(4)        radius = r;
(5)    }
(6)    // ...
(7)    public double area()
(8)    { return Math.PI * radius * radius; }

(9)    private double radius;
(10) }

(11) public class Rectangle extends ClosedFigure
(12) { public Rectangle (Point c, double w, double h)
(13)    { super(c);
(14)      width = w;
(15)      height = h;
(16)    }
(17)    // ...
(18)    public double area()
(19)    { return width * height; }

(20)    private double width;
(21)    private double height;
(22) }
```

Figure 10.5   A second pass at a definition of `Circle` and `Rectangle` in
             Java using inheritance and the `ClosedFigure` abstract class

Note in this code that the `Circle` and `Rectangle` constructors cannot initialize `center` directly, since it is private in `ClosedFigure`. Instead, the constructors must call the `ClosedFigure` constructor, and this is done in lines 3 and 13 of Figure 10.5 using the special syntax `super(c)` (the keyword `super` is used to indicate operations on the current object interpreted as a member of the parent class, while `this` refers to the current object as a member of its defining class).

An alternative to the use of `super` is to relax the protection of `center` so that it is accessible within subclasses but not by clients, and that can be accomplished through the use of the keyword `protected`:[5]

```
public abstract class ClosedFigure
{  // ...

    protected Point center;
}
```

This would allow `center` to be initialized directly:

```
public class Circle extends ClosedFigure
{   public Circle( Point c, double r)
```

---

[5] Java's protected feature allows package access as well as subclass access.

```
        {   center = c;
            radius = r;
        }
        // ...
    }
```

The public features of a class represent its view from the code that uses the class; the private features are its internal implementation; and the protected features are its view from implementations that extend the class.[6]

Now given the following declarations and initializations,

```
(1)   Point x,y;
(2)   ClosedFigure f;
(3)   Rectangle r;
(4)   Circle c;

(5)   x = new Point(0,0);
(6)   y = new Point(1,-1);
(7)   r = new Rectangle(x,1,1);
(8)   c = new Circle(y,1);
(9)   f = r;
(10) f.area();
(11) f = c;
(12) f.area();
```

the first call to f.area() (line 10) calls the appropriate method of r (and returns the value 1.0), while the second call to f.area() (line 12) calls the appropriate method of c (and returns the value 3.141592 . . .).

Inheritance establishes a parent-child dependency relationship between superclasses and subclasses, so that the class inheritance relationship can be viewed as an **inheritance graph**. For example, the graphical figures in the example have the following inheritance graph (the arrows point from subclass to superclass):

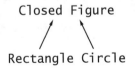

A more detailed inheritance graph along these same lines might be as in Figure 10.6.

---

[6] Java also has **package protection**, which is indicated by the absence of any protection keyword; this allows access by code from within a package but not elsewhere. (Packages were described in Chapter 9.)

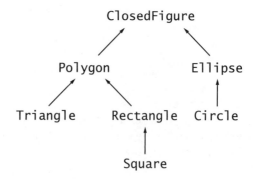

Figure 10.6   A possible inheritance graph for geometric figures

Inheritance provides many opportunities for polymorphism, since any method that applies to a base class can apply to a subclass as well, where it could also be redefined. This notion of polymorphism is in fact **subtype polymorphism** as we defined it in Chapter 6; here it is similar in effect to overloading—indeed, it can be thought of as overloading on the class of the implicit object parameter. For example, in an object-oriented language one might choose to define both integers and reals as subclasses of a class `number`:

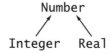

Now addition can be defined as a method of class `Number`, which acquires different implementations in subclasses `Integer` and `Real`.[7]

In each of the cases we have examined, the inheritance graph is a tree. This situation is called **single inheritance**, since each subclass class inherits from only one superclass. It is also possible to have **multiple inheritance**, in which a class may inherit from two or more superclasses. Some object-oriented languages such as C++ provide multiple inheritance. Java does not allow multiple inheritance because of its complexity. Instead, Java has an alternative, called multiple interface inheritance, which we describe later in this chapter.

As an example of multiple inheritance, consider the classes `Complex` and `LinkableObject` from Section 10.2. (For purposes of the example, we adapt the syntax of Java to allow multiple inheritance, even though it is not an actual part of the language.) A `LinkableObject` as defined in Figure 10.3 of Section 10.2 contains no data other than a link to another `LinkableObject`. To link together objects that contain complex numbers (for example, in a queue of complex numbers), we can create a new class

---

[7] Indeed, in the functional language Haskell, a similar mechanism is used to introduce overloading into Hindley-Milner polymorphic type checking. The "inheritance" there is at the level of types, not of objects; see Chapter 11.

LinkableComplex that is derived from both LinkableObject and Complex:

```
class LinkableComplex extends Complex, LinkableObject
{
    ...
}
```

Now an object of class LinkableComplex can appear anywhere an object of class LinkableObject or Complex can appear. In particular, if x and y are two objects of class LinkableComplex, then it is possible both to link them and add them:

```
x.add(y);
x.linkTo(y);
```

To see why multiple inheritance adds substantial complexity to a language, note first that, in a language with multiple inheritance, inheritance graphs can be directed acyclic graphs instead of being restricted to trees. This means that methods may be inherited in more than one way. For example, a method from class A is inherited by class D in two different ways in the following inheritance graph:

This creates difficulties in resolving references to methods. For instance, what happens if B, but not C, redefines a method of A? In addition, there may be situations where what is wanted is actually *two* copies of A in class D, not just one as the above diagram implies. The diagram then would be:

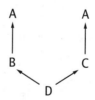

This is called **repeated inheritance**, and is an option in C++ (see Section 10.5).

For these reasons, Java does not allow multiple class inheritance, but it *does* allow a more restricted mechanism called **multiple interface inheritance**. We will briefly consider this and related issues using the following example.

Consider the case of a queue of linkable objects, with several possible data items as subclasses of LinkableObject as previously defined using multiple inheritance. That design is somewhat suspicious, since a

LinkableObject really has two purposes—not just to link other LinkableObjects together, but also to contain some data, and to express containment by inheritance is a well-known pitfall of object-oriented design. Instead, a LinkableObject should be redefined to allow it to contain an arbitrary object:

```
(1)   public class LinkableObject
(2)   { public LinkableObject( Object d )
(3)     { link = null;
(4)       item = d;
(5)     }

(6)     public LinkableObject( Object d, LinkableObject link)
(7)     { this.link = link;
(8)       item = d;
(9)     }

(10)    public LinkableObject next()
(11)    { return link; }

(12)    public void linkTo( LinkableObject p)
(13)    { link = p; }

(14)    public Object data()
(15)    { return item; }

(16)    private LinkableObject link;
(17)    private Object item;
(18) }
```

Figure 10.7   A Java definition of a LinkableObject class that contains
data (compare to Figure 10.3)

Here the use of the universal Java base class Object (lines 2, 6, 14, and 17 of Figure 10.7) allows any object to be contained in a LinkableObject, and we now can use a LinkableObject to store a Complex or an integer or a double (we must use the Java "wrapper" classes Integer and Double to store an int or double, because these latter are simple data, not objects in Java, for efficiency reasons):

```
LinkableObject r = new LinkableObject(new Double(1.2));
LinkableObject i = new LinkableObject(new Integer(42));
LinkableObject c = new LinkableObject(new Complex(1,-1));
```

We also say that a LinkableObject "has-a" data object, rather than the previous view, for example, that a LinkableComplex "is-a" Complex.

We now can define a Queue class (Figure 10.8) that uses the linking capabilities of LinkableObject to maintain itself internally as a circular singly-linked list with a rear pointer.

```
(1)   public class Queue
(2)   { public Queue()
(3)     { rear = null; }
```

```
(4)      public boolean empty()
(5)      { return rear == null; }

(6)      public LinkableObject front()
(7)      { return rear.next(); }

(8)      public void dequeue()
(9)      { if (front() == rear) rear = null;
(10)       else rear.linkTo(front().next());
(11)     }

(12)     public void enqueue( LinkableObject item)
(13)     { if (empty())
(14)        { rear = item;
(15)          rear.linkTo(item);
(16)        }
(17)      else
(18)        { item.linkTo(front());
(19)          rear.linkTo(item);
(20)          rear = item;
(21)        }
(22)     }

(23)     private LinkableObject rear;
(24) }
```

Figure 10.8   A Java definition of a Queue class using the
            LinkableObject class of Figure 10.7

Now we can store and retrieve the previously constructed
LinkableObjects:

```
Queue q = new Queue();
q.enqueue(r);
q.enqueue(i);
q.enqueue(c);
q.dequeue();
System.out.println(q.front().data()); // prints 42
```

This mechanism for storing objects of different classes using the universal
class Object is called the **based-object** approach to data structures, and is
typical of Java[8] and Smalltalk. The disadvantage to this mechanism is that
the actual class of the object retrieved from a data structure may not be
known, and both a test and a cast may need to be supplied if features of
the actual class the object belongs to are to be used. Java has a special

---

[8] As of this writing, Java does not have parametric polymorphism; however,
it is likely that this will be added to Java in the near future.

keyword `instanceof` for this situation. For example, suppose we wanted to double the value of each of the data items r, i, and c that were placed on q above. We would then have to use code such as

```
Object obj = q.front().data();
if (obj instanceof Double)
  System.out.println(((Double)obj).doubleValue()*2);
else if (obj instanceof Integer)
  System.out.println(((Integer)obj).intValue()*2);
else if (obj instanceof Complex)
  System.out.println(((Complex)obj).add((Complex)obj));
```

By contrast, C++ uses its template mechanism to establish uniform data structures that are type checked at compile-time, and the need for class membership tests and casts is reduced (see Section 10.5).[9]

An alternative to this design (that avoids questions of multiple inheritance) is to observe that the definition of class `Queue` requires only the existence of the methods `linkTo()` and `next()`, and any object with these methods can be stored in a `Queue`. Java has a mechanism for defining such constraints called an **interface**, which is like a class except that it only specifies the names and types (signatures) of methods, but gives no implementation, instance variables, or constructors. We could therefore define a `LinkableObject` as an interface:

```
interface LinkableObject
{  LinkableObject next();
   void linkTo( LinkableObject p);
}
```

An interface is like an abstract class, but unlike an abstract class an interface can give no details at all about an implementation—note in the above interface definition that even the keyword `public` is missing from the method definitions; methods in an interface are implicitly all `public`, since it makes no sense to have private ones.

With the above definition of `LinkableObject`, the previous `Queue` code works without change. Now, however, we can define a `LinkableComplex` class, since Java allows multiple inheritance involving interfaces (the aforementioned problems of multiple inheritance do not occur in the absence of any implementation details; see Exercise 10.32):

```
class LinkableComplex
      extends Complex implements LinkableObject
{ private LinkableObject link;
  public LinkableObject next() { return link; }
  public void linkTo( LinkableObject p)  { link = p; }
  public LinkableComplex( double re, double im)
```

---

[9] At the time of this writing, templates are a strong candidate for inclusion in future releases of Java for this reason.

```
        { super(re,im);
            link = null;
        }
    }
```

Interfaces in Java operate much as signatures do in ML or specification packages do in Ada (see Chapter 9).

10.4 Dynamic Binding

One of the principal features that distinguishes classes in an object-oriented language from modules or packages in a language like Ada or ML is the dynamic nature of classes versus the static nature of modules. This is visible already in the fact that objects from a class are allocated storage in a fully dynamic way, usually on a "heap."

Depending on the language, this dynamic allocation of objects may be under the manual control of the programmer (as in the C++ `new` and `delete` operations), or it may be fully automatic (as in most functional languages), or it may be a hybrid of the two. Allocation schemes have already been discussed in Chapter 8, but additional allocation issues for object-oriented languages are discussed in the next sections, particularly Section 10.9. We note here only that Java uses a hybrid scheme where the allocation (and initialization) of objects is under programmer control through the use of the `new` expression, but that there is no corresponding `delete`. Instead, objects are reclaimed automatically, either by exiting their scopes (in a stack-based fashion) or by some form of garbage collection.

However, the dynamic nature of classes goes beyond the allocation and deallocation of objects. Methods can also vary dynamically, and in this lies much of the power of the object-oriented approach. We have already seen examples of this in the last section. For example, the `area` method of class `ClosedFigure` is defined differently for each derived class. Then the appropriate area method is invoked for each object of `ClosedFigure`, depending dynamically on which derived class the object belongs to. Such methods are said to obey **dynamic binding**, and dynamic binding is one of the main sources of the power of an object-oriented language.

In the preceding example, the `area` method was in fact undefined for the class `ClosedFigure`, so it was necessary for appropriate methods of derived classes to be invoked. Dynamic binding can also occur when a method is **redefined** in a derived class. For example, the `Complex` class redefined the `toString` and `equals` methods of the universal `Object` class, and these methods are the ones that are called for a `Complex` object, no matter what the context is in which it occurs (otherwise, the `System.out.println` function would not work as advertised).

As an additional, more direct example of this phenomenon, consider a class `BorderedRectangle` that is derived from `Rectangle` and that redefines the method `area` to include the extra area covered by the border:

```
class BorderedRectangle extends Rectangle
{  public BorderedRectangle (Point c, double w,
                                    double h, double b)
    {  super(c,w,h);
       border = b;
    }
    // ...
    public double area()
    {  return (width+2*border) * (height+2*border);
    }

    private double border;
}
```

Now any `Rectangle` object that is actually a `BorderedRectangle` will call the new `area` method. For example, with the declarations

```
Rectangle r =
        new BorderedRectangle(new Point(1,1),3,4,0.5);
...
r.area()
...
```

the call to `r.area()` will compute the area according to the new `area` function.

It is possible to offer both static and dynamic binding of methods in an object-oriented language. In languages that represent more of a compromise between the object-oriented paradigm and standard imperative languages (such as C++), there is often a choice of whether to use static or dynamic binding, with static binding as the default. This is, for example, the case in C++, where methods to which dynamic binding apply must be declared to be `virtual` (a keyword and behavior inherited from Simula). In most "pure" object-oriented languages, such as Java and Smalltalk, all methods are implicitly "virtual"—that is, dynamic binding always applies. If necessary, static binding of methods can be achieved by appropriate use of the `super` keyword.[10] We offer an additional example of this behavior.

Consider the Java program of Figure 10.9.

```
(1)   class A
(2)   { void p()
(3)     { System.out.println("A.p");
(4)     }

(5)     void q()
(6)     { System.out.println("A.q");
(7)     }
```

---

[10] Static binding in Java can also happen when calling `static`, `final`, or private methods; we do not discuss these cases here.

```
(8)      void f()
(9)      { p();
(10)       q();
(11)     }
(12) }
(13) class B extends A
(14) { void p()
(15)     { System.out.println("B.p");
(16)     }
(17)     void q()
(18)     { System.out.println("B.q");
(19)       super.q();
(20)     }
(21) }
(22) public class VirtualExample
(23) { public static void main(String[] args)
(24)     { A a = new A();
(25)       a.f();
(26)       a = new B();
(27)       a.f();
(28)     }
(29) }
```

Figure 10.9   A Java program illustrating dynamic and static binding of methods

The program of Figure 10.9 prints

```
A.p
A.q
B.p
B.q
A.q
```

Dynamic binding says that, in the second call to a.f() (line 27 of Figure 10.9), B.p and B.q are called, since a at that point is a B. Note that this is true even though p and q are called through A.f (lines 9 and 10). The reason is that the calls on lines 9 and 10 are still implicitly calls through the object reference—in other words, the calls are interpreted as this.p() and this.q(), and of course this = a. Note also that the call super.q() on line 19 has the effect of a nondynamically bound call, so that this kind of behavior can be imitated in Java.

A further issue in the use of dynamic binding in an object-oriented language is how to implement dynamic binding as part of the runtime environment, since dynamic method calls cannot be resolved at compile-time as ordinary function calls are. Superficially, it appears that during execution the runtime environment must check the class to which each object belongs to determine which method is meant, and this can cause significant runtime overhead. However, it is possible to offer dynamic binding while retaining static typing, and paying only a small constant penalty for dynamic method invocation. See Section 10.9 for more detail.

10.5 C++

In the last sections we have used Java as our sample language while discussing the basic concepts of object-oriented languages. In this and the following section, we survey two other object-oriented languages—C++ and Smalltalk—and discuss the differences in terminology and available features of each. The examples we will use are the ones that have featured strongly in our previous discussions: complex numbers, queues, closed figures, and linkable objects.

C++ was originally developed by Bjarne Stroustrup at AT&T Bell Labs (where C was developed) as an extension of C with Simula-like classes, but in the late 1980s and 1990s it grew well beyond its origins into a language containing a large number of features, some object-oriented, some not. It is a compromise language in that it contains most of the C language as a subset (as Simula contains Algol60 as a subset). C++ was also designed to be an efficient, practical language, developing out of the needs of its users. As such it became the primary object-oriented language of the early 1990s and remains extremely popular for non-web applications. Since the first reference manual was published in 1986, many new features have been added, including multiple inheritance, templates, operator overloading, and exceptions. The language has now stabilized since the adoption of an international standard in 1998.

C++ contains class and object declarations similar to those of Java. Instance variables and methods are both called **members** of a class: Instance variables are referred to as **data members**, and methods are referred to as **member functions**. Subclasses are referred to as **derived classes** and superclasses are called **base classes**. One basic difference between C++ and most other object-oriented languages, including Java, is that objects are not automatically pointers or references. Indeed, except for inheritance and dynamic binding of member functions, the class data type in C++ is essentially identical to the struct (or record) data type.

Similar to Java, three levels of protection are provided for class members in C++: public, private, and protected. **Public** members are those accessible to client code, as well as to derived classes. **Protected** members are inaccessible to client code but are still accessible to derived classes. **Private** members are accessible neither to clients nor to derived classes. In a class declaration the default protection is private, while in a struct declaration the default is public. Additionally, the keywords private, public, and protected establish blocks in class declarations, rather than apply only to individual member declarations as in Java:

```
class A
{ // A C++ class
public:
    // all public members here
protected:
    // all protected members here
private:
    // all private members here
};
```

(Note the final semicolon after the closing bracket, which is a vestige of C syntax that is unnecessary in Java.)

In C++, initialization of objects is given as in Java by **constructors** that have the same name as that of the class. Constructors are automatically called when an object is allocated space in memory, and actual parameters to the constructor function are specified at that time. Thus, constructors are similar to Java, except that in C++ objects need not be references, and so a constructor can be called as part of a declaration, as well as in a new expression. Unlike Java, C++ does not have required built-in garbage collection, and so C++ also has **destructors**, which like constructors have the same name as the class, but which are preceded by the tilde symbol "~" (sometimes used in logic to mean "not"). Destructors are automatically called when an object is deallocated (either by going out of scope or through the use of the delete operator), but they must be provided by the programmer and so represent a manual approach to memory deallocation.

A class declaration in C++ does not always contain the implementation code for all member functions. Member functions can be implemented outside the declaration by using the **scope resolution operator** indicated by a double colon "::" after the class name. It gets its name from the fact that it causes the scope of the class declaration to be reentered. Member functions that are given implementations in a class declaration are automatically assumed to be **inline** (that is, a compiler may replace the function call by the actual code for the function).

As an example of the foregoing features, let us write out the code for a Queue data type in C++ using a circular linked list implementation similar to the Java code of Figure 10.8, Section 10.3. We first must write out the declaration for a LinkableObject, as in Figure 10.10.

```
(1)   class LinkableObject
(2)   {
(3)   public:
(4)      LinkableObject()
(5)      : link(0) { }

(6)      LinkableObject (LinkableObject* p)
(7)      : link(p) { }                          (continues)
```

(continued)

```
(8)     LinkableObject* next()
(9)     { return link; }

(10)    void linkTo( LinkableObject* p)
(11)    { link = p; }

(12) private:
(13)    LinkableObject* link;
(14) };
```

Figure 10.10   A C++ definition of a `LinkableObject` class (compare to the Java code of Figure 10.3)

Figure 10.10 declares a `LinkableObiect` with a `link` field as a pointer to a `LinkableObject` (but no data) and constructors that initialize the link field.

The syntax for instance variable initialization in a C++ constructor is somewhat unusual: The instance variable names are listed after a colon in a comma-separated list between the constructor declaration and body, with the initial values in parentheses after each instance name. Thus, the `LinkableObject` constructor declaration of Figure 10.10:

```
(6)     LinkableObject (LinkableObject* p)
(7)     : link(p) { }
```

means that `link` is initialized to the value of p. In other words, the above code has essentially the same meaning as

```
LinkableObject (LinkableObject* p)
{ link = p; }
```

Similarly, a class A with instance variables `int  a` and `char  b`, could initialize these in a default constructor as follows:

```
A()  : a(0), b(' ') { }
```

The reason for this notation in C++ is efficiency: C++ insists that all instance variables be initialized *prior* to the execution of the body of any constructor; thus, initialization would be performed *twice* if it were expressed as regular code inside the body of the constructor (once by the system and once by the actual code).

Note also that the first `LinkableObject` constructor (lines 4 and 5 of Figure 10.10) initializes the `link` field to 0—the C++ equivalent to `null` in Java.[11]

If we want to create a pointer to a `LinkableObject`, we can do so using the two different constructors as follows:

```
LinkableObject* p = new LinkableObject;
                    //same as new LinkableObject();
LinkableObject* q = new LinkableObject(p);
```

[11] Many C++ implementations provide the name NULL as a synonym for 0.

Note that the empty parentheses are not necessary in the call to the first constructor (the default constructor).

We now define a Queue of LinkableObjects in C++ as in Figure 10.11.

```
(1)   class Queue
(2)   {
(3)   public:
(4)      Queue() : rear(0) { }

(5)      int empty()
(6)      { return rear == 0; }

(7)      void enqueue(LinkableObject* item);

(8)      void dequeue();

(9)      LinkableObject* front()
(10)     { return rear->next(); }

(11)     ~Queue();

(12) protected: // demo - may not be appropriate
(13)     LinkableObject* rear;
(14)   };

(15) void Queue::enqueue(LinkableObject* item)
(16) { if (empty())
(17)    { rear = item;
(18)      rear->linkTo(item);
(19)    }
(20)    else
(21)    { item->linkTo(front());
(22)      rear->linkTo(item);
(23)      rear = item;
(24)    }
(25) }

(26) void Queue::dequeue()
(27) { if (front() == rear) rear = 0;
(28)    else rear->linkTo(front()->next());
(29) }

(30) Queue::~Queue()
(31) // demo code - may result in dangling refs
(32) { while (!empty())
(33)    { LinkableObject* temp = front();
(34)      dequeue();
(35)      delete temp;
(36)    }
(37) }
```

Figure 10.11   A C++ Queue definition using the LinkableObject class of Figure 10.10

The sample code of Figure 10.11 shows the use of the scope resolution operator "::" to allow member functions to have their implementation given outside the declaration of a class. The code also illustrates the existence of a destructor (called ~Queue), which frees all LinkableObjects remaining in a Queue object if it is released from memory (such as on exit from a local scope).[12] Note that the member functions empty and front are inline functions, and calls to them are replaced by the actual code for the functions. Note also the use of the protected keyword to allow access to the rear pointer for derived classes, but not for clients.

We can now create LinkableObjects and put them in and take them off a queue as follows:

```
Queue q;
LinkableObject* x = new linkableObject;
q.enqueue(x);
q.enqueue(new LinkableObject);
LinkableObject* y = q.front(); // now y is x
q.dequeue();
q.dequeue(); // q is now empty
```

A class Deque can inherit the operations of Queue and provide the extra operations addfront and deleterear using the following declaration:

```
class Deque : public Queue
{
public:
    void addfront(LinkableObject* x);
    void deleterear();
};
```

The use of the keyword public before the base class Queue of derived class Deque is to indicate that all access to members of Queue remains as declared in Queue. Thus, all public members of Queue remain public in Deque and similarly for protected members (private members are unavailable in any case). In other words, the subtype principle holds for Deque. C++ also allows private (and protected) derivation (for which the subtype principle does *not* hold), as for example,

```
class B : private A { ... };
```

Now class B has private access to the public and protected members of A, but must reexport any members it wishes to make public, as in the following example:

---

[12] Since the LinkableObjects are created outside the control of a Queue object, deleting these objects is inherently unsafe; an "industrial strength" Queue implementation would use its own internal LinkableObjects, as described later.

```
class Stack : private Queue
{
public:
   Queue::empty; //adjust access - no type info
   void pop()
   { dequeue(); } // rename dequeue as pop
   ...
};
```

As in Java, inheritance can be used to insert actual data into a Queue object, as in the following code:

```
class LinkableInt : public LinkableObject
{
public:
  LinkableInt(int d) : item(d) { }

  int data()
  { return item; }

private:
  int item;
};
  ...
Queue q;
LinkableInt* x = new LinkableInt(42);
q.enqueue(x);
x = static_cast<LinkableInt*>(q.front());
cout << x->data() << endl; // prints 42
  ...
```

This is a use of inheritance to achieve polymorphism, as described in Section 10.3. One can instead use the C++ template mechanism as described in Chapter 6 to achieve parametric polymorphism with type checking. Such polymorphism would be defined at the level of the Queue class, as in Figure 10.12 (we also make LinkableObjects into a local class for use only by the Queue class in this code).

```
(1)   template<typename T> class Queue
(2)   {
(3)   public:
(4)     Queue() : rear(0) { }

(5)     int empty()
(6)     { return rear == 0; }

(7)     void enqueue (T item);

(8)     void dequeue ();
```

(continued)

```
(9)     T front()
(10)    { return rear->next->data;

(11)    ~Queue();

(12) protected:
(13)    class Linkable
(14)    {
(15)    public:
(16)       T data;
(17)       Linkable* next;
(18)    };

(19)    Linkable* rear;
(20) };

(21) template <typename T>
(22) void Queue<T>::enqueue(T item)
(23) { Linkable* temp = new Linkable;
(24)    temp->data = item;
(25)    if (empty())
(26)    { rear = temp;
(27)       rear->next = temp;
(28)    }
(29)    else
(30)    { temp->next = rear->next;
(31)       rear->next = temp;
(32)       rear = temp;
(33)    }
(34) }

(35) template <typename T>
(36) void Queue<T>::dequeue()
(37) { Linkable* temp = rear->next;
(38)    if (temp == rear) rear = 0;
(39)    else rear->next = rear->next->next;
(40)    delete temp;
(41) }

(42) template <typename T>
(43) Queue<T>::~Queue()
(44) { while (!empty()) dequeue();
(45) }
```

Figure 10.12   A C++ Queue definition using templates (compare to the code of Figures 10.10 and 10.11)

With the code of Figure 10.12 a queue of integers can be declared and used as follows:

```
Queue<int> q;
q.enqueue(42);
int x = q.front();
q.dequeue();
```

Dynamic binding of member functions is provided as an option in C++, but it is not the default. Only methods defined using the keyword virtual are candidates for dynamic binding. For example, if we want to redefine an area function for a square derived from a rectangle, we would do so as follows in C++:

```
class Rectangle
{
public:
  virtual double area()
  { return length * width; };
  ...
private:
  double length,width;
};

class Square : public Rectangle
{
public:
  double area()
  // redefines rectangle::area dynamically
  { return width * width; }
  ...
};
```

Of course, what we really want in this example is an abstract area function in an abstract class ClosedFigure, and this can be achieved in C++ by the use of a so-called **pure virtual declaration**:

```
class ClosedFigure // an abstract class
{
public:
  virtual double area() = 0; // pure virtual
  ...
};

class Rectangle : public ClosedFigure
{
public:
  double area()
  { return length * width; }
  ...
private:
  double length,width;
};
```

(continues)

(continued)

```
class Circle : public ClosedFigure
{
public:
   double area()
   { return PI*radius*radius; }
   ...
private
   double radius;
};
```

The 0 in a virtual function declaration indicates that the function is null at that point, that is, has no body (and cannot be called) hence is abstract (and also renders the containing class abstract). Pure virtual functions must be declared `virtual`, since they must be dynamically bound during execution and overriden in a derived class.

Note in the above code that the overriding definitions of area in `Circle` and `Rectangle` do not repeat the keyword `virtual` (although it is permissible to do so). This is because, once a function is declared `virtual`, it remains so in all derived classes in C++.

Returning to the issue of dynamic binding in C++, it is not only necessary to declare methods `virtual` to enable dynamic binding; in addition, objects themselves must be either dynamically allocated or otherwise accessed through a reference. To see this in action, consider the code of Figure 10.13, which is a modification of the Java example of Figure 10.9 (Section 10.4).

```
(1)  class A
(2)  {
(3)  public:
(4)     void p()
(5)     { cout << "A::p\n" ;
(6)     }

(7)     virtual void q()
(8)     { cout << "A::q\n" ;
(9)     }

(10)    void f()
(11)    { p();
(12)       q();
(13)    }
(14) };

(15) class B : public A
(16) {
(17) public:
(18)    void p()
(19)    { cout << "B::p\n" ;
(20)    }
```

```
(21)    void q()
(22)    { cout << "B::q\n" ;
(23)    }
(24) };

(25) int main()
(26) { A a;
(27)    B b;
(28)    a.f();
(29)    b.f();
(30)    a = b;
(31)    a.f();
(32) }
```

Figure 10.13   A C++ program illustrating dynamic and static binding
             (compare to the Java program of Figure 10.9)

The somewhat surprising output from this program is:

```
A::p
A::q
A::p
B::q
A::p
A::q
```

In the call b.f() (Figure 10.13, line 29) the inherited function A.f is
called. Inside this function in A are calls to p and q (lines 11 and 12).
Since p is not virtual, dynamic binding does not apply, and this call is
resolved at compile-time to A::p(). On the other hand, the call to q is
virtual, and the implicit object parameter is used to dynamically resolve
the call during execution. Thus, the call to q is implicitly a call this->q(),
and in the the call b.f(), this is the address of b, so B::q appears on the
fourth line of the above output. On the other hand, the assignment a = b
(line 30) simply copies the data of b to a, and does not change the address
of a or the this pointer in the call to a.f() (line 31). Thus, A::p and
A::q are again called.

    If, on the other hand, we had changed the main program above to

```
(33) int main()
(34) {    A* a = new A;
(35)      B* b = new B;
(36)      a->f();
(37)      b->f();
(38)      a = b;
(39)      a->f();
(40)      return 0;
(41) }
```

we would now see the output

```
A::p
A::q
A::p
B::q
A::p
B::q
```

since now the assignment a = b (line 38) copies a pointer and changes the this pointer in the call to a->f() to point to b's object (which is a B) instead of the previous object pointed to by a (which was an A).

C++ offers multiple inheritance using a comma-separated list of base classes, as in

```
class C : public A, private B {...};
```

Multiple inheritance in C++ ordinarily creates *separate* copies of each class on an inheritance path. For example, the declarations

```
class A {...};
class B : public A {...};
class C : public A {...};
class D : public B, public C {...};
```

provides any object of class D with *two* separate copies of objects of class A, and so creates the following inheritance graph:

This is **repeated inheritance**. To get a single copy of an A in class D, one must declare the inheritance using the virtual keyword:

```
class A {...};
class B : virtual public A {...};
class C : virtual public A {...};
class D : public B, public C {...};
```

This achieves the following inheritance graph:

This is called **shared inheritance**. Resolution of method conflicts created by multiple (shared) inheritance (see Section 10.3) is explored in Exercise 10.16.

As a final example in C++, we offer the declaration of a complex number class in Figure 10.14.

```
(1)   class Complex
(2)   {
(3)   public:
(4)     Complex(double r = 0, double i = 0)
(5)     : re(r), im(i) { }

(6)     double realpart() { return re; }

(7)     double imaginarypart() { return im; }

(8)     Complex operator-() // unary minus
(9)     { return Complex( -re, -im); }

(10)    Complex operator+( Complex y)
(11)    { return Complex( re + y.realpart(),
(12)                      im + y.imaginarypart());
(13)    }

(14)    Complex operator-(Complex y) // subtraction
(15)    { return Complex( re - y.realpart(),
(16)                      im - y.imaginarypart());
(17)    }

(18)    Complex operator*(Complex y)
(19)    { return Complex(re * y.realpart() - im * y.imaginary-
        part(),
(20)                     im * y.realpart() + re * y.imaginary-
                         part());
(21)    }

(22)    Complex operator/(Complex y)
        // division, details omitted
(23)    { ... }

(24) private:
(25)    double re,im;
(26) };
```

Figure 10.14   A C++ complex number class

Figure 10.14 uses operator overloading in C++, as described in Chapter 5, so that now complex arithmetic can be written just as built-in arithmetic, for example:

```
Complex z(1,2);
Complex w(-1,1);
Complex x = z + w;
```

There is one new C++ feature in the code for the Complex class of Figure 10.14 that we have not previously mentioned: The constructor is defined with default values given for its parameters

```
Complex(double r = 0, double i = 0)
```

This allows `Complex` objects to be created with 0, 1, or 2 parameters (and avoids the need to create different overloaded constructors, as we did in the example of `LinkableObject`):

```
Complex i(0,1); // i constructed as (0,1)
Complex y; // y constructed as default (0,0)
Complex x(1); // x constructed as (1,0)
```

10.6   Smalltalk

Smalltalk arose out of a research project, called the Dynabook Project, begun by Alan Kay at Xerox Corporation's Palo Alto Research Center in the early 1970s. Influenced by both Simula and LISP, a series of stages marked its development, with its principal early versions being Smalltalk-72 and Smalltalk-76. The final version is Smalltalk-80, and we will use the name Smalltalk as a synonym for Smalltalk-80. Other major contributors to the design of Smalltalk were Adele Goldberg and Daniel Ingalls.

Of all the object-oriented languages, Smalltalk has the most thorough and consistent approach to the object-oriented paradigm. In Smalltalk, almost every language entity is an object, including constants such as numbers and characters. Thus, Smalltalk can be said to be **pure** object oriented in essentially the same sense that a language can be called pure functional (Java is often called a pure object-oriented language as well, and with some justification, but it is not as pure as Smalltalk, since basic data entities such as integers and characters are not objects).

Because the Smalltalk language has a somewhat unusual syntax, and because it is intimately connected to (and has no separate existence from) the Smalltalk runtime system, it has not experienced the popularity that it probably deserved. Additionally, it is difficult to present language issues in Smalltalk without getting into a lengthy discussion of the interactive runtime system, especially the **user interface**, through which programs are created and executed. We will, however, try to give some of the flavor of the language, in the following way. We will first give a brief overview of the Smalltalk system. Then we will discuss a few central language features. We will finish the discussion with two of the standard examples we have been using in other sections, namely, complex numbers and queues.

Smalltalk was innovative not only from the language point of view, but also in that, from the beginning, it was envisioned as a complete system for a personal workstation, such as the Unix workstations that only became available in the late 1980s, many years after the development of the language. The user interface was also novel in that it included a windowing system with menus and a mouse, long before such systems became common for personal computers. (It had in fact a major influence on the development of such systems.)

Smalltalk as a language is interactive and dynamically oriented. All classes, objects, and methods are created by interaction with the system, using windows and screen templates provided by the system. New classes are entered into a class dictionary, and the interaction of objects is also managed by the system. The Smalltalk system comes with a large hierarchy of preexisting classes, and each new class must be a subclass of an existing class. The class hierarchy is a tree, since Smalltalk-80 has only single inheritance. The class `Object` is the root of the class hierarchy, just as it is in Java. In Smalltalk, class names must begin with uppercase letters, while object and method names begin with lowercase letters (this has become the convention in Java and C++ as well, although it is not enforced by those languages). A sketch of the Smalltalk class hierarchy is given in Figure 10.15.

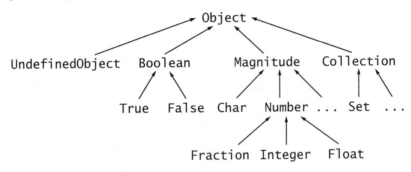

Figure 10.15 Simplified Smalltalk Class Hierarchy

A class is specified in Smalltalk by giving its superclass, its instance variables, and its methods at appropriate places within the Smalltalk system. There is no specific syntax for the layout of a class definition. All methods of a class are available to clients. In other words, there is no export or privacy control of methods in Smalltalk. However, access to instance variables is restricted to methods: Instance variables may not be accessed directly by clients. This provides adequate protection, since the state of an object can be changed only by invoking a method of that object. It also means that enough methods must be supplied for clients to query an object about the values of its instance variables and to modify those variables suitably.

Method names are called **selectors** in Smalltalk, and they are divided into categories: **unary** selectors correspond to operations without parameters, and **keyword** selectors correspond to operations with parameters. A message, or method invocation, in Smalltalk consists of the name of an object followed by the method selector and parameter names, if any. Dot notation is not used.

A couple of examples should make clear how object methods are invoked in Smalltalk. The C++ or Java method call to a `Queue` object q,

    q.front()

would correspond to the Smalltalk,

    q front

and the C++/Java call,

```
q.enqueue(x)
```

would correspond to the Smalltalk

```
q enqueue: x
```

In Smalltalk parlance, `front` is a **unary selector**, and `enqueue:` is a **keyword selector**. (Note the necessary colon at the end of a keyword selector.) The reason that method names are called keyword selectors is that, when a method takes several parameters, keywords must separate all the parameters. Thus, the Smalltalk message

```
table insert: anItem at: anIndex
```

means the same as the C++/Java call:

```
table.insert(anItem,anIndex)
```

In other words, the full name of the `insert` method in Smalltalk is actually `insert:at:`, and the suffix `at:` must separate the two parameters. Note also the use of `anItem` and `anIndex` as parameter names to achieve some resemblance to an English sentence. A name such as `anItem` is by convention any object from class `Item`. Parameters do not have their classes explicitly given in a message selector.

Actually, there is one other category of selector: **Binary selectors**, which are used for binary operations and must consist of one or two non-alphabetic characters. A good example is the name "+," which is a binary selector for the addition operation. Thus, the expression

```
2 + 3
```

in Smalltalk means the same as 2. + (3) and is a message to the object 2 requesting that it add 3 to itself. And

```
2 + 3 + 4
```

is a message to the result of the message 2 + 3 requesting that 4 be added to it, thus achieving the sum (2 + 3) + 4.

We will now give the definition of the class `LinkableObject` in Smalltalk, similar to the example of previous sections. Since Smalltalk has no direct syntax for class and method definitions, but uses screen windows, we will simply list the class, its superclass, its instance variables, and its methods in the following format:

```
Class name: <name>
Superclass: <name>
Instance variables: <list-of-names>
Methods: <name>
        <implementation>
      <name>
        <implementation>
```

Instance variables, like parameters, do not get types in Smalltalk as they do in a statically typed language, since Smalltalk, like LISP, is dynamically typed (and the only typing is class membership; see Exercise 10.15).

According to these conventions, the example of LinkableObject in Smalltalk appears in Figure 10.16.

```
(1) Class name: LinkableObject
(2) Superclass: Object
(3) Instance variables: link
(4) Methods: next
(5)           ↑ link
(6)           linkTo: anObject
(7)           link <- anObject
```

Figure 10.16   A representation of a LinkableObject class in Smalltalk

In the declaration of method next (lines 4–5 of Figure 10.16), the symbol ↑ means "return this value" in Smalltalk, like return in C or C++. If no return value is specified, then the method returns the current object; this is true, for example, for the definition of the linkTo method (lines 6–7). The symbol <- (line 7) is assignment in Smalltalk, like := in Ada or = in C/C++/Java.

Now an object of class LinkableObject can be created as follows:

```
x <- LinkableObject new
```

This sends the unary message new to the class LinkableObject, returning a new object of the class, which is then assigned to x. It also initializes the instance variable link to the nil object. Note that new is a **class method**: it is sent to the class LinkableObject. Smalltalk views classes themselves as objects of a "metaclass" Class. Fortunately, metaclass Class has a default new method that LinkableObject inherits. If, however, extra initialization is required, then the definition of a class must contain a redefinition of this class method, as well as the instance methods, such as next and linkTo:. For example, the following class method definition would initialize a new instance of LinkableObject to point to the parameter aLinkableObject:

```
new: aLinkableObject
  ↑ (self new) linkTo: aLinkableObject
```

In this code, self refers to the current object, just as this does in C++ or Java. The message self new selects the existing new class method of class LinkableObject (without parameters) and returns a reference to a LinkableObject with its link field initialized to nil. This new linkableObject is then sent the message linkTo: aLinkableObject, which reassigns the link field to aLinkableObject.

This definition of new: will always apply when sent to LinkableObject, since dynamic binding of methods is always observed in Smalltalk.

Now let us look at a definition of class Queue in Smalltalk, as given in Figure 10.17.

```
(1)   Class name: Queue
(2)   Superclass: Object
(3)   Instance variables: rear
(4)   Methods: empty
(5)                ↑ rear == nil
(6)          front
(7)             ↑ rear next
(8)          enqueue: aLinkableObject
(9)            self empty
(10)             ifTrue: [ rear <- aLinkableObject.
(11)                       rear linkTo: rear ]
(12)             ifFalse: [aLinkableObject linkTo: rear next.
(13)                rear linkTo: aLinkableObject.
(14)                rear <- aLinkableObject ]
(15)          dequeue
(16)             | temp |
(17)             temp < front.
(18)             (rear == temp)
(19)                ifTrue: [ rear <- nil ]
(20)                ifFalse: [ rear linkTo: (temp next) ]
```

Figure 10.17   A representation of a Queue class in Smalltalk

There are a couple of new features in the code of Figure 10.17. First, local variables within a method body are declared within vertical bars (line 16 of Figure 10.17) (note again that variables are untyped). Second, the period "." is used to separate statements, instead of the semicolon of Pascal-like languages (e.g., line 17 and others). Third, the operator "==" (a binary selector) tests for identity of objects, returning an object of class True if it succeeds and False otherwise (lines 5 and 18).

Finally, the code contains examples of a Smalltalk **block**, which is a code sequence surrounded by square brackets [...]. A block represents "unevaluated code," much as a pass by name parameter does in Algol60 (see Chapter 8). When an object is passed a block, it may choose to evaluate it by sending it the **value** message. This allows Smalltalk to handle control in a purely object-oriented fashion: The class True responds to the message ifTrue: by evaluating the passed block, and False responds to ifTrue: by doing nothing. Conversely, True does nothing when sent the message ifFalse:, while False evaluates the passed block. In other words, we can visualize class True as having the following method definitions,

```
ifTrue : aBlock
  ↑ aBlock value
ifFalse: aBlock
  ↑ nil
```

and similarly for class `False`. Note, finally, in the code for class `Queue` that a message must always have a target object, even if an object is passing the message to itself. Thus, a queue can find out if itself is empty by sending the message

```
self empty
```

This is different from C++ and Java, where inside the code for a class or method there is an implicit `this` object reference.

As an example of the use of class `Queue`, here is some demonstration code that adds two items to a queue, gets the front of the queue, and removes the two items again (the quoted strings are comments):

```
q <- Queue new.
x <- LinkableObject new.
y <- LinkableObject new.
q enqueue: x.
q enqueue: y.
y <- q front.
"now y == x"
q dequeue.
q dequeue.
"now q is empty"
```

Finally, we present in Figure 10.18 a Smalltalk implementation of a class `Complex` similar to that of previous sections.

```
Class name: Complex
Superclass: Object
Instance variables: re im
Methods:
  realPart
    ↑ re
  imagPart
    ↑ im
  setReal: x
    re <- x
  setImag: y
    im <- y
  + y
    ↑ (Complex new setReal: (re + (y realPart)))
                  setImag: (im + (y imagPart))
  ... etc.
```

Figure 10.18   A representation of a `Complex` class in Smalltalk

The `Complex` class of Figure 10.18 can be used as follows:

```
x <- (Complex new setReal: 1.0) setImag: 1.0.
y <- (Complex new setReal: 1.0) setImag: -1.0.
z <- x + y.
```

10.7 Design Issues in Object-Oriented Languages

In this section we survey a few of the issues surrounding the introduction of object-oriented features into a programming language and summarize the different approaches taken in the three languages we have studied.

Object-oriented features represent at their heart dynamic rather than static capabilities (such as the dynamic binding of methods to objects), so one aspect of the design of object-oriented languages is to introduce features in such a way as to reduce the runtime penalty of the extra flexibility. In a dynamically oriented (and usually interpreted) language like Smalltalk, this is less important, but in languages like C++ and to a certain extent in Java, the runtime penalty of their object-oriented features over the non-object-oriented features of their cousins (such as C and Algol) is an important aspect of their overall design. Particularly C++ was designed with efficiency as a primary goal.

One feature promoting efficiency has already been mentioned in the section on C++: Member functions whose implementations are included in the class definition are automatically inline functions in C++. This avoids the penalty of function call during execution.

Other issues that arise in connection with the efficient design of object-oriented languages involve the proper organization of the runtime environment as well as the ability of a translator to discover optimizations. Discussion of such implementation issues is delayed until the next section.

We note also that this section discusses design issues only as they relate to overall language design, not program design. Object-oriented design of programs to take maximum advantage of an object-oriented language is not within the scope of this book, but involves complex software engineering issues, and we have mentioned only a very few such issues in this chapter. Several of the references at the end of the chapter contain more information on object-oriented software design.

10.7.1 Classes versus Types

The introduction of classes into a language with data types means that classes must be incorporated in some way into the type system. There are several possibilities, three of which we catalog.

1. Classes could be specifically excluded from type checking. Objects would then become typeless entities, whose class membership would be maintained separately from the type system—generally at runtime

using a tagging mechanism. This method of adding classes to an existing language is the simplest and has been used in a few languages, such as Objective-C (see the references at the end of the chapter).

2. Classes could become type constructors, thus making class declarations a part of the language type system. This is the solution adopted by C++ and a number of other languages that add object-oriented facilities to an existing language. In C++ a class is just a different form of record, or structure, type. In this case, the assignment compatibility of objects of descendant classes to objects of ancestor classes must be incorporated into the type-checking algorithms. Specifically, if x is an object of a descendant class of the class of object y, then type checking must permit the assignment y = x but must flag the assignment x = y as an error. This complicates the type-checking algorithm.

3. Classes can also simply *become* the type system. That is, all other structured types are excluded from the language. This is the approach of many languages designed from the beginning as object-oriented, such as Smalltalk. This is also almost true of Java, where the class and the array are the only two structured types; however, there are still the basic types such as boolean, int, double, char, and their variants, and type checking must also involve these types. Using classes as the basis for the type system means that, under static typing, the validity of all object assignments can be checked prior to execution, even though exact class membership is not known until execution time.[13]

10.7.2   Classes versus Modules

Classes provide a versatile mechanism for organizing code that also encompasses some of the desired features of abstract data type mechanisms as studied in the previous chapter: Classes provide a mechanism for specifiying interfaces, for localizing code that applies to specific collections of data, and for protecting the implementation through the use of private data. Unfortunately, classes do not allow the clean separation of implementation from interface, nor do classes protect the implementation from exposure to client code, so that code that uses a class becomes (compilation) dependent on the particular implementation of the class even if it cannot make use of the details of that implementation. The use of pointers and indirection can remove some of these dependencies at a certain cost, as we have noted in the previous chapter. But the problem still exists. It is a particular problem for makers of libraries, where implementation details are often best left completely hidden. C and C++ manage this problem somewhat uncomfortably through the use of header files and

---

[13] There are always situations, such as the downcasting mentioned previously, where exact class membership must be tested in some way. We mentioned the Java instanceof operation. C++ has a related dynamic_cast operation that tests class membership while performing a cast during execution.

linkers, while Java relies entirely on machine-generated documentation to describe interfaces to users in an implementation-independent way.

Another problem with the use of classes alone to structure programs is that classes are only marginally suited for controlling the import and export of names in a fine-grained way. In simple cases a class can be used as a namespace or scope for a collection of utilities. For example, the Java `Math` class consists entirely of static constants and methods, and is therefore really a module or namespace masquerading as a class. However, it is not possible to import names from other classes and re-export a selection of them without some effort, so that classes do not function well as static namespaces or modules.

For this reason, object-oriented languages often include module mechanisms that are independent of the object-oriented mechanisms. The principle example is C++, which has the namespace mechanism, which is orthogonal to the class mechanism. Java, too, has a package mechanism that allows classes to be collected into groups and given special names by which their contents can be accessed (typically these names are also associated with a directory structure).

Sometimes object-oriented mechanisms are more closely related to a module structure. For instance, Ada95 introduced a number of object-oriented mechanisms (which we have not studied in this text), and the semantics of declarations using these mechanisms often depend on their relationship to the Ada packages in which they are defined.

Thus, the issue of what kind of module mechanism fits best in an object-oriented setting, and how best to integrate the two notions of class and module, remains to a certain extent open.

C++ also has a mechanism that allows a class to open up details of its implementation to another class or function: The other class or function is listed by the class as a `friend`. For example, in a C++ implementation of a complex data type, the problem arises that a binary operation such as addition acquires an unusual syntax when written as a method of class `Complex`, namely,

```
x.operator+(y)
```

(Fortunately, C++ does allow the substitute syntax x + y.) An alternative solution (and the only one in some earlier C++ implementations) is to declare the "+" operation outside the class itself as a `friend` (so that it can access the internal data of each `Complex` object) as follows:

```
class Complex
{
private:
   double re,im;
public:
   friend Complex operator+(Complex,Complex);
   ...
};

Complex operator+(Complex x, Complex y)
{ return Complex (x.re+y.re,x.im+y.im); }
```

10.7.3   Inheritance versus Polymorphism

There are three basic kinds of polymorphism:

1. Parametric polymorphism, where type parameters may remain unspecified in declarations. ML type variables, Ada generic packages, and C++ templates are examples of parametric polymorphism.

2. Overloading, or ad-hoc polymorphism, where different function or method declarations share the same name and are disambiguated through the use of the types of the parameters in each declaration (and sometimes the types of the returned values). Overloading is available in C++, Java, Haskell, and Ada, but not C or ML.

3. Subtype polymorphism, where all the operations of one type can be applied to another type.

Inheritance (including dynamic binding) is a kind of subtype polymorphism (as long as the subtype relationship can be guaranteed for subclasses; see Exercise 10.10). Inheritance can also be viewed as a kind of overloading on the type of the implicit object parameter (the `this` pointer). However, this form of overloading is restricted in that it overloads only on this one parameter. Thus, most object-oriented languages also provide overloading on the explicit parameters of methods as well.

The problem with the mixture of inheritance and overloading is that it does not account for binary (or n-ary) methods that may need overloading based on class membership in two or more parameters. This is called the **double-dispatch** or **multi-dispatch** problem.

The problem has already been mentioned in this chapter when defining the `Complex` class, which is a good example of this phenomenon. Take, for example, complex addition, which can be written in Java as `x.add(y)`, for x and y `Complex` objects. This can be written even more appropriately as `x.operator+(y)` or x + y in C++. Using overloading, this can even be extended to the case where y is no longer `Complex`, but might be a `double` or an `int`. But how might we define `Complex` addition if x is a `double` and y is a `Complex`? In Java this cannot be done, and in C++ it cannot be done if the + operator is defined as a method of the `Complex` class. The way C++ solves this problem is to define a separate, ordinary (overloaded) + operation taking two `Complex` parameters see the previous subsection, and then to provide conversions from `int` and `double` to `Complex` (which actually can come simply from the constructors alone).[14]

This has the decidedly unpleasant effect of splitting up the definition of complex numbers into a class definition and a number of separate, independent "ordinary" function definitions.

---

[14] Constructors taking a single parameter in C++ are called copy constructors. Such constructors provide automatic conversions in ways that we have not studied here; see the C++ references at the end of the chapter.

Several attempts have been made to design an object-oriented language that solves this problem via so-called **multimethods**: methods that can belong to more than one class and whose overloaded dispatch can be based on the class membership of several parameters. One of the more successful attempts in this direction is the **Dylan programming language**, whose development was begun at Apple Computer in the early 1990s. In Dylan, methods do not belong to a single class, but are part of a more generic mechanism allowing multidispatching to be precisely controlled by the programmer. Unfortunately, after the advent of Java, Apple abandoned its support of this language, and while it continues to be used and developed, interest in it has faded as Java's popularity has increased.

While overloading and inheritance are related concepts, and, except for the multiple dispatch problem, appear to mesh well in languages such as Java and C++, parametric polymorphism is more difficult to integrate, and C++ (and perhaps Ada) remain somewhat solitary examples of languages that attempt an integration of the two concepts. As we have noted, Java, Smalltalk, and many other object-oriented languages imitate parametric polymorphism using the based-object approach, but this removes the security of static typing from code that uses this form of polymorphism (a similar style of programming is possible in C++ using `void*` pointers that also circumvents static type checking). The problem here is that parametric polymorphism and inheritance appear to resist any simple kind of integration. For example, in C++ templates, if B is a derived class of A, and C is a class that is parameterized by a template,

```
template<typename T>
class C
{ ... }
```

then, to preserve secure static type checking, there is no inheritance (or other) relationship between C<A> and C<B>. Nevertheless, templates are proving to be one of the most powerful features of C++, with new uses of templates for abstraction still being discovered at an astonishing rate. How these uses of templates can be most effectively integrated with the object-oriented features of C++ is probably still not well understood.

10.8 Implementation Issues in Object-Oriented Languages

In this section we discuss a few of the issues encountered when implementing an object-oriented language, and we present several methods that allow object-oriented features to be implemented in an efficient way. Since these are primarily issues of efficient code generation by a compiler, they are less applicable to a dynamic, primarily interpreted language such as Smalltalk.

10.8.1 Implementation of Objects and Methods

Typically, objects are implemented exactly as record structures would be in C or Ada, with instance variables representing data fields in the structure. For example, an object of the following class (using Java syntax),

```
class Point
{ ...
  public void moveTo(double dx, double dy);
  { x += dx;
    y += dy;
  }
  ...
  private double x,y;
}
```

could be allocated space for its instance variables x and y just as the structure

```
struct
{ double x;
  double y;
};
```

by allocating space for x and y sequentially in memory:

space for x
space for y

An object of a subclass can be allocated as an extension of the preceding data object, with new instance variables allocated space at the end of the record. For example, given the declaration (again in Java syntax),

```
class ColoredPoint extends Point
{ ...
  private Color color;
}
```

an object of class ColoredPoint could be allocated as follows:

Point part:

space for x
space for y

ColoredPoint part:

space for color

Now the instance variables x and y inherited by any `ColoredPoint` object from `Point` can be found at the same offset from the beginning of its allocated space as for any point object. Thus, the location of x and y can be determined statically, even without knowing the exact class of an object—just that it belongs to a descendant class of `Point`.

Methods can also be implemented as ordinary functions. Methods do differ from functions in two basic ways. The first is that a method can directly access the data of the current object of the class. For example, the `moveTo` method of class `Point` changes the internal state of a point by assigning to the instance variables x and y. To implement this mechanism, one simply views a method as a function with an implicit extra parameter, which is a pointer that is set to the current instance at each call. For example, the `moveTo` method of class `Point` given can be viewed as implicitly declared in the following way

```
procedure moveTo(Point* p, double dx, double dy);
```

and each call `p.moveTo(dx,dy)` would be interpreted by the translator as `moveTo(p,dx,dy)`. Note that, as before, the instance variables of the object pointed to by p can be found by static offset from p, regardless of the actual class membership of the object at the time of execution.

A more significant problem arises with the dynamic binding of methods during execution, since this certainly does depend on the class membership of the current object when the call is made. This is dealt with in the next subsection.

10.8.2 Inheritance and Dynamic Binding

In the implementation of objects that we have described, only space for instance variables is allocated with each object; allocation of methods is not provided for. This works as long as methods are completely equivalent to functions, and the location of each is known at compile time, as is the case for ordinary functions in an imperative language.

A problem arises with this implementation when dynamic binding is used for methods, since the precise method to use for a call is not known except during execution. A possible solution is to keep all dynamically-bound methods[15] as extra fields directly in the structures allocated for each object. For example, given the declaration of Figure 10.19 (this time in C++ syntax, to show the distinction between a dynamically-bound and non-dynamically-bound method),

```
class A;
{
public:
  void f();
```

---

[15] Recall that *all* methods are (potentially) dynamically bound in Java and Smalltalk, but not in C++.

```
    virtual void g();
    ...
private:
    double x,y;
};
class B : public A
{
public:
    void f();
    virtual void h();
    ...
private:
    double z;
};
```

Figure 10.19 C++ Example for Implementing Dynamic Binding

an object a of class A would be allocated space as follows:

space for **x**
space for **y**
space for **g**

while an object b of class B would be allocated space as follows:

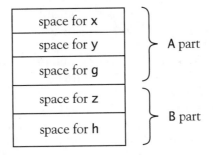

Here space for each method contains a code pointer (and perhaps environment pointers, see Chapter 8) that can be copied from an initialization table for each class when an object is created. Now an assignment a = b would make a point to the structure of b, and a call to a.g would find the g of b at the (statically fixed) offset from the beginning of a's record.

The problem with this is that each object structure must maintain a list of all virtual functions available at that moment, and this list could be very large, thus wasting considerable space. An alternative to this strategy is to maintain a table of "virtual" methods for each class at some central location, such as the global storage area, that can be statically loaded with code pointers and have a single pointer to this table stored in each object structure. Such a table is called a **virtual method table** or VMT, and the declarations of classes A and B in Figure 10.19 with objects a and b would result in the allocation picture of Figure 10.20.[16]

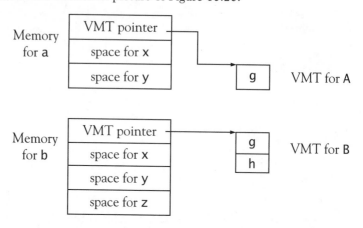

Figure 10.20   Object allocation following the definitions in Figure 10.19 using a VMT

Using the layout of Figure 10.20, a call to each virtual method is achieved by an extra indirection through the VMT pointer. And an object assignment a = b would just make a's VMT pointer point to the VMT for class B, thus ensuring that B's (virtual) methods will be called.

Note that none of these implementation possibilities requires that the inheritance graph be maintained during execution. In fact, as we have seen in the previous section, compatibility of assignments such as a = b can be viewed purely as a type-checking issue and can be determined statically by a compiler. Nevertheless, it is often necessary to be able to recover exact class membership information at runtime, and even to ask such questions as whether a particular object has a method with a particular name available. We saw simple examples of this in the Java instanceof and the C++ dynamic_cast operation (see Footnote 13 on page 453). Even more information about class membership can be obtained in these languages using what is called **reflection** in Java and **Run-Time Type Information** (or **RTTI**) in C++ (dynamic_cast can be viewed as a simple example of RTTI).

For example, in Java each object has a getClass method that returns a representation of the Class it belongs to, and this Class object itself has methods that can be used to find specific information about what methods, fields, and constructors may be defined. Here is a simple example:

```
class Funny
{}
```

---

[16] C++ requires that the VMT field only be allocated if virtual functions are actually present, for compatibility with C; see Exercise 10.43. C++ also requires that the objects a and b be dynamically allocated for there to be a VMT (thus a must have type A* in C++, and similarly for b).

```
class Funnier extends Funny
{}
 public class ReflectionTest
{ public static void main(String[] args)
   { Funny x = new Funnier();
     System.out.println(x.getClass().getName());
   }
}
```

This code prints "Funnier," which is the name of the class that x actually belongs to during execution.

This same example using RTTI in C++ is as follows:[17]

```
#include <typeinfo>
#include <iostream>

using namespace std;

class Funny
{ public: virtual void f() {}
};

class Funnier : public Funny
{ public: void f() {}
};

int main()
{ Funny* x = new Funnier;
  cout << typeid(*x).name() << endl;
  return 0;
}
```

Note the need in C++ to include a definition of a virtual function, since otherwise there would be no need for the compiler to distinguish a Funny object from a Funnier one, as far as dynamic binding is concerned (i.e., no virtual method table is constructed, and the typeid information is computed statically).

Runtime information on the class structure can still be maintained efficiently using a statically constructed representation of the class hierarchy, typically some kind of table, with an extra pointer in the VMT to give access to the appropriate position in the table. If it is possible to create classes dynamically, then this table must be dynamically maintained, but it is still possible to make this reasonably efficient using hash tables.

10.8.3   Allocation and Initialization

Object-oriented languages can maintain a runtime environment in the traditional stack/heap fashion of C as described in Chapter 8. For example,

---

[17] What actually gets printed by this C++ example is implementation-defined, but usually includes the class name as well as perhaps some additional information, such as a table or hash index.

this is true of C++. Within such an environment it is possible to allocate objects on either the stack or the heap, but since objects are generally dynamic in nature, it is more common for them to be allocated on the heap than the stack, and that is the approach adopted in Java and Smalltalk.

C++, however, permits an object to be allocated either directly on the stack or as a pointer. In the case of stack allocation, the compiler is responsible for the automatic generation of constructor calls on entry into a block and destructor calls on exit, while in the case of heap allocation of pointers, explicit calls to `new` and `delete` cause constructor and destructor calls to be scheduled. This means that C++ can maintain exactly the same runtime environment as C, but with the added burden to the compiler that it must schedule the constructor and destructor calls, as well as create and maintain locations for temporary objects.

Java, on the other hand, has no explicit deallocation routines, but requires the use of a garbage collector to return inaccessible storage to the heap. The execution overhead and added runtime complexity of such a requirement are significant, but techniques such as generational garbage collection can be used to reduce the penalty. See Section 8.5 for a further discussion.

During the execution of initialization code, it is necessary to execute the initialization code of an ancestor class before current initializations are performed. A simple example of this is when instance variables defined in an ancestor need to be allocated space before they can be used in the initialization of a descendant. In C++ and Java the calls to initialization code of ancestors are scheduled automatically by a compiler. In C++, where multiple inheritance can create several different paths from a descendant class to an ancestor class, initialization code is performed according to the topological sort of the dependency graph determined by the order in which parent classes are listed in each derived class declaration.

In addition to the question of the order of initializations, especially in a language with multiple inheritance, there can be problems related to the existence of appropriate constructors when they are to be supplied automatically. For example, in Java when there is no default constructor for a superclass, an explicit constructor call must be supplied in all constructors of subclasses. Thus, the code in Section 10.3 for a `Circle` and `Rectangle` required explicit constructor calls to the nondefault constructor of their base class `ClosedFigure` (as long as the `center` instance variable in `ClosedFigure` was kept private).

Exercises

10.1   Describe how object-oriented programming languages solve the problems with abstract data type mechanisms listed in Section 9.7.

10.2 Describe the differences in the definitions of an object in object-oriented languages and an object as given in Chapter 5. Is it possible for an entity to be an object under one definition but not the other? Why?

10.3 Describe the difference between inheritance and import.

10.4 Describe the difference between inheritance and overloading.

10.5 Give an example to show that protection and modifiability can be mutually conflicting requirements.

10.6 How does dynamic binding support reuse? Protection?

10.7 Why is it not possible for a class such as complex numbers to be adequately imitated by a C `struct`?

10.8 If x is an object of class A and y is an object of a class B that is a subclass of A, after the assignment x = y, why is x.m illegal when m is a method of B but not A? Why does this not violate the subtype principle?

10.9 Describe the differences among the protection mechanisms of (a) Java, (b) C++, and (c) Smalltalk.

10.10 (Snyder [1986]) A problem exists in the relationship of the subtype principle to private inheritance in C++.
(a) Describe the problem.
(b) Can you think of a way of revising either the subtype principle or protection mechanisms in C++ to avoid it?
(c) How does Java address this problem?

10.11 (a) Should a derived class be able to make an unprotected inherited feature protected? Why?
(b) Should a derived class be able to make a protected inherited feature hidden? Why?
(c) Should the reverse of (a) and (b) also be possible? Why?

10.12 Why is it not possible to create an object of an abstract class? Does this mean that variables of abstract class types cannot be declared? Explain.

10.13 Should abstract methods always be dynamically bound?

10.14 Describe the two meanings of the keyword **virtual** in C++ discussed in the text.

10.15 What is the difference between a type and a class?

10.16 Suppose class D inherits from both classes B and C, and classes B and C both inherit a method m from class A, but B redefines m. If d is an object of class D, then d.m could be either B.m or A.m. Describe how C++ solves this problem. (You will need to consult a C++ reference such as Stroustrup [1997]).

10.17 During the initialization of objects, it is possible that initialization routines of ancestor classes may need to be called. Under multiple inheritance this can result in questions about the order of initializations and the duplication of initializations. Describe these problems and outline a possible solution.

10.18 A `print` procedure is a good candidate for a dynamically bound method. Why?

10.19 Given the following code in Java:

```java
class A
{ public void p()
  { System.out.println("A.p"); }
  public void q()
  { System.out.println("A.q"); }
  public void r()
  { p(); q(); }
}

class B extends A
{ public void p()
  { System.out.println("B.p"); }
}

class C extends B
{ public void q()
  { System.out.println("C.q"); }
  public void r()
  { q(); p(); }
}
...
A a = new B();
a.r();
a = new C();
a.r();
```

What does this code print? Why?

10.20 Given the following code in C++:

```cpp
class A
{
public:
  virtual void p()
  { cout << "A.p" << endl; }
  void q()
  { cout << "A.q" << endl ; }
  virtual void r()
  { p(); q(); }
};

class B : public A
{
public:
```

```
      void p()
      { cout << "B.p" << endl;  }
};
class C : public B
{
public:
   void q()
   {  cout << "C.q" << endl; }
   void r()
   { q(); p(); }
};
...
A  a;
C  c;
a = c;
a.r();
A* ap = new B;
ap->r();
ap = new C;
ap->r();
```

What does this code print? Why?

10.21 Describe how the expression 2 + 3 * 4 is evaluated in Smalltalk.

10.22 Describe how Smalltalk accommodates multiple messages in the same expression, as in for example,

```
(q enqueue: x) enqueue: y
```

10.23 Write a Smalltalk implementation for the class False.

10.24 In Section 10.6 we mentioned that new is a "class method" rather than an "object method" in Smalltalk. What is the difference between these two kinds of methods?

10.25 The following question refers to the definition of the method new: on page 449. Explain how the expression

```
(self new) linkTo: aLinkableObject
```

is evaluated.

10.26 **(a)** If we try to redefine a new method in Smalltalk that initializes linkable objects to point to themselves (see Figure 10.3 and associated discussion in Section 10.2), we might try the following:

```
new
   ↑ (self new) linkTo: self
```

This will not work. Why?

(b) Suggest a way of writing a correct new method.

10.27 Similar to the `ifTrue` and `ifFalse` messages of Figure 10.17, Smalltalk has `whileTrue` and `whileFalse` messages.
   (a) To what class should these messages apply? What parameters should they have?
   (b) Write an implementation of `whileTrue`. (*Hint:* Use `ifTrue`.)

10.28 The C++ implementation of `Queue` in Figure 10.12 used a local `Linkable` class similar to the `LinkableObject` class of Sections 10.2 and 10.3. Local ("inner") classes are also possible in Java. Rewrite the Java implementation of the `Queue` class in Figure 10.8 to use a local `Linkable` class.

10.29 The equivalent in Java and C++ of the Smalltalk class method or instance variable is the `static` method or instance variable, which has no implicit `this` parameter and must be called using the class name:

```
public class A
{   static void f()
    {  ...  }
}
... A.f() // call to static f of class A
```

Compare a class with only static methods and instance variables with a C++ namespace (Chapter 9). How is it different? How is it the same?

10.30 Suppose we wanted to define a `SortedList` class that would store `LinkableObjects` in sorted order. Describe how to define an abstract class `ComparableObject` that can be used to force any object stored in a `SortedList` to have a comparison operation, and then describe an implementation of `SortedList` that uses it.

10.31 **(a)** Implement your design of the previous exercise in Java, using an interface for `ComparableObject`.
   (b) Implement your design of the previous exericse in C++ using multiple inheritance.

10.32 Explain in detail why multiple interface inheritance in Java does not suffer from the same problems as multiple (class) inheritance in C++.

10.33 We noted that the first `Queue` implementation in C++ in Section 10.5 had a memory allocation problem that made it difficult to write a destructor. Describe the problem in detail, and explain why the `Queue` version using a local `Linkable` class does not have the same problem.

10.34 The implementations of class `Complex` in C++ (Section 10.5) did not use pointers. Explain why.

10.35 Suppose we have a queue containing data of different classes. Introduce `PrintLinkable` and `PrintQueue` methods into the declarations of `LinkableObject` and `Queue` to allow for printing of a queue.

10.36 The following class definition in Java is from Chapter 1:

```
public class IntWithGcd
{ public IntWithGcd( int val ) { value = val; }
  public int intValue() { return value; }
  public int gcd ( int v )
  { int z = value;
    int y = v;
    while ( y != 0 )
    { int t = y;
      y = z % y;
      z = t;
    }
    return z;
  }
  private int value;
}
```

Rewrite this class in **(a)** C++; **(b)** Smalltalk.

10.37 Write a class definition for an `IntWithFactorial` class in **(a)** Java; **(b)** C++; **(c)** Smalltalk.

10.38 An abstract syntax tree for simple integer arithmetic expressions was described in Chapter 4. Syntax tree nodes can either be numbers or binary operator nodes, and a syntax tree could either produce an (integer) value, or be converted to a string by inserting parentheses to express grouping. An abstract class describing the capabilities of an abstract syntax tree might look as follows (in Java syntax):

```
public abstract class SyntaxTree
{   public abstract String toString();
    public abstract int value();
}
```

(a) Write two concrete subclasses `OperatorTree` and `NumberTree`.
(b) Would it make more sense for `SyntaxTree` to be an interface? Discuss.

10.39 Write the code for the previous exercise in **(a)** C++; **(b)** Smalltalk.

10.40 A recursive-descent parser (Chapter 4) is a collection of mutually recursive functions that could be viewed as taking a string as input and producing an abstract syntax tree as a result.
(a) Describe a possible object-oriented design of a parser.
(b) Implement your design of (a) in Java, C++, or Smalltalk.
(c) Compare your object-oriented version to the functional version. In what ways is it better?

10.41 Use Java reflection to write a utility method that will print out the names of the available methods of an object.

10.42 An alternative to the inheritance graph for geometric figures of Figure 10.6, which interprets inheritance as **specialization**, is to turn the graph upside down and interpret inheritance as **generalization**. For example, if we define square as follows,

```
class Square
{  public double area()
   { return side * side; }
   ...
   private Point center;
   private double side;
}
```

we could define a rectangle by extending square as follows:

```
class Rectangle extends Square
{ public double area()
  { area = side * height; }
   ...
  private double height;
}
```

Describe the advantages of this view of inheritance. Describe its disadvantages. Which is preferable?

10.43 In Figure 10.20, the VMT pointer field is placed before the space for any data. However, in C++ this field should not be allocated if there are no virtual functions (see the footnote on page 460). Thus, a C++ compiler may not allocate this field until a virtual function is enountered. Describe how this would affect Figure 10.20 if the code of Figure 10.19 were changed to the following:

```
class A;
{
public:
  void f();
  ...
private:
  double x,y;
};

class B : public A
{
public:
  void f();
  virtual void h();
  ...
private:
  double z;
};
```

10.44 In Figure 10.20 and the pictures that precede it, space for objects of class A and B did not include a field for procedure f. Why? How is f found?

10.45 Multiple inheritance causes complications for the description of the allocation of objects in Section 10.8.2. Describe a way of extending the mechanism described there so that it will handle multiple inheritance.

10.46 Instead of having a VMT for each class that includes all available dynamically bound methods for that class, it is possible to store only newly defined methods for each class and include pointers to parent classes in the VMT.

   (a) Give details on method invocation and VMT layout using this structure.

   (b) What are the advantages and disadvantages of this implementation method?

10.47 In the use of a parameterized class definition, runtime savings are achieved only if the same code for methods can be used, regardless of the parameter. If the size of the parameter's data can vary arbitrarily, this creates a problem for the compiler. What is it? Describe why code reuse for parameterized types would be easier in Java than it is in C++.

10.48 Assuming the following C++ declarations,

```cpp
class A
{
public:
    virtual void f();
    virtual void g();
private:
    int a;
};

class B : public A
{
public:
    void f();
    void h();
private:
    int b;
};

class C : public B
{
public:
    void g();
private:
    int c;
};
```

draw the VMT of each class and the layout of memory for a dynamically-allocated object of each class.

10.49 Meyer [1997] distinguishes overloading from parametric polymorphism as follows (Ibid., p. 38): "Overloading is a facility for client programmers: it makes it possible to write the same client code when using different implementations of a data structure provided by different modules. Genericity [parameterization] is for module implementors: it allows them to write the same module code to describe all instances of the same implementation of a data structure, applied to various types of objects." Discuss this view of polymorphism.

Notes and References

A good general reference for object-oriented programming techniques is Meyer [1997], which uses the interesting object-oriented language Eiffel, which we have not studied in this chapter. Budd [1997] and Booch [1994] describe object-oriented principles in a language-independent way. Liu [2000] discusses object-oriented mechanisms using Smalltalk. Java has of course many references, but two that emphasize object-oriented principles are Arnold et. al [2000] and Horstmann and Cornell [1999]. C++ is described in Stroustrup [1997] and Lippman and Lajoie [1998]. Books on Smalltalk proper include Lalonde [1994], Lewis [1995], and Sharp [1997]. Budd [1987] describes an interesting implementation of a subset of Smalltalk without the graphics user interface.

Other interesting object-oriented languages that are not studied here are described in the following references. The Dylan language mentioned in Section 10.6 is described in Feinberg et al. [1996]. Eiffel is a carefully designed language with a Pascal-like syntax (Meyer [1997]). Modula-3 is a Modula-2 derivative with object-oriented extensions (Cardelli et al. [1989], Nelson [1991], Cardelli et al. [1992]). Objective C is an extension of C with object-oriented features designed by Cox [1984, 1986]. An object-oriented extension of Pascal is described in Tesler [1985]. Object-oriented versions of LISP include CLOS (Gabriel, White, and Bobrow [1991]; Bobrow et al. [1988]); Loops (Bobrow and Stetik [1983]), and Flavors (Moon [1986]). Oberon (Wirth [1988b,c]) is an attempt to design a minimal Pascal-based language with significant object-oriented features. A complete introduction to the language with windows applications is presented in Muhlbacher et al. [1997].

Information on the use of C++ templates and their interaction with object-oriented techniques can be found in Alexandrescu [2001], Koenig and Moo [1996], Josuttis [1999], and Stroustrup [1997].

Many research papers, as well as reports on object-oriented programming techniques, have appeared in OOPSLA [1986ff]. An interesting application of object-oriented techniques to the sieve of Eratosthenes in C++ is given in Sethi [1996].

11 Functional Programming

The functional approach to programming, and functional programming languages, provide a substantially different view of programming than do the more traditional imperative or object-oriented programming languages. Functional programming has a number of distinct advantages over imperative programming, which have traditionally made it popular for prototyping, artificial intelligence, mathematical proof systems, and logic applications. These include the uniform view of programs as functions, the treatment of functions as data, the limitation of side effects, and the use of automatic memory management. A functional programming language has as a result great flexibility, conciseness of notation, and simple semantics.

The major drawback has traditionally been the inefficiency of execution of functional languages. Because of their dynamic nature, such languages historically were interpreted rather than compiled, with a resulting substantial loss in execution speed. Even when compilers became available, the speedups obtained were inadequate. In the last twenty years, however, advances in compilation techniques for functional languages, plus advances in interpreter technology in cases where compilation is unsuitable or unavailable, have made functional languages very attractive for general programming (although efficiency can still be a problem), and their semantic simplicity and orthogonality of design have made them a reasonable alternative to imperative languages in situations where execution efficiency is not a primary requirement. Additionally, functional languages such as those we discuss in this chapter have developed mature application libraries, such as windowing systems, graphics packages, and networking capabilities, and they also allow code from other languages such as C to be linked into functional programs for the most speed-critical code. Thus, there is no reason today not to choose a functional language to implement complex systems— even web applications—particularly in situations where development time is short and there is a need for clear, concise code with predictable behavior.

A reasonable question to ask, though, is whether functional languages can compete with object-oriented languages such as Java and C++ in areas other than their traditional niche of education, research, artificial intelligence, and prototyping. After all, functional languages have been around since the 1950s, yet they have never become "mainstream" languages, perhaps even retreating further into the background with the rise of object-orientation. One might wish to speculate on the reasons for this. One possible reason is that programmers typically learn to program using an imperative or object-oriented language, and that functional programming is foreign and intimidating to them. Another is that object-oriented languages build on traditional imperative concepts, providing a strong organizing principal for structuring code and controlling complexity in ways that mirror daily experience. Functional programming, too, has strong mechanisms for controlling complexity and structuring code, but they are more abstract and mathematical, and thus not as easily approached. Studies such as this chapter should make functional techniques more accessible.

There is in fact sufficient reason to study functional programming even if one never expects to write "real" applications in a functional language, and that is that functional methods such as recursion, functional abstraction, and higher-order functions, have influenced and/or become part of most programming languages and should be part of every professional programmer's arsenal of techniques.

In this chapter, we review the concept of a function and how programs can be viewed as functions. We give a brief introduction to functional techniques using C (showing that you do not need a "functional" language to do functional programming). We then survey three modern functional languages—Scheme, ML, and Haskell—and discuss some of their properties. Following that, we give a somewhat more mathematical look at function definition, including the definition of recursive functions, and conclude with a short introduction to lambda calculus, the underlying mathematical model for functional languages.

11.1   Programs as Functions

A program is a description of a specific computation. If we ignore the details of the computation—the "how" of the computation—and focus on the result being computed—the "what" of the computation—then a program becomes simply a "black box" for obtaining output from input. From this point of view, a program is essentially equivalent to a mathematical function:

> **Definition:** A *function* is a rule that associates to each x from some set X of values a unique y from another set Y of values. In mathematical terminology, if f is the name of the function, we write
>
> $$y = f(x)$$
>
> or
>
> $$f: X \rightarrow Y$$

The set X is called the **domain** of f, while the set Y is called the **range** of f. The x in $f(x)$, which represents any value from X, is called the **independent variable**, while the y from the set Y, defined by the equation $y = f(x)$, is called the **dependent** variable. Sometimes f is not defined for all x in X, in which case it is called a **partial function** (and a function that is defined for all x in X is called **total**).

We can think of programs, procedures, and functions in a programming language as all being represented by the mathematical concept of a function. In the case of a program, x represents the input and y represents the output. In the case of a procedure or function, x represents the parameters and y represents the returned values. In either case we can refer to x as "input" and y as "output." Thus, the functional view of programming makes no distinction between a program, a procedure, and a function. It always makes a distinction, however, between input and output values.

In programming languages we must also distinguish between **function definition** and **function application:** The former is a declaration describing how a function is to be computed using formal parameters (see Chapter 8), while function application is a call to a declared function using actual parameters, or arguments. In mathematics a distinction is often not clearly made between a "variable" and a parameter: The term "independent variable" is often used for both actual and formal parameters. For example, in mathematics one writes

$$\text{square}(x) = x * x$$

for the definition of the squaring function and then frequently applies the function to a variable x representing an actual value:

$$\text{Let } x \text{ be such that square}(x) = 2 \ldots$$

In mathematics, variables always stand for actual values, while in imperative programming languages, variables refer to memory locations as well as values. In mathematics there is no concept of memory location, or l-values of variables, so that a statement such as

$$x = x + 1$$

makes no sense. The functional view of programming must therefore eliminate the concept of variable, except as a name for a value. This also eliminates assignment as an available operation. Thus, in functional programming, there are no variables (in the usual programming sense as a name for a memory location), only constants, parameters, and values.[1]

Practically speaking, this view of functional programming is referred to as **pure functional programming**. Most functional programming languages retain some notion of assignment, and so are "impure," but it is still possible to program effectively using the pure approach—indeed, as we noted in Chapter 1, pure functional programming is Turing complete in that any computation may be described using functions alone.

One consequence of the lack of assignment in functional programming is that there also can be no loops. Indeed, a loop must have a control variable that is reassigned as the loop executes, and this is not possible without assignment. How do we write repeated operations in functional form? The essential feature is recursion. For example, in Chapter 1 we wrote a greatest common divisor calculation in both imperative and functional form, as shown in Figure 11.1 (written in C).

```
void gcd ( int u, int v, int* x)        int gcd ( int u,  int v)
{ int y, t, z;                          { if (v == 0) return u;
  z = u ; y = v;                            else return gcd(v, u % v);
  while (y != 0)                        }
  { t = y;
    y = z % y;
    z = t;
  }
  *x = z;
}
(a) Imperative version using a loop     (b) Functional version with
                                            recursion
```

Figure 11.1   C code for a greatest common divisor calculation

---

[1] Of course, named parameters are indeed "variables" in the mathematical sense, but the functional paradigm implies that these should not be used as "ordinary" variables, that is, assigned new values within a function body.

The second form (Figure 11.1(b)) is close to the (recursive) mathematical definition of the function as

$$gcd(u, v) = \begin{cases} u & \text{if } v = 0 \\ gcd(v, u \bmod v) & \text{otherwise} \end{cases}$$

Another consequence of the lack of variables and assignment is that there is no notion of the internal state of a function: The value of any function depends only on the values of its arguments (and possibly non-local constants), and not on whatever computations may have preceded the function call, including previous calls to the same function (thus requiring each call to represent a different "activation," as described in Chapter 8). The value of any function also cannot depend on the order of evaluation of its arguments, a fact that has been proposed as a reason to use functional programming for concurrent applications. The property of a function that its value depends only on the values of its arguments (and nonlocal constants) is called **referential transparency**.[2] For example, the gcd function is referentially transparent since its value depends only on the value of its arguments. On the other hand, a function rand, which returns a (pseudo) random value, cannot be referentially transparent since it depends on the state of the machine (and previous calls to itself). Indeed, a referentially transparent function with no parameters must always return the same value and, thus, is no different from a constant. In fact, a functional language is free to consider a function of no parameters to not be a function at all.[3]

The lack of assignment and the referential transparency of functional programming make the semantics of functional programs particularly straightforward: There is no explicit notion of state, since there is no concept of memory locations with changing values (a memory location would imply the existence of a variable). The runtime environment associates names to values only (not memory locations), and once a name enters the environment, its value can never change. Such a notion of semantics is sometimes called **value semantics**, to distinguish it from the more usual storage semantics or pointer semantics. Indeed, the lack of local state in functional programming makes it in a sense the opposite of object-oriented programming, where computation proceeds by changing the local state of objects.

Finally, in functional programming we must be able to manipulate functions in arbitrary ways, without arbitrary restrictions—functions must be general language objects. In particular, functions must be viewed as values themselves, which can be computed by other functions and which can also be parameters to functions. We express this generality of functions in functional programming by saying that functions are **first-class values**.

---

[2] A slightly different but equivalent definition, called the substitution rule, was given in Chapter 7.

[3] Both ML and Haskell (languages discussed later in this chapter) take this approach; Scheme does not: In Scheme a parameterless function is different from a constant.

As an example, one of the essential operations on functions is **composition**. Mathematically, the composition operator "o" is defined as follows: If $f: X \rightarrow Y$ and $g: Y \rightarrow Z$, then $g \circ f: X \rightarrow Z$ is given by $(g \circ f)(x) = g(f(x))$.

Composition is itself a function that takes two functions as parameters and produces another function as its returned value. Functions like this—that have parameters that are themselves functions, or that produce a result that is a function, or both—are called **higher-order functions**.

We summarize the qualities of functional programming languages and functional programs as follows:

1. All procedures are functions and clearly distinguish incoming values (parameters) from outgoing values (results).
2. There are no variables or assignments—variables are replaced by parameters.
3. There are no loops—loops are replaced by recursive calls.
4. The value of a function depends only on the value of its parameters and not on the order of evaluation or the execution path that led to the call.
5. Functions are first-class values.

11.2 Functional Programming in an Imperative Language

Functional programming style and techniques can to a surprising extent be used in an imperative language like C, Pascal, or Ada. This approach is being used more and more widely in imperative programming, for the same reasons that functional languages themselves are increasing in use: the simplicity of the semantics and the resultant clarity of the programs.

The basic requirement for functional programming in any language is the availability of recursion and a suitably general function mechanism. We have already seen examples of writing procedures in functional style in languages like C and Ada in Chapter 1 and the last section.

As a further example of functional-style programming, consider a function that returns the sum of integers between i and j:

$$\text{sum}(i, j) = i + (i + 1) + \cdots + (j - 1) + j$$

This is usually written in an imperative language as a loop as in Figure 11.2(a). A functional version of this function is given in Figure 11.2(b).

```
int sum( int i, int j)
{ int k, temp;
  temp = 0;
  for(k = i; k <= j; k++)
    temp += k;
  return temp;
}
```

```
int sum( int i, int j)
{ if (i > j) return 0;
  else return i + sum(i+1, j);
}
```

(a) Imperative version using a loop   (b) Functional version with recursion

Figure 11.2   C code for a sum function

A typical problem in functional-style programming is the cost of performing all loops by recursion. Even with modern processors, which substantially reduce the overhead of a procedure call, recursive implementations are slower than those that use standard loops. There is, however, one form of recursion that is easy to discover during translation, that can be easily converted internally to a standard loop structure, and that is **tail recursion**, where the last operation in a procedure is to call itself with different arguments. For example, the functional version of the gcd procedure of Figure 11.1(b) is tail recursive and can be automatically converted by a translator into a loop by reassigning the parameters and starting over, as indicated by the code of Figure 11.3 (compare this code to the previous nonrecursive version of the gcd procedure in Figure 11.1(a)).

```
int gcd (int u, int v)
{ int t1, t2; /* temps introduced by translator */
  for(;;)
  { if (v == 0) return u;
    else
    { t1 = v;
      t2 = u % v;
      u = t1;
      v = t2;
    }
  }
}
```

Figure 11.3   C code giving a possible automatic conversion of the tail recursive gcd function of Figure 11.1(b) into loop code without recursion

Unfortunately, many simple uses of recursion for looping are not tail recursive—the sum procedure earlier, for example, is not. As a consequence, functional programmers have invented techniques for converting functions into tail-recursive ones, with so-called **accumulating parameters** that are used to precompute operations performed after the recursive call, and to pass the results to the recursive call. As an example, we rewrite sum as a sum1 function using an additional accumulating parameter in Figure 11.4. In that figure the original sum procedure is also written as a single call to sum1, which initializes the accumulating parameter to 0 (sum1 is called a **helping procedure**).

```
int sum1(int i, int j, int sumSoFar)
{ if (i > j) return sumSoFar;
  else
     return sum1(i+1,j,sumSoFar+i);
};

int sum(int i, int j)
{ return sum1(i,j,0);
}
```

Figure 11.4   C code showing the conversion of the sum function of Figure 11.2(b) into a tail-recursive version

Lest one think that languages like C or Ada can be used to write perfectly pure functional programs, we note that imperative languages contain a number of restrictions that make it difficult or impossible to translate all programs into this style. In particular, the following restrictions are common in imperative languages:[4]

1. Structured values such as arrays and records cannot be returned values from functions.

2. There is no way to build a value of a structured type directly.

3. Functions are not first-class values, so higher-order functions cannot be written.

To understand how these restrictions can affect our ability to program in functional style (and how the functional methods can be simulated using occasional imperative constructs), we consider two examples: a sorting program and the composition higher-order function described earlier.

In functional style a sort procedure needs to return a sorted array given an input array. In a language like Ada, where arrays can be returned as values of functions, we can write (assuming the data to be sorted are integers)

```
function intSort(A: in IntArray) return IntArray
is
-- type IntArray is array (integer range <>) of integer
begin
   ...
end intSort;
```

In C, however, an array cannot be the returned value of a function. In addition, the size of an array parameter cannot be determined in C, so it must be separately passed. Thus, the IntSort function must be declared as follows:

```
void intSort (int a[], int b[], int size)
{
   ...
}
```

---

[4] This is somewhat less true as time goes on. For example, both C and Ada permit structured values to be returned from functions (C does not allow arrays). Ada also allows the direct construction of structured values (at least in limited form). And C and Ada have function variables and parameters (but not return values except under special conditions).

An additional problem in C is that any array is automatically passed by reference, so this procedure could have changed a. Of course, that is the most common imperative view of a sort procedure, that it should sort a in place:

```
void intSort (int a[], int size)
{
  ...
}
```

While this form may be more efficient, it violates the rule of functional programming that the input to a function should always be distinguished from its output. In fact, this form of the sort procedure destroys the original values of the array a.

Even when a language can return values of arbitrary types from a function, it is usually not possible to construct these values without the use of a local variable. In C, for example, an array cannot even be copied without using variables and a loop. In Ada arrays can be copied, but we would still need to declare a local variable to contain the copy, and then sort the local array:

```
function intSort(a: in IntArray) return IntArray
is
-- type IntArray is array (integer range <>) of integer
  temp: IntArray(a'first..a'last) := a;
begin
  ...
  return temp;
end IntSort;
```

The third restriction in the list—the non-first-classness of functions in imperative languages—is a little more difficult to overcome by using such simple expedients. In C and Ada95, functions and function types are available, but their use is severely restricted. For example, we could attempt the following definition of composition in C:

```
typedef  int (*IntProc) (int);

IntProc compose (IntProc f, IntProc g)
{  int tempProc (int x)
   {  return f(g(x));
   }
   return tempProc;
}
```

Of course, since C does not allow local function definitions, this is not even syntactically legal. The corresponding Ada95 program *is* syntactically legal:

```
type IntProc is access function (x: in integer) return
integer;

function compose (f, g: in IntProc) return IntProc
is

    function tempProc (x: in integer) return integer
    is
    begin
        return f(g(x));
    end tempProc;

begin
    return tempProc'access;
end compose;
```

but violates the Ada95 rule that a function value cannot be propagated outside its scope (if it did allow this, the standard stack-based runtime environment would have to be abandoned, a fact we discussed in Chapter 8). To make such a function possible, it is necessary to retain the activation of compose as long as the function tempProc can be called, thus requiring a fully dynamic runtime environment as described in Section 8.4.3.

As a final example of functional programming in an imperative language, let us consider a function for computing the maximum value of an array of integers, as shown in Figure 11.5(a).

```
int intArrayMax ( int a[], int size)
/* size must be > 0 */
{   int i, max = a[0];
    for (i = 1; i < size; i++)
        if (max < a[i]) max = a[i];
    return max;
}
```

Figure 11.5(a)   C code for a function intArrayMax that computes the maximum value in a nonempty array of integers

To convert this into a functional-style program, we must eliminate the local variables i and max, the loop, and the assignments. We do this by introducing a new accumulating parameter sofar which records the current maximum value, by using recursion to perform the loop, and by traversing the array in reverse order.[5] We also introduce an intMax function to simplify the computation of a maximum.[6] The resulting code is shown in Figure 11.5(b).

---

[5] Using address arithmetic in C, the forward array traversal order could actually be preserved.

[6] The C library often supplies this function as a macro.

```
int intMax (int x, int y)
{ return x > y ? x : y;
}

int intArrayMax1 ( int a[], int size, int sofar )
{ if (size == 0) return sofar;
  else
    return intArrayMax1(a, size-1,intMax(sofar,a[size-1]));
}

int intArrayMax ( int a[], int size )
/* size must be > 0 */
{ return intArrayMax1(a,size-1,a[size-1]);
}
```

Figure 11.5(b)   C code for a functional version of the intArrayMax function given in Figure 11.5(a) that uses a helping procedure
intArrayMax1 with recursion and an accumulating
parameter

11.3   Scheme: A Dialect of LISP

In the late 1950s and early 1960s, a team at MIT led by John McCarthy
developed the first language that contained many of the features of modern functional languages. Based on ideas from mathematics, in particular
the lambda calculus of Church, it was called LISP (for LISt Processor)
because its basic data structure is a list. LISP first existed as an interpreter
on an IBM 704 and incorporated a number of features that, strictly speaking, are not aspects of functional programming per se but that have been
closely associated with functional languages because of the enormous
influence of LISP. These include:

1. The uniform representation of programs and data using a single general
   data structure—the list.
2. The definition of the language using an interpreter written in the language itself—called a **metacircular interpreter**.
3. The automatic management of all memory by the runtime system.

Unfortunately, no single standard evolved for the LISP language,
and many different LISP systems have been created over the years. In
addition, the original version of LISP and many of its successors did not
have a uniform treatment of functions as first-class values, and used
dynamic scoping for nonlocal references. Two dialects of LISP have, however, become standard that use static scoping and give a more uniform
treatment of functions: Common LISP, developed by a committee in the
early 1980s and Scheme, developed by a group at MIT in the mid-1970s.
In the following we will use the definition of the Scheme dialect of LISP
given in Abelson et al. [1998], which is the current standard at the time
of this writing.

11.3.1 The Elements of Scheme

All programs and data in Scheme are expressions, and expressions are of two varieties: atoms and lists (actually, there is a slightly more general form of list, called an S-expression, but we will ignore this complication in the following discussion). Atoms are like the constants and identifiers of an imperative language: They include numbers, strings, names, functions, and a few other constructs we will not mention here. A list is simply a sequence of expressions separated by spaces and surrounded by parentheses. Thus the syntax of Scheme is particularly simple:[7]

$$expression \rightarrow atom \mid list$$

$$atom \rightarrow number \mid string \mid identifier \mid character \mid boolean$$

$$list \rightarrow \text{'('}expression\text{-}sequence\text{')'}$$

$$expression\text{-}sequence \rightarrow expression\ expression\text{-}sequence$$
$$\mid expression$$

Some examples of Scheme expressions are the following:

42	—a number
"hello"	—a string
#T	—the Boolean value "true"
#\a	—the character 'a'
(2.1 2.2 3.1)	—a list of numbers
a	—an identifier
hello	—another identifier
(+ 2 3)	—a list consisting of the identifier "+" and two numbers
(* (+ 2 3) (/ 6 2))	—a list consisting of an identifier followed by two lists

Since programs in Scheme are expressions, and programs need to be executed or evaluated, the semantics of Scheme are given by an **evaluation rule** for expressions. The standard evaluation rule for Scheme expressions is as follows:

1. Constant atoms, such as numbers and strings, evaluate to themselves.
2. Identifiers are looked up in the current environment and replaced by the value found there. (The environment in Scheme is essentially a dynamically maintained symbol table that associates identifiers to values.)
3. A list is evaluated by recursively evaluating each element in the list as an expression (in some unspecified order); the first expression in the list must evaluate to a function. This function is then applied to the evaluated values of the rest of the list.

---

[7] The current Scheme definition (R^{5}RS, Abelson et al. [1998]) gives a more explicit syntactic description that includes some built-in functions and that specifies the precise position of definitions; however, the rules given here still express the general structure of a Scheme program.

We can apply these rules to the sample Scheme expressions as follows: 42, "hello", #T and #\a evaluate to themselves; a and hello are looked up in the environment and their values returned; (+ 2 3) is evaluated by looking up the value of "+" in the environment—it returns a function value, namely, the addition function, which is predefined—and then applying the addition function to the values of 2 and 3, which are 2 and 3 (since constants evaluate to themselves). Thus the value 5 is returned. Similarly, (* (+ 2 3) (/ 6 2)) evaluates to 15. The list (2.1 2.2 3.1), on the other hand, cannot be evaluated, since its first expression 2.1 is a constant that is not a function. This list does not represent a Scheme program and results in an error if evaluation is attempted.

The Scheme evaluation rule implies that all expressions in Scheme must be written in prefix form. It also implies that the value of a function (as an object) is clearly distinguished from a call to the function: The function value is represented by its name, while a function call is surrounded by parentheses. (A similar situation exists in Java and C.) Thus, a Scheme interpreter would show behavior similar to the following:

```
> +
#[PROCEDURE: +]

> (+)
0 ; a call to the + procedure with no arguments[8]
```

A comparison of some expressions in C and Scheme is given in Figure 11.6.

C	Scheme
3 + 4 * 5	(+ 3 (* 4 5))
(a == b) && (a! = 0)	(and (= a b) (not (= a 0)))
gcd(10,35)	(gcd 10 35)
gcd	gcd
getchar()	(read-char)

Figure 11.6   Some Expressions in C and Scheme

The Scheme evaluation rule represents **applicative order evaluation** as discussed in Chapter 7: All subexpressions are evaluated first so that the expression tree is evaluated from leaves to root. Thus, the Scheme expression (* (+ 2 3) (+ 4 5)) is evaluated by first evaluating the two additions and then evaluating the resultant expression (* 5 9), as indicated by a bottom-up traversal of the expression tree

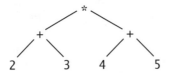

---

[8] A Scheme comment begins with a semicolon and continues to the end of the line.

This corresponds to the evaluation of (2 + 3) * (4 + 5) in a language like C, where expressions are written in infix form.

Since data and programs in Scheme follow the same syntax, a problem arises when data are represented directly in a program. As we noted above, we can represent a list of numbers in Scheme by writing it inside parentheses, with spaces separating the numbers, as in

```
(2.1 2.2 3.1)
```

but this list will generate an error if written directly, since Scheme will try to evaluate it as a function call. Thus, the need arises to *prevent* the evaluation of a list, and to consider it to be simply the list itself (much as simple constants evaluate to themselves). This is accomplished in Scheme by a built-in function whose sole purpose is to prevent evaluation—the quote function:

```
> (2.1 2.2 3.1)
Error: the object 2.1 is not a procedure
> (quote (2.1 2.2 3.1))
(2.1 2.2 3.1)
```

Since this function is used so often, there is a special short-hand notation for it—the single quote, or apostrophe:

```
> '(2.1 2.2 3.1)
(2.1 2.2 3.1)
```

Since all Scheme constructs are expressions, we need expressions that govern the control of execution. Loops are provided by recursive call, but selection must be given by explicit functions. The basic functions that do this are the if function, which is like an if-then-else construct, and the cond function, which is like an if-elsif construct (cond stands for **conditional expression**):

```
(if (= a 0) 0          ; if a = 0 then return 0
    (/ 1 a))           ; else return 1/a

(cond((= a 0) 0)       ; if a=0 then return 0
     ((= a 1) 1)       ; elsif a=1 then return 1
     (else (/ 1 a)))   ; else return 1/a
```

The semantics of the expression (if *exp1 exp2 exp3*) are that *exp1* is evaluated first; if the value of *exp1* is the Boolean value false (#f), then *exp3* is evaluated and its value returned by the if expression; otherwise, *exp2* is evaluated and returned. Also, *exp3* may be absent; in that case, if *exp1* evaluates to false, the value of the expression is undefined.

Similarly, the semantics of (cond *exp1* ... *expn*) are that each *expi* must be a pair of expressions: *expi* = (*fst snd*). Each expression *expi* is considered in order, and the first part of it is evaluated. If *fst* evaluates to #T (true), then *snd* is evaluated, and its value is returned by the cond expression. If none of the conditions evaluate to #T, then the expression in the else clause is evaluated and returned as the value of the cond expression (i.e., the keyword else in a cond can be thought of as always evaluating to #T). If there is no else clause (the else clause is optional) and none of the conditions evaluate to #T, then the result of the cond is undefined.

Notice that neither the if nor the cond function obeys the standard evaluation rule for Scheme expressions: If they did, all of their arguments would be evaluated each time, regardless of their values, which would render them useless as control mechanisms. Instead, the arguments to such control procedures are **delayed** until the appropriate moment. Delayed evaluation was already studied briefly in Chapters 7 and 8 (where it was called pass by name parameter passing). Ordinary Scheme functions use pass by value, while functions in Scheme and LISP that use delayed evaluation (such as if and cond) are called **special forms**.[9] Delayed evaluation is an important issue in functional programming, and it is discussed further in Section 11.5.

Two other important special forms are the quote function and the let function. We have already discussed the need for the quote function. It is a special form for obvious reasons: Its whole reason for existing is to *prevent* the evaluation of its argument.

The let function allows values to be given temporary names within an expression:

```
> (let ((a 2) (b 3)) (+ a b))
5
```

The first expression in a let is a **binding list**, which associates names to values. In this binding list of two bindings, a is given the value 2 and b the value 3. The names a and b can then be used for their values in the second expression, which is the body of the let and whose value is the returned value of the let.

To complete the process of creating a Scheme program, we must also have a way of declaring functions, or entering them into the environment, so that they may be called. This is done using the define function (which is also a special form). There are two ways of using define, either to define names directly by giving their values, as in

```
(define a 2)
(define emptylist '())
```

or by defining a function name (with its parameters) and then giving the function body:

```
(define (gcd u v)    ; function name and parameters
   (if (= v 0)        ; function body
      u
      (gcd v (remainder u v)))))
```

---

[9] In the latest Scheme report (Abelson et al. [1998]) special forms are called **syntactic keywords** or just **keywords**.

Given these definitions, we can then refer to the values of a, emptylist, and gcd and also call the function gcd:

```
> a
2

> emptylist
()

> gcd
#[PROCEDURE:GCD]

> (gcd 25 10)
5
```

The gcd function implements Euclid's algorithm in Scheme. To use the function we could simply "load" the function into the environment by evaluating the define expression and then entering the parameter values directly into a call from within the interpreter as in the evaluation of (gcd 25 10), or we could provide a further function with input and output operations to ask the user explicitly for values, as we would need to do in a compiled program. To finish this example of Scheme programming, we provide such an outer-level I/O function.

Scheme has two basic built-in I/O functions: read and display (princ is the more usual function in other LISPs). The read function has no parameters—it returns whatever value the keyboard provides:

```
> read
#PROCEDURE READ

> (read)
234 ; user types this
234 ; the read function returns this

> (read)
"hello, world"
"hello, world"
```

The display function similarly prints its parameter to the screen:

```
> (display "hello, world")
hello, world

> (display 234)
234
```

In Figure 11.7 we give an outer-level function to go with the gcd function just defined (note that define and let allow sequences of expressions in their bodies; this is also true of cond alternatives).

```
(define (euclid)
    (display "enter two integers:")
    (newline) ; goes to next line on screen
    (let ((u (read)) (v (read)))
```

```
(display "the gcd of ")
(display u)
(display " and ")
(display v)
(display " is ")
(display (gcd u v))
(newline)))
```

Figure 11.7   A "main" program `euclid` in Scheme that performs explicit
user input and output for the `gcd` function

11.3.2 Data Structures in Scheme

In Scheme as with other LISPs, the basic data structure is the list; all other
structures must be put into the form of lists. This is not hard, as a list can
represent an array, record, or any other data. For example, the following is
a list representation of a binary search tree:

```
("horse" ("cow" () ("dog" () ()))
         ("zebra" ("yak" () ()) () ))
```

A node in this tree is a list of three items (`name left right`), where
`name` is a string, and `left` and `right` are the child trees, which are also
lists. Thus, the given list represents the tree of Figure 11.8.

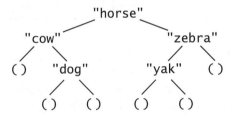

Figure 11.8   A binary search tree containing string data

To use lists effectively we must have an adequate set of functions
that operate on lists. Scheme has many predefined list functions, but the
basic functions that are common to all LISP systems are the selector functions `car` and `cdr`, which compute the head and the tail of a list, and the
constructor function `cons`, which adds a new head to an existing list.
Thus, if `L` is the list (1 2 3), then

```
> (car L)
1
> (cdr L)
(2 3)
> (cons 4 L)
(4 1 2 3)
```

The names `car` and `cdr` are a historical accident. The first machine
that LISP was implemented on was an IBM 704, and addresses or pointers
were used to represent lists in such a way that the head of a list was the

"Contents of the Address Register," or car, and the tail of a list was the "Contents of the Decrement Register," or cdr. This historical accident persists in all modern LISPs, partially because of the normal resistance to change by programmers, but more important because of another accident: On account of the single letter difference in the names of the operations, repeated applications of both can be combined by combining the letters "a" and "d" between the "c" and the "r." Thus, (car (cdr L))) becomes (cadr L), (cdr (cdr L)) becomes (cddr L), and (car (cdr (cdr L))) becomes (caddr L). For clarity, however, we will avoid these abbreviations.

The view of a list as a pair of values represented by the car and the cdr has also continued to be useful as a representation or visualization of a list. According to this view a list L is a pointer to a "box" of two pointers, one to its car and the other to its cdr.

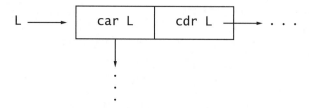

This "box notation" for a simple list such as (1 2 3) is as follows:

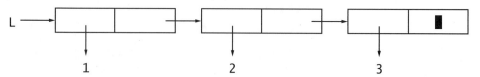

(The symbol ∎ in the box at the end stands for the empty list ().)
For a more complex example, see Figure 11.9.

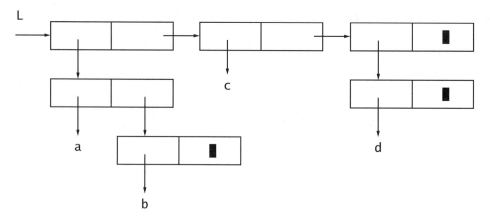

Figure 11.9   Box notation for the list L = ((a b) c (d))

A box diagram is useful for interpreting the list operations: The car operation represents following the first pointer, while the cdr operation represents following the second pointer. Thus, for the L of Figure 11.9, (car (car L)) = a, (cdr (car L)) = (b), and (car (cdr (cdr L)) = (d).

All the basic list manipulation operations can be written as functions using the primitives[10] car, cdr, and cons. For example, an append operation that returns the appended list of two lists can be written as follows:

```
(define (append L M)
  (if (null? L) M
      (cons (car L) (append (cdr L) M))))
```

and a reverse operation is as follows:

```
(define (reverse L)
  (if (null? L) '()
      (append (reverse (cdr L)) (list (car L)))))
```

In the reverse function we use the primitive function list, which makes an item into a list:

```
> (list 2 3 4)
(2 3 4)

> (list '(a b) '(c d))
((a b) (c d))
```

In fact, in the reverse function, we could have used (cons (car L) '()) instead of (list (car L)), since (list a) is the same as (cons a '()).[11]

Finally, we offer the example of the use of car and cdr to access the elements of a binary search tree defined as a list with structure (data leftchild rightchild):

```
(define (leftchild B) (car ( cdr B)))
(define (rightchild B) (car (cdr (cdr B))))
(define (data B) (car B))
```

Now we can write a tree traversal procedure print-tree that prints out the data in the tree as follows:

```
(define (print-tree B)
  (cond ((null? B) '() )
        (else (print-tree (leftchild B))
              (display (data B))
              (newline)
              (print-tree (rightchild B)))))
```

---

[10] A primitive is a built-in procedure that is implemented at a lower level. Most built-in procedures required by the Scheme standard are primitives, so we will not emphasize this distinction.

[11] Actually, append and reverse are also really built-in primitives, although as we have seen, they could be implemented in Scheme itself.

11.3.3 Programming Techniques in Scheme

Programming in Scheme, as in any functional language, relies on recursion to perform loops and other repetitive operations. One standard technique for applying repeated operations to a list is to "cdr down and cons up"—meaning we apply the operation recursively to the tail of a list and then collect the result with the cons operator by constructing a new list with the current result. One example is the append procedure code of the previous section. Another example is a procedure to square all the members in a list of numbers:

```
(define (square-list L)
   (if (null? L) '()
       (cons (* (car L) (car L)) (square-list (cdr L)))))
```

An example of a loop that is not applied to a list is a procedure that simply prints out the squares of integers from 1 to n:

```
(define (print-squares low high)
  (cond ((> low high) '())
        (else (display (* low low))
              (newline)
              (print-squares (+ 1 low) high))))
```

A call to (print-squares 1 100) will generate the desired result.

In the print-squares example we had to use the extra parameter low to control the recursion, just as a loop index controls repetition. At the end of the last section we noted that, in such cases, tail-recursive procedures are preferred because of the relative ease with which translators can optimize them into actual loops. In fact, the print-squares function is tail recursive. In Scheme, however, the language goes one step farther: The language *defines* tail recursion as equivalent to a loop in an imperative language. That is, a Scheme compiler or interpreter *must* perform tail recursion more efficiently than a standard call. This means that in Scheme one should program as much as possible using tail-recursive procedures.

In the last section we also demonstrated the technique of using an accumulating parameter to turn a non-tail-recursive procedure into a tail-recursive one. As an example in Scheme, we apply this technique to the square-list function by defining a helping procedure square-list1 with an extra parameter to accumulate the intermediate result:

```
(define (square-list1 L list-so-far)
   (if (null? L) list-so-far
       (square-list1 (cdr L)
              (append list-so-far
                      (list (* (car L) (car L)))))))
```

Now we define square-list as a call to square-list1 with () as its first accumulated value:

```scheme
(define (square-list L) (square-list1 L '()))
```

Similarly, for `reverse` one defines `reverse1` and `reverse` as follows:

```scheme
(define (reverse1 L list-so-far)
   (if (null? L) list-so-far
          (reverse1 (cdr L) (cons (car L) list-so-far))))

(define (reverse L) (reverse1 L '()))
```

11.3.4 Higher-Order Functions

Since functions are first-class values in Scheme, we can write functions that take other functions as parameters and functions that return functions as values. (Such functions are called higher-order functions.)

To give a simple example of a function with a function parameter, we can write a function map[12] that applies another function to all the elements in a list and then pass it the `square` function to get the `square-list` example:

```scheme
(define (map f L)
   (if (null? L) '()
          (cons (f (car L)) (map f (cdr L)))))

(define (sqr x) (* x x))

(define (square-list L) (map square L))
```

Here is an example of a function that has a function parameter and also returns a function value:

```scheme
(define (make-double f)
   (define (doublefn x) (f x x))
   doublefn)
```

This function assumes that `f` is a function with two parameters and creates the function that repeats the parameter `x` in a call to `f`. The function value `doublefn` returned by `make-double` is created by a local `define` and then written at the end to make it the returned value of `make-double`. Note that `x` is not a parameter to `make-double` itself but to the function created by `make-double`.

We can use `make-double` to get both the `square` function and the `double` function (a function that doubles its numerical value):

```scheme
(define square (make-double *))
(define double (make-double +))
```

The symbols "*" and "+" are the names for the multiplication and addition functions. Their values—which are function values—are passed to the `make-double` procedure, which in turn returns function values that are assigned to the names `square` and `double`. Note that we are using here

---

[12] The map function is in fact a standard Scheme function, with behavior somewhat more general than what we describe here.

the simple form of the `define`, which just assigns computed values rather than defining a function with a given body. Just as

```
(define a 2)
```

assigns the value 2 to the name a, the expression

```
(define square (make-double *))
```

assigns the function value returned by `make-double` to the name `square`.

Indeed, we have until now always used the function version of `define` to create functions with a given name. Scheme also has a way of creating function values directly, without having to give them a name. The expression that creates a function value in Scheme is called a **lambda expression**—the word *lambda* is the name of the Greek symbol "λ" and is borrowed from lambda calculus (Section 11.8).

A `lambda` expression has the following form

```
(lambda param-list body)
```

and can be used to define functions directly, as in

```
(define square (lambda (x) (* x x)))
```

or

```
(define gcd (lambda (u v)
              (if (= v 0) u
                  (gcd v (remainder u v)))))
```

Thus, the second version of `define` is just a different way of writing the first version:

```
(define (square x) (* x x))
```

is completely equivalent to

```
(define square (lambda (x) (* x x)))
```

Lambda expressions can also be used directly, without giving a name to the function value, as in

```
((lambda (x) (* x x)) 2)
```

This applies the function constructed by the `lambda` expression—the square function—directly to 2, returning the value 4. The same process can be applied to construct function parameters directly:

```
(define (square-list L)
  (map (lambda (x) (* x x)) L))
```

In this example, the `square` function is constructed by a `lambda` expression right in the call to `map`. Functions created directly using `lambda`s, as in these examples, are called **anonymous functions**.

We can also use `lambda`s in `let` expressions to assign local names to functions. For example, the following code represents a local construction and application of the square function:

```
(let ((square (lambda (n) (* n n))))
    (display (square (read))))
```

Unfortunately, the let cannot be used to define recursive functions, since let bindings cannot refer to themselves or each other. Thus, the following code will generate an error:

```
(let ((fact (lambda (n) (if (= n 0) 1
                            (* n (fact (- n 1)))))))
    (display (fact (read))))
```

For such situations there is a different construct, called letrec, that is just like a let, except that it allows arbitrary recursive references within the binding list:

```
(letrec ((fact (lambda (n) (if (= n 0) 1
                               (* n (fact (- n 1)))))))
    (display (fact (read))))
```

Finally, we can also use lambdas to return constructed function values in higher-order functions, thus making the use of a local define unnecessary. For example, the make-double function can be written as follows:

```
(define (make-double f)   (lambda (x) (f x x)))
```

The composition function for two functions with a single parameter can be written using a lambda to construct the returned value, as follows:

```
(define (compose g f)
    (lambda (x) (g (f x))))
```

As we have noted at the end of Section 11.2 and in Chapter 8, this ability of functional languages, including Scheme, to return function values from higher-order functions means that the runtime environment of functional languages is more complicated than the stack-based environment of a standard block-structured imperative language. Indeed, since the activation record of a function cannot in general be returned to free storage on exit from a call without causing dangling references, activations must be retained until all references to them have disappeared. Returning activations to free storage then requires the use of automatic memory management techniques, such as **garbage collection**, which are studied in Section 8.5.

As a final example of a higher-order function, we can rewrite the example of Section 8.4.3 of a make-new-balance function with a local variable that persists after the call that allocates it:

```
(define (make-new-balance balance)
    (lambda (amount)
        (if (< balance amount) "Insufficient funds"
        (begin
            (set! balance (- balance amount))
            balance))))
```

This function uses two features we have not yet discussed. The first is the `begin` function, which allows sequences of expressions to be grouped and evaluated in succession, with the value of the `begin` the value of the last expression to be evaluated. We did not see this before because many Scheme expressions, such as `define`s, `lambda`s, `let`s, and `cond`s (but not `if`s) have implicit `begin`s. The second new feature of Scheme in `make-new-balance` is the nonfunctional construct `set!`, which is Scheme's assignment function. Its use signals that `balance` is being used as a variable instead of as an (unchangeable) value parameter. Every call to `make-new-balance` creates a new environment that persists as long as its local state, represented by the variable `balance`, is accessible through its returned function value:

```
> (define withdraw1 (make-new-balance 100))
withdraw1

> (define withdraw2 (make-new-balance 100))
withdraw2

> (withdraw1 20)
80

> (withdraw2 50)
50

> (withdraw1 20)
60

> (withdraw2 60)
"Insufficient funds"
```

Persistent local environments in Scheme can be used to control the scope of variables and the access to those variables. In the preceding example the variable `balance` cannot be changed except by calling the function returned by the `make-new-balance` function. Thus, Scheme can encapsulate functions and variables in local environments. This is no longer functional programming, since it uses variables and assignments. It is really object-oriented programming, and such methods can be used in Scheme to achieve implementations of abstract data types (although Standard Scheme does not have facilities for separating specification from implementation).

11.4 ML: Functional Programming with Static Typing

As we have noted previously, ML is a functional programming language that is quite different from versions of LISP, such as Scheme. First, it has a more Algol-like syntax, which avoids the use of many parentheses. Second, it is strongly typed, so that the type of every expression is determined before execution, and types can be checked for consistency. While traditional LISP programmers may dislike the constraints of a strong type system, there are significant advantages, as noted in Chapter 6: The language is more secure, in that more errors can be found prior to execution, especially important in instructional settings and for good software engineering. There is also the efficiency to be gained by being able to predetermine size and allocation requirements. Additionally, ML's type system, which we studied in detail in Chapter 6, is extremely flexible: It does not insist, as with C or Ada, that *all* types be declared by the programmer, and it also allows for parametric polymorphism, where types can contain type variables that can range over the set of all types.

ML (for MetaLanguage) began in the late 1970s as part of a system for proving the correctness of programs: the Edinburgh Logic for Computable Functions (LCF) system developed by a team led by Robin Milner. Milner also helped develop the strong type inference system based on pattern matching that is now called Hindley-Milner type checking; it is a key feature of ML and also of Haskell (studied later in this chapter). A revision of the ML language occurred during the 1980s, combining features of the earlier language and the HOPE language, developed by Rod Burstall, also at Edinburgh, and was named Standard ML, or SML. Another minor revision to the language occurred in 1997, and the current standard is referred to as SML97 or just ML97. We use that revision in this text.

In this section, we will first review the basics of ML, including comparisons with Scheme. Then we will provide an introduction to ML data structures and programming techniques (some ML data structure information was already covered in Chapter 6).

11.4.1   The Elements of ML

In ML the basic program is, as in Scheme, a function declaration, as in:

```
> fun fact n = if n = 0 then 1 else n * fact(n - 1);
val fact = fn: int -> int
```

The reserved word `fun` in ML introduces a function declaration. The identifier immediately after `fun` is the name of the function, and the names of the parameters follow, up to the equal sign. After the equal sign is the body of the function.

The ML system responds to a declaration by returning the data type of the value defined. In this example, `fact` is a function, so ML responds that the value of fact is `fn`, with type `int -> int`, which means that `fact` is a function from integers to integers. Indeed, we could have given type declarations for the type of `fact` and the type of its parameter as follows:

```
> fun fact (n: int): int = if n = 0 then 1
                               else n * fact (n - 1);
val fact = fn: int -> int
```

Once a function has been declared it can be called as follows:

```
> fact 5;
val it = 120 : int
```

ML responds with the returned value and its type ("it" is the name of the current expression under evaluation). ML has essentially the same evaluation rule as Scheme: fact must evaluate to a function; then 5 is evaluated, and its type must agree with the parameter type of the function. The function is then called and its returned value printed together with its type. ML, however, does not need a quote function as in Scheme to prevent evaluation, since data is distinct from programs. There is also almost no need for parentheses in ML, as the system can determine the meaning of items based solely on their position.

One can also define values in ML using the val keyword:

```
> val Pi = 3.14159;
val Pi = 3.14159 : real
```

In ML arithmetic operators are written as infix operators as they are in C or Ada, rather than the uniform prefix notation of Lisp. This means that operator precedence and associativity are an issue in ML (see Chapter 4); of course, ML adheres to the standard mathematical conventions for the usual arithmetic operators: for example, $2 + 3 * 4$ means $2 + (3 * 4)$.[13] In ML it is also possible to turn infix operators into prefix operators using the op keyword, so that $2 + 3 * 4$ can be written as

```
> op + (2 , op * ( 3,4));
val it = 14 : int
```

Note here that the binary arithmetic operators take *pairs* of integers as their arguments, which are elements of the Cartesian product type, or **tuple type** int * int:

```
> (2,3);
val it = (2,3) : int * int
> op +;
val it = fn : int * int -> int
```

Lists are an important feature of ML (as they are in almost every functional language), though they are not as universal as they are in Lisp, since programs are not themselves lists. A list in ML is indicated by square brackets, and elements are separated by commas. For example, a list of the integers 1, 2, and 3 is represented as [1, 2, 3]:

```
> [1,2,3];
val it = [1,2,3] : int list
```

ML determines the type of this list to be int list; because of strong typing, ML lists may only contain elements that all have the same type:

```
> [1,2,3.1];
Error: operator and operand don't agree [literal]
```

---

[13] On the other hand, the unary minus or negation operator, which is usually written in mathematics with the same "−" symbol as subtraction, is written using a tilde in ML: ~5 is negative 5.

```
operator domain: int * int list
operand:         int * real list
in expression:
   2 :: 3.1 :: nil
```

If we want to mix data of different types, we must use a **tuple**:

```
> (1,2,3.1);
val it = (1,2,3.1) : int * int * real
```

The previous error message also gives us a hint as to how ML constructs
lists (in much the same way as Scheme): the operator :: corresponds to
cons in Scheme, and constructs a list out of an element (which becomes
the head of the list) and a previously constructed list (which becomes the
tail of the list):

```
> op :: ;
val it = fn : 'a * 'a list -> 'a list
> 2 :: [3,4];
val it = [2,3,4] : int list
```

Note that the type of the :: operator contains a **type variable** 'a, since ::
can be applied to a list containing values of any type. Thus, :: is a function from the tuple consisting of any type 'a and any list of type 'a to a
list of type 'a.

In ML every list is viewed as constructed by a series of applications
of the :: operator:

```
> 1 :: 2 :: 3 :: [];
val it = [1,2,3] : int list
```

Here [] is the empty list, which can also be written as the keyword nil.

ML has operations corresponding to Scheme's car and cdr operators
as well, except that they are called hd and tl (for **head** and **tail**):

```
> hd [1,2,3];
val it = 1 : int
> tl [1,2,3];
val it = [2,3] : int list
```

In fact, these functions are used much less in ML than their equiva-
lents in Scheme, because of ML's pattern matching ability; if we want to
identify the head and tail of a list L, we simply need to write h::t for the
list, and ML will extract h as the head and t as the tail by matching the
pattern against the list L (of course, if L is empty, the pattern will not
match, which is the reason for the warning below):

```
> val h::t = [1,2,3];
Warning: binding not exhaustive
          h :: t = ...
val h = 1 : int
val t = [2,3] : int list
```

Pattern matching is more typically used in function definitions and in `case` expressions. For example, a list `append` function in ML can be defined as follows:[14]

```
> fun append ([] , L) = L
  | append (h :: t , L) = h :: append (t , L);
val append = fn : 'a list * 'a list -> 'a list
```

This is equivalent to the following definition using a `case` expression:

```
> fun append (x,y) =
      case x of
      []      => y |
      (h::t) => h :: append (t,y);
```

Pattern matching can be used in virtually all function definitions where a case analysis is called for, and can eliminate most uses of `if` expressions. For example, the recursive factorial function defined previously can also be written using pattern matching:

```
fun fact 0 = 1 | fact n = n * fact (n - 1);
```

Here the second pattern—the variable n—matches anything, but its position as the second pattern implies that it must not be zero, since if it were, the first pattern (the integer literal 0) would have matched.

Patterns in ML can also contain wildcards, written as the underscore character; these are patterns that match anything, like variables, but whose contents we don't care about. For example, we could define our own version of the `hd` function as follows:

```
fun hd (h::_) = h;
```

In fact, this definition will generate a warning message ("match nonexhaustive"), since we have not included a definition of what `hd` is to do in the case of the empty list. A better definition is the following (see Chapter 7 for more on ML exceptions), which is essentially exactly what the predefined `hd` does:

```
fun hd (h::_) = h | hd [] = raise Empty;
```

ML's strong typing, while secure and flexible, does put important constraints on what is acceptable to the language. A typical example is a square function, which we define here for real (floating point) values:

```
> fun square x: real = x * x;
val square = fn : real -> real
```

An error will now be generated if we try to call this function with an integer, since ML will (like Ada) not automatically convert an integer into a real:

---

[14] In fact, ML has a built-in infix append operator @: `[1,2,3] @ [4,5,6] = [1,2,3,4,5,6]`.

```
> square 2;
Error: operator and operand don't agree [literal]
   operator domain: real
   operand:          int
   in expression:
     square 2
```

Instead, we need to manually convert the integer using a conversion function (in this case the function has the same name as the data type we are converting to):

```
> square (real 2);
val it = 4.0 : real
```

We might think that we could define a similar function with the same name for integers:

```
> fun square x: int = x * x;
val square = fn : int -> int
```

But ML does not allow overloading, and this definition will just replace the previous one. We might also try defining a "generic" version of square by not specifying the type of the parameter:

```
> fun square x = x * x;
val square = fn : int -> int
```

But ML simply assumes then that we meant x to be an integer.[15] The problem is that, while the built-in arithmetic functions are overloaded for arithmetic types like int and real, we cannot make use of that fact to define any overloaded user-defined functions. This problem has been largely removed in the language Haskell (see later in this chapter).

A related issue is that certain values in ML do not contain enough type information for ML to properly type check an expression before it is evaluated. The main example of this is the empty list [], which has type 'a list. If ML is to evaluate a polymorphic function on the empty list, ML will, in certain cases, complain that not enough information is known about the type of []:

```
> rev [];
  type vars not generalized because of value
  restriction are instantiated to dummy types (X1,X2,...)
  val it = [] : ?.X1 list
```

Here rev is the built-in reverse function that reverses a list, and has type 'a list -> 'a list. However, when rev is applied to the empty list, ML wants to instantiate the type variable 'a to a specific type, and it cannot because not enough information is available. Nevertheless, ML compensates by supplying a "dummy" type, and gets the right answer, despite

---

[15] Older versions of ML made this function definition into an error.

the annoying message. If we wish, supplying a specific type avoids the problem:

```
- rev []:int list;
val it = [] : int list
```

A further unusual type checking phenomenon is that ML makes a strong distinction between types that can be compared for equality and types that cannot. In particular, functions and real numbers cannot be compared for equality:

```
> 2.1 = 2.1;
Error: operator and operand don't agree [equality type
required]
  operator domain: ''Z * ''Z
  operand:          real * real
  in expression:
    2.1 = 2.1
```

When a polymorphic function definition involves an equality comparison, the type variable(s) can only range over the **equality types**, which are written with two quotes rather than a single quote:

```
> fun constList [] = true
      | constList [a] = true
      | constList (a::b::L) =
          a = b andalso constList (b::L);
val constList = fn : ''a list -> bool
```

Indeed, the equality function itself can only be applied to equality types:

```
> op =;
val it = fn : ''a * ''a -> bool
```

This somewhat awkward state of affairs has also been given an elegant solution in Haskell.

We conclude this section with a brief description of simple input and output in ML, and write an ML version of the Euclid program written in Scheme earlier in the chapter.

ML's version of the library package is the **structure** (see Chapter 9), and there are several standard predefined structures that are useful in performing input and output. The principle I/O functions are in the TextIO structure, and the simplest of these are the inputLine and output functions:[16]

```
> open TextIO; (* dereference the TextIO structure *)
... (* ML interpreter lists contents of TextIO *)
> output(stdOut,inputLine(stdIn));
                    (* reads and writes a line of text *)
Hello, world!
Hello, world!
val it = () : unit
>
```

---

[16] We are ignoring the simpler print function in the interest of uniformity.

Note that the returned value of an `output` operation is the value `()`, which is of type `unit`. This is somewhat akin to the `void` type of C, but in ML every function must return *some* value, so the `unit` type has exactly one value `()` that represents "no actual value."[17]

Now, these two I/O functions only read and write strings. To convert between strings and numbers, we must use the `toString` and `fromString` functions from the utility structures for the appropriate types (for example, the `Int` structure for `int`s):

```
> Int.toString;
val it = fn : int -> string
> Int.fromString;
val it = fn : string -> int option
```

Here there is yet another small hurdle: The `fromString` function may fail to extract any number, and so it returns a value of `option` type, which is defined as follows (see the next section on data structures):

```
datatype 'a myoption = NONE | SOME of 'a;
```

Finally, when performing a series of input and output operations, it is convenient to collect these operations in an **expression sequence** (like the `begin` construct of Scheme), which is a semicolon-separated sequence of expressions surrounded by parentheses, and whose value is the value of the last expression listed:

```
> fun printstuff () =
        ( output(stdOut,"Hello\n");
          output(stdOut,"World!\n")
        );
val printstuff = fn : unit -> unit
> printstuff ();
Hello
World!
val it = () : unit
```

Now we are ready for the `euclid` program in ML:[18]

```
> fun gcd (u,v) = if v = 0 then u
                            else gcd (v, u mod v) ;
val gcd = fn : int * int -> int
> fun euclid () =
        ( output(stdOut, "Enter two integers:\n");
          flushOut(stdOut);
          let val u = Int.fromString(inputLine(stdIn));
              val v = Int.fromString(inputLine(stdIn))
```

(continues)

---

[17] Unit can also be used to imitate parameterless functions in ML, since ML requires every function to have at least one parameter.

[18] There is one further quirk to be mentioned: We must use the `flushOut` function after the prompt string to make sure its printing is not delayed until after the input.

(continued)

```
                in
                case (u,v) of
                (SOME x, SOME y) =>
                        ( output(stdOut,"The gcd of ");
                          output(stdOut,Int.toString(x));
                          output(stdOut," and ");
                          output(stdOut,Int.toString(y));
                          output(stdOut," is ");
                          output(stdOut,Int.toString(gcd(x,y)));
                          output(stdOut,"\n")
                        ) |
                  _ => output(stdOut, "Bad input.\n")
              end
          )
    val euclid = fn : unit -> unit
    > euclid ();
    Enter two integers:
    15
    10
    The gcd of 15 and 10 is 5
    val it = () : unit
```

11.4.2   Data Structures in ML

Unlike Scheme, ML has a rich set of data types, from enumerated types to records to lists. We have already seen lists and tuples (Cartesian products) above. In Chapter 6 we saw additional examples of type structures in ML. We will review some of those and some additional structures briefly here. While Scheme relies primarily on lists to simulate other data structures, ML has many options for user-defined data types, similar to C++ or Ada.

First, it is possible to give synonyms to existing data types using the keyword **type**:

```
> type Salary = real;
type Salary = real
> 35000.00: Salary;
val it = 35000.0 : Salary
> type Coords = real * real;
type Coords = real * real
> (2.1,3.2):Coords;
val it = (2.1,3.2) : Coords
```

ML also has new user-defined data types, introduced by the **datatype** keyword. For example, an enumerated type can be defined as follows:

```
> datatype Direction = North | East | South | West;
```

The vertical bar is used for alternative values in the declaration and the names, such as North and East, are called **value constructors** or **data con-**

structors. Data constructors can be used as patterns in declarations or case expressions, as in the following function definition:

```
> fun heading North = 0.0 |
      heading East = 90.0 |
      heading South = 180.0 |
      heading West = 270.0 ;
val heading = fn : Direction -> real
```

Recursive types such as binary search trees can also be declared using a `datatype` declaration:

```
> datatype 'a BST = Nil
                  | Node of 'a * 'a BST * 'a BST;
```

Note that this `datatype` is parameterized by the type of data stored in the tree. We can now construct the tree of Figure 11.8 as follows:

```
> val tree = Node("horse",
            Node( "cow", Nil, Node("dog",Nil,Nil) ),
            Node("zebra",Node("yak",Nil,Nil), Nil));
val tree = Node ("horse",Node ("cow",Nil,Node #),Node
("zebra",Node #,Nil))
  : string BST
```

We can define `data`, `leftchild`, and `rightchild` functions on BSTs by pattern matching. For example,

```
> fun leftchild (Node(data,left,right)) = left
      | leftchild Nil = raise Empty;
val leftchild = fn : 'a BST -> 'a BST
```

A traversal function for binary search trees that prints out the string nodes is as follows:

```
> fun print_tree Nil = () |
    print_tree (Node (data,left,right)) =
            ( print_tree left;
              output(stdOut,data);
              output(stdOut,"\n");
              print_tree right);
val print_tree = fn : vector BST -> unit
> print_tree tree;
cow
dog
horse
yak
zebra
val it = () : unit
```

11.4.3   Higher-order Functions and Currying in ML

Higher-order functions and the use of expressions whose values are functions are as possible in ML as in Scheme, and can be made even more useful and powerful through a process known as Currying, which we will describe shortly.

ML's keyword for a function expression is `fn` rather than Scheme's `lambda`, and is used with a special arrow (an equals followed by a greater than) to indicate the body of the function:

```
> fn x => x * x;
val it = fn : int -> int
> (fn x => x * x) 4;
val it = 16 : int
```

A `fn` expression can be used to build anonymous functions and function return values. Indeed a `fun` definition is, similar to Scheme, just "syntactic sugar" for the use of a `fn` expression:

```
fun square x = x * x;
```

is equivalent to

```
val square = fn x => x * x;
```

One difference with Scheme is that, if we use a `fn` expression to declare a recursive function, we must add the `rec` keyword in ML (similar to a Scheme `letrec`):

```
val rec fact = fn n => if n = 0 then 1
                       else n * fact (n - 1);
```

Function expressions can be used to create function return values as well as function arguments, as for example a `make_double` function that repeats an argument to a two-parameter function:

```
> fun make_double f = fn x => f (x,x);
val make_double = fn : ('a * 'a -> 'b) -> 'a -> 'b
> val square = make_double (op * );
val square = fn : int -> int
> val double = make_double (op +);
val double = fn : int -> int
> square 3;
val it = 9 : int
> double 3;
val it = 6 : int
```

ML has a number of built-in higher-order functions, including function composition, given by the letter o (lowercase "Oh"):

```
> val double_square = double o square;
val double_square = fn : int -> int
> double_square 3;
val it = 18 : int
```

We can also use ML's nonfunctional variables (`ref` types), as in:

```
> val x = ref 0.0; (* create a variable *)
val x = ref 0.0 : real ref
> x := 1.0; (* assign it a new value *)
val it = () : unit
> !x; (* fetch its value using the dereference operator *)
val it = 1.0 : real
```

to imitate object-oriented techniques using higher-order functions (see the corresponding Scheme code in Section 11.3.4):

```
> fun make_new_balance (newbalance: real) =
      let val balance = ref newbalance in
          fn amount =>
              if !balance < amount then
                      raise Fail "Insufficient funds!"
              else
              ( balance := !balance - amount;
                !balance
              )
      end;
val make_new_balance = fn : real -> real -> real
> val withdraw1 = make_new_balance 100.00;
val withdraw1 = fn : real -> real
> val withdraw2 = make_new_balance 100.00;
val withdraw2 = fn : real -> real
> withdraw1 20.00;
val it = 80.0 : real
> withdraw2 50.00;
val it = 50.0 : real
> withdraw1 20.00;
val it = 60.0 : real
> withdraw2 60.00;
uncaught exception Fail: Insufficient funds!
```

Note the type of the higher-order function `make_new_balance: real -> real -> real`. This says that `make_new_balance` takes a parameter of type `real` and returns a function that itself takes a parameter of type `real` and returns a `real` result. It also means that we could actually supply both `real` parameters at once (though separately rather than as a tuple):

```
> make_new_balance 100.00 50.00;
val it = 50.0 : real
```

(Of course, it would not make a lot of sense to do so in this situation, since the withdrawal function, and with it the account, is then lost.)

A function of multiple parameters that can be viewed as a (higher-order) function of a single parameter that returns a function of the remaining parameters is said to be **Curried**, after the logician Haskell B. Curry.

For example, the following definition of a map function is Curried, because the parameters can be supplied separately[19] (or together):

```
> fun map f [] = [] | map f (h::t) = (f h):: map f t;
val map = fn : ('a -> 'b) -> 'a list -> 'b list
> val square_list = map square;
val square_list = fn : int list -> int list
> square_list [1,2,3];
val it = [1,4,9] : int list
> map (fn x => x + x) [1,2,3];
val it = [2,4,6] : int list
```

Note that in ML we have the choice of using a tuple to get an "uncurried" version of a function, or two separate parameters to get a Curried version:

```
(* uncurried version of a gcd function: *)
> fun gcd (u,v) = if v = 0 then u else gcd (v , u mod v);
val gcd = fn : int * int -> int
(* curried version of a gcd function: *)
> fun gcd u v = if v = 0 then u else gcd v (u mod v);
val gcd = fn : int -> int -> int
```

In fact, in ML the "uncurried" version of a function using a tuple is really just a function of a single parameter as well, except that its parameter is a tuple.

We will call a language **fully Curried** if function definitions are automatically treated as Curried, and if all multiparameter built-in functions (such as the arithmetic operators) are Curried. ML is not fully Curried according to this definition, since all built-in binary operators are defined as taking tuples:

```
> op +;
val it = fn : int * int -> int
> op ::;
val it = fn : 'a * 'a list -> 'a list
> op @;
val it = fn : 'a list * 'a list -> 'a list
```

However, we could if we wish define Curried versions of these functions, but they must be used as prefix functions rather than operators:

```
> fun plus x y = x + y;
val plus = fn : int -> int -> int
> plus 2 3;
val it = 5 : int
> val plus2 = plus 2;
val plus2 = fn : int -> int
> plus2 3;
val it = 5 : int
```

---

[19] The map function as defined here is in fact predefined in ML.

```
> fun append L1 L2 = L1 @ L2;
val append = fn : 'a list -> 'a list -> 'a list
> val append_to_one = append [1];
val append_to_one = fn : int list -> int list
> append_to_one [2,3];
val it = [1,2,3] : int list
```

11.5   Delayed Evaluation

An important problem that arises in the design and use of functional languages is the distinction between "ordinary" functions and special forms. As we have already noted, in a language with an applicative order evaluation rule, such as Scheme and ML, all parameters to user-defined functions are evaluated at the time of a call, even though it may not be necessary to do so—or even wrong to do so.

Typical examples that we have mentioned before are the Boolean functions and and or and the if function. In the case of the and function, the Scheme expression (and a b) or the infix expression a && b in a language like C or Java, need not evaluate the parameter b if a evaluates to false. This is called short-circuit evaluation of Boolean expressions, and it is an example of the usefulness of delayed evaluation. In the case of the if function, it is not a case of just usefulness, but of necessity: For the expression (if a b c) in Scheme to have the proper semantics, the evaluation of b and c must be delayed until the result of a is known, and based on that, either b or c is evaluated, but never both. For this reason, an if function cannot be written as a standard user-defined function in Scheme, ML, or C. It also means that Scheme and ML must distinguish between two kinds of predefined functions, those that use standard evaluation and those that do not (the special forms). This compromises the uniformity and extendibility of these languages, since programmers cannot use standard mechanisms to extend the language.[20]

A possible argument for restricting function evaluation to applicative order evaluation is that the semantics (and the implementation) are simpler. Consider the case of a function call in which one parameter may have an undefined value, such as in the Scheme expression (and (= 1 0) (=1 (/ 1 0))) or its C equivalent (1 == 0) && (1 == 1 / 0). In this case delayed evaluation can lead to a well-defined result, even though subexpressions or parameters may be undefined. Functions with this property are called **nonstrict**, and languages with the property that functions are strict are easier to implement. In essence, strict languages satisfy a strong form of the GIGO principle (garbage in, garbage out), in that they will consistently fail to produce results when given incomplete or malformed

---

[20] In Scheme this is in fact not quite true: Scheme allows the definition of new special forms using special definition mechanisms called macros. However, the use of these mechanisms is more complex than ordinary function definition.

input. Strictness also has an important simplifying effect on formal semantics (formal semantics are discussed in Chapter 13).

Nevertheless, as we have seen, nonstrictness can be a desirable property. Indeed, one can argue in favor of nonstrictness on essentially the same basis as the argument against it in the previous paragraph: Nonstrict functions can produce results even in the presence of incomplete or malformed input—as long as there is enough information to make the result reasonable. It is interesting to note that the language Algol60 included delayed evaluation in its pass by name parameter passing convention, discussed in Chapter 8. According to pass by name evaluation, a parameter is evaluated only when it is actually used in the code of the called procedure. Thus, the function

```
function p(x: boolean; y: integer): integer;
begin
  if x then p := 1
  else p := y;
end;
```

will, using pass by name evaluation, return the value 1 when called as p(true, 1 div 0), since y is never reached in the code of p, and so the value of y—the undefined expression 1 div 0—will never be computed.

In a language that has function values, it is possible to delay the evaluation of a parameter by putting it inside a function "shell" (a function with no parameters). For example, in C, we can achieve the same effect as pass by name in the previous example by writing

```
typedef int (*IntProc) (void);

int divByZero (void)
{   return 1 / 0;
}

int p(int x, IntProc y)
{ if (x) return 1;
  else return y();
}
```

and calling p(1,divByZero). (Sometimes such "shell" procedures as divByZero are referred to as **pass by name thunks**, or just thunks, for somewhat obscure historical reasons.) In Scheme and ML, this process of surrounding parameters with function shells is even easier, since the lambda and fn function value constructors can be used directly, as in the following Scheme definition:

```
(define (p x y) (if x 1 (y)))
```

which can be called as follows:

```
(p #T (lambda () (/ 1 0)))
```

Note that the code of p must change to reflect the function parameter y— y must be surrounded by parentheses to force a call to y. Otherwise the function itself and not its value will be returned.

Indeed, Scheme has two functions that do precisely what we have been describing. The special form delay delays the evaluation of its arguments and returns an object that can be thought of as a lambda "shell," or **promise** to evaluate its arguments. The corresponding procedure force causes its parameter, which must be a delayed object, to be evaluated. Thus, the function p would be written as

```
(define ( p x y) (if x 1 (force y)))
```

and called as

```
(p #T (delay (/ 1 0)))
```

Inefficiency results from delayed evaluation when the same delayed expression is repeatedly evaluated. For example, in the delayed version of the square function,

```
(define (delayed-square x) (* (force x) (force x)))
```

the parameter x will be evaluated twice in the body of delayed-square, which is inefficient if x is a complicated expression. In fact, Scheme has an improvement to pass by name built into the force function. Scheme uses a **memoization** process, where the value of a delayed object is stored the first time the object is forced, and then subsequent calls to force simply return the previous value rather than recomputing it. (This kind of parameter evaluation is sometimes referred to as **pass by need**.)

Pass by name delayed evaluation is helpful in that it allows parameters to remain uncomputed if not needed and permits special forms such as if and cond to be defined as ordinary functions. However, pass by name is not able to handle more complex situations where only parts of each parameter are needed in a computation. Consider the following simple example of a take procedure that returns the first n items of a list:

```
(define (take n L)
   (if (= n 0) '()
       (cons (car L) (take (- n 1) (cdr L)))))
```

If we write a version in which the computation of L is delayed,

```
(define (take n L)
   (if (= n 0 ) '()
       (cons ( car (force L)) (take (- n 1)
                                    (cdr (force L))))))
```

then a call (take 1 (delay L)) will force the evaluation of the entire list L, even though we are interested in the very first element only. This can be disastrously inefficient if L happens to be a very long list produced by a list generation procedure such as

```
(define (intlist m n)
   (if (> m n) '() (cons m (intlist (+ 1 m) n))))
```

Now a call (take 1 (delay (intlist 2 100))) will still construct the entire list (2..100) before taking the first element to produce the list (2). What is needed is a delay in the second parameter to cons in intlist as well:

```
(define (intlist m n)
  (if (> m n) '()
      (cons m (delay (intlist (+ 1 m) n)))))
```

so that taking (cdr (cons m (delay ...))) returns a delayed object to the recursive call to take. Thus, we have the following sequence of events in this computation, where each delayed object is represented by the computation it "promises" to perform enclosed in quotes:

1. The call (take 1 (delay (intlist 2 100))) causes the delayed object "(intlist 2 100)" to be passed as L to

   ```
   (cons (car (force L)) (take (- 1 1) (cdr (force L))))
   ```

2. The first call to (force L) in the cons causes L to be evaluated to

   ```
   (cons 2 ((delay (intlist (+ 1 2) 100))))
   ```

   which causes the construction of the list with head 2 and tail the delayed object "(intlist (+ 1 2) 100)."

3. The car of (force L) returns 2 from the cons, leaving the following expression to be evaluated:

   ```
   (cons 2 (take (- 1 1) (cdr (force L))))
   ```

4. The call to (take (- 1 1) (cdr (force L))) causes (- 1 1) to be evaluated to 0, and the cdr of (force L) to be evaluated to the delayed object "(intlist (+ 1 2) 100)" as constructed in step 2. Then the expression (take 0 "(intlist (+ 1 2) 100)") is evaluated, which returns the empty list '() without forcing the evaluation of (intlist (+ 1 2) 100).

5. The result of (cons 2 '()) is finally evaluated, returning the list (2). Thus, the rest of the integer list is never computed.

The scenario we have just described, together with memoization, is called **lazy evaluation**. It can be achieved in a functional language without explicit calls to delay and force by requiring the runtime environment to evaluate expressions according to the following rules:

1. All arguments to user-defined functions are delayed.

2. All bindings of local names in let and letrec expressions are delayed.

3. All arguments to constructor functions (such as cons) are delayed.

4. All arguments to other predefined functions, such as the arithmetic functions "+," "*," and so on are forced.

5. All function-valued arguments are forced.

6. All conditions in selection functions such as if and cond are forced.

These rules allow operations on long lists to compute only as much of the list as is necessary. It is also possible to include potentially infinite lists in languages with lazy evaluation, since the "infinite" part will never be computed, but only as much of the list as is needed for a particular computation. To express the potentially infinite nature of such lists, lists that obey lazy evaluation rules are often called **streams**. A stream can be thought of as a partially computed list whose remaining elements can continue to be computed up to any desired number. Streams are an important issue in functional programming: To eliminate side effects completely, one has to introduce input and output into functional languages as streams, and both Scheme and ML have ad hoc stream constructions (besides the manual `delay` and `force` procedures mentioned earlier), which we do not study here.[21]

The primary example of a functional language with lazy evaluation is Haskell (again, named after Haskell B. Curry), which we study in the next section, and which has a number of advanced features, including a mechanism for fitting overloaded functions into Hindley-Milner type checking.

Lazy evaluation permits a style of functional programming that allows us to separate a computation into pieces, consisting of procedures that generate streams and other procedures that take streams as arguments, without worrying about the efficiency of each step. Procedures that generate streams are called **generators**, and procedures that modify streams are called **filters**, and we will call this style of programming **generator-filter programming**. For example, the `intlist` procedure in a previous Scheme example is a generator, and the `take` procedure is a filter.

A famous problem in functional programming that requires generator-filter programming is the **same-fringe** problem for lists. Two lists have the same fringe if they contain the same non-null atoms in the same order, or to put it another way, when written as trees, their non-null leaves taken in left-to-right order are the same. For example, the lists ((2 (3)) 4) and (2 (3 4 ())) have the same fringe. To determine whether two lists have the same fringe, we must **flatten** them to just lists of their atoms:

```
(define (flatten L)
  (cond ((null? L) '())
        ((list? L) (append (flatten (car L))
                   (flatten (cdr L))))
        (else (cons L '()) )))
```

In the case of both lists in the previous paragraph, `flatten` returns the list (2 3 4). Flatten can be viewed as a filter, which then can be used as the input to the `samefringe` procedure, as follows:

```
(define (samefringe? L M) (equal? (flatten L)
                                  (flatten M)))
```

---

[21] Haskell has replaced I/O streams with a more general construct called a monad, which we also do not study here.

The problem with this computation under the usual Scheme evaluation rule is that `flatten` will produce complete lists of the elements of L and M, even if L and M differ already in their first fringe elements. Lazy evaluation, on the other hand, will compute only enough of the flattened lists as necessary before their elements disagree. (Of course, if the lists actually do have the same fringe, the entire lists must be processed.)

A similar situation arises when using the sieve of Eratosthenes to compute prime numbers. In this method, a list of consecutive integers from 2 is generated, and each successive remaining number in the list is used to cancel out its multiples in the list. Thus, beginning with the list (2 3 4 5 6 7 8 9 10 11), we first cancel multiples of 2, leaving the list (2 3 5 7 9 11). Then we cancel the multiples of 3, giving (2 3 5 7 11), and now we cancel all remaining multiples of 5, 7, and 11 (of which there are none) to obtain the list of primes from 2 to 11 as (2 3 5 7 11). Each cancellation step can be viewed as a filter on the list of the previous cancellation step. We will see in the next section how both of the previous problems can be easily solved in Haskell.

Why don't all functional languages use delayed evaluation? Part of the answer is contained in the remarks at the beginning of this section: It complicates the semantics of the language. In practical terms, this translates into an increased complexity in the runtime environment that must maintain the evaluation rules 1–6 listed earlier. But there is another reason: Because of the interleaving of `delays` and `forces`, it is difficult to write programs with side effects, in particular, programs with variables that change as computation proceeds. In a way, this is similar to the synchronization problem for shared memory in parallel processing (studied in Chapter 14). Indeed, delayed evaluation has been described as a form of parallelism, with `delay` as a form of process suspension, and `force` a kind of process continuation. The principal point is that side effects, in particular assignment, do not mix well with lazy evaluation. This is in part the reason that Haskell is purely functional, with no variables or assignment, and why Scheme and ML are strict languages, with some ad hoc stream and delayed evaluation facilities.

11.6 Haskell—A Fully-Curried Lazy Language with Overloading

Haskell is a pure functional language whose development began in the late 1980s, primarily at Yale University and the University of Glasgow. Its current standard is Haskell98, which we follow in our discussion here. Haskell builds on and extends a series of purely functional lazy languages developed in the late 1970s and 1980s by David A. Turner culminating in the Miranda programming language. Haskell also contains a number of novel features, including function overloading and a mechanism called **monads** for dealing with side effects such as I/O (always a problem for pure functional languages). We will not describe the monad or I/O features here (but see the Notes and References); instead, we will focus in the following description on Haskell's lazy evaluation and overloading.

Haskell's syntax is very similar to that of ML, but there are some notable differences. Haskell reduces the amount of syntax to an absolute minimum using internal program clues including the **layout rule** (Chapter 1) that uses indentation and line formatting to resolve ambiguities. As a result it is rare for a Haskell program to require a semicolon or bracketing of any kind. Indeed, there is even no special syntax for definitions, and no vertical bar needs to be used for functions defined using pattern matching. Here are a few examples of function definitions in Haskell:

```
fact 0 = 1
fact n = n * fact (n - 1)
square x = x * x
gcd1 u v = if v == 0 then u else gcd1 v (mod u v)
reverse1 [] = []
reverse1 (h:t) = reverse1 t ++ [h]
```

In these definitions we note the following differences from ML. First, Haskell does not allow the redefinition of functions that already are predefined (however, it is easy to change what is actually predefined). Thus, we append a "1" to the functions reverse and gcd above, since they are already predefined. Next, we note that the "cons" operator for lists (list construction) is written as a single colon (types, on the other hand, are given using a double colon, exactly the reverse of ML). Pattern matching, as already mentioned, does not require the use of the "|" symbol. Finally, list concatenation in Haskell is given by the ++ operator.

Haskell is a fully Curried language: All predefined binary operators are Curried, and in fact, can be partially applied to either argument using parentheses (this is called a **section** in Haskell). Thus,

```
plus2 = (2 +)
```

defines a function that adds 2 to its argument on the left, while

```
times3 = (* 3)
```

defines a function that multiplies 3 times its argument on the right:

```
> plus2 3
5
> times3 4
12
```

Infix functions can also be turned into prefix functions by surrounding them with parentheses (no op keyword is required):

```
> (+) 2 3
5
> (*) 4 5
20
```

Haskell has anonymous functions (lambda expressions), with the backslash representing the "lambda":

```
> (\ x -> x * x ) 3
9
```

There are many predefined higher-order functions, such as map, and they are all in Curried form (as noted above), so they can be partially applied to construct further higher-order functions. For example, the map function has type

```
(a -> b) -> [a] -> [b]
```

and a square_list function can be defined as follows (leaving off the list parameter by Currying):

```
square_list = map (\ x -> x * x)
```

As another example, the function composition operator in Haskell is denoted by the dot ".":

```
> ((*3) . (2+)) 5
21
```

Haskell, like ML, has built-in lists and tuples, as well as type synonyms and user-defined polymorphic types:

```
type ListFn a = [a] -> [a]
type Salary = Float
type Pair a b = (a,b)
data BST a = Nil | Node a (BST a) (BST a)
```

Note that type variables in Haskell (such as a and b in the above definitions) are written without the quote of ML, and are also written after the datatype name, rather than before (the keyword data replaces the ML keyword datatype, and new user-defined types are written in a slightly different syntax without the "of" keyword). Type and constructor names in Haskell are also required to be uppercase, while function and value names must be lowercase.

Functions on new data types can use data constructors as patterns as in ML:

```
flatten:: BST a -> [a]
flatten Nil = []
flatten (Node val left right) =
            (flatten left) ++ [val] ++ (flatten right)
```

Note that we have preceded the definition with the type of the flatten function; this is permitted, although not required, and can be used to resolve ambiguities or restrict the type of the function beyond what Hindley-Milner type checking would infer (similar to the way ML allows the types of the parameters and returned types to be specified within the definition itself, something not allowed in Haskell98).

Haskell additionally has a special notation for operations that are applied over lists, called **list comprehensions**, which are designed to look like set definitions in mathematics. For example, if we wanted to square a list of integers, we could write the following:

```
square_list lis = [ x * x | x <- lis]
```

This is really just syntactic sugar for map (\ x -> x * x) lis, but can make programming with lists even easier and more transparent. The notation can also be extended to include Boolean conditions, such as

```
square_list_positive lis = [ x * x | x <- lis, x > 0]
```

which is also syntactic sugar for map (\ x -> x * x) (filter (>0) lis), where filter is a predefined list function defined as follows:

```
filter:: (a -> Bool) -> [a] -> [a]
filter pred [] = []
filter pred (h:t) =
    if pred h then h : filter pred t else filter pred t
```

As another example of the use of list comprehensions, a highly compact definition for quicksort can be given (using the first element of a list as the pivot):

```
qsort [] = []
qsort (h:t) = qsort [x | x <- t, x <= h] ++
                   [h] ++ qsort [x | x <- t, x > h]
```

Haskell is, as noted, a lazy language, so no value is computed unless it is actually needed for the computation of a program. Thus, given the definition

```
f x = 2
```

any call to f will never evaluate its argument, since it is not needed for the result. Similarly, the following function will behave exactly like the built-in if-then-else expression:

```
my_if x y z = if x then y else z
```

Lazy evaluation also means that lists in Haskell are the same as streams, and are capable of being potentially infinite. Thus, we could define an infinite list of ones as follows, without danger of getting into an immediate infinite loop:

```
ones = 1 : ones
```

Haskell has, in fact, several short-hand notations for infinite lists. For example, the notation [n..] stands for the list of integers beginning with n. This same list can also be written as [n, n+1..], and the list of ones can also be defined as [1,1..]. As a final example of this notation, the list of even positive integers can be written as [2,4..].

Given a potentially infinite list, it is of course impossible to display or process the entire list. Thus, functions that partially compute the list become useful. Two such functions are take and drop; take extracts the first n items from a list, and drop discards the first n items (the underscore is the wildcard pattern, as in ML):

```
take 0 _ = []
take _ [] = []
take n (h:t) = h : take (n - 1) t
drop 0 lis = lis
drop _ [] = []
drop n (_:t) = drop (n - 1) t
```

For example, take 5 (drop 4 [2..]) gives the result [6,7,8,9,10].

Using lazy evaluation, it is possible to get an extremely compact representation of the Sieve of Eratosthenes (see page 512):

```
sieve (p : lis) = p : sieve [n | n <- lis , mod n p /= 0]
primes = sieve [2..]
```

With this definition of the (infinite) list of primes, take can be used to compute any desired number of primes:

```
> take 100 primes
[2,3,5,7,11,13,17,19,23,29,31,37,41,43,47,53,59,61,67,71,
73,79,83,89,97,101,103,107,109,113,127,131,137,139,149,
151,157,163,167,173,179,181,191,193,197,199,211,223,
227,229,233,239,241,251,257,263,269,271,277,281,283,
293,307,311,313,317,331,337,347,349,353,359,367,373,
379,383,389,397,401,409,419,421,431,433,439,443,449,
457,461,463,467,479,487,491,499,503,509,521,523,541]
```

The last topic we discuss in this short overview of Haskell is its unique approach to overloading. Recall that in ML functions could not be overloaded, and this either led to unresolved ambiguities or strong assumptions that ML had to make to avoid them. In particular, we could not define an arithmetic function such as square that would work for both integers and real numbers. Haskell has no such problem. Indeed, we can define a square function as usual:

```
square x = x * x
```

and then use it on any numeric value:

```
> square 2
4
> square 3.5
12.25
```

The type of `square` gives us a hint as to how Haskell does this:

```
square :: Num a => a -> a
```

This type is called a **qualified type**, and it says essentially that `square` can be applied to any type a as long as a is a Num. But what is a Num? It is not a type, but a **type class**: a set of types that all define certain functions. Here is a possible (incomplete) definition of the Num type class:

```
class Num a where
     (+), (-), (*)   :: a -> a -> a
     negate          :: a -> a
     abs             :: a -> a
```

Essentially, a type class definition states what the names and types of the functions are that every type belonging to it must define (so type classes are a little like Java interfaces). By itself, of course, this definition does nothing. For any types to belong to this class, we must give an instance definition, in which actual working definitions for each of the required functions are provided. For example, in the standard library, the data types Int, Float, and Double are all instances of Num. A (partial) instance definition for Int in the standard library looks as follows:

```
instance Num Int where
     (+)           = primPlusInt
     (-)           = primMinusInt
     negate        = primNegInt
     (*)           = primMulInt
     abs           = absReal
```

(The functions to the right of the equal signs are all built-in definitions that are hidden inside the standard library modules.)

Haskell determines the type of the `square` function by looking for the symbol * in a class definition (because the body of `square` depends on the availability of *) and applying the appropriate qualification. Then, the `square` function can be applied to any value whose type is an instance of the Num class.

There is, however, more structure to type classes than this simple description. In the case of Int, for example, the Num class does not describe all of the functions that need to be available, such as equality tests and order functions like < , not to mention `div` and `mod` (note that the Num class above does not require any division operation). Of course, there are further type classes requiring these functions: Eq for the equality operator ==, Ord for the less-than operator <, and Integral for the `div` and `mod` operations. Not only must Int be defined to be an instance of all of these type classes, but many of the type classes themselves should be required to be part of other type classes (so that any instances are forced to be

instances of these other classes as well). This dependency of type classes
on other type classes is called **type class inheritance**, and establishes a
hierarchy of type classes. Two type classes at the base of this hierarchy are
the Eq and Show classes. Show is used to establish the existence of a show
function, which is used to display values of member types (all predefined
Haskell types are instances of the Show class). The Eq class establishes
the ability of two values of a member type to be compared using the
== operator. Most types are instances of Eq, but not function types, for
example, since equality of functions cannot be defined in a way that
would provide useful information.

Here is a complete definition of the Eq class from the Haskell standard library:

```
class Eq a where
    (==), (/=) :: a -> a -> Bool
    x == y     = not (x/=y)
    x /= y     = not (x==y)
```

This class definition shows an additional feature: the use of default definitions for the required functions. Such default definitions are typically
based on other required functions. In the above code, the default definition of /= (not equal) depends on the definition of == being available, and
the default definition of == depends on the definition of /= being available. This apparent circularity means that, for a type to be declared an
instance of Eq, only one of the two required functions needs to be defined,
and the other will be implicitly defined by the default. For example, Int
is defined to be an instance of Eq as follows:

```
instance Eq Int where (==) = primEqInt
```

To establish the inheritance requirements for each type class,
Haskell uses a notation similar to type qualification. For example, the definition of the Num class in the Haskell standard library begins as follows:

```
class (Eq a, Show a) => Num a where ...
```

And the definition of the Ord class is as follows (with the default function
definitions removed):

```
class (Eq a) => Ord a where
    compare                  :: a -> a -> Ordering
    (<), (<=), (>=), (>)     :: a -> a -> Bool
    max, min                 :: a -> a -> a
```

The numeric class hierarchy of Haskell is shown in Figure 11.10, along
with sample functions that are required by some of the type classes.

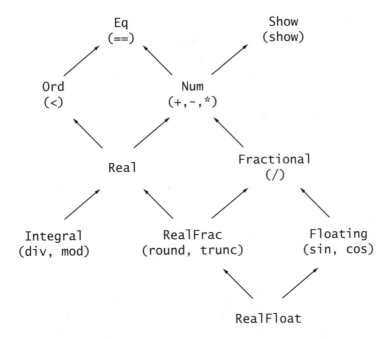

Figure 11.10   The numeric type class hierarchy in Haskell (sample functions required by some of the classes are in parentheses)

As a last example of the use of type classes in Haskell, when a program defines a new data type, such as the BST type defined previously:

```
data BST a = Nil | Node a (BST a) (BST a)
```

then such trees cannot in general either be displayed or compared for equality, since we have not defined BST to be an instance of the Show or Eq type classes. For example, if we define:

```
tree = Node "horse"
            (Node "cow" Nil (Node "dog" Nil Nil))
            (Node "zebra" (Node "yak" Nil Nil) Nil)
```

then a Haskell interpreter will respond as follows when we try to display or compare tree:[22]

```
> tree
ERROR: Cannot find "show" function for:
*** Expression : tree
*** Of type    : Tree [Char]
> tree == tree
```
(continues)

---

[22] This is the output from the HUGS Haskell interpreter—see the Notes and References.

(continued)

```
ERROR: Illegal Haskell 98 class constraint in inferred
type
*** Expression : tree == tree
*** Type        : Eq (BST [Char]) => Bool
```

In order to make a user-defined datatype useful, we typically must define it to be an instance of Eq and Show (Show requires a function show that converts the data type in question into a String so that it can be displayed):

```
instance Eq a => Eq (BST a)
    where
    Nil == Nil = True
    Node x a b == Node y c d =
        x == y && a == c && b == d
    _ == _ = False

instance Show (BST a) where show = ...
```

Note in particular how the definition of equality for a BST depends on the membership of the type parameter a in Eq, since otherwise the equality of the stored data cannot be tested.

Since it is such a common problem to need to define a new data type to be a member of certain classes like Eq, Show, and Ord, Haskell offers a way to automatically generate these definitions: Haskell simply assumes that the "natural" definitions are desired (a data type is shown by printing it out as a string, and equality is defined componentwise). To accomplish this, a deriving clause is added to the data definition:

```
data BST a = Nil | Node a (BST a) (BST a)
              deriving (Show,Eq)
```

With this definition of BST, Haskell has no trouble displaying a BST or comparing two BSTs for equality:

```
> tree
Node "horse" (Node "cow" Nil (Node "dog" Nil Nil))
   (Node "zebra" (Node "yak" Nil Nil) Nil)
> tree == tree
True
```

11.7 The Mathematics of Functional Programming I: Recursive Functions

In Section 11.1 we stated that a function f is a rule that associates to each element of a domain set X a unique element of a range set Y, and we write $f: X \rightarrow Y$. An alternative view is that f defines a collection of pairs of elements (x, y) of X and Y with the property that $y = f(x)$ and that each x is contained in at most one pair of such elements. (If (x, y) is such a pair and so is (x, y'), then $y = f(x)$ and $y' = f(x)$, so $y = y'$ and the pairs are the same.)

Thus, a function can be viewed as a **set of pairs** (x, y) such that $y = f(x)$ or as a subset of the Cartesian product $X \times Y$:

$$f \equiv \{(x, y) \in X \times Y \mid y = f(x)\}$$

where $\equiv$ means "is equivalent to" and $\in$ means "is contained in."

Viewing a function as a set has certain advantages for the study of the definition of functions in programming languages. In particular, there are two standard methods for defining sets. First, we can list all its elements. Thus, for example,

$$\text{digit} = \{0, 1, 2, 3, 4, 5, 6, 7, 8, 9\}$$

represents the set of all digits. This method of set definition is sometimes called **definition by extension**. It is possible to define functions this way also. For example, the function on the set of digits that adds one to each digit (wrapping around at 9 in a modulo fashion) can be defined as follows:

$$\{(0,1), (1,2), (2,3), (3,4), (4,5), (5,6), (6,7), (7,8), (8,9), (9,0)\}$$

In a program this would be an unusual way of defining functions, since it would need to be a giant case-statement taking up many lines of code. Instead, the more common definition of a function is by a **formula** or **property**. For example, a formula expressing the definition of the previous function would be

$$f(x) = (x + 1) \bmod 10$$

or in set terminology

$$f \equiv \{(x, y) \in \text{digit} \times \text{digit} \mid y = (x + 1) \bmod 10\}$$

Definition by formula is sometimes called **definition by comprehension**.

In a purely functional language the body of a function given in its definition typically represents an equation that gives its definition by comprehension. For example, in the ML function definition

```
fun square x = x * x
```

we are saying that the square function is given as the set square $\equiv \{ (x, y) \in \text{int} \times \text{int} \mid y = x * x\}$.

Now let us consider recursive functions. The first thing to note is that the recursion can be thought of as purely part of the equation representing the definition of the function, as in the recursive definition of the factorial function:

$$\text{fact } n = \text{if } n = 0 \text{ then } 1 \text{ else } n * \text{fact } (n - 1)$$

Nothing in this equation expresses anything about the nature of the runtime environment required to implement it, or even that the use of fact on the right-hand side represents a call, while the left-hand side represents a definition. Thus, to be mathematically precise, we speak of a **recursive definition** rather than a recursive function.

Can we give a mathematical meaning to a recursive definition? In Chapters 4 and 6 we saw that recursive definitions of language syntax and data types were common and could be represented as particular solutions to certain recursive set equations. But functions are also sets, so we might expect that the same kind of theory would apply in this case too. And indeed it does, but with complications. If we want to write the equation for the fact function in set form, we must rewrite the right-hand side in terms of sets. One way to do this is to realize that the expression "if $n = 0$ then 1 else $n * f(n - 1)$" represents the union of two functions. The then-part represents the function $\{(0, 1)\}$, that is, the function with the value 1 at 0, and no other values. The else-part represents the function $f'(n) = n * f(n - 1)$, which takes the value of f at $n - 1$ and multiplies it by n. For example, if $f = \{(0, 1), (1, 2)\}$ (i.e., f has the two values $f(0) = 1$ and $f(1) = 2$), then

$$\begin{aligned} f' &= \{(n, n * f(n - 1)) \mid n - 1 \in \text{domain of } f\} \\ &= \{(n, n * f(n - 1)) \mid n - 1 = 0 \text{ or } n - 1 = 1\} \\ &= \{(n, n * f(n - 1) \mid n = 1 \text{ or } n = 2\} \\ &= \{(1, 1 * f(1 - 1)), (2, 2 * f(2 - 1)\} \\ &= \{(1, 1 * 1), (2, 2 * 2)\} = \{(1,1), (2,4)\} \end{aligned}$$

and the expression "if $n = 0$ then 1 else $n * f(n - 1)$" is the function represented by the set $\{(0,1)\} \cup \{(1,1), (2,4)\} = \{(0,1), (1,1), (2,4)\}$. With this interpretation, the set equation for fact is

$$\text{fact} = \{(0, 1)\} \cup \text{fact'}$$

where $\text{fact'}(n) = n * \text{fact}(n - 1)$ is constructed as outlined.

There is another interpretation of the function equation, however, that is based on higher-order functions (and that is more common in the theoretical literature). We think of the left-hand and right-hand sides of the equation as representing possibly two different functions f and g:

$$f(n) = \text{if } n = 0 \text{ then } 1 \text{ else } n * g(n - 1)$$

Now the right-hand side of the equation has two parameters, namely, n and g. We can think of this as defining a higher-order function H as follows:

$$H(g)(n) = \text{if } n = 0 \text{ then } 1 \text{ else } n * g(n - 1)$$

(The use of the name H is traditional for this function; see the next section.) Thus H is a function that takes a function as a parameter and returns a new function; that is, H is a higher-order function.

Now consider the factorial function. The definition of fact implies that:

$$H(\text{fact})(n) = \text{fact}(n)$$

for all n, or that $H(\text{fact}) = \text{fact}$. Thus, the factorial function is a **fixed point** of the function H. Of course, this equation for H contains the same information as the set equation, and as with previous such equations in

Chapters 4 and 6, we want the **smallest solution** to this equation to be the chosen definition of the fact function. For this reason, recursive function definitions are said to have **least-fixed-point semantics**, and fact is taken to be the least fixed point of the function H.

How can a least fixed point solution be constructed for fact? If we go back to the equation

$$\text{fact} = \{(0, 1)\} \cup \text{fact}'$$

we can see a way of building up fact as a set. Start with a function with no values at all, that is, the empty set $\varnothing$. Call this function fact_0. Then consider fact'_0. This function can have no values either, since it is based on the domain of fact_0. Now we construct a new function fact_1, using the equation, as follows:

$$\text{fact}_1 = \{(0,1)\} \cup \text{fact}'_0 = \{(0,1)\} \cup \varnothing = \{(0,1)\}$$

We now have a function fact_1 that has one value, namely, $\text{fact}_1(0) = 1$. Now let us compute fact'_1 from fact_1:

$$
\begin{aligned}
\text{fact}'_1 &= \{(n, n * \text{fact}_1(n-1)) \mid n-1 \in \text{domain of } \text{fact}_1\} \\
&= \{(n, n * \text{fact}_1(n-1)) \mid n-1 = 0\} \\
&= \{(n, n * \text{fact}_1(n-1)) \mid n = 1\} \\
&= \{(1, 1 * \text{fact}_1(1-1))\} \\
&= \{(1, 1 * 1)\} = \{(1, 1)\}
\end{aligned}
$$

Finally, $\text{fact}_2 = \{(0,1)\} \cup \text{fact}'_1 = \{(0,1)\} \cup \{(1,1)\} = \{(0,1), (1, 1)\}$. We now have a function with two points! Continuing in this way we get

$$\text{fact}_3 = \{(0,1), (1,1), (2,2)\}$$

and

$$\text{fact}_4 = \{(0, 1), (1, 1), (2,2), (3,6)\}$$

The fact function is now the union of all these partial fact functions:

$$\text{fact} = \text{fact}_0 \cup \text{fact}_1 \cup \text{fact}_2 \cup \ldots$$

It is possible to show that this is indeed a smallest solution to the given set equation.

Note that the fact function we have constructed does indeed represent exactly those values of the fact function that would be computed by a series of recursive calls. Indeed, the definition we used gave fact only as a partial function with domain equal to the set of integers $> = 0$ (if a negative value is passed to fact, an infinite recursive loop results). It is possible to find a fixed point for the equation for fact that is defined for more values. For example, if we define $\text{fact}(n)$ as usual for $n > = 0$, and $\text{fact}(n) = 0$ for all $n < 0$, then fact still satisfies the equation $\text{fact}(n) = $ if $n = 0$ then 1 else $n * \text{fact}(n-1)$. This is the reason for taking the least fixed point solution to this equation: The least solution has exactly those function values that will be constructed by a runtime system implementing recursive calls.

11.8   The Mathematics of Functional Programming II: Lambda Calculus

Lambda calculus was invented by Alonzo Church as a mathematical formalism for expressing computation by functions, similar to the way a Turing machine is a formalism for expressing computation by a computer. In fact, lambda calculus can be used as a model for (purely) functional programming languages in much the same way that Turing machines can be used as models for imperative programming languages (see Chapter 1). Thus, it is an important result for functional programming that lambda calculus as a description of computation is equivalent to Turing machines. This implies the result that was stated in Chapter 1, namely, that a purely functional programming language (no variables and no assignment) with an if-then-else construct and recursion is Turing complete—any computation performed by a Turing machine can be described by such a language.

It is useful for anyone interested in functional programming to have at least some knowledge of lambda calculus, since many functional languages, including LISP, ML, and Haskell, have been based on lambda calculus, and since lambda calculus provides a particularly simple and clear view of computation. Therefore, we offer this section as a basic introduction to the subject. For those with more than a superficial interest in functional programming, we recommend consulting one of the texts listed at the end of the chapter.

The essential construct of lambda calculus is the **lambda abstraction:**

$$(\lambda x . + 1 x)$$

This can be interpreted exactly as the lambda expression

```
(lambda (x) (+ 1 x))
```

in Scheme, namely, as representing an unnamed function of the parameter x that adds 1 to x. Note that, like Scheme, expressions such as $(+ 1 x)$ are written in prefix form.

The basic operation of lambda calculus is the **application** of expressions such as the lambda abstraction. The expression

$$(\lambda x . + 1 x) 2$$

represents the application of the function that adds 1 to x to the constant 2. Lambda calculus expresses this by providing a **reduction rule** that permits 2 to be substituted for x in the lambda (and removing the lambda), yielding the desired value:

$$(\lambda x . + 1 x) 2 \Rightarrow (+ 1 2) \Rightarrow 3$$

The syntax for lambda calculus is very simple:

$$exp \rightarrow constant$$
$$|\ variable$$
$$|\ (exp\ exp)$$
$$|\ (\lambda\ variable\ .\ exp)$$

Constants in this grammar are numbers like 0 or 1 and certain predefined functions like + and *. Variables are names like x and y. The third rule for expressions represents function application $(f\ x)$ as noted earlier. The fourth rule gives lambda abstractions. Note that only functions of a single variable are allowed, but since lambda expressions provide for higher-order functions, this is not a significant restriction, as the notion of Currying discussed earlier in this chapter allows for functions of several variables to be interpreted simply as functions of a single variable returning functions of the remaining variables. Thus, lambda calculus as defined here is fully Curried.

Variables in lambda calculus are not like variables in a programming language—they do not occupy memory, since lambda calculus has no concept of memory. Lambda calculus variables correspond instead to function parameters as in purely functional programming. The set of constants and the set of variables are not specified by the grammar. Thus, it is more correct to speak of many **lambda calculi**. Each specification of the set of constants and the set of variables describes a particular lambda calculus. Lambda calculus without constants is called pure lambda calculus.

Parentheses are included in the rules for function application and lambda abstraction to avoid ambiguity, but by convention may be left out, in case no ambiguity results. Thus, according to our grammar, we should have written $(\lambda x.\ ((+\ 1)\ x))$ for $(\lambda x.\ +\ 1\ x)$ and $((\lambda x.\ ((+\ 1)\ x)\ 2)$ for $(\lambda x.\ +\ 1\ x)\ 2$. However, no ambiguity results from the way they were written.

The variable x in the expression $(\lambda x.E)$ is said to be **bound** by the lambda. The scope of the binding is the expression E. An occurrence of a variable outside the scope of any binding of it by a lambda is a **free occurrence**. An occurrence that is not free is a **bound** occurrence. Thus, in the expression $(\lambda x.\ E)$, all occurrences of x in E are bound. For example, in the expression

$$(\lambda x.\ +\ y\ x)$$

x is bound and y is free. If we try to apply the function specified by this lambda abstraction, we substitute for x, but we have no way of determining the value of y:

$$(\lambda x.\ +\ y\ x)\ 2 \Rightarrow (+\ y\ 2)$$

The variable y is like a nonlocal reference in the function—its value must be specified by an external environment.[23]

---

[23] Supplying an environment to bind free variables results in a pair consisting of a lambda expression and an environment; such a pair is called a **closure**, similar to the closures in Chapter 8.

Different occurrences of a variable can be bound by different lambdas, and some occurrences of a variable may be bound, while others are free. In the following expression

$$(\lambda x. + ((\lambda y. ((\lambda x. * x\ y)\ 2))\ x)\ y)$$

the occurrence of x after the $*$ is bound by a different lambda than the outer x. Also, the first occurrence of y is bound, while the second occurrence is free. In fact, applying the functions defined by the lambdas gives the following reduction:

$$(\lambda x. + ((\lambda y. ((\lambda x. * x\ y)\ 2))\ x)\ y) \Rightarrow$$
$$(\lambda x. + ((\lambda y. (* 2\ y))\ x)\ y) \Rightarrow$$
$$(\lambda x. + (* 2\ x)\ y)$$

When reducing expressions that contain multiple bindings with the same name, care must be taken not to confuse the scopes of the bindings—sometimes renaming is necessary (discussed shortly).

We can view lambda calculus as modeling functional programming by considering a lambda abstraction as a function definition and the juxtaposition of two expressions as function application. As a model, however, lambda calculus is extremely general. For example, nothing prevents us in lambda calculus from applying a function to itself or even defining a function that takes a function parameter and applies it to itself: $(x\ x)$ and $(\lambda x.\ x\ x)$ are legal expressions in lambda calculus. A more restrictive form of lambda calculus, called the **typed lambda calculus**, includes the notion of data type from programming languages, thus reducing the set of expressions that are allowed. We will not consider the typed lambda calculus further.

Since lambda calculus is so general, however, very precise rules must be given for transforming expressions, such as substituting values for bound variables. These rules have historical names, such as "alpha-conversion" and "beta-conversion." We will give a short overview to show the kinds of operations that can occur on lambda expressions.

The primary method for transforming lambda expressions is by **substitution**, or **function application**. We have seen a number of examples of this already: $((\lambda x. + x\ 1)\ 2)$ is equivalent to $(+ 2\ 1)$ by substituting 2 for x and eliminating the lambda. This is exactly like a call in a programming language to the function defined by the lambda abstraction, with 2 substituted for x as a value parameter. Historically, this process has been called **beta-reduction** in lambda calculus. One can also view this process in reverse, where $(+ 2\ 1)$ becomes $((\lambda x. + x\ 1)\ 2)$, in which case it is called **beta-abstraction**. **Beta-conversion** refers to either beta-reduction or beta-abstraction and establishes the equivalence of the two expressions. Formally, beta-conversion says that $((\lambda x.E)\ F)$ is equivalent to $E[F/x]$, where $E[F/x]$ is E with all free occurrences of x in E replaced by F.

Care must be taken in beta-conversion when F contains variable names that occur in E. Consider the expression

$$((\lambda x.(\lambda y. + x\ y))\ y)$$

The first occurrence of y is bound, while the second is free. If we were to replace x by y blindly, we would get the incorrect reduction $(\lambda y. + y\ y)$. This is called the **name capture** problem. What we have to do is change the name of y in the inner lambda abstraction so that the free occurrence will not conflict, as follows:

$$((\lambda x.(\lambda y. + x\ y))\ y) \Rightarrow ((\lambda x.(\ \lambda z. + x\ z))\ y) \Rightarrow (\lambda z. + y\ z)$$

Name change is another available conversion process in lambda calculus, called **alpha-conversion**: $(\lambda x.E)$ is equivalent to $(\lambda y.E[y/x])$, where as before, $E[y/x]$ stands for the expression E with all free occurrences of x replaced by y. (Note that if y is a variable that already occurs in E there can be trouble similar to the substitution problem just discussed.)

Finally, there is a conversion that allows for the elimination of "redundant" lambda abstractions. This conversion is called **eta-conversion**. A simple example is the expression $(\lambda x. (+ 1\ x))$. Since $+$ is Curried, the expression $(+ 1)$ is a function of one argument, and the expression $(+ 1\ x)$ can be viewed as the application of the function $+ 1$ to x. Thus, $(\lambda x. (+ 1\ x))$ is equivalent to the function $(+ 1)$ without the lambda abstraction. In general, $(\lambda x. (E\ x))$ is equivalent to E by eta-conversion, as long as E contains no free occurrences of x. As a further example of eta-conversion, we have

$$(\lambda x. (\lambda y.(+ x\ y))) \Rightarrow (\lambda x. (+ x)) \Rightarrow +$$

which is to say that the first expression is just another notation for the $+$ function.

It is worth noting that eta-reduction is helpful in simplifying Curried definitions in functional languages. For example, the ML definition

```
fun square_list lis = map (fn x => x * x) lis ;
```

can be simplified by eta-reduction to

```
val square_list = map (fn x => x * x) ;
```

The order in which beta-reductions are applied to a lambda expression can have an effect on the final result obtained, just as different evaluation orders can make a difference in programming languages. In particular, it is possible to distinguish applicative order evaluation (or pass by value) from normal order evaluation (or pass by name). For example, in the following expression

$$((\lambda x. * x\ x) (+ 2\ 3))$$

we could either use applicative order, replacing $(+ 2\ 3)$ by its value and then applying beta-reduction, as in

$$((\lambda x. * x\ x) (+ 2\ 3)) \Rightarrow ((\lambda x. * x\ x)\ 5) \Rightarrow (* 5\ 5) \Rightarrow 25$$

or we could apply beta-reduction first and then evaluate, giving normal order evaluation:

$$((\lambda x. * x\ x) (\ + 2\ 3)) \Rightarrow (* (+ 2\ 3) (+ 2\ 3)) \Rightarrow (* 5\ 5) \Rightarrow 25$$

Normal order evaluation is, as we have noted several times, a kind of **delayed** evaluation, since the evaluation of expressions is done only after substitution.

Normal order evaluation can have a different result than applicative order, as we have also previously noted. A striking example is when parameter evaluation gives an undefined result. If the value of an expression does not depend on the value of the parameter, then normal order will still compute the correct value, while applicative order will also give an undefined result.

For example, consider the lambda expression $((\lambda x.\ x\ x)\ (\lambda x.\ x\ x))$. Beta-reduction on this expression results in the same expression all over again. Thus beta-reduction goes into an "infinite loop," attempting to reduce this expression. If we use this expression as a parameter to a constant expression, as in

$$((\lambda y.\ 2)\ ((\lambda x.\ x\ x)\ (\lambda x.\ x\ x)))$$

then using applicative order, we get an undefined result, while using normal order we get the value 2, since it does not depend on the value of the parameter y.

Functions that can return a value even when parameters are undefined are said to be **nonstrict**, while functions that are always undefined when a parameter is undefined are **strict**. In lambda calculus notation, the symbol $\perp$ (pronounced "bottom") represents an undefined value, and a function f is strict if it is always true that $(f\ \perp) = \perp$. Thus, applicative order evaluation is strict, while normal order evaluation is nonstrict.

Normal order reduction is significant in lambda calculus in that many expressions can be reduced using normal order to a unique normal form that cannot be reduced further. This is a consequence of the famous **Church-Rosser theorem**, which states that reduction sequences are essentially independent of the order in which they are performed. The equivalence of two expressions can then be determined by reducing them using normal order and comparing their normal forms, if they exist. This has practical applications for translators of functional languages, too, since a translator can use normal forms to replace one function by an equivalent but more efficient function.

Finally, in this brief overview of lambda calculus, we wish to show how lambda calculus can model recursive function definitions in exactly the way we have treated them in the previous section. Consider the following definition of the factorial function:

$$\text{fact} = (\lambda n.\ (\text{if}\ (=\ n\ 0)\ 1\ (*\ n\ (\text{fact}\ (-\ n\ 1)))))$$

We remove the recursion by creating a new lambda abstraction as follows:

$$\text{fact} = (\lambda F.\lambda n.\ (\text{if}\ (=\ n\ 0)\ 1\ (*\ n\ (F\ (-\ n\ 1)))))\ \text{fact}$$

In other words, the right-hand side can be viewed as a lambda abstraction, which, when applied to fact, gives fact back again.

If we write this abstraction as

$$H = (\lambda F.\lambda n.\ (\text{if}\ (=\ n\ 0)\ 1\ (*\ n\ (F\ (-\ n\ 1)))))$$

then the equation becomes

$$\text{fact} = H \text{ fact}$$

or that fact is a **fixed point** of H. In the last section we constructed a least-fixed-point solution by building up a set representation for the function. However, in the lambda calculus, lambda expressions are primitive; that is, we cannot use sets to model them. Thus, to define a recursive function fact in the lambda calculus, we need a function Y for constructing a fixed point of the lambda expression H. Y needs therefore to have the property that $Y H = \text{fact}$ or $Y H = H (Y H)$. Such a Y can indeed be defined by the following lambda expression:

$$Y = (\lambda \, h. \, (\lambda \, x. \, h \, (x \, x)) \, (\lambda \, x. \, h \, (x \, x))).$$

Y is called a **fixed-point combinator**, a combinator being any lambda expression that contains only bound variables. Such a Y actually constructs a solution that is in some sense the "smallest." Thus, one can refer to the **least-fixed-point semantics** of recursive functions in lambda calculus, as well as in the ordinary set-based theory of functions.

Exercises

11.1 The following C function computes the power a^b, where a is a floating-point number and b is a (non-negative) integer:

```
double power(double a, int b)
{   int i;
    double temp = 1.0;
    for (i = 1; i <= b; i++) temp *= a;
    return temp;
}
```

(a) Rewrite this procedure in functional form.
(b) Rewrite your answer to (a) using an accumulating parameter to make it tail recursive.

11.2 A function that returns the maximum value of a 0-ended list of integers input from a user is given by the following C procedure:

```
int readMax(void)
{   int max, x;
    scanf("%d",&x);
    if (x != 0)
    {   max = x;
        while (x != 0)
        { scanf("%d",&x);
          if (x > max) max = x;
```

(continues)

(continued)

```
            }
            return max;
        }
    }
```

Rewrite this procedure as much as possible in functional style using tail recursion (the `scanf` procedure prevents a complete removal of variables).

11.3 Recursive sorts are easier to write in functional style than others. Two recursive sorts are Quicksort and Mergesort. Write functional versions of **(a)** Quicksort; **(b)** Mergesort in an imperative language of your choice (e.g., C, Ada, C++, Pascal), using an array of integers as your basic data structure.

11.4 It is possible to write nonrecursive programs that implement recursive algorithms using a stack, but at the cost of extra complexity (a necessary overhead of using a nonrecursive language like FORTRAN). Write nonrecursive versions of **(a)** Quicksort; **(b)** Mergesort. Discuss the difficulties of the added complexity. **(c)** Which of the two sorts is easier to implement nonrecursively? Why?

11.5 State which of the following functions are referentially transparent, and give reasons:
   (a) The factorial function
   (b) A function that returns a number from the keyboard
   (c) A function p that counts the number of times it is called (see the problem at the end of Section 5.5)

11.6 Is a function that has no side effects referentially transparent? Explain.

11.7 The binomial coefficients are a frequent computational task in computer science. They are defined as follows for $n >= 0, 0 <= k <= n$ (! is factorial and $0! = 1$):

$$B(n, k) = \frac{n!}{(n - k)! \, k!}$$

   (a) Write a procedure using a loop to compute $B(n, k)$. Test your program on $B(10, 5)$.
   (b) Use the following recurrence and the fact that $B(n, 0) = 1$ and $B(n, n) = 1$ to write a functional procedure to compute $B(n, k)$:

$$B(n, k) = B(n - 1, k - 1) + B(n - 1, k)$$

   Test your program on $B(10, 5)$.
   (c) Can you write a more efficient program than your program of **(b)** and still preserve the functional style? (*Hint:* Think of pass by need memoization as discussed in Section 11.5.)

11.8 The following functional programming exercises can be solved in any of the languages studied in the text (Scheme, ML, Haskell) or in a functional language of your choice:

(a) Write a tail-recursive procedure to compute the length of an arbitrary list.

(b) Write a procedure that computes the maximum and minimum of a list of integers.

(c) Write a procedure that collects integers from the user until a 0 is encountered and returns them in a list in the order they were input. (Scheme or ML only)

(d) Use your procedures of (b) and (c) to write a program to input a 0-ended list of integers, print the list in the order entered, and print the maximum and minimum of the list (Scheme or ML only).

(e) Write Quicksort for a list of integers (Scheme or ML only).

(f) Write Mergesort for a list of integers.

(g) A Pythagorean triple is a tuple of integers (x, y, z) such that $x * x + y * y = z * z$. Write a procedure with a parameter n to print all Pythagorean triples such that $1 \leq x < y \leq z \leq n$.

(h) Write a higher-order function `twice` that takes as a parameter a function of one argument and returns a function that represents the application of that function to its argument twice. Given the usual definition of the `square` function, what function is (`twice (twice square)`)?

(i) Write a higher-order function `inc_n` that takes an integer n as a parameter and returns an n-th increment function, which increments its parameter by n. Thus, in Scheme syntax, ((`inc_n 3) 2`) = 5 and ((`inc_n -2) 3`) = 1.

11.9 Consider the problem of designing a syntax tree for simple integer arithmetic expressions with the three operations $+$, $-$, and $*$, and an evaluator for such expressions that evaluates by traversing the syntax tree.

(a) Write a data structure definition for a syntax tree in ML or Haskell. Use an enumerated type for the operations.

(b) Write a function `eval` that computes the integer value of a syntax tree by tree traversal in Scheme, ML, or Haskell. If you are using ML or Haskell, use your data structure of (a). If you are using Scheme, describe in words the tree structure assumed by your function.

11.10 Suppose you want to use a list data structure to implement a `Set` data type. Write `insert` and `member` operations in (a) Scheme; (b) ML; (c) Haskell. Make sure in ML and Haskell that your `Set` data type is distinct from a list. (d) In Haskell, define your `Set` type to be an instance of classes `Eq` and `Show`.

11.11 Given the definition of a binary search tree in Haskell as given in the text:

```
data BST a = Nil | Node a (BST a) (BST a)
```

write a show function (show:: (BST a) -> String) as it would be generated by a Haskell deriving Show clause.

11.12 Many procedures we have seen are not tail recursive but "almost" so, in that the recursive call comes just before an arithmetic operation, which is the last operation in the procedure. For example, factorial and length of a list are almost tail recursive in this sense. Describe a general pattern for turning an almost tail-recursive procedure into a loop, in the same way a tail-recursive procedure can be so transformed, as described in Section 11.1. Can a translator recognize almost tail recursion as easily as tail recursion? How might it do so?

11.13 Draw box diagrams for the following Scheme lists:

```
((((a))))
(1 (2 (3 4)) (5))
((a ( )) ((c) (d) b) e)
```

11.14 Use the box diagrams of the last exercise to compute the following for each Scheme list for which they make sense:

```
(car (car L))
(car (cdr L))
(car (cdr (cdr (cdr L))))
(cdr (car (cdr (cdr L))))
```

11.15 Represent the following elements as car/cdr expressions of the lists of Exercise 11.13:

a of the first list

3 of the second list

c of the third list

11.16 Scheme's basic data structure is actually a little more general than the lists described in this chapter. Indeed, since the car of a list can be a list or an atom, it is also possible for the cdr to be an atom as well as a list. In the case when the cdr is not a list, the resulting structure is called a **pair** or **S-expression** instead of a list and is written (a . b), where a is the car and b is the cdr. Thus, (cons 2 3) = (2 . 3), and (cdr '(2 . 3)) = 3. The list (2 3 4) can then be written in pair notation as (2 . (3 (4 . ()))). Discuss any advantages you can think of to having this more general data structure.

11.17 The Scheme function reverse described in the text reverses only the "top level" of a list: if L = ((2 3) 4 (5 6)) then (reverse L) = ((5 6) 4 (2 3)). Write a Scheme function deep-reverse that also reverses all sublists: (deep-reverse L) = ((6 5) 4 (3 2)).

11.18 Write a Scheme list representation for the binary search tree:

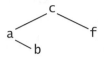

11.19 Write an `insert` procedure in Scheme for the binary search tree data structure described in Section 11.3.2.

11.20 Try to write a tail-recursive version of the `append` function in Scheme. What problems do you encounter? Can you think of a list representation that would make this easier?

11.21 Scheme has two functions that test equality of values: `eq?` and `equal?`. The first tests identity of memory location, while the second tests "structural equality," that is, identity of structure. Use these two versions of equality to show that Scheme uses pointer semantics for assignment of lists, as described in Section 5.6.

11.22 The Scheme `let` expression is actually syntactic sugar for a `lambda` that is immediately applied to a set of arguments.
(a) Rewrite `(let ((x 2) (y 3)) E)` as a lambda application.
(b) Can a `letrec` be given a similar interpretation?
(c) Why is the following `let` binding not legal (assuming a is not in the environment of the `let`):

   `(let ((a 2) (b (+ 1 a))) ...)`

(d) How could the `let` expression of (c) be made legal, using a similar interpretation to that of (a)?

11.23 (a) Give an algebraic specification for the ADT `List` with the following operations, and with properties as in Scheme: `car`, `cdr`, `cons`, `null?`, `makenull`.
(b) Write a C++ or Java class, or an Ada package to implement the ADT of (a).
(c) Use your implementation of the `List` ADT in (b) to write a "tiny Scheme" interpreter, that is, an interpreter that has only the ADT list functions as available operations and only has numbers as atoms.

11.24 In Section 11.3.4 we defined the `make-double` higher-order function in Scheme. What functions are returned by `(make-double - )` and `(make-double / )`?

11.25 The Scheme `make-new-balance` function defined in Section 11.3.4 used a local variable and assignment (`set!`) to keep and reset the value of the account balance, thus violating functional programming principles. Rewrite the definition of `make-new-balance` to eliminate the nonfunctional features. Discuss the effect this has on protection.

11.26 (a) Give an example to show that Scheme does not Curry its functions.

(b) Write a Scheme higher-order function that takes a function of two parameters as its parameter and returns a Curried version of the function.

11.27 List the ML types for all the functions in Exercise 11.8.

11.28 Write an ML function that determines the length of any list. Show how an ML system can determine the type of the length function using pattern matching.

11.29 List the Haskell types for all the functions in Exercise 11.8.

11.30 Write Haskell list comprehensions for the following lists: **(a)** all integers that are squares, **(b)** all Pythagorean triples (see Exercise 11.8), and **(c)** all perfect numbers (a perfect number is the sum of all of its proper factors).

11.31 **(a)** Write functions to test whether ML and Scheme use short-circuit evaluation for Boolean expressions.
  (b) Why do we not need to test Haskell to answer this question for that language?

11.32 When a function is defined using pattern matching in ML, the text mentions that an ML system may complain if cases are left out of the definition. Such missing cases imply the function is partial. Discuss the advantages and disadvantages of requiring all functions to be total in a programming language.

11.33 The `fact` function defined in this chapter for ML and Scheme is in fact partial, yet an ML translator will not discover this. Why?

11.34 ML and Haskell do not have general list structures like Scheme, but require the elements in a list to have all the same data type. Why is this? What data structure in an imperative language do such lists imitate?

11.35 Write a Scheme program to show that the Scheme procedures `force` and `delay` actually use pass by need memoization.

11.36 **(a)** Write a sieve of Eratosthenes in Scheme or ML using generators and filters, similar to the Haskell version in Section 11.6 (page 516).
  (b) Rewrite the Scheme version to use `force` and `delay`.

11.37 Rewrite the Scheme `intlist` function in Section 11.5 so that it takes only a lower bound as a parameter and produces a stream of integers from that point on: `(intlist 5) = (5 6 7 8 ...)`.

11.38 Haskell list comprehensions are actually compact expressions for generator-filter programs as noted in the text. For example, the list comprehension

```
evens = [ n | n <- [2..], mod n 2 == 0]
```

is equivalent to a generator procedure that produces the stream of integers beginning with 2 (represented by [2..]) and sends its output to the selector procedure of the predicate mod n 2 = 0 that passes on the list whose elements satisfy the predicate. Write a Scheme procedure that uses force and delay to produce the stream of even integers in a similar generator-filter style.

11.39 Rewrite the flatten Scheme procedure of Section 11.5 (page 511) to use force and delay.

11.40 (From Abelson and Sussman [1996]) Define a delayed version of the map procedure from Section 11.3.4 (page 491) as follows:

```
(define (delayed-map f L)
  (if (null? L) '()
      (cons (f (car (force L))) (delayed-map (cdr
      (force L))))))
```

Now define a show procedure that prints a value and returns the same value:

```
(define (show x) (display x) (newline) x)
```

Finally, define a delayed list as follows:

```
(define L (delay (delayed-map show (delay
  (intlist 1 100)))))
```

where intlist is the delayed version from Section 11.5 (page 510). What will the Scheme interpreter print when given the following expressions to evaluate in the order given (take is also the delayed version in Section 11.5):

```
> (take 5 L)
... some output here
> (take 7 L)
... some more output here
```

(*Hint*: The answer depends on whether Scheme uses pass by need or not; see Exercise 11.35.)

11.41 Show that the fact function as computed in Section 11.7 is the smallest solution to the set equation fact = $\{(0, 1)\} \cup$ fact'.

11.42 (a) Write out the definition of the higher-order function H as described in Section 11.7 for the recursive definition of the gcd function.

(b) Give a mathematical description of the sets gcd_0, gcd_1, and gcd_2 in the least-fixed-point construction as described in Section 11.7.

11.43 Write lambda calculus expressions for the higher-order functions twice and inc_n. (See Exercise 11.8.)

11.44 Assume square = $(\lambda x. * x x)$ in lambda calculus. Show the steps in an applicative order and normal order reduction of the expression (twice (twice square)). (See the previous exercise.)

11.45 Give applicative and normal order reductions for the following lambda expressions. State which steps use which conversions and which variables are bound and which are free.

(a) $(\lambda x. ((\lambda y.(* \ 2 \ y)) \ (+ \ x \ y))) \ y$

(b) $(\lambda x. \ \lambda y. \ (x \ y)) \ (\lambda z. \ (z \ y))$

11.46 It is a surprising fact in lambda calculus that lists can be expressed as lambda abstractions. Indeed, the list constructor cons can be written as $(\lambda x. \ \lambda y. \ \lambda f. \ f \ x \ y)$. With this definition one can write car as $(\lambda z. \ z \ (\lambda x. \ \lambda y. \ x))$ and cdr as $(\lambda z. \ z \ (\lambda x. \ \lambda y. \ y))$. Show that using these definitions the usual formulas (car (cons $a \ b$)) = a and (cdr (cons $a \ b$)) = b are true.

11.47 (From Abelson and Sussman [1996]) It is also possible to express the integers as lambda abstractions:

$$zero = \lambda f.\lambda x.x$$
$$one = \lambda f.\lambda x.(f \ x)$$
$$two = \lambda f.\lambda x.(f \ (f \ x))$$

$$\cdots$$

These are called Church numbers, after Alonzo Church.

(a) Given the following definition of the successor function:

$$successor = \lambda n.\lambda f.\lambda x.(f \ ((n \ f) \ x))$$

show that (successor zero) = one and (successor one) = two.

(b) Generalize (a) to any Church number.

(c) Define addition and multiplication for Church numbers.

(d) Write out an implementation of your lambda expressions in (c) as procedures in a functional language, and write an output procedure that shows they are correct.

11.48 Use the lambda expression $H = (\lambda F.\lambda n. \ (if \ (= \ n \ 0) \ 1 \ (* \ n \ (F \ (- \ n \ 1)))))$ and the property that the fact function is a fixed point of H to show that $fact \ 1 = 1$.

11.49 We noted that the fixed-point combinator Y can itself be written as the lambda abstraction $(\lambda h. \ (\lambda x. \ h \ (x \ x)) \ (\lambda x. \ h \ (x \ x)))$. Show that this expression for Y does indeed give it the property that $Y \ H = H \ (Y \ H)$, for any H.

11.50 Consider writing the fixed-point combinator in Scheme, ML, or Haskell by using the fixed-point property $y \ h = h \ (y \ h)$ as the definition.

(a) What is the type of y in ML or Haskell?

(b) Using the definition of h for the factorial function:

$$h \ g \ n = if \ n = 0 \ then \ 1 \ else \ n * g(n - 1)$$

does $y \ h$ actually produce the correct factorial function in Scheme, ML, or Haskell? Explain.

Notes and References

There are many books on functional programming. We list only a few here that are directly related to the languages and issues discussed in the chapter. For an overview of functional programming languages, including historical perspectives, from a somewhat different viewpoint from this chapter, see Hudak [1989]. Reade [1989] is a comprehensive text on functional programming, with many examples from ML. Abelson and Sussman [1996] is also a good reference for much of this chapter, as well as for the Scheme language (Section 11.3). The bank balance example in Section 11.3.4 is adapted from that book, as are a couple of the exercises. Friedman et al. [1996] is an advanced reference for Scheme. The (current) definition of Scheme is published in Abelson et al. [1998]. The ANSI and IEEE standards for Scheme (which are now somewhat out of date) are given in IEEE P1178 [1991].

Functional programming with the ML language (Section 11.4) is treated in Paulson [1996] and Ullman [1998]. Milner et al. [1997] gives the definition of Standard ML97, and Milner and Tofte [1991] provides a description of some of the theoretical issues surrounding the design of ML; see also Mitchell and Harper [1988].

The Haskell language (Section 11.6) is presented in Hudak [2000], Thompson [1999], and Bird et al. [1998]. The influential predecessor language Miranda is described in Turner [1986], with underlying ideas presented in Turner [1992].

General techniques for functional programming are studied in Okasaki [1999] and Lapalme and Rabhi [1999]. Implementation techniques for functional languages are studied in Peyton Jones [1987] and Appel [1992].

Delayed evaluation is studied in Henderson [1980]; parts of Section 11.5 are adapted from that reference.

Interest in functional programming increased dramatically following the ACM Turing Award lecture of Backus [1978], in which he describes a general framework for functional programming, called FP. A significant modern version of LISP not discussed in this chapter is Common LISP, which is described in Steele [1982] and defined in Steele [1984]. The ANSI Standard for Common Lisp is ANSI X3.226 [1994].

The explanation of least-fixed-point semantics of recursive functions in Section 11.7 was inspired by Meyer [1990]. The lambda calculus (Section 11.8) began with Church [1941] and is studied in Curry and Feys [1958], Barendregt [1982], and Hankin [1995]. Overviews of lambda calculus are presented in Peyton Jones [1987], where the use of normal forms in compiling Miranda is discussed; parts of the presentation in Section 11.8 are patterned after that text. Gunter [1992] and Sethi [1995] also survey the lambda calculus and study a statically typed version called the typed lambda calculus. Paulson [1996] describes an interpreter for lambda calculus. A history of the lambda calculus and the Church-Rosser theorem is given in Rosser [1982]. Currying is apparently originally due not to Curry but to Schönfinkel [1924].

Traditionally, functional programming has been thought to be highly inefficient because of its reliance on function call and dynamic memory management. Advances in algorithms, such as generational garbage collection, and advances in translation techniques make this less true. Some references dealing with these issues are Steele [1977] and Gabriel [1985]. Using recursive calls to do functional programming in an imperative language is also less expensive than one might imagine, and the techniques in Section 11.1 are usable in practice. An example of this is discussed in Louden [1987].

Logic as the science of reasoning and proof has existed since the time of the philosophers of ancient Greece. Mathematical or symbolic logic as the theory of mathematical proofs began with the work of George Boole and Augustus De Morgan in the middle of the 1800s. Since then logic has become a major mathematical discipline, and has played a significant role in the mathematics of the twentieth century, particularly with respect to the famous incompleteness theorems of Kurt Gödel. (See the Notes and References.)

Logic is closely associated with computers and programming languages in a number of ways. First, computer circuits are designed with the help of Boolean algebra (named after George Boole), and Boolean expressions and data are almost universally used in programming languages to control the actions of a program. (See Chapters 5 and 7.)

Logical statements have also been used to describe the semantics of programming language constructs: such semantics are called **axiomatic semantics** and are studied in Chapter 13. Logical statements can also be used as formal specifications for the required behavior of programs, and together with the axiomatic semantics of the language they can be used to prove the correctness of a program in a purely mathematical way.

In a different direction, computers have been used as tools to implement the principles of mathematical logic, and programs have been written that will construct proofs of mathematical theorems using the principles of logic. Such **automatic deduction systems** or **automatic theorem provers** turn proofs into computation. Experience with such programs in the 1960s and 1970s led to the major realization that the reverse is also true: Computation can be viewed as a kind of proof. Thus, logical statements, or at least a restricted form of them, can be viewed as a programming language and executed on a computer, given a sophisticated enough interpretive system. This work, primarily by Robinson, Colmerauer, and Kowalski (see the Notes and References), led to the programming language **Prolog**. The development of efficient Prolog interpreters in the late 1970s, particularly at the University of Edinburgh, Scotland, resulted in a tremendous increase in interest in logic programming systems.

Then, in 1981, Prolog achieved almost instant fame when the Japanese government announced that it would serve as the base language for the Fifth Generation Project, whose goal was the development of advanced computer systems incorporating reasoning techniques and human language understanding. The project ended somewhat inconclusively in 1992, and the use of Prolog has since then declined, except in the area of natural language understanding and expert systems. Nevertheless, a significant amount of research and development of logic programming systems had occurred as a result (see the Notes and References).

Prolog remains today the most significant example of a logic programming language, although a number of extensions have also become popular, especially the so-called constraint logic programming languages. Attempts have also been made to design even more powerful systems incorporating logic-like techniques. Among these are equational systems that use equations instead of logic to describe computation.

In the following sections we will first give a brief introduction to mathematical logic and the way logic can be used as a programming language. Next we turn our attention to a description of Prolog and the techniques of writing Prolog programs. We also give a brief description of the principles behind the operation of a Prolog system, and some of the weaknesses of these systems. Finally, we describe some of the additional work on equational and constraint logic systems.

12.1 Logic and Logic Programs

To describe what is meant by logic programming, we need to know a little bit about mathematical logic. The kind of logic used in logic programming is the **first-order predicate calculus**, which is a way of formally expressing **logical statements**, that is, statements that are either true or false.

EXAMPLE 1

The following English statements are logical statements:
  0 is a natural number.
  2 is a natural number.
  For all x, if x is a natural number, then so is the successor of x.
  -1 is a natural number.
A translation into predicate calculus is as follows:

>   natural(0).
>
>   natural(2).
>
>   For all x, natural(x) $\rightarrow$ natural (successor (x)).
>
>   natural(-1).   ∎

  Among these logical statements, the first and third statement can be viewed as **axioms** for the natural numbers: statements that are assumed to be true and from which all true statements about natural numbers can be **proved**. Indeed, the second statement can be proved from these axioms, since $2 =$ successor(successor(0)) and natural(0) $\rightarrow$ natural (successor(0)) $\rightarrow$ natural (successor(successor (0))). The fourth statement, on the other hand, cannot be proved from the axioms and so can be assumed to be false.
  First-order predicate calculus classifies the different parts of such statements as follows:

1. *Constants.* These are usually numbers or names. Sometimes they are called atoms, since they cannot be broken down into subparts. In Example 1, 0 is a constant.

2. *Predicates.* These are names for functions that are true or false, like Boolean functions in a program. Predicates can take a number of arguments. In Example 1, the predicate natural takes one argument.

3. *Functions.* First-order predicate calculus distinguishes between functions that are true or false—these are the predicates—and all other functions, like successor in Example 1, which represent non-Boolean values.

4. *Variables that stand for as yet unspecified quantities.* In Example 1, x is a variable.

5. *Connectives.* These include the operations and, or, and not, just like the operations on Boolean data in programming languages. Additional connectives in predicate calculus are implication "$\rightarrow$" and equivalence

"↔." These are not really new operations: $a \rightarrow b$ means that b is true whenever a is, and this is equivalent to the statement b or not a; see Exercise 12.1. Also $a \leftrightarrow b$ means the same as $(a \rightarrow b)$ and $(b \rightarrow a)$.

6. *Quantifiers.* These are operations that introduce variables. In Example 1, "for all" is the quantifier for x; it is called the **universal quantifier**. There is also the **existential quantifier** "there exists" as in the following statement:

there exists x, natural(x).

This statement means that there exists an x such that x is a natural number. A variable introduced by a quantifier is said to be **bound** by the quantifier. It is possible for variables also to be **free**, that is, not bound by any quantifier.

7. *Punctuation symbols.* These include left and right parentheses, the comma, and the period. (Strictly speaking, the period isn't necessary, but we include it since most logic programming systems use it.) Parentheses are used to enclose arguments and also to group operations. Parentheses can be left out based on common conventions about the precedence of connectives, which are usually assumed to be the same as in most programming languages. (Thus, the connectives in order of decreasing precedence are not, and, or, →, and ↔.)

In predicate calculus, arguments to predicates and functions can only be **terms**, that is, combinations of variables, constants, and functions. Terms cannot contain predicates, quantifiers, or connectives. In Example 1, terms that appear include constants 0, −1, 2, the variable x, and the term successor(x) consisting of the function successor with argument x. Some examples of additional terms that can be written are successor(0) and successor(successor(successor(x))).

EXAMPLE 2

The following are logical statements in English:

A horse is a mammal.

A human is a mammal.

Mammals have four legs and no arms, or two legs and two arms.

A horse has no arms.

A human has arms.

A human has no legs.

A possible translation of these statements into first-order predicate calculus is as follows:

mammal(horse).

mammal(human).

for all x, mammal(x) →

      legs(x,4) and arms(x,0) or legs(x,2) and arms(x,2).

arms(horse,0).

not arms(human,0).

legs(human,0).

∎

In this example, the constants are the integers 0, 2, and 4 and the names horse and human. The predicates are mammal, arms, and legs. The only variable is x, and there are no functions.

As in the previous example, we might consider the first five statements to be axioms—statements defining true relationships. Then, as we shall see shortly, arms(human,2) becomes provable from the axioms. It is also possible to prove that legs(human,2) is true, so the last statement is false, given the axioms.

Note that we have used precedence to leave out many parentheses in the preceding statements, so that, for example, when we write

$$\text{legs}(x,4) \text{ and } \text{arms}(x,0) \text{ or } \text{legs}(x,2) \text{ and } \text{arms}(x,2)$$

we mean the following:

$$(\text{legs}(x,4) \text{ and } \text{arms}(x,0)) \text{ or } (\text{legs}(x,2) \text{ and } \text{arms}(x,2)).$$

In addition to the seven classes of symbols described, first-order predicate calculus has **inference rules**: ways of deriving or proving new statements from a given set of statements.

EXAMPLE 3

A typical inference rule is the following:
From the statements $a \rightarrow b$ and $b \rightarrow c$, one can derive the statement $a \rightarrow c$, or written more formally,

$$\frac{(a \rightarrow b) \text{ and } (b \rightarrow c)}{a \rightarrow c}$$ ∎

Inference rules allow us to construct the set of all statements that can be derived, or proved, from a given set of statements: These are statements that are always true whenever the original statements are true. For example, the first five statements about mammals in Example 2 allow us to derive the following statements:

> legs(horse,4).
>
> arms(horse,0).
>
> legs(human,2).
>
> arms (human, 2).

Stated in the language of logic, if we take the first five statements of Example 2 to be axioms, then the preceding four statements become **theorems**. Notice that proving these statements from the given statements can be viewed as the computation of the number of arms and legs of a horse or a human. Thus, the set of statements in Example 2 can be viewed as representing the potential computation of all logical consequences of these statements.

This is the essence of logic programming: A collection of statements are assumed to be axioms, and from them a desired fact is derived by the application of inference rules in some automated way. Thus, we can state the following definition:

> **Definition:** A *logic programming language* is a notational system for writing logical statements together with specified algorithms for implementing inference rules.

The set of logical statements that are taken to be axioms can be viewed as the **logic program**, and the statement or statements that are to be derived can be viewed as the "input" that initiates the computation. Such inputs are also provided by the programmer and are called **queries** or **goals**. For example, given the set of axioms of Example 2, if we wanted to know how many legs a human has, we would provide the following query,

Does there exist a y such that y is the number of legs of a human?
or, in predicate calculus,

there exists y, legs(human,y)?
and the system would respond with something like

yes: $y = 2$

For this reason, logic programming systems are sometimes referred to as **deductive databases**, databases consisting of a set of statements and a deduction system that can respond to queries. Notice that these are different from ordinary databases, since they contain not only facts like mammal(human) or natural(0), but also more complex statements like natural(x) → natural (successor(x)), and the system can answer not only queries about facts but also queries involving such implications.

In a pure logic programming system, nothing is said about how a particular statement might be derived from a given set of statements. The specific path or sequence of steps that an automatic deduction system chooses to derive a statement is the **control problem** for a logic programming system. The original statements represent the logic of the computation, while the deductive system provides the control by which a new statement is derived. This property of logic programming systems led Kowalski to state the logic programming paradigm as the pseudoequation

$$\text{algorithm} = \text{logic} + \text{control}$$

as a contrast to Niklaus Wirth's expression of imperative programming as

$$\text{algorithms} + \text{data structures} = \text{programs}$$

(See the Notes and References.) Kowalski's principle points out a further feature of logic programming: Since logic programs do not express the control, operations (in theory at least) can be carried out in any order or simultaneously. Thus logic programming languages are natural candidates for parallelism.

Unfortunately, automated deduction systems have difficulty handling all of first-order predicate calculus. First, there are too many ways of expressing the same statements, and second, there are too many inference rules. As a result, most logic programming systems restrict themselves to a particular subset of predicate calculus, called Horn clauses, that we will briefly study.

12.2 Horn Clauses

A **Horn clause** (named after their inventor Alfred Horn) is a statement of the form

$$a_1 \text{ and } a_2 \text{ and } a_3 \ldots \text{ and } a_n \to b$$

where the a_1 are only allowed to be simple statements involving no connectives. Thus, there are no "or" connectives and no quantifiers in Horn clauses. The Horn clause here says that a_1 through a_n imply b or that b is true if all the a_i are true. b is called the **head** of the clause, and the $a_1 \ldots$, a_n the **body** of the clause. In the Horn clause, the number of a_i's may be 0, in which case the Horn clause has the form

$$\to b$$

Such a clause means that b is always true, that is, b is an axiom and is usually written without the connective $\to$. Such clauses are sometimes also called **facts**.

Horn clauses can be used to express most, but not all, logical statements. Indeed, there is an algorithm that can perform a reasonable translation from predicate calculus statements to Horn clauses, but it is beyond the scope of this book to describe. (See the Notes and References.) The basic idea is to remove "or" connectives by writing separate clauses and to treat the lack of quantifiers by assuming that variables appearing in the head of a clause are universally quantified, while variables appearing in the body of a clause (but not in the head) are existentially quantified.

EXAMPLE 4

The following statements from Example 1 are written in first-order predicate calculus:

> natural(0).
> for all x, natural(x) $\to$ natural (successor (x)).

These can be very simply translated into Horn clauses by dropping the quantifier:

> natural(0).
> natural(x) $\to$ natural (successor(x)).   ∎

EXAMPLE 5

Consider the logical description for the Euclidian algorithm to compute the greatest common divisor of two positive integers u and v:

The gcd of u and 0 is u.

The gcd of u and v, if v is not 0, is the same as the gcd of v and the remainder of dividing v into u.

Translating this into first-order predicate calculus gives

> for all u, gcd($u,0,u$).
>
> for all u, for all v, for all w,
> not zero(v) and gcd(v,u mod v,w) $\rightarrow$ gcd(u,v,w).

(Remember that gcd(u,v,w) is a predicate expressing that w is the gcd of u and v.)

To translate these statements into Horn clauses, we need again only drop the quantifiers:

> gcd($u,0,u$).
>
> not zero(v) and gcd(v,u mod v, w) $\rightarrow$ gcd(u,v,w). ∎

EXAMPLE 6

The foregoing examples contain only universally quantified variables. To see how an existentially quantified variable in the body may also be handled, consider the following statement:

> x is a grandparent of y if x is the parent of someone who is the parent of y.

Translating this into predicate calculus, we get

> for all x, for all y, (there exists z, parent(x,z) and parent(z,y)) $\rightarrow$ grandparent (x,y).

As a Horn clause this is expressed simply as

> parent(x,z) and parent(z,y) $\rightarrow$ grandparent(x,y). ∎

EXAMPLE 7

To see how connectives are handled, consider the following statement:

> For all x, if x is a mammal then x has two or four legs.

Translating in predicate calculus, we get

> for all x, mammal(x) $\rightarrow$ legs($x,2$) or legs($x,4$).

This may be approximated by the following Horn clauses:

> mammal(x) and not legs($x,2$) $\rightarrow$ legs($x,4$).
>
> mammal(x) and not legs($x,4$) $\rightarrow$ legs($x,2$). ∎

In general, the more connectives that appear to the right of a "$\rightarrow$" connective in a statement, the harder it is to translate into a set of Horn clauses; see Exercise 12.8.

Horn clauses are of particular interest to automatic deduction systems such as logic programming systems, because they can be given a **procedural interpretation**. If we write a Horn clause in reverse order

$$b \leftarrow a_1 \text{ and } a_2 \text{ and } a_3 \ldots \text{ and } a_n$$

we can view this as a definition of procedure b: the body of b is given by the body of the clause, namely, the operations indicated by the a_i's. This is very similar to the way context-free grammar rules were interpreted as procedure definitions in recursive descent parsing in Chapter 4. There is more than a passing similarity here, since logic programs can be used to directly construct parsers. (See the Notes and References.) In fact, the parsing of natural language was one of the motivations for the original development of Prolog. The major difference between parsing and logic programming is that in pure logic programming, the order in which the a_i are called is not specified.

Nevertheless, most logic programming systems are deterministic in that they perform the calls in a certain prespecified order, usually left to right, which is exactly the order indicated by context-free grammar rules. The particular kind of grammar rules used in Prolog programs are called **definite clause grammars**.

Horn clauses can also be viewed as **specifications** of procedures rather than strictly as implementations. For example, we could view the following Horn clause as a specification of a sort procedure:

$$\text{sort}(x,y) \leftarrow \text{permutation}(x,y) \text{ and sorted}(y).$$

This says that (assuming that x and y are lists of things) a sort procedure transforms list x into a sorted list y such that y is a permutation of x. To complete the specification, we must of course supply specifications for what it means for a list to be sorted and for a list to be a permutation of another list. The important point is that we may think of the Horn clause as not necessarily supplying the algorithm by which y is found, given an x, but only the properties such a y must have.

With the foregoing procedural interpretation in mind, most logic programming systems not only write Horn clauses "backward," but also drop the "and" connectives between the a_i and just separate them with commas. Thus, the greatest common divisor clauses in Example 5 would appear as follows:

$$\text{gcd}(u,0,u).$$
$$\text{gcd}(u,v,w) \leftarrow \text{not zero}(v), \text{gcd}(v,u \bmod v,w).$$

This is beginning to look suspiciously like a more standard programming language expression for the gcd, such as

$$\text{gcd}(u,v) = \text{if } v = 0 \text{ then } u \text{ else gcd}(v,u \bmod v).$$

From now on we will write Horn clauses in this form.

There is the question of the scope of the variables in a procedural interpretation of Horn clauses. As with procedure definitions in a block-structured language, the assumption is that all variables are local to each "call" of the procedure. Indeed, variables used in the head can be viewed as "parameters," while variables used only in the body can be viewed as "local temporaries." This is only an approximate description, as the algorithms used to implement the "execution" of Horn clauses treat variables in a more general way, as we will see in Section 12.3.

We haven't yet seen how queries or goal statements can be expressed as Horn clauses. In fact, a query is exactly the "opposite" of a fact—a Horn clause with no head:

$$\text{mammal(human)} \leftarrow. \qquad \text{— a fact}$$
$$\leftarrow \text{mammal(human)}. \qquad \text{— a query or goal}$$

A Horn clause without a head could also include a sequence of queries separated by commas:

$$\leftarrow \text{mammal}(x), \text{legs}(x,y).$$

Why queries correspond to Horn clauses without heads should become clear when we understand the inference rule that logic programming systems apply to derive new statements from a set of given statements, namely, the resolution rule or principle studied next.

12.3 Resolution and Unification

Resolution is an inference rule for Horn clauses that is especially efficient. Resolution says that if we have two Horn clauses, and we can match the head of the first Horn clause with one of the statements in the body of the second clause, then the first clause can be used to replace its head in the second clause by its body. In symbols, if we have Horn clauses

$$a \leftarrow a_1, \ldots, a_n.$$
$$b \leftarrow b_1, \ldots, b_m.$$

and b_i matches a, then we can infer the clause

$$b \leftarrow b_1, \ldots, b_{i-1}, a_1, \ldots, a_n, b_{i+1}, \ldots, b_m.$$

The simplest example of this is when there are only single statements in the body of the Horn clauses, such as in

$$b \leftarrow a.$$

and

$$c \leftarrow b.$$

Then resolution says that we may infer the following clause:

$$c \leftarrow a.$$

This is precisely the inference rule that we gave in Example 3 in Section 12.1.

Another way of looking at resolution is to combine left-hand and right-hand sides of both Horn clauses and then cancel those statements that match on both sides. Thus, for the simplest example,

$$b \leftarrow a.$$

and

$$c \leftarrow b.$$

give

$$b, c \leftarrow a, b.$$

and canceling the b,

$$\cancel{b}, c \leftarrow a, \cancel{b}$$

gives

$$c \leftarrow a.$$

Now we can see how a logic programming system can treat a goal or list of goals as a Horn clause without a head. The system attempts to apply resolution by matching one of the goals in the body of the headless clause with the head of a known clause. It then replaces the matched goal with the body of that clause, creating a new list of goals, which it continues to modify in the same way. The new goals are called **subgoals**. In symbols, if we have the goal

$$\leftarrow a.$$

and the clause $a \leftarrow a_1, \ldots, a_n$, then resolution replaces the original goal a by the subgoals

$$\leftarrow a_1, \ldots, a_n.$$

If the system succeeds eventually in eliminating all goals—thus deriving the empty Horn clause—then the original statement has been proved.

EXAMPLE 8

The simplest case is when the goal is already a known fact, such as

$$mammal(human).$$

and one asks whether a human is a mammal:

$$\leftarrow mammal(human).$$

Using resolution, the system combines the two Horn clauses into

$$mammal(human) \leftarrow mammal(human).$$

and then cancels both sides to obtain

$$\leftarrow.$$

Thus, the system has found that indeed a human is a mammal and would respond to the query with "Yes." ∎

EXAMPLE 9

A slightly more complicated example is the following. Given the rules

$$legs(x,2) \leftarrow mammal(x), arms(x,2).$$
$$legs(x,4) \leftarrow mammal(x), arms(x,0).$$
$$mammal(horse).$$
$$arms(horse,0).$$

if we supply the query

$$\leftarrow \text{legs(horse,4)}.$$

then applying resolution using the second rule, we get

$$\text{legs}(x,4) \leftarrow \text{mammal}(x), \text{arms}(x,0), \text{legs(horse,4)}.$$

Now, to cancel the statements involving the predicate legs from each side, we have to match the variable x to horse, so we replace x by horse everywhere in the statement:

$$\text{legs(horse,4)} \leftarrow \text{mammal(horse)}, \text{arms(horse,0)}, \text{legs(horse,4)}.$$

and cancel to get the subgoals

$$\leftarrow \text{mammal(horse)}, \text{arms(horse,0)}.$$

Now we apply resolution twice more using the facts mammal(horse) and arms(horse,0) and cancel:

$$\text{mammal(horse)} \leftarrow \text{mammal(horse)}, \text{arms(horse,0)}.$$
$$\leftarrow \text{arms(horse,0)}.$$
$$\text{arms(horse,0)} \leftarrow \text{arms(horse,0)}.$$
$$\leftarrow.$$

Since we have arrived at the empty statement, our original query is true.

■

Example 9 demonstrates an additional requirement when we apply resolution to derive goals: To match statements that contain variables, we must set the variables equal to terms so that the statements become identical and can be canceled from both sides. This process of pattern matching to make statements identical is called **unification**, and variables that are set equal to patterns are said to be **instantiated**. Thus, to implement resolution effectively, we must also provide an algorithm for unification. A very general unification algorithm does exist (it was already described briefly in Chapter 6 in relation to Hindley-Milner type infererence), but most logic programming systems use a slightly weaker algorithm that we discuss in Section 12.4.

EXAMPLE 10

To show in more detail the kind of unification that takes place in a logic programming language, consider the greatest common divisor problem (Euclid's algorithm, Example 5):

$$\text{gcd}(u,0,u).$$
$$\text{gcd}(u,v,w) \leftarrow \text{not zero}(v), \text{gcd}(v,u \bmod v,w).$$

Now given the goal

$$\leftarrow \text{gcd}(15,10,x).$$

resolution fails using the first clause (10 does not match 0), so using the second clause and unifying gcd(u,v,w) with gcd(15,10,x) gives

gcd(15,10,x) ← not zero(10), gcd(10,15 mod 10,x), gcd(15,10,x).

Assuming that the system knows that zero(10) is false, so that not zero(10) is true, and simplifying 15 mod 10 to 5, we cancel gcd (15,10,x) from both sides and obtain the subgoal

← gcd(10,5,x).

Note that this is just another goal to be resolved like the original goal. This we do by unification as before, obtaining

gcd(10,5,x) ← not zero(5), gcd(5,10 mod 5,x), gcd(10,5,x).

and so get the further subgoal

← gcd(5,0,x).

Now this matches the first rule

gcd(u,0,u).

so instantiating x to 5 results in the empty statement, and the system will reply with something like

Yes: $x = 5$

Resolution and unification have performed the computation of the greatest common divisor of 10 and 15 using Euclid's algorithm!   ■

There is one other problem that must be solved before a working resolution implementation can be achieved. To achieve efficient execution a logic programming system must apply a fixed algorithm that specifies (1) the order in which the system attempts to resolve a list of goals and (2) the order in which clauses are used to resolve goals. As an example of (1), consider the goal

← legs(horse,4).

In Example 9 this led to the two subgoals

← mammal(horse), arms(horse,0).

A logic programming system must now decide whether to try to resolve mammal(horse) first or arms(horse,0) first. In the example given, both choices lead to the same answer, but, as we shall see in the examples that follow, the order can have a significant effect on the answers found.

The order in which clauses are used can also have a major effect on the result of applying resolution. For example, given the Horn clauses

ancestor(x,y) ← parent(x,z), ancestor(z,y).
ancestor(x,x).
parent(amy,bob).

if we provide the query

$$\leftarrow \text{ancestor}(x, \text{bob}).$$

there are two possible answers: $x = \text{bob}$ and $x = \text{amy}$. If the assertion ancestor(x,x) is used, the solution $x = \text{bob}$ will be found. If the clause ancestor(x,y) $\leftarrow$ parent(x,z), ancestor(z,y) is used, the solution $x = \text{amy}$ will be found. Which one is found first, or even if any is found, can depend on the order in which the clauses are used, as well as the order in which goals are resolved.

Logic programming systems using Horn clauses and resolution with prespecified orders for (1) and (2) therefore violate the basic principle that such systems set out to achieve: that a programmer need worry only about the logic itself, while the control (the methods used to produce an answer) can be ignored. Instead, a programmer must always be aware of the way the system produces answers. It is possible to design systems that will always produce all the answers implied by the logic, but they are (so far) too inefficient to be used as programming systems.

12.4 The Language Prolog

Prolog is the most widely used logic programming language. Prolog uses Horn clauses and implements resolution using a strictly linear "depth-first" strategy and a unification algorithm described in more detail shortly. Although an ISO standard for Prolog now exists, for many years there was no standard, and implementations contained many variations in the details of their syntax, semantics, built-in functions, and libraries. This is still the case, but the most widely used implementation (so-called **Edinburgh Prolog** developed in the late 1970s and early 1980s at the University of Edinburgh) was somewhat of a de facto standard and indeed was used as the basis for the ISO standard. We use its notation for the clauses and goals in our examples below. We discuss the essential features of Prolog in the sections that follow.

12.4.1 Notation and Data Structures

Prolog uses almost the identical notation developed earlier for Horn clauses, except that the implication arrow "$\leftarrow$" is replaced by a colon followed by a dash (or minus sign), "`:-`". Thus the sample ancestor program from the previous section would be written in Prolog syntax as follows:

```
ancestor(X,Y) :- parent(X,Z), ancestor(Z,Y).
ancestor(X,X).
parent(amy,bob).
```

and Example 4 would be written as follows:

```
natural(0).
natural(successor(X)) :- natural(X).
```

Note that the variables X and Y are written in uppercase. Prolog distinguishes variables from constants and names of predicates and functions by using uppercase for variables and lowercase for constants and names. It is also possible in most Prolog systems to denote a variable by writing an underscore before the name, as in ancestor(_x,_x).

In addition to the comma connective that stands for "and," Prolog uses the semicolon ";" for "or." However, the semicolon is rarely used in programming, since it is not a standard part of Horn clause logic.

Basic data structures are terms like parent(X,Z) or successor(successor(0)). Prolog also includes lists as a basic data structure, which uses square brackets (like ML and Haskell): The list consisting of items x, y, and z is written as [x,y,z].

It is also possible to specify the head and tail of a list using a vertical bar: [H|T] means that H is the first item in the list and T is the tail of the list. Thus, if [H|T] = [1,2,3], then H = 1 and T = [2,3]. It is also possible to write as many terms as one wishes before the bar: [X,Y|Z] = [1,2,3] gives X = 1, Y = 2, and Z = [3]. The empty list is denoted by [] and does not have a first element.

Prolog has a number of standard predicates that are always built in, such as not, =, and the I/O operations read, write, and nl (for newline). One anomaly in Prolog is that the "less than or equal to" operator is usually written "=<" instead of "<=" (perhaps because the latter is too easily confused with implication).

12.4.2 Execution in Prolog

There exist compilers for Prolog, but most systems are run as interpreters. A Prolog program consists of a set of Horn clauses in Prolog syntax, which is usually entered from a file and stored in a dynamically maintained database of clauses. Once a set of clauses has been entered into the database, goals can be entered either from a file or from the keyboard to begin execution. Thus, once a Prolog system has begun to execute, it will provide the user with a prompt for a query, such as

    ?-_

Note that, while Prolog syntax is now standardized for clauses and queries, the responses from a Prolog interpreter (including the prompt as shown above) are *not* standardized; we give these responses in a plausible notation, but different ISO-compliant interpreters may behave slightly differently.

EXAMPLE 11

If the clauses

```
ancestor(X,Y) :- parent(X,Z), ancestor(Z,Y).
ancestor(X,X).
parent(amy,bob).
```

have been entered into the database, then the following queries would cause the indicated response:

```
?- ancestor(amy,bob).
yes.

?- ancestor(bob,amy).
no.

?- ancestor(X,bob).
X = amy ->_
```

In the last query there are two answers. Most Prolog systems will find one answer and then wait for a user prompt before printing more answers. If the user supplies a semicolon at the underscore (meaning "or"), then Prolog continues to find more answers:

```
?- ancestor(X,bob).
X = amy ->;
X = bob

?-_
```

A carriage return usually cancels the continued search.   ■

12.4.3 Arithmetic

Prolog has built-in arithmetic operations and an arithmetic evaluator. Arithmetic terms can be written either in the usual infix notation or as terms in prefix notation: 3 + 4 and +(3, 4) mean the same thing. However, Prolog cannot tell when to consider an arithmetic term as a term itself (that is, strictly as data), or when to evaluate it. Thus,

```
?- write(3+5).
3+5
```

To force the evaluation of an arithmetic term, a new operation is required: the is built-in predicate. Thus, to get Prolog to evaluate 3 + 5, we need to write

```
?- X is 3+5, write (X).
X=8
```

A further consequence of this is that two arithmetic terms may not be equal as terms even though they have the same value:[1]

```
?- 3+4 = 4+3.
no
```

To get equality of values we must force evaluation using is, for example, by writing the predicate

---

[1] We write a space between the 3 and the period in the following goal, since 3. could be interpreted as the floating-point number 3.0.

```
valequal(Term1, Term2) :-
        X is Term1, Y is Term2, X=Y.
```

We would then get

```
?- valequal(3+4, 4+3).
yes
```

Now we can see how to write Euclid's algorithm for the greatest common divisor from Example 10 in Prolog. We wrote this algorithm in generic Horn clauses as

$$gcd(u,0,u).$$
$$gcd(u,v,w) \leftarrow \text{not } zero(v), gcd(v,u \bmod v,w).$$

In Prolog this translates to

```
gcd(U,0,U).
gcd(U,V,W) :-
      not(V=0) , R is U mod V, gcd(V,R,W).
```

The middle statement R is U mod V is required to force evaluation of the mod operation.

12.4.4 Unification

Unification is the process by which variables are instantiated, or allocated memory and assigned values, so that patterns match during resolution. Unification is the process of making two terms "the same" in some sense. The basic expression whose semantics is determined by unification is equality: in Prolog the goal s = t attempts to unify the terms s and t. It succeeds if unification succeeds and fails otherwise. Thus, we can study unification in Prolog by experimenting with the effect of equality:

```
?- me = me.
yes

?- me = you.
no

?- me = X.
X = me

?- f(a,X) = f(Y,b).
X = b
Y = a

?- f(X) = g(X).
no

?- f(X) = f(a,b).
no
```

(continues)

(continued)

```
?- f(a,g(X)) = f(Y,b).
no

?- f(a,g(X)) = f(Y,g(b)).
X = b
Y = a
```

From these experiments we can formulate the following unification algorithm for Prolog:

1. A constant unifies only with itself: me = me succeeds but me = you fails.

2. A variable that is uninstantiated unifies with anything and becomes instantiated to that thing.

3. A structured term (i.e., a function applied to arguments) unifies with another term only if it has the same function name and the same number of arguments, and the arguments can be unified recursively. Thus, f(a,X) unifies with f(Y,b) by instantiating X to b and Y to a.

A variation on case 2 is when two uninstantiated variables are unified:

```
?- X = Y.
X = _23
Y = _23
```

The number printed on the right-hand side—in this case, 23—will differ from system to system and indicates an internal memory location set aside for that variable. Thus, unification causes uninstantiated variables to share memory, that is, become aliases of each other.

We can use unification in Prolog to get very short expressions for many operations. As examples, let us develop Prolog programs for the list operations **append** and **reverse**. We note again that because Prolog allows a list to be represented by a term such as [X|Y], where X and Y are variables, there is no need for a built-in function to return the head of a list or the tail of a list: just setting [X|Y] = [1,2,3] with uninstantiated variables X and Y returns the head as X and the tail as Y by unification. Similarly, there is no need for a list constructor like the cons operation of LISP: if we want to add 0, say, to the list [1, 2, 3], we simply write [0 | [1,2,3]], as for example,

```
?- X = [0|[1,2,3]].
X = [0,1,2,3]
```

However, we could, if we wanted, write the following clause

```
cons(X,Y,L) :- L = [X|Y].
```

and then use it to compute heads, tails, and constructed lists, depending on how we instantiate the variables on the left-hand side:

```
?- cons (0,[1,2,3],A).
A = [0,1,2,3]

?- cons (X,Y,[1,2,3]).
X = 1
Y = [2,3]
```

Thus, we can use variables in a term as either input or output parameters, and Prolog clauses can be "run" backward as well as forward—something the procedural interpretation of Horn clauses did not tell us!

Indeed, unification can be used to shorten clauses such as cons further. Since the " = " operator is there only to force unification, one can let resolution cause the unification automatically by writing the patterns to be unified directly in the parameters of the head. Thus, the following definition of cons has precisely the same meaning as the previous definition:

```
cons(X,Y,[X|Y]).
```

The appearance of the pattern [X|Y] in place of the third variable automatically unifies it with a variable used in that place in a goal. This process could be referred to as **pattern-directed invocation**. The functional languages ML and Haskell studied in Chapter 11 have a similar mechanism, and both the runtime systems and the type checkers of these two languages use forms of unification similar to Prolog's (for unification in type checking, see Section 6.8).

Now let's write an append procedure:

```
append(X,Y,Z) :- X = [], Y = Z.
append(X,Y,Z) :-
            X = [A|B], Z = [A|W], append(B,Y,W).
```

The first clause states that appending any list to the empty list just gives that list. The second clause states that appending a list whose head is A and tail is B to a list Y gives a list whose head is also A and whose tail is B with Y appended.

Rewriting this using pattern-directed invocation, we get the following extremely concise form:

```
append([],Y,Y).
append([A|B], Y, [A|W]) :- append(B,Y,W).
```

This append can also be "run" backward and can even find all the ways to append two lists together to get a specified list:

```
?- append(X,Y,[1,2]).
X = []
Y = [1,2] ->;

X = [1]
Y = [2] ->;

X = [1,2]
Y = []
```

Prolog does this by first using the first clause and matching X to the empty list [] and Y to the final list. Then it continues the search for solutions by using the second clause, matching X to [A|B] and setting up the subgoal append(B,Y,W) with W = [2] .This begins the search over again with B in place of X, so B is first matched with [] and Y with [2], giving X = [1|[]] = [1]. Then B is matched with a new [A|B] by the second clause, and so on.

Finally in this section, we give a Prolog definition for the reverse of a list:

```
reverse([],[]).
reverse([H|T],L) :- reverse(T,L1),
                    append(L1,[H],L).
```

Figure 12.1 collects the three principal Prolog examples of this section, for ease of reference.

```
gcd(U,0,U).
gcd(U,V,W) :- not(V=0) , R is U mod V, gcd(V,R,W).

append([],Y,Y).
append([A|B], Y, [A|W]) :- append(B,Y,W).

reverse([],[]).
reverse([H|T],L) :- reverse(T,L1),
                    append(L1,[H],L).
```

Figure 12.1   Prolog clauses for gcd, append, and reverse

12.4.5 Prolog's Search Strategy

Prolog applies resolution in a strictly linear fashion, replacing goals left to right and considering clauses in the database in top-to-bottom order. Subgoals are also considered immediately once they are set up. This search strategy can be viewed as a depth-first search on a tree of possible choices.

To see this, consider the following clauses:

(1) ancestor(X,Y) :- parent(X,Z), ancestor(Z,Y).
(2) ancestor(X,X).
(3) parent(amy,bob).

Given the goal ancestor(X,bob), Prolog's search strategy is left to right and depth first on the tree of subgoals shown in Figure 12.2. Edges in that figure are labeled by the number of the clause above used by Prolog for resolution, and instantiations of variables are written in curly brackets.

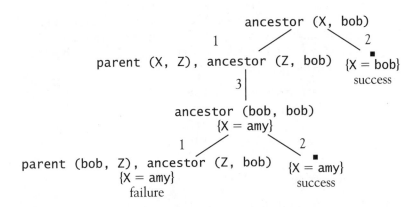

Figure 12.2   A Prolog search tree showing subgoals, clauses used for reso-
                 lution, and variable instantiations

Leaf nodes in this tree occur either when no match is found for the leftmost clause or when all clauses have been eliminated, thus indicating success. Whenever failure occurs, or the user indicates a continued search with a semicolon, Prolog **backtracks** up the tree to find further paths to a leaf, releasing instantiations of variables as it does so. Thus, in the tree shown, after the solution X = amy is found, if backtracking is initiated this instantiation of X will be released, and the new path to a leaf with X = bob will be found.

This depth-first strategy is extremely efficient, since it can be implemented in a stack-based or recursive fashion using an approach similar to that of a stack of activation records as described in Chapter 8. However, it means also that solutions may not be found if the search tree has branches that have infinite depth. For example, suppose we had written the clauses in a slightly different order:

```
(1) ancestor(X,Y) :- ancestor(Z,Y), parent(X,Z).
(2) ancestor(X,X).
(3) parent(amy,bob).
```

Now Prolog will go into an infinite loop attempting to satisfy ances-tor(Z,Y), continually reusing the first clause. Of course, this is a result of the "left-recursive" way the first clause was written and the fact that no other clauses precede it, but in true logic programming, the order of the clauses should not matter. Indeed, a logic programming system that adopts breadth-first instead of depth-first search will always find solutions if there are any. Unfortunately, breadth-first search is far more expensive than depth-first search, so few logic programming systems use it. Prolog always uses depth-first search.

12.4.6   Loops and Control Structures

We can use the depth-first search with backtracking of Prolog to perform loops and repetitive searches. What we must do is force backtracking even when a solution is found. We do this with the built-in predicate `fail`. As an example, we can get Prolog to print all solutions to a goal such as append without needing to give semicolons to the system as follows. Define the predicate

```
printpieces(L) :-append(X,Y,L),
                   write(X),
                   write(Y),
                   nl,
                   fail.
```

Now we get the following behavior:

```
?- printpieces([1,2]).
[][1,2]
[1][2]
[1,2] []
no
```

Backtracking on failure forces Prolog to write all solutions at once.

We can also use this feature to get repetitive computations. For example, the following clauses generate all integers ≥ 0 as solutions to the goal num(X):

(1) num(0).
(2) num(X) :- num(Y), X is Y+1.

The search tree is displayed in Figure 12.3. In this tree, it has an infinite branch to the right. (The different uses of Y from clause (2) in the tree are indicated by adding quotes to the variable name.)

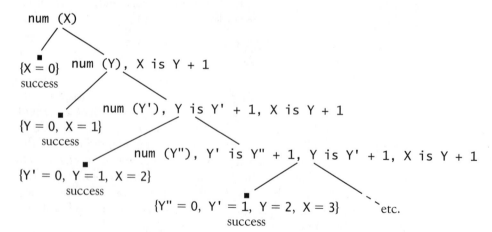

Figure 12.3 An infinite Prolog search tree showing repetitive computations

Now we could try to generate the integers from 1 to 10, say, by writing

```
writenum(1,J) :- num(X),
                 I =< X,
                 X =< J,
                 write(X),
                 nl,
                 fail.
```

and giving the goal writenum(1,10). Unfortunately, this will go into an infinite loop after X = 10, generating ever-larger integers X even though X =< 10 will never succeed.

What is needed is some way of stopping the search from continuing through the whole tree. Prolog has an operator to do this: the **cut**, usually written as an exclamation point. The cut "freezes" the choice made when it is encountered. If a cut is reached on backtracking, the search of the subtrees of the parent node of the node containing the cut stops, and the search continues with the "grandparent" node. In effect, the cut "prunes" the search tree of all other siblings to the right of the node containing the cut.

EXAMPLE 12

Consider the tree of Figure 12.2. If we rewrite the clauses using the cut as follows:

    (1) `ancestor(X,Y):- parent(X,Z), !, ancestor(Z,Y).`
    (2) `ancestor(X,X).`
    (3) `parent(amy,bob).`

then only the solution x = amy will be found, since the branch containing X = bob will be pruned from the search, as shown in Figure 12.4.

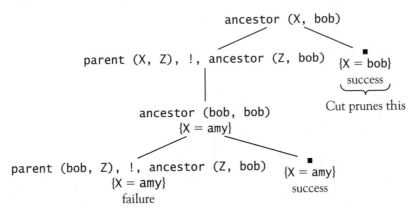

Figure 12.4 Consequences of the cut for the search tree of Figure 12.2

On the other hand, if we place the cut as follows,

    (1) `ancestor(X,Y) :- !, parent(X,Z), ancestor(Z,Y).`
    (2) `ancestor(X,X).`
    (3) `parent(amy,bob).`

then no solutions at all will be found, as shown in Figure 12.5.

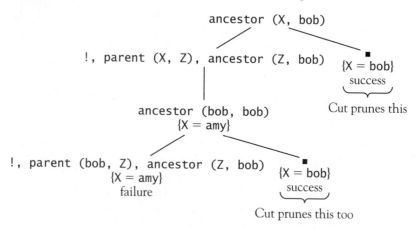

Figure 12.5 A further use of the cut prunes all solutions from Figure 12.2

Finally, if we place the cut as follows,

```
(1) ancestor(X,Y) : - parent(X,Z), ancestor(Z,Y).
(2) ancestor(X,X) : - !.
(3) parent(amy,bob).
```

both solutions will still be found, since the right subtree of ancestor(X,bob) is not pruned (in fact nothing at all is pruned in this example).   ∎

The cut can be used as an efficiency mechanism to reduce the number of branches in the search tree that need to be followed. The cut also allows us to solve the problem of the infinite loop in the program to print numbers between I and J. The following is one solution:

```
num(0).
num(X) : - num(Y), X is Y+1.
writenum(I,J) :- num(X),
                 I =< X,
                 X =< J,
                 write(X), nl,
                 X = J, !,
                 fail.
```

In this code, X = J will succeed when the upper bound J is reached, and then the cut will cause backtracking to fail, halting the search for new values of X.

The cut can also be used to imitate if-then-else constructs in imperative and functional languages. To write a clause such as

$$D = \text{if } A \text{ then } B \text{ else } C$$

we write the following Prolog:

```
D :- A, !, B.
D :- C.
```

Note that we could have achieved almost the same result without the cut,

```
D :- A, B.
D :- not(A), C.
```

but this is subtly different, since A is "executed" twice. Of course, if A has no side effects, then the two forms are equivalent. Nevertheless, the cut does improve the efficiency.

Finally, we give in Figure 12.6 a longer program that uses most of the features discussed so far. It is a program to compute primes using the sieve of Eratosthenes and is adapted from an example in Clocksin and Mellish [1994]).

```
primes(Limit, Ps) :- integers(2,Limit,Is),
                       sieve(Is,Ps).
integers(Low, High, [Low|Rest]) :-
           Low =< High, !, M is Low+1,
           integers(M,High,Rest).
integers(Low,High,[]).
sieve([],[]).
sieve([I|Is],[I|Ps]) :- remove(I,Is,New),
                          sieve(New,Ps).
remove(P,[],[]).
remove(P,[I|Is],[I|Nis]) :-
      not(0 is I mod P), !, remove(P,Is,Nis).
remove (P,[I|Is],Nis) :-
      0 is I mod P, !, remove(P,Is,Nis).
```

Figure 12.6   The Sieve of Eratosthenes in Prolog (adapted from Clocksin and Mellish [1994])

12.5 Problems with Logic Programming

The original goal of logic programming was to make programming into a specification activity—to allow the programmer to specify only the properties of a solution and to let the language system provide the actual method for computing the solution from its properties. Logic programming languages, and Prolog in particular, have only partially met this goal. Instead, the nature of the algorithms used by logic programming systems, such as resolution, unification, and depth-first search, have introduced many pitfalls into the specifics of writing programs, which a programmer must be aware of to write efficient, or even correct, programs. We have mentioned this occasionally, but we want now to collect some of these problems together, including a number of problems that have not yet been mentioned. The problems we will discuss are the "occur-check" problem in unification, problems with negation (the **not** operator), the limitations of Horn clauses in logic, and the need for control information in a logic program.

12.5.1   The Occur-Check Problem in Unification

The unification algorithm used by Prolog is actually incorrect: When unifying a variable with a term, Prolog does not check whether the variable itself occurs in the term it is being instantiated to. This is the "occur-check" problem. The simplest example is expressed by the following clause:

```
is_own_successor :- X = successor(X).
```

This will be true if there exists an X for which X is its own successor. However, even in the absence of any other clauses for successor, Prolog still answers "yes;" that is, any X will do! That this is incorrect becomes apparent only if we make Prolog try to print out such an X–, as with

```
is_own_successor(X) :- X = successor(X).
```

Now Prolog will respond with an infinite loop:

```
?- is_own_successor(X).
X = successor(successor(successor(successor(
    successor(successor(successor(successor(
    successor(successor(successor(successor(
    successor(successor(successor(successor(
    successor(successor(successor(successor(
    successor(successor(successor(successor(
    successor(successor(successor(successor(
    successor(successor(successor(successor ....
```

The reason is that unification has constructed X as a circular structure indicated by the following picture:

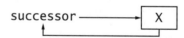

X is finite, but the attempt to print X is infinite. Thus, what should be logically false now becomes a programming error.

Why doesn't Prolog's unification contain a check for such occurrences? The answer is that unification without the occur-check can be relatively easily implemented in an efficient way, while efficient algorithms that include the occur-check are more complex. (For a discussion, see Lloyd [1984, p. 23].)

12.5.2   Negation as Failure

All logic programming systems have the basic property that something that cannot be proved to be true is assumed to be false. This is called the **closed-world assumption**. We saw an example of this already in Example 1, where we noted that, since natural(−1) cannot be proved from the axioms for the predicate "natural," it is assumed to be false. This property of logic programming, together with the way negation is implemented, results in further surprises in the behavior of logic programs.

How can one implement the not operator in logic programming? The straightforward answer is that the goal not(X) succeeds whenever the goal X fails. This is what is meant by "negation as failure." As a simple example, consider the following program consisting of one clause:

```
parent(amy,bob).
```

If we now ask,

```
?- not(mother(amy,bob)).
```

the answer is yes, since the system does not know that amy is female, and that female parents are mothers. If we were to add these facts to our program, not(mother(amy,bob)) would no longer be true.

The foregoing property of logic programs—that adding information to a system can reduce the number of things that can be proved—is called **nonmonotonic reasoning** and is a consequence of the closed-world assumption. Nonmonotonic reasoning has been the subject of considerable study in logic programming and artificial intelligence. (See the Notes and References.)

A related problem is that failure causes instantiations of variables to be released by backtracking, so that after failure, a variable may no longer have an appropriate value. Thus, for example, not(not(X)) does not have the same result as X itself (we assume the fact human(bob) in this example):

```
?- human(X).
X = bob

?- not(not(human(X))).
X = _23
```

The goal not(not(human(X))) succeeds because not(human(X)) fails, but when not(human(X)) fails, the instantiation of X to bob is released, causing X to be printed as an uninstantiated variable.

A similar situation is shown by the following:

```
?- X = 0, not(X = 1).
X = 0

?- not (X = 1), X = 0.
no
```

The second pair of goals fails because X is instantiated to 1 to make X = 1 succeed, and then not(X = 1) fails. The goal X = 0 is never reached.

12.5.3 Horn Clauses Do Not Express All of Logic

Not every logical statement can be turned into Horn clauses. In particular, statements involving quantifiers may not be expressible in Horn clause form. A simple example is the following:

$$p(a) \text{ and (there exists } x, \text{not}(p(x))).$$

We can certainly express the truth of $p(a)$ as a Horn clause, but the second statement cannot be written in Horn clause form. If we try to do so in Prolog, we might try something like:

```
p(a).
not(p(b)).
```

but the second statement will result in an error (trying to redefine the not operator). Perhaps the best approximation would be simply the statement p(a). Then the closed-world assumption will force not(p(X)) to be true for all X not equal to a, but this is really the logical equivalent of

$$p(a) \text{ and (for all } x, \text{not}(x = a) \rightarrow \text{not}(p(a))).$$

which is not the same as the original statement.

12.5.4 Control Information in Logic Programming

We have already talked about the cut as a useful, even essential, explicit control mechanism in Prolog. But because of its depth-first search strategy, and its linear processing of goals and statements, Prolog programs also contain implicit information on control that can easily cause programs to fail. One example is the ancestor program used earlier:

```
ancestor(X,Y) : - parent(X,Z), ancestor(Z,Y).
ancestor(X,X).
parent(amy,bob).
```

If we accidentally wrote the right-hand side of the first clause backward, as

```
ancestor(X,Y) :- ancestor(Z,Y), parent(X,Z).
```

we would immediately get into an infinite loop: Prolog will try to instantiate the variable Z to make ancestor true, causing an infinite descent in the search tree using the first clause. On the other hand, if we changed the order of the clauses to

```
ancestor(X,X).
ancestor(X,Y) :- ancestor(Z,Y), parent(X,Z).
parent(amy,bob).
```

the search will now find both solutions X = amy and X = bob to the query ancestor(amy, X), but will still go into an infinite loop searching for further (nonexistent) solutions. A similar situation exists if we write the clauses for the program to generate natural numbers in reverse order:

```
num(X) : - num (Y), X is Y + 1 .
num(0).
```

Now the goal num(X) will go into an infinite loop. Nothing at all will be generated.

A more complicated logical question is the representation of algorithmic logic using Horn clauses. We mentioned in Section 12.3 that a specification for a sorting procedure could be given as follows, for two lists S and T:

```
sort(S,T) :- permutation(S,T), sorted(T).
```

We can now give specifications for the meaning of permutation and sorted in Prolog syntax, in Figure 12.7.

```
sorted([]).
sorted([X]).
sorted([X,Y|Z]) :- X =< Y, sorted([Y|Z]).

permutation([],[]).
permutation(X,[Y|Z]) :- append(U,[Y|V],X),
                        append(U,V,W),
                        permutation(W,Z).
```

Figure 12.7   The definitions of the permutation and sorted properties in Prolog

This represents a mathematical definition for what it means for a list of numbers to be sorted in increasing order, but as a program, it represents almost the slowest sort in the world: Permutations of the unsorted list are generated until one of them happens to be sorted!

In the best of all possible worlds, one would want a logic programming system to accept the mathematical definition of a property and find an efficient algorithm to compute it. Of course, in Prolog or any other logic programming system, we not only provide specifications in our programs, we must also provide algorithmic control information. Thus, in the gcd program of Example 10, we specified explicitly the steps used by Euclid's algorithm instead of providing a mathematical definition of the greatest common divisor. Similarly, to get a reasonably efficient sorting program in Prolog, we must specify the actual steps an algorithm must take to produce the result. For example, a quicksort program in Prolog is given in Figure 12.8.

```
qsort([],[]).
qsort([H|T],S) :- partition(H,T,L,R),
                  qsort(L,L1),
                  qsort(R,R1),
                  append(L1,[H|R1],S),
partition(P, [A|X], [A|Y], Z) :- A < P,
                                 partition(P,X,Y,Z).
partition(P, [A|X], Y, [A|Z]) :- A >= P,
                                 partition(P,X,Y,Z).
partition(P,[],[],[]).
```

Figure 12.8   A quicksort program in Prolog (adapted from Clocksin and Mellish [1994])

In this program, the standard method of partitioning is shown by the clauses for the predicate partition, and the two recursive calls to qsort in the second clause are readily evident. Thus, in specifying sequential algorithms such as sorting, Prolog is not so different from imperative or functional programming as one might think.

There is, however, one useful aspect to being able to execute a specification for a property, even if it is not acceptable as an algorithm for computing that property: It lets us test whether the specification is correct. Prolog has in fact been used successfully as a basis for running such specifications during the design of a program. (See the Notes and References.)

12.6   Extending Logic Programming: Constraint Logic Programming and Equational Systems

12.6.1   Constraint Logic Programming

One of the chief failings of Prolog is its special treatment of arithmetic: Operations are not applied until forced by the "is" operation, and the use of this operation makes a program behave more like an imperative program than a logic program—for example, it can no longer be run backwards. Additionally, inequality tests such as X >= 0 require that all variables in the test be fully instantiated when the test is encountered or it will fail (the "is" operator also requires that all of the variables in its right-hand expression be fully instantiated).

A big improvement in the properties and behavior of programs involving such computation could be achieved if these instantiation requirements and the "is" operator were removed altogether. Indeed, there are a growing number of logic languages that do exactly that; such languages are generically called **constraint logic programming** languages, or **CLP** languages. The cost of this improvement lies in the extra complexity and reduced efficiency of the runtime system, but this cost has been decreasing with time, and constraint languages are now a reasonable alternative to Prolog. Several important CLP languages that are in use at the time of this writing are Prolog IV (by the inventors of Prolog), CLP(R), and CHIP. (See the Notes and References for more on these languages.)

The reason such languages are called *constraint* languages is that they turn uninstantiated arithmetic and inequalities into **constraints** that are accumulated as program resolution proceeds, and which are then solved by an attached **constraint solver** to produce a solution, or, if they still involve uninstantiated variables, are reported as part of the solution.

The need for a constraint solver means that CLP languages are restricted in their handling of constraints to one or more specific value domains for which constraint solvers exist in the language. Typical examples of value domains are the integers, the rationals, and various kinds of trees. Unification in such languages is replaced by a system that tests the solvability of a set of constraints, using either heuristics or calling on the constraint solver to actually find a specific solution, which is then used by the constraint system for variable instantiation. Examples of constraint solver algorithms include Gauss elimination (for systems of linear equations) and the simplex method (for inequalities). Indeed, unification itself can be viewed as a equality constraint solver over the domain of terms.

To see how a CLP language works, consider the Prolog program in Figure 12.9 for the mathematical factorial function.

```
fact(0,1).
fact(N,R) :-
     N > 0, N1 is N - 1, fact(N1,R1), R is N * R1.
```

Figure 12.9   A factorial program in Prolog

In a CLP language, this same program would be written as[2]

```
fact(0,1).
fact(N,N * R1) :- N > 0, fact(N - 1,R1).
```

This will work exactly as the previous Prolog program to compute factorials, but it can also be run in reverse to produce N given R:

```
?- fact(X,6).
X = 3
```

Here is how a CLP language would produce this result. Given the goal fact(X,6), a match is attempted first with fact(0,1), producing the constraints $X = 0, 6 = 1$. The second constraint is false (i.e., unsolvable), so this match is abandoned, and a match is attempted with the second clause. This produces the subgoal fact(N1,R1) and the constraints

```
6 = X * R1
X > 0
N1 = X - 1
```

Since none of these constraints are unsolvable, the system goes on to satisfy the subgoal fact(N1,R1). The first match is with fact(0,1), yielding $N1 = 0$ and $R1 = 1$. These values are substituted back into the constraints to get

```
6 = X * 1
X > 0
0 = X - 1
```

The last equation produces $X = 1$, which in turn is used to produce the constraints

```
6 = 1 * 1
1 > 0
```

The first constraint is false, so this match fails. The system then continues by matching fact(N1,R1) to the second clause in the factorial definition. Eventually, the system will correctly infer $X = 3$.

---

[2] Since there is no standard notation for CLP languages, this particular syntax may or may not work for a specific CLP language.

12.6.2 Equational Systems

One of the principal features of a logic programming language is that it can be used to write **executable specifications** for a programming system. Such specifications can be tested to verify that they are not only correct, but that they adequately represent the user's requirements. Thus, logic programming languages can be used as **rapid prototyping systems** for software development.

Unfortunately, the Horn clause logic of Prolog, or even predicate calculus, is not able to express the kinds of specifications that have been developed for a major area of programming, namely, the specification of abstract data types. In Chapter 9 we described the algebraic specification of abstract data types as developed by Goguen and Guttag, which uses equations to specify the behavior of the data type. For example, the specification of a stack of integers from that chapter is written as follows (we restrict ourselves here to integer stacks for simplicity):

type intstack **imports** boolean, integer

operations:
> createstk: intstack
> push: intstack $\times$ integer $\rightarrow$ intstack
> pop: intstack $\rightarrow$ intstack
> top: intstack $\rightarrow$ integer
> emptystk: intstack $\rightarrow$ boolean

variables: s: intstack; x: integer

axioms:
> top(createstk) = error
> top(push(s,x)) = x
> pop(createstk) = error
> pop(push(s,x)) = s
> emptystk(createstk) = true
> emptystk(push(s,x)) = false

The equations given in the axiom section completely define the behavior of the functions given in the operations section. It would be nice if these **equational specifications** could be written directly in a logic programming language.

However, Prolog and other Horn clause systems do not accept equations as rules, so an algebraic specification cannot be translated directly into Prolog. It is possible to give an approximate translation of some specifications into Prolog. For example, the `intstack` specification can be approximated by the following Prolog clauses:

```
intstack(createstk).
intstack(push(S,X)) :- intstack(S), integer(X).
pop(push(S,X),S) :- intstack(push(S,X)).
```

```
top(push(S,X),X) :- intstack(push(S,X)).
emptystk(createstk).
```

These clauses essentially define an `intstack` to be of the form `push(push(push(...push(createstk,Xn) .... X3),X2),X1)`, where all the `Xi` are integers. They rely on the closed-world assumption to make `top(createstk,X)`, `pop(createstk,S)`, and `emptystk(push(S,X))` false. A similar translation scheme could be used for other equational specifications in which the data type could be put into a standard form, such as a sequence of `push` applications (such a form was called a canonical form in Chapter 9).

It would be much better, however, if the equational specifications could be written directly in a logic programming language, and this has been a partial motivation for the development and study of **equational logic** programming languages, such as the **OBJ3** language developed by Goguen and the **Equation Interpreter Project** of O'Donnell. (See the Notes and References.) Equational logic languages allow the axioms for an abstract data type to be interpreted directly, or with small modifications, by the language system, without any underlying assumptions about the representation of such data types. Inference rules for such systems generally include the usual properties of equality, such as reflexivity, symmetry, and transitivity. Equational logic systems allow for the specification of a data type to be tested directly for consistency and applicability for a particular purpose.

Here, for example, is an OBJ3 specification for the intstack abstract data type:

```
obj STACK-OF-INT is sorts Stack NeStack .
      subsort NeStack < Stack .
      protecting INT .
      op empty : -> Stack .
      op push : Int Stack -> NeStack .
      op top_ : NeStack -> Int .
      op pop_ : NeStack -> Stack .
      var I : Int .
      var S : Stack .
      eq top push(I,S) = I .
      eq pop push(I,S) = S .
   endo
```

(The need for two types, nonempty stack = `NeStack` and ordinary stack `Stack`, comes from the error conditions in the algebraic specification.)

Equational logic programming languages have been difficult to implement, since the algorithms for inference are complex. However, OBJ3 and other equational languages have been used effectively for specification, prototyping, and theorem proving, and their use is increasing in the research and teaching community.

Exercises

12.1 A standard method for analyzing logical statements is the truth table: Assigning truth values to elementary statements allows us to determine the truth value of a compound statement, and statements with the same truth tables are logically equivalent. Thus the statement "p and not p" is equivalent to "false" by the following truth table:

p	not p	p and not p	false
false	true	false	false
true	false	false	false

Use truth tables to show that $p \rightarrow q$ is equivalent to (not p) or q (remember that $p \rightarrow q$ is false only if p is true and q is false).

12.2 A **tautology** is a statement that is always true, no matter what the truth values of its components. Use a truth table to show that false $\rightarrow p$ is a tautology for any statement p.

12.3 A **refutation system** is a logical system that proves a statement by assuming it is false and deriving a contradiction. Show that Horn clause logic with resolution is a refutation system. (*Hint*: The empty clause is assumed to be false, so a goal $\leftarrow a$ is equivalent to $a \rightarrow$ false. Show that this is equivalent to not(a).)

12.4 Write the following statements in the first-order predicate calculus:

If it is raining or snowing, then there is precipitation.

If it is freezing and there is precipitation, then it is snowing.

If it is not freezing and there is precipitation, then it is raining.

It is snowing.

12.5 Write the statements in Exercise 12.4 as Prolog clauses, in the order given. What answer does Prolog give when given the query "Is it freezing?" The query "Is it raining?" Why? Can you rearrange the clauses so that Prolog can give better answers?

12.6 Write the following mathematical definition of the greatest common divisor of two numbers in first-order predicate calculus: the gcd of u and v is that number x such that x divides both u and v, and, given any other number y such that y divides u and v, then y divides x.

12.7 Translate the definition of the gcd in Exercise 12.6 into Prolog. Compare its efficiency to Euclid's gcd algorithm as given in Figure 12.1.

12.8 Write the following statement as Prolog clauses: Mammals have four legs and no arms, or two arms and two legs.

12.9 Add the statement that a horse is a mammal and that a horse has no arms to the clauses of Exercise 12.8. Can Prolog derive that a horse has four legs? Explain.

12.10 Write Prolog clauses to express the following relationships, given the parent relationship: grandparent, sibling, cousin.

12.11 Write a Prolog program to find the last item in a list.

12.12 Write a Prolog program to find the maximum and minimum of a list of numbers.

12.13 Write a Prolog program that reads numbers from the standard input until a 0 is entered, creates a list of the numbers entered (not including the 0), and then prints the list in the order entered, one number per line. (read(X) can be used to read integer X from the input if the integer is entered on its own line and is terminated by a period.)

12.14 Write a Prolog program that will sort a list of integers according to the mergesort algorithm.

12.15 Compare the Prolog program for quicksort in Figure 12.8 with the Haskell version in Section 11.6 (page 515). What are the differences? What are the similarities?

12.16 Prolog shares some features with functional languages like Scheme, ML, and Haskell, studied in Chapter 11. Describe two major similarities. Describe two major differences.

12.17 In Prolog it is possible to think of certain clauses as representing tail recursion, in which the final term of a clause is a recursive reference, and a cut is written just before the final term. For example, the gcd clause

```
gcd(U,V,W) :- not(V=0), R is U mod V, !,
              gcd(V,R,W).
```

can be viewed as being tail recursive. Explain why this is so.

12.18 Write a Prolog program to print all Pythagorean triples (x, y, z) such that $1 \leq x < y \leq z \leq 100$. ($(x, y, z)$ is a Pythagorean triple if $x * x + y * y = z * z$.)

12.19 Write Prolog clauses for a member predicate: member(X,L) succeeds if X is a member of the list L (thus member(2,[2,3]) succeeds but member(1,[2,3]) fails). What happens if you use your clauses to answer the query member(X,[2,3])? The query member(2,L)? Draw search trees of subgoals as in Section 12.4.5 to explain your answers.

12.20 Rewrite the factorial Prolog program of Figure 12.9 to make it tail recursive (see Exercise 12.17).

12.21 Draw search trees of subgoals and explain Prolog's responses based on the trees for the following goals (see Figure 12.1):

(a) gcd(15,10,X).

(b) append(X,Y,[1,2]).

12.22 Rewrite the Prolog clauses for Euclid's algorithm (gcd) in Figure 12.1 to use the cut instead of the test not(V = 0). How much does this improve the efficiency of the program? Redraw the search tree of Exercise 12.21(a) to show how the cut prunes the tree.

12.23 Explain using a search tree why the cut in the following program has no effect on the solutions found to the query ancestor(X,bob). Does the cut improve the efficiency at all? Why or why not?

```
ancestor(X,Y) :- parent(X,Z), ancestor(Z,Y).
ancestor(X,X) :- !.
parent(amy,bob).
```

12.24 If we use cuts to improve the efficiency of the Prolog append program, we would write

```
append([],Y,Y) :- !.
append([A|B],Y,[A|W]) :- append(B,Y,W).
```

Now given the goal append(X,Y,[1,2]) Prolog only responds with the solution X = [], Y = [1,2]. Explain using a search tree.

12.25 Rewrite the sieve of Eratosthenes Prolog program of Figure 12.6 to remove all the cuts. Compare the efficiency of the resulting program to the original.

12.26 Explain the difference in Prolog between the following two definitions of the sibling relationship:

```
sibling1(X,Y) :- not(X = Y), parent(Z,X),
                 parent(Z,Y).
sibling2(X,Y) :- parent(Z,X), parent(Z,Y),
                 not(X = Y).
```

Which definition is better? Why?

12.27 Given the following Prolog clauses,

```
ancestor(X,Y) :- ancestor(Z,Y), parent(X,Z).
ancestor(X,X).
parent(amy,bob).
```

explain using a search tree of subgoals why Prolog fails to answer when given the goal ancestor(X,bob).

12.28 Given the following Prolog clauses,

```
ancestor(X,X).
ancestor(X,Y) :- ancestor(Z,Y), parent(X,Z).
parent(amy,bob).
```

explain Prolog's response to the query ancestor(amy,X) using a search tree of subgoals.

12.29 What is wrong with the following Prolog specification for a sort procedure:

```
sort(S,T) :- sorted(T), permutation(S,T).
```

Why?

12.30 Given only the following Prolog clause:

```
human(bob).
```

Prolog will respond as follows:

```
?- human(X).
X = bob

?- not(human(X)).
no
```

Why did Prolog respond to the last goal as it did? Is Prolog saying that there are no X that are not human, that is, that all X are human? Why?

12.31 The following is a possible implementation of a for-loop construct in Prolog, similar to the statement `for(I=L,I<=H,I++)` in C:

```
for(I,I,I) : - !.
for(I,I,H) .
for(I,L,H) :- L1 is L + 1, for(I,L1,H).
```

Using this definition, we can repeat operations over I, such as printing all integers between L and H as follows:

```
printint(L,H) :- for(I,L,H), write(I), nl, fail.
```

Explain how backtracking causes the for predicate to behave like a loop.

12.32 In the brief explanation of the difference between free and bound variables in Section 12.1, the details about potential reuse of names were ignored. For example, in the statement

$$a(x) \rightarrow \text{there exists } x, b(x)$$

the x in b is bound, while the x in a is free. Thus, the **scope of a binding** must be properly defined to refer to a subset of the uses of the bound variable. Develop scope rules for bindings from which it can be determined which uses of variables are free and which are bound.

12.33 Compare the definition of free and bound variables in logical statements with the definition of free and bound variables in the lambda calculus (Chapter 11). How are they similar? How are they different?

12.34 The occur-check was left out of Prolog because simple algorithms are inefficient. Describe using the **append** clauses of Figure 12.1 why the occur-check can be inefficient.

12.35 We have seen that Prolog can have difficulties with infinite data sets, such as that produced by the clauses

```
int(0).
int(X) :- int(Y), X is Y + 1 .
```

and with self-referential terms such as

```
X = [1|X]
```

which causes an occur-check problem. In Haskell (Chapter 11) infinite data constructions such as the foregoing are possible using delayed evaluation. Does delayed evaluation make sense in Prolog? Can you think of any other ways infinite data structures might be dealt with?

12.36 Complete the resolution of the goal fact(X,6) in the constraint logic example of Section 12.6.1 to show that X = 3 is indeed inferred.

12.37 Suppose instead of using the constraint methods described in Section 12.6.1 to find a solution to fact(X,6), we were to simply adopt a trial-and-error mechanism, that is, compute fact(n,Y) for n = 0, 1, 2, etc. Would this be any less efficient than solving constraints? Discuss.

12.38 Suppose we were to try the query gcd(X,10,5) (using the gcd Prolog program of Figure 12.1) in a CLP language. How is the system likely to behave in this case? What solutions will it find?

12.39 Give a Prolog implementation for the following intqueue abstract data type specification similar to the specification for an intstack in Section 12.6.2:

type intqueue **imports** boolean, integer

> createq: intequeue
>
> enqueue: intqueue $\times$ integer $\rightarrow$ intqueue
>
> dequeue: intqueue $\rightarrow$ intqueue
>
> frontq: intqueue $\rightarrow$ integer
>
> emptyq: intqueue $\rightarrow$ boolean

variables: q:intqueue; x: integer

axioms:

> emptyq(createq) = true
>
> emptyq(enqueue(q,x)) = false
>
> frontq(createq) = error
>
> frontq (enqueue (q, x)) = if emptyq(q) then x else frontq(q)
>
> dequeue(createq) = error
>
> dequeue(enqueue(q,x)) = if emptyq(q) then q else enqueue(dequeue(q),x)

12.40 Kowalski [1988] makes the following statement about his pseudoequation A(lgorithm) = L(ogic) + C(ontrol): "With Prolog we have a fixed C and can improve A only by improving L. Logic programming is concerned with the possibility of changing both L and C." Explain why he says this. Explain why it is not completely true that Prolog cannot change C.

12.41 In Chapter 11 we described a unification method used by ML and Haskell to perform type inference. Compare this unification with the unification of Prolog. Are there any differences?

12.42 Unification can be described as a substitution process that substitutes more specific values for variables so that equality of two expressions is achieved. For example, in Prolog the lists [1|Y] = [X] can be unified by substituting 1 for X and [] for Y. It is possible for different substitutions to cause equality. For instance, if [1|Y] is unified with X, one could set X = [1] and Y = [], or one could set X = [1|Y] and leave Y uninstantiated. This latter substitution is **more general** than the first because the additional substitution Y = [] transforms the first into the second. A substitution is a **most general unifier** of two expressions if it is more general than every other substitution that unifies the two expressions. Why does the unification algorithm of Prolog produce a most general unifier? Would it be useful for a logic programming language to have a unification algorithm that does not produce a most general unifier? Why?

Notes and References

Logic programming arose out of work on proof techniques and automated deduction. The resolution principle was developed by Robinson [1965], and Horn clauses were invented by Horn [1951]. Kowalski [1979b] gives a general introduction to logic and the algorithms used in logic programming, such as unification and resolution. Lloyd [1984] gives a mathematical treatment of general unification techniques and negation as failure.

The early history of the development of Prolog is discussed in a pair of companion articles by Kowalski [1988] and Cohen [1988]. Both mention the importance of the first interpreters developed by Alain Colmerauer and Phillipe Roussel in Marseilles and the later systems written by David Warren, Fernando Pereira, and Luis Pereira in Edinburgh. For a further perspective, see Colmerauer and Roussel [1996].

For a perspective and overview of the Japanese Fifth Generation Project (1981–1992), see Shapiro and Warren [1993].

Kowalski [1979a] introduced the famous formulation of Prolog's basic strategy as "Algorithm = Logic + Control" and gives a detailed account of how computation can be viewed as theorem proving, or "controlled deduction." (Niklaus Wirth's formulation of imperative programming "Algorithms + Data Structures = Programs" is the title of Wirth [1976] and is discussed in Chapters 1 and 6.)

Clocksin and Mellish [1994] is a basic reference for Prolog programming. Some of the examples in this chapter are based on examples in that text. Other references for programming techniques in Prolog are Sterling and Shapiro [1986] and Bratko [2000]. A Prolog standard was adopted by the ISO and ANSI in 1995 (ISO 13211-1 [1995]).

Davis [1982] describes how Prolog can be used as a runnable specification in the design of a software system. Warren [1980] shows how Prolog can be used in language translation and compilers. Clocksin and Mellish [1994] provide a chapter on the use of Prolog to parse grammars and a chapter on the relation of logic programming to logic, in particular the translation of statements in predicate calculus into Horn clauses. For an approach to infinite data structures in Prolog (Exercise 12.35), see Colmerauer [1982].

Nonmonotonic reasoning, mentioned in Section 12.5.2, has been the subject of considerable ongoing research; see for example Minker [2000] or Antoniou and Williams [1997].

Constraint Logic Programming (Section 12.6.1) is studied in Marriott and Stuckey [1997]. See also Pountain [1995], and Jaffar and Maher [1994]. The language CLP(R) (R = "real") is described in Jaffar et al. [1992]. The language Prolog III (a predecessor to Prolog IV) is described in Colmerauer [1990]. The language CHIP (Constraint Handling In Prolog) is described in Aggoun and Beldiceanu [1991].

The Equation Interpreter Project mentioned in Section 12.6.2 is described in O'Donnell [1985]. The OBJ3 language is described in Goguen and Malcolm [1997] and Goguen and Malcolm [2000]; the stack example in that section was adapted from the latter work.

13 Formal Semantics

In Chapters 5 through 8 we discussed the semantics, or meaning, of programs from an informal, or descriptive, point of view. Historically, this has been the usual approach, both for the programmer and the language designer, and it is typified by the language reference manual, which explains language features based on an underlying model of execution that is more implied than explicit.

Over the last 25 years, however, many computer scientists have emphasized the need for a more mathematical description of the behavior of programs and programming languages. The advantages of such a description are to make the definition of a programming language so precise that programs can be **proven** correct in a mathematical way and that translators can be **validated** to produce exactly the behavior described in the language definition. In addition, the work of producing such a precise specification aids the language designer in discovering inconsistencies and ambiguities.

Attempts to develop a standard mathematical system for providing precise semantic descriptions of languages have not met with complete acceptance, so there is no single method for formally defining semantics. Instead, there are a number of methods that differ in the formalisms used and the kinds of intended applications. No one method can be considered universal and most languages are still specified in a somewhat informal way. Formal semantic descriptions are more often supplied after the fact, and only for a part of the language. Also, the use of formal definitions to prove correct program behavior has been confined primarily to academic settings, although formal methods have begun to be used as part of the specification of complex software projects, including programming language translators. The purpose of this chapter is to survey the different methods that have been developed and to give a little flavor of their potential application.

Three principal methods that have been developed by researchers to describe semantics formally are

1. *Operational semantics.* This method defines a language by describing its actions in terms of the operations of an actual or hypothetical machine. Of course, this requires that the operations of the machine used in the description also be precisely defined, and for this reason a very simple hypothetical machine is often used that bears little resemblance to an actual computer. Indeed, the machine we use for operational semantics in Section 13.2 is more of a mathematical model, namely, a "reduction machine," which is a collection of permissible steps in reducing programs by applying their operations to values. It is similar in spirit to the notion of a Turing machine, in which actions are precisely described in a mathematical way.

2. *Denotational semantics.* This approach uses mathematical functions on programs and program components to specify semantics. Programs are translated into functions about which properties can be proved using the standard mathematical theory of functions.

3. *Axiomatic semantics.* This method applies mathematical logic to language definition. Assertions, or predicates, are used to describe desired outcomes and initial assumptions for programs. Language constructs are associated with **predicate transformers** that create new assertions out of old ones, reflecting the actions of the construct. These transformers can be used to prove that the desired outcome follows from the initial conditions. Thus, this method of formal semantics is aimed specifically at correctness proofs.

All these methods are syntax directed in that the semantic definitions are based on a context-free grammar or Backus-Naur Form (BNF) rules as studied in Chapter 4. Formal semantics must then define all properties of a language that are not specified by the BNF.

These include static properties such as static types and declaration before use, which a translator can determine prior to execution. Although some authors consider such static properties to be part of the syntax of a language rather than its semantics, formal methods can describe both static and dynamic properties, and we will continue to view the semantics of a language as everything not specified by the BNF.

As with any formal specification method, two properties of a specification are essential. First, it must be **complete**; that is, every correct, terminating program must have associated semantics given by the rules. Second, it must be **consistent**; that is, the same program cannot be given two different, conflicting semantics. Finally, though of much less concern, it is advantageous for the given semantics to be minimal, or **independent**, in the sense that no rule is derivable from the other rules.

Formal specifications written in the operational or denotational style have a nice additional property, in that they can be translated relatively easily into working programs in a language suitable for prototyping, such as Prolog, ML, or Haskell.

In the sections that follow we will give an overview of each of these approaches to formal semantics. To make the differences in approach clearer, we will use a sample small language as a standard example. In the operational semantics section, we also show briefly how the semantics of this example might be translated into a Prolog program (Prolog is closest in spirit to operational semantics). In the denotational semantics section, we also show briefly how the semantics of the example might be translated into a Haskell program (Haskell is closest in spirit to denotational semantics).

But first we give a description of the syntax and informal semantics of this language.

13.1 A Sample Small Language

The basic sample language that we will use throughout the chapter is a version of the integer expression language used in Chapter 4 and elsewhere. BNF rules for this language are given in Figure 13.1.

expr → *expr* '+' *term* | *expr* '−' *term* | *term*
term → *term* '*' *factor* | *factor*
factor → '(' *expr* ')' | *number*
number → *number digit* | *digit*
digit → '0' | '1' | '2' | '3' | '4' | '5' | '6' | '7' | '8' | '9'

Figure 13.1   Basic Sample Language

The semantics of such arithmetic expressions are particularly simple: The value of an expression is a complete representation of its meaning. Thus, $2 + 3 * 4$ means the value 14, and $(2 + 3) * 4$ means 20. Since this language is a little too simple to demonstrate adequately all the aspects of the formal methods, we add complexity to it in two stages, as follows.

In the first stage, we add variables, statements, and assignments, as given by the grammar in Figure 13.2.

A program in the extended language consists of a list of statements separated by semicolons, and a statement is an assignment of an expression to an identifier. The grammar of Figure 13.1 remains as before, except that identifiers are added to factors.

factor → '(' *expr* ')' | *number* | *identifier*
program → *stmt-list*
stmt-list → *stmt* ';' *stmt-list* | *stmt*
stmt → *identifier* ':=' *expr*
identifier → *identifier letter* | *letter*
letter → 'a' | 'b' | 'c' | . . . | 'z'

Figure 13.2   First Extension of the Sample Language

The semantics of such programs are now represented not by a single value, but by a set of values corresponding to identifiers whose values have been defined, or bound, by assignments. For example, the program

```
a := 2+3;
b := a*4;
a := b-5
```

results in the bindings $b = 20$ and $a = 15$ when it finishes, and so the set of values representing the semantics of the program is $\{a = 15, b = 20\}$. Such a set is essentially a function from identifiers (strings of lowercase letters according to the foregoing grammar) to integer values, with all identifiers that have not been assigned a value undefined. For the purposes of this chapter we will call such a function an **environment**, and we will write

$$Env: \text{Identifier} \rightarrow \text{Integer} \cup \{undef\}$$

to denote a particular environment Env. For example, the Env function given by the program example can be defined as follows:

$$Env(I) = \begin{cases} 15 \text{ if } I = a \\ 20 \text{ if } I = b \\ undef \text{ otherwise} \end{cases}$$

The operation of looking up the value of an identifier I in an environment Env is then simply described by function evaluation $Env(I)$. The operation of adding a new value binding to Env can also be defined in functional terms. We will use the notation $Env \ \& \ \{I = n\}$ to denote the adding of the new value n for I to Env. In terms of functions,

$$(Env \& \{I = n\})(J) = \begin{cases} n \text{ if } J = I \\ Env(J) \text{ otherwise} \end{cases}$$

Finally, we also need the notion of the **empty environment**, which we will denote by Env_0:

$$Env_0(I) = \text{undef for all } I$$

This notion of environment is particularly simple and differs from what we called the environment in Chapters 5 and 8. Indeed, an environment as defined here incorporates both the symbol table and state functions from Chapter 5. We note that such environments do not allow pointer values, do not include scope information, and do not permit aliases. More complex environments require much greater complexity and will not be studied here.

This view of the semantics of a program as represented by a resulting, final environment has the effect that the consistency and completeness properties stated in the introduction have the following straightforward interpretation: Consistency means that we cannot derive two different final environments for the same program; and completeness means that we must be able to derive a final environment for every correct, terminating program.

The second extension to our sample language will be the addition of "if" and "while" control statements to the first extension. Statements can now be of three kinds, and we extend their definition accordingly; see Figure 13.3.

stmt → *assign-stmt* | *if-stmt* | *while-stmt*
assign-stmt → *identifier* ':=' *expr*
if-stmt → 'if' *expr* 'then' *stmt-list* 'else' *stmt-list* 'fi'
while-stmt → 'while' *expr* 'do' *stmt-list* 'od'

Figure 13.3   Second Extension of the Sample Language

The syntax of the if-statement and while-statement borrow the Algol68 convention of writing reserved words backward—thus od and fi—to close statement blocks rather than using the begin and end of Pascal and Algol60.

The meaning of an *if-stmt* is that *expr* should be evaluated in the current environment. If it evaluates to an integer greater than 0, then the *stmt-list* after 'then' is executed. If not, the *stmt-list* after the 'else' is executed. The meaning of a *while-stmt* is similar: As long as *expr* evaluates to a quantity greater than 0, *stmt-list* is repeatedly executed, and *expr* is re-evaluated. Note that these semantics are nonstandard!

Here is an example of a program in this language:

```
n := 0 - 5;
if n then i := n else i := 0 - n fi;
fact := 1;
while i do
   fact := fact * i;
   i := i - 1
od
```

The semantics of this program are given by the (final) environment $\{n = 5, i = 0, fact = 120\}$.

Loops are the most difficult of the foregoing constructs to give formal semantics for, and in the following we will not always give a complete solution. These can be found in the references at the end of the chapter.

Formal semantic methods frequently use a simplified version of syntax from that given. Since the parsing step can be assumed to have already taken place, and since semantics are to be defined only for syntactically correct constructs, an ambiguous grammar can be used to define semantics. Further, the nonterminal symbols can be replaced by single letters, which may be thought to represent either strings of tokens or nodes in a parse tree. Such a syntactic specification is sometimes called **abstract syntax**. An abstract syntax for our sample language (with extensions) is the following:

$$P \rightarrow L$$
$$L \rightarrow L_1 \text{ ';' } L_2 \mid S$$
$$S \rightarrow I \text{ ':=' } E \mid \text{ 'if' } E \text{ 'then' } L_1, \text{ 'else' } L_2 \text{ 'fi'}$$
$$\mid \text{ 'while' } E \text{ 'do' } L \text{ 'od'}$$
$$E \rightarrow E_1 \text{ '+' } E_2 \mid E_1 \text{ '-' } E_2 \mid E_1 \text{ '*' } E_2$$
$$\mid \text{ '(' } E_1 \text{ ')' } \mid N$$
$$N \rightarrow N_1 D \mid D$$
$$D \rightarrow \text{ '0' } \mid \text{ '1' } \mid \ldots \mid \text{ '9'}$$
$$I \rightarrow I_1 A \mid A$$
$$A \rightarrow \text{ 'a' } \mid \text{ 'b' } \mid \ldots \mid \text{ 'z'}$$

Here the letters stand for syntactic entities as follows:

P : Program
L : Statement-list
S : Statement
E : Expression
N : Number
D : Digit
I : Identifier
A : Letter

To define the semantics of each one of these symbols, we define the semantics of each right-hand side of the abstract syntax rules in terms of the semantics of their parts. Thus, syntax-directed semantic definitions are recursive in nature. This also explains why we need to number the letters on the right-hand sides when they represent the same kind of construct: Each choice needs to be distinguished.

We note finally that the tokens in the grammar have been enclosed in quotes. This becomes an important point when we must distinguish between the symbol '+' and the operation of addition on the integers, or $+$, which it represents. Similarly, the symbol '3' needs to be distinguished from its value, or the number 3.

We now survey the different formal semantic methods.

13.2 Operational Semantics

Operational semantics define the semantics of a programming language by specifying how an arbitrary program is to be executed on a machine whose operation is completely known.

We have noted in the introduction that there are many possibilities for the choice of a defining machine. The machine can be an actual computer, and the operational semantics can be specified by an actual translator for the language written in the machine code of the chosen machine. Such **definitional interpreters** or **compilers** have in the past been de facto language definitions (FORTRAN and C were originally examples). However, there are drawbacks to this method: The defining translator may not be available to a user, the operation of the underlying computer may not be completely specified, and the defining implementation may contain errors or other unexpected behavior.

By contrast, operational semantics can define the behavior of programs in terms of an **abstract machine** that does not need to exist anywhere in hardware, but that is simple enough to be completely understood and to be simulated by any user to answer questions about program behavior.

In principle, an abstract machine can be viewed as consisting of three parts: a program, a control, and a store or memory:

An operational semantic specification of a programming language specifies how the control of this abstract machine reacts to an arbitrary program in the language to be defined, and in particular, how storage is changed during the execution of a program.

The particular form of abstract machine that we will present is that of a **reduction machine**, whose control operates directly on a program to reduce it to its semantic "value." For example, given the expression (3 + 4) * 5, the control of the reduction machine will reduce it to its numeric value (which is its semantic content) using the following sequence of steps:

$$(3 + 4) * 5 => (7) * 5 \qquad \text{— 3 and 4 are added to get 7}$$
$$=> 7 * 5 \qquad \text{— the parentheses around 7 are dropped}$$
$$=> 35 \qquad \text{— 7 and 5 are multiplied to get 35}$$

In general, of course, the semantic content of a program will be more than just a numeric value, but as we will see, the semantic content of a program can be represented by a data value of some structured type, which operational semantic reductions will produce.

To specify the operational semantics of our sample language, we give **reduction rules** that specify how the control reduces the constructs of the language to a value. These reduction rules are given in a mathematical notation similar to logical inference rules, so we discuss such logical inference rules first.

13.2.1 Logical Inference Rules

Inference rules in logic are written in the following form:

$$\frac{\text{premise}}{\text{conclusion}}$$

That is, the premise, or condition, is written first; then a line is drawn, and the conclusion, or result, is written. This indicates that whenever the premise is true, the conclusion is also true. As an example, we can express the commutative property of addition as the following inference rule:

$$\frac{a + b = c}{b + a = c}$$

In logic, such inference rules are used to express the basic rules of propositional and predicate calculus. As an example of an inference rule in logic, the transitive property of implication is given by the following rule:

$$\frac{a \rightarrow b, \, b \rightarrow c}{a \rightarrow c}$$

This says that if a implies b and b implies c, then a implies c.

Axioms are inference rules with no premise—they are always true. An example of an axiom is $a + 0 = a$ for integer addition. This can be written as an inference rule with an empty premise:

$$\overline{a + 0 = a}$$

More often, this is written without the horizontal line:

$$a + 0 = a$$

13.2.2 Reduction Rules for Integer Arithmetic Expressions

We use the notation of inference rules to describe the way the control operates to reduce an expression to its value. There are several styles in current use to how these rules are written. The particular form we use for our reduction rules is called **structural operational semantics**; an alternative form, called **natural semantics**, is actually closer to the denotational semantics studied later; see the Notes and References.

We base the semantic rules on the abstract syntax for expressions in our sample language:

$$E \rightarrow E_1 \text{ `+' } E_2 \mid E_1 \text{ `−' } E_2 \mid E_1 \text{ `*' } E_2 \mid \text{`(' } E_1 \text{ `)'}$$
$$N \rightarrow N_1 D \mid D$$
$$D \rightarrow \text{`0'} \mid \text{`1'} \mid \ldots \mid \text{`9'}$$

For the time being we can ignore the storage, since this grammar does not include identifiers. We use the following notation: E, E_1, and so on are used to denote expressions that have not yet been reduced to values; V, V_1, and so on will stand for integer values; $E \Rightarrow E_1$ states that expression E reduces to expression E_1 by some reduction rule. Reduction rules for expressions are the following, each of which we will discuss in turn.

(1) We collect all the rules for reducing digits to values in this one rule, all of which are axioms:

$$\text{`0'} \Rightarrow 0$$
$$\text{`1'} \Rightarrow 1$$
$$\text{`2'} \Rightarrow 2$$
$$\text{`3'} \Rightarrow 3$$
$$\text{`4'} \Rightarrow 4$$
$$\text{`5'} \Rightarrow 5$$
$$\text{`6'} \Rightarrow 6$$
$$\text{`7'} \Rightarrow 7$$
$$\text{`8'} \Rightarrow 8$$
$$\text{`9'} \Rightarrow 9$$

(2) We collect the rules for reducing numbers to values in this one rule, which are also axioms:

$$V \,\text{`0'} \Rightarrow 10 * V$$
$$V \,\text{`1'} \Rightarrow 10 * V + 1$$
$$V \,\text{`2'} \Rightarrow 10 * V + 2$$
$$V \,\text{`3'} \Rightarrow 10 * V + 3$$
$$V \,\text{`4'} \Rightarrow 10 * V + 4$$
$$V \,\text{`5'} \Rightarrow 10 * V + 5$$
$$V \,\text{`6'} \Rightarrow 10 * V + 6$$
$$V \,\text{`7'} \Rightarrow 10 * V + 7$$
$$V \,\text{`8'} \Rightarrow 10 * V + 8$$
$$V \,\text{`9'} \Rightarrow 10 * V + 9$$

(3) $\qquad\qquad V_1 \,\text{`+'}\, V_2 \Rightarrow V_1 + V_2$

(4) $\qquad\qquad V_1 \,\text{`−'}\, V_2 \Rightarrow V_1 - V_2$

(5) $\qquad\qquad V_1 \,\text{`*'}\, V_2 \Rightarrow V_1 * V_2$

(6) $\qquad\qquad \text{`('}\, V \,\text{`)'} \Rightarrow V$

(7) $\qquad\qquad \dfrac{E \Rightarrow E_1}{E \,\text{`+'}\, E_2 \Rightarrow E_1 \,\text{`+'}\, E_2}$

(8) $\qquad\qquad \dfrac{E \Rightarrow E_1}{E \,\text{`−'}\, E_2 \Rightarrow E_1 \,\text{`−'}\, E_2}$

(9)
$$\frac{E => E_1}{E \; `*' \; E_2 => E_1 \; `*' \; E_2}$$

(10)
$$\frac{E => E_1}{V \; `+' \; E => V \; `+' \; E_1}$$

(11)
$$\frac{E => E_1}{V \; `-' \; E => V \; `-' \; E_1}$$

(12)
$$\frac{E => E_1}{V \; `*' \; E => V \; `*' \; E_1}$$

(13)
$$\frac{E => E_1}{`(' \; E \; `)' => `(' \; E_1 \; `)'}$$

(14)
$$\frac{E => E_1, \; E_1 => E_2}{E => E_2}$$

Rules 1 through 6 are all axioms. Rules 1 and 2 express the reduction of digits and numbers to values: '0' $=> 0$ states that the **character** '0' (a syntactic entity) reduces to the **value** 0 (a semantic entity). Rules 3, 4, and 5 say that whenever we have an expression that consists of two values and an operator symbol, we can reduce that expression to a value by applying the appropriate operation whose symbol appears in the expression. Rule 6 says that if an expression consists of a pair of parentheses surrounding a value, then the parentheses can be dropped.

The remainder of the reduction rules are inferences that allow the reduction machine to combine separate reductions together to achieve further reductions. Rules 7, 8, and 9 express the fact that, in an expression that consists of an operation applied to other expressions, the left subexpression may be reduced by itself and that reduction substituted into the larger expression. Rules 10 through 12 express the fact that, once a value is obtained for the left subexpression, the right subexpression may be reduced. Rule 13 says that we can first reduce the inside of an expression consisting of parentheses surrounding another expression. Finally, rule 14 expresses the general fact that reductions can be performed stepwise (sometimes called the **transitivity rule** for reductions).

Let us see how these reduction rules can be applied to a complicated expression to derive its value. Take, for example, the expression $2 * (3 + 4) - 5$. To show each reduction step clearly, we surround each character with quotes within the reduction steps.

We first reduce the expression $3 + 4$ as follows:

$$
\begin{aligned}
\text{'3' '+' '4'} &=> 3 \text{ '+' '4'} &&\text{(Rules 1 and 7)} \\
&=> 3 \text{ '+' } 4 &&\text{(Rules 1 and 10)} \\
&=> 3 + 4 = 7 &&\text{(Rule 3)}
\end{aligned}
$$

Hence by rule 14, we have '3' '+' '4' $=> 7$. Continuing,

$$
\begin{aligned}
\text{'(' '3' '+' '4' ')'} &=> \text{'(' 7 ')'} &&\text{(Rule 13)} \\
&=> 7 &&\text{(Rule 6)}
\end{aligned}
$$

Now we can reduce the expression $2 * (3 + 4)$ as follows:

'2' '*' '(' '3' '+' '4' ')' => 2 '*' '(' '3' '+' '4' ')'	(Rules 1 and 9)
=> 2 '*' 7	(Rule 12)
=> 2 * 7 = 14	(Rule 5)

And, finally,

'2' '*' '(' '3' '+' '4' ')' '−' '5' => 14 '−' '5'	(Rules 1 and 8)
=> 14 '−' 5	(Rule 11)
=> 14 − 5 = 9	(Rule 4)

We have shown that the reduction machine can reduce the expression $2 * (3 + 4) - 5$ to 9, which is the value of the expression.

13.2.3   Environments and Assignment

We want to extend the operational semantics of expressions to include environments and assignments, according to the following abstract syntax:

$$P \to L$$
$$L \to L_1 \text{ ';' } L_2 \mid S$$
$$S \to I \text{ ':=' } E$$
$$E \to E_1 \text{ '+' } E_2 \mid E_1 \text{ '−' } E_2 \mid E_1 \text{ '*' } E_2$$
$$\mid \text{ '(' } E_1 \text{ ')' } \mid N$$
$$N \to N_1 D \mid D$$
$$D \to \text{ '0' } \mid \text{ '1' } \mid \ldots \mid \text{ '9' }$$
$$I \to I_1 A \mid A$$
$$A \to \text{ 'a' } \mid \text{ 'b' } \mid \ldots \mid \text{ 'z' }$$

To do this we must include the effect of assignments on the storage of the abstract machine. Our view of the storage will be the same as in other sections; that is, we view it as an environment that is a function from identifiers to integer values (including the undefined value):

$$Env\text{: Identifier} \to \text{Integer} \cup \{undef\}$$

To add environments to the reduction rules, we need a notation to show the dependence of the value of an expression on an environment. We use the notation $<E \mid Env>$ to indicate that expression E is evaluated in the presence of environment Env. Now our reduction rules change to include environments. For example, rule 7 with environments becomes

(7) $$\frac{<E \mid Env> \; => \; <E_1 \mid Env>}{<E \text{ '+' } E_2 \mid Env> \; => \; <E_1 \text{ '+' } E_2 \mid Env>}$$

This states that if E reduces to E_1 in the presence of environment Env, then E '+' E_2 reduces to E_1 '+' E_2 in the same environment. Other rules are modified similarly. The one case of evaluation that explicitly involves the environment is when an expression is an identifier I:

(15)
$$\frac{Env(I) = V}{< I \mid Env> \; => \; <V \mid Env>}$$

This states that if the value of identifier I is V in environment Env, then I reduces to V in the presence of Env.

It remains to add assignment statements and statement sequences to the reduction rules. First, statements must reduce to environments instead of integer values, since they create and change environments. Thus, we have

(16)
$$<I \text{ ':=' } V \mid Env> \; => \; Env \; \& \; \{I = V\}$$

which states that the assignment of the value V to I in environment Env reduces to a new environment where I is equal to V.

The reduction of expressions within assignments proceeds via the following rule:

(17)
$$\frac{<E \mid Env> \; => \; <E_1 \mid Env>}{<I \text{ ':=' } E \mid Env> \; => \; <I \text{ ':=' } E_1 \mid Env>}$$

A statement sequence reduces to an environment formed by accumulating the effect of each assignment:

(18)
$$\frac{<S \mid Env> \; => \; Env_1}{<S \text{ ';' } L \mid Env> \; => \; <L \mid Env_1>}$$

Finally, a program is a statement sequence that has no prior environment; it reduces to the effect it has on the empty starting environment:

(19)
$$L \; => \; <L \mid Env_0>$$

(recall that $Env_0(I) = $ undef for all identifiers I).

We leave the rules for reducing identifier expressions to the reader; they are completely analogous to the rules for reducing numbers (see Exercise 13.4).

Let us use these rules to reduce the following sample program to an environment:

```
a := 2+3;
b := a*4;
a := b-5
```

To simplify the reduction, we will suppress the use of quotes to differentiate between syntactic and semantic entities. First, by rule 19, we have

$$a := 2 + 3; b := a * 4; a := b - 5 =>$$
$$<a := 2 + 3; b := a * 4; a := b - 5 \mid Env_0>$$

Also, by rules 3, 17, and 16,

$<a := 2 + 3 \mid Env_0> \Rightarrow$
$<a := 5 \mid Env_0> \Rightarrow$
$Env_0 \ \& \ \{a = 5\} = \{a = 5\}$

Then, by rule 18,

$<a := 2 + 3; b := a * 4; a := b - 5 \mid Env_0> \Rightarrow$
$<b := a * 4; a := b - 5 \mid \{a = 5\}>$

Similarly, by rules 15, 9, 5, 17, and 16,

$<b := a * 4 \mid \{a = 5\}> \Rightarrow <b := 5 * 4 \mid \{a = 5\}> \Rightarrow$
$<b := 20 \mid \{a = 5\}> \Rightarrow \{a = 5\} \ \& \ \{b = 20\} = \{a = 5, b = 20\}$

Thus, by rule 18,

$<b := a * 4; a := b - 5 \mid \{a = 5\}> \Rightarrow$
$<a := b - 5 \mid \{a = 5, b = 20\}>$

Finally, by a similar application of the rules, we get

$<a := b - 5 \mid \{a = 5, b = 20\}> \Rightarrow$
$<a := 20 - 5 \mid \{a = 5, b = 20\}> \Rightarrow$
$<a := 15 \mid \{a = 5, b\ 20\}> \Rightarrow$
$\{a = 5, b = 20\} \ \& \ \{a = 15, b = 20\}$

and the program reduces to the environment $\{a = 15, b = 20\}$.

13.2.4 Control

It remains to add the if- and while-statements to our sample language, with the following abstract syntax:

$$S \to \text{'if' } E \text{ 'then' } L_1 \text{ 'else' } L_2 \text{ 'fi'}$$
$$\mid \text{ 'while' } E \text{ 'do' } L \text{ 'od'}$$

Reduction rules for if-statements are the following:

(20)
$$\frac{<E \mid Env> \Rightarrow <E_1 \mid Env>}{<\text{'if' } E \text{ 'then' } L_1 \text{ 'else' } L_2 \text{ 'fi' } \mid Env> \Rightarrow}$$
$$<\text{'if' } E_1 \text{ 'then' } L_1 \text{ 'else' } L_2 \text{ 'fi' } \mid Env>$$

(21)
$$\frac{V > 0}{<\text{'if' } V \text{ 'then' } L_1 \text{ 'else' } L_2 \text{ 'fi' } \mid Env> \Rightarrow <L_1 \mid Env>}$$

(22)
$$\frac{V \le 0}{<\text{'if' } V \text{ 'then' } L_1 \text{ 'else' } L_2 \text{ 'fi' } \mid Env> \Rightarrow <L_2 \mid Env>}$$

Reduction rules for while-statements are as follows:

(23)
$$\frac{<E \mid Env> => <V \mid Env>, V \le 0}{<\text{'while'} \ E \ \text{'do'} \ L \ \text{'od'} \mid Env> => Env}$$

(24)
$$\frac{<E \mid Env> => <V \mid Env>, V > 0}{<\text{'while'} \ E \ \text{'do'} \ L \ \text{'od'} \mid Env> => < L \ ; \text{'while'} \ E \ \text{'do'} \ L \ \text{'od'} \mid Env>}$$

Note that the last rule is recursive. It states that if, given environment Env, the expression E evaluates to a positive value, then execution of the while-loop under Env reduces to an execution of L, followed by the execution of the same while-loop all over again.

As an example, let us reduce the while-statement of the program

```
n := 0 - 3;
if n then i := n else i := 0 - n fi;
fact := 1;
while i do
   fact := fact * i;
   i := i - 1
od
```

to its environment value. The environment at the start of the while-loop is $\{n = -3, i = 3, \text{fact} = 1\}$. Since $<i \mid \{n = -3, i = 3, \text{fact} = 1\}> => <3 \mid \{n = -3, i = 3, \text{fact} = 1\}>$ and $3 > 0$, rule 24 applies, so by rule 18 we must compute the environment resulting from the application of the body of the loop to the environment $\{n = -3, i = 3, \text{fact} = 1\}$:

$<\text{fact} := \text{fact} * i \mid \{n = -3, \ i = 3, \text{fact} = 1\}> =>$
$<\text{fact} := 1 * i \mid \{n = -3, i = 3, \text{fact} = 1\}> =>$
$<\text{fact} := 1 * 3 \mid \{n = -3, i = 3, \text{fact} = 1\}> =>$
$<\text{fact} := 3 \mid \{n = -3, i = 3, \text{fact} = 1\}> =>$
$\{n = -3, i = 3, \text{fact} = 3\}$

and

$<i := i - 1 \mid \{n = -3, i = 3, \text{fact} = 1\}> =>$
$<i := 3 - 1 \mid \{n = -3, i = 3, \text{fact} = 3\}> =>$
$<i := 2 \mid \{n = -3, i = 3, \text{fact} = 3\}> =>$
$\{n = -3, i = 2, \text{fact} = 3\}$

so

$<\text{while} \ i \ \text{do} \ldots \text{od} \mid \{n = -3, i = 3, \text{fact} = 1\}> =>$
$< \text{fact} := \text{fact} * i \ ; i := i - 1; \text{while} \ i \ \text{do} \ldots \text{od} \mid \{n = -3, i = 3, \text{fact} = 1\}> =>$
$< i := i - 1; \text{while} \ i \ \text{do} \ldots \text{od} \mid \{n = -3, i = 3, \text{fact} = 3\}> =>$
$< \text{while} \ i \ \text{do} \ldots \text{od} \mid \{n = -3, i = 2, \text{fact} = 3\}>$

Continuing in this way, we get

<while i do . . . od | {$n = -3, i = 2$, fact $= 3$}> =>
<while i do . . . od | {$n = -3, i = 1$, fact $= 6$}> =>
<while i do . . . od | {$n = -3, i = 0$, fact $= 6$}> =>
{$n = -3, i = 0$, fact $= 6$}

so the final environment is {$n = -3, i = 0$, fact $= 6$}.

13.2.5   Implementing Operational Semantics in a Programming Language

It is possible to implement operational semantic rules directly as a program to get a so-called **executable specification**. This is useful for two reasons. First, it allows us to construct a language interpreter directly from a formal specification. Second, it allows us to check the correctness of the specification by testing the resulting interpreter. Since operational semantic rules as we have defined them are similar to logical inference rules, it is not surprising that Prolog is a natural choice as an implementation language. In this section, we briefly sketch a possible Prolog implementation for the reduction rules of our sample language.

First consider how we might represent a sample language program in abstract syntax in Prolog. This is easy to do using terms. For example, $3 * (4 + 5)$ can be represented in Prolog as

```
times(3,plus(4,5))
```

and the program

```
a := 2+3;
b := a*4;
a := b-5
```

as

```
seq(assign(a,plus(2,3)),
        seq(assign(b,times(a,4)),assign(a,sub(b,5))))
```

Note that this form of abstract syntax is actually a tree representation, and that no parentheses are necessary to express grouping. Thus, all rules involving parentheses become unnecessary. Note that we could also take the shortcut of letting Prolog compute the semantics of integers, since we could also write, for example, `plus(23,345)` and Prolog will automatically compute the values of 23 and 345. Thus, with these shortcuts, rules 1, 2, 6, and 13 can be eliminated.

Consider now how we might write reduction rules. Ignoring environments for the moment, we can write a general reduction rule for expressions as

```
reduce(X,Y) :- ...
```

where X is any arithmetic expression (in abstract syntax) and Y is the result of a single reduction step applied to X. For example, rule 3 can be written as

```
reduce(plus(V1,V2),R) :-
            integer(V1), integer(V2), !, R is V1 + V2.
```

Here the predicate integer tests its argument to make sure it is an (integer) value, and then R is set to the result of the addition.

In a similar fashion, rule 7 can be written as

```
reduce(plus(E,E2),plus(E1,E2)) :- reduce(E,E1).
```

and rule 10 can be written as

```
reduce(plus(V,E),plus(V,E1)) :-
            integer(V), !, reduce(E,E1).
```

Rule 14 presents a problem. If we write it as given

```
reduce(E,E2) :- reduce(E,E1), reduce(E1,E2).
```

then infinite recursive loops will result. Instead, we make a distinction between a single reduction step, which we call reduce as before, and multiple reductions, which we will call reduce_all. Then we write rule 14 as two rules (the first is the stopping condition of the recursion):

```
reduce_all(E,V) :- integer(V), !.
reduce_all(E,E2) :- reduce(E,E1), reduce_all(E1,E2).
```

Now if we want the final semantic value of an expression E, we must write reduce_all(E).

Finally, consider how this program might be extended to environments and control. First, a pair <E | Env> or < L | Env> can be thought of as a *configuration* and written in Prolog as config(E,Env) or config(L,Env). Then rule 15 can be written as

```
reduce(config(I,Env),config(V,Env)) :-
                    atom(I), !, lookup(Env, I, V).
```

(atom(I) tests for a variable, and the lookup operation finds values in an environment). Rule 16 can be similarly written as

```
reduce(config(assign(I,V),Env),Env1) :-
            integer(V), !, update(Env, value(I,V), Env1).
```

where update inserts the new value V for I into Env, yielding new environment Env1.

Any dictionary structure for which lookup and update can be defined can be used to represent an environment in this code. For example, the environment $\{n = -3, i = 3, \text{fact} = 1\}$ can be represented as the list [value(n,-3), value(i,3), value(fact,1)]. The remaining details are left to the reader.

13.3 Denotational Semantics

Denotational semantics use functions to describe the semantics of a programming language. A function describes semantics by associating semantic values to syntactically correct constructs. A simple example of such a function is a function that maps an integer arithmetic expression to its value, which we could call the *Val* function:

$$Val : \text{Expression} \to \text{Integer}$$

For example, $Val(2 + 3 * 4) = 14$ and $Val((2 + 3) * 4) = 20$. The domain of a semantic function such as *Val* is a **syntactic domain**. In the case of *Val* it is the set of all syntactically correct integer arithmetic expressions. The range of a semantic function is a **semantic domain**, which is a mathematical structure. In the case of *Val*, the set of integers is the semantic domain. Since *Val* maps the syntactic construct $2 + 3 * 4$ to the semantic value 14, $2 + 3 * 4$ is said to **denote** the value 14. This is the origin of the name denotational semantics.

A second example may be useful before we give denotational semantics for our sample language from Section 13.1. In many programming languages a program can be viewed as something that receives input and produces output. Thus the semantics of a program can be represented by a function from input to output, and a semantic function for programs would look like this:

$$P : \text{Program} \to (\text{Input} \to \text{Output})$$

The semantic domain to which *P* maps programs is a set of functions, namely, the functions from Input to Output, which we represent by Input → Output, and the semantic value of a program is a function. For example, if *p* represents the C program

```
main()
{ int x;
  scanf("%d",&x);
  printf("%d\n",x);
  return 0;
}
```

that inputs an integer and outputs the same integer, then *p* denotes the identity function *f* from integers to integers: $P(p) = f$, where f: Integer → Integer is given by $f(x) = x$.

Very often semantic domains in denotational descriptions will be function domains, and values of semantic functions will be functions themselves. To simplify the notation of these domains, we will often assume that the function symbol "→" is right associative and leave off the parentheses from domain descriptions. Thus,

$$P : \text{Program} \to (\text{Input} \to \text{Output})$$

becomes

$$P : \text{Program} \rightarrow \text{Input} \rightarrow \text{Output}$$

In the following we will give a brief overview of a denotational definition of the semantics of a programming language and then proceed with a denotational definition of our sample language from Section 13.1. A denotational definition of a programming language consists of three parts:

1. A definition of the **syntactic domains**, such as the sets Program and Expression, on which the semantic functions act

2. A definition of the **semantic domains** consisting of the values of the semantic functions, such as the sets Integer and Integer $\rightarrow$ Integer

3. A definition of the semantic functions themselves (sometimes called **valuation functions**)

We will consider each of these parts of the denotational definition in turn.

13.3.1 Syntactic Domains

Syntactic domains are defined in a denotational definition using notation that is almost identical to the abstract syntax described in Section 13.1. The sets being defined are listed first with capital letters denoting elements from the sets. Then the grammar rules are listed that recursively define the elements of the set. For example, the syntactic domains Number and Digit are specified as follows:

$$D: \text{Digit}$$
$$N: \text{Number}$$

$$N \rightarrow N\,D \mid D$$
$$D \rightarrow \text{`0'} \mid \text{`1'} \mid \ldots \mid \text{`9'}$$

A denotational definition views the syntactic domains as sets of syntax trees whose structure is given by the grammar rules. Semantic functions will be defined recursively on these sets, based on the structure of a syntax tree node.

13.3.2 Semantic Domains

Semantic domains are the sets in which semantic functions take their values. These are sets like syntactic domains, but they also may have additional mathematical structure, depending on their use. For example, the integers have the arithmetic operations "+," "−," and "∗." Such domains are **algebras**, which need to be specified by listing their functions and properties. A denotational definition of the semantic domains lists the sets and the operations but usually omits the properties of the operations. These can be specified by the algebraic techniques studied in Chapter 9, or they can simply be assumed to be well known, as in the case of the arithmetic operations on the integers. A specification of the semantic domains also lists only the basic domains without specifically including domains that are constructed of functions on the basic domains.

Domains sometimes need special mathematical structures that are the subject of **domain theory** in programming language semantics. In particular, the term "domain" is sometimes reserved for an algebra with the structure of a complete partial order. Such a structure is needed to define the semantics of recursive functions and loops. See the references at the end of the chapter for further detail on domain theory.

An example of a specification of a semantic domain is the following specification of the integers:

Domain v: Integer $= \{\ldots, -2, -1, 0, 1, 2, \ldots\}$
Operations
$\qquad +$: Integer $\times$ Integer $\rightarrow$ Integer
$\qquad -$: Integer $\times$ Integer $\rightarrow$ Integer
$\qquad *$: Integer $\times$ Integer $\rightarrow$ Integer

In this example we restrict ourselves to the three operations "$+$," "$-$," and "$*$," which are the only operations represented in our sample language. In the foregoing notation the symbols "v:" in the first line indicate that the name v will be used for a general element from the domain, that is, an arbitrary integer.

13.3.3   Semantic Functions

A semantic function is specified for each syntactic domain. Each semantic function is given a different name based on its associated syntactic domain. A common convention is to use the boldface letter corresponding to the elements in the syntactic domain. Thus the value function from the syntactic domain Digit to the integers is written as follows:

$$\mathbf{D} : \text{Digit} \rightarrow \text{Integer}$$

The value of a semantic function is specified recursively on the trees of the syntactic domains using the structure of the grammar rules. This is done by giving a **semantic equation** corresponding to each grammar rule.

For example, the grammar rules for digits

$$D \rightarrow \text{`0'} \mid \text{`1'} \mid \ldots \mid \text{`9'}$$

give rise to the syntax tree nodes

```
    D        D     . . .     D
    |        |               |
   '0'      '1'             '9'
```

and the semantic function **D** is defined by the following semantic equations,

$$
\mathbf{D}(\underset{\text{'0'}}{\overset{D}{|}}\,) = 0, \qquad \mathbf{D}\,(\underset{\text{'1'}}{\overset{D}{|}}\,) = 1, \ldots, \qquad \mathbf{D}\,(\underset{\text{'9'}}{\overset{D}{|}}\,) = 9
$$

representing the value of each leaf.

This cumbersome notation is shortened to the following:

$$\mathbf{D}[['0']] = 0, \mathbf{D}[['1']] = 1, \ldots, \mathbf{D}[['9']] = 9$$

The double brackets [[...]] indicate that the argument is a syntactic entity consisting of a syntax tree node with the listed arguments as children.

As another example, the semantic function

$$N : \text{Number} \rightarrow \text{Integer}$$

from numbers to integers is based on the syntax

$$N \rightarrow N\,D \mid D$$

and is given by the following equations:

$$N[[ND]] = 10 * N[[N]]] + N[[D]]$$
$$N[[D]] = D[[D]]$$

Here [[ND]] refers to the tree node $\overset{N}{\diagup \diagdown}_{N\ D}$ and [[D]] to the node $\overset{N}{\underset{D}{|}}$. We are now ready to give a complete denotational definition for the expression language of Section 13.1.

13.3.4   Denotational Semantics of Integer Arithmetic Expressions

Here is the denotational definition according to the conventions just described.

Syntactic Domains

E: Expression
N: Number
D: Digit

$$
\begin{aligned}
E &\rightarrow E_1 \text{ '+' } E_2 \mid E_1 \text{ '−' } E_2 \mid E_1 \text{ '*' } E_2 \\
&\quad \mid \text{ '(' } E \text{ ')' } \mid N \\
N &\rightarrow N\,D \mid D \\
D &\rightarrow \text{'0'} \mid \text{'1'} \mid \ldots \mid \text{'9'}
\end{aligned}
$$

Semantic Domains

Domain v: Integer = $\{\ldots, -2, -1, 0, 1, 2, \ldots\}$
Operations
$$+ : \text{Integer} \times \text{Integer} \to \text{Integer}$$
$$- : \text{Integer} \times \text{Integer} \to \text{Integer}$$
$$* : \text{Integer} \times \text{Integer} \to \text{Integer}$$

Semantic Functions

$$E : \text{Expression} \to \text{Integer}$$

$$\textbf{E}[[E_1\ `+'\ E_2]] = \textbf{E}[[E_1]] + \textbf{E}[[E_2]]$$
$$\textbf{E}[[E_1\ `-'\ E_2]] = \textbf{E}[[E_1]] - \textbf{E}[[E_2]]$$
$$\textbf{E}[[E_1\ `*'\ E_2]] = \textbf{E}[[E_1]] * \textbf{E}[[E_2]]$$
$$\textbf{E}[['('\ E\ `)']] = \textbf{E}[[E]]$$
$$\textbf{E}[[N]] = \textbf{N}[[N]]$$

$\textbf{N}$: Number $\to$ Integer

$$\textbf{N}[[ND]] = 10 * \textbf{N}[[N]]] + \textbf{N}[[D]]$$
$$\textbf{N}[[D]] = \textbf{D}[[D]]$$

$\textbf{D}$: Digit $\to$ Integer

$$\textbf{D}[['0']] = 0, \textbf{D}[['1']] = 1, \ldots, \textbf{D}[['9']] = 9$$

In this denotational description we have retained the use of quotes to distinguish syntactic from semantic entities. In denotational semantics this is not as necessary as in other semantic descriptions, since arguments to semantic functions are always syntactic entities. Thus, we could drop the quotes and write $\textbf{D}[[0]] = 0$, and so on. For clarity, we will generally continue to use the quotes, however.

To see how these equations can be used to obtain the semantic value of an expression we compute $\textbf{E}[[(2 + 3)*4]]$ or, more precisely, $\textbf{E}[['('\ `2'\ `+'\ `3'\ `)'\ `*'\ `4']]$:

$$\textbf{E}[['('\ `2'\ `+'\ `3'\ `)'\ `*'\ `4']]$$
$$= \textbf{E}[['('\ `2'\ `+'\ `3'\ `)']] * \textbf{E}[['4']]$$
$$= \textbf{E}[['2'\ `+'\ `3']] * \textbf{N}[['4']]$$
$$= (\textbf{E}[['2']] + \textbf{E}[['3']]) * \textbf{D}[['4']]$$
$$= (\textbf{N}[['2']] + \textbf{N}[['3']]) * 4$$
$$= \textbf{D}[['2']] + \textbf{D}[['3']]) * 4$$
$$= (2 + 3) * 4 = 5 * 4 = 20$$

13.3.5 Environments and Assignment

The first extension to our basic sample language adds identifiers, assignment statements, and environments to the semantics. Environments are functions from identifiers to integers (or undefined), and the set of environments becomes a new semantic domain:

Domain Env: Environment = Identifier $\rightarrow$ Integer $\cup$ {undef}

In denotational semantics the value undef is given a special name, *bottom*, taken from the theory of partial orders, and is denoted by a special symbol, "$\perp$." Semantic domains with this special value added are called **lifted domains** and are subscripted with the symbol "$\perp$." Thus Integer $\cup$ {$\perp$} is written as Integer$_\perp$. The initial environment Env_0 defined in Section 13.1, in which all identifiers have undefined values, can now be defined as $Env_0(I) = \perp$ for all identifiers I.

The evaluation of expressions in the presence of an environment must include an environment as a parameter, so that identifiers may be associated with integer values. Thus, the semantic value of an expression becomes a function from environments to integers:

$$E : \text{Expression} \rightarrow \text{Environment} \rightarrow \text{Integer} \perp$$

In particular, the value of an identifier is its value in the environment provided as a parameter:

$$E[[I]](Env) = Env(I)$$

In the case of a number the environment is immaterial:

$$E[[N]](Env) = N[[N]]$$

In other expression cases the environment is simply passed on to subexpressions.

To extend the semantics to statements and statement lists, we note that the semantic values of these constructs are functions from environments to environments. An assignment statement changes the environment to add the new value assigned to the identifier; in this case we will use the same "&" notation for adding values to functions that we have used in previous sections. Now a statement-list is simply the composition of the functions of its individual statements (recall that the composition $f \circ g$ of two functions f and g is defined by $(f \circ g)(x) = f(g(x))$. A complete denotational definition of the extended language is given in Figure 13.4.

Syntactic Domains

P: Program
L: Statement-list
S: Statement
E: Expression
N: Number
D: Digit
I: Identifier
A: Letter

$$P \to L$$
$$L \to L_1 \text{ ';' } L_2 \mid S$$
$$S \to I \text{ ':=' } E$$
$$E \to E_1 \text{ '+' } E_2 \mid E_1 \text{ '−' } E_2 \mid E_1 \text{ '*' } E_2$$
$$\mid \text{ '(' } E \text{ ')' } \mid I \mid N$$
$$N \to N D \mid D$$
$$D \to \text{'0'} \mid \text{'1'} \mid \ldots \mid \text{'9'}$$
$$I \to I A \mid A$$
$$A \to \text{'a'} \mid \text{'b'} \mid \ldots \mid \text{'z'}$$

Semantic Domains

Domain v: Integer = {. . ., $-2, -1, 0, 1, 2,$. . .}
Operations

$$+ : \text{Integer} \times \text{Integer} \to \text{Integer}$$
$$- : \text{Integer} \times \text{Integer} \to \text{Integer}$$
$$* : \text{Integer} \times \text{Integer} \to \text{Integer}$$

Domain Env: Environment = Identifier $\to$ Integer$_\perp$

Semantic Functions

P : Program $\to$ Environment

$$P[[L]] = L[[L]](Env_0)$$

L : Statement-list $\to$ Environment $\to$ Environment

$$L[[L_1 \text{ ';' } L_2]] = L[[L_2]] \circ L[[L_1]]$$
$$L[[S]] = S[[S]]$$

S : Statement $\to$ Environment $\to$ Environment

$$S[[I \text{ ':=' } E]](Env) = Env \ \& \ \{I = E[[E]](Env)\}$$

E : Expression $\to$ Environment $\to$ Integer$_\perp$

$$E[[E_1 \text{ '+' } E_2]](Env) = E[[E_1]](Env) + E[[E_2]](Env)$$
$$E[[E_1 \text{ '−' } E_2]](Env) = E[[E_1]](Env) - E[[E_2]](Env)$$
$$E[[E_1 \text{ '*' } E_2]](Env) = E[[E_1]](Env) * E[[E_2]](Env)$$
$$E[['(' E ')']](Env) = E[[E]](Env)$$
$$E[[I]](Env) = Env(I)$$
$$E[[N]](Env) = N[[N]]$$

N: Number $\to$ Integer

$$N[[ND]] = 10*N[[N]] + N[[D]]$$
$$N[[D]] = D[[D]]$$

D : Digit $\to$ Integer

$$D[['0']] = 0, D[['1']] = 1, \ldots, D[['9']] = 9$$

Figure 13.4 A Denotational Definition for the Sample Language Extended with Assignment Statements and Environments

13.3.6 Denotational Semantics of Control Statements

To complete our discussion of denotational semantics, we need to extend the denotational definition of Figure 13.4 to if- and while-statements, with the following abstract syntax:

$$S: \text{Statement}$$
$$S \to I\ ':='\ E$$
$$| \ \text{'if'}\ E\ \text{'then'}\ L_1\ \text{'else'}\ L_2\ \text{'fi'}$$
$$| \ \text{'while'}\ E\ \text{'do'}\ L\ \text{'od'}$$

As before, the denotational semantics of these statements must be given by a function from environments to environments:

$$\textbf{S} : \text{Statement} \to \text{Environment} \to \text{Environment}$$

We define the semantic function of the if-statement as follows:

$$\textbf{S}[[\text{'if'}\ E\ \text{'then'}\ L_1\ \text{'else'}\ L_2\ \text{'fi'}]](Env) =$$
$$\quad \text{if } \textbf{E}[[E]](Env) > 0 \text{ then } \textbf{L}[[L_1]](Env) \text{ else } \textbf{L}[[L_2]](Env)$$

Note that we are using the if-then-else construct on the right-hand side to express the construction of a function. Indeed, given F: Environment $\to$ Integer, G: Environment $\to$ Environment, and H: Environment $\to$ Environment, then the function "if F then G else H:" Environment $\to$ Environment is given as follows:

$$(\text{if } F \text{ then } G \text{ else } H)\ (Env) = \begin{cases} G(Env), \text{ if } F(Env) > 0 \\ H(Env), \text{ if } F(Env) \le 0 \end{cases}$$

The semantic function for the while-statement is more difficult. In fact, if we let $F = \textbf{S}[[\text{'while'}\ E\ \text{'do'}\ L\ \text{'od'}]]$, so that F is a function from environments to environments, then F satisfies the following equation:

$$F(Env) = \text{if } \textbf{E}[[E]](Env) \le 0 \text{ then } Env \text{ else } F(\textbf{L}[[L]](Env))$$

This is a recursive equation for F. To use this equation as a specification for the semantics of F, we need to know that this equation has a unique solution in some sense among the functions Environment $\to$ Environment. We saw a very similar situation in Section 11.6, where the definition of the factorial function also led to a recursive equation for the function. In that case we were able to construct the function as a set by successively extending it to a so-called **least-fixed-point solution**, that is, the "smallest" solution satisfying the equation. A similar approach will indeed work here too, and the solution is referred to as the least-fixed-point semantics of the while-loop. The situation here is more complicated, however, in that F is a function on the semantic domain of environments rather than the integers. The study of such equations and their solutions is a major topic of domain theory. For more information, see the references at the end of the chapter.

Note that there is an additional problem associated with loops: non-termination. For example, in our sample language the loop

```
i := 1 ;
while i do i := i + 1 od
```

does not terminate. Such a loop does not define any function at all from environments to environments, but we still need to be able to associate a semantic interpretation to it. One does so by assigning it the "undefined" value $\bot$ similar to the value of an undefined identifier in an environment. In this case the domain of environments becomes a lifted domain,

$$\text{Environment}_\bot = (\text{Identifier} \rightarrow \text{Integer}_\bot)_\bot$$

and the semantic function for statements must be defined as follows:

$$S : \text{Statement} \rightarrow \text{Environment}_\bot \rightarrow \text{Environment}_\bot$$

We shall not discuss such complications further.

13.3.7 Implementing Denotational Semantics in a Programming Language

As we have noted previously, it is possible to implement denotational semantic rules directly as a program. Since denotational semantics is based on functions, particularly higher-order functions, it is not surprising that a functional language is a natural choice as an implementation language. In this section, we briefly sketch a possible Haskell implementation for the denotational functions of our sample language. (We choose Haskell because of its minimal extra syntax; ML or Scheme would also be good choices.)

First, consider how one might define the abstract syntax of expressions in the sample language, using a data declaration:

```
data Expr = Val Int | Ident String | Plus Expr Expr
                | Minus Expr Expr | Times Expr Expr
```

Here, as with the operational semantics, we are ignoring the semantics of numbers, and simply letting values be integers (Val Int).

Suppose now we have defined an Environment type, with a lookup and update operation (a reasonable first choice for it, as in operational semantics, would be a list of string-integer pairs). Then the "E" evaluation function can be defined almost exactly as in the denotational definitions:

```
exprE :: Expr -> Environment -> Int
exprE (Plus e1 e2) env = (exprE e1 env) + (exprE e2 env)
exprE (Minus e1 e2) env = (exprE e1 env) - (exprE e2 env)
exprE (Times e1 e2) env = (exprE e1 env) * (exprE e2 env)
exprE (Val n) env = n
exprE (Ident a) env = lookup env a
```

Note that there is no rule for parentheses. Again in this case, the abstract syntax is in tree form, and parentheses simply do not appear.

Similar definitions can be written for statements, statement-lists, and programs. We leave the details as an exercise.

13.4 Axiomatic Semantics

Axiomatic semantics define the semantics of a program, statement, or language construct by describing the effect its execution has on assertions about the data manipulated by the program. The term "axiomatic" is used because elements of mathematical logic are used to specify the semantics of programming languages, including logical axioms. We discussed logic and assertions in the introduction to logic programming in Chapter 12. For our purposes, however, it suffices to consider logical assertions to be statements about the behavior of a program that are true or false at any moment during execution.

Assertions associated with language constructs are of two kinds: Assertions about things that are true just before execution of the construct and assertions about things that are true just after the execution of the construct. Assertions about the situation just before execution are called **preconditions**, and assertions about the situation just after execution are called **postconditions**. For example, given the assignment statement

    x := x + 1

we would expect that, whatever value x has just before execution of the statement, its value just after the execution of the assignment is one more than its previous value. This can be stated as the precondition that $x = A$ before execution and the postcondition that $x = A + 1$ after execution. Standard notation for this is to write the precondition inside curly brackets just before the construct and to write the postcondition similarly just after the construct:

$$\{x = A\}\ x\ :=\ x\ +\ 1\ \{x = A + 1\}$$

or

$$\{x = A\}$$
$$x\ :=\ x\ +\ 1$$
$$\{x = A + 1\}$$

As a second example of the use of precondition and postcondition to describe the action of a language construct, consider the following assignment:

    x := 1 / y

Clearly a precondition for the successful execution of the statement is that $y \neq 0$, and then x becomes equal to 1/y. Thus we have

$$\{y \neq 0\}$$
$$x := 1/y$$
$$\{x = 1/y\}$$

Note that in this example the precondition establishes a restriction that is a requirement for successful execution, while in the first example the precondition x = A merely establishes a name for the value of x prior to execution, without making any restriction whatever on that value.

Precondition/postcondition pairs can be useful in specifying the expected behavior of programs—the programmer simply writes down the conditions he or she expects to be true at each step in a program. For example, a program that sorts the array a[1]..a[n] could be specified as follows:

$$\{n \geq 1 \text{ and for all } i, 1 \leq i \leq n, a[i] = A[i]\}$$

sort-program

$$\{\text{sorted}(a) \text{ and permutation}(a, A)\}$$

Here the assertions sorted(a) and permutation(a, A) mean that the elements of a are sorted and that the elements of a are the same, except for order, as the original elements of the array A.

Such preconditions and postconditions are often capable of being tested for validity during execution of the program, as a kind of error checking, since the conditions are usually Boolean expressions that can be evaluated as expressions in the language itself. Indeed, a few languages such as Eiffel and Euclid have language constructs that allow assertions to be written directly into programs. The C language also has a rudimentary but useful macro library for checking simple assertions: assert.h. Using this library and the macro assert allows programs to be terminated with an error message on assertion failure, which can be a useful debugging feature:

```
#include <assert.h>
...
assert(y != 0);
x = 1/y;
...
```

If y is 0 when this code is executed, the program halts and an error message, such as

```
Assertion failed at test.c line 27: y != 0
Exiting due to signal SIGABRT
...
```

is printed. One can get this same kind of behavior by using exceptions in a language with exception handling:

```
if (y != 0) throw Assertion_Failure();
```

An **axiomatic specification** of the semantics of the language construct C is of the form

$$\{P\}\ C\ \{Q\}$$

where P and Q are assertions; the meaning of such a specification is that, if P is true just before the execution of C, then Q is true just after the execution of C.

Unfortunately, such a representation of the action of C is not unique and may not completely specify all the actions of C. In the second example, for instance, we did not include in the postcondition the fact that y ≠ 0 continues to be true after the execution of the assignment. To specify completely the semantics of the assignment to x, we must somehow indicate that x is the only variable that changes under the assignment (unless it has aliases). Also, y ≠ 0 is not the only condition that will guarantee the correct evaluation of the expression 1/y: y > 0 or y < 0 will do as well. Thus, writing an expected precondition and an expected postcondition will not always precisely determine the semantics of a language construct.

What is needed is a way of associating to the construct C a general relation between precondition P and postcondition Q. The way to do this is to use the property that programming is a **goal-oriented activity**: We usually know what we want to be true after the execution of a statement or program, and the question is whether the known conditions before the execution will guarantee that this becomes true. Thus, postcondition Q is assumed to be given, and a specification of the semantics of C becomes a statement of which preconditions P of C have the property that $\{P\}\ C\ \{Q\}$. To the uninitiated this may seem backward, but it is a consequence of working backward from the goal (the postcondition) to the initial requirements (the precondition).

In general, given an assertion Q, there are many assertions P with the property that $\{P\}\ C\ \{Q\}$. One example has been given: For 1/y to be evaluated, we may require that y ≠ 0, or y > 0, or y < 0. There is one precondition P, however, that is the **most general** or **weakest** assertion with the property that $\{P\}\ C\ \{Q\}$. This is called the **weakest precondition** of postcondition Q and construct C and is written $wp(C,Q)$.

In our example, y ≠ 0 is clearly the weakest precondition such that 1/y can be evaluated. Both y > 0 and y < 0 are stronger than y ≠ 0 since they both imply y ≠ 0. Indeed, P is by definition weaker than R if R implies P (written in logical form as $R \rightarrow P$). Using these definitions we have the following restatement of the property $\{P\}\ C\ \{Q\}$:

$$\{P\}\ C\ \{Q\}\ \text{if and only if}\ P \rightarrow wp(C,Q)$$

Finally, we define the axiomatic semantics of the language construct C as the function $wp(C,\_)$ from assertions to assertions. This function is a **predicate transformer** in that it takes a predicate as argument and returns a predicate result. It also appears to work backward, in that it computes the weakest precondition from any postcondition. This is a result of the goal-oriented behavior of programs as described earlier.

Our running example of the assignment can now be restated as follows:

$$wp(x := 1/y, \; x = 1/y) = \{y \neq 0\}$$

As another example, consider the assignment x := x + 1 and the postcondition x > 0:

$$wp(x := x + 1, \; x > 0) = \{x > -1\}$$

In other words, for x to be greater than 0 after the execution of x := x + 1, x must be greater than -1 just prior to execution. On the other hand, if we have no condition on x but simply want to state its value, we have

$$wp(x := x + 1, \; x = A) = \{x = A - 1\}$$

Again, this may seem backward, but a little reflection should convince you of its correctness. Of course, to determine completely the semantics of an assignment such as x := E, where x is a variable and E is an expression, we need to compute $wp(x := E, Q)$ for any postcondition Q. This is done in Section 13.4.2, where the general rule for assignment is stated in terms of substitution. First, we will study wp a little further.

13.4.1   General Properties of wp

The predicate transformer $wp(C,Q)$ has certain properties that are true for almost all language constructs C, and we discuss these first, before giving axiomatic semantics for the sample language. The first of these is the following:

Law of the Excluded Miracle

$$wp(C, \text{false}) = \text{false}$$

This states that nothing a programming construct C can do will make false into true—if it did it would be a miracle!

The second property concerns the behavior of wp with regard to the "and" operator of logic (also called conjunction):

Distributivity of Conjunction

$$wp(C, P \text{ and } Q) = wp(C,P) \text{ and } wp(C,Q)$$

Two more properties regard the implication operator "$\rightarrow$" and the "or" operator (also called disjunction):

Law of Monotonicity

$$\text{if } Q \rightarrow R \text{ then } wp(C,Q) \rightarrow wp(C,R)$$

Distributivity of Disjunction

$$wp(C,P) \text{ or } wp(C,Q) \rightarrow wp(C,P \text{ or } Q)$$

with equality if C is deterministic.

The question of determinism adds a complicating technicality to the last law. Recall that some language constructs can be nondeterministic, such as the guarded commands discussed in Chapter 7. An example of the need for a weaker property in the presence of nondeterminism is discussed in Exercise 13.35. However, the existence of this exception serves to emphasize that, when one is talking about *any* language construct C, one must be extremely careful. Indeed, it is possible to invent complex language mechanisms in which all of the foregoing properties become questionable without further conditions. (Fortunately, such situations are rare.)

13.4.2   Axiomatic Semantics of the Sample Language

We are now ready to give an axiomatic specification for our sample language.

We note first that the specification of the semantics of expressions alone is not something that is commonly included in an axiomatic specification. In fact, the assertions involved in an axiomatic specificator are primarily statements about the side effects of language constructs; that is, they are statements involving identifiers and environments. For example, the assertion $Q = \{x > 0\}$ is an assertion about the value of x in an environment. Logically, we could think of Q as being represented by the set of all environments for which Q is true. Then logical operations can be represented by set theoretic operations. For example, $P \to Q$ is the same as saying that every environment for which P is true is in the set of environments for which Q is true—in other words, that P is contained in Q as sets.

We will not pursue this translation of logic into set theory. We will also skip over the specification of expression evaluation in terms of weakest preconditions and proceed directly to statements, environments, and control.

The abstract syntax for which we will define the *wp* operator is the following:

$$P \to L$$
$$L \to L_1 \text{ ';' } L_2 \mid S$$
$$S \to I \text{ ':=' } E$$
$$\mid \text{ 'if' } E \text{ 'then' } L_1 \text{ 'else' } L_2 \text{ 'fi'}$$
$$\mid \text{ 'while' } E \text{ 'do' } L \text{ 'od'}$$

Syntax rules such as $P \to L$ and $L \to S$ do not need separate specifications,[1] since these grammar rules simply state that the *wp* operator for a program P is the same as for its associated statement-list L, and similarly, if a statement-list L is a single statement S, then L has the same axiomatic semantics as S. The remaining four cases are treated in order. To simplify

---

[1] If we did have to write semantics for a program, we would have to change its designation from P to *Prog*, say, since we have been using P to refer to a precondition.

the description we will suppress the use of quotes; code will be distinguished from assertions by the use of a different typeface.

Statement-lists.   For lists of statements separated by a semicolon, we have

$$wp(L_1 ; L_2 , Q) = wp(L_1, wp(L_2, Q))$$

This states that the weakest precondition of a series of statements is essentially the composition of the weakest preconditions of its parts. Note that since *wp* works "backward" the positions of L_1 and L_2 are not interchanged, as they are in denotational semantics.

Assignment Statements.   The definition of *wp* for the assignment statement is as follows:

$$wp(I := E, Q) = Q[E/I]$$

This rule involves a new notation: $Q[E/I]$. $Q[E/I]$ is defined to be the assertion Q, with E replacing all free occurrences of the identifier I in Q. The notion of "free occurrences" was discussed in Chapter 12; it also arose in Section 11.8 in connection with reducing lambda calculus expressions. An identifier I is **free** in a logical assertion Q if it is not **bound** by either the existential quantifier "there exists" or the universal quantifier "for all." Thus, in the following assertion, j is free, but i is bound (and thus not free):

$$Q = (\text{for all } i, a[i] > a[j])$$

In this case $Q[1/j] = (\text{for all } i, a[i] > a[1])$, but $Q[1/i] = Q$. In commonly occurring assertions, this should not become a problem, and in the absence of quantifiers, one can simply read $Q[E/I]$ as replacing all occurrences of I by E.

The axiomatic semantics $wp(I := E, Q) = Q[E/I]$ simply says that, for Q to be true after the assignment $I := E$, whatever Q says about I must be true about E before the assignment is executed.

A couple of examples will help to explain the semantics for assignment.

First, consider the previous example $wp(x := x + 1 , x > 0)$. Here $Q = (x > 0)$ and $Q[x + 1/x] = (x + 1 > 0)$. Thus,

$$wp(x := x + 1, x > 0) = (x + 1 > 0) = (x > -1)$$

which is what we obtained before. Similarly,

$$\begin{aligned} wp(x := x + 1, x = A) &= (x = A)[(x + 1)/x] \\ &= (x + 1 = A) \\ &= (x = A - 1) \end{aligned}$$

If-statements.   Recall that the semantics of the if-statement in our sample language are somewhat unusual: if E then L_1 else L_2 fi means that L_1 is executed if the value of $E > 0$, and L_2 is executed if the value of $E \leq 0$. The weakest precondition of this statement is defined as follows:

$$wp(\text{if } E \text{ then } L_1 \text{ else } L_2 \text{ fi}, Q) =$$
$$(E > 0 \rightarrow wp(L_1,Q)) \text{ and } (E \leq 0 \rightarrow wp(L_2,Q))$$

As an example, we compute

$$wp(\text{if } x \text{ then } x := 1 \text{ else } x := -1 \text{ fi}, x = 1) =$$
$$(x > 0 \rightarrow wp(x{:=}1, \ x = 1)) \text{ and } (x \leq 0 \rightarrow wp(x := -1, x = 1))$$
$$= (x > 0 \rightarrow 1 = 1) \text{ and } (x \leq 0 \rightarrow -1 = 1)$$

Recalling that $(P \rightarrow Q)$ is the same as Q or not $P)$ (see Exercise 13.1), we get

$$(x > 0 \rightarrow 1 = 1) = ((1 = 1) \text{ or } \text{not}(x > 0)) = \text{true}$$

and

$$(x \leq 0 \rightarrow 1 = 1) = (-1 = 1) \text{ or } \text{not}(x \leq 0) =$$
$$\text{not}(x \leq 0) = (x > 0)$$

so

$$wp(\text{if } x \text{ then } x :=1 \text{ else } x := -1 \text{ fi}, x = 1) = (x > 0)$$

as we expect.

While-statements.   The while-statement $\text{while } E \text{ do } L \text{ od}$, as defined in Section 13.1, executes as long as $E > 0$. As in other formal semantic methods, the semantics of the while-loop present particular problems. We must give an inductive definition based on the number of times the loop executes. Let $H_i(\text{while } E \text{ do } L \text{ od}, Q)$ be the statement that the loop executes i times and terminates in a state satisfying Q. Then clearly

$$H_0(\text{while } E \text{ do } L \text{ od}, Q) = E \leq 0 \text{ and } Q$$

and

$$H_1(\text{while } E \text{ do } L \text{ od}, Q) = E > 0 \text{ and } wp(L,Q \text{ and } E \leq 0)$$
$$= E > 0 \text{ and } wp(L,H_0(\text{while } E \text{ do } L \text{ od}, Q))$$

Continuing in this fashion we have in general that

$$H_{i+1}(\text{while } E \text{ do } L \text{ od}, Q) =$$
$$E > 0 \text{ and } wp(L,H_i(\text{while } E \text{ do } L \text{ od}, Q))$$

Now we define

$$wp(\text{while } E \text{ do } L \text{ od}, Q)$$
$$= \text{there exists an } i \text{ such that } H_i(\text{while } E \text{ do } L \text{ od}, Q)$$

Note that this definition of the semantics of the while requires the while-loop to terminate. Thus, a nonterminating loop always has false as its weakest precondition; that is, it can never make a postcondition true. For example,

$$wp(\text{while } 1 \text{ do } L \text{ od}, Q) = \text{false, for all } L \text{ and } Q$$

The semantics we have just given for loops has the drawback that it is very difficult to use in the main application area for axiomatic semantics, namely, the proof of correctness of programs. In the next section we will describe an approximation of the semantics of a loop that is more usable in practice.

13.5 Proofs of Program Correctness

The theory of axiomatic semantics was developed as a tool for proving the correctness of programs and program fragments, and this continues to be its major application. In this section we will use the axiomatic semantics of the last section to prove properties of programs written in our sample language.

We have already mentioned in the last section that a specification for a program C can be written as $\{P\} \, C \, \{Q\}$, where P represents the set of conditions that are expected to hold at the beginning of a program and Q represents the set of conditions one wishes to have true after execution of the code C. As an example, we gave the following specification for a program that sorts the array `a[1]..a[n]`:

> $\{n \geq 1 \text{ and for all } \mathtt{i}, 1 \leq \mathtt{i} \leq \mathtt{n}, \mathtt{a[i]} = \mathtt{A[i]}\}$
>
> sort-program
>
> $\{\text{sorted}(\mathtt{a}) \text{ and permutation}(\mathtt{a}, \mathtt{A})\}$

Two easier examples of specifications for programs that can be written in our sample language are the following:

1. A program that swaps the value of x and y:

> $\{\mathtt{x} = X \text{ and } \mathtt{y} = Y\}$
>
> swapxy
>
> $\{\mathtt{x} = Y \text{ and } \mathtt{y} = X\}$

2. A program that computes the sum of integers less than or equal to a positive integer n:

> $\{n > 0\}$
>
> sum_to_n
>
> $\{\text{sum} = 1 + 2 + \cdots + n\}$

We will give correctness proofs that the two programs we provide satisfy the specifications of (1) and (2).

Recall from the last section that C satisfies a specification $[P] \, C \, [Q]$ provided $P \rightarrow wp(C, Q)$. Thus, to prove that C satisfies a specification we need two steps: First, we must compute $wp(C,Q)$ from the axiomatic semantics and general properties of wp, and, second, we must show that $P \to wp(C,Q)$.

1. We claim that the following program is correct:

$$\{x = X \text{ and } y = Y\}$$
$$t := x;$$
$$x := y;$$
$$y := t$$
$$\{x = Y \text{ and } y = X\}$$

We first compute $wp(C,Q)$ as follows:

$wp(t := x \; ; \; x := y \; ; \; y := t, x = Y \text{ and } y = X)$
$\quad = wp(t := x, wp(x := y; \; y := t, x = Y \text{ and } y = X))$
$\quad = wp(t := x, wp(x := y, wp(y := t, x = Y \text{ and } y = X)))$
$\quad = wp(t := x, wp(x := y, wp(y := t, x = Y)$
$\qquad\qquad\qquad\qquad\qquad \text{and } wp(y := t, y = X)))$
$\quad = wp(t := x, wp(x := y, wp(y := t, x = Y))$
$\qquad\qquad\qquad \text{and } wp(x := y, wp(y := t, y = X)))$
$\quad = wp(t := x, wp(x := y, wp(y := t, x = Y)))$
$\qquad\qquad \text{and } wp(t := x, wp(x := y, wp(y := t, y = X)))$

by distributivity of conjunction and the axiomatic semantics of statement-lists. Now

$wp(t := x, wp(x := y, wp(y := t, x = Y))) =$
$wp(t := x, wp(x := y, x = Y)) = wp(t := x, y = Y) = (y = Y)$

and

$\quad wp(t := x, wp(x := y, wp(y := t, y = X))) =$
$\quad wp(t := x, wp(x := y, t = X)) = wp(t := X, t = x) = (x = X)$

by the rule of substitution for assignments. Thus,

$wp(t := x; x := y; \; y := t, \; x = Y \text{ and } y = X) = (y = Y \text{ and } x = X)$

The second step is to show that $P \to wp(C,Q)$. But in this case P actually equals the weakest precondition, since $P = (x = X \text{ and } y = Y)$. Since $P = wp(C,Q)$, clearly also $P \to wp(C,Q)$. The proof of correctness is complete.

2. We claim that the following program is correct:

```
{n > 0}
i := n;
sum := 0;
while i do
```

```
     sum := sum + i;
      i := i - 1
  od
  {sum = 1 + 2 + ··· + n}
```

The problem is now that our semantics for while-statements are too difficult to use to prove correctness. To show that a while-statement is correct, we really do not need to derive completely its weakest precondition $wp(\text{while} \ldots, Q)$, but only an **approximation**, that is, some assertion W such that $W \rightarrow wp(\text{while} \ldots, Q)$. Then if we can show that $P \rightarrow W$, we have also shown the correctness of $\{P\} \text{ while} \ldots \{Q\}$, since $P \rightarrow W$ and $W \rightarrow wp(\text{while} \ldots, Q)$ imply that $P \rightarrow wp(\text{while} \ldots, Q)$.

We do this in the following way. Given the loop while E do L od, suppose we find an assertion W such that the following three conditions are true:

(a) W and $(E > 0) \rightarrow wp(L,W)$

(b) W and $(E \leq 0) \rightarrow Q$

(c) $P \rightarrow W$

Then if we know that the loop while E do L od terminates, we must have $W \rightarrow wp(\text{while } E \text{ do } L \text{ od}, Q)$. This is because every time the loop executes, W continues to be true, by condition (a), and when the loop terminates, condition (b) says Q must be true. Finally, condition (c) implies that W is the required approximation for $wp(\text{while} \ldots, Q)$.

An assertion W satisfying condition (a) is said to be a **loop invariant** for the loop while E do L od, since a repetition of the loop leaves W true. In general, loops have many invariants W, and to prove the correctness of a loop, it sometimes takes a little skill to find an appropriate W, namely, one that also satisfies conditions (b) and (c).

In the case of our example program, however, a loop invariant is not too difficult to find:

$$W = (\text{sum} = (i + 1) + \cdots + n \text{ and } i \geq 0)$$

is an appropriate one. We show conditions (a) and (b) in turn:

(a)   We must show that W and $i > 0 \rightarrow wp(\text{sum} := \text{sum} + i \text{ ; } i := i - 1, W)$. First, we have

$wp(\text{sum} := \text{sum} + i; i := i - 1, W)$

$= wp(\text{sum} := \text{sum} + i; i := i - 1, \text{sum} = (i + 1) + \cdots + n$
   $\text{and } i \geq 0)$

$= wp(\text{sum} := \text{sum} + i, wp(i := i - 1, \text{sum} = (i + 1) + \cdots + n$
   $\text{and } i \geq 0))$

$= wp(\text{sum} := \text{sum} + i, \text{sum} = ((i - 1) + 1) + \cdots + n$
   $\text{and } i - 1 \geq 0)$

$= wp(\text{sum} := \text{sum} + i, \text{ sum} = i + \cdots + n \text{ and } i - 1 \geq 0)$

$= (\text{sum} + i = i + \cdots + n \text{ and } i - 1 \geq 0)$

$= (\text{sum} = (i + 1) + \cdots + n \text{ and } i - 1 \geq 0)$

Now $(W \text{ and } i > 0) \to (W \text{ and } i - 1 \geq 0)$, since

$$W \text{ and } i > 0 = (\text{sum} = (i + 1) + \cdots + n \text{ and } i \geq 0 \text{ and } i > 0)$$
$$= (\text{sum} = (i + 1) + \cdots + n \text{ and } i > 0) \to$$
$$(W \text{ and } i - 1 \geq 0)$$

Thus, W is a loop invariant.

(b)   We must show that $(W \text{ and } (i \leq 0)) \to (\text{sum} = 1 + \cdots + n)$. But this is clear:

$$W \text{ and } (i \leq 0) = (\text{sum} = (i + 1) + \cdots + n \text{ and } i \geq 0 \text{ and } i \leq 0)$$
$$= (\text{sum} = (i + 1) + \cdots + n \text{ and } i = 0)$$
$$= (\text{sum} = 1 + \cdots + n \text{ and } i = 0)$$

It remains to show that conditions just prior to the execution of the loop imply the truth of W.[2] We do this by showing that $n > 0 \to wp(i := n; \text{sum} := 0, W)$. We have

$$wp(i := n; \text{sum} := 0, W)$$
$$= wp(i := n, wp(\text{sum} := 0, \text{sum} = (i + 1) + \cdots + n \text{ and } i \geq 0))$$
$$= wp(i := n, 0 = (i + 1) + \cdots + n \text{ and } i \geq 0)$$
$$= (0 = (n + 1) + \cdots + n \text{ and } n \geq 0)$$
$$= (0 = 0 \text{ and } n \geq 0)$$
$$= (n \geq 0)$$

and of course $n > 0 \to n \geq 0$. In this computation we used the property that the sum $(i + 1) + \cdots + n$ with $i \geq n$ is 0. This is a general mathematical property: Empty sums are always assumed to be 0. We also note that this proof uncovered an additional property of our code: It works not only for $n > 0$, but for $n \geq 0$ as well.

This concludes our discussion of proofs of programs. A few more examples will be discussed in the exercises.

Exercises

13.1 Our sample language used the bracketing keywords "fi" and "od" for if-statements and while-statements, similar to Algol68. Was this necessary? Why?

13.2 Add unary minuses to the arithmetic expressions of the sample language, and add its semantics to (a) the operational semantics and (b) the denotational semantics.

---

[2] In fact, we should also prove termination of the loop, but we ignore this issue in this brief discussion. Proving correctness while assuming termination is called proving **partial correctness**, which is what we are really doing here.

13.3 Add division to the arithmetic expressions of the sample language, and add its semantics to **(a)** the operational semantics and **(b)** the denotational semantics. Try to include a specification of what happens when division by 0 occurs.

13.4 The operational semantics of identifiers was skipped in the discussion in the text. Add the semantics of identifiers to the operational semantics of the sample language.

13.5 The denotational semantics of identifiers was also (silently) skipped. What we did was to use the set Identifier as both a syntactic domain (the set of syntax trees of identifiers) and as a semantic domain (the set of strings with the concatenation operator). Call the latter set Name, and develop a denotational definition of the semantic function **I**: Identifier → Name. Revise the denotational semantics of the sample language to include this correction.

13.6 A problem that exists with any formal description of a language is that the description itself must be written in some "language," which we could call the **defining language,** to distinguish it from the defined language. For example, the defining language in each of the formal methods studied in this chapter are as follows:

> operational semantics: reduction rules
>
> denotational semantics: functions
>
> axiomatic semantics: logic

For a formal semantic method to be successful, the defining language needs to have a precise description itself, and it must also be understandable. Discuss and compare the defining languages of the three semantic methods in terms of your perception of their precision and understandability.

13.7 One formal semantic method not discussed in this chapter but mentioned in Chapter 11 is the use of the defined language itself as the defining language. Such a method could be called **metacircular,** and metacircular interpreters are a common method of defining LISP-like languages. Discuss the advantages and disadvantages of this method in comparison with the methods discussed in this chapter.

13.8 The grammar of the sample language included a complete description of identifiers and numbers. However, a language translator usually recognizes such constructs in the scanner. Our view of semantics thus implies that the scanner is performing semantic functions. Wouldn't it be better simply to make numbers and identifiers into tokens in the grammar, thus making it unnecessary to describe something done by the scanner as "semantics?" Why or why not?

13.9 The axiomatic semantics of Section 13.4 did not include a description of the semantics of expressions. Describe a way of including expressions in the axiomatic description.

13.10 Show how the operational semantics of the sample language describes the reduction of the expression $23 * 5 - 34$ to its value.

13.11 Compute $E[[23 * 5 - 34]]$ using the denotational definition of the sample language.

13.12 Show how the operational semantics of the sample language describes the reduction of the program a := 2; b := a + 1; a := b * b to its environment.

13.13 Compute the value $Env(a)$ for the environment Env at the end of the program a := 2; b := a + 1; a := b * b using the denotational definition of the sample language.

13.14 Repeat Exercise 13.12 for the program

```
a := 0 - 11;
if a then a := a else a := 0 - a fi
```

13.15 Repeat Exercise 13.13 for the program of Exercise 13.14.

13.16 Use operational semantics to reduce the following program to its environment:

```
n := 2;
while n do n := n - 1 od
```

13.17 The sample language did not include any input or output statements. We could add these to the grammar as follows:

$$stmt \rightarrow \ldots \mid \text{'input'} \; identifier \mid \text{'output'} \; expr$$

Add input and output statements to the **(a)** operational semantics and **(b)** denotational semantics. (*Hint for denotational semantics:* Consider a new semantic domain IntSequence to be the set of sequences of integers. Then statement sequences act on states that are environments plus an input sequence and an output sequence.)

13.18 An often useful statement in a language is an empty statement, which is sometimes denoted by the keyword **skip** in texts on semantics. Add a **skip** statement to the sample language of this chapter, and describe its **(a)** operational, **(b)** denotational, or **(c)** axiomatic semantics. Why is such a statement useful?

13.19 The sample language has unusual semantics for if- and while-statements, due to the absence of Boolean expressions. Add Boolean expressions such as x = 0, **true**, y > 2 to the sample language, and describe their semantics in **(a)** operational and **(b)** denotational terms.

13.20 Revise the axiomatic description of the sample language to include the Boolean expressions of Exercise 13.19.

13.21 Find $wp($a := 2; b := a + 1; a := b * b, $a = 9)$.

13.22 Find $wp($if x then x := x else x := 0 - x fi, $x \le 0)$.

13.23 Show that the following program is correct with respect to the given specification:

```
{true}
if x then x := x else x := 0 - x fi
{x ≥ 0}
```

13.24 Which of the following are loop invariants of the loop `while i do sum := sum + i; i := i - 1 od`:
(a) sum = i + ··· + n
(b) sum = (i + 1) + ··· + n and i > 0
(c) sum ≥ 0 and i ≥ 0

13.25 Prove the correctness of the following program:

```
{n > 0}
i := n;
fact := 1;
while i do
   fact := fact * i;
   i := i - 1
od
{fact = 1 * 2 * ... * n}
```

13.26 Write a program in the sample language that computes the product of two numbers n and m by repeatedly adding n m-times. Prove that your program is correct.

13.27 In Section 13.4 and 13.5 we used the following example of a program specification using preconditions and postconditions:

{n ≥ 1 and for all i, 1 ≤ i ≤ n, a[i] = A[i]}

sort-program

{sorted(a) and permutation(a, A)}

Write out the details of the assertions sorted(a) and permutation (a, A).

13.28 Show the correctness of the following program using axiomatic semantics:

```
{n > 0}
while n do n := n - 1 od
{n = 0}
```

13.29 Show using general properties of wp that $wp(C, \text{not } Q) \rightarrow \text{not } wp(C,Q)$ for any language construct C and any assertion Q.

13.30 Show that the law of monotonicity follows from the distributivity of conjunction. (*Hint:* Use the fact that $P \rightarrow Q$ is equivalent to $(P \text{ and } Q) = P$.)

13.31 We did not describe how operations might be extended to lifted domains (domains with an undefined value) such as Integer$_\perp$. Give a definition for "+," "−," and "*" that includes the undefined value $\perp$.

13.32 Sometimes operations can ignore undefined values and still return a defined value. Give an example where the "*" operation can do this. (Such operations are called nonstrict. Strictness was discussed in Chapter 11.)

13.33 The formal semantic descriptions of the sample language in this chapter did not include a description of the semantics in the presence of undefined values (such as the use of an identifier without an assigned value or a loop that never terminates). Try to extend the semantic descriptions of each of the three methods discussed in this chapter to include a description of the effect of undefined values.

13.34 We might be tempted to define an environment in denotational terms as a semantic function from identifiers to integers (ignoring undefined values):

$$\textbf{Env}: \text{Identifier} \rightarrow \text{Integer}$$

Would this be wrong? Why or why not?

13.35 The text mentions that in the presence of nondeterminism it is not true that $wp(C,P \text{ or } Q) = wp(C,P) \text{ or } wp(C,Q)$. Let C be the following guarded if, in which either statement might be executed,

```
if
      true => x := x + 1
      true => x := x - 1
fi
```

Show that $wp(C, (x > 0) \text{ or } (x < 0))$ is not equal to $wp(C, \ x > 0)$ or $wp(C, \ x < 0)$.

13.36 The operational semantics in Section 13.2 specified a left-to-right evaluation for expressions. Rewrite the reduction rules so that no particular evaluation order is specified.

13.37 The rule for reducing parentheses in operational semantics was written as the axiom '(' V ')' => V, where V stands for a numeric value. Why is it wrong to write the more general rule '(' E ')' => E, where E can be any expression?

13.38 In Section 13.2 we wrote three reduction rules for if-statements, but only two for while-statements.
(a) Rewrite the rules for if-statements as only two rules.
(b) Can one write three rules for the while-statement? Why?

13.39 Using the `skip` statement (Exercise 13.18), write a *single* reduction rule for the operational semantics of the while statement.

13.40 Is it possible to express the evaluation order of expressions in denotational semantics? Explain.

13.41 In operational semantics, an environment must be given before an abstract machine can perform any reductions. Thus, one (extremely abstract) view of operational semantics is as a function Φ: Program × Environment → Environment. In this sense, denotational semantics can be viewed as a Curried version (see Section 11.4.3) of operational semantics. Explain what is meant by this statement.

13.42 Complete the Prolog program sketched in Section 13.2.5 implementing the operational semantics for expressions in the sample language.

13.43 Extend the Prolog program of the previous exercise to include the full sample language.

13.44 Complete the Haskell program sketched in Section 13.3.7 implementing the operational semantics for expressions in the sample language.

13.45 Extend the Haskell program of the previous exercise to include the full sample language.

Notes and References

Formal semantic methods are studied in greater depth in Winskel [1993], Reynolds [1998], Gunter [1992], and Mitchell [1996]. A different operational method is the Vienna definition language, which is surveyed in Wegner [1972]. An outgrowth of VDL is the Vienna development method, or VDM, which is denotational in approach. A description of this method appears in Harry [1997], which includes a description of a related method, called Z.

Denotational semantics as they are presented here began with the early work of Scott and Strachey (see Stoy [1977]). An in-depth coverage of denotational semantics, including domain theory and fixed-point semantics, is given in Schmidt [1986]. Axiomatic semantics began with a seminal paper by Hoare [1969]. Weakest preconditions were introduced by Dijkstra [1975, 1976]. An in-depth coverage is given in Dijkstra and Scholten [1990] and Gries [1981]. For a perspective on nondeterminism and the law of the excluded miracle, see Nelson [1989].

Formal semantic methods as they apply to object-oriented languages are studied in Gunter and Mitchell [1994]. Perhaps the only production language for which a complete formal description has been given is ML (Milner et al. [1997]); a partial formal semantics for Ada83 can be found in Björner and Oest [1981].

One topic not studied in this chapter is the formal semantics of data types and type checking, which are usually given as a set of rules similar to the reduction rules of operational semantics. Details can be found in Hindley [1997] or Schmidt [1994].

14 Parallel Programming

The idea of **parallel processing**, or executing many computations in parallel, has been around at least since the 1960s, when the first **multiprogramming** or **pseudoparallel systems** became available: systems in which many processes share a single processor and appear to execute simultaneously. Pseudoparallelism represented a considerable advance in computer technology, and it is still the standard way most larger machines operate today. It has also long been clear that **true parallelism**, in which many processors are connected together to run in concert, either as a single system incorporating all the processors (a **multiprocessor system**) or as a group of stand-alone processors connected together by high-speed links (a **distributed system**), represents an even greater advance in computer technology, since this is one way of solving the problem of the von Neumann bottleneck (see Chapter 1).

However, this seemingly simple idea has not been simple to put into practice, and truly parallel systems, in which a single process can share different processors, are even at the time of this writing relatively uncommon, despite extensive study of the issues involved.[1] Thus, a comprehensive study of parallel processing is beyond the scope of this text.

---

[1] Larger computers often have multiple processors, but it is still rare for a single process to have access to more than one processor at a time.

The situation has become even more complex with the advent of high-speed networks, including the Internet, in that physically distant computers are now capable of working together using the same or similar programs to handle large problems. Thus, organized networks of independent computers can also be viewed as a kind of distributed system for parallel processing, and, indeed, may have already become more important than traditional styles of parallel computing.[2] Obviously, many of the issues involved in networked parallel processing are also beyond the scope of this text (see the Notes and References for networking texts that provide more information).

Nevertheless, programming languages have been intimately involved in the implementation of parallelism in a number of ways. First, programming languages have been used to express algorithms to solve the problems presented by parallel processing systems. Second, programming languages have been used to write operating systems that have implemented these solutions on various architectures. Also, programming languages have been used to harness the capabilities of multiple processors to solve application problems efficiently. Finally, programming languages have been used to implement and express communication across networks.

A survey of the principles and practice of programming language design would therefore not be complete without a study of the basic approaches that programming languages have taken to expressing parallelism. In this study we must also distinguish between the parallelism as expressed in a programming language and the parallelism that actually exists in the underlying hardware. Programs that are written with parallel programming constructs do not necessarily result in actual parallel processing, but could simply be implemented by pseudoparallelism, even in a system with multiple processors. Thus, parallel programming is sometimes referred to as **concurrent programming** to emphasize the fact that parallel constructs express only the **potential** for parallelism, not that parallel processing actually occurs (which is decided by the architecture of the particular system, the operating system, and the pragmatics of the translator interface). However, we will suppress this distinction and will refer to concurrent programming as parallel programming, without implying that parallel processing must occur.

---

[2] Indeed, the Internet can be viewed as a kind of gigantic parallel computer, and several initiatives have successfully used the Internet in that way; see the Notes and References.

In this chapter we briefly survey the basic concepts of parallelism, without which an understanding of language issues is impossible. We then survey basic language issues and introduce the standard approaches to parallelism taken by programming language designers. These include threads; semaphores and their structured alternative, the monitor; and message passing. Java and Ada are used for most of the examples. Finally, a brief look is taken at some proposed ways of expressing parallelism in functional and logic programming languages.

14.1 Introduction to Parallel Processing

The fundamental notion of parallel processing is that of the **process**: It is the basic unit of code executed by a processor. Processes have been variously defined in the literature, but a simple definition is the following:

> A process is a program in execution.

This is not quite accurate, since processes can consist of parts of programs as well as whole programs, more than one process can correspond to the same program, and processes do not need to be currently executing to retain their status as processes. A better definition might be the following:

> A process is an instance of a program or program part that has been scheduled for independent execution.

Processes used to be called **jobs**, and in the early days of computing, jobs were executed in purely sequential, or **batch** fashion. Thus, there was only one process in existence at a time, and there was no need to distinguish between processes and programs.

With the advent of pseudoparallelism, several processes could exist simultaneously. A process now could be in one of **several states**: It could be **executing**, that is, in possession of the processor; it could be **blocked**, waiting for some activity such as input-output to finish, or some event such as a keypress to occur; or it could be **waiting** for execution by the processor.[3] In such a system the operating system needs to apply some algorithm to schedule processes for execution, and to manage a data structure, usually a queue, to maintain waiting and blocked processes. It also needs a method to cause processes to relinquish the processor, or timeout. The principal method for accomplishing this is the **hardware interrupt**.

With the existence of multiple processes, a distinction can also be made between **heavyweight processes** and **lightweight processes**. A heavyweight process corresponds to the earlier notion of a program in execution: It exists as a full-fledged independent entity, together with all of

---

[3] This is a simplified description. Actual operating systems have a more complex state structure.

the memory and other resources that are ordinarily allocated by the operating system to an entire program. A lightweight process, on the other hand, shares its resources with the program it came from: It does not have an independent existence except insofar as it executes a particular sequence of instructions from its parent program independently of other execution paths, while sharing all memory and other resources. A lightweight process is also called a **thread**. Lightweight processes can be particularly efficient, since there is less overhead in their creation and management by the operating system.

In a true parallel processing system, where several processors are available, the notion of process and process state is retained much as in the pseudoparallel system. The complication is that each processor may individually be assigned to a process, and a clear distinction must be made between process and processor. Each processor may or may not be assigned its own queues for maintaining blocked and waiting processes.

The organization of the different processors is a critical issue to the operation of processes in a parallel processing system. Two primary requirements for the organization of the processors are

1. There must be a way for processors to synchronize their activities.
2. There must be a way for processors to communicate data among themselves.

For example, in a typical situation, one processor will be handling the input and sorting of data, while a second processor performs computations on the data. The second processor must not begin processing data before it is sorted by the first processor. This is a synchronization problem. Also, the first processor needs to communicate the actual sorted data to the second processor. This is a communication problem.

In some machines one processor is designated as a controller, which manages the operation of the other processors. In some cases this central control extends even to the selection of instructions, and all the processors must execute the same instructions on their respective registers or data sets. Such systems are called **single-instruction, multiple-data** or **SIMD systems** and are by their nature multiprocessing rather than distributed systems. Such systems are also often synchronous, in that all the processors operate at the same speed and the controlling processor determines precisely when each instruction is executed by each processor. This implicitly solves the synchronization problem.

In other architectures all the processors act independently. Such systems are called **multiple-instruction, multiple-data** or **MIMD systems** and may be either multiprocessor or distributed processor systems. In an MIMD system the processors may operate at different speeds, and therefore such systems are asynchronous. Thus, the synchronization of the processors in an MIMD system becomes a critical problem.

Hybrid systems are also possible, with each processor retaining some but not complete independence from the other processors. The difference between an SIMD and an MIMD system is illustrated in Figure 14.1.

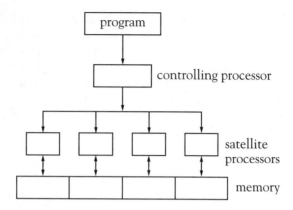

Figure 14.1a   Schematic of an SIMD Processor

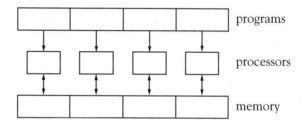

Figure 14.1b   Schematic of an MIMD Processor

In a similar way to the sharing of instructions in an SIMD system, memory may be shared. A system in which one central memory is shared by all the processors is called a **shared-memory system** and is also by nature a multiprocessor rather than a distributed system, while a system in which each processor has its own independent memory is called a **distributed-memory system** (and may be either an actual distributed system or a multiprocessor system).

In a shared-memory system the processors communicate through the changes each makes to the shared memory. If the processors operate asynchronously, they may also use the shared memory to synchronize their activities. For this to work properly, each processor must have exclusive access to those parts of memory that it is changing. This is the **mutual exclusion problem**. Without mutual exclusion, different processes may be modifying the same memory locations in an interleaved and unpredictable way, a situation that is sometimes called a **race condition**. Solving the mutual exclusion problem typically means blocking processes when another process is already accessing shared data using some kind of locking mechanism. This can cause a new problem to arise, namely, **deadlock**, where processes end up waiting forever for each other to unblock. Detecting or preventing deadlock is typically one of the most difficult problems in parallel processing.

Distributed-memory systems do not have to worry about mutual exclusion, since each processor has its own memory inaccessible to the other processors. On the other hand, distributed processors have a **communication problem**, in that each processor must be able to send messages to and receive messages from all the other processors asynchronously. Communication between processors depends on the configuration of links between the processors. Sometimes processors are connected in sequence, and processors may need to forward information to other processors farther along the link. If the number of processors is small, each processor may be fully linked to every other processor. Note that communicating processes may also block while waiting for a needed message, and this, too, can cause deadlock. Indeed, solving deadlock problems in a distributed system can be even more difficult than for a shared memory system, because each process may have little information about the status of other processes. For example, if another process is running on another computer connected to a network, and that computer crashes, it may be difficult to learn anything about what happened.

Again, it is possible for a system to be a hybrid between a shared memory and a distributed-memory system, with each processor maintaining some private memory in addition to the shared memory and the processors having some communication links separate from the shared memory. Figure 14.2 illustrates the difference between a shared-memory system and a fully linked distributed-memory system.[4]

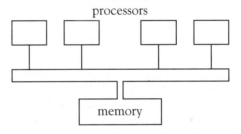

Figure 14.2a   Schematic of a Shared-Memory System

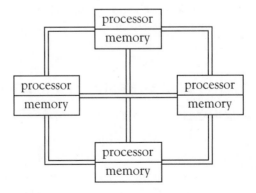

Figure 14.2b   Schematic of a Fully Linked Distributed-Memory System

---

[4] Figures adapted from Karp [1987], p. 44. Copyright 1987, IEEE. Used by permission.

Regardless of the organization of the underlying machine, it is the task of the operating system to integrate the operation of the processors and to shield the user from needing to know too much about the particular configuration. The operating system can also change the view the user has of the hardware, depending on the utilities it makes available. For example, the operating system could assign distinct parts of memory in a shared-memory system for exclusive use by each processor and use other parts of memory to simulate communications channels, thus making a shared-memory system appear to be a distributed-memory system. The operating system can even shield the user entirely from the fact that there is more than one processor and schedule users or processes on different processors automatically, according to an internal algorithm that attempts to allocate resources in an efficient way. However, automatic allocation of multiple processors is almost always less than optimal, and there is usually a need for operating systems to provide facilities for users to manage processes and processors manually. In general, an operating system will need to provide:

1. A means of creating and destroying processes.

2. A means of managing the number of processors used by processes (for example, a method of assigning processes to processors or a method for reserving a number of processors for use by a program).

3. On a shared-memory system, a mechanism for ensuring mutual exclusion of processes to shared memory. Mutual exclusion is used for both process synchronization and communication.

4. On a distributed-memory system, a mechanism for creating and maintaining communication channels between processors. These channels are used both for interprocess communication and for synchronization. A special case of this mechanism is necessary for a network of loosely connected independent computers, such as computers cooperating over the Internet.

In the next section, we will see how similar facilities must be provided by programming languages to make parallel processing available to programmers.

14.2 Parallel Processing and Programming Languages

Programming languages are like operating systems in that they need to provide programmers with mechanisms for process creation, synchronization, and communication. However, a programming language has stricter requirements than an operating system: Its facilities must be machine independent and must adhere to language design principles such as readability, writability, and maintainability. Nevertheless, most programming languages have adopted a particular model of parallel organization in providing parallel facilities. Thus, some languages use the shared-memory model and provide facilities for mutual exclusion, typically by providing a built-in thread mechanism or thread library, while others assume the distributed model and provide communication facilities. A few languages have included both models, the designers arguing that sometimes one model and sometimes the other will be preferable in particular situations.

A language designer can also adopt the view that parallel mechanisms should not be included in a language definition at all. If this is done, there are still ways that parallel facilities can be provided. Since this is the easiest approach to parallelism (from the point of view of the language designer), we will study this first. Also in this section, we will consider some approaches to process creation and destruction, since these are (more or less) common to both the shared-memory and the distributed models of parallelism. Model-specific facilities will be left to later sections. In particular, Section 14.3 will discuss **threads**, especially the Java thread implementation. Sections 14.4 and 14.5 will discuss **semaphores** and **monitors**, two approaches to the shared-memory model. Section 14.6 will study **message passing**, a mechanism that follows the distributed model, with examples from Ada. That section will also briefly mention a few of the issues surrounding the network model (which is a kind of distributed model).

We will also need a number of standard problems in parallel processing to demonstrate the use of particular mechanisms. We will use the following two problems throughout the remainder of this chapter (other problems are discussed in the exercises):

1. *The bounded buffer problem.* This problem assumes that two or more processes are cooperating in a computational or input-output situation. One (or more) process produces values that are consumed by another process (or processes). An intermediate buffer, or buffer process, stores produced values until they are consumed. A solution to this problem must ensure that no value is produced until there is room to store it and that a value is consumed only after it has been produced. This involves both communication and synchronization. When the emphasis is not on the buffer, this problem is called the *producer-consumer problem.*

2. *Parallel matrix multiplication.* This problem is different from the previous one in that it is an example of an algorithmic application in which the use of parallelism can cause significant speedups. Matrices are essentially two-dimensional arrays, as in the following declaration of integer matrices (we consider only the case where the size of both dimensions is the same, given by the positive integer constant N):

   ```
   typedef int Matrix [N][N];
   Matrix a,b,c;
   ```

   The standard way of multiplying two matrices a and b to form a third matrix c is given by the following nested loops:

```
for (i = 0; i < N; i++)
    for (j = 0; j < N; j++)
        c[i][j] = 0;
        for (k = 0; k < N; k++)
            c[i][j] = c[i][j] + a[i][k] * b[k][j];
```

This computation, if performed sequentially, takes N^3 steps. If, however, we assign a process to compute each c[i][j], and if each process executes on a separate processor, then the computation can be performed in the equivalent of N steps. Algorithms such as this are studied extensively in courses on parallel algorithms. In fact, this is the simplest form of such an algorithm, since there are no write conflicts caused by the computation of the c[i][j] by separate processes. Thus, there is no need to enforce mutual exclusion in accessing the matrices as shared memory. There is, however, a synchronization problem in that the product c cannot be used until all the processes that compute it have finished. A programming language, if it is to provide useful parallelism, must provide facilities for implementing such algorithms with a minimum of overhead.

14.2.1 Parallel Programming without Explicit Language Facilities

As we have noted, one possible approach to parallelism is simply not to express it explicitly at all in the language. This is especially possible in functional, logic, and object-oriented languages, which have a certain amount of inherent parallelism implicit in the language constructs. (We have mentioned this before, but we will review it again in Section 14.7.)

In theory it is possible for language translators, using optimization techniques, to make use automatically of operating system utilities to assign different processors to different parts of a program. However, as with operating systems, the automatic assignment of processors is likely to be suboptimal, and manual facilities are needed to make full use of parallel processors. In addition, a programming language may be used for purposes that require explicitly indicating the parallelism, such as the writing of operating systems themselves or the implementation of intricate parallel algorithms.

A second alternative to defining parallel constructs in a programming language is for the translator to offer the programmer **compiler options** to allow the explicit indicating of areas where parallelism is called for. This is usually better than automatic parallelization. One of the places where this is most effective is in the use of nested loops, where each repetition of the inner loop is relatively independent of the others. Such a situation is the matrix multiplication problem just discussed.

Figure 14.3 shows an example of a parallel loop compiler option in FORTRAN code for the matrix multiplication problem. The example is for a FORTRAN compiler on a Sequent parallel computer. The compiler option is

```
C$doacross share(a, b, c), local(j, k)
```

that causes a preprocessor to insert code that parallelizes the outer loop. The share and local declarations indicate that a, b, and c are to be accessed by all processes, but that j and k are local variables to each process. The call to m_set_procs sets the number of processes (and processors) that are to be used, returning an error code if not enough processors are available. (Note that in the example the number of processes is ten, far below the number needed to compute optimally the matrix product; see Exercise 14.4.) The call to m_kill_procs synchronizes the processes, so that all processes wait for the entire loop to finish and that only one process continues to execute after the loop.

```
      integer a(100, 100), b(100, 100), c(100, 100)
      integer i, j, k, numprocs, err
      numprocs = 10
C code to read in a and b goes here
      err = m_set_procs(numprocs)
C$doacross share(a, b, c), local(j, k)
      do 10 i = 1,100
        do 10 j = 1,100
          c(i, j) = 0
          do 10 k = 1,100
            c(i, j) = c(i, j) + a(i, k) * b(k, j)
   10 continue
      call m_kill_procs
C code to write out c goes here
      end
```

Figure 14.3   FORTRAN Compiler Options for Parallelism

A third way of making parallel facilities available without explicit mechanisms in the language design is to provide a library of functions to perform parallel processing. This is a way of passing the facilities provided by an operating system directly to the programmer. This way, different libraries can be provided, depending on what facilities an operating system or parallel machine offers. Of course, if a standard parallel library is required by a language, then this is the same as including parallel facilities in the language definition.

Figure 14.4 is an example in C where library functions are used to provide parallel processing for the matrix multiplication problem. (C itself has no parallel mechanisms.) We note that the example of the use of a translator option to indicate parallelism (Figure 14.3) also used some of the same library procedures. (This example is also for a Sequent computer, for comparison purposes.)

```
#include <parallel/parallel.h>
#define SIZE 100
#define NUMPROCS 10

shared int a[SIZE][SIZE], b[SIZE][SIZE], c[SIZE][SIZE];

void multiply(void)
{ int i, j, k;
  for (i = m_get_myid(); i < SIZE; i += NUMPROCS)
   for (j = 0; j < SIZE; j++)
    for (k = 0 ; k < SIZE; k++)
        c[i][j] += a[i][k] * b[k][j];
}
main()
{ int err;
  /* code to read in the matrices a and b goes here */
  m_set_procs(NUMPROCS);
  m_fork(multiply);
  m_kill_procs();
  /* code to write out the matrix c goes here */
  return 0;
}
```

Figure 14.4   Use of a Library to Provide Parallel Processing

In Figure 14.4 the four procedures m_set_procs, m_fork, m_kill_procs, and m_get_myid are imported from a library (the parallel/parallel library). m_set_procs and m_kill_procs are as in the previous example. m_fork creates the ten processes, which are all instances of the procedure multiply (the name fork comes from the Unix operating system, discussed shortly). In procedure multiply, m_get_myid gets the number of the process instance (from 0 to 9). The remainder of the code then divides the work among the processes, so that process 0 calculates c[0][i], c[10][i], ..., c[90][i] for all i, process 2 calculates c[21[i], c[12][i], ..., c[92][i], and so on.

A final alternative to introducing parallelism into a language is to simply rely on operating system features directly to run programs in parallel. Essentially, this requires that a parallel program be split up into separate, independently executable pieces and then set up to communicate via operating system mechanisms (thus allowing only program-level parallelism as described shortly). A typical example of this is to string programs together in a Unix operating system through the use of **pipes**, which is a method of streaming text input and output from one program to another without storing to intermediate files (which could be inefficient or impossible if these files are large). A simple example is the following, which will list all file names in the current directory containing the string "java:"[5]

```
ls | grep "java"
```

---

[5] This can actually be condensed to the single command "ls *java*" in Unix.

This command runs the two Unix utility programs `ls` and `grep` in parallel (`ls` is the directory listing program, `grep` is the "global regular expression print" program that finds string patterns in text). The output of `ls` is piped to `grep` using the pipe symbol (the vertical bar), and becomes the input to `grep`. As a more complex example, the pipe

```
cat *.java | tr -sc A-Za-z '\012' | sort | uniq -c | sort -rn
```

will list all of the words in Java programs in the current directory, with a count of their usage, and sorted in order of decreasing number of uses (we leave as an exercise the explanation of each of the five programs used in this pipeline).

14.2.2   Process Creation and Destruction

A programming language that contains explicit mechanisms for parallel processing must have a construct for creating new processes. We have seen this informally already in Figure 14.4, where calls to the library procedures `m_set_procs` and `m_fork` together created a fixed number of processes.

There are two basic ways that new processes can be created. One is to split the current process into two or more processes that continue to execute copies of the same program. In this case, one of the processes is usually distinguished as the **parent** while the others become the **children**. The processes can execute different code by a test of process identifiers or some other condition, but the basic program is the same for all processes. This method of process creation resembles the SIMD organization of Section 14.1 and is therefore called **SPMD programming** (for single program multiple data). Note, however, that SPMD programs may execute different segments of their common code and so do not necessarily operate synchronously. Thus there is a need for process synchronization.

In the second method of process creation, a segment of code (commonly a procedure) is explicitly associated with each new process. Thus, different processes have different code, and we can call this method **MPMD programming**. A typical case of this is the so-called **fork-join** model, where a process creates several child processes, each with its own code (a fork), and then waits for the children to complete their execution (a join). Unfortunately, the name is confusing, because the Unix system called `fork()` (studied shortly) is really an SPMD process creator, not a fork-join creator. We will therefore refer to MPMD process creation rather than a fork-join creation. Note that Figure 14.4 is an example of MPMD programming (with `m_kill_procs` taking the place of the join).

An alternative view of process creation is to focus on the size of the code that can become a separate process. In some designs, individual statements can become processes and be executed in parallel. A second possibility is for procedures to be assigned to processes. This was the case in Figure 14.4, where the procedure multiply was assigned to processes via the call `m_fork(multiply)`. A third possibility is for processes to represent whole programs only. Sometimes the different size of the code assignable to separate processes is referred to as the **granularity** of processes. The three choices of constructs for parallel execution that we have just listed could be described as follows:

1. statement-level parallelism: fine-grained
2. procedure-level parallelism: medium-grained
3. program-level parallelism: large-grained

Granularity can be an issue in program efficiency: Depending on the kind of machine, many small-grained processes can incur significant overhead in their creation and management, thus executing more slowly than fewer larger processes. On the other hand, large-grained processes may have difficulty in exploiting all opportunities for parallelism within a program. An intermediate case that can be very efficient is that of a thread, which typically represents fine-grained or medium-grained parallelism without the overhead of full-blown process creation.

Regardless of the method of process creation, it is possible to distinguish between process creator (the parent process) and process created (the child process), and for every process creation mechanism, the following two questions must be answered:

1. Does the parent process suspend execution while its child processes are executing, or does it continue to execute alongside them?
2. What memory, if any, does a parent share with its children or the children share among themselves?

In Figure 14.4 the assumption was that the parent process suspends execution while the child processes compute. It was also necessary to indicate explicitly that the global variables a, b, and c are to be shared by all processes, using the keyword shared.

In addition to process creation, a parallel programming language needs a method for process termination. In the simplest case, a process will simply execute its code to completion and then cease to exist. But in more complex situations, a process may need to continue executing until a certain condition is met and then terminate. It may also be necessary to select a particular process to continue execution.

We will briefly study process creation and destruction mechanisms for each kind of granularity.

14.2.3   Statement-Level Parallelism

A typical construct for indicating that a number of statements can be executed in parallel is the **parbegin-parend** block:[6]

---

[6] This example is taken from the programming language **Occam**, which is based on CSP—see the Notes and References.

```
parbegin
  S1;
  S2;
  ...
  Sn;
parend;
```

In this statement the statements S1, . . ., Sn are executed in parallel. It is assumed that the main process is suspended during their execution, and that all the processes of the Si's share all variables not locally declared within an Si.

An extension of this mechanism is the parallel loop construct of Fortran95, or **forall** construct, which indicates the parallel execution of each iteration of a loop, as in

```
    forall(i = 1:100, j = 1:100)
      c(i, j) = 0
      do 10 k = 1,100
        c(i, j) = c(i, j) + a(i, k) * b(k, j)
10      continue
    end forall
```

This is similar to the $doacross compiler option of Figure 14.3.

14.2.4 Procedure-Level Parallelism

In this form of process creation/destruction, a procedure is associated with a process, and the process executes the code of the procedure. Schematically, such a mechanism has the form

```
x = newprocess(p);
...
...
killprocess(x);
```

where p is a declared procedure and x is process designator—either a numeric process number or a variable of type **process**. Figure 14.4 uses library procedures that create processes essentially this way. An alternative to this is to use declarations to associate procedures to processes:

```
process x(p);
```

Then the scope of x can be used as the region where x is active: x begins execution when the scope of its declaration is entered, and x is terminated on exit from its scope (if it has not already executed to completion). This is the method used by Ada in the declaration of tasks and task types, which is discussed more fully in Section 14.5 (the **task** is Ada's term for a process).

14.2.5 Program-Level Parallelism

In this method of process creation only whole programs can become processes. Typically, this occurs in MPMD style, where a program creates a new process by creating a complete copy of itself. The typical example of this method is the `fork` call of the Unix operating system. A call to `fork` causes a second child process to be created that is an exact copy of the calling process, including all variables and environment data at the moment of the fork. Processes can tell which is the child and which is the parent by the returned value of the call to `fork`: A zero value indicates that the process is the child, while a nonzero value indicates the process is the parent (the value itself is the process number of the child just created). By testing this value the parent and child processes can be made to execute different code:

```
if (fork() == 0)
   {/* ... child executes this part ...*/}
else
   {/* ... parent executes this part ...*/}
```

After a call to `fork`, a process can be terminated by a call to `exit`. Process synchronization can be achieved by calls to `wait`, which causes a parent to suspend its execution until a child terminates.

Figure 14.5 gives sample C code for parallel matrix multiplication using `fork`, `exit`, and `wait`. In this code, a `fork` is performed for each of the NUMPROCS child processes, and a `wait` is performed for each of the child processes as well. For simplicity, this code assumes that global variables are shared by all processes. (Warning! This is not true of processes in a standard Unix implementation. See Exercises 14.15 and 14.16 for a discussion.)

```
#define SIZE 100
#define NUMPROCS 10
int a[SIZE][SIZE], b[SIZE][SIZE], c[SIZE][SIZE];
void multiply (int myrid)
{ int i, j, k;
  for (i = myid; i < SIZE; i+= NUMPROCS)
    for (j = 0; j < SIZE; ++j)
    { c[i][j] = 0;
      for (k = 0; k < SIZE; ++k)
      c[i][j] += a[i][k] * b[k][j];
    }
}
```

Figure 14.5   Sample C Code for the Fork Construct

14.3 Threads

As we have noted, threads can be an efficient mechanism for fine- or medium-grained parallelism in the shared memory model. Since Java has a widely used thread implementation, we shall study the thread implementation in Java in some detail here, as a good illustration of the principles we have discussed so far. In particular, we will describe process creation, destruction, synchronization, and mutual exclusion in Java, and illustrate these facilities with a variation of the bounded buffer problem.

14.3.1   Threads in Java

Threads are built into the Java language, in that the `Thread` class is part of the `java.lang` package, and the reserved word `synchronize` is used to establish mutual exclusion for threads.[7] A Java thread is created by instantiating a `Thread` object and by defining a `run` method that will be executed when the thread starts. This can be done in two ways, either by extending `Thread` through inheritance and overriding the (empty) `Thread.run` method,

```
class MyThread extends Thread
{ public void run()
   { ... }
}
...
Thread t = new MyThread();
...
```

or by defining a class that implements the `Runnable` interface (which only requires the definition of a `run` method), and then passing an object of this class to the `Thread` constructor

```
class MyRunner implements Runnable
{ public void run()
   { ... }
}
...
MyRunner m = new MyRunner();
Thread t = new Thread(m);
...
```

This latter mechanism is more versatile, so we use it in our examples.

Defining a thread does not begin executing it. Instead, a thread begins running when the `start` method is called:

```
t.start(); // now t will execute the run method
```

The `start` method in turn will call `run`. Although one could call the `run` method directly, this will in general not work, since the system must perform some internal bookkeeping before calling `run`. Note also that every Java program already is executing inside a thread whose `run` method is `main`.

---

[7] Actually, Java offers two thread packages, called **green threads** and **native threads**. Green threads (the default) do not use mechanisms provided by the underlying operating system, but all parallelism is managed by the Java Virtual Machine itself. Native threads, on the other hand, use special features of the underlying operating system, and may therefore operate more efficiently by taking advantage of system features, including hardware parallelism. Green threads are necessary if threads are to operate securely across an Internet connection.

Thus, when a new thread's execution is begun by calling start, the main program will still continue to execute to completion in its own thread (in other words, the start method of a thread immediately returns, while the thread itself continues to execute). However, the entire *program* will not finish execution until all of its threads complete the execution of their run methods.[8]

How are threads destroyed? As we have just noted, the simplest mechanism is to let each thread execute its run method to completion, at which time it will cease to exist without any programmer intervention. Threads can also wait for other threads to finish before continuing by calling the join method on the thread object:

```
Thread t = new Thread(m);
t.start(); // t begins to execute
// do some other work
t.join(); // wait for t to finish
// continue with work that depends on t being finished
```

Thus, Java threads exhibit fork-join parallelism as previously defined (with the fork operation given by the start method).

An alternative to waiting for a thread to finish executing is to *interrupt* it using the interrupt method:

```
Thread t = new Thread(m);
t.start(); // t begins to execute
// do some other work
t.interrupt(); // tell t that we are waiting for it
t.join(); // continue to wait
// continue
```

The interrupt method, as this code indicates, does not actually stop the interrupted thread from executing, but simply sets an internal flag in the thread object that can be used by the object to test whether some other thread has called its interrupt method. This allows a thread to continue to execute some cleanup code before actually exiting. The semantics of the interrupt method are somewhat complex, so we defer a fuller discussion temporarily.

Note that, when t.join() is called, the current thread (i.e., the thread that makes this call) becomes blocked, and will only unblock once t exits its run method. If t is also in a blocked state waiting for an event, then deadlock can result. If there is a real potential for deadlock, then we could try to avoid it by waiting only a specified amount of time, and then timing out:

```
t.join(1000); // wait 1 second for t, then give up
```

---

[8] There is also an alternative kind of thread in Java, called a **daemon**, which is killed off when the main program exits, regardless of whether it has completed execution. See the Notes and References.

In general, any Java method such as join that blocks the current thread has a time-out version such as the above, because the Java runtime system makes no attempt to discover or prevent deadlock. It is entirely up to the programmer to ensure that deadlock cannot occur.

So far we have not discussed how to enforce mutual exclusion for shared data in Java. But even with only the mechanisms described so far, Java threads can be useful, and indeed parallel matrix multiplication can already be written (see Exercise 14.17), since there is no need for mutual exclusion.

In general, Java threads will share some memory or other resources, typically by passing the objects to be shared to constructors of the Runnable objects that are used to create the threads.[9] For example, suppose several distinct threads are adding and removing objects using a shared queue:

```
class Queue
{   ...
    public Object dequeue()
    { if (empty()) throw EmptyQueueException ;
       ...
    }
    public void enqueue(Object obj) { ... }
    ...
}

class Remover implements Runnable
{   public Remover(Queue q) { ... }
    public void run() { ... q.dequeue() ... }
    ...
}

class Inserter implements Runnable
{   public Inserter(Queue q) { ... }
    public void run() { ... q.enqueue(...) ... }
    ...
}

Queue myqueue = new Queue(...);
...
Remover r = new Remover(q);
Inserter i = new Inserter(q);
Thread t1 = new Thread(r);
Thread t2 = new Thread(i);
t1.start();
t2.start();
...
```

---

[9] It is also possible to create inner Runnable classes and share data via nonlocal access.

Now the queue q is shared between threads t1 and t2, and some mechanism for ensuring mutual exclusion within q is necessary, so that it is not possible for one thread to be executing q.dequeue() while the other is executing q.enqueue(). In Java this is done using the synchronized keyword[10] in the definition of class Queue:

```
class Queue
{    ...
     synchronized public Object dequeue()
     { if (empty()) throw EmptyQueueException ;
       ...
     }
     synchronized public void enqueue(Object obj) { ... }
     ...
}
```

In Java every object has a single **lock** (see Section 14.4) that is available to threads. When a thread attempts to execute a synchronized method of an object, it must first acquire the lock on the object. If the lock is in possession of another thread, it waits until the lock is available, acquires it, and then proceeds to execute the synchronized method. After exiting the method, it releases the lock before continuing its own execution.[11] Thus, no two threads can be simultaneously executing any synchronized methods of the same object. (Unsynchronized methods are not affected.) This solves the above mutual exclusion problem.

There is one more thread mechanism in Java that we discuss here before considering an extended example: how to cause threads to wait for certain explicit conditions and then resume execution. For example, suppose, in the above queue example, that we know that if dequeue is ever called, then an object will eventually exist for the calling thread to remove from the queue. Then it is undesirable to generate an exception on an empty queue—the thread should simply wait for the object to appear in the queue.

If a condition is testable in the code for a synchronized method, a thread executing that method can be manually stalled by calling the wait() method of the object (wait is a method of class Object, so every object has this method). Once a thread is waiting for a certain condition, it also needs to be manually reawakened by another thread (typically the thread that establishes the desired condition). This is done using either

---

[10] In this text we only discuss method synchronization. In fact, in Java any block of code can be synchronized on any object for which a local reference exists (synchronized methods implicitly synchronize on the current object this). Method synchronization is a special case of block synchronization; a method such as enqueue above can be synchronized by the following equivalent code: public void enqueue(Object obj) { synchronized(this) { ... } }

[11] This is the simplest case; in fact, a thread can acquire multiple locks, or even the same lock multiple times; each synchronized exit releases only one "hold" on one lock.

the notify() or the notifyAll() methods of the object. Note that each
object in Java has a wait-list containing all threads who have called wait
on this object, in some unspecified order. The notify() method will wake
up only one (arbitrary) thread in this list, while notifyAll() will wake up
all threads in the list. Typically notifyAll() is used in preference to
notify(), since it is impossible to predict which thread will be awakened
by notify(), and a thread in the wait-list may be waiting on a different
condition than the one that has just been established.

Now let us reconsider the above queue example. Instead of generating an exception on an empty queue, the dequeue method should call
wait, and the enqueue operation should call notifyAll, since it makes
the queue non-empty:

```
(1)   class Queue
(2)   {   ...
(3)       synchronized public Object dequeue()
(4)       { try  // wait can generate InterruptedException
(5)           {  while (empty()) wait();
(6)              ...
(7)           }
(8)         catch (InterruptedException e) // reset interrupt
(9)           { Thread.currentThread().interrupt(); }
(10)      }
(11)      synchronized public void enqueue(Object obj)
                     // tell waiting threads to try again
(12)      { // add obj into the queue
(13)          ...
(14)          notifyAll();
(15)      }
(16)      ...
(17) }
```

Two things deserve special mention here. First, a while loop is used on
line 5 in dequeue, because empty() should be retested after a wake-up:
Another thread may have already emptied the queue before this thread
acquires the lock. Second, a call to wait can generate an
InterruptedException, which must be handled or rethrown. This exception will be generated if another thread calls interrupt on a thread that
is in the wait-queue, causing it to wake up and resume execution as
though the exception occurred in the usual way.

We have noted previously that a call to interrupt does not actually
stop a thread from executing, but sets a flag that can be tested by the
thread code, so that it may perform cleanup before exiting. However, if a
thread is waiting for a lock prior to executing a synchronized method, or
is in a wait-list, then it is not executing and so cannot test for an interrupt. This problem is solved by having a call to interrupt generate an
exception if the thread is not currently executing and simultaneously
wake the stalled thread. Also, the interrupt flag is cleared when the

exception is generated. Thus, a thread typically will want to test for both the interrupt flag and `interruptedException`, if it is to handle `InterruptedException` itself. Alternatively (and this is often the simplest), the synchronized method itself can handle the exception, in which case it is reasonable to reset the interrupt flag before exiting, as in line 9 above, so that the client thread can still discover that it has been interrupted. Then the client thread code could be as follows:

```
class Remover implements Runnable
{   public Remover(Queue q) { ... }
    public void run()
    {   while (!Thread.currentThread().isInterrupted())
        {   ... q.dequeue() ...
        }
        // perform some cleanup up
        }
    } // and now exit
    ...
}
```

Note how the interrupt flag is set and tested by calls to the `interrupt` and `isInterrupted` methods of `Thread.currentThread()`. Indeed, `currentThread` is a static method of the `Thread` class (i.e., a class method) and must be called on the `Thread` class object, in which case it returns the current `Thread` object. This is necessary, since the `run` code inside a `Runnable` class has no way of identifying the actual thread that has been interrupted, but it will always be the *currently executing* thread.

14.3.2   A Bounded Buffer Example in Java

To finish our discussion of Java threads, we discuss in some detail a solution to the bounded buffer problem mentioned in Section 14.2. We will cast this problem as an input-output problem, with the producer reading characters from standard input and inserting them into the buffer, and the consumer removing characters from the buffer and writing them to standard output. To add interest to this example, we set the following additional requirements:

- The producer thread will continue to read until an end of file is encountered, whence it will exit.

- The consumer thread will continue to write until the producer has ended and no more characters remain in the buffer. Thus, the consumer should echo all the characters that the producer enters into the buffer.

The complete code for this Java program is given in Figure 14.6. We make the following explanatory remarks about this code.

```
(1) import java.io.*;
(2) class BoundedBuffer {
(3)     public static void main(String[] args) {
(4)         Buffer buffer = new Buffer(5); // buffer has size 5
(5)         Producer prod = new Producer(buffer);
(6)         Consumer cons = new Consumer(buffer);
(7)         Thread read = new Thread(prod);
(8)         Thread write = new Thread(cons);
(9)         read.start();
(10)        write.start();
(11)        try {
(12)           read.join();
(13)           write.interrupt();
(14)        }
(15)        catch (InterruptedException e) {}
(16)    }
(17) }
(18) class Buffer {
(19)     private final char[] buf;
(20)     private int start = -1;
(21)     private int end = -1;
(22)     private int size = 0;
(23)     public Buffer(int length) {
(24)         buf = new char[length];
(25)     }
(26)     public boolean more()
(27)     { return size > 0; }
(28)     public synchronized void put(char ch)
(29)     { try {
(30)         while (size == buf.length) wait();
(31)         end = (end+1) % buf.length;
(32)         buf[end] = ch;
(33)         size++;
(34)         notifyAll();
(35)       }
(36)       catch (InterruptedException e)
(37)       { Thread.currentThread().interrupt(); }
(38)     }
(39)     public synchronized char get()
(40)     { try {
(41)         while (size == 0) wait();
(42)         start = (start+1) % buf.length;
(43)         char ch = buf[start];
(44)         size--;
(45)         notifyAll();                                    (continues)
```

Figure 14.6   Java Code for a Bounded Buffer Problem

(continued)

```
(46)              return ch;
(47)          }
(48)          catch (InterruptedException e)
(49)          { Thread.currentThread().interrupt(); }
(50)          return 0;
(51)      }
(52) }
(53) class Consumer implements Runnable {
(54)      private final Buffer buffer;

(55)      public Consumer(Buffer b)
(56)      { buffer = b;
(57)      }

(58)      public void run() {
(59)        while (!Thread.currentThread().isInterrupted())
(60)        {    char c = buffer.get();
(61)             System.out.print(c);
(62)        }
(63)        while(buffer.more()) // clean-up
(64)        {    char c = buffer.get();
(65)             System.out.print(c);
(66)        }
(67)      }
(68) }
(69) class Producer implements Runnable {
(70)      private final Buffer buffer;
(71)      private final InputStreamReader in
(72)            = new InputStreamReader(System.in);

(73)      public Producer(Buffer b) { buffer = b; }

(74)      public void run() {
(75)        try {
(76)        while (!Thread.currentThread().isInterrupted()) {
(77)          int c = in.read();
(78)          if (c == -1) break; // -1 is end of file
(79)          buffer.put((char)c);
(80)        }
(81)        }
(82)        catch (IOException e) {}
(83)      }
(84) }
```

Figure 14.6 Java Code for a Bounded Buffer Problem

     The main program creates a buffer of 5 characters, a reader (the producer) for the buffer and a writer (the consumer) that prints characters. Two threads are created, one for the producer and one for the consumer (so that three threads in all exist for this program, including the main thread). The main thread then waits for the reader to finish (line 12), and then interrupts the writer (line 13). (Since `join` can, like `wait`, generate `InterruptedException`, we must also handle this exception.)

The bounded buffer class itself uses an array to hold the characters, along with two indices that traverse the array in a circular fashion, keeping track of the last positions where insertions and removals took place (this is a standard implementation technique discussed in many data structures books). Both the `put` (insert) and `get` (remove) operations are synchronized to ensure mutual exclusion. The `put` operation delays a thread if the buffer is full (line 30), while the `get` operation delays a thread if the buffer is empty (line 41). As a result, both operations must handle the `InterruptedException`. Both also call `notifyAll` after performing their respective operations (lines 34 and 45).

The `Producer` class (lines 69–84) is relatively simple: Its `run` method checks for an interrupt—even though `interrupt` will never be called on its thread in this program, it is reasonable to write general code such as this. Its only other behavior is to check for an end of file (line 78, where EOF $= -1$), whence it exits.

The `Consumer` class is almost symmetrical to the `Producer` class. The major difference is that, when a `Consumer` is interrupted, we want to make sure that the buffer has been emptied before the `Consumer` exits. Thus, on reaching line 63, we know that the producer has finished, so we simply test for more characters in the buffer and write them before exiting.

14.4   Semaphores

A **semaphore** is a mechanism to provide mutual exclusion and synchronization in a shared-memory model. It was first developed by E. W. Dijkstra in the mid-1960s and included in the languages Algol68 and PL/I. A semaphore is a shared integer variable that may be accessed only via three operations: **InitSem**, **Signal**, and **Delay**. The *Delay* operation tests the semaphore for a positive value, decrementing it if it is positive and suspending the calling process if it is zero or negative. The *Signal* operation tests whether processes are waiting, causing one of them to continue if so and incrementing the semaphore if not. (These operations were originally called *P* and *V* by Dijkstra, but we will use the more descriptive names as given; note that *Signal* is analogous to `notify` in Java, and *Delay* is analogous to `wait`.)

Given a semaphore S, the *Signal* and *Delay* operations can be defined in terms of the following pseudocode:

Delay(S): if $S > 0$ then $S := S - 1$ else suspend the calling process

Signal(S): if processes are waiting then wake up a process else $S := S + 1$

Unlike ordinary code, however, the system must ensure that each of these operations executes **atomically**, that is, by only one process at a time. (If two processes were to try to increment S at the same time, the actual final value of S would be unpredictable; see Exercise 14.52.)

Given a semaphore S, we can ensure mutual exclusion by defining a **critical region**, that is, a region of code that can be executed by only one process at a time. If S is initialized to 1, then the following code defines such a critical region:

Delay(S);

{critical region}

Signal(S);

A typical critical region is code where shared data is read and/or updated. Sometimes semaphores are referred to as **locks**, since they lock out processes from critical regions.

Semaphores can also be used to synchronize processes. If, for example, process *p* must wait for process *q* to finish, then we can initialize a semaphore S to 0, call *Delay(S)* in *p* to suspend its execution, and call *Signal(S)* at the end of *q* to resume the execution of *p*.

An important question to be addressed when defining semaphores is the method used to choose a suspended process for continued execution when a call to *Signal* is made. Possibilities include making a random choice, using a first-in, first-out strategy, or using some sort of priority system. This choice has a major effect on the behavior of concurrent programs using semaphores.

As defined, a semaphore can be thought of as abstract data type, with some added requirements. Indeed, semaphores can be defined using a Java class definition as given in Figure 14.7:[12]

```
class Semaphore
{ private int count;

  public Semaphore(int initialCount)
  { count = initialCount; }

  public synchronized void delay()
              throws InterruptedException
  { while (count <= 0) wait();
    count--;
  }

  public synchronized void signal()
  { count++;
    notify();
  }
}
```

Figure 14.7   Simplified Java Code for a Semaphore

---

[12] This simplified code ignores several Java issues, particularly those surrounding interrupts (as indicated by the `throws InterruptedException` declaration for `delay`); see Exercise 14.28.

This code uses a call to notify rather than notifyAll, because each semaphore's wait list is waiting on a single condition—that count should be greater than 0—so that only one waiting thread needs to be awakened at a time.

14.4.1 A Bounded Buffer Using Semaphores

We can write a version of the bounded buffer class that uses semaphores to enforce synchronization and mutual exclusion, as shown in Figure 14.8. (The rest of the program of Figure 14.6 can remain exactly the same.) We note a number of things about this solution.

The solution uses three semaphores. mutEx provides mutual exclusion to code that changes the private state of a Buffer. The semaphores nonEmpty and nonFull maintain the status of the number of stored items available. Note that all Java synchronization mechanisms—synchronized methods, calls to wait and notifyAll—are now gone from the Buffer code itself, since they are indirectly supplied by the semaphores.

```
(1)    class Buffer {
(2)         private final char[] buf;
(3)         private int start = -1;
(4)         private int end = -1;
(5)         private int size = 0;
(6)         private Semaphore nonFull, nonEmpty, mutEx;

(7)         public Buffer(int length) {
(8)             buf = new char[length];
(9)             nonFull = new Semaphore(length);
(10)            nonEmpty = new Semaphore(0);
(11)            mutEx = new Semaphore(1);
(12)        }

(13)        public boolean more()
(14)        { return size > 0; }

(15)        public void put(char ch)
(16)        { try {
(17)            nonFull.delay();
(18)            mutEx.delay();
(19)            end = (end+1) % buf.length;
(20)            buf[end] = ch;
(21)            size++;
(22)            mutEx.signal();
(23)            nonEmpty.signal();
(24)         }
(25)         catch (InterruptedException e)
(26)         { Thread.currentThread().interrupt(); }
(27)    }                                                       (continues)
```

Figure 14.8   The Bounded Buffer Problem Using Semaphores

(continued)

```
(28)        public char get()
(29)        { try {
(30)            nonEmpty.delay();
(31)            mutEx.delay();
(32)            start = (start+1) % buf.length;
(33)            char ch = buf[start];
(34)            size--;
(35)            mutEx.signal();
(36)            nonFull.signal();
(37)            return ch;
(38)        }
(39)        catch (InterruptedException e)
(40)        { Thread.currentThread().interrupt(); }
(41)        return 0;
(42)     }
(43) }
```

Figure 14.8   The Bounded Buffer Problem Using Semaphores

14.4.2   Difficulties with Semaphores

The basic difficulty with semaphores is that, even though the semaphores themselves are protected, there is no protection from their incorrect use or misuse by programmers. For example, if a programmer incorrectly writes

$$Signal(S);$$
$$. . .$$
$$Delay(S);$$

then the surrounded code is not a critical region and can be entered at will by any process. On the other hand, if a programmer writes

$$Delay(S);$$
$$. . .$$
$$Delay(S);$$

then it is likely that the process will block at the second *Delay*, never to resume execution. It is also possible for the use of semaphores to cause deadlock. A typical example is represented by the following code in two processes, with two semaphores S_1 and S_2:

Process 1: $Delay(S_1);$
          $Delay(S_2);$
          $. . .$
          $Signal(S_2);$
          $Signal(S_1);$

$$Process\ 2: Delay(S_2);$$
$$Delay(S_1);$$

$$. . .$$

$$Signal(S_1);$$
$$Signal(S_2);$$

If Process 1 executes $Delay(S_1)$ at the same time that Process 2 executes $Delay(S_2)$, then each will block waiting for the other to issue a *Signal*. Deadlock has occurred.

To remove some of the insecurities in the use of semaphores, the monitor was invented; see Section 14.5.

14.4.3   Implementation of Semaphores

Generally, semaphores are implemented with some form of hardware support. Even on single-processor systems this is not an entirely trivial proposition, since an operating system may possibly interrupt a process between any two machine instructions. One common method for implementing semaphores on a single-processor system is the **TestAndSet** machine instruction, which is a single machine instruction that tests a memory location and simultaneously increments or decrements the location if the test succeeds. Assuming that such a *TestAndSet* operation returns the value of its location parameter and decrements its location parameter if it is > 0, we can implement *Signal* and *Delay* with the following code schemas:

$$Delay(S): while\ TestAndSet(S) <= 0\ do\ \{nothing\};$$
$$Signal(S) : S : = S + 1;$$

This implementation causes a blocked process to **busy-wait** or **spin** in a while-loop until S becomes positive again through a call to *Signal* by another process. (Semaphores implemented this way are sometimes called **spin-locks**.) It also leaves unresolved the order in which waiting processes are reactivated: It may be random or in some order imposed by the operating system. In the worst case, a waiting process may be preempted by many incoming calls to *Delay* from new processes and never get to execute despite a sufficient number of calls to *Signal*. Such a situation is called **starvation**. Starvation is prevented by the use of a scheduling system that is **fair**, that is, guarantees that every process will execute within a finite period of time. In general, avoiding starvation is a much more difficult problem to solve than avoidance of deadlock (which itself is not trivial). For example, neither Java nor Ada automatically provide for fair scheduling, although it is possible to achieve it with some effort (see the Notes and References).

Modern shared-memory systems often provide facilities for semaphores that do not require busy-waiting. Semaphores are special memory locations that can be accessed by only one processor at a time, and a queue is provided for each semaphore to store the processes that are waiting for it.

14.5 Monitors

A monitor is a language construct that attempts to encapsulate the mutual exclusion and synchronization mechanisms of semaphores. The idea is that a more structured construct will reduce programming errors and improve the readability and correctness of code. Originally designed by Per Brinch-Hansen and C. A. R. Hoare in the early 1970s, it has been used in the languages Concurrent Pascal and Mesa. It is also the basis for the concurrency mechanisms of both Java and Ada95, as we shall see shortly.

A **monitor** is an abstract data type mechanism with the added property of mutual exclusion. It encapsulates shared data and operations on these data. At most one process at a time can be "inside" the monitor, that is, using any of the monitor's operations. To keep track of processes waiting to use its operations, a monitor has an associated wait queue, which is organized in some fair fashion (so that processes do not wait in the queue forever as other processes arrive)—for example, as a regular first-in, first-out queue.

A monitor therefore can be viewed as a language entity with the following schematic structure:

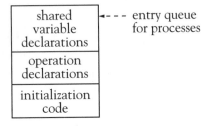

This organization of a monitor provides for mutual exclusion in accessing shared data, but it is not adequate by itself to synchronize processes that must wait for certain conditions before continuing to execute. For example, in the bounded buffer problem, a consumer process must wait if no items are in the buffer, and a producer must wait if the buffer is full.

For this reason a monitor must also provide **condition variables**, which are shared variables within the monitor resembling semaphores: Each has an associated queue with processes waiting for the condition, and each has associated *suspend* and *continue* operations, which have the effect of enqueuing and dequeuing processes from the associated queue (as well as suspending and continuing execution). Sometimes (unfortunately) these operations are also called signal and delay as for semaphores, but their operation is different. If a condition queue is empty, a call to *continue* will have no effect, and a call to *suspend* will **always** suspend the current process.

One question that must be answered to describe the behavior of a monitor completely is what happens when a *continue* call is issued to a waiting process by a process in the monitor. There are now potentially two processes active in the monitor, a situation that is forbidden. Two possibilities exist: Either the suspended process that has just been awakened by the *continue* call must wait further until the calling process has left the monitor or the process that issued the *continue* call must suspend until the awakened process has left the monitor.

It is possible to imitate the behavior of a monitor using semaphores. (Indeed, in the last section we saw how to implement a semaphore in Java using what amounts to a monitor, and then used the semaphore to implement a bounded buffer monitor). Thus, monitors and semaphores are equivalent in terms of the kinds of parallelism they can express. But monitors provide a more structured mechanism for concurrency than semaphores, and they ensure mutual exclusion. Monitors cannot guarantee the absence of deadlock, however (see Exercise 14.26).

Both Java and Ada have monitor-like mechanisms. In the next subsection we will describe how Java synchronized objects fit into the above monitor description, using the bounded buffer code of Figure 14.6 as our example. In the final subsection of this section, we will briefly describe Ada's concurrency and monitor mechanisms, and provide an Ada bounded buffer example. Further Ada concurrency mechanisms will also be studied in Section 14.6 (message passing).

14.5.1   Java Synchronized Objects as Monitors

Java objects all of whose methods are `synchronized` are essentially monitors; for the purposes of this discussion we will call such Java objects **synchronized objects**. There is an entry queue for each synchronized object in Java, and a thread that is "inside" the synchronized object (that is, executing a synchronized method of the object) is said to have acquired the lock on the synchronized object. One immediate problem with these queues in Java, however, is that they do not operate in a "fair" fashion: There is no order imposed on which thread is chosen on a wait queue when the executing thread leaves a method (hence the tendency in Java to call `notifyAll()` instead of `notify()`). Also, in Java an object may have both synchronized and unsynchronized methods, and any of the unsynchronized methods may be executed without acquiring the lock or going through the entry queue.

Additionally, Java's synchronized objects do not have separate condition variables. There is only one wait queue per synchronized object for any and all conditions (which is of course separate from the entry queue). A thread is placed in a synchronized object's wait queue by a call to `wait` or `sleep`; threads are removed from an object's wait queue by a call to `notify` or `notifyAll`. Thus, `wait` and `sleep` are *suspend* operations as described previously, while `notify` and `notifyAll` are *continue* operations.

Note that a thread may only be placed in a synchronized object's wait queue if it has the lock on the synchronized object, and it gives up the lock at that time. When it comes off the wait queue, it must again acquire the object's lock, so that in general it must go back on the entry queue from the wait queue. Thus, awakened threads in Java must wait for the awakening thread to exit the synchronized code before continuing (and are given no priority over threads that may have just arrived at the entry queue).

14.5.2   Ada95 Concurrency and Monitors

Concurrency in Ada is provided by independent processes called **tasks**, which are similar to Java threads. A task is declared using specification and body declarations similar to the package mechanism (see Chapter 9):

```
task T; -- task specification
-- see next section for more elaborate versions of this

task body T is
-- declarations
begin
-- code executed when task runs
end;
```

Unlike Java, an Ada task begins to execute as soon as the scope of its declaration is entered. It executes the code of its body in sequential fashion. When the end of the scope of the task declaration is reached, the program waits for the task to terminate before continuing execution. A task terminates by reaching the end of its code or by executing a **termi-nate** statement (discussed in Section 14.6). It is also possible to declare task types and variables to get more than one task of a particular type or to get dynamic control over task execution. For example,

```
task type T is
...
end;

task body T is
...
begin
...
end T;

p,q: T;
```

declares a task type T and two tasks p and q of type T.

In addition to tasks, which are part of Ada83, Ada95 also has monitors, called **protected objects**, that correspond to the synchronized objects of Java. There is a similar separation of a protected type or object declaration into specification and body. For example, a protected queue type can be declared as follows:

```
protected type Queue is -- specification
   procedure enqueue (item: in ...);
   entry dequeue (item: out ...);
   function empty return boolean;
private:
   -- private data here
   size: natural;
   ...
end Queue;

protected body Queue is
   -- implementation of services here
end Queue;
```

As we see in this example, operations within a protected object are of three different kinds: functions, procedures, and **entries**. All three are synchronized in the Java sense, but with the following differences: Functions are not allowed to change the local state of a protected object, but can be executed by any number of callers, provided no procedures or entries are currently executing. Procedures and entries, however, can only be executed by a single caller at a time, and no functions can be executing simultaneously with a procedure or entry (this is a standard multireader, single-writer protocol).

The difference between a procedure and an entry in a protected object is that a procedure can always be executed (subject to the mutual exclusion rules), while an entry can only be executed under a certain condition, called the **entry barrier**. For example, the dequeue operation is an entry because it can only be executed if the queue is nonempty, while an enqueue operation is a procedure because it can always execute (assuming the queue size can be arbitrarily expanded). If a task calls an entry whose barrier is closed (i.e., false), then the task is suspended and placed in a wait queue *for that entry* until the barrier becomes open (i.e., true), when a task in that entry's wait queue is reactivated. (Closed entries are reevaluated each time another task exits a procedure or entry that may have changed the value of the entry barrier.) Thus, Ada protected object entries correspond to monitor condition variables (and associated code to execute when the condition is true).

Ada entries are similar to Java synchronized methods that call wait or sleep. The difference is that in Java there is only one wait queue per object, while in Ada there is a wait queue for each entry. Also, the Ada runtime system automatically recomputes the entry barrier at appropriate times and wakes a waiting task, so there are no notify or notifyAll calls in Ada.

As an example of an entry declaration, we can flesh out the previous Queue body a bit as follows:

```
protected body Queue is
    procedure enqueue (item: in ...) is
    begin
        ...
    end enqueue;

    entry dequeue (item: out ...) when size > 0 is
    begin
        ...
    end dequeue;

    function empty return boolean is
    begin
        return size > 0;
    end empty;

end Queue;
```

As a complete example of the use of protected types and tasks in Ada, Figure 14.9 gives a solution to the bounded buffer problem.

```
(1)   with Text_IO; use Text_IO;

(2)   procedure BoundedBuffer is

(3)   type StoreType is array (positive range <>) of character;

(4)   protected type Buffer (MaxBufferSize: positive) is
(5)      entry insert(ch: in character);
(6)      entry delete(ch: out character);
(7)      function more return boolean;
(8)   private
(9)      store: StoreType(1..MaxBufferSize);
(10)     bufferStart: integer := 1;
(11)     bufferEnd: integer := 0;
(12)     bufferSize: integer := 0;
(13)  end Buffer;

(14)  protected body Buffer is

(15)     entry insert(ch: in character)
(16)        when bufferSize < MaxBufferSize is
(17)     begin
(18)        bufferEnd := bufferEnd mod MaxBufferSize + 1;
(19)        store(bufferEnd) := ch;
(20)        bufferSize := bufferSize + 1;
(21)     end insert;

(22)     entry delete(ch: out CHARACTER)
(23)        when bufferSize > 0 is
(24)     begin
(25)        ch := store(bufferStart);
(26)        bufferStart := bufferStart mod MaxBufferSize + 1;
(27)        bufferSize := bufferSize - 1;
```

```
(28)    end delete;

(29)    function more return boolean is
(30)    begin
(31)       return bufferSize > 0;
(32)    end more;

(33) end Buffer;

(34) buf: Buffer(5); -- buffer of size 5

(35) task producer;
(36) task body producer is
(37) ch: character;
(38) begin
(39)    loop
(40)      if (end_of_file) then exit;
(41)      end if;
(42)      if (end_of_line) then
(43)        skip_line;
(44)        -- use carriage return in buf to indicate new line:
(45)        buf.insert(character'(Standard.Ascii.CR));
(46)      else
(47)        get(ch);
(48)        buf.insert(ch);
(49)      end if;
(50)    end loop;
(51) end producer;

(52) task consumer;
(53) task body consumer is
(54) ch: character;
(55) begin
(56)    while (not producer'terminated or buf.more) loop
(57)       buf.delete(ch);
(58)       -- carriage return indicates new line:
(59)       if ch = character'(Standard.Ascii.CR) then
(60)             new_line;
(61)       else put(ch);
(62)       end if;
(63)    end loop;
(64) end Consumer;

(65) begin
(66)    null; -- no code needed, tasks execute automatically
(67) end BoundedBuffer;
```

Figure 14.9   A Bounded Buffer Solution Using Ada Tasks and Protected
             Types

14.6 Message Passing

Message passing is a mechanism for process synchronization and communication using the distributed model of a parallel processor. It was introduced around 1970 by Brinch-Hansen and others.

In its most basic form, a message passing mechanism in a language consists of two operations, **send** and **receive**, which may be defined in C syntax as follows:

```
void send(Process to, Message m);
void receive(Process from, Message m);
```

In this form, both the sending process and the receiving process must be named. This implies that every sender must know its receiver, and vice versa. In particular, the sending and receiving processes must have names within the scope of each other. A less restrictive form of *send* and *receive* removes the requirement of naming sender and receiver:

```
void send(Message m);
void receive(Message m);
```

In this case, a sent message will go to any process willing to receive it, and a message will be received from any sender. More commonly, a message passing mechanism will require *send* to name a receiver, but allow *receive* to receive from any process. This is asymmetrical, but it mimics the situation in a procedure call, where only the caller must know the name of the called procedure, while the called procedure has in general no knowledge of its caller.

Other questions that must be answered about the *send* and *receive* operations revolve around the synchronization of processes that wish to communicate via *send* and *receive*:

1. Must a sender wait for a receiver to be ready before a message can be sent, or can a sender continue to execute even if there is no available receiver? If so, are messages stored in a buffer for later receipt?

2. Must a receiver wait until a message is available to be sent, or can a receiver receive a null message and continue to execute?

In the case where both sender and receiver must wait until each other is ready, the message passing mechanism is sometimes called **rendezvous**. When messages are buffered, additional questions arise. For example, is there a size limit on the number of messages that can be buffered? And what process manages the buffer? If a separate process manages the buffer, then sometimes the buffer (or its managing process) is named in the *send* and *receive* calls, instead of the sending and receiving processes. In this case, we have a **mailbox** mechanism, where processes "drop off" and "retrieve" messages from named (or numbered) mailboxes. Sometimes mailboxes are assigned **owners** (for example, a process that creates a mailbox can become its owner). In this case the mailbox may be managed by its owner instead of a separate process.

Essential to any message passing mechanism are **control facilities** to permit processes to test for the existence of messages, to accept messages only on certain conditions, and to select from among several possible messages. Often these control structures are influenced by or are based on Dijkstra's **guarded if** and **guarded do** commands (see Chapter 7).

In the following, we will discuss Ada's version of message passing, which is a form of rendezvous. Other forms of message passing include Hoare's **Communicating Sequential Processes** (CSP) language framework, and its implementation in the language **occam**; mechanisms for distributing computation over a large network, such as **Remote Procedure Call** (RPC) or **Remote Method Invocation** (RMI), which is supported by the Java networking library; and various forms of interfacing standards to facilitate the uniform sharing of code execution among different computers and operating systems, such as **MPI** (Message Passing Interface), **CORBA** ("Common Object Request Broker Architecture") and **COM** ("Common Object Model"). See the Notes and References for information on these mechanisms, which are beyond the scope of this introductory chapter.

Task Rendezvous in Ada

So far we have seen Ada tasks as similar to Java threads, each executing a body of code, and communicating via protected (synchronized) code inside monitors. However, Ada tasks can also pass messages to each other via a rendezvous mechanism. Indeed, Ada83 did not have monitors, so rendezvous was the only way to share data among tasks in a synchronized way (we will return to this issue shortly).

Rendezvous points are defined by **task entries**, which are similar in appearance to protected type entries, but are used (confusingly) in a completely different way. Entries are defined in a task's specification just as they are for protected types:

```
task userInput is
    entry buttonClick (button: out ButtonID);
    entry keyPress (ch: out character);
end userInput;
```

A task exports entry names to the outside world just as protected types do. Thus, another task can rendezvous with `userInput` by "calling" `userInput.buttonClick(b)` or `userInput.keyPress(c)`. However, entries do not have code bodies. Instead, entries must appear inside an `accept` statement, which provides the code to execute when the entry is called. `Accept` statements can only appear inside the body of a task, and their position inside the body determines when they will be executed. The caller of an entry will wait for the task to reach a corresponding `accept` statement, and, similarly, if no call has occurred, a task that reaches an `accept` statement will wait for a corresponding call. Thus, a rendezvous occurs at the point in the called task's body where the corresponding `accept` statement appears, and the message that is passed at the rendezvous is represented by the entry parameters. Each entry has an associated queue to maintain processes that are waiting for an `accept` statement to be executed. This queue is managed in a first-in, first-out fashion.

To continue with the previous example, the `userInput` body might therefore look as follows:

```
task body userInput is
begin
    ...
    -- respond to a button click request:
    accept buttonClick (button: out ButtonID) do
        -- get a button click while the caller waits
    end buttonClick; -- caller can now continue
    -- continue with further processing
    ...
    -- now respond to a keypress request:
    accept keyPress (ch: out character) do
        -- get a keypress while the caller waits
    end keyPress; - caller can now continue
    -- continue with further processing
end userInput;
```

An `accept` statement has the following form (in EBNF notation):

accept *entry-name* [*formal-parameter-list*]

[do *statement-sequence* end [*entry-name*]] ;

When an `accept` statement is executed, the caller remains suspended while the code in the accept body is executed (the statements between the `do` and the `end`). An `accept` statement does not need to name the caller of the entry. Thus, Ada's message passing mechanism is asymmetric, like procedure calls. The entry/accept mechanism can be used entirely for synchronization, in which case a body of code for the entry is unnecessary.

Typically, a task that operates as a server for other client tasks will want to maintain a set of possible entries that it will accept, and wait for one of these entries to be called, whereupon it will process the entry and loop back to wait for the next entry. Which entries can be selected can depend on a number of conditions (such as whether a queue is empty, or a buffer is full). Maintaining a set of entries to accept is done through the `select` statement. The EBNF for a `select` statement is

select

[when *condition* =>] *select-alternative*

{or [when *condition* =>] *select-alternative*}

[else *statement-sequence*]

end select ;

where a *select-alternative* is an `accept` statement followed by a sequence of statements, or a `delay` statement (not described here) followed by a sequence of statements, or a `terminate` statement.

The semantics of the `select` statement are as follows. All the conditions in the `select` statement are evaluated, and those that evaluate to true have their corresponding select alternatives tagged as **open**. An open `accept` statement is selected for execution if another task has executed an entry call for its entry. If several accepts are available, one is chosen arbitrarily. If no open accepts are available and there is an `else` part, the statement sequence of the `else` part is executed. If there is no `else` part, the task waits for an entry call for one of the open accepts. If there are no open accepts, then the `else` part is executed if it exists. If there is no `else` part, an exception condition is raised (see Chapter 7).

Looping back to a set of `select` alternatives is not part of the basic select command, but can easily be achieved by surrounding a `select` statement with a loop.

Continuing with the previous example, the `userInput` body might be structured as follows to allow it to behave as a server for `keyPress` and `buttonClick` requests:

```
(1)    task body userInput is
(2)    begin
(3)      loop
(4)        select
(5)          when buttonClicked =>
(6)             -- respond to a button click request:
(7)             accept buttonClick (button: out ButtonID) do
(8)                -- get and return a button click
(9)                -- while the caller waits
(10)            end buttonClick; -- caller can now continue
(11)            -- do some buttonClick cleanup
(12)          or when keypressed =>
(13)             -- now respond to a keypress request:
(14)             accept keyPress (ch: out character) do
(15)                -- get a keypress while the caller waits
(16)            end keyPress; -- caller can now continue
(17)            -- do some keyPress cleanup
(18)          or terminate;
(19)        end select;
(20)      end loop;
(21) end userInput;
```

Note the `terminate` alternative in the select statement (line 18). Termination of tasks in Ada can occur in one of two ways. Either the task executes to completion and has not created any dependent tasks (i.e., child processes) that are still executing, or the task is waiting with an open `terminate` alternative in a `select` statement, and its **master** (the block of its parent task in which it was created) has executed to completion. In that case, all the other tasks created by the same master must also have terminated or are waiting at a `terminate` alternative, in which case they all `terminate` simultaneously. This avoids the necessity of writing explicit synchronizing statements (such as `join` or `wait`) in a parent task that must wait for the completion of its children.

Of course, a task with the above behavior might, depending on circumstances, be better written as a protected type in Ada. For example, we can write a version of the bounded buffer (Figure 14.9) that uses a task and rendezvous to provide mutual exclusion and synchronization, even though a protected type is likely to be more appropriate. The code is in Figure 14.10. Note that, because tasks, unlike protected types, cannot have functions that return values, but must return values through out parameters in entries, the buffer code in Figure 14.10 requires a small modification in the consumer code of Figure 14.9. We leave the details to the reader (Exercise 14.39).

We offer two additional examples of tasks in Ada. The first (Figure 14.11) is an implementation of a semaphore type as a task type. Note in that example that the code block in an **accept** of a parameterless entry such as **signal** or **delay** can be empty, in which case the **do ... end** can be omitted. The second example (Figure 14.12) is an Ada package using tasks for parallel matrix multiplication.

```
task buf is
  entry insert(ch: in character);
  entry delete(ch: out character);
  entry more (notEmpty: out boolean);
end;

task body buf is
    MaxBufferSize: constant integer := 5;
    store: array (1..MaxBufferSize) of character;
    bufferStart: integer := 1;
    bufferEnd: integer := 0;
    bufferSize: integer := 0;
begin
    loop
      select
        when bufferSize < MaxBufferSize =>
          accept insert(ch: in character) do
              bufferEnd := bufferEnd mod MaxBufferSize + 1;
              store(bufferEnd) := ch;
          end insert;
          bufferSize := bufferSize + 1;
      or when bufferSize > 0 =>
          accept delete(ch: out character) do
            ch := store(bufferStart);
          end delete;
          bufferStart := bufferStart mod MaxBufferSize + 1;
          bufferSize := bufferSize - 1;
      or
          accept more(notEmpty: out boolean) do
              notEmpty := bufferSize > 0;
          end more;
      or terminate;
```

```
      end select;
   end loop;
end buf;
```

Figure 14.10   A Bounded Buffer as an Ada Task

```
task type Semaphore is
   entry initSem (n: in integer);
   entry delay;
   entry signal;
end;
task body Semaphore is
   count : integer;
begin
   accept initSem (n: in integer) do
    count := n;
   end initSem;
   loop
    select
     when count > 0 =>
      accept wait;
      count := count - 1 ;
    or
      accept signal;
      count := count + 1;
    or
      terminate;
    end select;
   end loop;
end Semaphore;
```

Figure 14.11   A Semaphore Task Type in Ada

```
generic Size: INTEGER;
package IntMatrices is
   type IntMatrix is array (1..Size,1..Size) OF INTEGER;
   function ParMult(a,b: in IntMatrix) return IntMatrix;
end;

package body IntMatrices is
 function ParMult(a,b: in IntMatrix) return IntMatrix is
   c:IntMatrix;

   task type Mult is
     entry DoRow (i: in INTEGER);
   end;
   task body Mult is
     iloc: INTEGER;
   begin                                              (continues)
```

Figure 14.12   Parallel Matrix Multiplication in an Ada Package

(continued)

```
    accept DoRow (i: in INTEGER) do
      iloc := i;
    end;
    for j in 1..Size loop
      c(iloc,j) := 0;
      for k in 1.. Size loop
        c(iloc,j) := c(iloc,j) + a(iloc,k) * b(k,j);
      end loop;
    end loop;
  end Mult;

begin -- ParMult
  declare m: array (1..Size) of Mult;
  begin
    for i in 1..Size loop
      m(i).DoRow(i);
    end loop;
  end;
  return c;
end ParMult;
end IntMatrices;
```

Figure 14.12   Parallel Matrix Multiplication in an Ada Package

14.7 Parallelism in Non-Imperative Languages

Parallel processing using functional or logic programming languages is still in an experimental and research phase, despite a significant amount of work since the mid-1980s. Nevertheless, a number of good implementations of research proposals exist, and we discuss several of these, including MultiLisp, QLisp, Parlog, and FGHC, after a brief general introduction to the area. The reader is encouraged to consult the references at the end of the chapter for more information.

In earlier chapters we have mentioned that non-imperative languages such as LISP and Prolog offer more opportunities for automatic parallelization by a translator than do imperative languages. The opportunities for parallel execution in such languages fall into two basic classes:

1. **And-parallelism.** In this form of parallelism, a number of values can be computed in parallel by child processes, while the parent process waits for the children to finish and return their values. This type of parallelism can be exploited in a functional language in the computation of arguments in a function call. For example, in LISP, if a process executes a function call

    (f a b c d e)

it can create six parallel processes to compute the values f, a, ..., e. It then suspends its own execution until all values are computed, and then calls the (function) value of f with the returned values of a through e as arguments. Similarly, in a let-binding such as

```
(let ((a e1) (b e2) (c e3)) ( ... ))
```

the values of e1, e2, and e3 can be computed in parallel.

In Prolog a similar and-parallel opportunity exists in executing the clause

```
q :- p1, p2, ..., pn.
```

The p1 through pn can be executed in parallel, and q succeeds if all the pi succeed.

Implicit in this description is that the computations done in parallel do not interfere. In a purely functional language, the evaluation of arguments and let-bindings causes no side effects, so noninterference is guaranteed. However, most functional languages are not pure, and side effects or state changes require that and-parallelism be synchronized. In Prolog, the instantiation of variables is a typical and necessary side effect that can affect the behavior of and-parallelism. For example, in the clause

```
process(N,Data) :-
            M is N - 1,
            Data = [X|Data1],
            process(M,Data1).
```

the three goals on the right-hand side cannot in general be executed in parallel, since each of the first two contribute instantiations to the last. Thus, synchronization is also necessary here.

2. *Or-parallelism.* In this type of parallelism, execution of several alternatives can occur in parallel, with the first alternative to finish (or succeed) causing all other alternative processes to be ignored (and to terminate). In LISP, an example of such parallelism can occur in the evaluation of a cond expression:

```
(cond (p1 e1) (p2 e2) ... (pn en))
```

In this situation it may be possible for the ei that correspond to true pi conditions to be evaluated in parallel, with the first value to be computed becoming the value of the cond expression. (It may also be possible to compute the pi themselves in parallel.) In this case it may also be necessary to synchronize the computations. But there is another problem as well: or-parallel computation makes the cond into a nondeterministic construct (similar to Dijkstra's guarded if), which may change the overall behavior of the program if the order of evaluation is significant. For example, an else-part in a cond should not be evaluated in parallel with the other cases.

In Prolog, or-parallelism is also possible in that a system may try to satisfy alternative clauses for a goal simultaneously. For example, if there are two or more clauses for the same predicate,

```
p(X) :- q(X).
p(X) :- r(X).
```

a system may try to satisfy q and r in parallel, with p succeeding with X instantiated according to the one that finishes first (or perhaps even saving other instantiations in a queue). In fact, this is consistent with the semantics of pure logic programming, since alternative goals are satisfied nondeterministically. However, in common Prolog implementations, the correct execution of a program may depend on the order in which alternatives are tried. In this case, a strict ordering may need to be applied. For example, in a common program for factorial in Prolog,

```
fact (X, Y) := X = 0 , ! , Y = 1.
fact (X, Y) := Z is X - 1, fact (Z, Y1), Y is X * Y1.
```

the first clause needs to be tried before the second (or reaching the cut in the first should terminate the second).

The synchronization and order problems we have mentioned for both and-parallelism and or-parallelism are difficult to solve automatically by a translator. For this reason, language designers have experimented with the inclusion of a number of manual parallel constructs in non-imperative languages. In some cases these are traditional constructs like semaphores or mailboxes, with modified semantics to provide better integration into the language. In other cases more language-specific means are used to indicate explicit parallelism.

There is, however, another argument for the inclusion of explicit parallelism in non-imperative languages. In many situations one may wish to suppress the creation of small (i.e., fine-grained) processes when the computational overhead to create the process is greater than the advantage of computing the result in parallel. This may be the case, for example, in highly recursive processes, where as one approaches the base case, one may not want to create new processes, but switch to ordinary computation. Or one may wish to suppress parallel computation altogether when the values to be computed have a small computational overhead.

In the following we will briefly indicate a few of the explicit parallel mechanisms employed in some of the parallel LISPs and Prologs mentioned at the beginning of this section.

14.7.1   LISP Parallelism

The more natural form of parallelism for LISP seems to be and-parallelism, and this is the kind most often implemented. In the language Multilisp, which like Scheme (see Chapter 10) has static scoping and first-class function values, parallel evaluation of function calls is indicated by the syntax

```
(pcall f a b c ...)
```

which is equivalent to the evaluation of (f a b c ...) but with parallel evaluation of its subexpressions. Even more parallelism can be achieved in Multilisp by the use of a "future:" If f has already been computed in the function call (f a b c), then the execution of f can proceed even before the values of a, b, and c have been computed, at least up to the point in f where those values are used. For example, in an f defined by

```
(define (f a b) (cond ((= a 0) ...)
                      ((> b 0) ...) ...))
```

the value of b is never used if a evaluates to 0, so the computation can proceed regardless of how long it takes to compute b.

A **future** is a construct that returns a pointer to the value of a not yet finished parallel computation. A future resembles (but is not identical to) delayed evaluation, as represented in the `delay` primitive of Scheme, studied in Section 10.5. In Multilisp a call

```
(pcall f (future a) (future b) ...)
```

allows the execution of f to proceed before the values of a and b have been computed. When the execution of f reaches a point where the value of a is needed, it suspends execution until that value is available. Futures have been included in other parallel LISPs besides Multilisp—for example, Qlisp.

Qlisp includes a parallel let-construct called `qlet` to indicate and-parallelism in let-bindings:

```
(qlet p (bindings) exp)
```

This construct will evaluate the bindings in parallel under the control of the predicate p. If p evaluates to `nil`, ordinary evaluation occurs. If p evaluates to a non-nil value, then the bindings will be computed in parallel. If p evaluates to the special keyword `:eager`, then futures will be constructed for the values to be bound.

14.7.2 Prolog Parallelism

The more natural form of parallelism for Prolog appears to be or-parallelism, although both forms have been implemented. In fact, or-parallelism fits so well with the semantics of logic programming (as noted above) that it is often performed automatically by a parallel Prolog system.

And-parallelism is more difficult in Prolog because of the interactions of instantiations mentioned earlier, and because there is no natural return point for backtracking. One version of and-parallelism uses guarded Horn clauses to eliminate backtracking. A guarded Horn clause is one of the form

```
h : - g1, ..., gn | p1, ..., pm.
```

The g1, ..., gn are **guards**, which are executed first and which are prohibited from establishing instantiations not already provided. If the guards succeed, the system **commits** to this clause for h (no backtracking to other clauses occurs), and the p1, ..., pm are executed in parallel. Such a system is FGHC (for flat guarded Horn clauses). A sample FGHC program is the following, which generates lists of integers:

```
generate(N,X)  :- N = 0 | X = [].
generate(N,X)  :- N > 0 | X = [N|T], M is N-1,
                  generate(M,T).
```

The problem with FGHC is that it places severe constraints on variable instantiation, and hence on unification. This results in a significant reduction in the expressiveness of the language. An alternative is to provide **variable annotations** that specify the kind of instantiations allowed and when they may take place. A language that does this is **Parlog**. In Chapters 10 and 11 we discussed the difference between input variables and output variables to a procedure: Input variables are like value parameters; that is, they have incoming values but no outgoing values. Output variables, on the other hand, have only outgoing values. In Prolog this means that input variables may be instantiated when initiating a goal, but may not be instantiated during the process of satisfying the goal, and similarly for output variables. Parlog distinguishes input variables from output variables in a so-called **mode declaration** by writing input variables with a "?" and output variables with a "^." If during the process of satisfying a goal, an uninstantiated input variable must be unified, the process suspends until such time as the variable becomes instantiated. A further tool for controlling instantiations is "directional" unification: The goal X = Y has a variant X <= Y, which only allows X to be instantiated, not Y.

As an example of and-parallelism in Parlog, consider the following quicksort program:

```
mode qsort (P?,S^).
qsort([],[]).
qsort([H|T] S) :- partition(H,T,L,R),
                  qsort(L,L1),
                  qsort(R,R1),
                  append(L1,[ H|R],S).
mode partition(P?,Q?,R^,S^).
partition(P,[A|X],[A|Y],Z) :- A < P:
                  partition(P,X,Y,Z).
partition(P,[A|X],Y,[A|Z]):- A >= P:
                  partition(P,X,Y,Z).
partition(P,[], [], []).
```

Parlog selects an alternative from among clauses by the usual unification process and also by using guards. It then commits to one alternative. In the foregoing qsort, the partition predicate has guards to prevent incorrect choices. After selecting a clause, Parlog creates a process for each goal on the right-hand side. Thus, Parlog will execute the four goals on the right-hand side of qsort in parallel. Since L and R are input variables to the two right-hand calls to qsort, their associated processes will suspend as soon as these are needed for unification, until the first parti-

tion process produces them. The **append** process (whose definition is not shown) will also suspend until its first two arguments become available.

This concludes our brief survey of non-imperative parallelism.

Exercises

14.1 How many links does a fully linked distributed system with n processors need? How do you think this affects the design of fully linked systems with many processors?

14.2 Some parallel processors limit the number of processes that a user can create in a program to one less than the number of processors available. Why do you think this restriction is made? Is such a restriction more or less likely on an SIMD or MIMD system? Might there be a reason to create more processes than processors? Explain.

14.3 It is possible to compute the sum of n integers in fewer than n steps. Describe how you could use k processors to do this, where $k < n$. Would there be any advantage to having $k \geq n$?

14.4 The text mentioned that matrix multiplication can be done in n steps using n^2 processors. Can it be done in fewer steps using more processors?

14.5 Describe the difference between SPMD and MPMD programming. Would you characterize the program of Figure 14.3 as SPMD or MPMD? Why?

14.6 Why did the text prefer to use the term MPMD instead of fork-join?

14.7 Explain why both large-grained and small-grained parallelism can be less efficient than medium grained. Try to give programming examples to support your argument.

14.8 The C code of Figure 14.4 assumes that NUMPROCS is less than SIZE. What happens if NUMPROCS > SIZE? Rewrite the code of Figure 14.4 to take advantage of the extra processors if NUMPROCS > SIZE.

14.9 (For Unix users) Explain what happens in each step of the following Unix pipeline:

```
cat *.java | tr -sc A-Za-z '\012' | sort | uniq -c | sort -rn
```

14.10 (For Windows users) Command line windows in versions of Microsoft Windows also allow certain commands to be piped, such as `dir | more`. Determine if these pipes are true pipes in the Unix sense (that is, each program in the pipe is a separate process, with no intermediate files saved to disk).

14.11 A typical process synchronization problem is that of resource allocation. For example, if a system has three printers, then at most three
processes can be scheduled to print simultaneously. Write a program
to allocate three printers to processes in
(a) Java
(b) Ada95
(c) Ada83

14.12 A standard problem (like the bounded buffer problem) that is used to
test a concurrent language mechanism is the **readers-writers** problem.
In this problem stored data are continuously accessed (read) and
updated (written) by a number of processes. A solution to this problem must allow access to the data by any number of readers, but by
only one writer at a time. Write a solution to this problem using (a)
Java; (b) Ada tasks.

14.13 The Java specification promises that getting the value of a single variable of any built-in type *except* `long` or `double`, or updating such a
variable, is an atomic operation, but that such operations on `long` or
`double` variables may not be atomic.
(a) Explain the reason for this difference.
(b) In what way did this fact affect the code for the bounded buffer
problem (Figure 14.6)?
(c) Does this fact have any effect on the solution to the readers-
writers problem? Explain.

14.14 Another standard concurrency problem is the **dining philosophers
problem** of Dijkstra. In this problem five philosophers spend their time
eating and thinking. When a philosopher is ready to eat, she sits at
one of five places at a table heaped with spaghetti. Unfortunately,
there are only five forks, one between every two plates, and a philosopher needs two forks to eat. A philosopher will attempt to pick up the
two forks next to her, and if she succeeds, she will eat for a while, leave
the table, and go back to thinking. For this problem,
(a) Describe how deadlock and starvation can occur.
(b) Why are there five philosophers and not four or three?
(c) Write a deadlock-free solution to this problem in either Java or
Ada.
(d) Is it possible to guarantee no starvation in your solution to part
(c)? Explain.

14.15 The C code for matrix multiplication in Figure 14.5 doesn't work in a
typical Unix implementation, since a fork does not cause memory to
be shared. This problem can be solved using files, since forked
processes continue to share files. Rewrite the code to compute the
matrix c correctly using files. Comment on the efficiency of your solution.

14.16 Can Figure 14.5 be corrected by using pointer variables to share the
addresses of the arrays among several processes? Explain why or why
not.

14.17 (a) Write a solution to the matrix multiplication problem in Java using one thread for each row and column of the answer.

(b) Write a solution to the matrix multiplication problem in Java that uses a fixed number of threads less than the number of elements in the answer matrix, where each thread looks for the next element in the answer matrix that has not yet been worked on.

14.18 Repeat the previous exercise in Ada.

14.19 Given two processes p and q, and a semaphore S initialized to 1, suppose p and q make the following calls:

$$p: delay(S);$$

$$\ldots$$

$$delay(S);$$
$$q: delay(S);$$

$$\ldots$$

$$signal(S);$$

Describe what will happen for all possible orders of these operations on S.

14.20 Describe how the busy-wait implementation of a semaphore can cause starvation.

14.21 In addition to deadlock and starvation, concurrent processes can experience **livelock**, where no process is blocked, all processes get to execute, but each continually repeats the same code without possibility of success. Write a simple program in **(a)** Java or **(b)** Ada that is an example of livelock.

14.22 Here is an alternative to the code for the semaphore operations:

$$Delay(S) : S : = S - 1;$$
> if $S < 0$ then suspend the calling process;

$$Signal(S): S : = S + 1;$$
> if $S > = 0$ then wake up a waiting process;

Compare this to the code in Section 14.4. Is there any difference in behavior?

14.23 Does it make any sense to initialize a semaphore to a negative value? Why or why not?

14.24 Sometimes a language will provide only a **binary semaphore** mechanism, in which the stored value is Boolean instead of integer. Then the operations wait and signal become

$$Delay(S) : \text{if } S = \text{true then } S := \text{false}$$
> else suspend the calling process

$$Signal(S): \text{if processes are waiting then wake up a process}$$
> else $S : = \text{true};$

(To distinguish them from binary semaphores, the semaphores described in the text are sometimes called **counting semaphores**.) Show how a counting semaphore can be implemented using binary semaphores.

14.25 A lock is sometimes distinguished from a semaphore by being non-blocking: Only one process can acquire a lock at a time, but if a process fails to acquire a lock, it can continue execution. Suppose that a lock L has two operations, a Boolean function **lock-lock(L)** that returns true if the lock has been acquired, false otherwise and **unlock-lock(L)** that unlocks the lock (having no effect if the lock is already unlocked). Write an implementation for a lock in **(a)** Java; **(b)** Ada.

14.26 If one monitor entry calls another monitor entry, deadlock may result. **(a)** Construct an example to show how this can happen. **(b)** How is this problem dealt with in Java? **(c)** In Ada?

14.27 Suppose the code for the signal operation in the Java implementation of a semaphore (Figure 14.7) was changed to

```
public synchronized void signal()
{ notify();
  count++;
}
```

Would this work? Explain.

14.28 The Java semaphore code in Figure 14.7 is overly simple, due to the possibility of interrupts. Here is an improved version for the `delay()` procedure:

```
// adapted from Lea [2000], p. 267
public void delay() throws InterruptedException
{ if (Thread.interrupted())
    throw new InterruptedException();
  synchronized (this)
  { try
    { while (count <= 0) wait();
      count--;
    }
    catch( InterruptedException ie)
    { notify(); throw ie; }
  }
}
```

Explain carefully the reason for each of the differences between this code and the code of Figure 14.7.

14.29 Explain the behavior of the Java code for the bounded buffer problem if the keyword `synchronized` is removed from the `put` operation (line 28 of Figure 14.6).

14.30 In Ada we saw that the bounded buffer could be represented either by task or a monitor. Is one of these solutions to be preferred over the other? Why?

14.31 A shared-memory system can imitate the mailbox version of message passing by defining a mailbox utility using mutual exclusion. Write a package to implement mailboxes (i.e., queues of data with *send* and *receive* primitives) in **(a)** Java; **(b)** Ada.

14.32 In Ada the caller of an entry must suspend execution during the execution of the corresponding accept-statement. Why is this necessary?

14.33 In an Ada select alternative, an accept-statement can be followed by more statements. For example, in the bounded buffer solution in Ada, we wrote

```
accept insert (ch: in character) do
    bufferEnd := bufferEnd mod MaxBufferSize + 1;
    store (bufferEnd) := ch;
end insert;
bufferSize := bufferSize + 1;
```

Note that bufferSize is incremented outside the accept statement. Is there a reason for this? Could the statement be put inside the accept? Could the statement store(bufferEnd) := ch be moved out of the accept? Why?

14.34 In Ada a task type can be used in the declaration of other types. In particular, pointer (or access) types to task types can be declared, as in

```
task type T is ... end;
type A is access T;
...
x: A;
```

The variable x now represents a pointer to a task. When does the associated task begin executing? When might it terminate?

14.35 In Ada a task is not automatically terminated when the end of the scope of its declaration is reached in its parent task. Instead, the parent suspends until the task completes. Why do you think this choice was made in the design of Ada?

14.36 In the Ada implementation of a semaphore, the Signal entry always incremented the semaphore value. Is this correct? Why?

14.37 An alternative for the Ada implementation of semaphores is to test for the existence of a waiting task using the attribute COUNT, which is predefined for entries. The code inside the loop would then read as follows:

```
select
  when count > 0 =>
    accept Wait;
    count := count - 1;
or
  accept Signal;
  if Wait'COUNT > 0 then
    accept Wait;
  else
```

(continues)

(continued)

```
            count := count + 1;
         end if;
      or
         terminate;
      end select;
```

Is this implementation preferable to the one given? Why or why not?

14.38 Write an implementation of a semaphore as an Ada protected type, and compare this with the task implementation of Figure 14.10.

14.39 Rewrite the Ada bounded buffer code of Figure 14.8 to use the buffer task of Figure 14.9.

14.40 In Figure 14.11 (parallel matrix multiplication in Ada), we used a local variable iloc inside task Mult to store the current row index of matrix multiplication for use outside the accept-statement. We could have avoided the need for iloc by writing the whole body of Mult inside the accept statement, as follows:

```
task body Mult is
begin
  accept DoRow (i: in INTEGER ) do
    for j in 1..Size loop
      c(i, j) := 0;
      for k in 1..Size loop
        c(i, j) := c(i, j) + a(i, k)*b(k, j);
      end loop;
    end loop;
  end;
end Mult;
```

What is wrong with this solution?

14.41 This chapter ignored the question of formal semantics for concurrent programs. (Some studies are mentioned in the references.) Can you think of problems that may be encountered in applying axiomatic semantics to concurrent programs? What about denotational semantics?

14.42 The matrix multiplication solution in Ada of Figure 14.11 uses the size of the matrix to determine the number of tasks. Rewrite the solution to use a number of tasks specified as an input parameter to the ParMult function.

14.43 Or-parallelism in Prolog can be viewed as a parallel search of the tree of alternatives (see Chapter 11), where at each node a new process is created to search each child. Describe how these processes can coordinate their activities to allow backtracking.

14.44 Write a procedure to perform a parallel search of an unordered binary tree in **(a)** Java; **(b)** Ada.

14.45 Discuss the claim made in the text that or-parallelism is more natural for Prolog, whereas and-parallelism is more natural for LISP.

14.46 Describe in detail the way or-parallel Prolog computes the three solutions to `delete([1,2,3],X,T)` in parallel. What time savings would you expect (in terms of numbers of steps)?

14.47 How much actual parallelism is performed in the and-parallel Prolog example of `generate` on page 664? Explain.

14.48 In and-parallel Prolog, if a guard encounters an uninstantiated variable, execution is suspended until the variable is instantiated (by another process). Why is this necessary? Are there any problems with this requirement?

14.49 Explain why backtracking is difficult in and-parallel Prolog.

14.50 In Figures 14.4 and 14.5 the main process creates new child processes to compute the matrix product and then suspends until all the child processes have finished. This is wasteful. Rewrite these programs so that the main process also performs some computations in parallel with its children.

14.51 Compare the notion of mailbox to that of a buffer.

14.52 Suppose two processes both attempt to increment a shared variable S that is unprotected by a mutual exclusion mechanism. Suppose the assignment

$$S := S + 1$$

consists within each process of three machine instructions:

> Load S into a reg
> Increment the *reg*
> Store the *reg* to S

What values might S have after both processes complete their increment operations? Show how each value can be obtained.

Notes and References

The field of parallel/concurrent programming is a huge one, involving operating system, architecture, and language issues; we have barely touched on specific language issues in this chapter, using primarily Java and Ada as our examples. Typically, an entire course is devoted to parallel programming, often using one of the language-independent protocols supported by third-party libraries. Two examples of useful texts in this area are Andrews [2000] and Wilkinson and Allen [1997].

Surveys of parallel programming languages include the September 1989 issue of ACM Computing Surveys (Vol. 21, no. 3) and the July 1989 issue of IEEE Software. Some individual articles from these issues are also mentioned in the following. Another survey article is Andrews and Schneider [1983].

Programming using Java threads is studied in Lea [2000], Horstmann and Cornell [1999] (Vol II), and Arnold et al. [2000]. For an alternative view of threads, see Butenhof [1997], which describes the Pthreads standard for Unix. Programming using Ada tasks and Ada95 protected types is studied in Cohen [1996]; see also Wegner and Smolka [1983].

A survey of parallel architectures appears in Duncan [1990]. The diagrams in Section 14.1 are adapted from Karp [1987], where several methods of adding parallelism to FORTRAN are also studied. See also Karp and Babb [1988] for examples similar to those of Section 14.2.

Semaphores were introduced by Dijkstra [1968b]. See Stallings [2000] for a study of their use in operating systems. Monitors were introduced by Hoare [1974] and made part of the Concurrent Pascal language designed by Brinch-Hansen [1975]. For a critique of the Java approach to monitors, see Brinch-Hansen [1999].

The question of scheduling policies, fairness, and starvation were only mentioned briefly in this chapter, and the associated issue of process priorities was not discussed at all. For a discussion of the Java approach, see Lea [2000], especially Sections 3.4.1 and 3.7. For a discussion of the Ada95 approach, see Cohen [1996], Section 18.6.

Message passing, including a theoretical framework called Communicating Sequential Processes, or CSP, was introduced by Hoare [1978]. CSP is often used as a basis for formal semantics and verification of concurrent programs; see Schneider [2000]. CSP was also the inspiration for the programming language **Occam**, designed to run on a proprietary parallel system called the **transputer**; see Jones and Goldsmith [1988]. For a different approach to formal semantics of concurrent programs using a technique called **process algebra**, see Milner [1994].

A description of Multilisp is in Halstead [1985]. QLisp is described in Goldman and Gabriel [1989]. Surveys of parallel logic programming include Kergommeaux and Codognet [1994], Ciancarini [1992], Shapiro [1989], and Tick [1991]. Parlog is studied in Conlon [1989], Gregory [1987], and Ringwood [1988]. FGHC is described in Ueda [1987]. Concurrency and constraints in logic programming (Chapter 12) are closely related; see Ueda [2000] or Saraswat and Van Hentenryck [1995].

Information on various protocols for distributed parallel computing on networks can be found in Horstmann and Cornell [1999], Vol. II (Java's RMI) and Pacheco [1996] (MPI). Books on CORBA and COM are too numerous to mention, since these protocols are used for program interoperability as well as concurrency. A brief introduction can be found in Horstmann and Cornell [1999].

Several projects have used the Internet as a large parallel processing system; perhaps the best known is the Great Internet Mersenne Prime Search Project (see www.mersenne.org), which currently holds the record for the largest known prime number.

Bibliography

Abelson et al. 1998. "Revised Report on the Algorithmic Language Scheme," *Higher-Order and Symbolic Computation* **11(1)**: 5–105, August 1998. (Also known as R^{5}RS.)

Abelson, H. and G. J. Sussman with Julie Sussman. 1996. *Structure and Interpretation of Computer Programs* (2nd ed.). Cambridge, Mass.: MIT Press.

Aggoun A. and N. Beldiceanu. 1991. "Overview of the CHIP Compiler System," in K. Furukawa (Ed.) *Logic Programming, Proceedings of the Eighth International Conference, Paris, France*, 775–789. Cambridge: MIT Press.

Aho, A. V., J. E. Hopcroft, and J. D. Ullman. 1983. *Data Structures and Algorithms*. Reading, Mass.: Addison-Wesley.

Aho, A. V., B. W. Kernighan, and P. J. Weinberger. 1988. *The AWK Programming Language*. Reading, Mass.: Addison-Wesley.

Aho, A. V., R. Sethi, and J. D. Ullman. 1986. *Compilers: Principles, Techniques and Tools*. Reading, Mass.: Addison-Wesley.

Alexandrescu, A. 2001. *Modern C++ Design: Generic Programming and Design Patterns Applied*. Addison-Wesley.

Andrews, G. R. 2000. *Foundations of Multithreaded, Parallel, and Distributed Programming*. Reading, Mass.: Addison-Wesley.

Andrews, G. R. and F. B. Schneider. 1983. "Concepts and Notations for Concurrent Programming." *ACM Computing Surveys* **15(1)**, 3–43.

ANSI-1815A. 1983. *Military Standard: Ada Programming Language*. Washington, D.C.: American National Standards Institute.

ANSI-X3.226. 1994. *Information Technology—Programming Language—Common Lisp*. Washington, D.C.: American National Standards Institute.

Antoniou, G. and M. Williams. 1997. *Nonmonotonic Reasoning*. Cambridge, Mass.: MIT Press.

Appel, A. 1992. *Compiling with Continuations*. Cambridge University Press.

Appel, A. and D. MacQueen. 1994. "Separate Compilation for Standard ML," *SIGPLAN Conference on Programming Language Design and Implementation*.

Apt, K. R., V. W. Marek, M. Truszczynski, and D. S. Warren (Eds.). 1999. *The Logic Programming Paradigm: A 25-Year Perspective*. New York: Springer-Verlag.

Arnold, K., J. Gosling, and D. Holmes. 2000. *The Java Programming Language* (3rd ed.). Reading, Mass.: Addison-Wesley.

Ashley, R. 1980. *Structured COBOL: A Self-teaching Guide*. New York: John Wiley & Sons.

Baase, S. 1988. *Computer Algorithms: Introduction to Design and Analysis* (2nd ed.). Reading, Mass.: Addison-Wesley.

Backus, J. W. 1981. "The History of FORTRAN I, II, and III." In Wexelblat [1981], pp. 25–45.

Backus, J. W. 1978. "Can Programming Be Liberated from the von Neumann Style? A Functional Style and Its Algebra of Programs." *Comm. ACM* **21(8)**, 613–641.

Backus, J. W. et al. 1957. "The FORTRAN Automatic Coding System." *Proceedings of the Western Joint Computing Conference*, pp. 188–198. Reprinted in Rosen [1967], pp. 29–47.

Barendregt, H. 1984. *The Lambda Calculus: Its Syntax and Semantics (Revised Edition)*. Amsterdam: North-Holland.

Barnes, J. 1998. *Programming in Ada 95* (2nd ed.). Reading, Mass.: Addison-Wesley.

Barnes, J. G. P. 1980. "An overview of Ada." *Software Practice and Experience* 10, 851–887. Also reprinted in Horowitz [1987].

Barron, D. W. 1977. *An Introduction to the Study of Programming Languages*. Cambridge U.K.,: Cambridge University Press.

Bergin, T. J., and R. G. Gibson. 1996. *History of Programming Languages—II*. New York: ACM Press and Reading, Mass.: Addison-Wesley.

Bird, R., T. E. Scruggs, and M. A. Mastropieri. 1998. *Introduction to Functional Programming*. Englewood Cliffs, N.J.: Prentice-Hall.

Birnes, W. J. (Ed.). 1989. *High-Level Languages and Software Applications*. New York: McGraw-Hill.

Birtwistle, G. M., O.-J. Dahl, B. Myhrhaug, and K. Nygaard. 1973. *Simula Begin*. Philadelphia: Auerbach.

Bishop, J. 1986. *Data Abstraction in Programming Languages*. Reading, Mass.: Addison-Wesley.

Björner, B. and O. N. Oest (Eds.). 1981. *Towards a Formal Description of Ada*, New York: Springer Verlag.

Bobrow, D. G., L. G. DeMichiel, R. P. Gabriel, S. Keene, G. Kiczales, and D. A. Moon. 1988. "The Common Lisp Object System Specification." *ACM SIGPLAN Notices* **23(9)** (special issue).

Bobrow, D. G. and M. Stefik. 1983. *The LOOPS Manual*. Palo Alto, Calif.: Xerox Palo Alto Research Center.

Böhm, C. and G. Jacopini. 1966. "Flow Diagrams, Turing Machines and Languages with Only Two Formation Rules." *Comm. ACM* **29(6)**, 471–483.

Booch, G. 1994. *Object-Oriented Analysis and Design with Applications* (Addison-Wesley Object Technology Series) Reading, Mass.: Addison-Wesley.

Booch, G., D. Bryan, and C. G. Petersen. 1993. *Software Engineering with Ada*. Addison-Wesley.

Bratko, I. 2000. *PROLOG Programming for Artificial Intelligence* (3rd ed.), Addison-Wesley.

Bridges, D. and F. Richman. 1987. *Varieties of Constructive Mathematics*, London Mathematical Society Lecture Note Series #97. Cambridge: Cambridge University Press.

Brinch-Hansen, P. 1999. "Java's Insecure Parallelism." *ACM SIGPLAN Notices* **34(4)**, pp. 38–45.

Brinch-Hansen, P. 1996. "Monitors and Concurrent Pascal: A Personal History." In Bergin and Gibson [1996], pp. 121–172.

Brinch-Hansen, P. 1981. "The Design of Edison." *Software Practice and Experience* **11**, pp. 363–396.

Brinch-Hansen, P. 1975. "The Programming Language Concurrent Pascal." *IEEE Transactions on Software Engineering* **SE-1(2)**, 199–207.

Brodie, L. 1981. *Starting FORTH: An Introduction to the FORTH Language*. Englewood Cliffs, N.J.: Prentice-Hall.

Brooks, F. 1996. "Language Design as Design." In Bergin and Gibson [1996], pp. 4–16.

Budd, T. 1987. *A Little Smalltalk*. Reading, Mass.: Addison-Wesley.

Budd, T. 1997. *An Introduction to Object-Oriented Programming*. Reading, Mass.: Addison-Wesley.

Burks, A. W., H. H. Goldstine, and J. von Neumann. 1947. "Preliminary Discussion of the Logical Design of an Electronic Computing Instrument." In *John von Neumann: Collected Works*, Vol. V, pp. 34–79. New York: Macmillan, 1973.

Burstall, R., D. MacQueen, and D. Sanella. 1980. *HOPE: An Experimental Applicative Language*. Report CSR-62-80, Computer Science Department, Edinburgh University, Scotland.

Butenhof, D. R. 1997. *Programming with POSIX Threads*. Reading, Mass.: Addison-Wesley.

Cardelli, L., J. Donahue, L. Glassman, M. Jordan, B. Kaslow, and G. Nelson. 1992. "Modula-3 Language Definition," *SIGPLAN Notices* **27(8)**, 15–42.

Cardelli, L., J. Donahue, M. Jordan, B. Kaslow, and G. Nelson. 1989. "The Modula-3 Type System." *Sixteenth Annual ACM Symposium on Principles of Programming Languages*, pp. 202–212.

Cardelli, L. and P. Wegner. 1985. "On Understanding Types, Data Abstraction, and Polymorphism." *ACM Computing Surveys* **17(4)**, 471–522.

Carriero, N. and D. Gelernter. 1990. *How to Write Parallel Programs: A First Course*. Cambridge, Mass.: MIT Press.

Carriero, N. and D. Gelernter. 1989a. "How to Write Parallel Programs: A Guide to the Perplexed." *ACM Computing Surveys* **21(3)**, 323–357.

Carriero, N. and D. Gelernter. 1989b. "Linda in Context." *Comm. ACM* **32(4)**, 444–458.

Chapman, S. J. 1997. *Fortran 90/95 for Scientists and Engineers*. New York: McGraw-Hill.

Chomski, N. A. 1956. "Three Models for the Description of Language." *I. R. E. Transactions on Information Theory* **IT-2(3)**, 113–124.

Church, A. 1941. *The Calculi of Lambda Conversion*. Princeton, N.J.: Princeton University Press.

Ciancarini, P. 1992. "Parallel Programming with Logic Languages." *Computer Languages* **17(4)**, 213–239.

Clark, R. L. 1973. "A Linguistic Contribution to GOTO-less Programming." *Datamation* **19(12)**, 62–63. Reprinted in *Comm. ACM* **27(4)**, April 1984.

Clark, K. L. and S.Å. Tärnlund (Eds.) 1982. *Logic Programming*. New York: Academic Press.

Cleaveland, J. C. 1986. *An Introduction to Data Types*. Reading, Mass.: Addison-Wesley.

Clocksin, W. F. and C. S. Mellish. 1994. *Programming in Prolog* (4th ed.). Berlin: Springer-Verlag.

Cohen, J. 1988. "A View of the Origins and Development of Prolog." *Comm. ACM* **31(1)**, 26–37.

Cohen, J. 1981. "Garbage Collection of Linked Data Structures." *ACM Computing Surveys* **13(3)**, 341–367.

Cohen, N. 1996. *Ada as a Second Language* (2nd ed.). New York: McGraw-Hill.

Colburn, D. R., C. H. Moore, and E. D. Rather. 1996. "The Evolution of FORTH." In Bergin and Gibson [1996], pp. 625–658.

Colmerauer, A. and P. Roussel. 1996. "The Birth of Prolog." In Bergin and Gibson [1996], pp. 331–352.

Colmerauer, A. 1982. "Prolog and Infinite Trees." In Clark and Tärnlund [1982].

Conlon, T. 1989. *Programming in PARLOG*. Reading, Mass.: Addison-Wesley.

Cooper, D. 1983. *Standard Pascal User Reference Manual*. New York: W. W. Norton.

Cox, B. 1986. *Object-Oriented Programming: An Evolutionary Approach*. Reading, Mass.: Addison-Wesley.

Cox, B. 1984. "Message/Object Programming: An Evolutionary Change in Programming Technology." *IEEE Software* **1(1)**, 50–69.

Curry, H. B. and R. Feys. 1958. *Combinatory Logic*, Vol. 1. Amsterdam: North-Holland.

Dahl, O.-J., E. W. Dijkstra, and C. A. R. Hoare. 1972. *Structured Programming*. New York: Academic Press.

Dahl, O.-J. and K. Nygaard. 1966. "SIMULA—An Algol-based Simulation Language." *Comm. ACM* **9(9)**, 671–678.

Dane, A. 1992. "Birth of an Old Machine." *Popular Mechanics*, March 1992, 99–100.

Davis, R. E. 1982. "Runnable Specifications as a Design Tool." In Clark and Tärnlund [1982].

Demers, A. J., J. E. Donahue, and G. Skinner. 1978. "Data Types as Values: Polymorphism, Type-checking, Encapsulation." *Conference Record of the Fifth Annual ACM Symposium on Principles of Programming Languages*, pp. 23–30. New York: ACM Press.

Dijkstra, E. W. and C. S. Scholten. 1990. *Predicate Calculus and Program Semantics (Texts and Monographs in Computer Science)*. New York: Springer-Verlag.

Dijkstra, E. W. 1976. *A Discipline of Programming*. Englewood Cliffs, N.J.: Prentice-Hall.

Dijkstra, E. W. 1975. "Guarded Commands, Nondeterminacy, and the Formal Derivation of Programs." *Comm. ACM* **18(8)**, 453–457.

Dijkstra, E. W. 1968a. "Goto Statement Considered Harmful" (letter to the editor). *Comm. ACM* **11(3)**, 147–148.

Dijkstra, E. W. 1968b. "Co-operating sequential processes." In F. Genuys (ed.), *Programming Languages: NATO Advanced Study Institute*. New York: Academic Press.

Donahue, J. E. and A. J. Demers. 1985. "Data Types Are Values." *ACM Transactions on Programming Languages and Systems* **7(3)**, 436–445.

Duncan, R. 1990. "A Survey of Parallel Computer Architectures." *IEEE Computer* **23(2)**, 5–16.

Dybvig, K. 1996. *The Scheme Programming Language: ANSI Scheme* (2nd ed.). Englewood Cliffs, N.J.: Prentice-Hall.

Ellis, M. A. and B. Stroustrup. 1990. *The Annotated C++ Reference Manual*. Reading, Mass.: Addison-Wesley.

Falkoff, A. D. and K. Iverson. 1981. "The Evolution of APL." In Wexelblat [1981], pp. 661–674.

Feinberg, N., Ed. 1996. *Dylan Programming : An Object-Oriented and Dynamic Language*. Reading, Mass.: Addison-Wesley.

Feldman, M. and E. Koffman. 1999. *ADA 95: Problem Solving and Program Design* (3rd ed.). Reading, Mass.: Addison-Wesley.

Flanagan, D. 1999. *Java in a Nutshell* (3rd ed.). O'Reilly & Associates, Inc.

Friedman, D. P., C. T. Haynes, and E. Kohlbecker. 1985. "Programming with Continuations." In P. Pepper (Ed.), *Program Transformations and Programming Environments*. New York: Springer-Verlag.

Futatsugi, K., J. Goguen, J.-P. Jouannaud, and J. Meseguer. 1985. "Principles of OBJ2." *In Proceedings of the ACM Symposium on Principles of Programming Languages*, pp. 52–66.

Gabriel, R. P. 1985. *Performance and Evaluation of Lisp Systems*. Cambridge, Mass.: MIT Press.

Gabriel, R. P., J. L. White, and D. G. Bobrow. 1991. "CLOS: Integrating Object-oriented and Functional Programming." *Comm. ACM* **34(9)**, 29–38.

Gehani, N. H. 1984. *Ada: Concurrent Programming*. Englewood Cliffs, N.J.: Prentice-Hall.

Gelernter, D. and S. Jagannathan. 1990. *Programming Linguistics*. Cambridge, Mass.: MIT Press.

Geschke, C., J. Morris, and E. Satterthwaite. 1977. "Early Experience with Mesa." *Comm. ACM* **20(8)**, 540–553.

Ghezzi, C. and M. Jazayeri. 1997. *Programming Language Concepts* (3rd ed.). New York: John Wiley & Sons.

Goguen, J. and G. Malcolm. 1997. *Algebraic Semantics of Imperative Programs*. Cambridge, Mass.: MIT Press.

Goguen, J. and G. Malcolm (Eds.). 2000. *Software Engineering with OBJ: Algebraic Specification in Action*. Amsterdam: Kluwer Academic Publishers.

Goguen, J. A., J. W. Thatcher, and E. G. Wagner. 1978. "An Initial Algebra Approach to the Specification, Correctness, and Implementation of Abstract Data Types." In Yeh [1978], pp. 80–149.

Goldman, R. and R. P. Gabriel. 1989. "Qlisp: Parallel Processing in Lisp." *IEEE Software*, July 1989, 51–59.

Goodenough, J. B. 1975. "Exception Handling: Issues and a Proposed Notation." *Comm. ACM* **16(7)**, 683–696.

Gosling J., B. Joy, G. Steele, and G. Bracha. 2000. *The Java Language Specification* (2nd ed.). Reading, Mass.: Addison-Wesley.

Gregory, S. 1987. *Parallel Logic Programming in PARLOG: The Language and Its Implementation*. Reading, Mass.: Addison-Wesley.

Gries, D. 1981. *The Science of Programming*. New York: Springer-Verlag.

Griswold, R. E. 1981. "A History of the SNOBOL Programming Languages." In Wexelblat [1981], pp. 601–645.

Griswold, R. E. and M. Griswold. 1996. "History of the ICON Programming Language." In Bergin and Gibson [1996], pp. 599–621.

Griswold, R. E. and M. Griswold. 1983. *The Icon Programming Language*. Englewood Cliffs, N.J.: Prentice-Hall.

Griswold, R. E. and M. Griswold. 1973. *A SNOBOL4 Primer*. Englewood Cliffs, N.J.: Prentice-Hall.

Griswold, R. E., J. F. Poage, and I. P. Polonsky. 1971. *The SNOBOL4 Programming Language* (2nd ed.). Englewood Cliffs, N.J.: Prentice-Hall.

Gunter, C. A. 1992. *Semantics of Programming Languages: Structures and Techniques (Foundations of Computing Series)*. Cambridge, Mass.: MIT Press.

Gunter, C. A. and J. C. Mitchell (Eds.). 1994. *Theoretical Aspects of Object-Oriented Programming: Types, Semantics, and Language Design (Foundations of Computing)*. Cambridge, Mass.: MIT Press.

Guttag, J. V. 1977. "Abstract Data Types and the Development of Data Structures." *Comm. ACM* **20(6)**, 396–404.

Halstead, R. H., Jr. 1985. "Multilisp: A Language for Concurrent Symbolic Computation." *ACM Transactions on Programming Languages and Systems* **7(4)**, 501–538.

Hankin, C. 1995. *Lambda Calculi : A Guide for Computer Scientists* (Graduate Texts in Computer Science, No 3). Oxford: Clarendon Press.

Hanson, D. R. 1981. "Is Block Structure Necessary?" *Software Practice and Experience* **11(8)**, 853–866.

Harper, R. and Mitchell, J. 1993. "On the Type Structure of Standard ML." *ACM Transactions on Programming Languages and Systems* **15(2)**, April 1993, 211–252.

Harry, A. 1997. *Formal Methods Fact File: Vdm and Z (Wiley Series in Software Engineering Practice)*, New York: John Wiley & Sons.

Henderson, P. 1980. *Functional Programming: Application and Implementation*. Englewood Cliffs, N.J.: Prentice-Hall.

Henglein, F. [1993] "Type Inference with Polymorphic Recursion." ACM *Transactions on Programming Languages and Systems* **15(2)**, April 1993, 253–289.

Hindley, J. R. 1997. *Basic Simple Type Theory (Cambridge Tracts in Theoretical Computer Science, No 42)*. Cambridge, England: Cambridge University Press.

Hindley, J. R. 1969. "The Principal Type-scheme of an Object in Combinatory Logic." *Trans. Amer. Math. Soc.* **146(12)**, 29–60.

Hoare, C. A. R. 1981. "The Emperor's Old Clothes." *Comm. ACM* **24(2)**, 75–83.

Hoare, C. A. R. 1978. "Communicating Sequential Processes." *Comm. ACM* **21(8)**, 666–677.

Hoare, C. A. R. 1974. "Monitors: An Operating System Structuring Concept." *Comm. ACM* **17(10)**, 549–557.

Hoare, C. A. R. 1973. "Hints on Programming Language Design." *ACM SIGACT/SIGPLAN Symposium on Principles of Programming Languages*. Reprinted in Horowitz [1987], pp. 31–40.

Hoare, C. A. R. 1969. "An Axiomatic Basis for Computer Programming." *Comm. ACM* **12(10)**, 576–580, 583.

Hoare, C. A. R. and N. Wirth. 1966. "A Contribution to the Development of ALGOL." *Comm. ACM* **9(6)**, 413–431.

Hopcroft, J. E. and J. D. Ullman. 1979. *Introduction to Automata Theory, Languages, and Computation*. Reading, Mass.: Addison-Wesley.

Horn, A. 1951. "On Sentences Which Are True of Direct Unions of Algebras." *J. Symbolic Logic* **16**, 14–21.

Horowitz, E. 1987. *Programming Languages: A Grand Tour* (3rd ed.). Rockville, Md.: Computer Science Press.

Horowitz, E. 1984. *Fundamentals of Programming Languages* (2nd ed.). Rockville, Md.: Computer Science Press.

Horowitz, E. and S. Sahni. 1984. *Fundamentals of Data Structures in Pascal*. Rockville, Md.: Computer Science Press.

Horstmann, C. and G. Cornell. 1999. *Core JAVA 1.2, Vols I and II*. Palo Alto, Calif.: Sun Microsystems Press/ Prentice-Hall PTR.

Hudak, P. 1989. "Conception, Evolution, and Application of Functional Programming Languages." ACM *Computing Surveys* **21(3)**, 359–411

Hudak, P. 2000. *The Haskell School of Expression: Learning Functional Programming through Multimedia*, New York: Cambridge University Press.

Hui, R. K. W. et al. 1990. "APL \ ?" in *APL90 Conf. Proc.*, **20(4)**, 192–200.

Ichbiah, J. D., J. G. P. Barnes, J. C. Heliard, B. Krieg-Brueckner, O. Roubine, and B. A. Wichmann. 1979. "Rationale for the Design of the Ada Programming Language." ACM *SIGPLAN Notices* **14(6)**, Part B.

IEEE. 1985. "ANSI/IEEE Std 754-1985: Standard for Binary Floating-Point Arithmetic." Reprinted in ACM *SIGPLAN Notices* **22(2)**, 9–25.

IEEE P1178. 1991. *IEEE Standard for the Scheme Programming Language*.

ISO 8652. 1995. ISO/IEC Standard—Information technology—Programming languages—Ada. International Organization for Standardization, Geneva, Switzerland.

ISO 9899. 1999. ISO/IEC Standard—Information technology—Programming languages—C. International Organization for Standardization, Geneva, Switzerland.

ISO 13211-1. 1995. ISO/IEC Standard—Information technology—Programming languages—Prolog-Part 1: General core. International Organization for Standardization, Geneva, Switzerland.

ISO 14882-1. 1998. ISO/IEC Standard—Information technology—Programming languages—C++. International Organization for Standardization, Geneva, Switzerland.

ISO 14977. 1996. ISO/IEC Standard—Information technology—Syntactic metalanguage—Extended BNF. International Organization for Standardization, Geneva, Switzerland.

Iverson, K. 1962. *A Programming Language*. New York: John Wiley & Sons.

Jaffar, J., S. Michaylov, P. Stuckey and R. Yap. 1992. "The CLP(R) Language and System," ACM *TOPLAS*, **14(3)**, 339–395.

Jaffar, J. and Maher, M. 1994. "Constraint Logic Programming: A Survey," *Journal of Logic Programming*, **19/20**, 503–581.

Johnson, S. C. 1975. "Yacc—Yet Another Compiler Compiler," Computing Science Technical Report No. 32. Murray Hill, N.J.: AT&T Bell Laboratories.

Jones, G. and M. Goldsmith. 1988. *Programming in Occam 2*. Englewood Cliffs, N.J.: Prentice-Hall.

Josuttis, N. 1999. *The C++ Standard Library—A Tutorial and Reference*. Reading, Mass.: Addison-Wesley.

Kamin, S. 1983. "Final Data Types and Their Specification." ACM *Trans. on Programming Languages and Systems* **5(1)**, 97–123.

Karp, A. H. 1987. "Programming for parallelism." *IEEE Computer* **21(5)**, 43–57.

Karp, A. H. and R. O. Babb II. 1988. "A Comparison of 12 Parallel Fortran Dialects." *IEEE Software*, September 1988, 52–67.

Kay, A. C. 1996. "The Early History of Smalltalk." In Bergin and Gibson [1996], pp. 511–579.

Kergommeaux, J. C. and P. Codognet. 1994. "Parallel LP Systems," ACM *Computing Surveys* **26(3)**, 295–336.

Kernighan, B. W. and D. M. Ritchie. 1988. *The C Programming Language* (ANSI Standard C) (2nd ed.). Englewood Cliffs, N.J.: Prentice-Hall.

King, K. N. 1988. *Modula-2: A Complete Guide*. Lexington, Mass.: D. C. Heath.

Knuth, D. E. 1974. "Structured Programming with GOTO Statements." ACM *Computing Surveys* **6(4)**, 261–301.

Knuth, D. E. 1972. "Ancient Babylonian Algorithms." *Comm.* ACM **15(7)**, 671–677.

Knuth, D. E. 1967. "The Remaining Trouble Spots in Algol60." *Comm.* ACM **10(10)**, 611–617. Also reprinted in Horowitz [1987], pp. 61–68.

Knuth, D. E. and L. Trabb Pardo. 1977. "Early Development of Programming Languages." In *Encyclopedia of Computer Science and Technology*, Vol. 7, pp. 419–493. New York: Marcel Dekker.

Koenig, A. and B. Moo. 1996. *Ruminations on C++: A Decade of Programming Insight and Experience*. Reading, Mass.: Addison-Wesley.

Koenig, A. and B. Stroustrup. 1990. "Exception Handling for C++," Proceedings of the USENIX C++ Conference" (pp. 149–176), San Francisco, April 1990; reprinted in *JOOP* Vol. 3, No. 2, July/Aug 1990, pp. 16–33.

Kowalski, R. A. 1988. "The Early Years of Logic Programming." *Comm.* ACM **31(1)**, 38–43.

Kowalski, R. A. 1979a. "Algorithm = Logic + Control." *Comm.* ACM **22(7)**, 424–436.

Kowalski, R. A. 1979b. *Logic for Problem Solving*. New York: Elsevier/North-Holland.

Kurtz, T. E. 1981. "BASIC." In Wexelblat [1981], pp. 515–537.

Lajoie, J. 1994a. "Exception Handling: Supporting the Runtime Mechanism." C *Report* (March/April 1994).

Lajoie, J. 1994b "Exception Handling: Behind the Scenes." C *Report* (June 1994).

Lalonde, W. 1994. *Discovering Smalltalk* (Addison-Wesley Object Technology Series). Reading, Mass.: Addison-Wesley.

Lampson, B. W. 1983. "A Description of the Cedar Language," Technical Report CSL-83-15. Palo Alto, Calif.: Xerox Palo Alto Research Center.

Lampson, B. W., J. J. Horning, R. L. London, J. G. Mitchell, and G. J. Popek. 1981. "Report on the Programming Language Euclid," Technical Report CSL-81-12. Palo Alto, Calif.: Xerox Palo Alto Research Center.

Lampson, B. W. and D. Redell. 1980. "Experience with Processes and Monitors in Mesa." *Comm.* ACM **23(2)**, 105–117.

Landin, P. J. 1966. "The Next 700 Programming Languages." *Comm.* ACM **9(3)**, 157–165.

Lapalme, G. and F. Rabhi. 1999. *Algorithms: A Functional Programming Approach*. Reading, Mass.: Addison-Wesley.

Lea, D. 2000. *Concurrent Programming in Java: Design Principles and Patterns*. (2nd ed.). Reading, Mass.: Addison-Wesley.

Lenkov, D., D. Cameron, P. Faust, and M. Mehta. 1992. "A Portable Implementation of C++ Exception Handling," Proceedings of the Usenix C++ Conference, Portland, Oreg.

Lesk, M. E. 1975. "Lex—A Lexical Analyzer Generator," Computing Science Technical Report No. 39. Murray Hill, N.J.: AT&T Bell Laboratories.

Lewis, J., M. Shields, E. Meijer, and J. Launchbury. 2000. "Implicit Parameters: Dynamic Scoping with Static Types." In *Proceedings of the 27th Annual ACM SIGPLAN-SIGACT Symposium on Principles of Programming Languages*, pp. 108–118. New York: ACM Press.

Lewis, S. 1995. *The Art and Science of Smalltalk*. Englewood Cliffs, N.J.: Prentice-Hall.

Lindsey, C. H. 1996. "A History of Algol 68." In Bergin and Gibson [1996], pp. 27–84.

Lippman, S. and J. Lajoie 1998. *C++ Primer* (3rd ed.). Reading, Mass.: Addison-Wesley.

Liskov, B. 1996. "A History of CLU." In Bergin and Gibson [1996], pp. 471–497.

Liskov, B., R. Atkinson, T. Bloom, E. Moss, J. C. Schaffert, R. Scheifler, and A. Snyder. 1984. *CLU Reference Manual*. New York: Springer-Verlag.

Liskov, B. and A. Snyder. 1979. "Exception Handling in CLU." *IEEE Translations on Software Engineering* **SE-5(6)**, 546–558. Also reprinted in Horowitz [1987], pp. 254–266.

Liskov, B., A. Snyder, R. Atkinson, and C. Schaffert. 1977. "Abstraction Mechanisms in CLU." *Comm. ACM* **20(8)**, 564–576. Also reprinted in Horowitz [1987], pp. 267–279.

Liu, C. 2000. *Smalltalk, Objects, and Design*. Lincoln, Nebraska: iUniverse.com.

Lloyd, J. W. 1984. *Foundations of Logic Programming*. New York: Springer-Verlag.

Louden, K. 1987. "Recursion versus Non-recursion in Pascal: Recursion Can Be Faster." *ACM SIGPLAN Notices* **22(2)**, 62–67.

Louden, K. 1997. *Compiler Construction: Principles and Practice*. Boston: PWS.

Louden, K. 1997b. "Compilers and Interpreters." In Tucker [1997], pp. 2120–2147.

Luckam, D. C. and W. Polak. 1980. "Ada Exception Handling: An Axiomatic Approach." *ACM Transactions on Programming Languages arid Systems* **2(2)**, 225–233.

MacQueen, D. B. 1988. "The Implementation of Standard ML Modules." *ACM Conference on Lisp and Functional Programming*, 212–223. New York: ACM Press.

Mandrioli, D. and C. Ghezzi. 1987. *Theoretical Foundations of Computer Science*. New York: John Wiley & Sons.

Marriott, K. and P. J. Stuckey (Eds.). 1997. *Programming with Constraints*. Cambridge, Mass.: MIT Press.

Martin-Löf, P. 1979. "Constructive Mathematics and Computer Programming." In L. J. Cohen et al. (Eds.) *Logic, Methodology and the Philosophy of Science*, Vol. VI. New York: North-Holland. 1982.

McCarthy, J. 1981. "History of LISP." In Wexelblat [1981], pp. 173–185.

Metcalf, M. and J. Reid. 1999. *Fortran 90/95 Explained* (2nd ed.). Oxford: Oxford University Press.

Meyer, B. 1997. *Object-Oriented Software Construction* (2nd ed.). Englewood Cliffs, N.J.: Prentice-Hall.

Milner, R. 1978. "A Theory of Type Polymorphism in Programming." *J. Computer and System Sciences* **17(3)**, 348–375.

Milner, R. 1994. *Communication and Concurrency*. Englewood Cliffs, N.J.: Prentice-Hall.

Milner, R. and M. Tofte. 1991. *Commentary on Standard ML*. Cambridge, Mass.: MIT Press.

Milner, R., M. Tofte, R. Harper, and D. MacQueen. 1997. *The Definition of Standard ML (Revised)*. Cambridge, Mass.: MIT Press.

Minker J. (Ed.). 2000. *Logic-Based Artificial Intelligence* (The Kluwer International Series in Engineering and Computer Science Volume 597). Amsterdam: Kluwer Academic Publishers.

Mitchell, J. C. 1996. *Foundations for Programming Languages (Foundations of Computing Series)*. Cambridge, Mass.: MIT Press.

Mitchell, J. C. and R. Harper. 1988. "The Essence of ML." *Fifteenth ACM Symposium on Principles of Programming Languages*, pp. 28–46. New York: ACM Press.

Mitchell, J. G., W. Maybury, and R. Sweet. 1979. "Mesa Language Manual, Version 5.0," Technical Report CSL-79-3. Palo Alto, Calif.: Xerox Palo Alto Research Center.

Moon, D. A. 1986. "Object-oriented Programming with Flavors." *OOPSLA 1986, ACM SIGPLAN Notices* **21(11)**, 1–8.

Moon, D. A. 1984. "Garbage Collection in Large Lisp Systems." *Proceedings of the 1984 ACM Symposium on Lisp and Functional Programming*, pp. 235–246. New York: ACM Press.

Moore, D. L. 1977. *Ada, Countess of Lovelace: Byron's Legitimate Daughter*. London: Murray.

Morrison, P. and E. Morrison (Eds.). 1961. *Charles Babbage and His Calculating Engines*. New York: Dover.

Muhlbacher, J. (Ed.). 1997. *Oberon-2 Programming with Windows*. New York: Springer-Verlag, 1997.

Naur, P. 1981. "The European Side of the Last Phase of the Development of Algol 60." In Wexelblat [1981], pp. 92–139.

Naur, P. (Ed.). 1963a. "Revised Report on the Algorithmic Language Algol 60." *Comm. ACM* **6(1)**, 1–17. Also reprinted in Horowitz [1987], pp. 44–60.

Naur, P. 1963b. "GOTO Statements and Good Algol Style." *BIT* **3(3)**, 204–208.

Nelson, G. (Ed.). 1991. *Systems Programming with Modula-3*. Englewood Cliffs, N.J.: Prentice-Hall.

Nelson, G. 1989. "A Generalization of Dijkstra's Calculus." ACM *Transactions on Programming Languages and Systems* **11(4)**, 517–561.

Nygaard, K. and O.-J. Dahl. 1981. "The Development of the SIMULA Languages." In Wexelblat [1981], pp. 439–480.

Okasaki, C. 1999. *Purely Functional Data Structures*. Cambridge, U.K.: Cambridge University Press.

O'Donnell, M. J. 1985. *Equational Logic as a Programming Language*. Cambridge, Mass.: MIT Press.

OOPSLA. 1986ff. ACM Conference on Object-Oriented Programming Systems and Languages. Also published as various issues of *ACM SIGPLAN Notices*.

Ousterhout, J. K. 1998. "Scripting: Higher-Level Programming for the 21st Century," *IEEE Computer* **31(3)**, pp. 23–30.

Pacheco, P. 1996. *Parallel Programming with MPI*. San Francisco: Morgan Kaufmann.

Pamas, D. L. 1985. "Software Aspects of Strategic Defense Systems." *Comm. ACM* **28(12)**, 1326–1335. Reprinted from the American Scientist **73(5)**, 432–440.

Paulson, L. 1996. *ML for the Working Programmer* (2nd ed.). Cambridge, U.K.: Cambridge University Press.

Perlis, A. J. 1981. "The American Side of the Development of Algol." In Wexelblat [1981], pp. 75–91.

Peyton Jones, S. L. 1987. *The Implementation of Functional Programming Languages*. Englewood Cliffs, N.J.: Prentice-Hall.

Popek, G. J., J. J. Homing, B. W. Lampson, J. G. Mitchell, and R. L. London. 1977. "Notes on the Design of Euclid." *ACM SIGPLAN Notices* **12(3)**, 11–19.

Pountain, D. 1995. "Constraint Logic Programming: A Child of Prolog Finds New Life Solving Programming's Nastier Problems," *BYTE*, February 1995.

Radin, G. 1981. "The Early History and Characteristics of PL/I." In Wexelblat [1981], pp. 551–575.

Randell, B. and L. J. Russell. 1964. *Algol 60 Implementation*. New York: Academic Press.

Reade, C. 1989. *Elements of Functional Programming*. Reading, Mass.: Addison-Wesley.

Reynolds, J. C. 1998. *Theories of Programming Languages*. Cambridge, U.K.: Cambridge University Press.

Richards, M. and C. Whitby-Strevens. 1979. *BCPL—The Language and Its Compiler*. Cambridge, U.K.: Cambridge University Press.

Ringwood, G. A. 1988. "Parlog86 and the Dining Logicians." *Comm. ACM* **31(1)**, 10–25.

Ripley, G. D. and F. C. Druseikis. 1978. "A Statistical Analysis of Syntax Errors." *Computer Languages* **3(4)**, 227–240.

Ritchie, D. M. 1996. "The Development of the C Programming Language." In Bergin and Gibson [1996], pp. 671–687.

Robinson, J. A. 1965. "A Machine-Oriented Logic Based on the Resolution Principle." *Journal of the ACM* **12(1)**, 23–41.

Rosen, S. 1972. "Programming Systems and Languages 1965–1975." *Comm. ACM* **15(7)**, 591–600.

Rosen, S. (Ed.). 1967. *Programming Systems and Languages*. New York: McGraw-Hill.

Rosser, J. B. 1982. "Highlights of the History of the Lambda Calculus." *Proceedings of the ACM Symposium on Lisp and Functional Programming*, pp. 216–225. New York: ACM Press.

Rubin, F. 1987. " 'GOTO Statement Considered Harmful' Considered Harmful" (letter to the editor). *Comm. ACM* **30(3)**, 195–196. Replies in the June, July, August, November, and December 1987 issues.

Sammet, J. E. 1981. "The Early History of COBOL." In Wexelblat [1981], pp. 199–243.

Sammet, J. E. 1976. "Roster of Programming Languages for 1974–75." *Comm. ACM* **19(12)**, 655–699.

Sammet, J. E. 1972. "Programming Languages: History and Future." *Comm. ACM* **15(7)**, 601–610.

Sammet, J. E. 1969. *Programming Languages: History and Fundamentals*. Englewood Cliffs, N.J.: Prentice-Hall.

Saraswat, V. and P. Van Hentenryck (Eds.). 1995. *Principles and Practice of Constraint Programming: The Newport Papers*. Cambridge, Mass.: MIT Press.

Schmidt, D. A. 1994. *The Structure of Typed Programming Languages (Foundations of Computing Series)*. Cambridge, Mass.: MIT Press.

Schmidt, D. A. 1986. *Denotational Semantics: A Methodology for Language Development*. Dubuque, Iowa: Wm. C. Brown.

Schneider, S. 2000. *Concurrent and Real-time Systems: The CSP Approach*. New York: John Wiley & Sons.

Schneiderman, B. 1985. "The Relationship between COBOL and Computer Science." *Annals of the History of Computing* **7(4)**, 348–352. Also reprinted in Horowitz [1987], pp. 417–421.

Schönfinkel, M. 1924. "Über die Bausteine der mathematischen Logik." *Mathematische Annalen* **92(3/4)**, 305–316.

Scott, M. L. 2000. *Programming Language Pragmatics*. San Francisco: Morgan Kaufmann.

Sebesta, R. W. 1996. *Concepts of Programming Languages* (3rd ed.). Reading, Mass.: Addison-Wesley.

Sethi, R. 1996. *Programming Languages Concepts and Constructs* (2nd ed.). Reading, Mass.: Addison-Wesley.

Shapiro, E. 1989. "The Family of Concurrent Logic Programming Languages." *ACM Computing Surveys* **21(3)**, 412–510.

Shapiro, E. and D. H. D. Warren (Eds.). 1993. "Special Section: The Fifth Generation Project: Personal Perspectives, Launching the New Era, and Epilogue," *Communications of the ACM*, **36(3)**, 46–103.

Sharp, A. 1997. *Smalltalk by Example: The Developer's Guide*. New York: McGraw-Hill.

Shaw, C. J. 1963. "A Specification of JOVIAL." *Comm. ACM* **6(12)**, 721–736.

Shaw, Mary (Ed.). 1981. *Alphard Form and Content*. New York: Springer-Verlag.

Sipser, M. 1997. *Introduction to the Theory of Computation*. Boston: PWS.

Snyder, A. 1986. "Encapsulation and Inheritance in Object-oriented Languages." *ACM SIGPLAN Notices* **21(11)**, 38–45.

Springer, G. and D. P. Friedman. 1989. *Scheme and the Art of Programming*. Cambridge, Mass.: MIT Press.

Stallings, W. 2000. *Operating Systems: Internals and Design Principles*. Englewood Cliffs, N.J.: Prentice-Hall.

Steele, G. L., Jr., and R. P. Gabriel. 1996. "The Evolution of Lisp." In Bergin and Gibson [1996], pp. 233–309.

Steele, G. 1984. *Common Lisp: The Language*. Burlington, Mass.: Digital Press.

Steele, G. 1982. "An Overview of Common Lisp." *Proceedings of the ACM Symposium on Lisp and Functional Programming*, pp. 98–107. New York: ACM Press.

Steele, G. 1977. "Debunking the 'Expensive Procedure Call' Myth." *Proceedings of the National Conference of the ACM*, pp. 153–162. New York: ACM Press.

Stein, D. 1985. *Ada: A Life and Legacy*. Cambridge, Mass.: MIT Press.

Sterling, L. and E. Shapiro. 1986. *The Art of Prolog*. Cambridge, Mass.: MIT Press.

Stoy, J. E. 1977. *Denotational Semantics: The Scott-Strachey Approach to Programming Language Semantics*. Cambridge, Mass.: MIT Press.

Stroustrup, B. 1997. *The C++ Programming Language* (3rd ed.). Reading, Mass.: Addison-Wesley.

Stroustrup, B. 1996. "A History of C++: 1979–1991." In Bergin and Gibson [1996], pp. 699–755.

Stroustrup, B. 1994. *The Design and Evolution of C++*. Reading, Mass.: Addison-Wesley.

Sussman, G. J., and G. L. Steele, Jr. 1975. "Scheme: An Interpreter for Extended Lambda Calculus." AI Memo 349. Cambridge, Mass.: MIT Artificial Intelligence Laboratory.

Swinehart, D. C., P. T. Zellweger, R. J. Beach, and R. B. Hagmann. 1986. "A Structural View of the Cedar Programming Environment." ACM *Transactions on Programming Languages and Systems* **8(4)**, 419–490.

Tanenbaum, A. S. 1976. "A Tutorial on Algol68." ACM *Computing Surveys* **8(2)**, 155–190. Also reprinted in Horowitz [1987], pp. 69–104.

Teitelman, W. 1984. "A Tour through Cedar." *IEEE Software*, April 1984, 44–73.

Tesler, L. 1985. "Object Pascal Report." *Structured Language World* **9(3)**, 10–14.

Thompson, S. 1999. *Haskell: The Craft of Functional Programming* (2nd ed.). Reading, Mass.: Addison-Wesley.

Tick, E. 1991. *Parallel Logic Programming*. Cambridge, Mass.: MIT Press.

Tucker, A. 1997. *The Computer Science and Engineering Handbook*. Boca Raton, Fla: CRC Press.

Turner, D. A. 1986. "An Overview of Miranda." ACM *SIGPLAN Notices* **21(12)**, 158–166.

Turner, D. A. 1982. "Recursion Equations as a Programming Language." In Darlington J. et al. (Eds.), *Functional Programming and Its Applications*. Cambridge, U.K.: Cambridge University Press.

Ueda, K. 1987. "Guarded Horn Clauses." In E. Y. Shapiro (Ed.), *Concurrent Prolog: Collected Papers*, pp. 140–156. Cambridge, Mass.: MIT Press.

Ueda, K. 1999. "Concurrent Logic/Constraint Programming: The Next 10 Years." In Apt et al. [1999].

Ullman, J. 1998. *Elements of ML Programming, ML97 Edition*. Englewood Cliffs, N.J.: Prentice-Hall.

Ungar, D. 1984. "Generation Scavenging: A Non-disruptive High Performance Storage Reclamation Algorithm." Proceedings of the ACM SIGSOFT/ SIGPLAN Symposium on Practical Software Development Environments, ACM *SIGPLAN Notices* **19(5)**, 157–167.

Ungar, D. and R. Smith. 1987. "SELF: The Power of Simplicity." *OOPSLA* 1987.

Wall, L., T. Christiansen, and J. Orwant. 2000. *Programming Perl* (3rd ed.). O'Reilly & Associates.

Warren, D. H. D. 1980. "Logic Programming and Compiler Writing." *Software Practice and Experience* **10(2)**, 97–125.

Wegner, P. 1976. "Programming Languages—The First 25 Years." *IEEE Transactions on Computers* **C-25(12)**, 1207–1225. Also reprinted in Horowitz [1987], pp. 4–22.

Wegner, P. 1972. "The Vienna Definition Language." ACM *Computing Surveys* **4(1)**, 5–63.

Wegner, P. and S. A. Smolka. 1983. "Processes, Tasks, and Monitors: A Comparative Study of Concurrent Programming Primitives." *IEEE Transactions on Software Engineering* **SE,9(4)**, 446–462. Also reprinted in Horowitz [1987], pp. 360–376.

Welch, B. B. 2000. *Practical Programming in Tcl and Tk*. Englewood Cliffs, N.J.: Prentice-Hall.

Wexelblat, R. L. 1984. "Nth Generation Languages." *Datamation*, September 1, 111–117.

Wexelblat, R. L. (Ed.). 1981. *History of Programming Languages*. New York: Academic Press.

Whitaker, W. A. 1996. "Ada—The Project: The DoD High Order Language Working Group." In Bergin and Gibson [1996], pp. 173–228.

Whitehead, A. N. 1911. *An Introduction to Mathematics*. Oxford, U.K.: Oxford University Press.

Wilkinson, B. and Allen, C. M. [1997]. *Parallel Programming: Techniques and Applications Using Networked Workstations and Parallel Computers*. Englewood Cliffs, N.J.: Prentice-Hall.

Wilson, P. R. 1992. "Uniprocessor Garbage Collection Techniques." In Bekkers et al. (Eds.), *International Workshop on Memory Management*, Springer Lecture Notes in Computer Science #637, 1–42. New York: Springer-Verlag.

Winograd, T. 1979. "Beyond Programming Languages." *Comm.* ACM **22(7)**, 391–401.

Winskel, G. 1993. *The Formal Semantics of Programming Languages: An Introduction (Foundations of Computing Series)*. Cambridge, Mass.: MIT Press.

Wirth, N. 1996. "Recollections about the Development of Pascal." In Bergin and Gibson [1996], pp. 97–111.

Wirth, N. 1988a. *Programming in Modula-2* (4th ed.). Berlin: Springer-Verlag.

Wirth, N. 1988b. "From Modula to Oberon." *Software Practice and Experience* **18(7)**, 661–670.

Wirth, N. 1988c. "The Programming Language Oberon." *Software Practice and Experience* **18(7)**, 671–690.

Wirth, N. 1976. *Algorithms + Data Structures = Programs*. Englewood Cliffs, N.J.: Prentice-Hall.

Wirth, N. 1974. "On the Design of Programming Languages." *Proc. IFIP Congress* 74, 386–393. Amsterdam: North-Holland. Reprinted in Horowitz [1987], pp. 23–30.

Wirth, N. and H. Weber. 1966a. "Euler: A Generalization of Algol, and Its Formal Definition," Part 1. *Comm. ACM* **9(1)**, 13–23.

Wirth, N. and H. Weber. 1966b. "Euler: A Generalization of Algol, and Its Formal Definition," Part II. *Comm. ACM* **9(2)**, 89–99.

Wulf, W. A., R. L. London, and M. Shaw. 1976. "An Introduction to the Construction and Verification of Alphard Programs." *IEEE Transactions on Software Engineering* **2(4)**, 253–265.

Wulf, W. A., D. B. Russell, and A. N. Habermann. 1971. "BLISS: A Language for Systems Programming." *Comm. ACM* **14(12)**, 780–790.

Yeh, R. T. (Ed.). 1978. *Current Trends in Programming Methodology, Vol. IV, Data Structuring.* Englewood Cliffs, N.J.: Prentice-Hall.

Zuse, K. 1972. "Der Plankalkül." *Berichte der Gesellschaft für Mathematik und Datenverarbeitung,* No. 63, Part 3, Bonn.

Index